John o. Kingston Mackay

The Celtic Monthly

A Magazine for Highlanders - Vol. 1

John o. Kingston Mackay

The Celtic Monthly
A Magazine for Highlanders - Vol. 1

ISBN/EAN: 9783337160128

Printed in Europe, USA, Canada, Australia, Japan

Cover: Foto ©Andreas Hilbeck / pixelio.de

More available books at **www.hansebooks.com**

THE

Celtic Monthly:

A Magazine for Highlanders.

EDITED BY

JOHN MACKAY, Kingston, Glasgow.

VOL. II.

GLASGOW: ARCHIBALD SINCLAIR, Celtic Press, 10 Bothwell Street;
HENRY WHYTE, JOHN MENZIES & CO., and WILLIAM LOVE.
EDINBURGH: NORMAN MACLEOD, and JOHN GRANT.
INVERNESS: WILLIAM MACKAY PORTREE: J. G. MACKAY.
OBAN: THOMAS BOYD, and HUGH MACDONALD.

1894.

❖ CONTENTS. ❖

CONTENTS.

CONTENTS.

(DEDICATION.)

To JOHN MACKAY, C.E., J.P.,

of Hereford,

ONE OF THE NOBLEST OF SUTHERLAND'S SONS.

As an acknowledgment of his life-long service in the cause of his fellow countrymen, his practical sympathy with every movement intended to improve the social condition of the people of his native county, and his intense love for, and generous support of, the literature of the Gael, this volume is respectfully dedicated by his clansman,

THE EDITOR.

ARCHIBALD SINCLAIR, Printer and Publisher, Celtic Press, 10 Bothwell Street, Glasgow.

THE CELTIC MONTHLY:
A MAGAZINE FOR HIGHLANDERS.

Edited by JOHN MACKAY, Kingston.

No. 1. Vol. II | OCTOBER, 1893. | Price Threepence.

THE VEN. WM. MACDONALD SINCLAIR, D.D., ARCHDEACON OF LONDON.

IF no account of the Colosseum at Rome be complete without the quotation "Butchered to make a Roman holiday," certainly no account of the subject of our present sketch is possible without a reference to "the lordly line of high St. Clair," which for ordinary readers has stamped the record of the Sinclair family on the page of Scottish history. A distinguished ancestry is not only a proud possession in itself, but it is also a splendid spur to individual effort, and surely no public man has a more inspiring record in this respect than the Archdeacon of London. According to the historian of the Clan Sinclair, the family of *de Sancto Claro* not only "came across with William the Conqueror, you know," but was intimately connected, both by blood relationship and by marriage, with the Conqueror himself. From the fourth Earl of Caithness the Sinclairs of Ulster are descended, the most distinguished and best known of the name being Sir John Sinclair, Bart. of Ulster, the grandfather of the present Archdeacon of London. A hundred years ago Sir John seems to have pervaded every department of public life with the genius of his original brain and untiring energy. The best known of his many achievements are the "Statistical Account of Scotland," a work of colossal proportions and the highest importance, and the institution of the Board of Agriculture. Besides these, however, he raised Highland regiments for the defence of his country (see our recent numbers for an account of these from the pen of Archdeacon Sinclair), he generously supported the Highland and Gaelic Societies both of London and Scotland, defended "Ossian" Macpherson, wrote voluminously on all sorts of subjects, and conducted a correspondence with most of the eminent men in Europe. His third son,

William, rector of Pulborough and prebendary of Chichester Cathedral, was the father of our Archdeacon. Besides his paternal ancestry, the Archdeacon has another distinguished line through his grandmother, the Hon. Diana, daughter of Lord Macdonald of the Isles.

Inheriting the handsome features, great stature and muscular frame of his historic race, the Archdeacon is every inch a man. Born in 1850, at Leeds, he received the first elements of his education at Malvern Wells, and later at the great Public School of Repton, from which he passed to Balliol College, Oxford. There he had a distinguished career, being elected to the high honour of President of the Union in 1872, a position occupied by his father before him. Ordained in 1874, he was resident chaplain to the Bishop of London from 1877 to 1880. For the following ten years he laboured hard as Vicar of St. Stephens, Westminster, and did noble work among the poor in that poor neighbourhood. In 1889 he was appointed Hon. Chaplain to the Queen, and later Archdeacon of London and Canon of St. Paul's. Not two out of every twenty Englishmen can tell what are the duties of an Archdeacon, and therefore it may be necessary to explain in a Celtic magazine that an archdeacon is a sort of sub-bishop, or, as Dr Sinclair aptly calls it, "a bishop's *aide-de-camp*," having direct oversight of every church and parish in the Diocese. Dr. Sinclair's life is one of incessant and exhausting labour, and the ever-varying character of his engagements taxes even his herculean strength. We have known him travel 200 miles back to London before 11 A.M., read through his heavy correspondence and dictate replies up to noon, attend a deputation to Mr. Gladstone, and make a speech thereat at 12.30 P.M.; snatch a hasty dinner at 2 P.M., attend a conference at Westminster Abbey at 3, and a vestry meeting at 3.30, address a Sunday School Union in North London at 5, preach at Kensington at 8 P.M., and arrive about 10.30 P.M. at a London Caithness concert at which he was down to take the chair, returning before midnight to his home with a sermon to write before indulging in a much-needed sleep. And this sort of thing goes on day after day, supplemented by two services daily at St. Paul's Cathedral, during his month of residence.

Theologically, Scotsmen will be pleased to learn that the Archdeacon is a thorough evangelical, Ritualism being as far from him on the one side as Broad-churchism on the other. He is indeed the leader of the Evangelical party in the Church of England, a position which has for some time been vacant and waiting for an able man to fill it. He edits *The Churchman*, the organ of the Evangelicals, and is a voluminous author besides.

His sermons are earnest and moving, as might be inferred from the character of his published works, and one cannot help attributing his solid and orthodox Christianity to his Caithness origin. It is unnecessary to remind Highlanders that whenever a Free Kirk Professor goes wrong, his heresy is scented out by the Caithness folks months before it comes between the wind and the nobility of more southern noses. We have tried the Archdeacon's sermons on the strictest of that fast diminishing race, "the Men," and have received their unqualified approval, than which no higher certificate is possible.

In addition to the high honours he has received in the Church, the Archdeacon is Hon. Chaplain to the Queen, the Scottish Corporation, the Highland Society of London, and the Caledonian Asylum, and, lastly, he is the ever active and enthusiastic President of the London Caithness Association.

London.   J. T. C.

DO NINEAG OIG.

Le Iain Caimbeul anns an Leideig.

Si mo ghaolsa 'mhaighdean uasal
A tha thall 's an eilean uaine ;
'S mi gu'n snàmhadh caol gun uallach
Ach mi dh' fhaotainn suas ri 'm mhàltaig.

T-fhalt na dhualan sios mu'd ghuaillean
'S iomadh buaidh tha fuaight' ri'd nàdur ;
Ciallach, stuama, rianail, suairce,
'S fhada uait tha fuath is àrdan.

Tha thu eutrom, aoidheil, cuantar,
'S brisg do cheum air leac nam fuar-bheann
'S mis' tha trom gach là, 's gach uair dheth,
Bho'n a chaidh thu tuath bho 'n àite.

'S tric a dh' fhàg e mise luaineach
Thu bhi uam, 's a nis air m' fhàgail ;—
'Sràid cha'n fhaigh mi 'm beul na h-oidhche
Ann an caoimhneas mar bu ghnàth leinn.

Bha mi uair is b'e mo mhiann-sa,
Bhi a' seòladh n' iar thar sàile ;
A' tarruing *ròp*, 's a' togail sheòl,
No cur gach bòrd an òrdaigh càraidh.

'S e'm peann a nis a tha ga'm chnuaradh
A h-uile latha a 'dol nis truaighe ;
Ri bòrd an sgriobhaidh tàthte, luaidhte,
'S cha'n fhaigh mi luaidh, bhi leat mar b'àbhaist.

'S tric mo chridh' le taing a' bualadh
Do'n cheud fhear chur am *post* air ghluasad ;
'S ged' tha'n mìonag fada uamsa
Ruigidh litir luath mo ghràdh sa.

'S ged a bhith's ar càirdean gruamach,
'S their iad gu bheil pòsadh luath dhuinn ;
Orm cha chuir e smuairean uair—
Bu truagh n'am b'aois a b'fhearr a thàthadh.

'S mo chead, a nis, do'n ribhinn chiatach,
A tha thall 's an eilean iosal ;
'S fhad 'sa' chi mi ghrian 'san iarmailt
Cha tig fiaradh air mo ghràdh dhi.

CAMANACHD.

Glasgow Cowal Shinty Club.—The annual business meeting was held in the Waterloo Rooms —Mr. John Mackay, Kingston, president, in the chair. The secretary's and treasurer's reports were very favourable, the balance on hand being £8 16s. The following office-bearers were then elected :— Patrons, Lord Archibald Campbell ; Mr. D. H. MacFarlane, M.P. ; Colonel Malcolm of Poltalloch ; Messrs. W. Sutherland Hunter, Magnus MacLean, M.A., F.R.S.E. ; J. MacNaught Campbell, Duncan Whyte, and James Mackellar ; hon. president, Alex. Mackellar ; president, John Mackay, editor, *Celtic Monthly* ; vice-president, Duncan Morrison ; captain, Archibald Campbell (Dr.) ; vice-captain, Peter Campbell (No. 2) ; secretary, Hugh Mac-Corquodale, 100 Cornwall Street, Plantation ; treasurer, Peter Campbell (No. 1) ; committee, Archd. Campbell (Leckie), Donald MacCorquodale, Thomas Scott, Cameron Henderson, R. Lawrie, D. Turner, W. Robertson, J. MacInnis, Duncan Robertson, and Donald MacInnis ; match committee, D. Morrison, Arch. Campbell (Dr.), Arch. Campbell (Leckie), Thomas Scott, and Peter Campbell ; umpire, Donald MacCorquodale. The forth-coming match with Kingussie was discussed, and a small committee appointed to make arrangements for same. Reports were also given in regarding the fund which is being raised to erect a suitable club-house on the ground, the lack of which has been much felt, especially on the occasion of matches. Should any of our readers interested in the national pastime feel disposed to contribute towards this deserving object, the Editor of the *Celtic Monthly*, 17 Dundas Street, Kingston, Glasgow, will gladly acknowledge any subscriptions sent to him.

GLENORCHY'S WIDOW:
A Legend of Lochawe.

BY THE EDITOR.

> BEN CRUACHAN is king of the mountains,
>   That gird the lonely Loch Awe,
> Loch Etive is fed from his fountains
>   By the stream of the dark-rushing Awe,
>   With his peak so high,
>   He cleaves the sky
>   That smiles on his old grey crown,
>   While the mantle green,
>   On his shoulders seen,
>   In many a fold flows down.
> —*Professor Buckie.*

A CERTAIN poet, who could speak wisdom in prose as well as in verse, once sarcastically remarked that nine-tenths of his countrymen travelled through the world with their eyes open but their ears shut. They were gifted with the power of seeing things, but seldom took the trouble to understand them. A picturesque object may attract their attention, its quaint appearance may extract from them an expression of admiration, but their interest goes no further. Wordsworth has very neatly portrayed such a character in the well-known lines:

> "A primrose by a river's brim,
>   A yellow primrose was to him,
> And it was *nothing more*."

How often in our holiday wanderings have we met the traveller from the sunny south. He is sometimes innocent, but nearly always amusing. He puts on his eye-glass to look at some grand old ruin, around which cling, as closely as the ivy itself, many of the most eventful episodes in our national history. Mr. Smith gazes at the crumbling towers for some time, then mutters laconically, "how pretty!" as if he were giving his valuable opinion regarding the latest design in painted tea cups. If this visitor from the south had been told that within those gloomy walls a Scottish king had been done to death, that its stones still show the marks of many a terrible siege, and that its courtyard had been the scene of many a bloody conflict, he would, no doubt, put on his eye-glass and remark, "Aw, how peculiar! Is that so? What did you say was the name of the place?" On such occasions a person feels, like one of Dickens's heroes, inclined to kick something.

For a hundred years and more these interesting visitors have been with us. They come to the cold north with the brave intention of "doing" the Highlands; they rush through the country like an express train, and on their return home they publish a volume of "Impressions," the principal feature of which is their discovery that Scotland is civilised, and that the Highlanders do not wear kilts, drink whisky all day, nor ask the loan of "saxpences." Also, that heather does not grow in the back greens in Glasgow. This is always a matter of surprise!

Not long ago I had occasion to visit Oban, and on the return journey, just as the train was rushing along the side of Loch Awe, under the shadow of the mighty Ben Cruachan, I looked out at the ruins of Kilchurn Castle, the ancient stronghold of the Campbells of Breadalbane. The sun had set, and the massive, roofless towers looked weird and gloomy in the mirky light. I thought of its romantic history, of the numberless legends associated with its vicinity, and wondered if these had ever been collected. Kilchurn Castle, for many years, has been the subject of inspiration to a host of painters and

KILCHURN CASTLE, LOCH AWE.

poets. A painting of it is to be seen in nearly
every picture shop window. Almost every
tourist who has written a book about the Highlands has visited it, and has told us as much
about it as his predecessors did. It is very
amusing. All these accounts are so meagre,
and bear such a close family resemblance to
each other, that there can be no doubt that each
was guilty of an attempt at literary plundering,
and that the only honest man among them was
the gentleman who wrote the first description.
He doubtless made a virtue of his necessity,
and was honest because there was no previous
account to steal from !

And yet what a halo of romance surrounds
that noble ruin. Had these Cockney book-
makers been in a less hurry, what a store of
interesting matter they could have collected.
Had one of them asked a Glenorchy man to tell
him something of the history of the old castle,
he would very likely have started at the beginning, and told him the story of the gallant
Knight Templar who, inspired with a holy
purpose, went abroad to take part in the wars
of the crusades in Spain, and how during his
long absence his good lady erected that great
fortress. Perhaps then he might have narrated
the well-authenticated legend of how Loch Awe
itself was formed by the overflowing of a little
spring on Ben Cruachan, which was usually
covered by a stone, and how Duncan Ban
MacIntyre hunted the deer and sung songs on
the slopes of Ben Dorain. If there is still an
Englishman thirsting to become famous by
writing a really attractive book on the Highlands, I would say to him, almost in the very
words of the genial *Mr. Punch*, "Go to Loch
Awe side at your earliest leisure, provide yourself with a well-filled flask of real ' Ardbeg'
and a snuff-box, write down all the stories you
hear, regarding the absolute truth of the most
improbable of which every Glenorchy man will
give his affidavit, and unless you are too clever
or a fool your *magnum opus* is as good as written,
and you may at once imagine yourself as good
as famous !"

There is one story which I shall save him the
trouble of writing, and which it is my intention
to give here. He has the consolation of knowing that one stone taken from a good-sized cairn
does not make it much smaller. Mr. Smith is
welcome to the other stones with my kindest
regards.

At a period when all the clans considered
themselves the greatest, and every chief the
most powerful, it would be only courteous that I
should describe Sir Colin Campbell, of Lochow,
as the most distinguished of the Highland chiefs.
He was the second son of Sir Duncan Campbell,
ancestor of the present ducal family of Argyll,

and his possessions extended over a large part of
the ancient district of Lorn. The Campbells
had ever the reputation of acting on the principle of "keeping what they have, and taking
what they can," and this may account for this
second son being so much better provided for
than the majority of the younger sons of whom
we read. At this time the long-continued
struggle between the supporters of the Cross
and the Crescent was raging with great fury in
Spain, and the order of Knight Templars had
established itself in Scotland, having opened an
hospital in Lothian, known as that of St. Ger-
mains. To this order of knight-errants many of
the most daring of the young Scots cavaliers
connected themselves, men who were ready to
draw their swords in support of a cause which
presented such easy opportunities of gaining
fame and honour and also, what was more
frequently found, a soldier's grave. Of this
body of gentlemen soldiers Sir Colin was a
member. It is not known what prompted him
to take this step—some say that it was because
of his love of adventure, while others assert
that his estates were embarrassed, and he chose
to go abroad for a time to improve his position.
Be that as it may, we may safely assume that
he was not likely to lose sight of his own personal interests, and that in going to Spain to
fight the Moors he had something more substantial in view than mere glory. Of the latter,
tradition says that he gained a great store, and
the memory of his warlike deeds liveth to this
day. He arranged that his lady during his
absence was to manage the affairs of the estate,
and, as the sequel shows, he could not have
chosen a more prudent factor.

As time rolled on the wealth of the family
increased, and the happy idea suggested itself to
Lady Glenorchy that, in anticipation of her
lord's home-coming, she should erect a grand
and stately castle, which would not only be
pleasing to Sir Colin, but would add dignity to
the family name for all time to come. The
work was at once commenced, and when completed the castle of Kilchurn was one of the
largest and most powerful fortresses in the
land.

During all this time no news had been received from the absent knight. Six years had
passed since he went abroad, and even the most
patient of wives might be excused for growing
a little impatient under the circumstances. At
first she had excused this neglect on the ground
that his heart was so much occupied in furthering the cause of the Cross that there was not
one little corner left for her. As the silence
was not broken, and it became at last clear to
her that the Cross had taken up its abode their
permanently, the good lady became a little des-

consolate, and felt that she was being rather badly treated. She was strengthened in this belief by a neighbouring chief, MacCorquodale, who, out of pure sympathy for the lonely lady, did not hesitate to say that Sir Colin's neglect was really "too bad." He was not an obtrusive person, and did not interfere much in other people's affairs, but he sometimes went the length of remarking that if he had been Sir Colin, and was blessed with such a beautiful and loving wife, not to speak of other desirable considerations, he would not have left her to lead such a lonely and cheerless life. Mr. MacCorquodale was a kind hearted old gentleman, and did not know how to flatter a lady, yet he condescended on various occasions to make this remark, while the fair object of his compliment did not pretend even to doubt the sincerity of his statement. In fact, the gallant chief of the Mac-Corquodale clan was at length of the opinion that the lady was rather pleased to hear him repeat it, and he was of too courteous a disposition not to humour her in such a trifling matter. It must not, of course, he imagined for one moment that he could, under any circumstances,

take the place of Sir Colin in her affections, or even hope that at some future time he could have all this love and beauty for himself.

It is difficult at times to account for a lady's whims, but, occasionally, they are more easy to understand than the puzzle of fifteen. The charming lady Glenorchy had now taken to "sighing," which, I fancy, was a sure sign that she was not quite well. Some people, who were learned in such matters, said that the trouble arose from the heart. It is not generally known what MacCorquodale thought, but as the symptoms were somewhat alarming he became a frequent visitor to the castle, and it was remarked that when he departed the sufferer appeared greatly improved in health, and the sighing was not quite so severe. This was usually explained by the genial atmosphere which his very presence created wherever he went. Nothing could excel or disturb his good nature. As an instance of this it may be mentioned that he has been known to sheath his dirk in the body of a menial for some trifling neglect and then spend the afternoon with the disconsolate lady, assuring her that Sir Colin's behaviour was "quite too bad!"

(To be concluded).

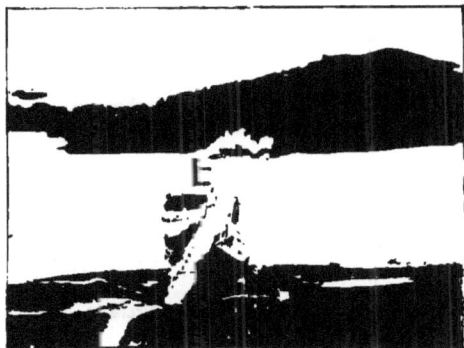

LOCH AWE.

KING ROBERT THE BRUCE IN KINTYRE.

By the DUKE OF ARGYLL, K.T.

MARK well that cove, for once of yore
  A boat was seen to beat her way
Coming through storm at close of day
  Until her bows had kissed the shore.

Then, leaping from the stranded bark,
  And moving up the copse-wood brae,
  A knight was seen to stride away
Until he vanished in the dark.

In one near opening of the wood
  Where wattled hazels of the time
  Kept out the rain of windy clime,
Quick stepping to the door he stood.

With courteous yet commanding air
  He asked the way to further shore:
  He asked for this, he asked no more,
Nor sought for rest or shelter there.

The farmer, though of humble lot,
  Looked at the king without surprise,
  Read all his meaning in his eyes,
With noble manners of the Scot.

" Sir knight, the moorlands you must cross
  Are high and bare—no friendly trees
  To break the blast of ocean seas,
With swollen streams and treacherous moss.

" My house is poor, but yet the bed
  Of heather and the blazing fire
  Are better than the shrieking choir
Of stormy spirits overhead."

"Scant time have I," the knight replied :
"You know the troubles of our land,
And how we're fighting hand to hand
'Gainst England, upon Scotland's side.

"Nor yet has fortune lent her smiles :
Until she does I cannot rest :
And now I go to farthest west
To rouse the clansmen of the Isles."

"No boat, Sir Knight, can cross the sea
Until the storm has passed away ;
It will have passed by break of day,
Then gladly I'll be guide to thee."

And so the Scot and Norman knight,
On middle floor around the fire,
Communed and slept in far Kintyre
Until the morning broke in light.

Then when the peaks of Arran stood
In cold dark grays against the sky,
More slowly drifted clouds on high,
More gently swayed the feathery wood.

Up pressed the two, without a stop,
Through tangled thickets of the hill,
Breasting its roughness with a will
Until, ere noon, they reached the top.

Beneath them the vast ocean lay,
Still heaving with a troubled breast ;
And many a wave with angry crest
Ran foaming on each rock and bay.

To north the scattered clouds had clung
Round lofty Jura's mountain line ;
Whilst silver vapours, thin and fine,
O'er hills of Islay softly hung.

And southward in broad fields of light,
In dazzling shimmers of the sun,
The Antrim coast in dark had won
The nearest hailings of their sight.

And chiefly did the Rathlin Isle
Seem close below them in the clear,
And as the knight perceived it near
He seemed to greet it with a smile.

Then, resting on broad-hilted blade,
Addressed his comrade of the day :
"Good friend, you've kindly led my way
Now when my fortunes are in shade.

"'Tis true thou dost not know my name
Nor hinted thou didst care to know,
With such as thou 'tis always so ;
All noble natures are the same.

"Nor did I tell thee all I meant,
Nor, closely, where I seek to go :
To hide, to wander to and fro
Till better days, I now am bent.

"My life of venture far and wide
Has taught me care, for fear of wile
Not from the Scots of leal Argyle
Yet still I lean to caution's side.

"I told thee what I seek alone :
With Edward's claims I know no truce :

Start not, good friend, I am the Bruce,
And I shall sit on Scotland's throne.

"The levies he has brought afield
Will melt like sun in western gale,
But our proud spirit shall not fail,
Again I'll raise the sword and shield.

"In that lone isle below us, now,
Hid in some hut beside the shore,
I'll bide my time, come out once more,
And wear the crown I held at Scone.

"I tell thee what, in visions seen,
Upholds me oft in hopeless hour ;
I know that I shall break the power
That Scotland's curse so long has been."

Then bowed the Scot, the son of Kay,
And hailed his comrade as his king:—
"Would I could wait beneath thy wing,
To lift old Scotland's Standard high."

"Come thou no further, friendly man,
I need no guide to what is seen,
Tell then none else where thou hast been
Until thou seest me in the van."

And when the king's recoming sail
Had brought him to his great return
And when he won at Bannockburn
He well remembered Ugadale.

The land that bore that sheltering roof,
Their rocks, their shore, their shingly cove,
In token of his kingly love,
Were chartered for Mackay's behoof.

For near six hundred years that land
Has held his children's children well :
Still o'er and o'er they love to tell
Of Bruce's foot-steps on its strand.

Nor thus alone can they approach
So nearly to those ancient days ;
For full accoutred on the ways
They're plaided with a noble brooch,

Such as were made in elder time,
Which Bruce had given to their sire
With coral, pearl, and crystal fire,
In memory of that morning climb.

And on that spot of parting ways,
Where Robert Bruce and proud Mackay
Had stood in light of ocean sky
A stone still marks heroic days.

THE UGADALE BROOCH.

J. LINDSAY MACKAY, M.A., LL.B.

WINNER OF THE "FRASER-MACKINTOSH PRIZE."

MR. J. LINDSAY MACKAY is a native of Glasgow, his father being Mr. George H. Mackay, accountant to the Savings' Bank, and a life-member of the Clan Mackay Society. Mr. Mackay was educated at the High School and Glasgow University, where, in addition to class prizes, he took the degrees of M.A. and LL.B. Although by profession a lawyer, Mr. Mackay has many tastes, having already earned considerable renown in the pleasant fields of music and literature. His favourite study, however, is music, and he has composed a large number of songs, part-songs, and pianoforte pieces, a collection of which will, I hope, be given to the public in the near future. He has also conducted several important musical societies in Glasgow, and is organist in Langside Free Church. Mr. Mackay is perhaps best known to the general public by his popular operetta, "Prince and Pedlar," and the Opera "Natalie," which have been performed with great success in various parts of the kingdom, and also in Australia and America. In connection with these Mr. Mackay has received flattering notices in the press, and handsome offers from London firms to publish his work. As an example of his versatility, I may mention that he not only composes the music for his pieces, but also the libretto, which usually takes the form of verse. Indeed, it may be truly said that he is gifted in a special degree with the poetical faculty as well as the musical. Mr. Mackay is very popular among the members of his clan, and on all social occasions he accompanies the singers at the piano, and renders other services to the society. The spirited air to which Miss Annie Mackay's beautiful song, "Lord Reay's Welcome," is sung was composed by the subject of our sketch. The splendid melody which has just gained the "Fraser-Mackintosh Prize" is well worthy of his reputation, and is sure to become popular among Highlanders. It has been said of Highlanders that all are born with the spirit of music and poetry in them, and that while a few possess the gift of giving suitable expression to their feelings, the greater number die with the music in their hearts. Mr. Mackay is undoubtedly one of those who soon found expression to his song, for his tastes lay in the direction of music from his earliest years. To him it is no undertaking to write a melody; he composes quickly and easily. As an instance of the rapidity with which he writes, I may mention that he composed the beautiful air to which the "Welcome to Lord Reay" is sung, and set it to four-part harmony, in one evening. Personally, Mr. Mackay is of the most kindly and obliging disposition. He is ever ready to render a service to a friend, whether it be to assist at a concert, to compose a melody to a song, or to conduct an orchestra. Nothing in the way of music comes amiss to him. Mr. Mackay belongs to the Reay country branch of the clan, and it is pleasant to know that the Mackays still cherish that love for song and music for which they were so famous in the days of Rob Donn and Iain Dall. In this respect it may be said of Mr. J. L. Mackay that he acts up to the spirit of the Ossianic injunction —"Leau gu dlùth ri cliù do shinnsir" (Follow closely the fame of your fathers).

Cambuslang.   CHARLES MACKAY.

OUR MUSICAL PAGE.

A SONG OF CLANRANALD.

THE following stirring and popular song—*Tha tigh'nn fodham éiridh*—is one of many composed in praise of *Ailein Deary*, red Allan, chief of Clanranald, and the part he took in the historic rising of 1715. The author of the song is *Iain mac Dhùghaill 'ic Lachainn*, and it was the proud boast of Boswell, the biographer of Johnson, that he could sing one verse of this ancient ditty.

Allan, chief of Clanranald, stands out, not only in the impassioned lays of the bards, but in the annals of the times, as the *beau-idéal* of a Highland chief. At an early age he was transferred from Castle Tirrim, the seat of the clan, to the island of Uist, and placed under the care of his brother-in-law, Macdonald of Benbecula. He was carefully trained, considering the turbulent times, and the steady discipline of his youth exercised a powerful influence over him throughout life. He was reputed to be "gentle, courteous even to the humblest of his people, and warm-hearted, and filled with a high sense of honour which rose superior to any feelings of egotism or mere self-interest." A devoted adherent of the Stuarts, he and his brother-in-law, at the head of five hundred followers, joined Claverhouse in the Braes of Lochaber, and took an active part in the Battle of Killiecrankie, 1689. Here Claverhouse fell, and his successor, Colonel Cannon, being quite unable to retain the clans together, young Clanranald and his brother-in-law returned to Uist. A few years later the Government, by very questionable means, succeeded in bringing the hostile chiefs into comparative submission, and garrisons and forts were established among the more refractory clans. A strong party from Fort-William was put in possession of Castle Tirrim, where they remained until a short time previous to the insurrection of 1715. So keenly did the spirited Clanranald feel the presence of these soldiers in the family stronghold, and despairing of seeing another opportunity to draw his sword in favour of the legitimate king, that he determined to forsake his native country and seek employment in France. He was well received at the French Court, and was given a commission under the Duke of Berwick. In France he distinguished himself in many engagements. After the brilliant victory of Almanza, Clanranald was left on the field covered with wounds. Fortunately, a search party found him and had him conveyed to a country house in the vicinity, where he was carefully nursed. During his convalescence he became acquainted with the lady whom he afterwards married Penelope MacKenzie, daughter of Colonel MacKenzie, at one time Governor of Tangiers. She accompanied Clanranald to Uist, where for some years they lived in retirement. About this time, 1715, another insurrection was planned in favour of the Stuarts, and *Ailean Muideartach* was among the first to be involved in it, "although his better judgment must have shown clearly how utterly hopeless and disappointing the result was likely to be." There can be little doubt Clanranald had a presentiment of coming disaster, for after crossing from Uist to Moidart he gave secret instructions to one of his followers to set Castle Tirrim on fire immediately after his departure for the seat of war. "As might be expected, the follower was loath to perform the task, and ventured to expostulate with his chief; but the latter removed his scruples by representing that the building was likely to fall into the hands of the Government troops again, who, upon their second visit, would certainly show little mercy to the district. 'Besides,' he gloomily added, 'I shall never come back again,—*cha till mise gu bràth tuilleadh*,—and it is better that our old family seat should be given to the flames than forced to give shelter to those who are about to triumph over our ruin.'" The deed was faithfully carried out, for Clanranald had scarcely reached Glenfinnan when Castle Tirrim was in flames, and became the sad ruin it at present remains. Clanranald and Glengarry mustered nine hundred Macdonalds between them, and marched under the Earl of Mar to Sheriffmuir. As is well known, the action that day was indecisive. This is how the old song puts it—[*]

> " There's some say that we wan,
>   And some say that they wan,
>   And some say that nane wan at a', man ;
>   But ae thing I'm sure, that at Sheriff-muir
>   A battle there was that I saw man."

The same song makes reference to Glengarry and Clanranald being in the heat of the engagement, with Drummond of Logie Almond, and proceeds—

> " Strathmore and Clanranald cried still, ' Advance, Donald !'
>   Till both of these heroes did fa', man ;
>   For there was sic hashing, and broadswords a-clashing,
>   Brave Forfar himsel' got a claw, man."

Clanranald's forebodings proved true. He was

---

[*] "Songs of Scotland prior to Burns," page 62.

hit on the chest by one of the enemies' bullets, and was carried away in a dying condition to another part of the field. His body was afterwards carried to Drummond Castle, and there, amid the lamentations of his devoted clansmen, was consigned to the dust.

"The Macdonalds," says the historian, "did act the part of men that are resolute and brave under the command of their chief, who, for his good parts and genteel accomplishments, was looked upon as the most gallant and generous young gentleman among the clans—maintaining a splendid equipage, keeping a just deference to the people of all sorts, void of pride or ill-humour. He performed the part of one that knew the part of a complete soldier."

The able writer of that fascinating work, "Moidart; or, Among the Clanranalds," to which I am indebted for much that precedes, concludes his sketch of this gallant chief as follows:—"The Macdonalds returned to their native hills, utterly disheartened at the calamity which had overtaken them. The evil news having preceded them, filled their friends among the Isles and in the Rough Bounds (*Garbh-chriochan*) with the deepest sorrow. Perhaps the gloom weighed heavier on Moidart than anywhere else, for the blackened, ruined walls of Castle Tirrim, and the sad circumstances under which they became so, impressed more vividly on the natives the irreparable loss which had come on the whole clan by the death of their brave and gallant chief. He left no issue, and with him terminated the direct line of the Clanranald succession."

The song from which the following verses are taken will be found complete in *The Beauties of Gaelic Poetry* and several other collections of Gaelic song

FIONN.

AILEAN MUIDEARTACH—ALLAN, LAIRD O' MOIDART.

Translation by MALCOLM MACFARLANE.

KEY G. *With spirit.*

Is ged a bhiodh tu fada ua n,
Gu'n eireadh suund 'us aigne orm
'Nuair chluinniun sgeul a b' aite leam
Air gaisgeach nan gniomh euchdach

Gur sgiobair ri là gaillinn thu
A sheòladh cuan nam marannan,
A bheireadh long gu calachan
Le spionnadh glac do threun-fhear.

Tha sgeul beag eil' a dhearbhadh leat,
Gur sea'gair sithne 'n garbhlaich thu,
Le d' chuilbhear caol nach dearmadach
Air dearg-ghreidh nan ceann eutrom.

B'e sud an leòghann aigearnach—
'Nuair nochdadh tu do bhardealan,
Lamh dhearg 'us long, 'us bradanan,
'Nuair lasadh meamn 'nad sudann.

Thae times when he was far awa'
Across the seas at war, an' a'
His fame for deeds o' daurin', O,
Was ringing a' thro' Moidart

His was the skill o' sailin' O ;
When tempests were prevailin' O,
And waves the bark assailin', O.
He steered us safe tae Moidart.

He hunted aye sae keenly, O,
And brocht down aye sae cleanly, O,
The stags and hinds sae queenly, O,
Amang the wilds o' Moidart.

When he spread forth his pennon, O,
Abune his warlike men an' a',
His foes were dauntit, kennin' a'
The red-hand badge o' Moidart.

TO CORRESPONDENTS.

All Communications, on literary and business matters, should be addressed to the Editor, Mr. JOHN MACKAY, 17 Dundas Street, Kingston, Glasgow.

—⊙—

TERMS OF SUBSCRIPTION.— The CELTIC MONTHLY will be sent, post free, to any part of the United Kingdom, Canada, the United States, and all countries in the Postal Union—for one year, 4s.

THE CELTIC MONTHLY.

OCTOBER, 1893.

CONTENTS.

TO OUR READERS.

WE trust that our readers are satisfied with our efforts to further improve the magazine. The contents of this number may be safely left to speak for themselves, and we presume the most satisfactory assurance which we can give our readers is that we expect to make the *C.M.* even more attractive in the near future. The Highland Societies and Shinty Clubs are now commencing the work of the season, and in our next issue we shall give short reports of their proceedings during the month. We regret that owing to the present pressure on our space we have been unable to give our "Notes and Queries" page, and other interesting contributions, but these will find a place in our next.

We trust that those of our readers who have not yet forwarded their annual contributions (1 post free) will do so at once, so that we may be able to make up a complete list of subscribers.

THE MÒD AT OBAN.

As a full report of this great Celtic Gathering appears in another place, it is not our intention here to do more than make a few general observations on the events of the day. The Mòd was a splendid success, and in every respect an improvement upon that of last year. The attendance was larger, the competitors were more numerous, and the talent was better than on the former occasion.

To an enthusiastic president and an energetic committee is mainly due the chief credit of the success of the meeting. We are greatly delighted with the hearty interest which LORD ARCHIBALD CAMPBELL manifests in the literature and music of our mountain-land, and his thoroughly Highland spirit. There is no half-heartedness about him, and Highlanders will like him the better for it. We were also glad to see one Highland M.P. present—Dr. Donald MacGregor. This reminds us to remark that surely the MEMBER FOR THE COUNTY could have spared one day from his Caithness shooting to countenance the great Gaelic event of the year in his own constituency. For our part we are glad that an attempt is to be made to hold the Mòd next year in PERTHSHIRE. If it is not taken up there enthusiastically no one need again complain of its being held in Oban. The offer has been made and it lies with Perthshire-men to accept or reject it. The EVENING CONCERT was a fitting termination to a successful gathering. Miss Jessie N. MacLachlan was in splendid voice, and was accorded a hearty reception. The other soloists acquitted themselves well, Miss Lizzie Mackay's rendering of the beautiful laments being worthy of special commendation. The combined CHOIRS sang with great taste and power, and gave an example of the capabilities of our Gaelic song when properly directed. The SUPPER after the concert was an enjoyable function, and Lord Archibald Campbell's declaration that he had had "many scrimmages with the War Office regarding the Highland Regiments, and that he was prepared at any moment to renew the contest should occasion demand," was received with loud applause. In this his lordship will find many supporters. We had also the usual "HIGHLAND HONOURS." Now, we confess we are altogether sceptical about these so-called "honours." To our mind they are not Highland. Logan, in the "Scottish Gael," refers to a custom among *Celtic Societies* which somewhat resembles this, but does not mention several features which are obnoxious in the variety with which we are at present afflicted. The custom, as presently practised, is not pretty, and we are not disposed to accept it as natural to our Highland soil without sufficient proof of its authenticity. Can any of our readers quote any reliable authority in which this custom is described as of Highland origin, or any work of last century in which it is referred to? The matter is worth looking into, and until we are satisfied on this point, we refuse to accept in good faith these so-called "Celtic Honours."

OUR NEXT ISSUE.—We will present our readers with a life-like plate portrait of Mr. Allan Cameron of Lundavra, Athlone, a chieftain of the Clan Cameron, and one of the most popular members of the historic clan. Portraits will also appear of Messrs. Robert Fergusson, Stirling (held over from this issue); George M. Sutherland, F.S.A. Scot., Wick; and Duncan MacLean, Manchester, the well known poet. We also expect to publish an interesting romance by Mr. John Mackay, Hereford, dealing with the expulsion of the Danes from the Reay country, and illustrated with views of places of historic interest in the land of the MacKays. A number of other illustrated contributions will also appear.

AN COMUNN GAIDHEALACH.

The Mod, or Gathering, at Oban.

THIS great Gaelic Gathering was held in the Argyllshire Gathering Hall, Oban, on Tuesday, 12th September. Lord Archibald Campbell occupied the chair, and among those present we noticed the following :—Lady Archibald Campbell and daughter; Provost MacIsaac, Oban; Campbell of Dunstaffnage; Rev. Messrs. MacDougall, Duror, and MacInnes, Oban; Dr. MacGregor, M.P.; Professor Mackinnon of the Celtic Chair; Rev. Dr. John MacLean; Rev. Dr. Stewart, Nether-Lochaber; Bishop Smith; Rev. Father MacDonald, Dahbrog, Uist; Dr. MacDiarmid, Glasgow; Dr. MacNicoll, Dalmally; Dr. N. M. Campbell, Oban; Mr. Magnus MacLean, M.A., Glasgow; Mr. A. Mackenzie Mackay, London; Miss Annie Mackay, Bardess to the Clan Mackay Society; Mr. John Campbell, Ledaig; Mr. Alexander MacDonald, Thedford, Ont., Canada; Mr. Donald Mackay, Ledaig; Ex. Bailie Stuart, Inverness; Mr. Robert Ferguson, Stirling; Mr. John Campbell, Secretary; Mr. John Mackintosh, Asst. Secretary.

The following were the judges —For reading and reciting—Messrs. Henry Whyte ('Fionn') Glasgow; Malcolm MacFarlane, Paisley; and Dr. MacNicol, Dalmally. Sgeulachd—Rev. James MacDougall, Duror; and Rev. D. MacInnes, Oban. Prose and Poetry—Rev. Dr. Stewart, Nether Lochaber; and Messrs. D. Reid, Glasgow; and M. MacFarlane. Music—Principal MacBeth, of the Athenæum College of Music, Glasgow; and Messrs. Whyte and MacFarlane.

The chairman, in opening the proceedings, referred to the success which had attended their efforts, and was satisfied that the present gathering already promised so well. The Mod, next year, might possibly be held in some other locality, but no matter where held it would have his hearty support. He then announced the first competition.

The following is the prize list : — *Gaelic Sgeulachd* — 1 ("Fionna-Chointeach"), J. MacFadyen, Glasgow; 2 ("Gleamm-ach"), A. Stewart, Glenlyon. *Translation from Gaelic* — 1 ("Carnbath"), Alexander Stewart, police station, Polmont; 2 ("Skeena"), Miss J. MacGregor, Kilmore, Oban. *Writing to Gaelic dictation*—1, John Black, Oban. *Gaelic Prose Competition* - 1 ("Bhruth-Chorean"), J. MacFadyen, Glasgow; 2 ("Conal"), Neil Ross, Glendale. *Gaelic Poetry*—1 ("Conal"), Neil Ross, Glendale; 2 ("Garbhag-hath"), J. MacFadyen, Glasgow; 3 ("Monach"), A. Stewart, Glenlyon.

Gaelic Recitation (first prize, £2; second, £1).—1, Mr. Neil Ross; 2, Mr. Arch. Munn, Oban.

Gaelic Reading (first prize £2; second, £1).—1, Mr. Munn; 2, Mr. Neil Ross.

Choral Competition for Juniors (first prize, £4; second, £2).—1, Oban Junior Gaelic Choir; 2, St. Columba (R.C.) School Choir, Oban.

Solo Competition for Juniors (two prizes of £1 1s. offered by St. Columba Gaelic Choir, Glasgow).—1, Miss Ella Lawrie, Ballachulish; 2, James Wilson, Jun., Lismore.

Choral Competition for Seniors (first prize, £10; second, £7 10s.) This event was very keenly contested, and it was only after repeated trials that the judges decided to award the first prize to the Glasgow St. Columba Choir, the second to Oban, and a special prize of £5 from Lord Archibald Campbell to the Ballachulish Choir.

Solo Competition for Seniors (first prize, Oban Burgh gold Medals and £1; 2nd £1, 3rd 10s.).—Seven ladies and twelve gentlemen took part in this competition. Ladies— 1, Miss M. A. MacKeehnie, Oban (last year's winner); 2. Miss M. MacKenzie, Morven; 3, Miss Margaret Mac-Donald, Glasgow. Gentlemen— 1, K. D. MacKenzie, Glasgow, (last year's winner); 2, Peter M. MacDonald, Glasgow; 3, Donald MacCallum, Oban.

Lady Archibald Campbell presented the prizes to the successful competitors, after which Lord Archibald referred to the difficult duty which the judges had to perform, and how necessary it was that those who had not won prizes should be

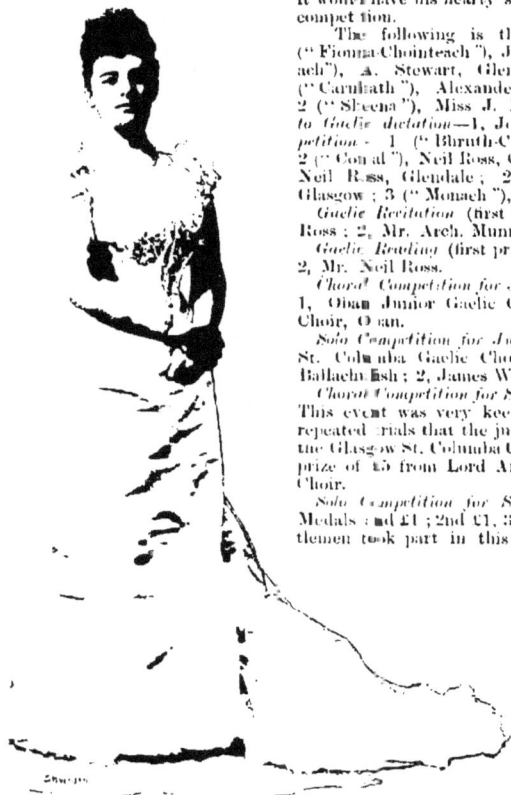

MISS J. N. MACLACHLAN. Gaelic Vocalist.

satisfied with the results, as the decisions were only arrived at after careful consideration. He hoped, now that his term of office had expired, that they would find a president as Highland in spirit as he was. Rev. Dr. Stewart intimated that Miss MacDonell of Glengarry had offered a prize of three guineas for competition at next Mòd for psalm singing in Gaelic, repeating the line in the old style.

ANNUAL BUSINESS MEETING.

This meeting took place immediately after the Mòd. Lord Archibald Campbell presided, and there was a good attendance of members. The Secretary and Treasurer gave very favourable reports of the work of the past year. An interesting discussion took place as to the advisability of holding the Gathering next year at Perth or Inverness, and it was finally decided to make enquiries, and should it be found that no sufficient inducement was forthcoming the secretaries were empowered to report to the executive, and hold the Mòd in Oban as before. The election of office-bearers followed. Lord Archibald Campbell was re-elected president, and Mr. John Mackay, C.E., J.P., Hereford ; Dr. MacGregor, M.P. ; and Mr. Birkmyre, M.P., were added to the list of vice-presidents. The other office-bearers were re-appointed.

EVENING CONCERT.

A grand Gaelic concert was held in the Gathering Hall, every seat being filled long before the advertised time to commence. The principal feature of the programme was the rendering of several songs by the combined choirs, under the leadership of Mr. Archibald Ferguson, and the spirit and taste with which these melodies were given evoked the enthusiasm of the audience. Miss Jessie N. MacLachlan rendered several songs in her usual excellent style, and solos were also given by Misses M. A. MacKechnie, Lizzie Mackay, Mary MacDonald, Kate MacDonald (with Clàrsach accompaniment) ; and Mr. Angus MacDonald, Glencoe, delighted the audience with his spirited rendering of "Gabhaidh sinn an rathad mòr."

PRESENTATIONS.

During the course of the evening Lord Archibald Campbell presented Mr. Archibald Ferguson, Conductor, Glasgow St. Columba Church Gaelic Choir, with a conductor's baton, which bore the following inscription—"To Archibald Ferguson, for invaluable services in the cause of Celtic music, from the President at Oban Mòd, 1893."

The members of the Inveraray Pipe Band, whose services were much appreciated during the day, were each presented with a silver medal by the executive of the Association.

Mr. John Campbell, Secretary, was also the recipient of a drinking cuach from his lordship.

The members of the executive and friends supped together in the Royal Hotel, Lord Archibald occupying the chair. Speeches were given and toasts drunk, and a very enjoyable time was spent. And so ended this eventful day !

SHIELDS IN THE SCOTTISH GAELIC KINGDOM IN THE SECOND AND THIRD CENTURIES.

By Lieut.-Colonel CHARLES STEWART ("Tigh'n Duin"), author of "The Gaelic Kingdom in Scotland and its Celtic Church ;" "Killin Collection of Poetry and Music," &c.

WHEN the Gaels (also known as Fion or Scot) settled in the Irish and Scottish Gaeldoms they brought with them the knowledge of iron, its workings and uses.

Their armourers were exceedingly expert in tempering steel and making it into swords and other weapons. The most noted of these armourers was the much approved *Luin*. He made a sword for Fingal which became so notable that it was styled, when spoken of, as "MacLuin," or the son of Luin. There would be no difficulty in getting ore, as there are places over the Highlands where it is palpable that it was extracted as for instance in Glenlochy, Breadalbane ; whilst the site of the armoury for working it is within a hundred yards from my own door. As I have already shown,[*] people in that age were in such comfortable circumstances that they could afford to buy them, and as their lives depended on their swords and shields there can be no doubt that, as to *swords* at anyrate the steel would soon replace the bronze. Indeed it may have done so in great part before their coming.

The shields were in a different category, as they were not only beautifully designed, but were most serviceable weapons. I have no doubt that with regard to them the bronze age considerably overlapped with the iron. In later eras, when Norman feudalism and other "isms" had done their evil work, the people could not afford to buy the best, and wood and leather were much used ; but, as will be seen, the shields of the era we are having in view were, necessarily from the uses they were put to, made of metal. These uses also necessitated the bosses not being soldered or affixed to the shield, but that they should be forced out from the metal of the shield. Thus when seen at the back they looked like cups, and at the front like bosses. It is also most worthy of notice that when mentioned in the ancient Gaelic historical poems they are usually called *cupped* and not *bossed* shields. They were round in form, with a very strong margin and several circles, which had bosses varying in size and number within them. The middle boss was larger than the rest, and sometimes had a socket for a spike in it.

* Vol. I., page 68.

The Gaelic shield was known as the *Sgiath-bullach*, Anglice, the spotted ring, *ballach* being applied to these cups or bosses.

What showed great skill in the armourers was—

I.—That each principal shield had a sound of its own, easily recognised, especially by the Bards.

II.—That some of the bosses also had sounds of their own.

III.—That necessarily all the shields must have been in harmony.* These qualities, both in shields and special bosses, enabled the king and his leading champions to signal to the whole host, or part of it, in presence of the enemy. For instance, Cathmore's shield had seven bosses, each of which had its own sound, and whereby he could signal to his own force.

We now come to the uses that the shields were put to—

First—before all others—was the guarding of the warrior from the swords, spears, and other weapons of his opponents.

Second—Before starting on a campaign, for three nights the Bards sang the war-song in the hall of assembly, accompanied by the sounding of a shield.

Third—Fingal was in the habit of devolving the command on one of his chief champions for the first day of the fight. A few of these were selected, who then took their position on the top of a knoll, and sounded their shields with all their might, and on the chiefs of the Bards fell the duty of fixing upon the one whose shield sounded the loudest. This they could do, as each shield had its own sound.

Fourth—The great national shield was at such times hung up between spears, or two boughs of a tree, beside the commander's temporary abode. When the champion selected to lead on the first day failed in achieving more than a drawn battle, this shield was sounded to intimate to the host that the commander in-chief himself would lead on the morrow. Fingal, as was his wont, would have intervened sooner if there was any risk of a defeat, but as there was not he delayed so as to give the chosen leader every chance on that day.

Fifth—It was sounded as a warning before the battle commenced.

Sixth—During the advance, which was led by the Bards, chanting the march, occasionally the whole host broke in, striking their shields with furious battle-clang.

Seventh—On the defeat of the enemy the host were recalled from the pursuit by the sound of the shield.

* Vol. I., page 69.

Eighth- Cups from their shields were laid beside the warriors in their graves. Toscar and Ossian did so when raising a memorial stone to those killed in battle. It is not said that cups were also cut on the memorial stones, but it is certain that they were. These cup-marked stones and rocks are found over all parts of Britain inhabited by Celts, and it is our tradition that they were cut in honour of departed heroes. In Breadalbane, to my own knowledge, a cup-marked stone was almost invariably found near our burial circles. I had myself the satisfaction of opening a mound at Dalraoch, Fortingal, on which one of these stones had stood, and found therein the remains of a skeleton.* Sometimes it is a stone with one cup mark, as in this case, and sometimes it is a rock with a very large number of cups. The two finest specimens of this I have met with was at Craggantoll, in Breadalbane, and Almais Rock, in Yorkshire.

Then the term *bullach* is both applied to shields and cup-marked stones. The invariable tradition of the Gaels is, as just said, that the cups were in honour of departed heroes. When on stones singly, they must represent one exceptionally distinguished hero, and when on rocks in great numbers, they must represent many heroes fallen in battle in some spot near by them. My explanation of the wherefore of the cup marks is intelligible, and, I think, satisfactory to any Gael who knows his own country thoroughly, with its history, annals, traditions, customs, names of places, and monuments. This intelligibility is very different from planet-worship and other imaginary theories of the haziest kind. The Gaels had no worship of the heavenly bodies. There was a race in our Gaeldom before we Gaels who *did* worship the sun and moon. This, too, seems to be nearly all we have got about them. Indeed, as far as I know, the skeleton which I found in the mound at Bruach, Glenlyon,† is the only nearly perfect one which has yet been found.

The bossed shields and cup-marked stones are still more closely allied to each other by the type of design that characterises both of them. Thus we have a metal shield with but one circle of bosses at the circumference, and others with several concentric circles of alternate bosses and spaces from the centre to the circumference. One found at Harlech, in Wales, has a number of bosses irregularly placed within the centre circle, and seven concentric circles (but no bossed ones) from thence to the circumference.‡ We have also

* Proc. Soc. Antiq., Scot., 1883-84, p. 376.
† Proc. Soc. Antiq., Scot., 1884-85, p. 39.
‡ See "Stone Monuments," by Waring (1878), plate. 79

leathern shields with the same manner of circles and spaces, the bosses being represented by nails with brass knobs, and with spiral and interlaced patterns on the spaces, as well as various other devices—all of them, however, conformable to the circular and circulo-spiral type of design.* The finest specimens of cup-markings that I have seen are in the neighbourhood of Ilkley, Yorkshire. For instance, some single cups with one or more circular lines cut around them, and clusters of cups, with spiral lines entwining amongst them.

There are some who hanker after the mystic, and find all manner of superstition in these. I see nothing in them but an evidence of that sense of the beautiful and the heroic, which is so important a part of the idiosyncrasy of the Celt, and especially of the Gaelic Celt.

I have in my possession a very old family dagger, a Scotch-made "Andrea Fararra," which has a brass-plate at the end of the handle with the ancient arms of the Stewarts of Appin engraved on it. Underneath is a copy of it from a drawing made for me by my friend, Dr. Brigham, of London.

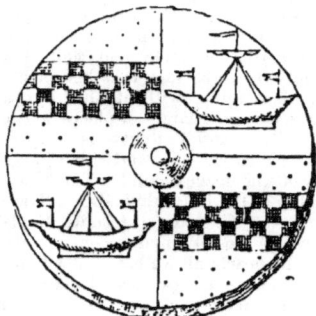

The execution of the original engraving shows how old it is. In each of two of the compartments we have a galley of Lorne. In other two we have the tesse cheque of the Appin Stewarts, representing the order in which they fought, and which seems to me to be a forestalling of our present mode of skirmishing. Then we have three compartments with cup marks. It is also interesting to state that the edges of this shield representative are dented, like those of one which had seen service

in the hands of a champion.† To have dents on the shield was honourable, to have it broken was looked upon as disgraceful. The Gael was from his infancy taught the use of the broadsword, and even so must it have been with regard to the shields, for unless he had the full knowledge and command of them he could not present the proper angle to receive the arrow in its flight, the spear in its cast, or the sword in its cut, and thus the shield would be broken. The most intensely beautiful use made of this cup marking is by Ossian, in a notable passage, in which he tells us that this earth is to pass away, leaving nought behind it but a mist, on which is recorded by cups the deeds of the good and mighty. The word he uses as to this mist is *ballach*, which we have seen was applied to cup marked rocks and stones, and also to shields. The cups on these represented during the existence of time, glorious deeds done on this earth, whilst those on the mist represented the same deeds when earth and earthly time had passed away for ever. Such at least was Ossian's wondrously beautiful conception, flowing from the Gael's sublime belief in the spirit's immortality. For it may be asked, "But who would be there to see these cups?" Who but those Gaels whom he believed would, when their "spirits," or "I ams," parted from their souls and bodies, pass into a heavenly region, not of mere contemplative idleness, but of glorious activity.

† Carried by Donald Stewart at Pinkie. 1547. See "Geneal. Stewarts of Appin," by J. H. J. Stewart and Col. Duncan Stewart (1880), p. 168.

CLAN MACKAY SOCIETY.—We have just received a cheque for £10 from Mr. John Mackay, C.E., J.P., Hereford, towards the clan Bursary Fund, for which truly handsome donation we beg to tender him our sincerest thanks. This is the third liberal contribution Mr. Mackay has made to this object.

A GAELIC AND ENGLISH CONCERT is to be held in the Assembly Rooms, Bath Street, on Friday, 6th October, in aid of the widow and orphans of the late J. Campbell, who was known to many Glasgow Celts. We hope there will be a large attendance.

THE GAELIC SOCIETY'S CONCERT takes place in the Lesser Waterloo Rooms, on Tuesday, 24th October.

NOTE.—As we go to press we observe that Archdeacon Sinclair, has just been appointed a chaplain-in-ordinary to the Queen.

QUERY.

MAC CRINDLE.—To what clan do the Mac Crindles belong? I have been told they belong to the clan Ranald—the name being a corruption of *Mac Raonuill*, or Mac Ranald.

A. RONALD.

* These, of course, are of a later period than the 3rd and 4th centuries, but, doubtless, the reproduction of the older designs.

JOHN MACFADYEN, GLASGOW.

THERE are few Celts in Glasgow better known to our countrymen than the genial author of *An t-Eileanach*. His presence is a familiar one at our Highland gatherings, and when he mounts the platform to sing one of his amusing songs, in his own inimitable way, his reception is always hearty and appreciative. Mr. John MacFadyen was born at Balivullen, in the Island of Mull, on 20th May, 1850. When about eighteen years of age he removed to Ardrishaig, where he entered the service of Mr. Angus Mac-Laine, late of Fascadale. It was at concerts held there, presided over by Provost Reid, that Mr. MacFadyen made his *début* as an exponent of our sweet Gaelic songs. His next appearance was at the Saturday evening Gaelic concerts in the Crown Halls, Glasgow, which were conducted under the auspices of the old *Comunn Gaidhealach Ghlaschu*. The great success which attended those splendid concerts was principally due to the enthusiasm and patriotism of Mr. Duncan Sharp, who not only originated the concerts, but for several years presided over them with much acceptance. Mr. Sharp's valuable services in the early days of the Gaelic revival in Glasgow will not soon be forgotten. In connection with these concerts, which were afterwards continued in the Assembly Rooms, Bath Street, where they are still held, it is interesting to remember the names of several popular singers, such as Donald Graham (now in Oban),

James Johnstone (Craignish), Malcolm MacFarlane (of Bonawe), Murdoch MacRae (Lochalsh), James Sinclair (now at Furnace), Hugh Stewart (Partick), and Pipe-Major A. R. MacLeod (London), who took part with John MacFadyen in these weekly gatherings. In 1890, Mr. MacFadyen published a handsome volume, entitled *An t-Eileanach*, which contained some eighty Gaelic songs, poems, and readings. That the work was welcomed by Highlanders is evidenced by the fact that the large edition is already nearly exhausted. Mr. MacFadyen has for several years been an office-bearer in the Mull and Iona Association, the Gaelic Society of Glasgow, and other Highland Societies. It may be also mentioned that Mr. MacFadyen won the first prize for original Gaelic prose at the *Mòd* competition last year. A complimentary concert was held on 22nd February, 1892, in honour of the subject of our sketch, which was a great success. On that occasion Mr. D. R. Mackinnon, a brother bard, composed a Gaelic toast, which very aptly expresses the best wishes of Mr. MacFadyen's many friends, and with which we may fitly conclude this brief sketch :

"Slàinte gu'n robh aig gach neach,
'S aig an neach a thubhairt e,
'S gu ma pailt' e aig a' mhac
Thug a mach cuideachd sinn,
Saoghal fada dha co-dhiu,
Cliù dha 's gun deireas air,
'S gu ma fada 'seinn a chliùil
Ughdar an "Eileinich."

Glasgow.   ARCHIBALD SINCLAIR.

AM FRAOCH.

O, fàilt' air do bhadan
Is cùbhraidh na'n caineal,
O, fàilt' air do bhalain
'S do mheangain air raon ;
Tha 'chòisir bhinn ghreannar
A' gleusadh gu fonnar,

'S an trusganaibh samhraidh
Air gleannta mo ghaoil.

'S tu sgeadaich na 'n àilleachd,
Na fuar-bheannaibh àrda, —
Gheibh feudag'us tàrmachan
Blàs o gach gaoth ;
'S tu fàs leis a' mhìslean,

Air còmhnard nam frìthean,
'S gu 'n còmhlaich thu 'n dìthein,
Aig ìsleach nan caol.

Gur sòghar mar bhiadh thu,
Dh-eòin ruadha, 's do'n liath-chirc,
Tha dèidh aig an fhiadh ort
Air riasgaibh nam maol;
Gur guanach a dh-fhàs thu,
Gun saothair nan làmhan,
'S na cluaineagan fàsail
Tha nàdurra saor.

Thèid fleasgach do 'n chòmhlan,
'S tu 'm broilleach a chòta,
Bad ùrail mu 'm pròiseil,
An òigridh 's an t-aosd';
'Nuair cheanglas an ribhinn,
A dualan 's an t-sìoda,
'Toirt buaidh air gach riomhadh
Tha min ghasan fraoich.

Tha t' fhailcas a' dealradh,
'Am fior-uisg' na steallaire,
Ri 'n leum am breac tara-gheal
Gu meamnach ri d' thaobh;
Ni do bhàrr gorm mireag,
'An cuairteig na linne,
Le luath-shruth an fhirich
'S fo shile nan craobh.

Fo chaoin dhealt nan speuran,
'S an òg mhaduinn chèitein,
No 'lasadh nan slèitibh
Ri grèin air gach taobh;
Bidh seillein le cùram
A' deoghal do chùirnein,
'S tu neamhnaid is mùirniche
'N dùthaich nan laoch.

Tha mòran ga 'm buaireadh,
An inbhe nan uaibhreach,
'S tric cadal glè luaineach
Air cluasagan maoth;
De shòlas cha d' fhuair iad
'N àm dùsgadh a 'm bruadar,
Na gheibh mu do bhruachan
Am buachaille laogh.

JOHN MACFADYEN.

[Mr. MACFADYEN, was successful in gaining three prizes at the Oban Mòd. We have much pleasure in giving above the poem which gained second prize in that competition.]

THE CLAN MACLEAN GATHERING takes place in the Queen's Rooms, Glasgow, on Friday, 27th Oct., Col. Sir Fitzroy D. MacLean, Bart., Chief of the Clan, in the Chair.

WE REGRET that we have been compelled to hold over till next issue a patriotic poem by Neil MacDonald, New York, entitled : " The awakening of the Gael," continuation of the " Roll of the Reay Fencibles," and other interesting contributions.

PRIZE COMPETITIONS.

THROUGH the characteristic generosity of Mr. Charles Fraser-Mackintosh of Drummond, we are enabled to offer prizes for two competitions one in Gaelic and the other in English, so that all our readers may have an opportunity of competing. The prizes are as follows :—

Gaelic Prize.

I. One Guinea for the Best Original Gaelic Biographical Sketch of any of the following bards, with examples from their works :— Duncan Ban MacIntyre, Rob Donn Mackay, Alistair MacDonald, William Ross, Dugald Buchanan, Dr. MacLachlan of Rahoy; or, if the competitors prefer, they may write an essay upon any of the following subjects: "Gaelic Humorous Songs," "Patriotic Songs," or "Laments."

The papers must be original, and not mere translations of biographies or sketches which have already appeared in print.

English Prizes.

II. One Guinea for the Best Tradition (hitherto unpublished) relating to any part of the Highlands and Islands.

(Essays for the above competitions must not exceed 2000 words.)

Miss Katherine Mackay, Fort-William, Belfast, kindly offers a special prize of

III Five Shillings for the Best Unpublished Tradition Relating to the Reay Country. Not to exceed 1000 words.

Rules.—Any reader of the *Celtic Monthly* may compete. All compositions must be signed by a *nom-de-plume* only, each MS. being accompanied by a sealed envelope with the *nom de-plume* written on the outside, and enclosing a slip bearing the competitor's name and address. The competition papers will be examined by impartial and competent judges, whose award will be final. All manuscripts must reach the Editor of the *Celtic Monthly*, 17 Dundas Street, Kingston, Glasgow, not later than Wednesday, 1st November, 1893.

The prize papers will be published in the *Monthly*, as well as any of the unsuccessful compositions which may be deemed worthy of insertion.

JOHN CAMPBELL, LEDAIG, TESTIMONIAL.—We beg to acknowledge, with thanks, a contribution of 10s. towards this worthy object from Mr. Neil MacLeod, 22 Viewforth Gardens, Edinburgh.

No. 2.—GLENFINNAN.

WHILE few are doubtless prepared to to deny that the designation "brilliant blunder," as applied to the historic rising of '45, is but too true and expressive, the episode has still a wonderful fascination for the Celt, and the localities which were the scene of any of the leading incidents in that brief drama possess an attraction unimpaired by years, and awaken sentiments akin to awe and reverence. Such a place is the lonely Glenfinnan, where Prince Charlie raised his standard on the 19th August, o.s., 1745. On crossing from Borro-dale to Moidart Prince Charlie learned that the more loyal clans were mustering throughout the various districts. Landing at Glenuig, he was met by a crowd of the loyal natives, including some of the oldest men in the district—and such was their enthusiasm that eight of the oldest ceatharnaich danced a reel in the presence of the Prince—the spirited tune which put metal in the heels of those octogenarians being long afterwards known as *Ochd fir Mhùideart*—"The Eight Men of Moidart." The Prince then made his way to Kinlochmoidart, where he remained

for a few days. It having been arranged that the Prince was to meet the loyal chiefs with their clansmen at Glenfinnan, by the shores of Loch Sheil, he proceeded thither and anxiously waited the arrival of Lochiel and his Cameron men. When the Prince's patience was well nigh exhausted the sound of the bagpipes was heard, announcing the approach of the "gentle Lochiel" with a strong following—

"Their swords are a thousand, their bosoms are one.'

These brave men advanced in two lines of three men deep, while between the lines were a party of soldiers unarmed, taken at High Bridge, trophies of the first victory of the Jacobites. The Camerons were immediately followed by the MacDonalds of Keppoch. The Prince was so elated by the presence of these gallant Highlanders that he immediately declared open war against the Elector of Hanover, and the royal standard having been blessed by Bishop Hugh MacDonald, was unfurled to the breeze. The army sent up a shout which rent the air, and a hundred hills echoed applause. The standard is said to have been of silk and twice the size of an ordinary banner, and its colours were red, white, and blue. The Marquis of Tullibardine was favoured by unfurling this historic gonfalon and it was afterwards carried back by him to the quarters of the Prince, surrounded by a guard of fifty Camerons.

What a contrast Glenfinnan of to-day presents to what it must have been at that eventful period. Then all was life and activity, pipers playing, banners flying, chiefs and clansmen in battle array—

> " Fierce in their native hardiness of soul,
> True to imagined right beyond control ! "

Now in that glen silence reigns supreme. Low down in the plain, near the silver waters of Loch Shiel, stands the stately cenotaph to Prince Charles Edward Stuart, erected by Alex. MacDonald, Glenaladale, in 1825. The statue which surmounts the column, represents him looking up the glen for the Camerons. It bears the following inscription in Gaelic :—

" 'Fhir astair, ma's miann leat luaidh air sgeul ainmeil nan làitheau a threig, thig dlùth agus dean ùmlachd : So an t-àite anns an d'fhoillsich Prionnsa Teàrlach a Bhratach, 'n uair a sgaoil am fìrean òg a sgiathan a'm mor chùis 'nnma a chosnadh na rìoghachd a chaill 'athraichean, agus a thilg se e féin gun chòmhnadh gun charaid an uchd fìughantach nam Flath meamnach, 's uan laoch treuna a thogair éiridh gun athadh, a dhìol a chòrach no 'chall am beatha. Mar chnimhne air an Rìoghalachd an dìlseached agus an cruadal aons gach gàbhadh a lean ; Chaidh an Tùr so thogail leis an òg-nasal urramach Alastair Dòmhnullach, Triath Ghlinnealadail ; a chaochail Beatha an Dùn-eidionn, Bliadhna MDCCCXXV. An Tùs 'Aidh."

There is a similar inscription in Latin and English, the latter of which is as follows :—

"On the spot where Prince Charles Edward first raised his standard, on the 19th day of August, 1745, when he made the daring and romantic attempt to recover a throne, lost by the imprudence of his ancestors, this column was erected by Alexander Macdonald, Esq. of Glenaladale, to commemorate the generous zeal, the undaunted bravery, and the inviolable fidelity of his forefathers, and the rest of those who fought and bled in that unfortunate enterprise.· This pillar is now, alas ! also become the monument of its amiable and accomplished founder, who, before it was finished, died in Edinburgh on the 4th day of January, 1825, at the early age of twenty-eight years."

Glenfinnan is about 17 miles from Fort-William, but perhaps the easiest way to get there is by taking Mr. MacBrayne's steamer from Oban to Salen, Loch Sunart, and drive to Sheil-bridge Hotel, a distance of some four miles. About two miles from this hotel is the famous Castle Tirrim, once the stronghold of Clanranald, hoary with age and steeped in historic associations. A steamer sails from the Sheil Bridge end of Loch Sheil to Glenfinnan at the other, and in this way tourists have a splendid opportunity of visiting the various places of interest in the vicinity and gazing on the romantic scenery of the district.

THE INFLUENCE OF GAELIC MUSIC ON LOWLAND SONG.

By Malcolm MacFarlane.

IT is not any part of my purpose to show the influence of Gaelic music on the poetical thought and feeling of Lowland song. That subject is of too intangible a nature to be grappled with except by those who have gone deeply into the study of the music and song of the three races which inhabit the United Kingdom. My wish in this brief article is merely to draw attention to a field of research which, being mostly of a technical nature, offers comparatively little difficulty, is interesting in itself and worthy of more consideration than it has, so far as I am aware, hitherto received.

There is nothing more patent to those who understand Gaelic music and song than that there is a singular rhythmical correspondence between the words and the music. So much is this the case that we are forced to the conclusion that the poetical and musical styles of Gaelic song grew up together. In the name "Gaelic" I include Irish. The Irish and Scottish sections of Gaelic music have a great deal in common ; and it is impossible in many cases to say whether a tune belongs primarily to Ireland or to Scotland. At the same time, the one people have predilections for certain styles, while the other people have predilections for others quite different. For instance, we find in Irish music the frequent occurrence of one note repeated three times in the final cadences of their tunes, as will be seen in the example following, named "Slàn beò." This peculiarity is rare in Scottish Gaelic music. Something like it is found in "Thug mi 'n oidhche 'n raoir sunndach." On the other hand, it may be noted as a peculiarity of Scottish Gaelic music, that its final cadences very frequently end on a non-rest note— *i.e.*, any note which is not *doh* or *lah*—commonly *ray* and *soh*, as the tune following, named " An teid thu leam," illustrates. It is a labour song—in fact a rowing song ; and it is felt that it is meant to go on and on, rest being the one thing not wanted. Another peculiarity of Scottish Gaelic song is the frequency with which lines end on the unaccented syllable. This is due to the fact that the words of the language are to a large extent disyllable and trisyllable, with the accent invariably on the first syllable. In consequence of this, musical cadences of — ‿ and — ‿ ‿ are very common. In contrast to this fact, the English language has a very large proportion of its words of one syllable, and prefers, in consequence, the strong note as a final one, as ‿ — and ‿ ‿ — . In regard to the style of musical stanza, the Irish people have a strong predilection for one consisting of two strains for the first two lines of the verse, reversed for the second two lines, as the following tune illustrates :—

SLAN BEO.

Key F.

:d .r | m : l₁ : t₁ | d :—: m .f | s :—: m .d | r : d : d᷁ : d :—:

:d .r | m : d : r | d'᷁ :—: t .d᷁ | l :—: l .s | m : d : r᷁ | m :—:

:m .r | m : d : r | d :—: t .d᷁ | l :—: l .s | m : d : r᷁ | m :—:

:m .r | m : l₁ : t₁ | d :—. r : m .f | s :—: m .d | r : d : d᷁ | d :—:

The style of which the above is a type is also found in the Scottish Highlands; but not to the large extent which prevails in Ireland. In the Highlands the third line is never an exact repetition of the second. Perhaps the nearest approach to this Irish type which I could suggest is " Eilean a' cheò," or " Muile nam beann àrda," by the writer (see Vol. I., page 131). Both in Ireland and Scotland there are numerous developments of this type which display little repetition beyond the final cadence of the tune being the same as that of the first line. But, nevertheless, it is perfectly evident that such tunes are developments of the simpler type referred to.

Turning now to the consideration of Scottish Gaelic music and song, we find the favourite stanza to be one in which the first three lines rhyme to one another and the last one rhymes to the final line of every succeeding verse. This is not a difficult kind of rhyme in a language which, like the Gaelic, only requires vowel rhyme. But in the case of English, which requires consonantal rhyme as well as vowel rhyme, it is much more difficult, particularly if the verses are numerous. The following little gem of a tune, already referred to, illustrates the type of stanza under consideration in its most primitive form :

AN TEID THU LEAM.

Key F.

: d' | l : 1 : — .s : l | r : — :

r .m | f : l : — .s | m : — :

: d' | l : — .s : l | r : — : —

| d : — : — | m : r :

Having said so much for Gaelic music and song, how does it bear upon Lowland song. Taking into consideration the linguistic differences between the Gaelic language and the English, previously referred to, we would expect that there would be a difficulty in adapting English words to Gaelic airs. This is just what we find to be the case; and numerous are the devices which are used to get over the difficulty. These will be seen in the following lines which

occur to me. " Where ha'e ye been sae braw, lad? where ha'e ye been sae brankie, O!" " Clavers and his Hieland men cam down upon the raw, man," " Ye're welcome, Whigs, tae Bothwell Brigs; your malice is but zeal, boys," and so on. All the "lad's," "O's," "man's" "boys," &c, are but devices to make up for the poverty of rhyming material capable of suiting the musical character of the tunes. Besides these devices, there is the other very common one of repeating the same word at the end of all the verses of a song, for which we need no quotation, as many examples will occur to the reader. But there is one song among those of Lowland Scotland, for which the author has not had to have recourse to any device to make up for the poverty of rhyming material. I mean " Scots wha ha'e." It is almost the only Lowland song exemplifying the favourite Scottish Gaelic stanza, which has not the final rhymes of each verse on the same word; and, even in its case, the rhyme is strained—" victory" and "slavery" not being particularly happy as rhymes for "free" and "flee." In connection with this tune, there is a still further evidence of the probability of its being Gaelic in the fact that it ends on soh, a non-rest note. Chambers, in his "Songs Prior to Burns," writes as follows :—" All that we know with any certainty of the history of Tuttie Taittie is, that it was the spirited air of a certain Jacobite song, which, from a historical allusion in one of its verses, may be presumed to have been composed about the year 1718." The song referred to is " Here's to the king, sir." Jacobitism is itself suggestive of a northern extraction. I might enumerate a large number of examples of the same nature, but space will not allow it. I therefore proceed to the illustration of the part which the Irish style of stanza plays in Lowland song.

Perhaps the tune best suited to my purpose is "Will ye go to Flanders, Mally, O!" I should like - but dare not encroach on the space at my disposal—to exhibit the various sets of this tune which are current in Ireland and and Scotland. I must content myself with giving the Lowland Scotch set, which is as follows :—

WILL YE GO TO FLANDERS, MALLY, O?

Key F.

| s .,l : s .m | l : d'.d' | s ,m. - : r .,d | d :

| d' .,t : d'.r' | t : l .s | l .,t : l .,s | s :

| d' .,t : d'.r' | d.t : l .s | l .d' : s .m | s :

| d' .,t : l .s | l .t : d'.d' | s ,m. - : r .,d | d :

This tune is no other than a form of our own well-known "Mo Mhaili bheag òg" and "Gu ma slàn a chì mi," the Irish "Gramachree," "The harp that once through Tara's hall," "Molly Astore," and "Little Molly, O." The evidences are all in favour of its Irish origin. In four songs sung to it, we find "Molly" or "Mally." "Mally" is not a Lowland Scotch name. Nor for that matter is it common in the Highlands. It is a form of "Mary," due to a tendency among Irish Gaels to confound the consonants *l* and *r* with one another, as may be seen in the use of the *le* for *ri*, which latter is the old Irish and the modern Scottish form of the word. Besides this it is perfectly evident that the tune is a modification of the Irish type previously illustrated by "Slàn beò." It is quite natural to expect Irish music in Lowland Scotland. There were two channels by which it could make an entrance for itself—one through the Highlands and the other through Galloway. It is a fact that numerous tunes belonging to the Borders and to Buchan are constructed much after Gaelic styles.

It is needless to continue the analysis further. It would require much research and considerable study to set forth the subject in a thorough manner. But I think I have demonstrated that there is plenty of scope for the expenditure of labour in both. It is quite possible a wider knowledge might cause some of the opinions put forward here to be modified; but it seems to me that, in the main, what may be termed Lowland Scottish style, in music and song, has its foundation in Gaelic music.

REVIEWS.

"SCOTTISH GAELIC AS A SPECIFIC SUBJECT" (Glasgow : A. Sinclair, price 1s) To anyone familiar with existing grammars of the Gaelic language the first glance at the present work is apt to give rise to some apprehension, for the arrangement of it is quite out of the beaten track of former compilers. Those who have hitherto sought to enlighten us regarding the grammar of our language have thought it proper to construct their efforts after the model of Latin grammars—paying little or no attention to modern progress, even in the way of presenting the construction of a language to learners. We are glad to find that the Committee entrusted with the preparation of the Gaelic hand-book have had the courage of their opinions, and have, as they themselves express it, "gone off' the beaten track, judging it best to exhibit the structure of the language in a way suited to itself, without having undue regard to conventional methods." The work is consequently no hash up of existing grammatical *dicta*, but is distinctly original in its treatment of the subject of Gaelic grammar, presenting it in a manner so attractive that no one interested in the language can fail to find the perusal of the work pleasant study. The matter is carefully arranged, each paragraph and section leading up to that which follows. Section I. is devoted to the leading principles of Gaelic spelling. It has been remarked that " Gaelic is a language which few can read and nobody can spell," but a careful study of the rules here laid down should make the spelling of the language a matter of easy acquisition by any person who speaks it freely. The second section deals with words in composition —*i.e.*, as they affect one another in speech. The mode of presenting this is very interesting ; and we here find many of the peculiarities of the language accounted for. The scope of other sections of the work may be learned from their headings:— Section III.—Word Formation and Development ; Section IV.— The Function of Words ; Section V.—The Inflections of Words. These are followed by an exhaustive Table of Numerals, which cannot fail to be valuable to pupils. There are numerous carefully graded exercises throughout the work, as well as copious Gaelic-English and English-Gaelic vocabularies. The work has been most carefully printed, and reflects great credit on the publisher. The *Comunn Gaidhealach*, under whose auspices the work appears, is to be congratulated on the manner in which their Committee have discharged the trying and difficult duty entrusted to them. It remains now for School Boards and teachers to do their part ; and we prophecy easy and rapid progress on the part of the children if the order of the work now before us is faithfully adhered to. After a careful, unprejudiced perusal of " Scottish Gaelic as a Specific Subject," we do not hesitate to say that Gaelic grammar has by its publication been raised to a higher platform and placed in line with the knowledge which obtains among scientific thinkers in the realm of language.

An Gaodhal (Brooklyn, N.Y., U.S.A.)—We cordially welcome our Celtic friend from New York. The August number is full of interesting matter, a good part of it being printed in Irish character. It prints a poem entitled *An Gaidheal air Leaba Bàis*, with the remark, " This beautifully pathetic lamentation was sent to us, among others, by Miss Jessie MacIntyre, of Grove Park, Kent, England. It is a question if there be a more beautiful or more sentimental song in the language." It may interest the editor of *The Gael* to know that the poem is by our well-known contributor "Fionn," and that it appears, with a translation by the author, in his popular volume, " The Celtic Garland." We cordially reciprocate the good wishes of *The Gael* towards ourselves.

The Gaelic Journal (Maynooth College, Ireland). —The number for July contains a rich collection of specimens of Irish as now spoken in various districts of the country. The provincialisms are not more marked than they are among the Gaelic-speaking people of Scotland. We have also several specimens of Irish poetry and a number of popular Irish proverbs, which are extremely interesting. From his " Notes on Scottish Gaelic," it is apparent that the learned editor, Professor O'Growney, is abreast of all that is going on among the " sea-divided Gael." *A h-uile latha dha.*

ALLAN CAMERON OF LUNDAVRA,
(Chieftain of the Clan Cameron.)

THE CELTIC MONTHLY:

A MAGAZINE FOR HIGHLANDERS.

Edited by JOHN MACKAY, Kingston.

No. 2. Vol. II | NOVEMBER, 1893. |Price Threepence.

ALLAN CAMERON OF LUNDAVRA.

MR. ALLAN CAMERON, whose portrait we have pleasure in presenting to our readers with this issue, is the lineal representative of the ancient House of Lundavra, and is, we believe, the senior hereditary Chieftain of the Clan Cameron. He traces his descent in an unbroken line from John, second son of *Ailean nan Creach*, chief of Lochiel, by his wife Mariot, daughter of Angus MacDonell, 2nd of Keppoch, grandson of the Lady Margaret, who was a daughter of King Robert the Second of Scotland.

Mr. Cameron was born in Ireland, in 1841, and is maternally connected with that country through the Coleloughs of Tintern Abbey, Co. Wexford.

When 19 years of age he became an officer in the Royal Irish Constabulary, in which corps he has done good service for his country, for which he has been thanked by Government, and rewarded with rapid promotion. He is now Assistant Inspector-General of the Royal Irish Constabulary, and also a Divisional Commissioner, in which latter capacity he is charged with the preservation of the peace, and is directly responsible to the Irish Government for the good order of his Division, which comprises one-fifth part of Ireland. He has at his disposal for this purpose all the forces of the Crown, civil and military, located within the bounds of his Division. It will therefore be seen that the subject of our sketch occupies a very responsible position in the "Sister Isle."

But it is with Mr. Cameron as a Highlander that we wish specially to deal, for although he has spent most of his life in Ireland his heart is Highland, and he clings with a tenacity, essentially Celtic, to the traditions of his race and clan. Lundavra never feels more thoroughly at home than when mingling with the members of his clan at their meetings, or when roaming o'er the hills of historic Lochaber. He supported his chief, Lochiel, like a true Cameron, at the memorable gathering which was held in the Queen's Rooms, Glasgow, two years ago, when there was such a re-union of Camerons as had not been seen in Glasgow since a former Lochiel led his men into the city in 1745; and it was only last winter that we had the pleasure of being present at the second gathering of the clan, over which Mr. Allan Cameron presided with his characteristic grace and ability, and at which he delivered an address so full of patriotic fervour that it could not fail to awaken a responsive chord in the breast of every Highlander present. Lundavra is extremely popular among the members of his clan, and indeed it may be truly said of him that he is loved by all who have come in contact with him, both in this country and in Green Erin across the waters. He has been always ready to help the deserving, and to lend a friendly hand to the weak.

We shall publish next month a Gaelic elegy composed by the famous bard, Ailean Dall, upon the death of Mr. Cameron's great grandfather, Allan of Lundavra, and for the benefit of those of our readers who do not understand Gaelic we will append an English translation by the late Mrs. Mary Mackellar, whose lamented death will be fresh in the recollection of our readers.

A few words regarding the father of the subject of this beautiful elegy may interest many. Allan of Lundavra was lieutenant to his chief, the "gentle Lochiel," on that historic occasion when, on the 19th of August, 1745, he marched with 800 of his clansmen to Glenfinnan, and was first among the Highland clans which arrayed themselves under the banner of Bonnie Prince Charlie. This brave chieftain fell at the eventful battle of Preston, on the 21st September following, in the very moment of victory.

Of Mr. Cameron we could write a great deal which, we feel sure, would interest our readers, but we daresay nothing could afford them greater satisfaction than to learn that at the termination of his public service Mr. Cameron hopes to spend the remainder of his days amongst the hills of Lochaber—the cradle of his race—and those lone glens where oft in the bygone days so

" Wild and high the Camerons' gathering rose."

EDITOR.

GLENORCHY'S WIDOW:
A Legend of Lochawe.

BY THE EDITOR.

ONE day this aged comforter called upon her, and found that she had been sighing more than usual. He condoled with her, and then said he was the unwilling bearer of sad news. Putting his handkerchief to his eyes in quite an affecting way, he exclaimed :

"My dear lady, word has just been received that your brave husband, Sir Colin, is dead. He was killed in battle with the Moors."

The fair widow gave way to a flood of tears, and showed symptoms of fainting.

"What shall I do," she murmured. "Alas! now that the hope that he lives no longer sustains me, what is there to live for ? What can I do alone ?"

"My sweet lady, do not give way to such weakness. There is still much that you can live for. There is—hem !—there is always the prospect of taking another husband to become the the sharer of your sorrows and joys. There are, I make no doubt, many who would be greatly honoured in gaining your affections, and—hem ! —if I might presume so far, if, in fact—hem !— I should be willing myself, very willing, my dear lady, to make you Mrs. MacCorquodale— if you would excuse my saying so."

The old gentleman was now deeply affected, and used his handkerchief frequently. As the lady paid no attention to his proposal, he repeated :

"Your husband did not know how to appreciate a loving wife. I have learnt to love you with all my heart, and I should, as I already mentioned, feel very proud to occupy in your affections that place which you so long reserved for one who was cruel enough not to value it as he should. I shall value it at its proper worth, my dear Lady Glenorchy !"

Such an example of disinterested kindness could not fail to touch the heart of such a susceptible woman ; but, although her first impulse was to close with the offer, the natural coyness of the sex asserted itself, and she remarked with a faint smile beaming through her tears, that she was not prepared at the moment to listen to

such a proposal, but that she fully appreciated the kindly feeling which prompted it.

Mr. MacCorquodale thought this was pretty good as a beginning, and again assuring her that his only desire was to serve her, to contribute, if possible, to her happiness, and to relieve her of the cares of managing such a large estate, which he felt confident he could do much better than she could, he wiped his eyes and took his departure. The suggestive smile that crept over his face, when he got outside of the castle, might have led people who did not know his kindly and disinterested ways to believe that he had played a part in an amusing comedy, and felt sure that he had acted well.

MacCorquodale was now assiduous in his attentions to the lonely widow, and so successfully did he conduct the matrimonial campaign that the lady consented to bestow upon him her heart and hand —not to mention the other substantial considerations which were to accompany them. The news soon spread throughout the country, and although the members of the clan did not manifest any degree of enthusiasm over the matter the happy day was fixed, and great preparations were made to celebrate the event with pomp and circumstance worthy of the occasion. In making the arrangements, MacCorquodale manifested his generosity to a remarkable degree —all the expense being defrayed from the lady's purse. This was only another instance of his unselfishness. Some narrow-minded people would have paid these accounts themselves, but not so this gentleman, who would not have deprived the fair lady the pleasure of paying these items of expense for anything.

CHAPTER II.

IT is usual, in the orthodox three-volume novel, to end the first book with a thrilling description of the heroine being carried down a wild mountain torrent to certain death ; or perhaps the villain stands over her with an uplifted dagger, which he is about to plunge into her breast, while, with calm fortitude, she braves him to do his worst. In the next volume, the hero appears on the scene, and we breathe more freely when the gallant youth rescues the fair maiden. This is not an orthodox novel, but it is just possible that my readers may consider that the time has now arrived when I should explain what Sir Colin had been doing all these years. Unless he can satisfactorily account for his conduct, we might judge him harshly.

I already mentioned that the Knight of Glenorchy had, with other members of the order, crossed over to Spain, where he had achieved great renown in the wars against the Moors. Each year he had sent a trusty page with letters to his lady, with strict injunctions to deliver them to herself only, and to hasten back with her reply. Not one of these messengers had ever returned. Their fate was involved in mystery. As might be expected, this ominous silence had caused him great pain and anxiety, especially as he had no means of learning its cause, and his oath as a Knight Templar precluded him from returning home until the cause of the Cross had triumphed.

At last, after six years had passed, Sir Colin joined a party of knights who were sent to Rome on an important mission. Here he hoped to meet some of his own countrymen, who would be able to give him news from home. His search was fruitless—he met no one who could tell him anything of his wife or people.

When one is in the greatest misery, it is then that the first glint of sunshine comes to dispel the gloom. One night Sir Colin lay in bed, and, in the midst of his troubled slumbers, a voice whispered distinctly in his ears. On such interesting occasions "a little bird" usually gets the credit of the whispering, but, in this instance, we must frankly admit that the real cause of the phenomenon was never satisfactorily explained. The owner of the voice was in no hurry, for he gave very particular instructions to the restless sleeper what to do. He was to rise at once, and well armed, to leave Rome and return to Scotland, without loss of time. A great danger threatened his wife and friends, which only he could avert. He was to assume the guise of a palmer, and to seek the home of his aged nurse, who would reveal to him the nature of the impending danger, and advise him what to do.

Sir Colin acted on the suggestion, and started on his journey next morning. In due course he arrived in Glenorchy, and on visiting the nurse's house learned then, for the first time, the strange events that had happened during his absence. His surprise may be imagined when he was told that his lady, in anticipation of his return, had built one of the noblest castles in the land; that MacCorquodale, a neighbouring chief, had shown letters proving that Sir Colin was dead, and that, believing her husband was no more, she had consented to honour MacCorquodale with her hand, the wedding having been arranged to take place, with great festivities, the next day.

It was bad enough to be mourned as dead, but Glenorchy thought that it was a cruel joke for another man to marry his beautiful wife, and calmly settle himself down to enjoy his (Sir Colin's) property.

MacCorquodale had played him a nasty trick, but he was determined to play him a better one on the morrow.

. . . .

The bridegroom and his party had arrived at the castle, and the marriage ceremony was about to begin. The bride, with her blushing bridesmaids, came tripping into the banquetting chamber, when a servant stopped her and exclaimed that a holy palmer was at the gate, and had asked the favour of a goblet of wine to drink the lady's health, and to bless her ere the ceremony took place. Such a kindness was not to be refused, and the lady filled a brimming cup of wine, with which she went to meet the stranger. He was an old man, supporting his tottering frame with a staff, and his shoes and clothes were worn with much travelling. He took the goblet, and before drinking the sparkling liquor, said in feeble tones of voice: "Lady, you have not yet vowed thyself to another?"

The bride, with merry laugh, answered that she had not, but that before long her vows would be given; and that she hoped that the holy man would accept of their hospitality, and grant his blessing.

Raising the cup to his lips he drained it, then touching the rim, he said in a strong, stern voice:

"Lady, 'tis well that thou hast sought my blessing ere thou gav'st thyself away. Behold thou shalt find my blessing in the cup. Wilt thou accept it now from me?"

Startled by the altered sound of the voice, and the upright figure of the supposed palmer, she glanced in the cup, and saw there the very ring which she had given to her husband when they last parted. Some ladies would, under such peculiar circumstances, have found it convenient to faint, others to show symptoms of hysterics, but not so our fair lady. Her countenance brightened with a new found joy, and rushing into the palmer's arms, she exclaimed:

"My dear husband! I know your voice and your smile. I knew it was you all along. And you have come back to me, my own dear husband!"

This was a most affecting scene to all except one. That was the unfortunate MacCorquodale, who realised that Glenorchy had presented himself at a most inconvenient moment. He was so indignant at this intrusion that he drew his dirk, and aimed a deadly blow at Sir Colin, exclaiming in loud, angry tones:

"This will help thee to return to that spirit world, where thou hast long pretended to have been."

The weapon glanced aside, and the supposed palmer, throwing off his disguise, revealed himself in full armour. Seeing how matters stood, the disappointed lover took to flight, and before the retainers could start in pursuit he had reached a place of safety among his own clan.

There is little now to add. It was discovered that three of MacCorquodale's retainers had each year waylaid Glenorchy's messenger, and, after securing the papers which he carried, tied stones round his mutilated body and sunk it in the unfathomed depths of Loch Etive. Having further explained that they did so at their chief's instigation, to whom they delivered the letters, they were, next day, hanged on a tree overlooking a precipice. A battle was fought between the followers of the rival chiefs, in which MacCorquodale was slain, and his army completely routed.

Such, then, was the romantic origin of Kilchurn Castle. The fortress is now a picturesque ruin, but Sir Colin's descendants have erected a still more palatial residence on Loch Tayside (Taymouth Castle), where the Marquis of Breadalbane now resides. Strange to say, the Marquis was installed not long ago as Grand Master of the Order of Knight Templars, of which his illustrious ancestor was a notable member.

[CONCLUDED.]

AINGEAL AN DOCHAIS.

1st PRIZE POEM AT OBAN MOD, 1893.

A' GHRIAN gu glòrmhor anns an iar
Chaidh sios air cùl a' chuain.
An oidhch' a falluinn ghruamach, chiar,
Ghrad dh' iath mu bheinn is cluain ;
Is dhealraich ann an uchd nan speur
Gach reul a's glaine tuar.

'S an uair sin fèin bho shaothair theann
Thug mi gu fann mo làmh.
Air cluasaig leig mi sios mo cheann
A chum gu 'm faighinn tàmh.
A doimhneachd suaimhneis dh' èirich suas
Gu h-aoibhneach bruadar àigh !

Ar leam gu 'n robh mi fèin a falbh
Air astar doirbh is mòr ;
Bha 'n turus deuchainneach is searbh,
Bha 'n t-ana-moch air mo thòir ;
Is àite-fasgaidh cha robh ann,
'S mi claoidhte, fann gu leòir.

Bha m' inneachd làmh ri amhainn shèimh,
Fodh sgàile sgeimh nan craobh.
A nuas air osaig thlàth nan neamh
Sheòl iomhaigh fhlathail chaomh.
Gu m' ioghnadh mòr, bha aingeal dheas
'N a seasamh ri mo thaobh !

'N uair 'phaisg i 'sgiathan riomhach glan
Fodh 'duail air dhreach an òir,
Dhealraich a gnùis 'bu shuairce gean.
Shin i a slat a' m' chòir
Is dhùisg i solas 'n a mo chliabh,
Le brìathran binn a beòil.

"Biodh agad misneach agus neart
Ged tha do thurus searbh.
Bu mhiann leam thu 'bhi siubhail ceart
'S an astar mhòr gu dearbh ;
Oir thàinig mi le bàigh is treòir ;
Aingeal an Dòchais m' ainm.

Tha mise 'gnàth a frithealadh
'Gach dùil breòite, sgìth,
Bho chian air feadh nan ginealach,
'An cogadh no 'an sìth.
A' m' bheachd tha 'n deòraidh iriosal
Co-ionann ris an rìgh.

An uair 'bhios trioblaidean na cràdh
'G a d' shàruchadh gu cruaidh ;
No 'dhuiteas t-inntinn sios gu làr
A mhàin air m' ainm-sa luaidh
Is thig mi fèin le thachd is deòin
'G a d' thrèòrachadh gu buaidh."

'Sin sgaoil i 'sgiathan glòrmhor geal,
'S gu ciatach sheòl i nam.
A h-iomhaigh eireachdail gun smal
Chaidh as mo shealladh suas.
An uair a dh' fhàg i beachd mo shùl
Ghrad dhùisg mi as mo shuain.

A nis a leughadair mo dhàin,
Ma thig ort àmghair ghèir,
Gairm air an Aingil ud 'tha 'tàmh
Le fàbhar dhuinn gu lèir.
A measg nan neul a's dorr h' tha 'snàmh
Thar fàsach gleann nan deur.

Glendale.   NEIL ROSS.

THE SEA-BIRD AND THE STORM.

BY THE LATE MARY MACKELLAR.

To the green shores of Muile* a sea-bird had come,
So dim-eyed and weary with terror and pain,
'Twas driven by tempests from kindred and home,
Afar o'er the foam-crested, wild-rolling main.

Now safe from the roar of the dark, surging wave,
So calmly at rest in the sunshine it lay,
Whilst its storm-ruffled bosom it gladly would lave,
In the soft rippling waters that shone in the bay.

The sea, in the light of the west, gleamed like gold,
And its murmur was soft as the sound of the shell,
And the sea-bird at rest, with its pinions afold,
To surges and tempests would fain say farewell.

Vain wish for ere night came the surges rose high,
The night winds were moaning afar on the sea,
No star could be seen to illumine the sky,
And the sob of the billow was loud on the lea.

The sea-bird again spread its wings for a flight,
Away from green Muile in terror and pain,
Away from the storm-cloud, in darkness of night,
O'er the foam crested, wild rolling breast of the main.

* Muile The Island of Mull, Argyllshire.

D. T. MACDONALD, J.P., CANADA.

WHEN Dr. Norman MacLeod *Caraid nan-Gaidheal* was writing his Gaelic dedication of "Leabhar nan Cnoc," in 1834, he took occasion to remark that even if Gaelic were driven from the Scottish Highlands that ancient tongue would find a comfortable home and receive a hearty welcome from thousands of warm-hearted Highlanders across the main.

We make no apology for introducing our readers to one of these leal hearted Celts who have gained distinction and honour in the land of their adoption. Mr. MacDonald is a native of Coll, Argyllshire. He left that island in 1836, at the age of 15, and became a bound apprentice to Messrs. Blackie & Sons, printers &c., Glasgow. Having met with an accident, he relinquished that business, and in 1839 entered the Glasgow Apothecaries' Hall, where he remained for over seven years. In 1846 he opened a drug shop at Inveraray, and remained in that burgh till 1856. During his residence he was elected Dean of Guild and Bailie of that ancient burgh. For about two years before leaving Inveraray he had the management of one of the Duke of Argyll's metal mines, then in active operation. On this mine becoming exhausted the lessees took Mr. MacDonald with them to England. Shortly after this he was sent to Norway, and we afterwards find him engaged in the management of extensive mines in Ireland, and in Hartz Mountains, Germany, and on the north shore of Lake Superior. Unfortunately, this latter mine belied expectations, and in eighteen months' time its further working was found to be unprofitable. Mr. MacDonald, nothing daunted, crossed the lake, and in 1869 built for himself a comfortable house and a drug store at Red Jacket, Calumet, Michigan, where we now find him. In 1872 he was appointed a Justice of the Peace and Coroner, which offices he has now held for over twenty years.

Here it may be interesting to state that Mr. MacDonald is a nephew of that literary Celt, man, the late Lachlan MacLean, author of the "History of the Celtic Language," &c. &c., and manifests a warm interest in all that pertains to the language and literature of the Celt. The following bit of autobiography cannot fail to interest our readers:

"Like my uncle, Lachlan MacLean, I take a great interest in Celtic literature. I joined the Clan MacDonald Society a couple of years ago, and the Clan MacLean, at Chicago, last June. I was proud to meet Sir Fitzroy D. MacLean and "Pennycross" at Chicago, with five pipers marching at their head, playing

'Gabhaidh sinn an rathad mór
Olc air mhath le càch e.'

The little education I received was at Arnabost School, Coll, but I attended chemistry classes in Glasgow, under Professor Penny and Dr MacGregor."

Although Mr. MacDonald is close upon the "allotted span," he is still hale and hearty, and we hope he may be spared to enjoy many years of that leisure to which an active life has made him justly entitled. FIONN.

THE CELTIC AWAKENING.

Our Gaelic race is rousing from the torpor of the
  past ;
The Celtic fire, long smothered, is flaming bright at
  last ;
The beauties of our ancient tongue, our bards', our
  heroes' fame,
Are dear, as ne'er before, to those who boast of High-
  land name.
They say 'tis disappearing, the language of our sires,
Which sounding once through Selma's hall inflamed
  pure hero-fires ;
That speech, recalling ages dim, as shell, the sound-
  ing sea,
Must soon become a memory of what has ceased to be.
They say 'tis fading, dying, that its end is nearing
  fast,
And is now but an echo, save to those who love the
  past.

From where the storm-swept Hebrides upraise a
  a towering crest,
Like emerald gems, above the swell of broad Atlantic's
  breast,
To where the Tay and Spey unite their waters with
  the sea,
Where'er true Highland hearts abide, they say, it
  shall not be!
From far Australia's southern clime, from India's
  torrid plain,
To where St Lawrence pours its flood into the
  surging main.
From east to west of our New World, from Lakes, to
  Mexique sea,
Where beats a loyal Celtic heart, they say it must
  not be,
Each wind that sweeps the ocean carries that voice
  along,
They knew not how we loved it, they shall know our
  love is strong.

Let progeny of caitiff race forget they had a past,
And in oblivion's darkest shade let speech of slaves
  be cast ;
But where's the man in all the world, though proud
  of Saxon name,
Would dare impugn our sires' renown, or blot our
  heroes' fame?
The fame of those who kept at bay the conquerors of
  the world,
And taught the Roman hosts their flag could not be
  there unfurled,
Behind that range of Highland hills, to freedom ever
  dear,
The citadel of high emprise, of deeds we must revere.
The voice of these, our fathers, is borne on every gale
That waves the heather on the hills, that sweeps o'er
  loch and vale.

There Ossian—Homer of our race—struck from the
  sounding lyre
Tones that still echo from our hearts, that raise the
  patriot's fire ?
Tones which resound from Morven's heights and
  Selma's vacant hall,
And echoing Lora, till we think Fingal and Ullin call.
And he gave words to thoughts which burn within the
  Celtic breast,

Their passion and their tenderness, their longing
  and unrest ;
Their feeling of the loveliness that over Nature broods,
The mystic charm and grandeur in all its various
  moods.
And he voiced their love of honour, their scorn for
  what is wrong,
As he swept the chords of feeling with his magic gift
  of song.

Can we forget those saintly men, who from Iona's
  isle
Diffused the light of purer faith among the heathen
  vile ?—
Who, to the Scandinavian fierce, and pagan Teuton,
  gave
The ideal of a nobler life—the Christ who came to
  save.
And down the ages as we come, however dark the
  page,
We find it brightened by the light of Celtic saint or
  sage ;
And never through the bygone years, as many cycles
  ran,
Have there been wanting to our race the pride and
  worth of man.
To-day takes up the story of that grand, effulgent
  past :—
We were not dead but sleeping ; we are rousing now,
  at last.

In eloquence and literature, in science and in art,
In halls of State, in marts of trade, we've played no
  minor part ;
And on the field of battle, 'mong the bravest in the
  van,
You have always found him foremost, the man of
  Highland clan.
Then let detractors of our race the Celtic name
  assail,—
Their prejudice and jealous rage can never much
  avail
We point to our distinguished sires, to deeds which
  they have done,
And feel, while true unto our past, assured for time
  to run.
Then reverence and cherish the Celtic tongue and
  fame :
Should the speech of Ossian perish, we Gaels must
  bear the blame.   NEIL MACDONALD.

New York, U.S.A.   Bard to the Celtic Society
                                        of New York.

HIGHLAND PLACES WORTH VISITING.

No. 3. ISLAND OF LEWIS.

THE Island of Lewis has sometimes been, very much to its disadvantage, compared with the neighbouring island of Skye as a tourist resort, but there are many who, like Dr. Johnson when he visited the "Isle of the Mist," do not care to be "always climbing or descending," and Lewis, in the words of old "Sixty One," is "a land with too many charms not to be able to bear criticism and truth." To the quiet visitor who really wants rest for mind and body it has attractions which ought to make even the growlings of the Minch tolerably pleasant. There is a breadth and expansiveness in its heath-covered *machars* not to be met with in all places where the freedom of the wilderness may allure the cramped-up city toiler to stretch his limbs. Then it is a place with a record whose beginnings are not of yesterday, like some more pretentious districts. Julius Cæsar's conquest of South Britain is a comparatively

From a Phot. by]　　　　　　　STORNOWAY　　　　　　　[J. Valentine & Son

modern achievement to the student of Long Island history. The first clear evidences of human occupation consist in the stone circles and monuments which are found here and there throughout the island, chiefly in the vicinity of Garynahine, about 12 miles from Stornoway. One of these circles, with the remains of two or three stone avenues leading towards it, is at Callernish, overlooking an arm of Loch Roag, and is said to be, next to Stonehenge, the most remarkable fragment of the kind in the British Islands. The number of stones now remaining is 45, and the height of some of them nearly 30 feet. Here it is said the Arch-Druid, whose uncanny art has passed into the language under the name of *Draidheachd* presided at the human sacrifices that were offered up periodically within the central enclosure.

The island is now universally allowed to have derived its name *Leodhus* from Leod, the traditional progenitor of the Clan MacLeod, although in the well-known work by "M. Martin, Gent.," it is traced to *Leog*, the Irish for water. The old Scandinavian mariners made it a frequent place of call, and at Ness still the bulk of the natives, in form and feature, bear a close resemblance to the Norwegian and Danish sailors who every season visit the port of Stornoway in their trading vessels. Created a free barony by James V. in 1541, shortly after the Royal visit, the whole lands, with the castle and other property, were conferred upon Roderick, the chief of the Clan Macleod, "and Barbara Stewart, his affianced spouse." This Roderick, or as he is half-affectionately known in the family annals, "Old Rory," was tenth in succession from Leod, the founder of the clan. His rule covers a period of half a century, and is one long, wild story of family strife and bloodshed, ending in disaster to all concerned in it, and the final loss to the clan of their island territory. Old Rory's first wife was a daughter of John Mackenzie of Kintail, and on her marriage with Macleod had been for some time a widow. Her attachments would appear to have been but fickle, for she soon transferred her person and affections to the Laird of Raasay, and Macleod, out of revenge his enemies said, though he himself gave a better reason, disinherited her son, who was thereupon adopted by his mother's relations at Strathconon, and came to be known as "Torquil Connanach." Macleod married twice after this, and had three sons by these wives, besides five illegitimate sons, whose appetite for plunder was like that of young lions. Jealous of what he conceived to be his rights, Torquil Connanach, backed up by the Kintail family, carried on a long and bitter conflict with his father, in the course of which he laid siege to the Castle of Stornoway, took it, captured the old chief, killed a number of his followers, and completed the sack by carrying away all the writs, charters, and other documents belonging to the family and handing them over to Colin, chief of Kintail. These civil disturbances, involving so much misery and bloodshed, were the direct cause of the Fife invasion. So far as the colonists were concerned it was a purely business adventure. They arrived there in October, 1599, with a force of 600 armed men, besides a number of private gentlemen, and skilled mechanics of all kinds, and were met by the islanders under Neil Macleod, one of Old Rory's illegitimate sons, but after a stubborn contest they succeeded in landing at Stornoway, "and in the end made up a bonny town there." From various causes, however, the undertaking proved a failure, and the settlers after a few years sold their interest to Mackenzie, who had set his heart upon obtaining possession of the island. Kintail soon disposed of the remaining scions of the *Siol Thorquil* Neil "was made short by the head" in Edinburgh; his son was banished from Scotland; his brother Norman, after pining for ten years in the Edinburgh Tolbooth, got permission to retire to Holland, where he died in the service of the Prince of Orange; two of his nephews were executed by Mackenzie, and the third is supposed to have died an exile in Spain. The Seaforths held the island until 1844, when it was sold to Sir James Matheson, whose widow now has it in life-rent.

In the old days, and amidst much that was rough and ready, a kind of rude attempt at dispensing justice continued to be kept up, the presiding authority being called Brieve or *Breitheamh*—a judge. There is a Gallows Hill at Stornoway; at Kneep, Uig; and at Shawbost, indicating the nature of the cases that often fell to be disposed of by this functionary.

The present century has witnessed an extraordinary change in the habits of the people, and, so far as their moral and social condition is concerned, it is not too much to say that a revolution has taken place. When the Ettrick Shepherd visited the place in 1800 he was struck with the absence of wheaten bread from the table at which he dined, and when he started to walk to Barvas the road on which he travelled led him for two or three miles into the moor and left him there. Now, every village has its baker, while locomotion by steam cars has become a question of "practical politics." Bad old customs are either dead or dying; funerals are conducted decently and reverently; weddings have none of the accompanying excesses which were at one time thought to be quite handsome and becoming. As regards the land question, tenant-right and landlord-right are twin brothers. In the town of Stornoway the stranger will find much to interest him, although almost everything that linked it with the past is gone, and it requires no vivid imagination to think of the Macleod warriors turning in their graves at Eye Churchyard in consequence, or mayhap occasionally revisiting by the glimpses of the moon the spot where their old fort stood.

Stornoway is now easily accessible from the south. Certainly the most pleasant route is that by Mr. MacBrayne's fine steamer "Claymore," which leaves Glasgow twice a week, and after passing through the majestic scenery of the Western Isles calls at Stornoway. Only those who have had the pleasure of enjoying this trip can fully appreciate its attractions.

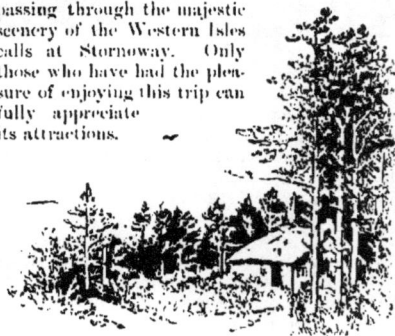

Stornoway.

R. J. MACLEOD.

OUR MUSICAL PAGE.

MO DHACHAIDH.

THE following is a translation of the song by Mr. Malcolm MacFarlane which appeared at page 102 of our first volume, entitled "Mo Dhachaidh." It is by Mr. Alexander Stewart, police constable, Polmont, Stirlingshire, and for it he was awarded first prize at the Mòd recently held at Oban. Mr. Stewart, it will at once be acknowledged, has made an excellent rendering of the original. His translation, assisted by the capital air to which it is set, will, we venture to think, be-come popular among those who are unable to sing the original Gaelic. We have seen few translations which so well illustrate the beauty of Gaelic assonance as this one—notice the rhyming word in the middle of every fourth line—and we see no reason why writers of original poetry in English should not occasionally imitate this style. It is in this case, un-doubtedly, an added charm. Mr. Stewart is a native of Balquhidder, and has before won prizes in literary contests in the *People's Journal* and *Dundee Weekly News*, and we trust to see more equally good work from his pen.

It may interest our readers to learn that another translation by the author of the Gaelic original is to appear, along with the music, in an early number of the *National Choir*, pub-lished by Messrs J. and R. Parlane, Paisley.

Lady Archibald Campbell was so charmed with the music that, on hearing it sung by the St. Columba Choir at Oban, she spared no efforts to acquire some verses of the song.

ED.

MY AIN HOOSE.

Translation by ALEXANDER STEWART, *Polmont*.

Ayont by the ferry, whaur woodlands are green,
My canty cot hoosie stan's tidy an' clean;
I envy nae laird in his castle, I ween,
    I'm happy an' bien in my ain hoose.

My cosy bit biggin' it's dear aboon a',
Surroonded wi' daisies an' primroses braw,
The hillock ahint it's a bield frae the snaw
    When winter win's blaw roon my ain hoose.

Kin' nature has scattered her gifts tarough the glen,
The lark is in tune as he soon's his refrain:
My wife hears the croon o' the burn in the den
    As she lilts to the wean in oor ain hoose.

May blessin's gang wi' ye, fond wifie o' mine,
The star o' my hame since I wooed ye langsyne,
Yer leal heart wad never to envy incline,
    Ye're canty an' kin' in yer ain hoose.

At fa' o' the gloamin', when darkness is near,
Oor hearth is surroonded wi' dattin' an' cheer,
The bairnies are singin' sae lichtsome an' clear,
    They're pleasant to hear in oor ain hoose.

Awa' wi' yer riches an' rank, wi' their glare,
They're naething but folly an' phantoms o' air;
The ha' o' the Queen an' the luxuries there
    Can never compare wi' my ain hoose.

TO CORRESPONDENTS

All Communications, on literary and business matters, should be addressed to the Editor, Mr. JOHN MACKAY, 17 Dundas Street, Kingston, Glasgow.

TERMS OF SUBSCRIPTION.—*The CELTIC MONTHLY will be sent, post free, to any part of the United Kingdom, Canada, the United States, and all countries in the Postal Union—for one year, 4s.*

THE CELTIC MONTHLY.

NOVEMBER, 1893.

CONTENTS.

TO OUR READERS.

"HIGHLAND HONOURS."

As the few remarks which we made in our last issue on this subject have greatly interested many of our readers, and been extensively quoted by the public press, it may not be out of place to again refer briefly to these so-called "Highland Honours." We invited the upholders of this custom to refer us to any work of last century in which it is described as of Highland origin, but we are not surprised that no one has been kind enough to quote an authority. On the contrary, we have received letters from several gentlemen learned in Highland lore, who agree in describing the "honours" as a modern invention, and have expressed their satisfaction that we have raised the question of its authenticity.

It seems quite clear that the custom of drinking a toast in the particular fashion described was adopted by certain Highland Societies in London about the year 1820. It is believed to have been first introduced for "stage effect" in a Highland play in the Theatre Royal, Edinburgh, by a Mr. Murray, who was then manager. This was at the time when Sir Walter Scott's novels had created an appetite for Highland excitements. Sir Walter himself tells us that the members of the Celtic Society of London attended the meetings armed with claymores! They were further characterised by what he humorously describes as "wild ways." Nothing could serve the purpose of these gentlemen better than the "stage effects" of Mr. Murray's "Highland Honours," and the custom was practised at their festive gatherings, and has been handed down to us as a venerable survival of the days of long ago, deserving all the respect paid to old age and antiquity. In our opinion it is a palpable fraud—a product of the enthusiasms of the Waverley novels period! The question then is, if we have no decided proof that it is a genuine Highland custom, but have good reasons to believe that it is a southern importation, would it not be better for Highlanders at their social gatherings to ignore it altogether? Surely we can honour a countryman without standing on chairs and tables, or by breaking glasses—which, by the way, few of our forefathers *had* to break. The genuine manners and customs of the Highlanders were beautiful, and compare favourably with those of any country, and we can surely have our "Highland Honours" without associating with them certain features which are neither pretty nor tasteful, nor natural to our Highland soil.

THE LONDON "GLOBE" ON THE GAELIC REVIVAL.—We thought that we had heard the last of those venomous attacks upon Highlanders and their language which not many years ago were a feature of, and a disgrace to, English newspapers. Evidently the desire to flout and ridicule the Celtic race is as strong as ever among a certain class of writers in what are known as *smart* journals. The *Globe* recently devoted over a column to the Gaelic revival, in which the Highlander, his language, literature, music, and national institutions, particularly the Oban Mòd, were made the objects of the clumsiest form of "wit" which we remember ever having seen in print. The whole idea of the writer seemed to resolve itself into this, that Sandy could not be a gentleman until he had discarded his national costume, language and accent, and developed into a full-fledged Englishman. We hope the day is far distant when the Highlander will be ashamed of his nationality, or seek to forget his mother tongue. The London press seem to have forgotten the crushing reply which the learned Dr. MacElheran gave to the *Times*, when it attempted to be-little the Celt. His closing sentence is still applicable to the *Globe*, and exactly states the truth in regard to these Cockney attacks on Celts. He says, "I don't hate *him* (the Saxon) for priding himself; but I do detest your vile race of mongrels, who would be Saxon or Hottentot because the Irish are Celtic." We may add that Professor Blackie replied to the article in a manner which effectually silenced the *Globe* on the subject of Highlanders.

OUR NEXT ISSUE.—We will present our readers with a life-like plate portrait of Mr. Alex. MacDonald, town-clerk, Govan, a Highlander whose contributions to Highland literature have made his name known in all parts of the world. Portraits will also appear of Mr. George M. Sutherland, Wick (held over from this issue); Mr. Alex. Mackellar, hon. president and first captain of the Glasgow Cowal Shinty Club; Mr. Donald MacDonald, hon. sec., Gaelic Society of New York, U.S.A.; Dr R. C. MacDiarmid, vice-president, Gaelic Society of Glasgow, and the late Mr. Duncan Campbell, of the Glasgow Skye Association.

DUNCAN MACLEAN, MANCHESTER.

FULL of restless energy and with that true poetic temperament that marks the Celt, Mr. Maclean from earliest days has made his personality felt wherever his lot was cast, and in whatever work he was engaged. Born, June 2nd, 1857, in Dunoon, of typical Highland parents, Mr. Maclean was fortunate when of school age to be placed under the care of a teacher who cared more for the mental and moral attainments of his pupils than for Government grants.

Leaving school Mr. Maclean was for four years engaged as assistant Inspector of the Poor in Dunoon and Kilmun parish.

Migrating to Glasgow, he was employed first in the G. P. O. there as Sorting Clerk, and then as Clerk in the Globe Parcel Express Company's Office. Being transferred to Manchester as assistant manager, he four and a half years ago succeeded to full control of the Manchester branch on the death of the then manager, and there he remains, winning alike the 'Golden' opinion of his employers and the general public with whom he comes into daily contact. As showing that his services were not forgotten but at once remembered and appreciated, the Commissioners of Dunoon asked Mr. Maclean to write an opening Ode, which was sung by the children of the Dunoon Grammar School, at the opening of the Dunoon Castle Recreation Grounds, in June, 1893. Since going to Manchester, Mr. Maclean has been instrumental along with a few kindred spirits, in bringing into existence the Caledonian Society, which as the name implies is the rallying ground for 'Brither Scots' once a fortnight during the year. Twice has the Society given Mr. Maclean tangible proof of their appreciation of his efforts as Secretary to make the Society a happy meeting place for 'exiles frae hame.'

As a writer Mr. Maclean has been most prolific. As far back as 1880, he issued his first book entitled "Hamely Rhymes," in which, whether in hamely Scotch or elegant English, Mr. Maclean gave utterance to many gems of thought. Ever since he has contributed to various periodicals and magazines. In the *Oban Times* and *Highland Magazine* Mr. Maclean advocated in trenchant language the cause of the Crofter. To the *Argyllshire Standard* he contributed a series of sketches entitled "Cracks frae Whinny Knowe," sketches which caused that newspaper to be eagerly looked for each Friday by interested and amused readers.

In all his writings the subject of our sketch exhibits a keen sense of the beautiful in nature and a perfect Carlylean hatred of sham in man. A true radical he ever has had the warmest sympathy for the Crofters and Cottars of the far North. In these days of self-seeking, and when so many would fain forget the land of their birth, it is encouraging to meet such an one as Mr. Maclean who, while making for himself a 'pile' and name in the Sassenach country, never forgets the burns and braes and heath-clad hills of Caledonia. Of him it may well be said—

"I live for those who love me,
  For those I know are true,
For the heaven that smiles above me
  And awaits my spirit, too ;
For all human ties that bind me,
For the task my God assign'd me,
For the bright hopes left behind me,
  And the good that I can do."

Dunoon.   THOMAS SMITH.

BUADHAN AN UISGE-BHEATHA.

SEISD:—Tha buaidh air an uisge-bheatha
'S a bhuadhan, cha chòir an cleith,
Ge b' e dh' òlas a bheag dheth
Gu 'n toir e iomadh truaigh air

An tighean bochd nam pòitearan
Cha 'n 'eil ni deagh-òrdail annt',
Tha clann is mnathan brònach annt'
Na'n deòraidh le droch shmuagh orr'.

Cha 'n 'eil biadh ri 'chòcaireachd,
No àirneis anns an t-seòmar ac',
No trusgan ac' gu 'n còmhdachadh
Oir dh' òl iad an cuid airgid.

Tha 'n t-uisge-beatha ro-èifeachdach,
Gu bhi ag àrach èucaile,
'S gu toirt air falbh am beusalachd
O dhaoine eagnaidh, geamnaidh.

Bheir e'n toil 's an tùr uapa,
Bheir e' meas 's an cliù uapa,
Bheir e' neart 's an lùth uapa,
Is bheir e dh' ionnsuidh 'n uaigh iad.

Mu théid thu dh' ionnsuidh 'Bhìobuill leis
A' chùis so chum a mìneachadh,
Is i teist is breith na Fìrinn
Nach fhaigh am misgear suaimhneas.*

Air 'n aobhar sin is barail leam
Gur sona iad a dh' fhanas uaith
'S a bhòidicheas nach bean iad da
'S e chaitheas beath' na stuamachd.

* Gal. v. 21. Isa. v. 11.

Govan.   ALEX. MACRAE.

LITIR AS A' CHEARDAICH.

A GHAIDHEIL RUNAICH,

Buaidh 'us piseach ort a ghoistidh !
'S fhad o 'n bha miann orm sgriobhadh 'g a
t ionnsuidh, ach bha mi air mo chunnail cho
dripeil le gnothaichean an t-saoghail 's nach
robh mi 'faotainn cothrom air peann a chur air
paipeir. Agus a nis le cion cleachdaidh tha mo
mheòirean air fàs cho rag ris na gàtachan iarninn
a tha agam anns a' cheàrdaich.

Tha mi anabarrach toilichte a chluinntinn cho
math 's a tha thu 'faotainn air t aghart. Gu 'n
bheil thu fàs mòr agus clìitreach, agus tha
dòchas agam gu 'n lean thu mar sin. Tha sinne
anns a' cheàrn iomallach so dhe 'n dùthaich ro
thoilichte t-aghaidh fhaicinn a tighinn an rathad
uair 's a' mhìos; le do chuibhreach bòidheach
gorm ort agus do dhuilleagan finealta làn dhe
gach seòrs' eòlais agus fiosrachaidh. Agus tha
sinn gu h-àraidh ro bhuidheach dhiot air son
nan dealbhan gasda tha thu 'toirt dhuinn do
Ghàidheil fhinealhail a tha làn airidh air gach

onair agus urram a tha iad a faotainn. Ach
na 'm biodh mo ghob 'n a do chluais bheirinn
rabhadh beag dhuit air son cho dearmadach 's a
tha thu air mo sheann sean-mhathair chòir a'
Ghàilig. Tha dòchas agam nach bi thusa coltach
ris gach comunn Gàilig, agus paipeir Gàidhealach
eile 'tha dol air chois thall 's a bhos air feadh
na rioghachd. Neo-ar-thaing nach toir iad
sin dhuinn geallaidhean mòra briagha 'n àm
tòiseachaidh. Cò ach iadsan ! 's iad fhéin na
gillean, a tha dol a chumail suas cainnt, ceòl,
agus bàrdachd nan Gàidheal ! Ach cha luaithe
a shuidheas iad aig an stiùir agus a gheibh iad
an long fo' h-uidheam, na theid a' Ghàilig a chur
'an cùl a chinn 's a' Bheurla 'an clàr an aodainn.
Agus ann am beagan ùine cha 'n fhaod a' Ghàilig
chòir a gnùis a nochdadh, no idir a guth a thogail aig a h-aon dhe 'n cuid choinneamhan. Mo
nàire air na Gàidheil, nach biodh seasmhach,
duineil, mar 'bu chòir dhoibh, 's mar bu dual
dhoibh.

Ach feumaidh mi aideachadh gu 'm bheil aon
Chomunn Gàidhealach a chaidh air chois bho
chionn ghoirid air am bheil fìor choltas gnoth-
aich—sin agad Mòd an Obain. Mo sheachd
beannachd air na daoine tapaidh a tha air a
cheann, tha dòchas agam gu 'n soirbhich leò.
Agus ma bhios mis' air mo chaomhnadh gus an
ath-bhliadhn' fhaicinn, théid mi gu Mòd an Obain
ge do thigeadh orm am balg-sèididh agam a reic
air son m' fharadh a phàidheadh.

A nis a ghoistidh, feuch gu 'm bi thu seasmhach dìleas air taobh nan Gàidheal, 's air taobh
na Gàilig. Agus tha dòchas agam gu 'm bi na
Gàidheil seasmhach dìleas air do thaobh-sa. Ma
bheir thu àite do 'n litir so cha 'n 'eil mi 'g ràdh
nach sgriobh mi 'g a t-ionnsuidh a rithist 'n uair
a bhios cothrom agam. Ach aig an àm so
feumaidh mi iarunn eile a chur 's an teallaich.
'S mi le mòr spèis do charaide dìleas,

"an latha chi 's mac fhaic,"
GIOBHA-NAN-DUAN.

IN our next issue will appear the illustrated article
by Mr John Mackay, Hereford, on the Danish expulsion from the Reay country, and an interesting article
by Mr. C. Fraser-Mackintosh, F.S.A. (Scot.), on "The
two last Macdonalds of Isla," giving some hitherto
unpublished documents connected with Angus Macdonald of Dunyvaig and the Glens, and his son, Sir
James Macdonald, last of Isla and their attempts to
retrieve the fortunes of the Clan Iain Mor. The
first prize Gaelic Sgeulachd at the Oban Mòd will
also appear. The following interesting contributions will also find a place :—"The Highland Ancestors of Dr. David Livingstone," by Rev. A. Maclean
Sinclair, Nova Scotia; "A Sutherland Shinty Match,"
by Miss Robina Findlater; "A Minor Poet," by Miss
K. S. Cameron; "The Reay Fencibles," by Mr. D.
M. Rose, and articles by Messrs. Malcolm MacFarlane,
Henry Whyte, A. B. Maclennan, and other well-
known writers.

STATE OF CAITHNESS FROM 1730 TO 1760, AND THE SHERIFF.

(An Old MS.).

IT may be assumed that the North of Scotland was not in a very settled condition during the above period, and it appears from an old manuscript, entitled "Information respecting the present peculiar position" of the County of Caithness, dated 17th June, 1760, that this county was in an exceptionally troubled state. The MS. referred to sets forth that more "riots and murders prevailed in Caithness than in any three counties in Scotland." To have an end put to this sad position of matters, the interposition of superior authority was called for, and this demand was couched in highly patriotic language. It asserted that Caithness was inferior to no county in Britain, "if not before them all, in furnishing men to His Majesty's armies in proportion to their rents, and from whence not one man ever went to oppose his armies." The protection of the law was therefore invoked to remedy the distresses of the people "in this dangerous, deplorable situation." But what rendered the condition of matters the more curious was the fact that Sinclair, the laird of Freswick, was accused of conniving at some of the proceedings, and that Mr. Sinclair, the then young laird of Freswick, who was appointed Sheriff-Depute of the county about 1718, did not trouble himself much about the deprecations that were going on.

"The information" contains a detailed narrative of the causes of complaint. It recites that robberies were unknown in Caithness until about 1730, and thereafter describes at length the principal incidents of the subsequent thirty years.

It would appear that about 1730 a stranger named Bernard Clunis came to Caithness, and he formed a gang of desperadoes who, it is said, "distresst the country." He is charged with having "seduced, trained, and headed a band of the most profligate of the people." This band apparently carried on their operations for some years in the county, robbing and murdering where it suited them. Their conduct, however, roused the temper of the county gentlemen, who assisted the Sheriff in capturing the whole gang. Two of the principal ringleaders were sentenced to death. One of them, Donald Miller, was hanged, while the other who had been sentenced to death was sent, through some influence, to undergo another trial in Edinburgh. On his way there, however, he made his escape. Another man, named Donald Banks, "was shot and thereafter killed with a sword or cutlass in open daylight, on the the Sands of Dunnet," while James Hunter, the murderer, who had left Caithness for a little time, returned to the county, where he lived "quite unconcernedly." What aggravated the people was the circumstance that Hunter was protected by old Freswick, who gave him the utmost countenance.

But, instead of getting better, matters were gradually getting worse. A new and more powerful gang appeared, under the leadership of a new comer to the county, named Samuel Campbell. He and his family were nicknamed "Jews." The inhabitants complained that the new comers "made no account of themselves, from whence they came or what they were about, nor were they called upon to do so." It seems that the Campbells went about with a lot of merchandise, which they sold under value, but certainly contrary to the methods of the Jewish fraternity. Old Campbell had ample supplies of money, and latterly his eldest son, John, "married a gentleman's daughter of character and credit—a first cousin of the Sheriff-Depute." This connection, although not countenanced by the Sheriff-Depute, increased the boldness of the

FRESWICK CASTLE IN 1760.

Campbells, because, as the MS. states, they "evidently presumed upon the connection, and were known to distress the inhabitants of the town of Thurso. The sufferers chose to put up with their losses rather than try an attack upon the character of these Campbells." After an investigation it became evident that there were about twenty men in the gang, and that old Campbell was the recognised leader, he being, in the words of the MS., possessed " of a large stock of sagacity and subtilty." A number of murders followed. Hugh Munro, merchant, Thurso, was killed in his own house " by thrusting a sharp iron in his ear through his head," and so was John Swanson, alias " Canny." The shop of James Mackay, merchant, in Thurso, was broken into and the goods taken away.

G. M. SUTHERLAND.

Wick.

(To be concluded.)

A MACKAY-LAND SPOT IN LONDON TOWN.

JUST imagine the sounds of the *Piob Mhor* rushing into your ears through the thick atmosphere of a London street on a dark, wet night. You look around and find that the surprise comes from under an end door several steps above the level of the pavement of one of the colonies of small streets away to the north of "The Angel." It was no imagination with me, but a delightful reality: and with very little hesitation I dashed up the half stair and knocked. The door was opened so quickly, that the bright little man who responded must have had a premonition that the knock was coming. Just as quick was the greeting in the Gaelic of a born Londoner, and a warm welcome to the man who had so much of the Highlander in him as to impel him to break through ceremony and make for where the voice of the mountains was heard. In I go, in response to the warmest of invitations, and on being presented to as bright a wife—busy as a bee among household affairs on Saturday night—we descend to the region whence the stirring melody of *Gille Calum* issues. Here we find Archie Mackay, a strapping lad of fifteen, playing the pipes with a pleasant, easy grace, and Donald, under thirteen, going through the sword dance with masterly ease and loving care. I do not know which to place first, the utter want of backwardness or equally marked absence of forwardness in the two lads. Never did I see anything which went to show the nativity of those qualities which have made the genuine Highlander be accepted as a born gentleman. There is love of the household gods there, and there is the hold on the young hearts which the

mountains and the waterfalls and the rocks of the land of heroes and of bards and pipers have taken during early pilgrimages to the Mackay country, and to the lands of Deirdre and the sons of Uisneach.

The pipes change hands by and bye, and the smaller boy puts the bigger one through the same performance among the sticks which serve for swords. This done, we have a spell of conversation, in Gaelic or English as happens, much of it in reference to the classic shores of Loch Etive, where they all had spent portions of recent summers, and ranging from John Campbell's poetry, and gardening and grotto Sunday class, over the remains of *Barr a Ghobhainn* and of *Grianan Dheard-'uil*, to the majestic brow and noble crown of *Cruachan-beann*. But the pipes are almost palpitating on their bed to be again allowed to throw their share into the feast of most delightfully excited reason and flow of pellucid patriotism; and Archie and John Mackay, descendants of remote Highland fathers, are asked to relieve the agonies of the instrument. Each takes up an instrument, and they are in an instant marching under the solemn drones, whose far off sounds mix so well with the sharper notes of the chanter. From slow to quick they change, and from quick to quicker, until we actually have the two agile performers dancing as well as playing the *Tulaichean*. This is irresistible, and the father taking up one angle of the figure, and Donald the other—like the rest, perfectly spontaneously—the pride and pomp of the great, the petty strifes of trade, and the foul atmosphere of the London shops are as completely excluded as if the whole scene had been away beneath the green waves which move over the tree tops of *Eilean na h-Oige*.

By and bye the father takes one of the instruments and gives us "Scots wha hae" and "Corn Riggs" with a power which sends us to the corn riggs of the Carse of Stirling, whence we behold the monument on the Abbey Craig in the light of a glorious moon which defies the mirky gloom of London. And so on, and so on all of which I must leave you to spell out in your own imagination until I myself could not resist the spell, and I must perform my little share on John Mackay's splendid instrument. Who could not play it, especially after all that had gone before and off I come, defying the rain and the soot, and the mud and the noise of the London streets, to efface one feature in the little picture of a corner of the Mackay country in the good old times, when clansmen were more valuable than deer, and clanswomen more precious than rubies.

The best Highlanders in London will have no difficulty in making out where this Mackay-land spot is situated. JOHN MURDOCH.

ROBERT FERGUSSON, STIRLING.

ROBERT FERGUSSON, now of Stirling, was born in 1819, at East Stronvar, Balquhidder. He is what would be considered an old man; yet though his locks are white his heart is young, and his nature buoyant and simple as that of a youth. Age cannot wither nor custom stale the infinite variety of his ways for promoting things Highland. A poet, he loves the music of the Gael, and learned early to sympathise with nature, as he roamed amid the hills and beside the mountain torrents of his native glen. The parish school—at that time close to the churchyard — received him as a faithful scholar, quick to learn, and well acquainted with the Gaelic tongue, which was taught him by his father. In the competition in that language in 1834 he gained the first prize. His education was continued in Stirling, the grey 'City of the rock,' and in 1856-7-8 he passed through the F.C. Training College in Edinburgh. His profession of a schoolmaster was, however, begun at Dalveich, Lochearnside, in 1836, where Mr. Ferguson had the honour of having two future poets as his pupils—the late Rev. Samuel Fergusson of Fortingall, author of "The Queen's visit, and other poems," and Mr Donald M'Laren, Ardveich, whose songs and poems are all in Gaelic. For some time Mr. Fergusson taught the school of Strathyre hallowed with memories of Dugald Buchanan the Cowper of the Highlands, whose Spiritual songs are well known to all lovers of Gaelic poetry, and in whose memory the subject of our sketch was instrumental in raising a memorial fountain, which has its site near to the railway station. From 1842 to 1846 he was a teacher in Stirling, and in the neighbourhood of Dunfermline from 1846 to 1856, where his love for song and poetry was greatly fostered through intercourse with D. K. Coutts, his then school assistant, and afterwards master of Dr. Bell's School, Leith. In this school he was again favoured with another poet in one of his pupils - Mr. J Millar, now of London, author of "Zig Zag" and "My Lawyer," &c. From 1858 to 1868 Mr Fergusson acted as a teacher in a mission school connected with the Free Church, near Fordoun Station. During this time he occasionally acted as local preacher, and officiated in almost all the Free Church pulpits within the Presbytery. The close of Mr. Fergusson's active career as a schoolmaster was spent in the little village of Raploch, which nestles under the steep grey crags of Stirling Castle. He has now retired and, having celebrated his jubilee, is well entitled to do so. His time is chiefly occupied in doing what he can to further the cause of Celtic literature and the continuation of the Gaelic language. As an ex-president of the Stirling Highlanders' Society, he has had no small influence in fostering Celtic sentiment, and the Clan Fergusson Society has in him, one of its original promoters. "His poetical productions," says Mr. Edwards, in his *Modern Scottish Poets*, "possess a remarkable roundness and completeness of thought and while graceful in their simplicity, and set in smooth and musical words, they ever manifest buoyancy and spontaneity of flow, and occasional quiet pathos."

R. MENZIES FERGUSSON, M.A.

HIGHLAND NOTES AND QUERIES.

THE MacAlpines claim to be the most ancient of the clans.

TWENTY-ONE Highland chiefs with their clans fought on the side of Bruce at Bannockburn.

THREE fought in the English ranks—the Mac-Dougalls, Cummings, and MacNabs.

THE HENDERSONS OF CAITHNESS are a sept of the Clan Gunn.

FOR a Highlander to lose his sword in battle was considered an everlasting disgrace.

THERE is a certain loch in Perthshire where, the people say, the great water-horse has been frequently *very nearly seen*!

IT is said that the MacPhersons were never defeated in battle. This was, perhaps, because they did not fight once a week as most other clans did!

THE FIXED BAYONET, which has been adopted by the armies of all European nations, was first introduced into warfare by General Hugh Mackay of Scourie.

MAC FEARN Can any one give me the origin of this surname? I am told there is an interesting song and story connected with it.

DUNVEGAN CASTLE, the seat of the Chief of the MacLeods, is the oldest inhabited fortress in the British Isles.

THERE is an old Highland superstition to the effect that those who parted on a bridge would never meet again.

SIR WILLIAM WALLACE, the Scottish hero, was of the Gaelic race, and his army which routed the English at the battle of Stirling Bridge was composed almost entirely of Highlanders.

WHEN THE HEREDITARY JURISDICTION ACT was passed after the '45, the Campbells got £45,800, and the Menzies £12,000 as compensation. There was a grand scramble for the plunder.

IN THE CRICKET TEAM which represented "England" against Australia recently there were two Gaels - Gunn and MacGregor. No wonder "England" won!

THE CAMERON CLAN.—The first regiment to scale the ramparts at Tel-el-Kebir was the Cameron Highlanders; and the first man to meet a soldier's death in the attack was Donald Cameron, a Lochaber man.

THE FIRST GAELIC SOIRÉE held in Glasgow, came off in the St. Clair Hall, Robertson Street, under the auspices of the Gaelic Lodge of Good Templars, on *9th October, 1873.*

THE FUNERAL OF LORD LOVAT, in 1632, was attended by 1000 Munros, 1000 Rosses, 1000 Frasers, 900 Mackenzies, and 800 Grants, all armed. The historian quaintly remarks that the "proceedings passed off peaceably!"

OF THE 800 MACLEANS who took part in the Battle of Inverkeithing, not more than 40 escaped with life. In attempting to shield the person of the chief (Sir Hector) from injury, no less than eight gentlemen of the name of Maclean lost their lives, hence the Gaelic proverb, "Fear eil' airson Eachainn!" another for Hector!

THE MACGREGOR'S SLOGAN, or war-cry, was "Ard-Choille"—the woody height; their gathering tune, "Ruaig Ghlinne Freoine" the chase of Glen Fruin; and their banner was of green, the famous "Pine-crested Banner."

THE MACKAYS did not accept a charter for their lands till 1889, and are supposed to have been the last clan to accept a "sheep skin" charter. The Strong Hand (*Manu-Forti*) had hitherto been their best right of possession.

THE LATE CHIEF OF THE GRANTS, the Earl of Seafield, had a truly chequered career. He was successively an auctioneer's clerk, a storeman at a salary of 30s. per week, and a bailiff in the town of Omaru, New Zealand.

THE DUKE OF SUTHERLAND has decided to increase the crofters' holdings by breaking up some of the large farms. I hope I shall be there to see the people entering the land of my forefathers—the "Promised Land" Strathnaver and Kildonan.

CLUNY MACPHERSON, who was out in 1745, declared, after the Battle of Falkirk, that the English cavalry must have very thick skulls, as he "struck at them till he was tired, and was scarcely able to break one." No wonder! The horsemen wore iron skull-caps in their hats!

WHILE SPENDING MY ANNUAL HOLIDAY in the romantic Reay country recently, I received the following lines from a poetic friend in London, who was evidently sighing for a sight of his own native mountains:—

> " And oft do I long,
> With a tear in my eye,
> For a glimpse of the hills
> In the land of Mackay."

"HIGHLAND" TROOPS IN INDIA. Two of the finest regiments at present stationed in India are, I believe, the Seaforth Highlanders, and the 93rd Sutherland Highlanders. Other crack Scotch regiments are there as well. Yet this is the impudent manner in which the London *Standard* insults their Scotch nationality. It says—" In regard to the armament of the *English* (?) troops in India, 70,000 magazine rifles have now been sent from *England*." And yet Scotch papers would reproduce this insult, and present it to their readers without protest! We had better all become "Englishmen" at once, if we wish to be in the fashion.

STRENGTH OF THE SUTHERLANDSHIRE CLANS The following list, compiled from the electoral roll of 1885, will interest many of our readers. The figures are instructive as showing the relative strength of the clans which have been specially identified with the past history of the county:—Mackays, 547; Macleods, 237; Sutherlands, 230; Rosses, 177; Mackenzies, 170; Munros, 126; Macdonalds, 119; Murrays, 117; Mathesons, 92; Campbells, 82; Gunns, 62; Morrisons, 62; Grants, 41; Gordons, 41; Sinclairs, 23; Macleans, 19; Kerrs, 19; Bannermans, 18. An analysis of the above figures shows some curious results. In the five parishes which comprise the Mackay country, we find that there are 354 Mackays, while the total of all other names only amounts to 156, which shows how strong the clan is still in its ancient territory. In Assynt, the Macleod country, the Macleods number 114, while the other names number 156. In the eight parishes in the south, where the Sutherlands would be expected to be strongest, we find they number only 193, while the Mackays, the northern clan, are 206. We shall give the Caithness clans in our next. Would any of our readers favour us by sending an analysis of the electoral rolls of the other Highland counties?

NEWS OF THE MONTH.

GLASGOW MULL AND IONA ASSOCIATION.—The annual meeting of this society was held in the St. Andrew's Hall on 3rd October—Mr Duncan Mackinnon in the chair. The annual reports showed the association to be in a flourishing condition. The following office-bearers were elected :- Hon. president, Sir Fitzroy D. MacLean; president, Donald MacPherson ; vice-president, Duncan Mackinnon ; treasurer, Edward Archer ; secretary, John M. Murray, 41 Breadalbane Street, and twelve directors. The social gathering will take place in the City Hall on the last Friday of February next.

EDINBURGH SUTHERLAND ASSOCIATION. — The monthly meeting was held on the 6th ult. Rev. Peter Dewar, M.A., North Bute, gave an interesting account of the enquiry now being carried on by the Psychical Research Society on the subject of "Second Sight" in the Highlands. Mr. Dewar mentioned that the belief in the supernatural still seems prevalent in Sutherland, and asked the members to send notes upon any instances which came under their observation.

GAELIC SOCIETY OF INVERNESS. The first meeting of the season was held in Inverness—Mr. Alex. Mackenzie presiding. Eleven new members were elected. At the close of the meeting Mr. Colin Chisholm, Namur Cottage, sang a Gaelic song.

NEW KINTYRE ASSOCIATION.— At an enthusiastic meeting of natives of Kintyre resident in Glasgow, held on 6th ult., a new society was formed, and office-bearers elected.—Hon. president, Rev. James C. Russell, D.D. ; president, David Andrews ; secretaries, Donald Fisher and Donald Stalker ; treasurer, Thomas MacPhail. The objects of the association are to form a bond of union among Kintyrians in Glasgow, to foster native interests and sentiment, and to promote the welfare of its members. The society has already received encouraging support. The meetings are held fortnightly in the Religious Institution Rooms, Buchanan Street, and all interested are cordially invited.

THE MENZIES CLAN SOCIETY.- On Saturday, 7th ult., the annual meeting was held at Aberfeldy. Mr. Walter Menzies presided. There was a large attendance. The secretary's report was most satisfactory, the total funds of the society being over £300, £270 of which were intended to form the nucleus of a clan bursary. Sir Robert Menzies, Bart., chief of the clan, on entering the meeting, received a hearty welcome, amidst cries of " The red and white for ever !" (the colours of the Menzies tartan). Office-bearers were then appointed as follows : Chief, Sir Robert Menzies, Bart. ; junior chief, Captain Neil James Menzies ; captain, Fetcher Norton Menzies ; chieftains, Lieut. W. G. S. Menzies of Culdares ; Major W. J. B. S. Menzies of Chesthill ; president, W. W. Graham Menzies ; convener, Walter Menzies ; secretary, D. P. Menzies, F.S.A. (Scot.); treasurer, Rector Thomas Menzies, F.E.I.S. ; and also local secretaries and pipers.

CLAN MACLEOD SOCIETY.—The opening meeting of the session was held on the 9th ult.—Mr. Brodie MacLeod presiding. Mr. Henry Whyte read a paper on "Gaelic Poetry and Music of the Clan MacLeod." He referred to the various bards of the clan, and to the poems which had been composed in its honour. He gave examples of the compositions of Mary MacLeod (Màiri nighean Alasdair Ruaidh), the lament for "Roary Mòr," and "MacCrimmon's Lament," &c. In the present century the clan has been well represented by capable poets, and he referred specially to Neil MacLeod, Murdo MacLeod, Peter MacLeod, and others. Several of those present having expressed their pleasure at listening to so interesting a lecture, a hearty vote of thanks was awarded to the lecturer. It may be mentioned that the chief of the clan is to pay a visit to this city in April, when he is to receive a Highland welcome from the members of the clan.

THE CLAN GRANT SOCIETY are to have a grand concert in Glasgow about the middle of November, Professor Sir Ludovic Grant, Edinburgh University, in the chair.

GLASGOW SUTHERLAND ASSOCIATION. The society met in the Assembly Rooms, on the 5th ult. Mr. Donald Mackenzie, president, in the chair. Dr. J. F. Sutherland delivered an instructive lecture on "Old Age Pensions," which led to an interesting discussion. Resolutions were passed condemning the sentences passed upon the Airdens Crofters, and in favour of an extension of the Crofters' Act to leaseholders. The association's funds amount to £35.

THE GLASGOW COWAL SOCIETY'S funds amount to £830.

THE CLAN MACKAY held their monthly meeting on the 19th ult. in Glasgow Mr. Alex. Mackay, president, in the chair. A paper was read on " A Mackay-Land Spot in London Town," which will be found in this issue of the Celtic Monthly. The meeting was a very enjoyable one. The Society's funds amount to £780, exclusive of a sum of over £500 which was raised for the fishing disaster in Sutherland.

THE CLAN MACMILLAN are to have a social gathering this month.

GLASGOW COWAL SHINTY CLUB.—We beg to acknowledge, with thanks, receipt of the following donations towards the club-house fund :— Lachlan Macdonald, Esq., of Skeabost, Skye (patron), £1 ; W. Sutherland Hunter, Esq., Pollokshields (patron), 5s. We shall be glad to receive and acknowledge further subscriptions.

MORE SUTHERLAND BURSARIES. - Mr. John Mackay, C.E., J.P., Hereford, has again shown his interest in his native parish in a practical way. He has provided a bursary of £25 for four years to Rogart lads, to be called the "Cromartie" Bursary, in honour of the late Duchess of Sutherland, and another of £15 for four years for girls, to be called the "Alexandra," in honour of the late Lady Alexandra.

JOHN MACKENZIE, of the "Beauties," and Mr. T. D. MacDonald, Canada, were very intimate friends, and Evan MacColl, the poet, and he were bed-fellows in Glasgow. Old Dr. Norman MacLeod was a constant visitor at Lachlan MacLean's shop.

TO MY HIGHLAND HOME.

On wavelet, playing at my feet,
  Seek thou the open sea,
And, mounted on a billow fleet,
  Bear a greeting back from me
To the Ben on whose brown heather
  I have frolicked when a child,
To the kindest foster-mother
  That e'er on nursling smiled.

Tell her, as in the hollow shell
  The music of the brine,
So doth the mountain spirit dwell
  In this lone heart of mine ;
As its fairy legend clingeth
  To yonder ruin grey,
So her haunting presence flingeth
  Its charm round me alway.

I greet her in the wild, wild sea
  That kneeleth at her feet,
Sinking his voice, caressingly,
  To murmurs low and sweet ;
In the wind that roams the hollow,
  And plays on her heathy crest,
I come on the wing of the swallow,
  For shelter, and Summer, and rest.

I greet the river from the glen,
  The rushy, flower-gemmed lea,
The cottage by the hazel den,
  And the gnarled, old oak tree ;
And, the children's feet caressing,
  As they gather shells by the tide,
I send on the breeze a blessing
  To the kirk on the green hillside.

Each ferny nook, and rocky height,
  Each bosky woodland grove
On mem'ry's tide lies mirrored bright
  In the magic light of love :
I see it all in the sunlight,
  When the rose and the hawthorn blow,
And I see it again when the moonlight
  Shines full on the ermine snow!

My home upon the mountain side,
  I dwell for aye in thee ;
Nymph-like, within my fount abide,
  As the mermaid in her sea ;
How oft, from the deeps of feeling,
  From her cave, hid far from the light,
An imprisoned thought comes stealing
  In the calm, sweet hours of night ;

She sings to me the cradle-song
  That lulled my early youth—
The love of freedom, hate of wrong,
  The praise of peace and truth,
And the spirit of the mountain
  Takes up the glad refrain,
Till my being's ice-bound fountain
  Springs joyously upward again.

The mists of sorrow roll away
  That wrapped my soul in gloom,
The light breaks forth, with mellow ray,
  My life to re-illume ;
The hopes that seemed to be shattered
  Take deeper, firmer root,
And the buds whose blossoms were scattered
  Change fast into ripening fruit.

Now say, oh wavelet, to the hill
  Upon whose breast I've played,
So precious to my heart is still
  Each dell, and rock, and glade,
E'en in death shall her child turn to greet her,
  As the spirit returns to its God.
And, methinks, I should slumber the sweeter
  If wrapped in her heathery sod !

                  K. W. G.

To the Editor, "Celtic Monthly."

"THE GARB OF OLD GAUL."

SIR,—Your remarks on the so called "Highland Honours" at festivals, &c., in your last issue, embolden me to call attention to one or two modern customs which are very common with thoughtless people when writing in English on Gaelic matters.

The first is—such writers are sure to use the words "Celt" and "Celtic," when they mean Gael and Gaelach, to use the short spelling. I have never seen or heard the word "Celt" in our own language, and for classification purposes it would be as correct to refer to a modern Lowlander or Sassanach as a Teuton. When the reader pronounces it "Selt" the absurdity is complete.

"The Garb of Old Gaul" is another misleading and favourite phrase, for which the author of that much-quoted song is responsible. I remember in my youthful days being under the firm belief that it meant the costume of old France, though at the time pretty well acquainted with stories of Goll or Gall Mac Morna, to whom, I believe, it refers, but which I never heard pronounced "Gaul," the vowel being sounded short.

"Fingal"—I wonder if any of your readers have ever heard this name in Gaelic—I never have, in either Ireland or Scotland. It was always Fionn, or Fionn Mac Cumhal. I notice that Lieut.-Colonel Stewart, in your last two issues, uses "Fingal" in the papers which he contributes, and also that he makes Cuchullainn a contemporary of the Fiana, upon what authority I do not know, as both the oral and written legends place them in two different epochs altogether.

I was much interested in the enjoyable paper on Gaelic music by Mr. M. Macfarlane, and apropos of the tendency in Irish Gaelic to substitute l for r. I remember hearing Gregalach for Gregorach, and is not the name Frazer Frizallach in Gaelic ?

                MAC RUAGHNUICH.

Barrow-on-Furnace.

A TALENTED CAITHNESS LADY.

SIR, Permit me to refer, in a few lines, to a distinguished lady of this county, whose recent death we deeply deplore. Mrs. Roger, Druid Hall, Durban, S. Africa, was the younger daughter of the late Mr. Donald Mackay, Upper Lybster, where her ancestors settled, when evicted from Strathnaver. She was nearly related to the well known and highly respected Mackays of Montreal. Born at Lybster in 1858, she was educated in the F. C. school there, and subsequently at Reay. At the age of 13, she entered the Queen Street Ladies' College, Edinburgh, where, in addition to other prizes, she carried off the £100 scholarship, which was regarded as the 'blue riband' of the institution. She afterwards passed the University examination in mathematics and English literature, for the degree of M.A. About 14 years ago, she accepted an appointment in the Ladies' College, Durban, where she laboured with ability and success. In 1884, she was married to Mr. George Roger. Her death, on the 1st April last, filled with sadness many an aching heart, both in the old and in her adopted country. Her whole life was devoted to acts of charity, and in furthering mission work, and the tribute which was paid her memory, by the Natal papers, was a fitting acknowledgment of a life nobly spent in doing good.

Reay.   HUGH CAMPBELL.

REVIEWS.

"FISHING INCIDENTS AND ADVENTURES." By Malcolm Ferguson. (Dundee: John Leng & Co.) Mr. Ferguson has added another volume to his interesting series of works on the Highlands, and we consider it the best which has yet come from his pen. Although it appeals specially to the followers of the gentle art, it contains many features which ought to make it welcome to the ordinary reader. His descriptions of Highland scenery are always true to nature ; and no one knows better than Mr. Ferguson how to tell a good story well. The volume is brimful of racy stories, some humorous, others exciting enough to enthrall the reader's attention. The book is also valuable from an historical point of view, for the author is deeply learned in the traditions, poetry, and folk-lore of his native Perthshire, and he has imparted into these sketches a good deal of his own rich store of knowledge. The printing and binding are excellent, and the portrait of the author, which appears as a frontispiece, and the other illustrations, are very artistic. Mr. Ferguson's name will be familiar to our readers. His portrait appeared in our February issue, and an article by him on the "Black Watch Memorial" found a place in the September number. We trust that the " Fishing Incidents and Adventures " will have a large sale.

THE ENGLISH ILLUSTRATED MAGAZINE for October is specially interesting to Highlanders on account of the exceedingly fine portrait of Lord Aberdeen the new Governor of Canada, which appears as the frontispiece. An interesting biographical sketch of this head of the "Gay Gordons" is also given. Some of the illustrations in this number of the English Illustrated are the finest specimens of zincography which we have ever seen.

"THE SCOTTISH CANADIAN" (Toronto) now appears in a new and neater form. Its contents are always varied and instructive, and we look forward each week to its arrival with much pleasure, the news of the Highland societies across the seas being of peculiar interest to us. We are sorry to learn that the talented editor, Mr. Alex. Fraser (our own Canadian correspondent), has been seriously ill for some time past—which accounts for the absence of our " Canadian Letter " of late—but we are glad to state that he is now convalescent and about to resume his editorial duties.

"SWEETHEART GWEN: A WELSH IDYLL." By William Tirebuck. (London : Longmans, Green & Co., 1893). —Those who want to read a charming, if sketchy, Welsh story will find such a thing here. If the name of the writer be new to many, "Sweetheart Gwen" affords a cordial means of introduction to one it is worth our while to know. Welsh farm life is faithfully and lovingly depicted; a child's feelings and recollections, with the light of romance-magic resting upon the smallest details, are most felicitously portrayed ; and —in Part III. especially, which is, alas, also the sand-bed in which the forceful and limpid river of narrative loses itself—wit and fancy play themselves between graver thoughts that are in turn pale with regret and red with desire. This pen, at least, runs to line issues, oftentimes, and even when it but toys with its own powers shows something of the diamond point. In a word, this is a tale wherein we may enjoy a singularly fresh presentment of a fascinating, and perhaps not altogether unusual, relationship between the sexes, which ends—ah, well, buy the book.

HIGHLAND CHARITY FUNERALS.—It has been the habit on the west coast for the Parochial Board to supply three bottles of whisky at the funerals of paupers. Recently, it was decided to restrict this magnificent allowance, and in future to supply only one bottle. After that, there was no genuine enthusiasm over pauper funerals in that district, and the Board had to defray the cost, which came to more than the value of the extra two bottles. It was then decided to go back on the old arrangement, and now that there is more whisky to be had, pauper funerals have become more popular than ever. A sarcastic friend has endeavoured to point out to us a connection between the quantity of whisky and the amount of enthusiasm, but we do not profess to recognise it. To us it only seems clear that the people have educated themselves up to an appreciation of pauper funerals !

"SECOND-SIGHT" IN SCOTLAND.—The Society for Psychical Research are at present engaged upon an inquiry into second-sight in Scotland, and we have been invited to give our personal experiences, or such authentic information as we possess on the subject. We fear that if we gave a circumstantial account of our own experiences, and those of persons of our acquaintance still living, some enterprising novelist would seize upon the facts and make a fortune out of them ! We intend shortly publishing a well authenticated case of second-sight in the Highlands, which, in its weird and startling details, will make even the members of the Psychical Society feel a little uncomfortable. However, some of our readers may be able to assist the committee in their inquiry, and for their information we append the following queries:—"(1) Is second-sight believed in by the people of your neighbourhood ? (2) Have you yourself seen or heard of any cases which appear to imply such a gift ? If so, will you send me the facts ? (3) Can you refer me to anyone who has had personal experience, and who would be disposed to make a statement to me on the subject ? (4) Do you know of any persons who feel an interest, and would be disposed to help, in this inquiry ?" The Rev. Peter Dewar, The Manse, North Bute, Rothesay, will be pleased to hear from anyone who has any information to communicate on the subject of second-sight.

CAMANACHD NOTES.

THE SHINTY ASSOCIATION.—The formation of a shinty association, which was duly inaugurated at Kingussie on the 10th ult., is the chief subject of discussion in camanachd circles at present. Fourteen clubs were represented at the meeting, office-bearers were appointed, and a code of rules was adopted. The clubs represented at the meeting were all located in the north, the place of meeting (Kingussie) being too far distant for clubs in the south and west to send delegates. Had Perth been chosen as a centre the meeting would have been more representative of the Highlands. The formation of an association is certainly a step in the right direction. It is a pity, however, that the west country clubs were not represented, because the rules adopted differ materially from those adhered to by many of the clubs in the west and south, and we fear they may not be ready to adopt in their entirety those arranged. We may also ask, is it wise to elect all the office-bearers from north country clubs alone, and ignore the west altogether? And why fix the annual business meeting for Inverness a year in advance? If the association is intended to represent the north only this may seem right and proper, but if it is to include the clubs at a distance it is foolishness to expect these clubs to send delegates so far. Why not make the meeting at Perth, which would be a central place for all parties? Was it necessary to fix a date for the next annual business meeting already—could this not have been left to the office-bearers to decide upon later on? There are, we daresay, as many clubs in the west and south as there are in the north, and the convenience and co-operation of these ought to receive some consideration. These suggestions occurred to us as soon as we read the report of the meeting, and we find that this feeling is shared by shinty players in general in this district. If it is not yet too late we would ask the office-bearers to give these matters their earnest consideration, and so avoid any appearance of localising the association to any one part of the country. If this is not done the probability is that an association will be started to represent the west and south of Scotland and England.

THE LONDON NORTHERN COUNTIES CAMANACHD CLUB held their annual business meeting on the 6th ult. The attendance was large and enthusiastic; and the treasurer's report showed a substantial balance at the credit of the club. We understand that a match has been arranged between the Camanachd and the Glasgow Cowal, which is to be played in London sometime in December, or on New-Year's Day. A contest between these well-known clubs should arouse some interest in shinty in the Metropolis. The following office bearers were elected for the year: Chief, Superintendent Colin Chisholm; hon. captain, Lieut. Neil Mackay; captain, W. Macgregor Stoddart; vice-captain, Ewen Cattanach; treasurer, A. Anderson; secretary, J. Mackenzie, 45 Wilton Square, Islington. Committee—Roderick Macleod, Kenneth Macaulay, Donald Macgillivray, J. M. Watson, Neil Maclaren, D. Forbes, Alexander Mackenzie, John MacLean, James Smith, W. A. Martin, C. F. Munro, and Walter Nichol. Pipers, Donald Mackay, John Mackenzie, and J. G. Mackay. Fourteen new members joined the Club.

THE GLASGOW COWAL SHINTY CLUB TOURNAMENT, which took place on the 7th October, was a great success. Twenty four members entered for the competitions, and these were balloted for in teams of six each. The matches were very keenly contested, and finally resulted in No. 4 team carrying off the honours. The following composed the winning team:—William Robinson (goal), Peter Campbell, vice-captain; Duncan Martin, Gilbert D. Gillies, Cameron Henderson, and John Campbell. There was a large number of spectators present, who declared that they never saw a better exposition of shinty on any field. The Cowal men certainly were never in better form than they are at present. In the evening a social meeting was held Mr John Mackay, editor, Celtic Monthly, occupying the chair. After a substantial supper, speeches were made, healths drank, and songs rendered by members and friends. The entertainment was very enjoyable, and others of a similar nature are to be arranged during the winter.

EDINBURGH CAMANACHD CLUB. — The annual general meeting of this club was held on Friday, the 6th October, and was well attended. Mr. W. G. Cumming occupied the chair. The minutes of of the last general meeting, as well as the annual detailed report, were read by the secretary and approved of. The following office-bearers were elected:—Chief, Mr. Patrick Cameron of Corrychoille; chieftain, Mr. W. G. Cumming; secretary and treasurer, Mr. T. H. Brodie. Committee Messrs. Donald Cameron, A. Mackay Robson, Donald Oliver, Alex. Kennedy, Wm. Murray, Jack Lawson, and D. Smith. The Inverleith Park, where the club meets for practice, is now open, and we hope the devoted band who compose the club will receive the well-deserved encouragement of all Highlanders resident in Edinburgh, and enthusiasts in their national pastime.

OBITUARY.

DEATH has laid its hand heavily of late among our subscribers. We regret to intimate the death of MR. MURDO MACLEOD, CHIEF MAGISTRATE OF STORNOWAY, a gentleman highly respected in his native island, and by all who had the pleasure of knowing him. Mr. Macleod was a liberal supporter of Gaelic literature, and was among the first to welcome the advent of the Celtic Monthly. His early death will be lamented by many friends at home and abroad.

Another typical member of the same clan, MR. MURDO MACLEOD, OF EDINBURGH, has also passed away. Mr. Macleod was a native of Assynt, Sutherland, and his services on behalf of his unfortunate countrymen will be long and gratefully remembered. He was an enthusiastic member of the Edinburgh Sutherland Association, and of the Clan Macleod Society. His manly form and genial presence will be missed by a large circle of friends.

ALEXANDER MACDONALD.

(Town Clerk, Govan).

THE CELTIC MONTHLY:
A MAGAZINE FOR HIGHLANDERS.
Edited by JOHN MACKAY, Kingston.

No. 3. Vol. II.] DECEMBER, 1893. [Price Threepence.

ALEXANDER MACDONALD, GOVAN.

LIKE his famous clansman, Marshal Macdonald, Duke of Tarentum, Mr Alexander Macdonald belongs to the Clanranald branch of the great Clan Donald. He was born at Irvine on 19th March, 1824, and while yet an infant was taken from the land of Burns to the equally renowned land of *Alasdair Mac-Mhaighstir Alastair*, whose songs will be sung while the Gaelic language is spoken. Mr. Macdonald commenced his legal studies in the town of Inverness, where he entered the office of Mr. Charles Stewart of Brin, who was confidential solicitor to many of the distinguished families of the north. Among the important cases which were attended to in Mr. Stewart's chambers was the celebrated Advocation of Brieves, between Lord Lovat, grandfather of the present baron, and the Rev. Alex. Gorden Fraser, of New York, who claimed the Lovat title and estates. Upwards of one hundred of the oldest men of the north were examined as witnesses, and Mr. Macdonald remembers many of the interesting tales of the risings of 1715 and '45 told by these witnesses. There are few people living now who can say that they have conversed with persons who had witnessed the closing events of the '45, and it is interesting to mention that as a boy, the subject of our sketch spoke to one—his own grand-uncle—who had heard the firing and seen the smoke of Culloden! Among Mr. Macdonald's school fellows at Inverness were the late Mr. Malcolm M'Lennan, Procurator-Fiscal at Wick, author of "Peasant Life in the North," and his talented brother, Mr. John F. M'Lennan, M.A., advocate, author of "Primitive Marriage," and other learned treatises.

Mr. Charles Fraser-Mackintosh, whose name is a household word wherever Highlanders are to be found, was another of his contem-

poraries. That gentleman gave early promise of the industry, ability, and gentlemanly conduct which have all along distinguished him through life. In 1844 Mr. Macdonald left Inverness to prosecute his studies in the University of Glasgow, and was successful in taking the first prize for Scots law. He afterwards matriculated in the University of Edinburgh, and acted as secretary to Mr. Allan Menzies, W.S., Professor of Conveyancing, whom he assisted in preparing his lectures.

While still a law student he did not neglect his literary studies. In 1849, on the occasion of the Queen's visit to Scotland, the *Glasgow Examiner* offered a prize for the best poem on the auspicious event. About one hundred compositions were sent in, which were submitted for adjudication to Sheriff Henry Glassford Bell, who awarded the prize to Mr. Macdonald. In this year he went to Germany to study Roman law, and public and international law. After remaining abroad for about a year he returned to Scotland, and became a member of the Faculty of Procurators in Greenock, where he practised for several years, and conducted several important church cases. In 1863 he went to New Zealand, intending to settle there, but finding the country in a very depressed condition he returned to Scotland, and began business in Glasgow.

In 1880 Mr. Macdonald was appointed to the important office of Town Clerk of Govan, a position which he has since filled with credit and distinction. He is also well-known as a successful author, and has written several legal treatises—one on "Justices of the Peace and other Magistrates in Scotland," another on the law relative to "Masters, Workmen, Servants, and Apprentices," and also a compendium of of "The Law with regard to National Education in Scotland," besides other minor works. In addition to these professional works, he wrote "A Student's Adventures in Turkey and the East," and founding on his experience of church cases—"The Story of a Disputed Settlement; or, Love, Law, and Theology," which were both published by Messrs. Dunn & Wright, Glasgow.

Both books—the latter in particular—show a keen sense of humour, and from each we get pleasant and intelligent glimpses of life under various conditions. His literary style manifests the shrewd perception and methodical training of the lawyer, touched and softened by the breadth and freedom given by world-wide travel. May we venture to hope for a book based on the Jacobite period, and embodying Mr. Macdonald's delightful and unique stories of the "Rebellion"? Mr. Macdonald is one of the vice-presidents of the Clan Macdonald Society, and is at present engaged in gathering materials with regard to the life and times of Marshal Macdonald, in which congenial undertaking we hope he may be assisted by the readers of the *Celtic Monthly.*

Edinburgh.   A. F. CARMICHAEL.

PRIZE STORY.

DONALD MACLEOD, THE SOLDIER:
A WEST HIGHLAND TRADITION.

THERE lived in Strathbran, in the Highlands of Ross-shire, about two hundred years ago, a scion of the Clan Macleod, called *Iain Bàn Mac Dhomhnuill Iain.* He had an only son named Donald, a tall, handsome, good-looking man, and as erect as a rash. Before Donald completed his twentieth year his father died; and about a year afterwards Donald married Mary Mackenzie, a beautiful girl of only eighteen summers, belonging to a neighbouring hamlet. Donald Macleod and his young wife pictured to themselves a long and happy future, but fate decided otherwise. They had only enjoyed the married state about six weeks when the affectionate husband was ruthlessly torn from the arms of the loving wife, and, like many other Highlanders of that period, sent abroad to fight in the wars. Having received little or no education, Donald, although he could read a little, could not write any, and, being of a haughty disposition, he would not deign to ask another to write for him, so he never sent or received a letter, or heard from his wife.

Mrs. Macleod, who was pregnant when her husband was taken from her, in due time gave birth to a strong, healthy son, whom she nursed with motherly care, and as he grew in years she trained him with tact for all that was necessary for one his position. As she never heard from her husband, she concluded that he had been killed in battle, the thought of which drew many a tear from her eyes, and wrung many a heavy sigh from her heart. She received many offers of marriage, but she declined them all. One night, some time after retiring to bed, about twenty-two years after her husband's departure, she was suddenly seized by a severe chill. Getting alarmed, she called her son, who was sleeping in another bed in the same apartment. He at once rose and did everything possible for her, without effect. As a last resort, in order to impart warmth to his mother, he lay down at her back and in a short time had the satisfaction to know that she was better; and soon afterwards both imperceptibly fell asleep.

Being a steady, active man, Donald Macleod became a favourite with his commanding officer. As he never drew any money, his officer took care of it all for him, putting it into a small bag which he procured for the purpose. On his arrival in England and receiving his discharge, his officer presented Donald with his (Donald's) sword, the bag of money, and five shillings, advising him at the same time not to touch the contents of the bag till he reached home; that the five shillings were for his requirements by the way, and that he should always choose the "long, safe" road in preference to the "short, dangerous" one, a counsel having a highly elevating moral. Donald was accompanied on his journey homeward by another discharged soldier belonging to Easter Ross. On their way they came to a point where the road branched off into two—one an even, good road, which, after a considerable detour, converged again with the other, which, though much shorter, was rough, and passed through a thick wood, said to be infested by robbers. Donald elected to take the "long, safe" one, while his companion proceeded by the other. Donald had not gone far when he heard cries of "murder." He ran to the spot whence the cries proceeded, and found two men robbing his companion. Donald, with two well-directed strokes of his sword, decapitated both.

Donald and his companion now proceeded together by the "long, safe" road. But they could not travel day and night continuously; so, arriving late one evening at a small country village where there was a little public-house, they went in to lodge for the night. It was conducted by a pretty young woman, whose husband, the landlord, was a diminutive, old creature, who had slept for some time previously in a little crib in a corner off the kitchen. Being somewhat fatigued, Donald and his com panion retired early, but, for some inexplicable reason, Donald failed to fall asleep, so after his companion fell into a profound slumber he rose and went outside. Shortly afterwards he noticed a man on horseback coming to the place. Arriving, he put his horse into the stable, and then went into the public-house. Being curious to know his business, Donald cautiously drew near, and for once in his life adopted the rôle of eavesdropper, the result proving the wisdom of the act on this occasion at any rate. Donald was not long acting in his new character when he discovered that the rider was making love with the young buxom landlady, who was at that moment telling her swain that the long-wished-for time to end the life of her old, useless husband had now come ; that he (the rider) might kill him at once, and they could easily blame the soldiers. This wicked suggestion was immediately acted upon, and after the horrible deed was committed the wanton land-lady proposed that they should get married as soon as possible after everything connected with the old man's death and funeral were satisfactorily disposed of, to which her wicked paramour assented. She also requested him to call upon her in course of the following afternoon, so as to learn how matters were proceeding. To this he also agreed. Then, after tenderly embracing each other, they parted. On taking his horse out of the stable, and when in the act of mounting, Donald, who stood concealed near the spot, sprang forward, and with one blow of his trusty blade struck off his right hand at the wrist. With his mutilated limb pained and bleeding, he galloped off as fast as his horse could go to the residence of a medical man, who soon bound it up for him. The soldier picked up the bleeding hand, and after wiping it put it into his pocket, and, re-entering the public-house, undressed and lay down beside his fellow-lodger, who was still in the land of Nod, and, therefore, knew nothing of what had occurred, either in the house or outside of it, since he retired to bed.

Next morning witnessed a great commotion at the little public-house. The old landlord was found dead in his crib, having been stabbed to death during the night. That the soldiers were the perpetrators of the deed there seemed to be no doubt, for the young widow, who was utterly prostrate with grief for her "dear husband," distinctly heard through the night the sound of footsteps between the bed in which they slept and that occupied by her "late darling," but it never occurred to her that such a dreadful deed was being committed. But, apart from the sorrowing woman's evidence, the fresh blood, on Donald's sword was conclusive proof of his guilt. The mob now became furious, and threatened the soldiers with instant death

unless they made a full confession of their crime and what prompted it. Donald, who all along declared their innocence, now produced the rider's hand, and solemnly vowed that its owner was the landlord's murderer. He also minutely described the manner in which it came into his possession. It was an open secret in the village that the district miller's son was on familiar terms with the young hostess, so, on hearing the soldier's story, a dozen men were despatched to the miller's house to prove or disprove his statement. On arriving there they were informed that the young man was unwell, that he was in bed, and that he could not be seen that day. This answer being unsatisfactory they proceeded to his bed and demanded to see his right hand. The mutilated arm was reluctantly shown, when it was found that the hand was amissing. He was consequently dragged out of bed and carried to the public-house, whence himself and his female accomplice were conveyed to the chief town of the county, to be dealt with according to law. Donald was complimented for the manner in which he acted in the matter.

Donald and his companion now proceeded on their journey. But owing to the stormy state of the weather—it was about the middle of November their progress was naturally slow. At length, however, Dingwall was reached, where, as the roads to their respective destinations led in different directions, they parted company, and a few hours afterwards Donald Macleod arrived at his house in Strathbran, where he left his sobbing wife twenty-two years previously. It was past midnight when he reached. The house presented no attraction in appearance, nor was there any change on the door-fastening since he left, so, opening it, he proceeded to the smouldering embers on the hearth, and, lighting the old, black cruisgean, he noiselessly entered the sleeping apartment. His wife, whom he readily recognised, was sound sleeping, and, though pale and careworn, she seemed as innocent, lovely, and beautiful as ever. But did she forget him—was she unfaithful—did she break her marriage vows? If not, why was that young man sleeping with her? The soldier's rage at that moment knew no bounds. He seized his sword, and was about to decapitate the offender, when by some mysterious influence he lowered the uplifted arm, and, returning his sword to its sheath, resolved to spare the man till morning, when he would deal with him as circumstances might suggest. Meantime he returned to the kitchen, and sat down beside the dying embers, and, extinguishing the lamp, began thinking over his wife's incontinency, whose face even now betrayed no signs of guilt.

Some time before daybreak he heard the young man addressing the woman thus "I hope you are all right now, mother. If so, I may go to my own bed." The woman answered —"Yes, dear, I am quite well now." The youth immediately arose, and, having gone to the other bed in the apartment, said—"Mother, what a strange dream I have just had. I dreamed that my father came home, and on his coming to the bedside he raised his sword above my head to kill me. On seeing which, I prayed to God for protection, and my father immediately disappeared. He seemed exactly as you used to describe him, but he wore a red coat. On hearing her son's dream and remarks she burst into tears and said if her dear husband had been alive he would long ere then have come home to see her and her dear son. Donald now grasped the situation and rushed into the bedroom, shouting —"My darling Mary, I have come to you at last, and nothing but death will again separate us.' After being locked in each others arms in the most affectionate manner, he turned to his son, who had meanwhile risen and dressed, and kissed him as tenderly as if he had still been a babe.

On opening the bag given him by his commanding officer, Donald found it contained one hundred sovereigns. This was a large sum of money in those days, and with it Donald Macleod rented a nice croft that on which his cottage stood—which he fully stocked. On this croft he and his loving wife lived during the remainder of their lives in comfort and happiness. When they died, which was at a great age, they left all they possessed to Donald Og, their son, who never left the paternal roof, and being, like his parents, wise and prudent, he managed his affairs so circumspectly that he became the most opulent and popular man in the district in his day. Donald Og married and had a family. His descendants are still in in Ross-shire.

A. B. M'Lennan (*Ben Wyvis*).

Lochboisdale.

CLANSMEN, DEAR TO ONE ANOTHER.

Tune.—Men of Harlech.

Dedicated to Col. Sir Fitzroy Donald Maclean, Bart. of Duart, Morven, and Brolas, chief of the Clan Maclean, and sung by Mr. Charles Maclean at the second annual gathering of the clan and friends, held in the Queen's Rooms, Glasgow, on Friday, 27th October, 1893.

Let me greet you as a brother,
Clansmen, dear to one another,
As the babe is to its mother,
    Smiling on her breast.
Clansmen from the purple heather,
Who have donned the kilt and feather,

Clansmen who now range together
From the north and west,
Lads from the glen and corrie,
Ye have all a story,
Both proud and true, untarnished too,
And wreathed with martial glory;
When the god of war was screaming,
Then Macleans, with banners streaming,
Broad claymores, both wild and gleaming,
    Fought, and fought their best.

When Prince Charlie's cause was waning,
When some chiefs were loud complaining,
Highland glens Macleans were training,
    Who would scorn to fly;
Clansmen brave as any lion,
Stalwart chiefs all ills defying,
Courted death, nor dreamt of flying,
    They would sooner die.
With their tartans streaming,
And their pibrochs screaming,
Macleans of old, both tough and bold,
Soon woke men from their dreaming;
When they proudly rushed to battle,
Men were stricken down like cattle,
While the deadly muskets' rattle,
    Told Macleans were nigh.

Clansmen by each Highland valley,
Scene of war, and war-like sally,
Where our fathers used to rally,
    With stern courage true,
Let us cherish deep the daring,
Of our gallant fathers' bearing,
While our sainted mothers' caring.
    Thrills us thro' and thro';
Rouse, my lads, like heroes,
Wrongs shall never fear us,
With Virtue deckt, we'll stand erect,
And smiling Right shall cheer us.
Let us guard our honour ever,
Let us love each glen and river,
Let us stoop to baseness never,
    But the right pursue.

Clansmen from the rugged Highlands,
Bens and glens, and mist-wrapt islands,
With your sons in far and nigh lands,
    Peace is in your train,
Lads with kilts and ribbons streaming
Maids with beauty sweetly beaming,
Chief whose brain with lore is teeming,
    You I greet again.
Let the pibroch thrilling,
All our hearts be filling,
With mem'ries grand, of our loved land
All strife and envy killing;
While our hearts with joy are beating,
At the pleasure of this meeting,
Let us ever be repeating,
    Health to Chief MacLean.

Manchester.

Duncan MacLean.

CAMANACHD.

ALEXANDER MACKELLAR,
FIRST CAPTAIN, GLASGOW COWAL SHINTY CLUB.

NOW that the ancient Highland game of shinty has again become popular, both in the straths in the north and towns in the south, it is interesting to refer to some of the prominent players of an older generation, who had done so much in their time to popularise our favourite pastime. Of these veterans few were better known ten or twelve years ago than Mr. Alex Mackellar, the first captain of the Glasgow Cowal Shinty Club. Mr. Mackellar is a native of Tighnabruaich, one of the most beautiful and favourite watering-places on the Cowal shore. In 1876 the subject of our sketch was the prime mover in forming the celebrated Glasgow Cowal Shinty Club, which, with the Edinburgh Camanachd, are the only clubs which have survived the vicissitudes of the intervening years. The Cowal men did wisely in electing Mr. Mackellar to the post of captain, for he guided the fortunes of his club so well that for a period of eight years after their formation the Cowal team were undefeated. Perhaps this may be partly accounted for by the fact that Mr. Mackellar induced his men to play the " passing game," and anyone who has seen a match played on this scientific principle will understand the advantage which it gives the players who practice it. He also substituted the leather ball for the old wooden one, which it will be admitted, was rather a dangerous article to play with.

Those were the palmy days of shinty in the south. The principal clubs at that time were the Edinburgh Camanachd, Vale of Leven, Ossian, Glasgow Camanachd, Glasgow Inverary, Fingalians (later Glenforsa), and the Skye. Mr. Mackellar captained his club in many stubborn contests during the eight years in which he held that office. Of these the most memorable, perhaps, were the match with the Glasgow Inveraray, on 26th April, 1879, for the Celtic Society's Challenge Cup, when the Cowal defeated their opponents by 6 hails to 0; and in the following year the game with the Renton on their own ground, when the Cowal won by 3 hails to 1. Although Mr. Mackellar no longer leads the Cowal men to the fray, he is the honorary president of the club, and feels proud that the Cowal team still hold their own on the shinty field, and are universally acknowledged to be " second to none" as exponents of the grand old game.

For ten years Mr. Mackellar was a member of the Glasgow Highlanders (late 105th), during five of which he carried the colours, and before he retired he was offered a commission. The above portrait represents him in the uniform of the regiment. It may be also mentioned that as an amateur all-round athlete he had few equals. The value of the silver plate trophies in his possession amounts to £100. He also possesses the championship medal for natives of Argyleshire, for putting the stone.

Mr Mackellar was for many years director of the Cowal Society, and latterly acted as treasurer. He recently retired from business, and is now residing at his Highland home in Cowal.

Glasgow. ROBERT MURRAY.

THE LAST MACDONALDS OF ISLA.

By CHARLES FRASER-MACKINTOSH, F.S.A. (Scot.).

PART I.

CERTAIN interesting documents, once the property of Sir James Macdonald, last of Isla, hitherto unpublished, having come into my hands, I purpose printing in the pages of the *Celtic Monthly*- some of them *in extenso*, with abstracts of others. To make my story complete and intelligible it is proper to give an account of the family, but only in the briefest form, so many well-known histories, accurate and inaccurate, having been written on the subject.

Seven generations from the time of Somerled, King of the Isles and Lord of Argyle and Kintyre, undoubted *stirps* of the great house and clan of Macdonald, bring us to John, for some time last independent Lord of the Isles. John, who succeeded about 1330, was first of his race to acknowledge the King of Scotland as overlord and superior. Attempts had often been made by the Scottish kings to curb the power of the Macdonalds, but hitherto without permanent success. John married his cousin, Amie nin Ruarie, a pious, excellent woman whose memory is still held in sweet reverence on the west mainland and islands of Inverness-shire—dowered with great possessions. Of this marriage the eldest son was Reginald, of whom Clanranald and others; the second Iain Mor, of whom the Macdonalds of Isla; and third Alexander, of whom the Macdonells of Keppoch. John may be said to have been the greatest man in Scotland, making treaties with foreign powers and fighting as an independent ally with the French at Poictiers, where he was wounded and taken prisoner by the Black Prince. Tempted by the high alliance into a second marriage with the daughter of Robert, Steward of Scotland, afterwards Robert II.,

John weakly submitted to the offspring of the second marriage having priority. He had to satisfy the natural claims of his elder sons by large grants of property, having the effect, as intended by the wily promoters of the marriage of greatly weakening, reducing, and finally destroying the predominant position of the ancient independent Lords of the Isles.

By the second marriage John had a son Donald, who succeeded as Lord of the Isles, and by marrying Margaret, daughter of the Countess of Ross, unltimately, in his wife's right, on failures of heirs male, and other heirs and after fighting the battle of Harlaw in 1411. was recognised as Earl of Ross. Donald, therefore, from his vast acquisition of estate, had become as serious a danger to the Crown as his predecessors, the independent Lords of the Isles, and every opportunity was seized upon—and many actually created—within the next seventy years to embroil him and his successors with the Crown and powerful neighbours. This, added to the haughty spirit of Donald, his son Alexander, and his grandson John, finally brought about the destruction of the second dynasty of the Lords of the Isles, also Earls of Ross, which only ran through three generations. So anxious were King and Parliament to stamp out the title of Earl of Ross, synonymous to them with turbulent power, that at the final forfeiture of John, last Earl of Ross and Lord of the Isles, this title was declared to be inalienably held by the Crown. A Duke of Ross was afterwards created, as if to emphasise the inalienation, which title soon fell; and when, as is sometimes noticed, so-and-so means to apply to make good his claim to the dignity of Earl of Ross, any such attempts are futile. Upon the downfall of the Macdonalds in the north and west, the the Mackenzies and Campbells arose, in no very creditable manner; and of them all that need be said (in this connection alone let it be kept in remembrance) is, that the Campbells are not now what they once were, particularly in Isla.

We now turn to the family with which these papers more particularly deal, viz., the Isla branch of the Macdonalds, styled after John, second son of John, Lord of the Isles, "Clann Iain Mhoir."

1.   This John married, about 1400, Marjory Byset, heiress of the Seven Lordships of the Glens, in Antrim, a lady of the good blood of the Bysets and O'Neills. After the marriage John is found styled Lord of Dunyvaig and the Glens, also Lord of Isla and Kintyre. The title of Dunyvaig and the Glens became the leading title of John's descendants. Dunyvaig castle, for centuries a ruin, stands on the estate

of Kildalton, in Isla. Great as the estate given to Iain Mor by his father was, it does not appear to have satisfied him. Instigated by evil advice, John rose against his younger brother, Donald of the Isles and of Harlaw, but was defeated, and fled to Ireland. Peace was made up betwixt the brothers, and heartily recognising the seniority conferred upon their younger brother consanguinean, both Reginald, first of Clanranald, and Iain Mor, first of Isla, gave hearty support to Donald, Lord of the Isles, at the battle of Harlaw. It was this Clanranald's bard who composed that magnificent martial address which, above all others, exhibits the depth and comprehensiveness of the Gaelic language. Iain Mor's fidelity to his nephew Alexander, son of Donald, cost him his life. The manner of Iain Mor's death has left a deep stain on the memory of James I. and his advisers.

According to the Clanranald history, privately printed at Edinburgh in 1819, Donald of Harlaw died in France in the year 1427, but according to others, including the late Mr. Hector Maclean, of Isla, a very competent writer, Donald died in 1425, at his own Castle of Ardtornish, in the forty-fifth year of his age, leaving his son Alexander, Lord of the Isles and Earl of Ross, in minority. The death of Donald seemed to the King and his advisers a good opportunity for seizing the person and lands of the minor.[2] He was accordingly entrapped into an interview, detained in prison for a considerable period, and meantime the

DUSYVAIG CASTLE (DUN NAOMHAIG), ISLAY.

authorities had the baseness to endeavour to enlist Iain Mor on their side with the bribe of a large portion of his nephew's estates. Their emissary, named Campbell, sought an interview, with a large retinue, and upon Iain Mor indignantly declining the offer, was declared King's prisoner, and after making all the resistance his small retinue could command, was overpowered and slain. Campbell was made a scapegoat, tried and executed for the murder of Iain Mor, his defence being a strong and earnest statement that what he did was by the King's orders, though unable to furnish written evidence of his assertion. Campbell doubtless knew too much for those in power, to warrant their allowing him his life.

II.—Donald (styled Donald Balloch), son of Iain Mor, succeeded and worthily maintained the reputation of his house in deeds of arms and valour. He was only twenty years of age at his father's death, but lost no time in revenging the foul deed, and making himself obnoxious to the ruling powers. Great part of his cousin Alexander's property had been given to Alexander, Earl of Mar, who endeavoured to establish himself in Lochaber and other parts. Donald Balloch gathered a considerable force,

"At the Isle of St. Finlagan, in Ic, Alexander of Yle, Lord of the Isles. Master of the Earldom of Ross, gave charter to Gilleonan mac Roderc vie Murchard Makneill, of the Islands of Barra and others. Dated in the 'Vigils of St. John the Baptist,' 1427." This shows that Donald of Harlaw was dead whilst his wife Margaret was living.

partly through his own influence, and partly through an urgent message from Alexander, again in prison, to his followers to rally round Donald. The Earl of Mar took means to detach a considerable portion of the proper following of Alexander, including the Keppochs and Camerons, an insult which afterwards cost these families dear at the hands of Alexander and his son John. Lord Mar had the support of his brother Allan (Lord Caithness), and many eastern and lowland gentlemen, together with that of certain Macdonalds and Camerons just mentioned, and both parties met at Inverlochy. Donald Balloch gained a complete victory, with the loss of fifty men against a thousand of the enemy. Lord Mar's pitiful state after his escape from the field of battle, is still talked of in the Brae of Lochaber He arrived late the night of the battle at Rynach, in the head of Glenroy, and asked for some refreshment. The people were so poor, or had lately been harried, that they had no dish, and the Earl, whose name and position were unknown, had to drink some milk, drawn from a goat, out of his shoe. Upon leaving he told the host, one O'Brien or O'Byrne, if he ever were in Aberdeenshire, to knock at the gate of Kildrummie Castle and ask for Alexander Stuart. He did so some time afterwards, and the Earl was told by his servants that a

FINLAGGAN CASTLE AND LOCH, ISLAY.*

stranger had knocked, asking for one Alexander Stuart. The Earl instantly ordered his admission, treated him well, told him who he was, and sent him homewards rejoicing, the happy possessor of twelve cows. Considering that the Camerons, with others, suffered a complete defeat, it seems not a little singular that their famous and somewhat defiant pibroch is commonly attributed to the first battle of Inverlochy. As it could hardly be composed after, or in commemoration of, the battle, it must have been composed, if then composed, on the march to Inverlochy. The highest credit is due to the Camerons for their valour at the second battle of Inverlochy, under Montrose. Donald Balloch, after the battle, which took place in 1431, sailed to Ireland. The king desired his head to be sent to him, and a head was accordingly sent in due time, but not that of Donald, who ingratiated himself with his powerful neighbours, the O'Neills, marrying O'Neill's daughter. By their intercession Donald's peace was made up with the king.

(To be continued.)

* Through the kindness of Mr. A. Ferguson, Cadila, Portaskaig, Isla, in photographing Finlagan Castle, and loch, one of the chief seats of the Macdonalds in Isla, an engraving is here given of this venerable structure.

REVIEWS.—We regret that our limited space prevents us this month from noticing Provost Macpherson's valuable work on "Badenoch," Mr. D. P. Menzies' "Book of Menzies," "The Irish Echo" (Boston), &c.

THE HIGHLANDERS were the only race the Romans could not conquer. They tried again and again, but failed. In 207 A.D., Severus, the Roman Emperor, lost 50,000 men in one campaign against the brave mountaineers, and had to retreat completely beaten.

THE RAID OF LOCH CARRON.

By Alexander Macdonald, Govan.

About the end of the sixteenth century, a deadly feud raged between the Macdonells and Mackenzies. Scarcely a month passed which did not witness some skirmish, raid, or act of violence. This predatory warfare was very active during the life of Sir Kenneth Mackenzie, created Lord Kintail in 1608 who at last procured letters of fire and sword against his enemies, whom he in the end completely humbled and dispossessed of part of their territory. Sometime before this, however, Glengarry, chief of the Macdonells, planned an enterprise against him, the execution of which he entrusted to his eldest son Angus. Sir Kenneth, suspecting that a storm was gathering, went to Mull to obtain assistance from his cousin Maclean. In his absence young Glengarry sailed to Loch Carron with his followers, where he committed the most horrible cruelties upon the defenceless inhabitants; but Lady Mackenzie, a woman of great energy and decision of character, planned and executed a stratagem by which, on the return of the Macdonells in their boats, through the Kyles of Skye, the Mackenzies, in ambuscade on the Bailigh Rock, succeeded in destroying a great number of them, including their savage leader. The incidents of the enterprise are related in the following ballad: --

"The merciless Macdonwald from the Western Isles."
Macbeth.

The "fiery cross" is speeding fast
O'er heathery hill and glen,
At fierce Glengarry's stern command
"Go! marshal all my men.
The hour of sweet revenge has come,
And Ellandonan's lord
Shall wail at many a coronach.
I swear by my good sword."

Now, o'er the banks of dark Loch Oich,
And Garry's birch-clad lake,
A wild and lurid gleam it sheds
From many a fiery flake,

Now blazing bright on some hill top,
Now glimmering from afar;
On, on it speeds with restless flight,
Dread harbinger of war.

Creag an Fhithich is the cry,
Borne down the rocky glen
From Corry side and bare hill top,
And barren, heath-clad fen;
Each mountain peak repeats the cry
To valley, hill, and dale,
And wafts the slogan of its chief
Across to bleak Kintail.

Now old men's dreams are broken,
Now young men start from sleep,
And waken at the warlike sound
And from their couches leap:
Now, through the gloom of midnight's hour
The "fiery cross" is seen:
Each man arms quick and hurriedly,
None ask "What can it mean?"

The morning's sun shone bright and clear
On Invergarry's walls,
And sounds of pibroch and of steel
Resound throughout its halls,
And full two hundred clansmen bold
Are ranged along the green,
In dark red tartan kilt and plaid,
A gallant sight I ween!

Claymores are belted by each side,
Sharp dirks sheathed at their knees,
And pistol stocks were seen to peep
As plaids waved in the breeze,
A deep, wild gleam shot from each eye,
And every look was stern,
For had not bold Sir Kenneth marked
Defeat by many a cairn?

Out spoke fierce Angus Macdonell,
Glengarry's eldest son,
"Come! follow me, my clansmen bold.
There's work now to be done."
A long, loud shout his clansmen gave,
Erect was every head,
A fiercer band than his ne'er marched,
Nor fiercer leader led.

Now, woe betide thee, Lord Kintail,
Thy kinsmen's fate is hard,
The wolf will come when thou art gone
And find no one on guard;
Oh! many a babe will he devour,
And many a mother slay,
And thou shalt bitter, bitter rue
The day thou went'st away.

In Ellandonan's Castle sat
Sir Kenneth's lady fair.
And on her knee a lovely boy
Is twining her brown hair;
But smiles she not upon her boy,
For care is on her brow,
Her gaze is fixed, her look is sad:
Good Lord! what ails her now?

(To be concluded.)

TO CORRESPONDENTS.

All Communications, on literary and business matters, should be addressed to the Editor, Mr. JOHN MACKAY, 17 Dundas Street, Kingston, Glasgow.

TERMS OF SUBSCRIPTION.—The CELTIC MONTHLY will be sent, post free, to any part of the United Kingdom, Canada, the United States, and all countries in the Postal Union—for one year, 4s.

THE CELTIC MONTHLY

DECEMBER, 1893.

CONTENTS.

"WHERE GAELIC IS SPOKEN."

SUCH is the attractive title of an article on the Gaelic language, and its influence upon the Highland people, which appeared last month in the *St. Louis Daily Globe-Democrat*. On reading it we were not quite sure at first whether the writer was preparing a supplement to the "Innocents Abroad," or was addressing the "Great Republic" in all seriousness. We are now inclined to the latter opinion, but must confess that a perusal of this literary curiosity afforded us as much genuine amusement as we ever derived from the works of a popular American humorist. It would be a pity were such an interesting composition lost in the pages of an American newspaper, and for the benefit of such of our readers as are fond of a good thing in the way of jokes, we will take the liberty of making a few extracts from it.

The article is in the form of a "letter," dated "Tobermory, Island of Mull, August 16," and is evidently the composition of one of those pilgrims from the American continent who favour our straths with their genial presence every autumn. He had evidently wandered a little, he had heard the Gaelic spoken, and he had also heard it spoken about, and, feeling burdened with the weight and value of his information, he presented over a column of his "impressions" to an unsuspecting newspaper. How much genuine amusement it created in the States may well be imagined, and acting on the principle of "passing on a good thing," our good friend, Mr. D. T. MacDonald, of Calumet, thoughtfully sent it on to us. We are

sorry that space will not allow us to print the letter in full, but as we know our readers are not above appreciating a few good jokes about themselves, we intend making some extracts from this precious production, which we hope they will enjoy as heartily as we did.

How will this do as a beginning? He says—"As long as the Gaelic continues to be the recognised language of the people, just so long must, in my judgment, the Highlanders remain a rude, barbaric people, enjoying few or none of the comforts of modern civilisation—just so long will race bitterness exist in the hearts of the Highland people," and so on. When this candid visitor was rusticating in the island of Mull, we wonder did he venture to express such an opinion to the "barbaric people" whom he met daily, and who, we are quite sure, treated him with a degree of courtesy which he certainly would not have received in his own country. We daresay not, for if he did the climate of Mull would suddenly become much too warm for such a delicately refined and civilised curiosity, and the people would almost deserve the description of being rude. Then he also learned that the language has a scant literature. "for, with the exception of Donald MacIntyre (?), I can find no trace of any real first class poets." Shades of Alastair MacDonald, Rob Donn Mackay, and the bards of a thousand years! And if he did find traces of the Gaelic bards, we wonder how much of them he could understand. He further gravely informs us that in the north-easterly part of Caithness "the native language is Scandinavian." This will be news for our Caithness readers. We hope they will manage to find these gifted persons, for although we know the county pretty well we never met one man in it yet who spoke Norse as his "native language." But, of course, it must be admitted that an American tourist ought to know far more about the people of Caithness than the natives of that county know themselves!

He also found that the Gaelic fosters prejudice and indolence among the people, it raises up a barrier which shuts off the Gael from participating in the comforts of civilisation, and "the attitude of each man towards his neighbour is—politically, ethnologically, socially, and commercially—determined by the fact whether that neighbour 'has' or 'has not the Gaelic.'" This is really very serious or very funny; it raises questions which simply appal us! How are we to explain the fact of so many Gaelic-speaking Highlanders having raised themselves to such high and responsible positions at home and abroad; to Highlanders and Lowlanders enjoying a social night together at the Highland gatherings without the ghost of the Gaelic "bogey" once obtruding itself, or —? It is too serious a question to reflect upon—let us pass on! But our Yankee pilgrim got at the root of this painful question, and declares that "the principal transgressor is the Church, and it is said upon competent authority that most extraordinary things go on at the Gaelic services, which, owing to the peculiar freemasonry existing among the Gaelic-speaking people, were never found out." Our Yankee critic has decreed that we ought to let the Gaelic die as quickly as possible—and why don't we set about arranging the funeral ceremony at once? Yes, we may well ask "Why?"

OUR MUSICAL PAGE.

LAMENT FOR RORY MOR MACLEOD, 1626.

RORY MOR, XIII. of Dunvegan succeeded his brother William, who died in 1590. He was called *Ruairidh Mòr*, big Rory, not so much from his size or stature as from his desire to do everything on a large scale. He was undoubtedly a born leader of men, possessing in a marked degree those qualities which went to constitute a true Highland chief in the turbulent times in which he lived. It is not our intention to give a detailed sketch of this warrior, or enumerate his deeds of prowess, as these are fully recorded by the historian of the clan.* In 1613 he received from James VI. of Scotland the honour of knighthood. During his chiefship he added to, and considerably improved the ancestral halls, in which he delighted to dispense princely hospitality. Among the many interesting relics in Dunvegan there are two at least which go to prove the munificence of his feasts. These are Rory Mòr's drinking horn, and Rory Mòr's cup. The horn, which probably once adorned the head of a kyloe bull, is destitute of ornament except a broad rim of silver, chased and carved, fixed round the edge. It is said to hold as much as three ordinary bottles, and quaffing off its contents, in claret, was one of the feats to be performed by each chief as he came of age.

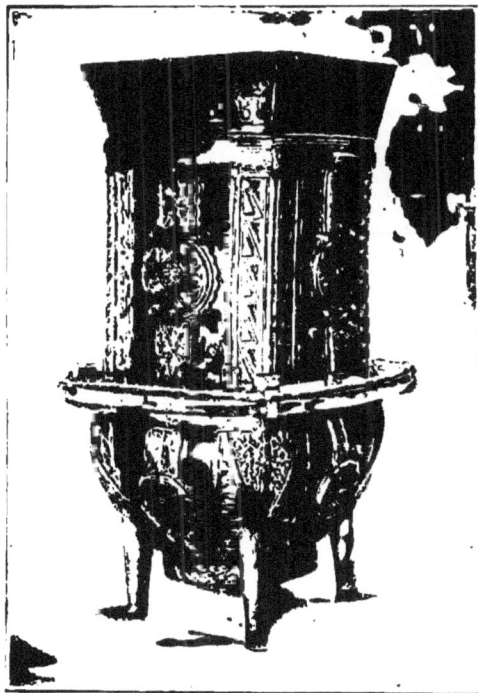

RORY MOR'S CUP.

Johnson, who visited Skye in 1773, refers to this horn, while Burns, in one of his songs, says —

" I'll conjure the ghost of the great Rory Mòr,
And bumper his horn to him twenty times o'er."

Rory Mòr's cup, however, is a much more interesting relic. Through the kindness of Rev. R. C. MacLeod, vicar of Bolney, Sussex, a son of the Venerable MacLeod of MacLeod, we are permitted to give a photograph of this very ancient piece of workmanship It is described as follows by Sir Walter Scott in his notes to "The Lord of the Isles": —

"This very curious piece of antiquity is nine inches and three-quarters in inside depth, and ten and a half in height on the outside, the extreme measure over the lips being four inches and a half. The cup is divided into two parts by a wrought ledge, beautifully ornamented, about three fourths of an inch in breadth. Beneath this ledge the shape of the cup is rounded off, and terminates in a flat circle, like that of a teacup: four short feet support the whole. Above the projecting ledge the shape of the cup is nearly square, projecting outward at the brim. The cup is made of wood (oak to all appearance), but most curiously wrought and embossed with silver work, which projects from the vessel. There are a number of regular projecting sockets, which appear to have been set with stones: two or three of them still hold pieces of coral, the rest are empty. At the four corners of the projecting ledge, or cornice, are four sockets, much larger, probably for pebbles or precious stones. The workmanship of the silver is extremely elegant, and appears to have been highly gilded. The ledge, brim, and legs of the cup are of silver. The family tradition bears that it was the property of Neil Glūndubh, or Black-knee. But who this Neil was no one pretends to say. Around

* "History of the Macleods," by Alex. Mackenzie, F.S.A. (Scot.). Inverness, 1889.

the edge of the cup is a legend, perfectly legible, in the Saxon black-letter, which seems to run thus :

Ulfo : Johis : Mich : || Mgn : Pncipis : De : Vir · : Manac : Mich : || Liahia : Mgrvneil : || Et : Spat : Bo : Jhu : Da : || Clea : Mlorm Opa : | Fecil : Ano . Di : Ar : 993 Onili : Oimi : ||

The inscription may run thus at length : *Ufo Johanis Mich Mayni Principis de Hr Manac Mich Liahia Magryueil et sperat Domino Ihesu dari clementiam illorum opera. Fecit Anno Domini 993 Onili Oimi.* Which may run in English : Ufo, the son of John, the son of Magnus, Prince of Man, the grandson of Liahia Macgryneil, trusts in the Lord Jesus that their works (*i.e.* his own and those of his ancestors) will obtain mercy. Oneil Oimi made this in the year of God nine hundred and ninty-three.

" But this version does not include the puzzling letters HR before the word Manac. Within the mouth of the cup the letters Jhs. (Jesus) are repeated four times. From this and other circumstances it would seem to have been a chalice. This circumstance may perhaps account for the use of the two Arabic numerals 93. These figures were introduced by Pope Sylvester, A.D 991, and might be used in a vessel formed for church service so early as 993. The workmanship of the whole cup is extremely elegant, and resembles, I am told, antiques of the same nature preserved in Ireland."

There is a lament for Neil *Gliun-dubh* in the " Book of the Dean of Lismore," and in a footnote we are informed that he succeeded to the throne of Ireland in 916, and was killed in battle by the Danes in 919. The lament was composed by his wife, who refers to her lord as follows : -

"Nocha n'fhac mi fear mar Niall,
Do bu gheal e ach a ghliun,
Fa maith a mhaise 's a mamh,
Taise a chiabh 'us glas a shuil."

" Never have I seen one like Nial,
Fair was he all except the knee,
Great were his beauty and his fame,
Soft were his locks and grey his eye."

The legend connecting the cup with this Neil *Gliun-dubh* seems to contradict the inscription, which says that this curious vessel was made for Magnus, Prince of Man.

"Few cups," remarks Sir Walter Scott, "were better, at least more actively employed in the rude hospitality of the period than those of Dunvegan. There is in the *Leabhar Deirg* a song intimating the overflowing gratitude of a bard of Clan-Ranald, after the exuberance of a Hebridean festival at the patriarchal fortress of MacLeod." The poem here referred to is entitled " *Laoidh do rinne Niall mor mac muiriche san dun do ruaidhraighe mor mac Leoid*," and is reproduced in the late Dr. Cameron's " *Reliquiæ Celticæ*," Vol. I. It may interest our readers to quote a few verses to show how the Gaelic of that period was written : -

"Se hoidhce dhamsa san dun
nior bhe ancoinnmhibh falsa fuar
cuirm lionmhur da hibhe abor
fion bhrugh mor is lionmhur sluagh
. . . . . .

Gair na gelairseach sna cuach throm
ag nach gnathach fuath na feall
gaire na miledh fleasgach fionn
lionn misgeach is teine theanu

Rio u odbhuir aignuibh ur
eunnbhuidh achuid ribh gach cliar
sanenbhrugh na haisling ol
da shluagh lionnmhur fairsaing fiall

Fichad misge leinn gach laoi
nibhudh treisi linne no le
fiu nert far metha do bhi
cethair athri · 7 · le · 6."

The poem has been translated by the great Irish annalist, Dr. O'Connor. We give his rendering of the Gaelic verses quoted :—

"Six nights I had been in Dun, it was not a fallacious entertainment I received ; plenty of *cuirm* (strong ale) was drunk at the board, there was a large *winebrugh* and a numerous host." . . . .

"The merriment of the harp and of the full bowls, with which hatred and treachery are not usually accompanied ; the laughter of the fair haired youngsters, we had inebriating ale and a blazing fire."

"A prince from whom a good disposition is acquired, he keeps the fellowship of all ecclesiastics ; in his regal court drinking is not a dream, to his numerous company he is plentiful and hospitable."

"We were twenty times drunk every day, to which we had no more objection than he had ; even our food was in abundance, which consisted of four, three, seven, along with six of varieties."

It is abundantly evident that Rory Mór's cup and horn must have inspired this tribute of praise from the Clan-Ranald bard.

The hereditary pipers at Dunvegan were the famous MacCrimmons. *Para Mór* (big Patrick) was piper to Rory Mór, and, as might be expected, he took his master's death very much to heart. Dunvegan had lost all its charms, he could no longer remain within its walls, so he shouldered his *piob-mhór* and marched off to his own home at Borreraig, consoling his grief by playing as he went a lament for his chief, which is one of the most melodious and plaintive pipe tunes on record. The Gaelic words associated with the tune are as follows :

Tog orm mo phiob 'us theid mi dhachaidh,
Is truagh leam fhein mo leir mar thachair ;
Tog orm mo phiob 's mi air mo chradh,
Mu Ruairidh Mor, mu Ruairidh Mor.

Tog orm mo phiob tha mi sgith,
'S mar faigh mi i theid mi dhachaidh ;
Tog orm mo phiob tha mi sgith,
'S mi air mo chradh mu Ruairidh Mor.

Tog orm mo phiob tha mi sgith,
'S mar faigh mi i theid mi dhachaidh ;
Clarsach mo phiob cha tog mo chridh,
Cha bheo fear mo ghraidh,'Ruairidh Mor.

A translation or paraphrase of these lines will be found underneath the music.

FIONN.

CUMHA RUAIRIDH MHOIR—RORY MOR'S LAMENT, 1626.

Key E♭.—*Slowly, with much feeling.*

```
.d : r ,m | l :— .l : s ,m | s .d  — .d : r ,m | l :—  .d : r ,m | r .d :—.
Tog orm mo | phiob 'us thei l mi|dhachaidh, Is truagh leam fhein,  mo  cir mar  thachair ;
Give me my | pipes, I'll home them carry,  In these sad halls  I  dare not  tarry ;
```

Rallantando.

```
.d : r ,m | l :— .l : s ,l  d' :— .d' : r' ,d' | l :— .s : m ,r | r :  . |
Tog orm mo  phiob 's mi air mo ,chràdh,  Mo Ruairidh | Mòr,  mu  Ruairidh Mòr.
My pipes hand o'er, my heart is  sore,  For  Rory  Mòr,  my  Rory  Mòr.
```

Fetch me my pipes, my heart is breaking
For Rory Mòr his rest is taking ;
He wakes no more, and to its core
My heart is sore for Rory Mòr.

Give me my pipes, I'm sad and weary,
These halls are silent, dark, and eerie ;
The pipe no more, cheers as of yore,—
Thy race is o'er, brave Rory Mòr.

THE LATE DUNCAN CAMPBELL.

By the death of Mr. Duncan Campbell, at the early age of twenty-four, the Glasgow Skye Association has lost one of its most esteemed and valued members. Mr. Campbell was well known to Highlanders in the city as an enthusiastic lover of everything Highland — pipe music, Gaelic singing, and Highland dancing had each a special attraction for him. He took a keen interest in the work of the Skye Association, and when applications for assistance were under discussion Mr. Campbell was always anxious that every deserving case should be dealt with generously, the outcome, no doubt, of his own kindly and generous disposition. He read two interesting papers before the association on "William Ross, the Gaelic Bard," and "Place-Names in Strath, Skye." It may be said, to his credit, that he was so keenly sensitive on questions affecting the good name of the Highlands that he could not even appreciate a joke when it reflected in any degree upon his countrymen. We heartily respect the feeling. Mr. Campbell was a member of the Glasgow Highland Regiment. He died at his native place, Broadford, Skye, where he had gone to recruit his health, and lies buried in Kil-a-chro, under the shadow of the hills he loved so well. Some of his friends in Glasgow propose erecting a memorial stone over his grave. His presence will be greatly missed at the annual gathering of the natives of Skye, which takes place on an early date.

Bearsden.   DONALD NICOLSON.

OUR NEXT ISSUE.

In our next issue we will present our readers with a life-like plate portrait of Sir James Colquhoun, Bart, chief of the clan, who is to preside at the social gathering of the Clan Colquhoun, in Glasgow, on 29th December, Also portaits of Dr. R. C. Macdiarmid, Dr W. Murray Mackay, North Shields, vice-president, Clan Mackay Society ; and Miss A. E. Murray-Macgregor, director, Clan Gregor Society. In addition to these, the second part of Mr. Fraser-Mackintosh's interesting article will be illustrated with a *fac-simile* of a charter dated 1550, granted by Archibald, 4th Earl of Argyll, with a fine reproduction of his seal. A view of Mingarry Castle will also be given. Mr. Mackay, Hereford's, concluding article will be illustrated with engravings of Borve Castle, Farr, and an ancient stone in Farr Churchyard, believed to belong to the Norse period. Mr. D. Murray Rose also contributes a valuable article on the "Earldom of Ross," which will be suitably illustrated. In addition to these, other pictures will be given.

We also intend presenting our readers with a four-page Supplement, containing the complete Muster-Roll of the Reay Fencible Regiment, which will be a valuable appendix to Mr. Mackay, Hereford's, volume on that regiment, recently published.

The next number will also contain interesting contributions from the pens of Mr. Malcolm MacFarlane, Col. Charles Stewart, and other well-known writers. Altogether, our "New Year Number" will be the best and most interesting budget of Celtic literature ever offered to Highlanders at the small charge of threepence.

EXPULSION OF THE NORSEMEN FROM SUTHERLAND - STRATHNAVER THE SCENE.

By John Mackay, C.E., J.P., Hereford.

THERE is no very authentic record in the annals of Scotland as to the exact era in which the dreaded "Lochlinnich" made settlements on the north and south coasts of Sutherland, or of Caithness or the Hebrides. In the Ossianic poems references are made to their predatory and hostile incursions under such leaders as Gorlo, Sarno, the father of Comal (Caomh-mhal), Swaran ; and Dubh-mhic-Roinne, who, it is said, lived in the north-east of Caithness, was one of the heroes who assisted Cumhal, the father of the renowned Fingal, in his wars with the sons of Morni, but, from his name, it may be conclusively said he was a Caledonian Pictish chief, not a Norse leader.

The sterility of their country, their continual feuds amongst themselves, the continuous wars for ascendancy and power amongst their leaders, inclined the Norsemen to be warriors, seafaring men, and pirates. In their own country they lived by hunting and fishing. In early days, when the tilling of the ground was little understood and practised, it must have been hard work tempting those yellow-haired lads eager, young adventurers—to stay at home when they could live upon the sea in their rude but staunch little ships as well, if not better, than on land, especially when they were told great stories of

" BONNIE STRATHNAVER " THE HOME OF THE MACKAYS.

sunshiny, fruitful lands that lay to the west and south, where plenty of silver and gold, bright clothes, and abundance of food could be obtained in the market of war for the blows of their axes, the strength of their arms, and the courage of their hearts. No wonder that it seemed to them a waste of time and energy to stay at home in bleak and sterile Norway.

Till the middle of the 8th century the expeditions of the Norsemen were more for plunder and adventure than for taking possessions and colonising. They sailed into bays and estuaries, plundering wherever they landed, fighting when resisted, and from these habits acquired in their own language the appellation of "Vikingr," bay frequenters, rovers, pirates, freebooters. In heathen times in Norway it was usual for young men of distinction, before settling down, to make warlike expeditions into foreign places, as a part of their education, and this voyage was called "viking" going into bays for a raid. It is possible these Norse raiders taught the Gael to imitate these practices in after years on land.

Gradually these expeditions led to permanent conquests in Scotland, Ireland, France, and Sicily, even to Greece and the gates of Constantinople. In 843 these bold, warlike warriors sailed up the Loire and plundered the country right and left. In 845 Rolf, the Ganger, sailed up the Seine and plundered Paris, and a few years thereafter took possession of Normandy and defied the King of France.

The north of Scotland, from its proximity to the Orkney Isles, the great seat of the Vikingr, severely felt the plunderings and extortions of these marauders, and hence, it may be presumed, the erection of those so-called Pictish towers so numerous in every fertile strath in Sutherland and parts of Caithness, for defence and warning in time of invasion by these fierce barbarian, seafaring hordes. No doubt many a bloody conflict took place between them and the natives, of which we have so many traditionary tales, in poetry and prose.

In 875 Sigurd Eysteinson, Earl of Orkney, with the aid of Thorstein the Red, subdued Caithness and Sutherland as far as Ekkialsbakki (Oy Kel), frequently defeating the armies sent against them by the King of Scots, and carrying their conquest into Ross-shire. Sigurd was buried at Siderha, now called Cyderhall, near Dornoch. In 995 this Sigurd, or Siward Hlodrerson, subdued the whole coast right away to Aberdeen, and obtained a daughter of the King of Scots in marriage. Siward fell at the great battle of Clontarf, near Dublin, in 1014, won by Brian Boroimhe (the cow distributor), and his son Thorfinn, at the age of five, was confirmed in the possessions of his father by the King of Scots. Disagreeing with Duncan, the successor of his grandfather, who demanded tribute from him, he defeated his armies, as the Sagas say, and ravaged the whole of the Lowlands as far south as Fife, burning, slaying, and subduing the land as he went. After Thorfinn's death in 1064, Caithness and the Orkneys were torn by internal dissensions and disputed successions, murders and assassinations amongst the Norse leaders, till 1150, when Harold Maddadson, a grandson of an Athole Earl, succeeded. He, too, had a competitor in Harold Wugi, or the younger, who was favoured by William the Lion, King of Scots, who bestowed upon him the title of Earl of Caithness, while the King of Norway confirmed to the other the title and possessions of the Orkney Isles. The younger Harold levied troops in Sutherland and Caithness, to make good the rights given him by the King of Scots, and a great battle was fought between the two Harolds at Clardon, near Thurso, in which the younger was slain and his army defeated. This event, and the cruelties to which the victor subjected the vanquished, having come to the ear of the Lion King of Scots, made him very wroth. He immediately set about punishing the cruel Harold, and arranged with Reginald of the Isles, son of the King of Man, the greatest warrior of his day, to levy and collect troops in Ireland, Galloway, Kintyre, and the Isles, expel Harold from Sutherland and Caithness, and reduce the country to the king's rule. Reginald accepted the king's mandate, collected his troops from these districts, and landing either in Lochbroom or Lochinver, marched through the morasses and forests of Sutherland, and debouched into Strathnaver by the south side of the famed Ben Chibric. Harold was kept well informed of Reginald's movements, knew from what quarter the storm of battle would burst upon him, and he prepared himself for it by collecting his Norsemen from Orkney and Caithness, and marching them into the heights of Strathnaver to meet the coming storm. He posted his army upon rising ground on the east side of the river Naver—since called Dal-harold, or Harold's field or meadow—about a mile below the east end of Loch Naver, sending out as far as the east end of Ben Chibric a strong detachment to watch the advance of the enemy, and, should the opportunity offer itself, to give them a taste of Norse valour and fighting qualities. This, it would appear, happened, for on Reginald's vanguard coming round the east end of Ben Chibric Norsemen were descried to the left, posted on the southern slope of Cnoc-lud-an-leathad (the hill of the tufty slope), north side of Loch Truderscaig. This advance division of Reginald's army at once made for the enemy, and an obstinate combat ensued. The Norsemen were defeated with great slaughter, and retired upon Harold's main army encamped upon Dal-harold. The scene of this conflict is still marked with twenty two tumuli, where the slain were interred.

Having ascertained the presence of the enemy, Reginald put his forces in order of battle and marched on for miles till he came in view of Harold's position by the side of the Naver river, which protected his right flank, his right centre strengthened by an ancient fort, into which he would probably post his archers. In his immediate front was a ravine, difficult to cross and easily defended; his centre was posted on ground rising into a terrace above the river, and his left posted on the slopes of a knoll, still called the "bloody knoll," a name given to it from the terrible slaughter made upon and around it. The position was well chosen for the fight of heroes, and extended from the river a distance of 1500 yards. Reginald's army was probably superior in numbers to Harold's, but the Norsemen were fresh, while the Islanders and Highlanders were tired and weary by their long March over the moors and morasses from Assynt to the Naver. The battle soon began, and we may be sure of it, that Harold, with his valiant and fierce veteran Norsemen, did their very best—they were fighting for hearth and home. The Islanders, Gallowegians, Irish, and the natives who joined were actuated by a spirit of deep revenge for injuries perpetrated upon them for several centuries by the ruthless Lochlinnich.

(To be concluded).

URUISG CHOIRE-NAN-NUALLAN.

First Prize Sgeulachd at Oban Mod.

By John MacFadyen.

THACHAIR 'o chionn a fada gu'n d'thàinig Righ Othaileam à Tùr Athaileam a shealg do Ghleann nam mang 's nam maoiseach, 's bha e chòmhnaidh

"Fo annart thar ghèig barraich,
'An scalladh sròl bair crannaibh a long."

Agus thachair air latha de na làithean 'n uair a bha iad a mach a' sealg, gu'n deachaidh mac an Righ, Talamsan nan dual òir, air seachran o chàch, 's gun na chuideachd ach dithis ghillean agus a chù " Luran," agus fhad' 'sa bha iad ag iarraidh an rathaid thàinig an t-anamoch orra, agus thachair gu'n robh an rathad dhachaidh 'g an toirt troimh Choire-nan-nuallan, agus 'n uair a bha iad a' dol seachad air bothan na h-àiridh aig Cailleach-bun-na-beinne, bha ise a mach agus thuirt i riutha :—" Tillibh a chlann, cha 'n 'eil an Coire glan roimhibh." " Cha till ach gealtaire a Chaillich chrom," arsa Talamsan. " Ciod is mò air Talamsan mac Righ Othaileam à Tùr Athaileam, thu féin na na bheil 'sa' Choire ?" " Is àrd d' inbh a dhiùlnaich, ach 's diù nach gabh comhairle," ars' a' Chailleach.

Ghabh na laoich air an aghaidh troimh Choire-nan-nuallan, gus an d'thàinig iad gu Sloc-nam-meall agus an sin chunnaic iad an ainnir 'bu luraiche air an do dhearc sùil riamh—

Bha sùil ghorm-mheallach mar dhrùchd meala
Air bhàrr fàillean nan lios,
Mar uchd cala, no clòimheid cannaich
Bha smuadh lannair a cneas.

Bha slatag sheilich 'na làimh dheis, agus bha a lamh chlì air a cùlaobh. Chaidh an cù ceum air thoiseach air na daoine, an sin sheas e, is thòisich e air comhartaich rithe. " Caisg do chù a Thalamsain," ars' ise, "bithidh coin nam flath air éill gus an tòisich an fhaoghaid."

" Laidh ' Luran,'" arsa Talamsan. " Se sin ' Luran ' do dhunach sa nochd," ars' an ainnir, nach robh 'na h-ainnir ni b'fhaide ach 'na caillich nualaidh, peimheil, ghuineach. Dh'fhàs an t-slatag sheilich a bha na làimh na shlacan draoidhneachd, 's bha nathair shligineach, theinnteach 'na cuaich 'na broilleach :—

Bha craicionn mar bhoicionn
Ciar-bhoc nan càrn,
Bhios eadar an ceàrd 'san t-sròsl ;
Chunap-bhristeadh i 'chnò
Eadar a sròn 's a smeig.

Cho luath 'sa fhuair i ainm a' choin ghairm i 'g a ionnsaidh e 's cha tugadh e feairt tuilleadh air a mhaighstir ; 's ann a chaidh e 'na charaibh leis an Uruisg, oir b'i sud Uruisg Choire-nan-nuallan, ged bu mhaiseach i air a cheud sheall-adh a fhuair iad dhi.

'N uair a chunnaic na gillean mar a thachair, theich iad dhachaidh leis an sgeul mhuladach gu'n do mharbh Uruisg Choire-nan-nuallan Talamsan, mac an Righ.

Thog an Righ a mach an lath'r-na-mhàireach, leis a h-uile duine 'bha mar mhilltean dha a shireadh a mhic. Fhuair iad an cù, " Luran," marbh 's gun ribe fionnadh air, ach cha 'n fhac' iad mac an Righ, no Uruisg, ach meall ùr 'an Sloc-nam-meall. Thill an Righ dhachaidh gu duthach, brònach ; cha robh do chloinn aige ach Talamsan agus aon nighean- Caol-mhala-dhonn - agus thug Caol-mhala-dhonn bòid nach pòsadh i fear gu bràth ach am fear a mharbhadh Uruisg Choire-nan-nuallan.

Chuala Breac-ghlùn, Mac Thorcuil, Righ Dhùnaid an Eirinn, mu'n bhòid a thug Caol-mhala-dhonn. B'e sud Breac-ghlùn nan seachd cath 's nan seachd buaidh, agus bhiodh seachd laoich a' cath air gach làimh dheth.

Air latha de na làithean thàinig e air tìr aig Amar-nan-eithear, agus thog e ris an aonach 's an anamoch, agus o'n nach robh aige ach Caill-each ri choinneachadh cha b' fhiach leis a chuid laoch a thoirt leis, ach thug e leis an t-Easgadach-luath-chasach :—

A' bheireadh air a' ghaoth luath Mhàirt
'S cha bheireadh a' ghaoth luath Mhairt air.

A' dol seachad air bothan na h-àiridh aig Cailleach-bun-na-beinne, bha 'Chailleach a mach, agus thuirt i -" Tillibh a chlann cha 'n eil an Coire glan roimhibh." " Gabh romhad a chrom Chaillich liath," arsa Breac-ghlùn, " cha till ach gealtaire, 'dé 's mò air Breac-ghlùn, mac Thorcuil Righ Dhùnaid nan còig stuadh, 'an taobh tuath na h-Eirionn, thu féin na na tha 'sa' Choire? " " Is àrd d' inbh a dhiùlnaich ach 's diù nach gabh comhairle," ars' a' Chailleach. 'N uair a ràinig Breac-ghlùn Coire-nan-nuallan chunnaic e an ainnir 'bu mhaisiche air an do dhearc sùil riamh —

Thar gach ainnir 'an snuadh,
A' toirt buaidh air mnai na h-Eirionn.

Bha slatag sheilich 'na làimh 's thuirt i ris :— " Cia d' às, 's có d'thuige a laoich, dé fàth do sheud 's do shiubhal ? " " Is mise," ars' esan Breac-ghlùn mac Thorcuil Righ Dhùnaid nan còig stuadh an taobh tuath na h-Eirionn, tha mi 'dol do Choire-nan-nuallan a' marbhadh Uruisg Shloc-nam-meall, a réir iarrtus Caol-mhala-dhonn, nighean Righ Othaileam an Tùr Athaileam." Ars' an ainnir - " An e gaol ainnir no fuath uruisg a thug Breac-ghlùn à Eirinn ? Ma 's e fuath uruisg lùbaidh a chruaidh* ri h-uchd, ma 's e gaol ainnir, is sleamhain an greum air an easgainn a h-earball.

---

* Lùbaidh a chruaidh- his steel shall bend, or his sword shall bend. Cruaidh—steel.

Tha ochd flathaibh le mòr fhir an Tùr Atl aileam
a nochd :--

Is sleamhain leac an dorus tùir,
Is sleamhna na sin ùdh 's na dh'aog.

"Is mise nighean righ garbh-shleagh, an
Talla-nan-sògh, 's tha maithibh m' atha~ aig
ròic a' nochd. Cuir do ghille a thirea B do
laoich, is thigibh uile do Thalla-nan-sògh is
gheibh sibh aoidheachd nach d'fhuair thu riamh
air talamh na h-Eirionn."

"Fallbh Easgadaich," arsa Breac-ghlùm. 's e
cur cagar na chluais, "greas a' so mo laoich ach
biodh iad na 'n èideadh."

Dh'fhalbh an t-Easgadach, 's mu 'n robh e
ach gann air falbh dh'atharaich an aimsir a
cruth, 's dh' aithnich Breac-ghlùm gur h-e a n a
bh'aige an Uruisg Dh'fhàs a slatag sheilich
'na shlacan-druidheachd is tharuinn Breac-ghlùm
a shleagh--

A bha sadadh air slacan na h-Uruisg
'S a' toirt Mac-talla à stùcan nam beann,

Ach 'n uair 'thill an t-Easgadach 's na laoich,
cha d' fhuair iad mac righ, ain ùr, no Uruisg,
ach meall ùr 'an Sloc nam meall.

(To be concluded).

STATE OF CAITHNESS FROM 1730 TO 1760, AND THE SHERIFF.

(An Old MS.).

THE shops of two merchants named Henderson and Miller were likewise robbed.
Robert Goldie, a merchant from Elgin,
was also robbed about three miles from
Thurso, and his money and merchandise taken
to the value of £150. The Meal Girnds
in Thurso were broken into in 1759, and
their contents stolen. It is unnecessary, however, to give further details from the MS. to
illustrate what was happening at the time,
as the instances given will amply suffice. It
may be mentioned, however, that latterly the
band developed the daring plot of robbing old
Freswick himself at Freswick Castle, where it
was believed he kept a large sum of money.
There have been several versions, traditionary
and otherwise, of this attempt given to the
public, to which much public interest has been
attached. But as the MS. on which this brief
article is based was written scarcely two months
after the incident itself, its contents may be
looked upon as authentic when compared with
all other statements. The robbery was to take
place on a certain night, and a female servant
at Freswick Castle was a party to the plot.
Two of the gang, named James Sutherland and
Alexander Rugg, relented, and divulged the
whole scheme to Freswick. At length the
Sheriff-Depute bestirred himself, and with the
assistance of his retainers and others he caused
the apprehension of Donald Rugg, John Swanson, and Andrew Keith. The Sheriff had a
private interview with John Campbell, the Jew,
whom he allowed to escape out of the county,
along with his father, Samuel Campbell. Freswick's female servant committed suicide, and
was buried in the Hill of Freswick. Her remains were found almost intact about ten years
ago in the same place.

The Sheriff came in for a great share of public
indignation, but as he was not on friendly terms
with the county gentlemen he cared little what
they said. It edged out that John Campbell
had informed the Sheriff of all the murders and
robberies which the band had committed. Further, Andrew Keith made a similar confession,
which he signed, and this confession was sent by
Mr. John Russell, the Procurator-Fiscal to the
Sheriff-Depute ! But, notwithstanding all this,
the latter worthy left the county and proceeded
to Edinburgh as if nothing unusual had been
taking place within his sheriffdom. Before
going he left no instructions, and, on the whole,
treated matters with absolute indifference.
Sutherland and Rugg had been dismissed by
himself, and allowed to go through the county
as they pleased. Through an act of indulgence
Donald Rugg was allowed to escape from prison.
He was visited while there several times by a
woman named Clark, who surreptitiously introduced some irons, through the instrumentality of
which he afterwards broke through the prison
and escaped.

The county gentry in their seats were
alarmed, as men with faces blackened were observed skulking around their houses in the
night time. Firearms had to be resorted to,
and things had been brought to such a pass
that gentlemen did not consider themselves
safe without having parties of men guarding
their houses, nor in travelling without an escort
at night. Some of the gang were even seen to
go to church. The MS. graphically sums up
the state of matters in one sentence—"Such is
the present situation of this very gross and
grave affair." The Sheriff took matters easy,
and suited himself. Andrew Keith, with some
others, broke into the prison and liberated his
sister, while all the time the Sheriff was spending the night in a public house, within thirty
yards distance. The public-house was kept by
the acting bailie of the town ; and the Sheriff
took no steps to assert his authority, but quietly
left for his country seat as if nothing had happened. The Sheriff allowed his own friends to
do as they liked, and on one occasion, on receiving a complaint from a Thurso merchant,
the Sheriff returned him an abusive and
threatening letter.

There were about twenty fairs in the county
at the time, at which, the MS. narrates, that
men, after getting drunk, thrashed and abused
one another with huge sticks, many being
killed, while many lingered for a time and died
of their bruises. It was laid at the door of the
Sheriff that he had not held a Sheriff Court for
a considerable period, and, in proof of this,
reference was made to the Sheriff Court books.
But, further, it was alleged that he had a large
estate in the county, parts of which were situated at considerable distances from each other;
that there were several large farms on his
estate, with several hundred small tenants, and
that he had no time for the discharge of the
duties of the sheriffdom. Besides, he was at
variance with all the county gentlemen, whom
he would not ask for assistance, and that in the
administration of justice all these differences
had their influences.

But, in conclusion, it is asked in the MS
why all this should be endured by men who
had assisted His Majesty's armies and paid
their taxes? It is satisfactory, however, to
know that not long after the date of the document in question a considerable improvement
had taken place in the peace and general security of the county. Had there not been ample
proof, it is scarcely possible to believe that so
much violence existed in the far north only
about one hundred and thirty years ago.

GEORGE M. SUTHERLAND.

Wick.

HIGHLAND NOTES AND QUERIES.

THE MACDONALDS are the most numerous of all
the clans.

THE GREAT *piob mhor* (bagpipe) is peculiar to Scotland only.

LORD BREADALBANE'S ESTATE stretches seventy
miles west from his own door.

ANGUS DUBH MACKAY could raise 4000 fighting
men.

KING ROBERT THE BRUCE addressed the Parliament of Ardchattan in the Gaelic tongue.

THE LAST WOLF IN SCOTLAND is said to have been
killed by Sir Ewen Cameron.

THE KING of one of the Pacific Islands is a
Highlander named Ross.

THE MACLEODS, Macaulays, Macaskills, Macivers,
and MacCorquodales are of Norse origin.

TWO HIGHLANDERS who refused a bribe of
£30,000 to betray Prince Charlie were afterwards
hanged for *stealing a cow!*

MUNRO OF FOWLIS holds his lands on condition
that he will be prepared to present his Sovereign
with a ball of snow when called upon to do so.

THE grandfather of Lord Macaulay, the historian,
had to flee the country for attempting to betray
Prince Charlie in the island of Uist.

THE ANCIENT SPELLING of the name Mackay was
"Macky." General Mackay of Scourie was the
first to adopt the present form.

THE FAVOURITE WEAPONS of the ancient Highlanders were the broadsword, Lochaber axe, and
dirk (*biodag*).

AMONG THE FIRST FAMILIES in Scotland to embrace the Protestant religion were the Sutherlands,
Mackays, Munros, and Roses.

FROM 1760 to 1814, the number of Highlanders
who joined the army has been estimated at from
80,000 to 100,000.

IN the Sutherland Fencible regiment of 1779
there were no fewer than 104 persons of the name
of William Mackay, 17 being in one company.

WHEN THE WEARING OF THE KILT was proscribed
in 1746, it was a common practice for Highlanders
to evade the law by stitching the kilt up the
middle!

THE MACDONALDS OF CLANRANALD'S MARCH is
Spaidsearachd Mhic Mhic-Ailein; their lament,
Cumha Mhic Mhic-Ailein; and their slogan or
war-cry, *Dhaibh Dh'onnaich*.

THE DAYS OF THE WEEK IN GAELIC.—Can anyone give the origin and derivation of the Gaelic
names for the days of the week. Are they Celtic?
—DI-LUAIN.

JOHN MACKENZIE, OF "THE BEAUTIES."—Can
anyone say if there is a likeness of this well-known
Celt in existence, and if so, where it is treasured?
It would be well worthy of a place in your gallery
of Celtic celebrities.—CAREREFEIDH.

IT is not generally known that Mr. Charles
Coborn, the well-known vocalist, is the son of a
Ross-shire Highlander. His real name is Mac-
Callum, and his father was at one time president of
the Gaelic Society of London.

THE MACLEANS declare that Spain will get "a
jolly good drubbing" in their war with Morocco,
for the commander-in-chief of the Moors, and confidential adviser to the Sultan, is a Maclean! The
Spaniards ought to be warned in time.

THE ANTIQUITY OF THE TARTAN.—The coat of
many colours bestowed by Jacob on his son Joseph
is held by a sanguine theorist to have been tartan,
for saith Zachary Boyd's Bible :—

"Jacob gave to his wee son Josie
A tartan coat to keep him cosie."

THE HIGHLANDERS OF LAST CENTURY are often
referred to as "a race of brawlers, murderers, and
robbers." The following statistics ought to silence
these slanderers for ever :- From 1747 to 1817 the
proportion of convicted criminals in the Highlands
was 1 to 301,677 of the inhabitants. In England
and Wales the proportion from 1810 to 1817 was 1
to 16,898. In the Inveraray circuit the proportion
was only 1 to 769,501 of the population.

THE NAME "CRAIG."—Sir, I would feel obliged
if you, or any of your readers, could inform me to
what clan (if any) the Craigs belonged, also what
tartan they wore? I am told the name is derived
from the Gaelic for a stone.—ONE OF THEM.—
Craig is a topographic surname from (Gaelic) *creag*
a rock ; Scotch, crag. It is hard to say where
the Craigs originally belong to. They are found in
various parts of the Lowlands. Cosmo Innes, in
his work, "Concerning some Scotch Surnames,"
refers at page 39 to the confusion occasioned by
translating names, and remarks, "We made De la
Roche and De Rupe into Craig."—FIONN.

CUMHA DO DH-FHEAR LONNDABHRA —LAMENT FOR ALLAN CAMERON OF LUNDAVRA.

GAELIC BY AILEAN DALL, TRANSLATION BY THE LATE MRS. MARY MACKELLAR.

AIR FONN—"*Mìle marbhaisg air an t-saoghal.*"

'S LIONMHOR sùil a tha galach,
　Dubhach, deurach, mu Fhear Lonndabhrà ;
'S goirt leam sgaradh do chéile,
　Bho 'n la thainig an t-eug ort gun dàil ;
Bhi ga d' mhilleadh b' e 'm beud ',
　Gun do ghillean ad réir 's tu 'n cruaidh-chàs,
Dhol a chumail do shréine
　'N uair a dh' fheargnaich a' bheist 'thug a lìd làth.

Tha do nighean fo ghruaman,
　Snaim a cridhe cha 'n fhuasgail ach mall,
'S e mar chudthrom na luaidhe
　Air tuiteam fo bhruaidhlein nach gann :
Sior-shnidhe le 'gruaidhibh,
　'S i drùghadh tromh 'cluasaig fo ceann ;
'S goirt an sgaradh a fhuair i,
　'N am dhi dùsgadh, 's cha bhruadar a bh' ann.

N uair a chaidh thu na d' dhlollaid,
　Moch an là ud a triall bho 'n Tigh-bhàn,
Lan tuigs' agus riasain,
　Fhir a chumadh an riaghailt air càch—
Faicleach, furachail, ciallach,
　'N uair a ghlac thu do shrian an n ad làimh
Mar stiùir luinge 'n uair fhiathuil,
　'S i gun eagal gun fhiamh roimh 'n ghaoith a rd.

Chaidh an t-ainmhidh gu dhùlan,
　'S cha ghabhadh a' bhrhid cur fo smachd ;
'S m' an deachaidh tu 'd chùram,
　'S ann thainig a' chùis ort gu grad ;
Leis an leum thug an cùrs-each,
　Mar gu'n lasadh am fudar fo 'n t-sraid,
Bha do phearsa, 's b' i 'n diùbhail
　Air dhroch càramh fo chruidhear a chas.

Bu tu marcaich nan steud-each,
　Gun nireasbhuidh céille na 'n dài ;
'S ged a thuislich do cheum ort,
　Cha 'n eil fios nach e 'n t-eug a bha 'n dàn ;
Ach sgeul cràiteach ri leughadh,
　Gun do chàirdean bhi leirsinn mar bhà.
'S tu call d' fhola, trom-chreuchdach,
　Gun aon duin' ach thu féin an gleann fàs.

'N uair a thainig do ghille,
　Bha sud nàdurra 'thioma bhi truagh ;
Dhoirt a shùilean air mhire
　'S bu dhùth 'dheoir a iad a' sileadh le ghruaidh :
Cha robh chòdhail ach sgiorrail,
　'S e gun chòmhnadh a' sileadh nam bruach,
Tigh'nn na ònrachd bho 'n fhìreach,
　'S gun fhear-sgeoil aige dh' innis nar fhuair.

Oh ! sore is our weeping,
　Lundavra, 'tis for thee that we mourn,
Thy loved spouse alone sleeping
　Sighs in vain for her chieftain's return ;
Would thy men had been near thee
　In the hour of thy sorest need,
Then no danger could fear thee
　Tho' restless and wayward thy steed.

Oh ! thy daughter's in anguish,
　Whatever can soothe her again,
In woe she will languish,
　And the tears from her eyelids will rain :
Rude and wild was the billow
　That woke her that morn from sleep,
Now bedewed is her pillow
　With the tears that she aye must weep.

The grey dawn was breaking
　When leaving the white house in the glen,
Thy last morn was breaking,
　Thou sagest in counsels of men ;
Sitting firm in thy saddle
　Thou wert without fear or qualm,
Holding lightly thy bridle,
　Like the helm of a ship in a calm.

As the tempest comes dashing,
　Oft uprooting the stateliest tree,
As the lightnings come flashing,
　The swift message of death came to thee ;
Thy charger had bounded
　Ere thou wert, brave chieftain, aware,
And bleeding and wounded
　Lay thy form, once so stately and fair.

Thou wert rider most fearless
　Although death in thy path lay in wait,
Among men thou wert peerless,
　Though dark and untoward thy fate ;
Had thy friends but been near thee
　When bleeding alone on the ground,
With no fond voice to cheer thee,
　And no kind hand to soothe thy deep wound.

Oh ! sad was the wailing
　Of him who came first of thy men,
Oh ! deep is the wailing
　O'er thee in the desolate glen ;
Oh ! well might he sorrow
　To find thee alone in thy pain,
And to know that no morrow
　Could restore him his chieftain again.

PRIZE COMPETITIONS.

THE prize of £1 1s., offered by Mr. Charles Fraser-Mackintosh for the best Highland tradition, has been awarded to Mr. A. B. M'Lennan, Lochboisdale (*Ben Wyvis*), for his contribution, entitled "Donald Macleod, the Soldier," which we have pleasure in printing in the present issue.

The prize of five shillings offered by Miss Mackay, Belfast, for the best Reay country tradition, has been awarded to Mr. George Mackay, Simon, Dar-ness, Sutherland (*Glen-Gollie*), for his story, "Lord Reay's Adventure on Fionaven," which will appear in next number.

We have decided to keep the Gaelic competition open till the 30th November, so that everyone who intends competing may have a fair chance. Papers for this competition should be forwarded to the editor not later than that date.

NEW YORK CELTIC SOCIETY.—At a meeting of this Society, held on 30th October, it was unanimously agreed, on the motion of Mr. Duncan MacGregor Crerar, seconded by Mr. Donald MacDonald—" That, in recognition of the many and valuable services rendered to the language, music, and traditions of the Scottish Highlands by Mr. Henry Whyte (" Fionn "), the honour and privileges of honorary membership be, and are hereby conferred upon him ; and that he, in virtue of this resolution, be elected an honorary member of this society."

CLAN MACKAY SOCIETY.—The Annual Business Meeting was held in Edinburgh on 16th ult., Dr. George Mackay in the chair. Mr. John Mackay, Kingston, (Secretary,) read a very favourable report of the year's work, and the Treasurer's statement showed that the Society's funds amounted to nearly £800. The following office-bearers were elected.—president, Alex. Mackay, J.P., F.S.A., Wilts ; vice-presidents, Colonel A. Forbes Mackay, Alex. Mackay, LL.D., Editor, *Educational News*, Dr. W. Murray Mackay, North Shields, George Mackay, Blairmore, and Alex. Mackay, and Lieut. William Mackay, Glasgow. The Secretaries, Treasurer, and a council of twenty-four were appointed. It was resolved to hold the competition for the Society's bursary next August. The Rev. J. Aberigh-Mackay was duly acknowledged chieftain of the Abruch branch of the clan, an honour which that gentleman will greatly appreciate, and which has given universal satisfaction to the members of the clan. It was decided to hold the Social Gathering in Edinburgh about the middle of February, when Lord Reay is expected to preside. It has also been arranged to hold a musical entertainment in Glasgow about the middle of this month, at which a lecture will be delivered by Mr. W. Gordon Campbell on " The Mackay Country," illustrated by a large number of views of historic places on the magic lantern. This entertainment will be open to friends of members, and a large attendance is expected.

GLASGOW COWAL SHINTY CLUB.—We have pleasure in acknowledging receipt of the following additional subscriptions for the club-house fund :— Charles Fraser-Mackintosh, Esq., London, £1 ; A. Brown, Esq., £1 ; Duncan Whyte, Esq., 10s ; Arch. M'Arthur, Esq., 5s ; Lieut. Black, £1 ; per Colin Macphail, £1 10s 6d.

THE NATIONAL CHOIR (J. & R. Parlane, Paisley) for November contained an excellent translation, with music, of " *Mo Dhachaidh*," by the author, Mr. Malcolm MacFarlane.

CAMANACHD NOTES.

THERE is little to report this month in connection with shinty. The match season has not yet commenced, but next month several interesting contests are expected to take place. The GLASGOW COWAL are arranging to play the LONDON NORTHERN COUNTIES on an early date, and during the course of the season they expect to meet EDINBURGH CAMANACHD, BALLACHULISH, and other prominent clubs.

We are glad to state that a strong club has been started in STORNOWAY, and the following office-bearers have been elected : - Captain, W. J. Mackenzie ; vice-captain, Mr. Cameron ; secretary, John Maclean ; treasurer, Mr. Chrystal ; and a committee of five.

INVERGORDON has also its shinty club now, and the following office-bearers have been appointed :— Captain, Mr. Black ; vice-captain, Arch. Watson ; secretary, A. Sutherland.

We wish these new clubs every success.

REVIEWS.

THE GAELIC JOURNAL. (Dublin).—The November number is to hand, and is specially attractive to all who are interested in Gaelic from an educational standpoint, containing as it does a number of examination papers in Irish Gaelic. We have also a fine-toned English article on the recently formed Gaelic League—a society " for the sole purpose of keeping the Irish language *spoken* in Ireland." There are also a variety of articles in Irish prose and verse. It is evident from the " Scottish Gaelic Notes " that the learned editor, Prof. O'Growney, is keeping himself abreast of all that is going on among the Scottish Gaels. We cordially reciprocate the editor's good wishes towards ourselves.

PERSONAL AND CLAN NAMES OF THE HIGHLANDS : THEIR ORIGIN AND MEANING.— Such is the title of a series of most interesting and valuable articles from the facile pen of our friend, Mr. Alexander MacBain, M.A., Inverness, which have appeared lately in the *Northern Chronicle*. This is the only treatise on this subject that is in any way exhaustive or scientific, and we could wish that it was given to the public in a permanent form. We are confident that the articles, revised and amplified, and with a copious index, would, in these days of clan societies, be eagerly bought, as we have really no authentic work on the subject of clan and personal names.

STRENGTH OF THE CAITHNESS CLANS.—We are indebted to Mr. Hector Sutherland, solicitor, Wick, for the following interesting statistics, compiled from the electoral roll of 1892 :—

Names.	Reay.	Thurso.	Halkirk.	Olrig.	Dunnet.	Bower.	Canisbay.	Wick.	Watten.	Latheron.	Total.
1. Campbells	11	30	16	5	4	6	3	7	5	18	102
2. Gunns	9	20	14	11	3	4	4	26	8	49	137
3. Hendersons	9	12	24	2	3	8	5	16	6	20	105
4. Keiths	1	5	1	3	3	2	3	0	0	8	24
5. Mackays	20	18	24	3	4	8	8	15	14	58	202
6. Sutherlands	14	41	29	9	13	10	13	28	21	142	320
7. Sinclairs	9	32	27	10	6	8	10	12	5	52	171
8. Swansons	1	41	1	18	6	14	4	2	6	2	98

It will certainly be a surprise to many to learn that the two strongest Sutherland clans, the Mackays and Sutherlands, occupy the leading place in Caithness as well, and the Sinclairs, who have figured so largely in the past history of the county, only take third place. The Mackays and Sutherlands settled in Caithness in large numbers at the time of the evictions, 1812 to 1820. Will any of our readers kindly favour us with an analysis of the Ross-shire clans?

SIR JAMES COLQUHOUN, BART.,
Chief of the Clan Colquhoun.

THE CELTIC MONTHLY:
A MAGAZINE FOR HIGHLANDERS.
Edited by JOHN MACKAY, Kingston.

No. 4. Vol. II.]   JANUARY, 1894.   Price Threepence.

SIR JAMES COLQUHOUN, BART.,
CHIEF OF THE CLAN COLQUHOUN.

SIR JAMES COLQUHOUN of Colquhoun and Luss, Baronet, whose portrait appears as the frontispiece of this number, was born in George Street, Edinburgh, on 30th March, 1844. After passing through preparatory training at Hatfield Rectory, and later at Hoddesdon, in Hertfordshire, under the Rev. C. G. Chittenden, he entered Harrow, where he concluded his school education. From Harrow Sir James went to Trinity College, Cambridge, and in 1871 graduated there, taking the M.A. degree. Sir James, who is Lord-Lieutenant of Dumbartonshire takes a keen interest in all public affairs. He married Miss Charlotte M. Douglas Munro, youngest daughter of Major Munro, late of the 79th Highlanders, and Elizabeth, his wife, a daughter of Sir Robert Abercromby, Bart., Banffshire,—and has two daughters.

As Chief of the Clan Colquhoun, a short account of the origin of the family, and a notice of one or two of the more famous members may be of interest to our readers in regard to the subject of our sketch, more particularly as the Clan Society holds its first annual gathering on the 29th of this month. At this gathering, which will be held in the Waterloo Rooms, Glasgow, it is hoped that all clansmen, who can, will attend, as it is now many a long day since the Colquhouns gathered as a clan under their chief; and, indeed, we have no doubt the clansmen would extend their welcome to their quondam enemies, and be glad to meet around the festive board the Clan Gregor, whom last they met in the "Vale of Sorrow."

The first member of this family of whom there is any written notice was Umphredus de

Kilpatrick, who, in the reign of Alexander II., obtained a grant of the barony of Colquhoun, "pro servitio tennis militas," and, as was the custom of the time, assumed the name of the lands so granted. The barony formed a portion of the parish of Kilpatrick, and on the most commanding portion of it—the rock of Dunglass—they erected a stronghold, upon the ruins of which their armorial bearings may still be seen. The great-grandson of this Humphrey was a Sir Robert Colquhoun, who married the heiress of Luss, and founded the present family.

Three generations later Sir John Colquhoun was appointed Governor of the Castle of Dumbarton during the minority of James II. At this time the post was one of great importance and no little danger, and it is recorded by Buchanan that Sir John was treacherously assassinated by a body of "lawless Highlanders."

The importance of the family at this period is further evidenced by the fact that Sir John's son, Malcolm, was one of the hostages for payment of the ransom of James I.

This Sir John's grandson was Sheriff of Dumbartonshire in 1471, and three years later received a Crown grant of Strone, Kilmun, Invercaple, and other places in Argyllshire, and in the same year was made Grand Chamberlain of Scotland. In this capacity, and accompanied by Bishop Spence of Aberdeen, the Laird of Sauchie, and the Lion-King-at-Arms, he went to the Court of England with powers to treat for a marriage between the Scottish heir apparent, and Princess Cecilia, daughter of Edward IV. of England.

This intended marriage never took place, but so well did he acquit himself of his mission that the king made him Governor of the Castle of Dumbarton for life. This Sir John was killed at the siege of the Castle of Dunbar (1477).

Sir Alexander Colquhoun, who succeeded to the estate in 1592, was chief of the clan at the time of the famous fray at Glenfruin with the Clan Gregor, in 1603. Passing over the succeeding generations, who were distinguished in various ways, we mention Sir John, who suc-ece led to the estates in 1645. We know that he was a warm adherent to the Royalist party in Scotland, and in that cause suffered many hardships, and that during the time that Cromwell was in power in Scotland he was fined the sum of £2000, though this sum was afterwards modified to a third of that amount.

In more modern times members of the Clan Colquhoun have gained celebrity in various ways—through Garscadden in the reckless old times of hard drinking and gay living; and still later, in the higher paths of literature and science, through Dr. Patrick Colquhoun, the able author of "The Population, Power, Wealth, and Resources of the British Empire," and through Mr. John Colquhoun, whose charming "Moor and Loch," and "Stray Shots and Salmon Casts," are still the envy of the literary sportsman.   H. COLQUHOUN HAMILTON,

Glasgow 12th Dec., 1893.   M.A., LL.B.

SHOTTY DOOLT'S COURTSHIP.

BY REID TAIT.

WONDER at ye mither; I canna think what ails ye. To think I wad tak' up wi' yon Shotty!" exclaimed Ailsa Cameron, angrily.

"Hout, tout," said her mother, "ye needna be sae haughty. Shotty wad mak' a gran' guidman to ony lass."

"Ye ken fine I'm no thinkin' o' men, and want none o' them," said Ailsa, with a sound of tears in her voice.

"There, lassie," said her mother, "I didna mean to vex ye. Ye shallna be made to tak' onybody ye dinna want; but if ye wad think o' Shotty I'd like it fine. He mayna be ower fine lookin', puir body, but he's honest and guid, wi' a fine hoose to tak' a wife tae."

But when did these attributes ever take a young girl's fancy? Mrs. Cameron forgot her own young days; it was not honesty or goodness, or even a "fine hoose," that weighed with her then.

Ailsa Cameron was a pretty girl, with eyes blue as forget-me-nots, yellow hair like the waving corn in autumn, and a face like a wild rose with the dew upon it.

These were the despised Shotty's similes, to himself, in secret. He had a vein of poetry running through his nature which no one suspected. He made verses on his sweetheart sometimes, but these no eye ever saw but his own. With all her beauty, Ailsa had had her troubles

—troubles which the neighbours knew about, and were not likely to forget.

She had been going to marry Donald Fraser, the handsomest lad in the village, but he had gone south and had not proved true. After he had been away a while, Ailsa heard he was taking up with a girl in the town where he was staying. She did not believe it at first, but his letters grew few and cold, and at last she taxed him with it; and he acknowledged it. This was more than a year ago, and Ailsa had heard no more from him, since she had written indignantly, giving him his freedom.

Shotty Doolt had come to the village, from the next parish, about six months before Donald went away, and he was as ugly as the other was handsome. Even his very name was against him. He had been a foundling, found on an old man's doorstep, and this old man, who was an eccentric character, had insisted, though remonstrated with by the minister himself, in giving the infant this preposterous name. He said, certainly with some show of reason, that as he was going to bring the child up, and make a man of him, he surely had a right to call him what he liked, and of course he had his own way.

After his adopted father died, which did not occur until Shotty was twenty-six years of age, he had come to Innisfair to live, as it was handier for the fishing. After he came, the bully of the village, a big, powerful fellow, with a long tongue, had set upon him, but Shotty took no notice of him, treated him with good-natured contempt, which the bully took for a sign of weakness.

At last things came to a crisis. There was a crowd of the men together, Shotty and James Hendrie amongst them, and James commenced to jeer at Shotty for his name. Shotty stood it for a few minutes, good temperedly, but by and by James said something that reflected on Shotty's mother, and Shotty's countenance changed. In a moment he had raised his fist, brought it down with crashing force on his adversary's head, and knocked him flat on the ground. The bully's blood was up, and he rose, vowing vengeance. Shotty was nothing loth, so coats were taken off, a ring was made, and there was a set-to fight. The old man had been a boxer in his youth, and had carefully taught his adopted son the noble art of self-defence, and Shotty's powerful and scientific blows soon told a tale, and James Hendrie lay stretched on the ground in a sorry plight.

"Have ye had enough?" asked Shotty, as unruffled as ever. "Yes, do ye say?" he added. "Well, mind ye and keep a civil tongue in your head for the future," and Shotty walked off and he was never molested again.

But though he was so bold in this way, Shotty was very "blate" in his wooing. He was so fully aware of his deficiencies. He looked upon Ailsa as such a personification of all beauty and goodness, that he was more awkward before her than was usual with him, and no one could call Shotty graceful at any time.

A big, burly figure stood in the open doorway of the Camerons' cottage, looking in.

"Good evening to ye," said the pleasant voice of Shotty himself.

"Come awa' in, Shotty, I'm gled to see ye," said Mrs. Cameron, who was always especially gracious to him, to make up for Ailsa's coolness. "Hoo are ye the night?"

Shotty came in as he was told, carrying several fine fish on a string in his hand.

There was no doubt about it, as he stepped into the light of the window, that Shotty was ugly. You could not smooth it over and call him plain; ugly was the only word for it. His features were about as irregular as they well could be—he had a big mouth, high cheek-bones, a flat nose, green-grey eyes, and a shambling, loose-jointed kind of figure. He was clad in a fisherman's rough, but smart, blue cloth suit, a blue guernsey, and long-legged boots. A physiognomist would have said there were lines round that big mouth that told of tenderness equal to a woman's, that there was a firmness and determination about the square chin that said its owner would get on in the world, and that in the broad forehead, on which the dark hair fell, a fine intellect lay hid. But girls as a rule, do not look so deep as this, and to Ailsa, Shotty was neither more nor less than an ugly young man, whom she disliked because he had the face to come after her, and her mother favoured him.

"Hoo's the fishin' been to-day, Shotty?" enquired Mrs. Cameron, plying her needles as she spoke.

"Just middlin'," he replied, awkwardly, "I brought you these two or three codlin', thinkin' ye might like them."

"Ye're ower guid, Shotty," said Mrs. Cameron. "What fine anes tae! Hang them up, Ailsa."

Ailsa put down her knitting and advanced to do her mother's bidding. But Shotty would not allow this. He followed the girl out into the little yard, hung up the fish himself, and because Ailsa was looking at him he nearly let them fall, at which she laughed.

"Your fingers are a' thumbs, Shotty," she said.

"Aye," he answered, "so it seems," and laughed himself, but still it hurt him, that Ailsa should laugh at him.

(To be continued.)

GAELIC AIRS TO LOWLAND SONGS.

By Malcolm MacFarlane.

IN the article by Mr. John Whyte, in this magazine (Vol. I., p. 186), on "Duncan Bàn's Musical Adaptations," the author is puzzled at the poet's taste in adapting *Cumha Choire Cheathaich* to "The Flowers of Edinburgh." The explanation given may be correct, but there is room for another. We find the same bard's song, *Oran a' champa*, adapted to "Sae will we yet," which was popular in Edinburgh in Duncan's day. At the St. Columba Gaelic Choir's concert two years ago, when Mr. Ferguson, the conductor of the choir, was singing *Oran a' champa*, it was remarked by some one behind me that the tune was familiar to him. "I have no doubt," rejoined the person addressed, "that is 'The Wearing of the Green.'" That is so. But it is "Sae will we yet," and *Oran a' champa* nevertheless. It is more. It is "The Captain with his Whiskers," which I well remember to have been popular over twenty years ago. In Maver's "Genuine Irish Melodies" is this note, which I quote entire:—

"'The Wearing of the Green'—in Scotland known as 'Sae will we yet.' This air was first published by James Oswald in 1747, amongst his 'Airs for the Season,' and called by him 'The Tulip (Spring).' Recently it has made its appearance (slightly altered) as a modern *English* comic song called 'The Captain with his whiskers.' Our German friends would fain claim this fine tune as theirs, judging from the following note addressed to the editor of the *London Daily News* a few years ago:— 'Sir, Your Metz correspondent, in his capital description of a military picnic, observes:— "It may interest the British music hall patrons to know that a translation of 'The Captain with his whiskers' is one of the chiefest favourites with the Prussian officers. They rattle away at its lively chorus with the greatest delight." May I venture to say that "The Captain with his whiskers" is merely a vulgarised version of an excellent ditty of the old French war, and that the melody is borrowed from the famous Blucher song. 'Was blazeu d e Trompeten, Husaren heraus.'" This is all very fine, and 'The Tulip' *may* have come across from 'Germanic,' but it is nevertheless the fact that the tune was first introduced to the British public by James Oswald 130 years ago.'"

Alongside of this place another fact. A friend, who can speak German and frequents the company of Germans, informed me that he had the greatest difficulty in convincing some German musical acquaintances that "The last rose of summer" was not German but Irish. Again, I was told that some one who had heard *Mo Dhachaidh* sung at the Mòd, pronounced the air a French one. That *may* be; but I stumbled across it a few weeks ago in Patrick McDonald's collection (1784), where it is given as a tune from the Western Isles, named *Posadh peathar luns bhain*. John Maclean, the Tiree bard, wrote a song to this air, called *Am Maraiche*

Gleusda. Let us turn now to a brother bard and contemporary of Duncan Bàn, namely, *Mac Mhaighstir Alastair* (Alexander MacDonald). We find his song, *Allt an t-siùcar*, adapted to "The Lass o' Patie's Mill." This air is said to have been first published in *Orpheus Caledonius* (1725) along with words by Allan Ramsay. It is also stated that it was known by the same name before his time. The original "Lass o' Patie's Mill" is claimed for Keithhall, Aberdeenshire, and also for Ayrshire. Let it be noted that these are places in touch with a Gaelic-speaking people. Do Highlanders sing *Allt an t-siùcar* to the "Lass o' Patie's Mill?" Not exactly. Turn to number 36 of *The Celtic Lyre* and compare the tune there given with the other. They are substantially the same. Which is the original? Perhaps neither. But which is the more primitive in style? Assuredly that in *The Celtic Lyre*. It is on the Irish model referred to in my article at p. 9, Vol. II. of this magazine. For my own part, I do not hesitate to say that the "Lass o' Patie's Mill" is an elaboration of the Gaelic air according to a style common to tunes published a century and a half ago. No one with knowledge would contend that the Gaelic air was a development of the other. In the light of all this, may it not be that "Sae will we yet" was a Gaelic or Irish air, and that Duncan composed his song to it, the English name having been given by the editor of his poems, as was the case with *Allt an t-siùcar*? The tune, apart from its being now an Irish national one, suggests an Irish origin. Similarly, may not "The Flowers of Edinburgh" be a dance set of some Highland or Irish tune which Duncan had in his mind when he composed his *Cumha*. Mr. Henry Whyte kindly supplies the following *Port à beul* which Highlanders often sing to the music. (See also Vol. I., p. 159, of *Celtic Monthly*):—

Reicidh mi mo sheannhair
Is gheibh mi beagan airgid ;
Reicidh mi mo sheannhair
O'n tha i fas sean.
Reicidh mi mo sheannhair
Is gheibh mi beagan airgid ;
Reicidh mi mo sheannhair
Is ceannaichidh mi bean, &c.

It is noted in "Hardiman's Irish Minstrelsy" that Carolan's "Nancy Cooper" is in the same measure as the "Flowers of Edinburgh;" and that measure agrees with the above lilt and Duncan Bàn's song. On the other hand, the song given to the air in Mayer's collection, p. 196, namely, "The Banks of Tarf," differs in point of measure from these. One quatrain of it covers as much of the music as two of the Scottish and Irish Gaelic versions, and the rhythmic movement of the tune is reproduced better on them than on the Lowland Scotch song.

These introductory remarks are chiefly suggestive, and meant to show, among other things, that all the sources of enquiry into the origin of tunes to Scottish songs have not been tapped. Hitherto research has been made principally by persons without a knowledge of Scottish Gaelic, not to speak of Irish Gaelic. The time has come when the results of that kind of research will not be accepted with the same confidence as formerly. It will not do to dogmatise, however; for it is perfectly evident that tunes travel far from their homes and become subject to changes to suit the musical taste of the people among whom they settle. It is, therefore, with a mind open to correction that I put forward the following list, which contains, among many tunes concerning which there can be no doubt, some others which afford room for discussion; and there are others besides, which are included here because they have Gaelic names, although it is questionable, at the same time, whether or not they are Gaelic tunes. The list will, if it does no other good, serve as a nucleus of information for those who may wish to make searching inquiry into the subject. That can only be done properly by persons having at their command a large number of appropriate books, plenty of leisure, some musical knowledge, an aptitude for research, and, above all, a cool judgment.

Fraser of Knockie's List.

1. Nighean donn nan gobhar—The maid that tends the goats. "Up amang the cliffy rocks" is sung to this air.

2. Nighean a' ghreusaich—Wilt thou be my dearie (Burns)? This tune is called in some books "The Sutor's Dochter," an exact translation of the Gaelic name. "Sutor" is Lowland Scotch for shoemaker. The Gaelic name is given in "The Scots Repository."

3. Banais aig a' mhuillear—Comin' thro' the rye. The older name is "Dinna ask me gin I lo'e thee."

4. O, tha mi tinn—Long, long the night.

5. Mac Griogair o Ruadhshruth—From the chase in the mountain.

6. Baile na craoibhe—My love's in Germanie.

(To be continued.)

Urquhart and Glenmoriston—Olden Times in a Highland Parish, by William Mackay, Solicitor, Inverness. The work will consist of sixteen chapters, and many interesting appendices, in all, 550 pages. It will also be suitably illustrated. Price, £1 1s.; Quarto copies on antique paper, £1 11s. 6d. The work is to be published by the Northern Counties Publishing Co., Ltd., Margaret Street, Inverness, and we cordially recommend it to our readers.

MISS A. G. MURRAY MACGREGOR, DUNKELD.

THE lady whose portrait is given in this number—Miss Amelia Georgiana Murray MacGregor—was born on the 18th of January, 1829, and is the youngest of the family of Major-General Sir Evan Murray MacGregor of MacGregor, K.C.B., and G.C.H., who died in 1841, Governor of Barbadoes. He was the only son of Sir John MacGregor Murray of MacGregor, created baronet 1795, nephew of Glencarnoch, who with his brothers bore a distinguished part in the Jacobite risings, and after 1745 lost all his possessions. Sir John, after his return home in 1798, from a most honourable career in India, was well known as a truly paternal chief, ever active in promoting the interests of young men belonging to his clan on their first start in life, by obtaining appointments for them, and afterwards corresponding with them. He was an excellent Gaelic scholar. Sir John married his second cousin, Anne M'Leod, great-granddaughter of Sir Norman M'Leod of Bernera, son of Sir Roderick M'Leod, XIII. of Dunvegan, "Rory Mor." * and died in June, 1822.

Sir Evan, a highly distinguished officer, was very severely wounded at the taking of Fort Tahore, when with the army of the Deccan in pursuit of Holkar, 1818. On the occasion of King George IV.'s visit to Edinburgh, in 1822, a body of the Clan Gregor turned out under Sir Evan's command, and were appointed as guard to the Knight Marischal in charge of the regalia. Sir Evan was strongly attached to his name and race, and it was at his suggestion that the Clan Gregor Society was founded in December, 1822. He married, in 1808, Lady Elizabeth Murray, youngest daughter of John, 4th Duke of Atholl. With such a thoroughly Highland descent, Miss Murray MacGregor naturally inherited a warm attachment to her country, its people, and especially to her clan. Both at Edinchip (parish of Balquhidder), now belonging to her grand nephew, Sir Malcolm Mac Gregor of Mac Gregor, and in Atholl, where she has lived for upwards of forty years, constant intercourse with Highland people has strengthened her taste for traditions, old customs, and genealogical and historical pursuits. Miss MacGregor joined the Clan Gregor Society soon after its resuscitation (which dates from May, 1886) and was present at the memorable expedition of the Society to Loch Katrine in July, 1888. As soon as the rule admitting ladies to be office-bearers was passed she was elected one of the directors of the Society, in the prosperity of which she takes a very great interest. Miss MacGregor is engaged in the preparation of a history of the Clan Gregor, to be eventually published under the auspices of the Society. The brooch shown in the portrait is of silver, with granite curling-stones, and was presented to Miss Macgregor by the Dunkeld Curling Club, the records of which she has kept for many years.

13 Grosvenor Crescent, Glasgow   ALEX. M'GRIGOR.

* Vide Celtic Monthly Vol. ii., p. 51.

THE LAST MACDONALDS OF ISLA.

By CHARLES FRASER-MACKINTOSH, F.S.A. (Scot.).

PART II.

A CHARTER by John de Yle, Earl of Ross and Lord of the Isles, to his brother Hugh (son of Alexander), of the Isles, Lord of Slete, and Fynvola nin Allister vic Iain of Ardnamurchan, spouses, of the 30 merk of Skirrichcugh, in Uist, which Donald Balloch is referred to, is not only curious in itself, but on account of a singular error in its own date, or in the King's confirmation which followed, or in the Register of the Great Seal, the date given being 28th June, 1409. There was only one John who was both Earl of Ross and Lord of the Isles, viz., the last, whose father Alexander died in 1448, or early in 1449. The correct date of the charter, therefore, in all probability is 1449, for not only the parties to it but the witnesses' names establish that 1409 must be erroneous. It bears to be signed at "our castle of Aros," and to be granted "with advice of our council." The Earl's kinsmen are declared to be Donald de Insulis, Lord of Dunyvaig and the Glens ; Celestine de Insulis of Lochalshe; Lachlan Maclean of Duart, and Alexander Mac Iain of Ardnamurchan. The witnesses, in addition to the above four kinsmen, are John Maclean of Lochbuie, Lachlan Maclean Master of Duart. William Macleod of Glenelg, Roderick Macleod of Lewis, John Lachlan Maclean of Coll, and Mr. Thomas Monro, secretary to the Earl and rector of Kilmonivaig. I find Donald Balloch at Inverness in 1466, and despite his early stormy career he died peacefully in Isla at an advanced age. His eldest son

III.— John married Sabina O'Neill, and he

DUNAVERTY, KINTYRE.

is placed as successor, though I think he died before his father. In the year 1461-2, during the negotiations of the Earl of Ross with the English King, Donald Balloch and his son John agreed to serve the King, they to receive respectively annually £40 and £20 sterling in time of war, and half these pensions in time of peace. The next chief was

IV.— John, and grandson of Donald, styled "Iain Cathanach," a distinguished warrior, incidents in whose chequered life formed the staple of many a story and song. Edward IV. sends him an embassy in 1481, wherein he is styled John of Isla, Lord of the Glens and Dunyvaig. He received the honour of knighthood from James IV., who granted him charters of a Luis Scottish estates. There was reserved, however, to the Crown, and strongly fortified, the Castle of Dunaverty, in South Kintyre, adjacent to Sir John's possessions. Sir John Cathanach at the earliest opportunity attacked, took, and destroyed in very aggravating circumstances the castle, with its garrison, a great humiliation to the proud spirited King James, unable at the time to retaliate.[*] At whatsoever time King or Council wished to attack a Macdonald or a Maclean, they always had an Argyle ready to hand. The Argyle open and fair-field attacks were few in number, and seldom successful, hence they employed others to do the hard and underhand work. In this case of Sir John's, John Macdonald of Ardnamurchan, who had a dispute with him regarding Sunart, was

[*] The castle was repeatedly taken and destroyed. Mrs. Margaret Fleming, afterwards Mackay, mother of the talented and energetic editor of the *Celtic Monthly*, lived for some time in the neighbourhood, and has often in her youth picked up bones of the slain in the adjoining sands. The configuration of large holes or pits dug at different times for wholesale interment was quite distinct there existing a feeling against the surface being broken up or interfered with. The sketch is by Miss Macdonell of Keppoch.—C. F.-M.

the instrument employed, a man of great ambition, who, as head of the powerful sept styled Mac Iain, had a strong following. Sir John Cathanach, with two of his sons, in a perfidious way, were taken prisoners and executed at Edinburgh, their bodies being buried within the Chapel of Saint Anthony. John Mac Iain received from the King, on 24th November, 1505, a ratification, for good services, of all charters formerly made in his favour of whatsoever lands in the islands of Isle and Jura and the low land (*bassa terra*) of Ardnamurchan and Suynart, with the Castle of Mingary, in Ardnamurchan, and Donavagan, in Isle, &c. The King, at Edinburgh, 19th November, 1506, confirmed to John Mac Iain, as heir of his grandfather, John vic Allister vic Iain, *inter alia*, two merks and 6s. 8d. worth of lands in Jura, viz., a large eighth part of Aridscarnula, and eighth part of Knock-na-scoloman, which held of the late Donald de Insulis, Lord of Dunyvaig and Glens, but now in the hands of the Crown through the forfeiture of the late John de Insulis of Dunyvaig, Knight, heir of the said Donald de Insulis, on account of Sir John's treason.

Sir John Cathanach, who married Sheela Savage, daughter of the then chieftain of that great family, settled at Portaferry, County Down, left two surviving sons, Alexander, and Angus, predecessor of the Macdonalds of Sanda. Sir John was succeeded by

V.—Alexander, who with his brother fled to Ireland, pursued by the implacable vengeance of the King, who caused pass an order that Alexander and his descendants be prohibited from ever setting foot in Scotland, or owning a foot of Scottish soil, and this decree stood in force until James IV.'s death at Flodden. Mac Iain was also sent to Ireland to capture or slay Alexander, but failed, after long search, as he reported to the King. In reality, Mac Iain seems to have relented, became reconciled to Alexander, and gave him his daughter Catherine in marriage, all unknown to the King. Alexander, after the accession of James V. of Scotland, was received by him into favour, and settled peacefully in Scotland. James V. entirely altered the course pursued by his immediate predecessors towards the Highland and Island chiefs, by giving them justice when in the right.

I have called the Isla family Macdonalds rather than Macdonells, although the Irish family of Antrim so called themselves at an early period. In reality the latter Islas sign "Konnel" ("M'Conil") and "M'Connal." This Alexander, the last head of the family, who could not write, signs thus, "Alexander Konnel de Dunoweg, with my hand on the pen," entered into a bond of gossipry with Sir John Campbell, first of the house of Calder named Campbell, wherein he is styled "Alex. the Illis, son of John Cathanach." The bond is dated at Glennay, in the Taraf, 7th May, 1522, and to endure for five years. Alexander is to serve Sir John by himself and all the branch of the Clan Donald that he is descended from, and he is bound not to harm such of the Mac Iains as hold of Sir John. On the other hand, Sir John gives Alexander 45 merks land in Isla, and the lands of Colonsay, free of mail, as also Jura, under certain conditions, during the foresaid space of five years. The reference to gossipry is curious: "Also for the final concord betwixt the said Sir John and the said Alexander, either of other, faithfully promise that what time or hour God sends them any bairns, that they shall baptize the bairn and be gossips, and aye until the said gossipry be completed, the said Sir John and Alexander shall keep leal, true, and a full part to other, as if it were completed."

Prior to his settling in Scotland, Alexander had made a great figure in Ireland, many of the flower of the Macdonalds resorting to his standard after the final forfeiture of John, Earl of Ross and Lord of the Isles. He thus not only maintained himself in his hereditary estate, but powerfully aided his native Irish allies against English oppression in Ulster. Alexander had by his wife six sons—James, Angus, Coll, Alexander, Donald Gorm, and Sorley—and three daughters, who all married well. Angus, Alexander, and Donald Gorm fell in battle in Ireland. James, the eldest son, succeeded; Coll, known as "Coll mac Capul," will be afterwards referred to; and Sorley, styled Sorley Buie, or "Somerled," otherwise "Samuel the Golden-haired," settled in Ireland, and was the first of the Great Irish house of the Macdonells of Antrim. Upon the death of Alexander, who had successfully upheld the fortunes of the family, he was succeeded by his eldest son,

VI.—James Macdonald, who married Lady Agnes Campbell, daughter of Colin, third Earl of Argyle, and some say had the honour of knighthood conferred upon him. The papers in my possession do not bear out this view. As regards his interests in Scotland, James Macdonald not only maintained, but increased his influence. In 1545 he received grants of lands from Queen Mary, which were renewed in 1558. In the insurrections of the Islanders under Donald Dubh, James was the only island chief who opposed. Yet having on Donald's death been elected Lord of the Isles, James accepted the position, and addressed a letter, dated Ardnamurchan, 24th January, 1546, to the Irish Privy Council, designing himself "James M'Conaill of Dunewack and ye Glennis, and apparent aeyr of ye Illis." It has been well said by an Irish historian that James "must have been very popular with both the contending parties in Scotland having been first elected Lord of the Isles by the persons whom he had previously opposed, and afterwards welcomed again by the Regent, even though he had assumed the obnoxious and then treasonable title of Lord of the Isles." Through the Argyle connection James received from his brother-in-law, Archibald, 4th Earl of Argyle, the 80 merks land of old extent of Ardnamurchan, which had come to the Earl through the resignation of Mariot Mac Iain. Notwithstanding the recent family connection, the acquisition of these lands must have been very welcome to Isla, but, whether well-intentioned or ill-intentioned, the grant ultimately helped the downfall of the Macdonalds, proving as fatal to Isla as the lands given for Sir John Cathanach's betrayal proved to the Mac Iains. We now arrive at the date 12th October, 1550—of the oldest documents in my possession, viz :— Charter of Alienation, endorsed in an old hand "Letter of Warrandice;" Precept of Sasine ; and Charter, all granted by Archibald, 4th Earl of Argyle, Lord Campbell and Lorne, in favour of James Maconell of Dunyvaught.

A *fac-simile* of the first-named charter, with the signature, "A Erle of Argyle," having greater part of the seal entire, is here given, having been done to my entire satisfaction expressly for these papers.

The three documents are of the same tenour, being charter and relative writs by the Earl of Argyle to James Macdonald of the 80 merks land of the old extent of Ardnamurchan, with the castle and fortalice of Mingary, tenants, tenantries, and service of free tenants, &c., &c., lying within the Sheriffdom of Inverness. The consideration is for good and thankful service done by James in time past, and to be done in time coming, and also for certain sums of money paid, the destination being to James and the heirs male of his body lawfully begotten, whom failing, to revert to the Earl ; and the holding, ward and relief ; signed at Edinburgh, the 12th day of October, 1550, in presence of Archibald, Master of Argyle; Sir John Lamont of Inveryne ; Mr. Neil Campbell, rector of Kilmartin ; Archibald Stewart, John Groung Mackay, and Mr. Cornelius Oneyght, the rector of Kilberhie.

---

* We have to express our indebtedness to Mr. Angus Mackay, Mount Pleasant, Cambuslang, for his kindness in photographing the charter, of which the above is a *fac-simile*.—ED.

DR. R. C. MACDIARMID, GLASGOW.

DR. MACDIARMID'S share in the movement for the intellectual and educational development of the Highlands has been a notable one, and the eve of his departure for a foreign sphere of labour is a fitting occasion for a brief record of his active and successful career. Dr. MacDiarmid was born at Dunvegan, Skye, in 1854. Having received a sound education he entered the Free Church Training College, Glasgow, where he qualified as a public school teacher. Successively Mr. MacDiarmid held charge of schools in Orkney and Islay, and the reports of Her Majesty's Inspectors testify to his assiduous devotion to duty, and the attainment of a high standard of educational work; but he early had aspirations towards the profession of medicine. Accordingly, he took the requisite curriculum in Glasgow University, and graduated in 1887 as M.B., C.M. For a few years he practised successfully at Whiteinch, and, taking a warm interest in the public affairs of the district, was for three years president of the Whiteinch Literary Association. About a year ago, ambitious of a wider field, he removed to the Anderston division of Glasgow, where he has already established a substantial practice. Recently Dr. MacDiarmid was offered, and he has accepted, a lucrative appointment as medical officer to the mining company of Messrs. Sopwith & Company, Limited, Linares and he proceeds to Spain early this month.

Dr. MacDiarmid, with Mr. Archibald M'Lean, Tiree, and the writer, originated the Gaelic Society of Glasgow, and has continuously assisted its progress to the position it now holds as one of the leading centres of Gaelic culture. An admirable paper on Donald MacLeod, the Skye bard, was read by him during the first session of the society, and deservedly occupies a place in the Society's transactions. At the present time the Doctor is one of the vice-presidents of the Gaelic Society. He is a zealous member of the Glasgow Skye Association, and he is also a member of the Executive Council of *An Comunn Gaidhealach*, the youngest, and, perhaps, the most energetic of our Highland societies. He has secured several lucrative appointments, conspicuous among which is that of Physician and Surgeon to the Highland Medical Aid Society of Glasgow. It may be said that Dr. MacDiarmid's influence has been exerted in every department of Celtic enterprise, and his removal to Spain will deprive his associates in the Celtic field of an earnest coadjutor. He will be accompanied to the sunny South by the good wishes of many friends, who bid his worthy lady, his family, and himself a prosperous sojourn in Spain, and, let us hope, a pleasant return, some day, to the rougher mountain land, which the Doctor loves so well.

Oban.   J. MACMASTER CAMPBELL.

OUR MUSICAL PAGE.

THE following song first appeared in the CELTIC GARLAND. The words and melody were taken down from the singing of a popular Gaelic vocalist. It is evidently the composition of some jilted lover who has placed his thoughts if not his name on record. In the last verse he accepts the situation with philosophic coolness—rendered literally it runs, " Why should I be now dejected, with my nets upon the shore, while there's as good fish beneath the sea as ever came above."

FIONN.

'S FHEUDAR DHOMH 'BHI TOGAIL ORM—I MAUN RISE AND GANG AWA.

Translation by MALCOLM MACFARLANE.

KEY A. *Moderato.*

SEISD :—
CHORUS:

r .,d : l₁ .d	l₁ .,f₁ : s₁	l₁ . d : r . m	s .,f : m
'S fheudar dhomh 'bhi	togail	orm	Fuireachd	cha dean	feum ach	falbh,
I maun	rise and	gang	awa,	Owre the	hills and	far a-	wa,

r .,d : l₁ .d	l₁ .,f₁ : s₁ .,l₁	d : s .,m	m,.r .— : d
'S fheudar dhomh 'bhi	togail	orm	A	dhir - eadh nam fuar - bheann.
I maun	rise and	gang	awa. Since gane	is my Ma - ry.

RANN :—
VERSE :—

s .,s : d .,d	m .,f : s .,f	m . m : r . r	m .s : l .,s
'Righ	gur mise	'tha fo	bhròn dheth	Air an	tulaich	so 'n am	ònar
On the	knowe a-	lane	I'm lyin',	Wistfully	the	ocean	eyein';

s .,f : m .m	r .,r : d .,d	r .r : m .s	f ,m .— : r
Fàth mo	mhulaid	thu 'bhi	poisde	Og-bhean	a'chuil	dual - aich.
Sick and	sad at	heart I'm	sighin'	For my	faithless	Ma - ry.

Do na h-Innsean 's tric a sheòl mi,
'S anns gach caladh tha mi eòlach
Té ni coimeas riut am bòidhchead,
Gus a so cha d' fhuair mi.

Ach cha mhaise 'rùin 's cha bhòidhchead
A chuir mi cho mór an tòir ort,
'S e mi bhi riut tric a' còmhradh,
'Us eòlach air do ghluasad.

'N uair chi mi 'n gleann 's an robh sinn còmhla
'Buain nan sòbhraichean 's nan neòinean
'S sinn le chéile aotrom gòrach,—
Ruithidh deòir ri m' ghruaidhean.

Dh'fhàg thu mise so gu brònach,
H-uile latha o'n a sheòl thu,
'S ged a théid mi 'measg nan òighean
Bith'dh mo chòmhradh fuar leò.

Ach c'uime 'm bithinnse fo smalan
'Us mo liontan air a' chladach,
'S iasg cho math an grunnd na mara
'S a thàinig riamh an uachdar.

I ha'e been tae mony places,
I ha'e seen fu' mony faces :
Never sic a wealth o' graces
As belang'd tae Mary.

'Twasna beauty a'thegither
Made me prize her 'bune a' ither ;
But sae aft's I did forgather
Wi' my lang-lo'ed Mary.

'Neath my view the glen reposes,
Whaur I've aften fashioned posies,
O' its daisies and primroses
For my charmin' Mary.

But her leavin's left me tearfu',
O' the future doubtfu', fearfu';
Mang the lasses nae mair cheerfu'
As I was wi' Mary.

But why should I be noo despairin'
And my sorrows thus be airin',
When there's tae be had for spierin'
Quite as guid as Mary?

DR. W. MURRAY MACKAY, NORTH SHIELDS.

VICE-PRESIDENT, CLAN MACKAY SOCIETY.

IT may seem strange to many that so large a proportion of the most enthusiastic members of the Clan Mackay Society are natives of Caithness. Although born in a county whose inhabitants in past times had no love for the Gaelic race, yet these Caithness Mackays are as proud of their name, their clan, and the beautiful land of their forefathers, *Duthaich Mhic Aoidh*, as any clansman born beneath the shadow of Ben Loyal, or by the side of the clear waters of the Naver. Many of them have risen to high and honourable positions in every part of the world, and in the county itself at the present time clansmen occupy many of the most responsible official positions.

It is, therefore, not to be wondered at that at last Annual Business Meeting of the Clan Mackay Society the members elected to the presidential chair Mr. Alex. Mackay, J.P., Wilts, a gentleman who has done credit to his native county; and as vice-presidents, other two Caithnessians — Dr. W. Murray Mackay, North Shields, and Lieut. William Mackay, Glasgow.

Dr. W. Murray Mackay, whose portrait we give herewith, is a clansman who, from its inception, has taken a deep interest in the work of the society, and has assisted it liberally in all its undertakings. A few particulars regarding the career of this distinguished member of the clan may prove interesting to many of our readers.

William Murray Mackay, L.R.C.P., L.R.C.S., and L.M. (Edin.), L.F.P.S. and L.M. (Glasgow), second son of Mr. James Mackay, farmer, Geeslittle House, Thurso, was born in 1859, and was educated at the Pulteneytown Academy, Wick, under Mr. Dick, who is still rector. He began the study of medicine in Glasgow University, was afterwards at Durham University, and the Surgeons' Hall, Edinburgh, where he became the most distinguished student of his year, having carried away nearly all the medals and first prizes, and in other ways so distinguished himself that he became the personal friend of many of his teachers. After qualifying, he for a short time acted as assistant to his brother, Dr. A. Davidson Mackay, of Eshe Hall, Durham, but soon afterwards began practice in North Shields on his own account, where in a very short time he established a large practice. Dr. Mackay took an active part in starting the Caledonian Association of North Shields, and is now vice-president. He has been twice elected a Guardian for the Tynemouth Union, and is a member of the British Medical Association. Dr. Mackay was present at the grand clan banquet which was given Lord Reay on his return from India. He is very proud of his name, and we trust he may be long spared to do credit to it.   EDITOR.

TO CORRESPONDENTS.

All Communications, on literary and business matters, should be addressed to the Editor, Mr. JOHN M.CKAY, 17 Dundas Street, Kingston, Glasgow.

TERMS OF SUBSCRIPTION.— The CELTIC MONTHLY will be sent, post free, to any part of the United Kingdom, Canada, the United States, and all countries in the Postal Union—for one year, 4s.

THE CELTIC MONTHLY
JANUARY. 1894.

CONTENTS.

We wish our many readers at home and abroad

A MERRY CHRISTMAS AND A HAPPY NEW YEAR.

OUR NEXT ISSUE.

In our next issue we will present our readers with a life-like plate portrait of Surgeon-Major J. MacGregor. M.D.. India, a distinguished native of Lewis, and a Gaelic poet of considerable repute. Also portraits of Messrs. Alex. M'Grigor, Glasgow, hon. secretary, Clan Gregor Society; John Mackenzie, secretary, London N.C. Camanachd Club; and Hugh MacCorquodale, secretary, Glasgow Cowal Shinty Club. In addition to these, the third part of "The Last Macdonalds of Isla" will be illustrated with a *fac-simile* of a charter, dated 1569, granted by Archibald, 5th Earl of Argyll, and also a full-size reproduction of the seal. A picture of Mingarry Castle, as it appeared about the middle of last century, will also be given. Mr. John Mackay, Hereford, will contribute another interesting paper on the Mackay country, entitled "Tongue; its History and Traditions," which will be illustrated by views of Ben Loyal, Kyle of Tongue, the Seat of the Lords of Reay, and other places of interest. The concluding part of the "Earldom of Ross" will have a picture of the Abbey of Fearn, with effigy of Earl Ferchar, and the seal of Alexander, Earl of Ross. Mr. Henry Whyte (*Fionn*) will contribute a biographical sketch of the late Lachlan MacLean, Coll, author of "Adam and Eve," and other curious Gaelic works, which will be accompanied with a picture of his birth-place, &c. We also intend giving a *fac-simile* reproduction of the famous Gaelic charter of 1408, in which the Lord of the Isles granted to Mackay the Rhinns of Islay for services rendered. This is a most interesting document, being the *only* Gaelic charter in existence. In addition to the above, there will be other fine illustrations, and several articles, poems, &c.

Of Interest to Clansmen.—It may interest our readers to learn that we intend giving in early issues life-like plate portraits of Lord Reay, chief of the Clan Mackay; Sir Malcolm MacGregor, Bart., chief of the Clan MacGregor; Mr. D. Reid Crow, hon. president, London Argyllshire Association; Captain James Mackay, Trowbridge, and other distinguished Highlanders. We are arranging to give a series of finely engraved portraits of the chiefs of the Highland clans.

ANSWERS TO CORRESPONDENTS.

John Livingstone, St. Boswells.—We will do our best to meet your wishes in regard to the Mackenzies and the Seaforth Highlanders. Our desire is to give as great a variety of contributions in each number as possible. We reciprocate your kind wishes.

"Ornun," Manchester.—Mr. Arch. Sinclair, 10 Bothwell Street, Glasgow, keeps in stock a large variety of Gaelic song books and other Gaelic publications. Send for his price-list. Mr. Norman Macleod, The Mound, Edinburgh, has also a good selection of Gaelic books. We are glad to learn that the bound copy of Vol. I. gave you so much pleasure.

Dr. J. C. MacA., Columbus, O., U.S.A.—We have sent copy of December issue, and hope you will become a subscriber. The following elementary works should suit your purpose:—"Gaelic as a Specific Subject," by the Highland Association; "Elementary Gaelic Grammar," by L. MacBean; "Practical Lessons in Gaelic for English-speaking Students," by D. C. Macpherson; "Gaelic and English Conversations," by Rev. D. M'Innes. A more advanced work is Stewart's "Gaelic Grammar." All the above works can be had from Mr. Archibald Sinclair, publisher, Glasgow.

Bound Copies of Volume I.

This handsome volume, consisting of 192 pages, and containing some fifty life-like portraits of well-known Highlanders, and other illustrations, can now be had bound in cloth, with gilt lettering, at **4s.** post free, or in fine, strong leather. **5s. 6d.** post free.

This valuable volume is specially suitable to send as a present to a Highland friend, or as a prize in schools in the Highlands.

As only a few copies can be had, those who wish the volume should apply at once to the EDITOR, *Celtic Monthly*, 17 Dundas Street, Kingston, Glasgow.

EXPULSION OF THE NORSEMEN FROM SUTHERLAND—STRATHNAVER THE SCENE.

By JOHN MACKAY, C.E., C.P., Hereford.

THE clash of sword upon sword and targe, the heavy thuds of the great battle-axe, the crashing of spears, were soon heard over the field of fight, mingled with the hoarse voices of commanders encouraging their men to redouble their efforts for victory, and the cries of the wounded who were falling in the terrible fray, resounded all over the field. The fight continued, and it would seem that Reginald, probably by superiority in numbers, out-generalled Harold, and eventually drove him across the river. Harold and his brave Norwegians retreated in good order down the west side of the Strath, pursued by Reginald, till "Ach cill na borgie" was reached, where, to cover their recrossing the Naver to the east side, their rearguard made a stand, and another conflict took place with Reginald's pursuing van. Again the Norsemen were defeated, losing many men and their commander, the gallant Bjorn, who was interred on the green knoll where he fell. A stone was placed over his grave, and from that day to this the spot is called "Leck-bairn," or "Leck-bjorn"—the flat stone of Bjorn. The others slain in the conflict were buried round the knoll. Some few years ago, one of the inhabitants thought of building a house upon this green knoll, a very nice site. He collected

DORVE CASTLE, FARR, SUTHERLAND.

stones for the purpose, when an ancient sage of the vicinity passing the way inquired what were the stones collected for. On being informed, he said, "Oh, man! do not build thy house over the graves of the slain, for if thou dost their ghosts will haunt it." The house was not built, though the collected stones are there still.

The battlefield of Dal-harold, where the Norsemen sustained so severe a defeat, is very interesting to the antiquary. Fought in 1198, it forms an epoch in Scottish history, as the commencement of the expulsion and wane of Norse rule in the North. It is singular that the chroniclers of the time make no mention of it. It is Torfæus who relates it, and from him the history of this eventful epoch is taken. The battlefield itself, with its erect stones marking the graves of commanders of distinction, and the numerous cairns along the whole line of battle mark the places where Norse and Scot were interred, and the memorial cairn raised over them.

As previously described, this battle was fought on the east bank of the Naver, and extended from 1500 to 1600 yards from the river, which gently flows by it. Along the river bank is meadow land, upon which Harold's right wing was posted. The meadow is flat for about 150 yards inland, till it ends at the foot of a terrace. On the edge of this terrace are the remains of an ancient fort, or Pictish tower, sixty yards in circumference, with an opening to the south, and fifteen yards inside diameter. The walls were apparently five to six feet thick,

From this fort, at a distance of sixty yards, and a little to its rear, are the standing stones marking where the heroic commanders fell, all in a circle, the highest in front being nine feet above ground and three feet in width; another to its right is of equal size, while the others diminish from eight to three feet in height. There are thirteen in all. In front of the stones are two large oval mounds, eight yards long by four yards wide, and in their rear are five cairns. Farther on in the line of battle are fourteen cairns, and on the extreme left, up to the "bloody knoll," are no less than forty-two cairns, marking where the slaughter was the greatest.

Harold, as previously mentioned, having recrossed the river during the conflict at Lech-bjorn, marched away about two miles towards Caithness, past the clachan of Farr, and with his defeated forces took post on the face and summit of Fiscary Hill, having probably received in the meantime reinforcements from Caithness, and there waited to stop Reginald's march farther east. He had not long to wait. Reginald followed, and came upon the formidable position taken up by Harold. Undeterred by the difficulties of its approach, and confiding in the bravery of his men, flushed, no doubt, with their previous victories, the assault was made in front and flank. Gradually the Scots pushed up the hillsides, each foot being desperately contested, till at last the hill-top was reached, where the fighting became still more fast and furious. The Norsemen were getting the worst of it, and, gradually yielding, they fled into Caithness, and Harold into the Orkneys, leaving the country at the mercy of his relentless opponents. Numberless cairns stud the top and slopes of Fiscary Hill, indicating the severity of the conflict, which for a time overthrew Norse influence in Sutherland and Caithness, though their rule was revived, as we shall see. Various articles of silver and gold were found on this battlefield, amongst them a splendid gold brooch.

In the Churchyard of Farr, which is situated near the foot of Fiscary Hill, the scene of the battle, is a remarkable monumental stone, carved with various devices, and of a kind of greenish granite, unknown in the North. It is supposed to have been reared in memory of a commander of great distinction who fell in the battle. A cross may still be distinctly traced on this stone.

ANCIENT STONE IN FARR CHURCHYARD.

The battle of Fiscary Hill gained, Reginald pursued his victorious career into Caithness, right away to Thurso, then the most important place in the district, and the seat of a bishop. All opposition having ceased with Harold's flight into the Orkneys, Reginald set himself to work in restoring order and bringing the country under the rule of the King of Scots. To preserve peace and order, he appointed three governors - one in Thurso, one in Tongue, and another in the southern part of Sutherland, whose abode was a fortalice, standing, it is said, where Dunrobin Castle is now situated. He was a Norse magnate named Rafn. He proved loyal to his trust, and was held in high esteem by William the Lion. The modest abode of this nobleman was named by the natives Dun-rafn, gradually mutated to Dun-rabyn and Dun-robin. Reginald remained in the country for several months, receiving the submission of the people, and seeing all peaceful and composed, went away southward to report his deeds to the King of Scots and receive his reward.

Harold having heard of his departure, and thinking the coast clear, sent spies over to see how the governors were affected towards him, and endeavour to assassinate them if they were found inimical. These spies came first to Rafn, who was found to be incorrigible, and as the same time well guarded. The Thurso Governor was next tried. He, too, would not side with Harold, was assassinated, and, for fear of being themselves slain, the spies immediately sailed away to report to Harold, who in a few months collected an army in the Orkneys, landed at Thurso, mutilated the bishop, who had been very friendly to Reginald, and took repossession of Caithness. The governors left by Reginald went off to report to William the Lion what happened, who in 1198 personally led an army into Caithness and finally disposed of Harold's pretensions, fined him for slaying the bishop, and allowed him to rule over Caithness only, paying tribute and giving William his eldest son as a hostage for his good behaviour in the future. With Harold the power and influence of the Norwegians passed away, although his two sons, David and John, succeeded him. The latter was the last of the race, and he, like many of his ancestors, met with a violent death, which finally ended the line of Norwegian Earls of Caithness.

(CONCLUDED).

[We have to express our thanks to Mr. W. Gordon Campbell, solicitor, Edinburgh, for the use of the negatives from which the preceding illustrations were engraved, and to Mr. Angus Mackay, Cambuslang, for kindly supplying us with prints of the same.—ED.]

THE EARLDOM OF ROSS.

By D. MURRAY ROSE.

I

ONE of the most historic of the old Scottish Earldoms is that of Ross, which was forfeited in 1476. The Earls of Ross attained an almost regal position in the north. For several centuries they took a prominent part in national affairs; consequently a brief account of these potent nobles, who, upon more than one occasion, made the kings of Scotland tremble upon their throne, may be of some interest. Unfortunately, no historian has yet undertaken to deal with the most interesting district in the north; and while Caithness, Sutherland, and Nairn have had their histories written up, Ross has scarcely been touched upon. Nowhere else, if we omit Sutherlandshire, has there been such a total extinction of the old aristocracy as in the Earldom of Ross.

The names of many of the great vassals who followed the banner of the Earls are still preserved, but only in connection with the lands of which they were once lords. Well may one ask where are the Tarrels of Tarrel, who possessed estates in Ross and Sutherland; the Tullochs of that ilk; the Baynes of Tulloch; the Dingwalls of that ilk and of Kildun; the Denoons of Cadboll; the Ferns of that ilk afterwards of Tarlogie; the MacCullochs of Tarrel, Plaids, Kindeace, and Glastullich? Where are the representatives of the fifty flourishing cadets of the house of Balnagown? Balnagown itself has long since passed into a family alien in name and blood. The Munroes still retain the old acres of their race, but the cadets of this ancient house have, like the others, all waned. Yet although these gentle families have disappeared they have left their names and their doings written largely in the records of the past.

No evidence has yet been forthcoming as to the actual date of the creation of the Earldom of Ross, and, as usual, the origin of the family ennobled under this title, has been the subject of much discussion. The first Earl of whom there is any mention is Malcolm, who (according to the register of Dunfermline) had a mandate from the King of Scots to protect the monks of Dunfermline between 1153 and 1165. Soon after the accession of Alexander II., Ferchar, Earl of Ross, comes upon the scene. He did some service in suppressing the rebellion which broke out in Ross and Moray, but there is no reason to believe in the origin assigned to him by Sir Robert Gordon and Skene. These writers are only held as authorities by those who never trouble to critically examine their statements, and who are possessed of a pious belief that they could not err. Into the question of origin we will not at this time enter; and only remark that Earl Ferchar was not paternally of Celtic descent, nor was he of "uncultured and savage disposition," as represented by some. He regularly attended the Court of Alexander II., and rendered valuable assistance in negotiations with England. It is much to his credit that he tried to forward Christianity and civilisation among the rude tribes of his Earldom. He founded the Abbey of Fearn, in the parish of Edderton, but owing to the savage disposition of the natives it had to be removed to another site. A stone effigy of the Earl still exists.

William, the next Earl, at the request of King Alexander, raised his vassals and led them against the men of Skye and Lewis, which Islands he brought into subjection, and received them as a reward from his sovereign. Dying in 1274, he was succeeded by his son, also William, who lived in stirring times. The death of the Maid of Norway plunged Scotland into the horrors of a disputed succession, and it is noteworthy that Brus, who afterwards was to prove the deliverer of his country, was the first to precipitate civil war. In the events which preceded the election of John Baliol to the kingly functions the Earl of Ross did not act a patriotic part : nor, indeed, did any of the Scots nobles. They preferred to sacrifice their country to their personal resentments. The Earl of Ross was commanded by Baliol to make war

Seal of William, Fourth Earl of Ross, attached to Deed of Homage by Baliol to Edward I of England.

upon the "foreign isles of Scotland and their chieftains," because they were quite opposed to

the king. At the head of a large body of his vassals Ross invaded the Isles, and in this expedition, which was crowned with success, he spent over £1000 : and having brought Lachlan and Roderic of the Isles prisoners to the king, the latter granted to him the lands of Dingwall and Ferrintosh.

In the troublous times which followed the deposition of Baliol, the Earl of Ross is found acting the part of a patriot. In 1296 he broke off with Edward of England, and led an army across the borders, devastating the country. This expedition terminated in disaster, for, the Scots meeting with an overwhelming defeat at Dunbar, the Earl of Ross was taken prisoner and confined in the Tower of London ; being allowed sixpence per day for his maintenance. He was set free three years later, and appointed warden beyond Spey by the English King, over whose interests he watched with vigilance. In 1304 he informed Edward that the Islesmen meant mischief. His old antagonist, Lachlan, had issued orders to his vassals that "each davoch of land should furnish a galley of twenty oars."

Robert the Brus was at this time actively engaged, in the English interest, in putting

CHURCH DEDICATED TO ST. DUTHAC, TAIN, ROSS-SHIRE.

down rebellion in Scotland. In the following February Brus met Sir John Comyn at Dumfries, and, perhaps, recollecting the scene and insult in Ettrick Forest in 1299 when Sir John seized him by the throat, the quarrel was renewed, with the result that the Comyn was stabbed, and Brus perforce had to raise the standard of revolt.

The Earl of Ross and "the men beyond the mountains" were bitterly opposed to Brus, and when the latter's queen and daughter sought refuge in the sanctuary of St. Duthac, at Tain, they were seized by the Earl and delivered prisoners to the

English King. After a time fortune smiled upon the Brus He did not forget nor forgive the Earl's conduct, and in 1307 he invaded Ross and Sutherland—an expedition to which none of our historians make any reference. The whole power of Ross, Sutherland, and Caithness was assembled to oppose the Brus, but his advance struck such terror into the inhabitants of these districts that they petitioned the English King to send assistance. Brus took signal vengeance upon the Earl, and ravaged his lands, which made him glad to sue for pardon and make a truce. They met at Auldearn, and here the

Earl swore fealty; this reconciliation being cemented by the marriage of the Earl's son, Hugh, with the Princess Maud, sister of the King. In 1312 Earl William appended his seal to the agreement between the Kings of Scotland and Norway. He led the men of Ross at the battle of Bannockburn, and was one of those who addressed the famous letter to the Pope, in 1320, asserting the independence of Scotland.

Hugh, the fifth Earl of Ross, commanded the reserve of the Scots army at Halidon Hill. He was of a superstitious nature, for the English found on his body the shirt of St. Duthac, which was supposed to possess miraculous powers, although it did not prevent him from being slain. The shirt, it may be mentioned, was restored to the chapel by the English. This Earl married a second time, the eldest son of his second wife (Margaret Graham) being Hugh Ross, ancestor of the Rosses of Balnagown, while a daughter, Euphemia, became the Queen of Robert II.

Seal of Euphemia Ross, Queen of Robert II.

William, the sixth Earl of Ross and Lord of Skye, assembled his feudal following in 1346 to assist King David in his expedition to England, but having basely murdered Ranald of the Isles, in the Monastery of Elcho, to escape the royal vengeance he returned with his men to the north. In 1366 he rose in rebellion, but was soon obliged to find security to keep the peace. King David Brus did not forget the conduct of the Earl of Ross and his desertion at Elcho, and refused to sanction his proposal of making his half-brother Hugh his heir. His only son had died, and his elder daughter, Euphemia, married Sir Walter Lesley against his will. The poor Earl seems to have been treated harshly, for he was compelled to resign all his lands in 1370, and they were conferred, failing heirs male of his body, upon his daughter Euphemia and her husband; whom failing, to his younger daughter Janet (who married Sir Alexander Fraser of Cowie) and her heirs.

Upon the death of the Earl of Ross, in 1372, the title devolved upon his daughter Euphemia, who had a son and daughter by Sir Walter Leslie, viz :—Alexander, Earl of Ross, and Margaret, who married Donald, Lord of the Isles.

URUISG CHOIRE-NAN-NUALLAN.
FIRST PRIZE SGEULACHD AT OBAN MOD.

By JOHN MACFADYEN

PART II.

ACH 's e thachair air latha àraidh---

'N uair a sheinn na h eòin bhuic he bhadanach
An ceòl binn feadanach,
Gu'n d'thàinig Fearchar og na faoghaid
Le 'chuid ghaotuar air eill.

'Nuair a bha esan a' dol seachad air bothan na h-àiridh aig Cailleach bun-na-beinne, 's an am-moch, bha 'Chailleach a mach 's thubhairt :—

"Tillibh a chlann, cha 'n 'eil an Coire glan romhaibh a' nochd."

"Cha do chill nach do thréig, a Mhuime chaomh na h-àiridh," arsa Fearchar. "Nach tig thu seachd ceumannan 'am chuideachd, thoir dhomh do bheannachadh, 's cuir air falbh mi 's caidlidh mi 'nochd fo sgàil an leamhain 'an Gleann nam mang 's nam maoiseach le m' thriuir ghillean ruadha, 's mo dhà chì lonach—

"'S mo ghallag bheag robach nan gonagan giar,*
'Bheir fuil air an fhiadh air gach beinn."

Fhreagair a' Chailleach -

"An do thog Fearchar a shùil
Ris an ainnir a's ciuine rosg?'

"Cha d' iarr mi ainnir no urram," arsa Fearchar, "tha mi dol do'n bheinn shidhionn 'us sheilg :—

"A ruagadh a' bhuic, a' bhuic, 's an fhéidh
Am maireach mu 'n éirich a' ghrian."

An sin thuirt Muime na h-àiridh—"Theid mi seachd ceum leat is bheir mi seachd beannachd dhuit, 'Fhearchair mhic Airt mhic Aillinn†—

Nighean righ Mhanainn a' chuan—
Thàinig thar snuadh Innis-thorc,—
Mac an athar nach d' thug càin
Eadhon 'o nàmh le an-iochd.

So agad mo lorg dhìreach nan tri meangan, de'n abhall nach crion, a chuir Manach, 's a bhuain Manach air taobh deas balla-cró na caibealt. 'Sa bheannaich Manach tri uairean—

'S troimh 'n lùb faobhar na h-umha
Ma bhuailear a bhuille le daoidh.

* Gonagan giar = sharp teeth. Gonagan or coin-chriche = canine teeth.
† Aillean = cleampane, a British perennial plant which grows in moist meadows. Also applied as a name to a beautiful woman. Aillean was Fearchar's mother, "nighean righ Mhanainn."

Cuir dhiot gartan na coise chì 's cuir coingheall*
dheth mu amhach na galla, thoir drüican fala à
cluais dheis an dà choin, 's na gairm a h-aon
diu air an ainm o'n a theid a' ghrian fodha gus
am blais an t-eun an t-uisge an la 'r-na-mhàireach, 's mo bheannachd a'd' chuideachd 's bi
triall."

Dh' fhalbh Fearchar le 'ghillean 's le choin, 's
bha soragt na h-oidhche 'seinn ciùil dha. An
uair a ràinig e Sloc-nam-meall thachair ainnir
air 's bu mhaiseach a snuadh :—

Bha h-àrd bhroilleach mìn
Mar shneachd fiorghlan air fonn,
Bha gucag a cioch
Mar bhlàth fearr-dhris 's a' choilleig
Am blàthas doire nan tom.

Bha slatag sheilich 'na laimh, agus thoisich na
coin air comhartaich rithe. "Caisg do choin a
a laoich," ars' ise. "Cha ghreas 's cha ghrab
mi iad," arsa Fearchar. Bha na coin 's a h-uile
rib a bh' orra 'na sheasamh cho direach ri
fridhein an tuire ; ach chas an ainnir greann is
dh' atharaich i 'cruth gu bhi 'na h-ùruisg cho
oillteil, agus na b' oillteala na 'bha i aona chuid
do Thalamsan no do Bhreac-ghlun. "Mur a
caisg thu do choin," ars' an Ùruisg. "caisge mis'
iad,"—'s i toirt ionnsuidh air a h-aon dhiu leis
an t-slacan. Tharuinn Fearchar a shleagh, is
thòisich an sheadh. Mur an robh nuallanaich
'an Coire-nan meallan riamh roimhe bha gu leòir
dheth 'n oidhch' ud ann eadar na coin 's an
Ùruisg :—

"A h-uile leum a bheireadh Bruid,‡
Thilleadh e le fhuil mu 'bhial,
A h-uile beum a bheireadh Speuch,
Thug an Ùruisg sgread dà sgriach."

Leum an uathair shligineach, theinndeach à
broilleach na h-Ùruisg 's thug i ionnsuidh air
Fearchar, ach bhuail esan i leis an lorg aig
Muime-na-h-àiridh 's chaidh i 'n a cuaich, dh' at
i, 's an sin sgàin i:-

Le fuaim faoghar 'chuir crith
Air gach ladhar 's a' ghleann.

Chaidh i 'n sin 'na lasair theine a' cur na h-
Ùruisg ri theine còmhla rithe agus ann am
prioba sùl cha robh aig Fearchar ach torran
luadha.

Chaidh e fo sgàil barraich 's thainig an cadal
air, oir bha e sgìth, agus dhùisgeadh 'am brist-

eadh na fàire e le "Brionn"* ag imlich aodainn,
's an sin sheinn—

Na h-eòin bhuidhe bhadanach
An ceòl binn feadanach.

'N uair a sheall Fearchar mu 'n cuairt air
chunnaic e gu 'n robh mòran de mhill chlach
iongantach ann an Sloc-nam-meall. Bhuail e 'n
lorg abhail air aon de na mill agus thionndaidh
an meall 'na dhuine, 's theich Fearchar. "Na
teich le abhall nam buadh 'Fhearchair," ars' an
duine. "tha feum ort fhathasd 'an Sloc-nam-
meall." Thill Fearchar agus bhuail e 'n lorg
air meall an dèigh mill, a' h-uile meall 'an Sloc-
nam-meall, 's a h-uile meall a' fàs 'na ghaisgeach
gusan robh naoidh naoidhnear laoch 'nan seasamh
ri 'thaobh, agus na 'm measg bha Talamsan mac
Righ Othaileam agus Breac-ghlùn mac Righ
Thorcuill agus thug Fearchar iad air fad gu Tùr
Athaileam

Is fhuair e nighean an Righ is dà ìmlachd,
'S a chòmhnuidh an Tùr Innis-stoth.

'S mar do shiùbhail iad bho sin tha iad beò
fhathasd.

(CONCLUDED).

CAMANACHD NOTES.—What promises to be a
great attraction to London Scotsmen is the match
which is to take place on 26th Dec. (Boxing Day),
in London, between the LONDON N.C. CAMANACHD
CLUB and the GLASGOW COWAL SHINTY CLUB.
The game will be well worth seeing, and we hope
that there will be a large attendance of our coun-
trymen. Both teams have a splendid record. On
Saturday, 30th, the COWAL have arranged to play
the BALLACHULISH SHINTY CLUB, at Moray Park,
Strathbungo. We hope to see a large gathering of
Glasgow Highlanders present. EDINBURGH UNI-
VERSITY v. ABERDEEN UNIVERSITY.—These teams
met in Inverleith Park, Edinburgh, on the 25th
November, and after a well contested game the
Aberdeen men won by 4 hails to 3.

GLASGOW COWAL SHINTY CLUB.—We have to
thank John Mackay, Esq., C.E., J.P., Hereford
(patron of the club) for a handsome donation of £3 3s.
towards the club's funds. The club-house is now
in course of erection.

THE JOHN MACKAY (HEREFORD) PRIZE OF £10.—
Our readers are reminded that this competition
closes on the 30th December, and all papers should
be sent in at once to the Secretaries of the Gaelic
Society of London. (See Advt.).

Two of our contributors—Miss Annie Mackay,
Eastbourne, and Mr. Duncan Maclean, Manchester
have each won a prize of one guinea for poems in
the Christmas number of the People's Journal.

PORTRAITS of Sir James Colquhoun, Bart., can
be had printed on stiff paper of a larger size, suitable for framing, at 6d each, post free, from the
Editor, 17 Dundas Street, Kingston, Glasgow.

* Coingheall   a turn or circle. In some places a
dog's collar is called coingheall.
† Sorag na h-oidhche   water sprite of the night.
Sora is a water sprite supposed to sing in the swirl
and wimple and hiss and splash of falling waters,
throughout the night.
‡ Bruid, the name of one of the dogs.
§ Speuch, the name of the bitch. "Spreud da sgriach"   bha da sgriach anns an aona sgread.

* "Brionn," one of his dogs.

THE RAID OF LOCH CARRON.

By Alexander Macdonald, Govan.

(Continued from page 49).

GLENGARRY CASTLE.

Lo! up she starts with frantic mein,
  Nor heeds her baby's cry,
Her stare is fearful, dark and wild
  The gleam that's in her eye.
"Come back, come back! Sir Kenneth, come!
  Your people will be slain!
Come back! come back! come back to-night,
  Or else 'tis all in vain!

Do not I see fierce Macdonell,
  And full two hundred men!
They're marching forth, on murder bent,
  Through Garry's birch-clad glen!
Its deep, dark fords they now have crossed,
  They march with quickened speed,
Ah woe is me! where's Seaforth now,
  In this dread hour of need?

Hold! stand thou back, grim-visaged ghost!
  Point not thy bony hand—
I know thee well, thou shadowy sprite;
  Begone, why dost thou stand?
"I've seen the 'Fiery Cross' go forth,
  While wandering in the night,
Across bleak Corryvarligan,
  And o'er Mam Cluany's height.

Glengarry's eldest-born will come,
  With full two hundred men,
And not a sheiling will he spare
  On bare hillside or glen,
And not a mother will he spare,
  Nor infant on her knee,—
A tiger's heart and bloodhound's scent
  Has he who's on the sea."

"Ha! ghost of dark Mam Cluany,
  Can'st thou not tell me more?
Say whither does fierce Angus sail?"—
  "'Tis to Loch Carron's shore."
"But what—ho spirit, where art thou?—
  'Tis but yon scutcheoned stone!
Good Heavens! what is this I've seen?
  Have I been, then, alone?

Yes! yes! alone, alone I've seen,
  But like some dream of night,
A death-cloud grey stole o'er my eyes—
  I've seen with second sight!"

'Twas on a lovely Sabbath morn,
  No sound disturbed the air
Save the dull moaning of the waves,
  And eke the sound of prayer,
A fleet of twenty boats was seen
  To steer for Carron's shore,
And eighty men were seen to ply
  The tough, unweildy oar.

"Now, who be they who sail so bold,
  And steer for Seaforth's land?
'Tis brave Sir Kenneth," is the cry
  Which rises from the strand,
"He comes from Mull with eighty men,
  And so he's safe and well,
We'll march by morning light to meet
  The rieving Macdonell."

Eftsoons the boats approach the shore,
  But hark! what means that cry?
Lo! like a herd of timid deer,
  The people quickly fly,
And piercing screams now rend the air,
  As on the solid ground
The keels of twenty boats are heard
  To strike with grating sound

As if by magic, up there springs
  A host of armed men,
Who crouching in their boats had lain,
  Like tigers in their den;
In dark red tartan they are dressed,
  Claymores are in each hand,
And, quick as lightning, from the boats
  They spring upon the land.

"Now, follow me," their leader cries,
  "We have them in our toils,
But first bind, hack, or slay the dogs!
  Before you think of spoils."
"Aye! aye!" they shout, and wildly rush,
  With claymores poised on high,
And midst their dreadful yelling shout—
  "Die, false Mackenzie, die!"

Oh! what a horrid sight was there!
  What cries now rend the air!
Old men and young grasped by the throat,
  And women by the hair.
Claymores are dripping with warm blood,
  Plaids which were red before
Are redder now than ere they were,
  With stains of human gore!

"Sad news, sad news, my lady fair!
  Sad news I bring to thee;
There's murder on Loch Carron's shore,
  And murder on the sea.
I only have escaped the sword,
  And hither come, forlorn,
For vengeance on the murderer,
  Glengarry's eldest born."

"My worthy kinsman, what can I,
  A frail, weak woman do?
Oh, Seaforth! Seaforth! where art thou?
  This day thou'lt surely rue;

But yet I'll try what can be done,
By poor weak woman's aid,
To wipe this stain from off our house,
And stop this murderous raid.

Ho! Seneschal, go round our men—
Dost hear?—call every man,
And bring them here with every speed—
We'll then devise a plan
To carry out a sweet revenge
For this most bloody deed;
Let them come armed and fit for war,
With all convenient speed."

Calm shone the moon, and many a star
Upon the Kyles of Skye,
As twenty boats, all laden deep,
Were slowly passing by;
But suddenly a darkening cloud
Obscured the moon's pale light,
And snowflakes fell, as rose the swell,
And darker grew the night.

Still on they sailed, and first there came
A boat before the rest.
It seemed the leader's galley,
And its course was for the west.
It proudly cut the crested wave,
And sailed full half a mile,
Ere the dull splashing of its sweeps
Were heard on Bailigh's Isle.

'Twas just abreast that lonely rock,
A voice called out—"Stand clear!"
A deafening volley belches forth,
And, hark! there bursts a cheer.
"Perdition seize me!" Angus cried,
"My galley's on the ground.
Ho! rowers, back her with your sweeps,
And pull her through the sound."

"She fills! she fills!" some wildly cry;
"They come! they come!" some call,
While, bursting from their ambuscade,
Mackenzies on them fall.
Now fierce they fight with dirk and sword,
Anon they fight pell mell,
Revengeful each Mackenzie looks,
And desperate, Macdonell.

"Keep them on board," their leader cried;
Let no one get to shore."
"Press on, my men, down with the dogs,"
Fierce Angus oft did roar.
Both met, and mutual was their hate—
They closed, and down they fell.
"Take that," Mackenzie fiercely said,
"Thou murderous Macdonell."

Out gushed the blood from Angus' heart,
He gave one piercing cry,
His men looked round, their chief was stark,
And death was in his eye.
But back to back they bravely stand,
And fight upon the deck,
For none there is among that band
Can leave the fatal wreck.

Keen swords guard every part around,
Dirks gleam in every hand,
Ah! little chance, fierce Macdonells,
Have you to reach the land.

The deck is slippery—soaked with blood—
And covered with dead men,
"No quarter give, no quarter take,"
Were both their watchwords then.

"Push out the boat, push out the boat,"
Is heard on every side.
'Tis done, she slowly leaves the rock,
And passes with the tide.
But hark! what horrid shriek was that
The midnight echoes gave?
Ah! 'tis a death-wail from the boat
They've sunk beneath the wave.

[The picture at the beginning of the above ballad represents Ellandonan Castle.—ED.]

NEWS OF THE MONTH.

GOVAN HIGHLAND ASSOCIATION.—The Annual Concert in connection with this vigorous society was held in the Broomloan Halls, on 7th December. Prof. Campbell Black occupied the Chair, and there was a large attendance. An attractive programme of Gaelic and English Songs, Highland Dancing, and Pipe Music, was gone through, and the committee are to be congratulated on the success which attended their efforts.

THE CLAN MACLEAN.—On 7th December, Mr. Henry Whyte ("Fionn") delivered a lecture to this clan society on "Lachlan Maclean, Coll," author of "Adhamh agus Eubh," "History of the Celtic Language, &c., &c. Mr. Magnus Maclean, M.A., presided, and there was a large attendance. The lecture, which lasted an hour, was listened to with marked attention, and a proposal to erect a Celtic cross over his remains was favourably received. We hope next month to give a synopsis of the lecture, with a sketch of the house in which this distinguished Collman was born.

THE AIRDRIE HIGHLAND ASSOCIATION held their first Gathering on 10th December. Mr G. B. Shearer presided, and the large hall was crowded to excess. The programme submitted was quite an exceptional one, and the audience enthusiastically applauded the various artistes. Miss J. W. Mac-Lachlan, who was in good voice, received quite an ovation for her rendering of the Gaelic songs. We were glad to see so many wearing the Highland dress. This association has already done excellent work, and we trust that the splendid gathering which has just been held will help to increase the membership roll, and encourage the members in the patriotic work they have undertaken.

The annual social gathering of the Clan Campbell was held in the Waterloo Rooms on 11th Dec. — Ex-Bailie Malcolm Campbell in the chair. There was a large attendance of members and friends, who thoroughly enjoyed the excellent programme submitted. An assembly followed.

CLAN MACMILLAN SOCIETY.—The first Annual Social Gathering of this clan was held on 28th Nov., in the St. Andrew's Halls. Rev. Hugh MacMillan, D.D., LL.D., occupied the chair, and the hall was crowded. The Chairman's Address was worthy of his great literary reputation, and speeches were also delivered by Messrs. Wm. M. C. MacMillan, J.P., of Lamloch, Daniel MacMillan, president, Rev. Donald MacMillan, M.A., and Mr John Mackay, Kingston, Secretary, Clan Mackay, who responded for the kindred societies. The after part of the evening was devoted to music and dancing, and altogether the MacMillan Gathering was one of the most successful and enjoyable of the season. Clansmen wishing to join the society should communicate with the Secretary, Mr Archibald MacMillan, 9 University Street, Glasgow.

THE STRENGTH OF THE CLANS IN THE ISLAND OF LEWIS IN 1861.

(To the Editor of the Celtic Monthly.)

SIR,—In response to your request for further information with respect to the strength of the clans in the several districts of the Highlands, I send you the following. Some thirty-two years ago two gentlemen in Stornoway had a discussion as to whether the Macleods or the Mackenzies were the more numerous clan in the Lewis, and to determine the question a census of the population was taken at the time, with the following result :—In a population of 21,059, there were 232 surnames. The following are the particulars of the "count":—Macleod, 3838 ; Macdonald, 2510 ; Mackenzie, 1482 ; Morrison, 1402 ; Maciver, 1198 ; Maclean, 956 ; Mackay, 857 ; Smith, 794 ; Macaulay, 727 ; Murray, 615 ; Campbell, 639 ; Graham, 392 ; Matheson, 376 ; Maclennan, 348 ; Nicolson, 300 ; Macrae, 280 ; Martin, 235 ; Montgomery, 227 ; Macritchie, 222 ; Macphail, 216 ; Macaskill, 212 ; Macarthur, 211 ; Macmillan, 206 ; Stewart, 171 ; Munro, 143 ; Mackinnon, 135 ; Finlayson, 124 ; Gillies, 113 ; Macinnes, 112 ; Ross, 104 ; Macsween, 103 ; Macfarlane, 102 ; Ferguson, 94 ; Gunn, 88 ; Kennedy, 77 ; Thomson, 73 ; Buchanan, 72 ; Macneil, 60 ; Beaton, 44 ; Young, 43 ; Fraser, 42 ; Macgregor, 37 ; Macpherson 41 ; Reid, 36 ; Chisholm, 33 ; Bethune, 32 ; Chrighton, 32 ; Macleay, 30 ; Watt, 30 ; Clark, 28 ; Grant, 26 ; Mitchell, 26 ; Robertson, 23 ; Chambers, 21 ; Cameron, 18 ; Carmichael, 18 ; Patterson, 18 ; Gordon, 16 ; Hunter, 15 ; Miller, 14 ; Macqueen, 14 ; Macdougall, 13 ; Macdiarmid, 13 ; Macfarquhar, 12 ; Macgillivray, 11 ; Mackintosh, 12 ; Saunders, 12 ; Lees, 11 ; Wilson, 11 ; Bain, 10 ; Humphrey, 10 ; Macnaughton, 9 ; Brown, 9 ; Calder, 9 ; Fleet, 9 ; Polson, 9 ; Sutherland, 9 ; Kerr, 8 ; Kackeegan, 8 ; Macbride, 8 ; Rigg, 8 ; Scott, 8 ; Anderson, 7 ; Adam, 7 ; Chapman, 7 ; Christie, 7 ; Russell, 7 ; Macrimmon, 7. It will doubtless be of some interest to your readers to know also the

SEVEN MOST PREVALENT SURNAMES

all over Scotland. According to a calculation made after the census of 1881, they were—Smith, the name of one person in every 69 ; Macdonald, one in every 78 ; Brown, one in every 79 ; Robertson, one in every 91 ; Campbell, one in every 92 ; Thomson, one in every 95 ; and Stewart, one in every 98. One person in every twelve in Scotland will answer to one or other of these names. The first of these, Smith, is, of course, a purely cosmopolitan name. In England and Wales they are calculated to be about one in every 73 of the population. Macdonald, therefore, heads the Highland clans by a good lead. Their calculated number in Scotland in 1881 was 36,000. The Campbells were at the same time 19,000. A very interesting account of the strength of the clans in the town of Inverness, where the Frasers have a very good lead, appeared in the Inverness Courier about the beginning of last September. Could you not prefix the account for us, Mr. Editor, by reproducing it in the Celtic Monthly?

GAELIC SPELLING.

I would here ask your permission to refer to the letter which appeared in your last issue over the signature "Mac Roughrigh." He recites a few Celtic grievances (would he write here "Gaelach grievances"—or, what else ?), some of which are to the point, and others of which are very far fetched, and he winds up by committing an error as grave as any of those he has complained of, viz :—writing "Fraser" and "Frizallach," instead of "Fraser" and "Frisealach." In English, as the name is said to be of Norwegian origin, the "z" might pass muster, but there is no such letter in the Gaelic alphabet.—I am, &c.   T. D. MACDONALD.

London.

REVIEWS.

NEW WORKS ON THE HIGHLANDS.—As an indication of the interest which is now being taken in histories of Highland Parishes, we have pleasure in announcing the early publication of the following valuable works by gentlemen whose names will be a guarantee of their completeness and correctness.

THE RED AND WHITE BOOK OF MENZIES, by D. P. Menzies, F.S.A., Scot., is a history of the Clan Menzies and its Chiefs. It is to contain a large number of portraits and other illustrations. Price, £2 2s. ; Edition de Luxe, £5 5s. Publishers, Messrs. John Menzies & Co., Edinburgh.

THE IRISH ECHO is a patriotic Gaelic Journal published in Boston, Mass., U.S.A. It contains a large variety of interesting reading in poetry and prose, in both languages. It is well printed and ably edited, and is very popular among the Irish Gaels across the Atlantic. We reciprocate the editor's kind wishes towards ourselves.

GLIMPSES OF CHURCH AND SOCIAL LIFE IN THE HIGHLANDS IN OLDEN TIMES, by Alexander Macpherson, F.S.A., Scot., Solicitor, Kingussie. This is an authoritative work on the famous district of Badenoch, and deals largely with the fortunes of the Macphersons and their chiefs. It also contains a selection from the MSS. of the late Captain Macpherson, and an interesting appendix. It is illustrated with sixteen fine portraits and pictures of historic places. Messrs. Blackwood & Sons, Edinburgh, are the publishers, and to subscribers the price is 22s., post free. We hope it will have a large sale.

"Dain Iain Ghobha" (Morrison's Poems), collected and edited, with a memoir, by George Henderson, M.A. Vol. I. (Glasgow : Archibald Sinclair ; Edinburgh, Norman Macleod. The Mound). Admirers of the Songsmith of Harris will be glad to have such a handsome volume of his poetry. Although some of his best known poems were published both in Canada and in this country, this is really the first attempt to give us a complete edition of his works. The editor has written a learned life-history of the Songsmith, extending to seventy-five pages, which will be read with interest by all interested in the poetry of Iain Gobha. Several of the poems given in this volume are set to music. The work is beautifully got up, reflecting much credit on the publisher—and all who admire Iain Gobha's life and poetry cannot but feel grateful to Mr. Henderson for his patriotic labours. We hope editor and publisher will receive the support they deserve from Gaelic-speaking Highlanders.

HIGHLAND NOTES AND QUERIES.

Will the Editor of the Celtic Monthly kindly enlighten me on the following points : Have the Morrisons a tartan and badge ? Are they affiliated to any clan ? Are they Highlanders by accident of birth only?—Balgan-peolach.

The Gilchrists or MacGilchrists. — Would you, or any of the readers of the Celtic Monthly, kindly inform me what is known of the Gilchrists or MacGilchrists ? To what clan or branch they belong, and what tartan, crest, badge, or motto they are entitled to wear?— A. G.

Chips from Cape Wrath.—(1) Days of the Week in Gaelic.—Diluain, di + luain ; di, a day; luna, moon. Dimairt, di + mart-is; Mars, god of war. Diciadaoin, di + ceud + aoin day of the First Fast. Diardaoin di + cadar , aoin day between the Fasts. Dihaoine, di + aoin, the Fast day. Disathuirne, di + Saturn, Saturn. Didomhnuich, di + dominicus = the day of the Lord. The prefix di for day is now obsolete in Gaelic; it is to be seen in an dingh, to-day. From the above it is clear we have got the first two days from heathen times ; the rest, through the Church. (2) Census of the Gaelic Race.—Here is a nut to crack for the American correspondent who longed for the extinction of the Celtic tongues. It is taken from a trustworthy source the Revue Celtique. The first column gives the number who can speak two languages, one of which is Celtic ; the second column, those who speak a Celtic dialect only :—

France (Brittany)....	1,240,000	700,000
Wales ..	296,530	304,110
Man ..	12,514	190
Ireland	867,574	103,560
Scotland .	309,254	48,878
	3,425,800	1,156,793

(Rev.) Adam Gunn, Durness.

The magazine this month consists of 24 pages, the "Muster-Roll of the Reay Fencibles" being given as a supplement.

MUSTER-ROLL OF THE REAY FENCIBLES, 1795.

Contributed by D. Murray Rose.

"Muster-Roll of His Majesty's Reay Fencible Highland Regiment of Foot for 236 days, from 25th October, 1794, to 17th June, 1795, both days inclusive :—

Attested 3rd November, 1794.—Sergeants—John Graham, Donald Mackay, Hugh Mackay, Angus Macdonald, Finlay M'Leod. 9th Nov.—John Cochran. 17th Nov.—Andrew M'Laren. 18th Nov.—Alex. M'Lean. 19th Nov.—Rupert Mackay. 20th Nov.—Hugh Mackay, John Mackay. 21st Nov.—Wm. Sutherland. 22nd Nov.—Hugh Grant, John Mackay, Hugh Mackay, John Mackay. 25th Nov.—Hugh Mackay. 26th Nov.—Charles Mackay. 28th Nov.—Donald Mackay. 1st Dec.—William Mackay. 2nd Dec.—Thomas Woode, Duncan Mackay. 3rd Dec.—Donald Munro. 11th Dec.—John M'Iver. 26th Dec.—Alexander Mackay. 2nd Jan., 1795.—Alexander Ross. 7th Feb. James Mitchell. 4th March. — Robert Willock. 6th March.—Archibald M'Arthur. 7th March.—Chas. M'Arthur, John Wilson. 10th March.—John M'Leod.

Attested 3rd Nov., 1794. - Corporals — Colin Sinclair, Donald Macdonald, Alexander Mackay. 4th Nov.—John Hepburn. 9th Nov.—Robert Ray. 15th Nov.—Donald Calder. 18th Nov. - Donald Mackay. 20th Nov.—Robert Mackay, James Mackay, Donald Munro. 21st Nov.—John Morrison. 22nd Nov.—John Munro, William Mackay, George Mackay, George M'Leod, Hugh M'Intosh. 28th Nov.—William Budge. 2nd Dec.—John Gunn. 4th Dec.—Hugh Morrison, Hugh M'Kenzie. 5th Dec.—William Morrison. 8th Dec.—Donald M'Arkle. 25th Dec.—Alex. Ross. 28th Dec.—James Gordon. 30th Jan., 1895.—Henry Hendon. 3rd Feb.—John Evans, Hugh Morrison. 16th Feb. Murdo Mackenzie. 24th April.- Alexander Murray. 25th April.—John M'Kenzie.

Attested 6th Nov., 1794.—Drummers—Fred. Hughes. 18th Nov.—John Mackay, Wm. M'Leod, Donald Morrison. 25th Nov.—Isaac Spyron. 28th Nov. Charles Mackay. 1st Dec.—Patrick Gallie. 2nd Dec. Archibald Wilson. 4th Dec.—Donald M'Leod, Donald Graham. 9th Dec.—Donald M'Intosh. 20th Dec.—Joseph Morrison. 21st Dec—Simon Hope. 25th Dec.—George Ross. 26th Dec.—John M'Donald. 3rd Feb., 1795.—Hugh Masson. 5th Feb. William Gordon, Adam Campbell. 6th Feb. William Mackenzie. 16th Feb.—John Macpherson. 23rd Feb.—Thomas Simpson. 1st March.—William Gunn.

Attested 30th Oct., 1794. Private Men—John Macdonald, Hugh Campbell. 3rd Nov.—Robert Anderson. 3rd Nov.—John Campbell, Angus Campbell, James Campbell, Alexander Gunn, John Gordon, Donald Gunn, Finlay Gunn, Angus Macdonald, John M'Donald, Hugh Mackenzie, John Macdonald, Donald Macleod, Hector Mackay, Donald Macleod, Neil Mackay, Neil Macpherson, George Mackay, Robert Mackay, Hugh M'Leod, Donald Mackay, Robert M'Leod, Angus Mackay, Alexander M'Donald, Alexander M'Donald, Alex. M'Kenzie, Roderick M'Donald, Angus M'Leod,

Colin Macleod, William M'Leod, Donald Mackay, Donald M'Leod, John M'Leod, John Malton, Angus M'Pherson, John M'Pherson, William Mackay. Hugh Mackay, Hugh Nicol, John Ross, William Sinclair, George Shanks, John White, James Finnie, William Horsburgh, John M'Callum, Hector Munro, William Ross, John Neilson, Thomas Ross, William Younglmsband, William Morrison, Alexander Ross. 10th Nov.—James Dunn, Thomas Grant, John Mackenzie. 11th Nov.—William Nairn. 12th Nov.—George Sutherland. 13th Nov.—Alexander Macleod. 14th Nov.—James Macdonald. 15th Nov.—Hugh Campbell, Robert Gunn, John Gordon, William Gunn, William Gunn, James Gunn, John Mackay, Hugh Mackay, Iye Mackay, John Mackay, Hugh Mackay, Hugh Mackay, Robert Mackay. George Mackay, John M'Leod, Robert M'Intosh, John Ross, John Sutherland, John Stewart. 16th Nov.—Hugh Mackay, George M'Kenzie. 17th Nov.—Angus Campbell, Angus Campbell, Donald Campbell, Angus Campbell, John Campbell, George Campbell, Kenneth Forbes, Alexander Mackay, John M'Culloch, George Mackay, Donald Mackay. John Mackay, Murdo Macpherson, William Macleod, Hugh Macleod, John Ross, Kenneth Sutherland, George Sutherland. 18th Nov.—Alexander Clarke, Hugh Gunn, James Graham, James Morrison, George M'Leod, George Mackenzie, Donald Mackay, George Morrison, Kenneth Mackay, Alexander Mackay, Alexander Macleod, Hugh Morrison, Robert Mackay, Angus Mackay, Roderick Mackay, John Matheson, Robert Mackay, John Mackay, William Morrison, Alexander Macleod, Angus Mcleod, William M'Kenzie, John Mackay, Hugh Macleod, John Macleod, John Macleod, John M'Leod, Hugh M'Leod, Kenneth Macleod, George M'Leod, Donald Mackay, John Mackenzie, Donald Mackenzie, William Macleod, Hugh Ross, Donald Sutherland. 19th Nov.—Hugh Sutherland, William Abrach, Alexander Mackay, Paul Macaul, Donald Macleod, John Mackay, Hugh Morrison. 20th Nov.—Donald Mackintosh, John Calder, Hugh Calder, John Calder, Alexander Calder, Donald Mackay, Donald Mackay, Murdo Mackay, Robert Mackay, William Mackay, Angus Mackay, Neil Mackay, Donald Munro, James Munro, Donald Mackay, James Mackay, Angus Mackay, Hugh Mackay, William Mackay, John Mackay. James Mackay, John Mackay, Angus Mackay, Angus Mackay, George Mackay, Donald Mackay, Donald Macleod, Angus Mackintosh, John Mackay, John Mackenzie, John Mackay, Robert Macpherson, William Munro, Donald Mackay, Angus Munro, Hector Mackay, William Mackay, William Mackay. James Munro, John Mackay, Kenneth Mackay, Hugh Mackay, Hector Mackay, Angus Mackay, Angus Rose, George Ross, John Sutherland, Peter Thomson, Alexander Munro, John Deans. 21st Nov.—Richard Green, Angus Gunn, Iye Gordon, Donald Mackay, Alexander Mackay, William Mackay, Alexander Macleod, William Mackay, Hugh Macdonald, William Mackay, Robert Mackay, George Gordon, Colin Munro, George Mackay, John Munro, Angus Mackay, Angus Macleod, Angus Mackay, Alexander Mackay, Angus Macdonald, Hugh Mackay, James Ross, Angus Sutherland, John Scobie, Robert Stewart, Hector Sutherland, Robert Sutherland, Hugh Sutherland. 22nd Nov.—William Mackay, Donald Campbell, Angus Campbell, Donald Campbell, George Forbes, Donald Mackay, William Mackintosh, Charles Mackay, Angus Mackay, John Mackenzie, Neil Mackay, Alexander Mackay. Hector Morrison, Alexander Mackay, Donald Munro, Hugh Morrison, William Mackay, Hugh Mackay, George Macleod, Murdo Mackay, William Mackay, George Macleod, Alex. Mackay, John Mackay, Angus Mackay, Donald Mackay, William Mackay, Alexander Macdonald, Angus Mackay, Alexander Macdonald, Hugh Mackenzie, Robert Mackenzie, Robert Mackay, Angus Macleod, Hugh Mackay, Hugh Mackenzie, Donald Mackay, John Mackay, William Mackay, William Mackay, Hugh Mackay, Adam Mackay, Angus Mackay, Andrew Munro, Alexander Mackay, John Ross, John Beattie. 23rd Nov.—Donald Munro, Donald Abrach. 24th Nov.—John Mackay. 25th Nov.—Allan Buchanan, William Gunn, Donald Gunn, George Mackay, George Mackay, Murdo Macdonald, William Mackay, Hugh Morrison, Alex. M'Raskle, Donald Mackay, George Matheson, Hugh Mackay, Donald M'Culloch, Alexander Mackay, James Mackay, Angus Morrison, William Mackay, Donald Macdonald, Angus Morrison, Neil Mackay, Alexander Mackenzie, James Mackay, Hugh Macleod, John Morrison, John Mackay, Robert Macleod, Hugh Mackenzie, Murdo Macleod, William Morrison, George Morrison, John Morrison, Robert Mackay, Donald Macleod, Hugh Mackay, William Mackay, Hugh Mackay, John Ross. 26th Nov.—Robert Sutherland, Hector Gunn, Angus Mackay. 27th Nov.—Alexander Cheshom, John M'Leod, William Mackay, John Ross. 28th Nov.—John Mackay, Neil Macpherson, Donald Mackay, William Mackay, Murdo Mackay, George Macdonald, Hugh Mackay. 29th Nov.—Murdo Mackay, Peter Campbell, William Mackay, Donald Macdonald. 1st Dec.—Angus Campbell, Robert Calder, Hugh Campbell, Alexander Lyal, Donald Morrison, Donald Mackenzie, William Morrison, John Mackay, George Mackay, George Munro, Peter Morrison, Donald Morrison, Kenneth Sutherland, John Wear. 2nd Dec. Thomas Hardie, Angus Munro, Alex. Munro, Hugh Mackay, Henry Anderson. 3rd Dec. John Mackintosh, William Sutherland. 4th Dec. Robert Campbell, James Dunn, Neil Mackintosh, Donald Mackay, James Mackay, Donald M'Leod, William Mackay, James Mackay, Donald Mackintosh, Robert Mackay, John Morrison, Robert Mackenzie, George Sutherland, George Sutherland, Donald White. 5th Dec.—George Gibb, John Budge, Samuel Cochran, Alexander Maclaren, John Morrison, Donald Mackenzie, Robert Mackay, William Murray, John Mackay, Roderick Morrison, Hugh Ross, William Sutherland, Hugh Sutherland, James Pringle. 6th Dec. Neil Buchanan, Archibald Campbell, George Mackay, John Murray, Donald Mackay, Donald Mackay, Thomas Leay, John Read, Alexander Sutherland, William Young. 7th Dec.—John Bruce, William Muckle. 9th Dec. James Beard, Richard Campbell, Murdo M'Leod, Hugh Mackintosh, Charles Mackay, John Macleod, William Macleod, John M'Caul. 10th Dec. Donald Gordon, Charles Wilson. 11th Dec.—Roderick Mackay, James Mackay, Alexander Mackay, Donald Mackay. 13th Dec.—John Beard, Alexander Henderson, Robert Johnstone (2), William Sutherland. 15th Dec.—John Logan, John Menzie, Neil

Macleod, Hugh Mackay, Donald Mackay, Hugh
Mackay. 16th Dec.—George Campbell, Walter
Douglas, Charles Murray, George M'Pherson,
Lewis Mackay, James M'Leod. 17th Dec.—Robert
Macpherson, Alexander Webster, William Mac-
donald, George Ireland, Turnbull Martin. 20th
Dec.—Malcom Mackay, Walter Campbell. 21st
Dec.—John M'Leod, George Hope, Hugh Munro.
22nd Dec.—John Tait. 23rd Dec.—James
Trumble. 24th Dec.—Robert Allan, Kenneth
Mackenzie, James Ramsay. 25th Dec.—James
Anderson, Hugh Fraser, William Gunn, Murdo
Mackintosh, Henry Beatson. 26th Dec.—Simon
Fraser. 27th Dec.—William Gunn, William
Hodge, William Macleod. 29th Dec.—Donald
Urquhart, James Murray. 30th Dec.—Colin Camp-
bell, John Mackay, Hugh Maclachlan, Robert
Sutherland. 31st Dec.—John M'Leod, Donald
Ross. 1st Jan., 1795.—James Mitchell. 2nd
Jan.—John M'Donald, John Morrison, Alexander
Sutherland, John Weir. 3rd Jan.—James Beattie,
Alexander Gunn. 4th Jan.—John M'Donald. 5th
Jan.—William Gordon, John Halliday. 6th Jan.—
George Innes, William Mackay, William Beard.
8th Jan.—John M'Leay, George Mackay. 9th
Jan.—David Ross, George Smith. 10th Jan.—
Robert Aldie, Alexander Mackay. 12th Jan.—
Robert Boyle, Daniel Douglas, Murdo M'Kenzie,
John M'Leay. 14th Jan.—James Robison, Alex.
Beatson, William Arden, John Murray, John Mac-
donald. 15th Jan.—John Urquhart, Adam Wallace.
18th Jan.—Archibald Fletcher, Ronald Macdonald.
19th Jan.—James Banner. 21st Jan.—Robert
Mackenzie, Joseph Smith. 22nd Jan.—George
Simpson. 24th Jan.—Archibald Brooks, John
Wilson, James Holmes. 26th Jan.—James Cleland,
William Mackay, Donald Henderson. 27th Jan.—
James Neil, John Sutter. 28th Jan.—Hugh Logan,
William Scott. 29th Jan.—William Dorsier. 30th
Jan.—Thomas Jones, Eason M'Laurin, Archibald
Murdoch. 31st Jan.—John Morrison, James Sharp.
2nd Feb.—James Gordon, Thomas Morrison, John
M'Leod, David Rendle. 3rd Feb.—Joseph
Badenoch, Peter Liddle, Donald Murray, Moses
Roffie, John Shelgrove, William Harris, John
Gibson, James Harne. 4th Feb.—John M'Caira.
6th Feb.—John Adams, William Collins, John
M'Kenzie. 11th Feb.—Archibald M'Aulay. 12th
Feb.—Andrew Hardie, Norman Mackay. 16th
Feb.—Walter Davidson, Donald Davidson, Daniel
Thomson. 17th Feb.—Thomas Baine, William
M'Laurin. 18th Feb.—William Wilson. 19th
Feb.—James Edward, James Denham, Hector
M'Kenzie, James Telford. 20th Feb.—John
M'Donald. 21st Feb.—Kenneth Cameron. 23rd
Feb.—Francis Barclay, William M'Kenzie, Andrew
Munro, Alexander M'Leod, David White. 24th
Feb.—John Joyce, Thomas Shaw. 25th Feb.—
Alexander Knight. 26th Feb.—Abner Sutherland.
27th Feb. Malcom M'Farlane. 28th Feb.—
William Mackay, John Mackay, William Martin,
John Munro. 2nd March. George Henderson,
Angus M'Leod, Sutherland Munro, William
M'Kenzie, John Sutherland, Hugh Sutherland,
William Telford, Philip Tole. 3rd March.—William
Campbell, James Mitchel, John Moffat, John
M'Donald, Alexander Matheson, Roderick Mackay,
Finlay M'Leod, David Urquhart. 4th March.—
James Dewart, Andrew Gibson, Alexander Suther-
land. 5th March.—George Mackay, William
Russel. 6th March.—Robert Farms. 7th March.—
George Holms. 8th March.—John M'Kenzie. 9th
March.—William M'Leod. 10th March.—James
Greig, William King. 11th March.—Donald
Henderson, John Mackay, Robert Mackay, Peter
Skillinglaw. 13th March.—William Gunn. 14th
March.—Alexander Aird, George Graham, David
Munro. 16th March.—Malcom Gillies, George
Matheson, William Ross. 18th March.—George
Gordon, William Laing, Alexander Mackay, Alex.
Mills, Donald Gordon. 20th March.—William
Grant, Hugh Mackay, James Mirillies, Neil Munro,
William Ross, James Russel. 21st March.—William
Gordon, William Sutherland. 22nd March.—John
M'Lean. 23rd March.—Donald Ross, John Suther-
land, William Clark. 24th March—John Gordon,
William Murdoch, Alexander Mackay, Angus
Mackay. 25th March.—Roderick Henderson,
Robert Mackay, Francis Webster. 26th March.—
Edward Spalding. 27th March.—John Ferguson,
Adam Mackay. 28th March.—John Mitchel. 30th
March.—Hugh Calder. 1st April.—Alexander
M'Lean. 2nd April.—Donald Mackay, Murdo
Mackay, Donald Nicol. 3rd April.—John Cush,
Andrew Russel. 4th April.—George M'Arthur,
Hugh Ross. 6th April. Angus Mackay, William
Young. 8th April.—Alexander Mackenzie, James
Mackay, Alexander Sinclair. 9th April.—James
Hamilton, Robert Allen. 10th April.—Donald
M'Kenzie, John M'Lean. 11th April.—Donald
Mackay. 14th April.—Hugh Campbell, Donald
M'Kenzie, Alexander Mackay. 15th April.—
Robert Dannewell. 16th April.—John Mackay,
Alexander Douglas. 18th April.—James Panics.
21st April.—John Murray. 23rd April.—Angus
M'Leod, George Sutherland. 25th April.—John
M'Leod, John M'Kenzie. 26th April.—George
M'Donald. 29th April. William Mackay. 1st
May.—Gilbert Sutherland. 2nd May.—Roderick
M'Leod. 13th May.—George Grant, John Suther-
land. 17th May. Murdo Sutherland, John
M'Kenzie. 21st May. Donald Mackay. 28th
May.—Hugh M'Leod. 2nd June.—James Munro,
Alexander Mackay, John M'Leod, Angus Mackay,
Robert Mackay, John Mackay, Hugh Mackay,
George Mackay, Donald Sutherland, Donald Suther-
land, Hector Mackay, William Mackay, Robert
Mackay, Alexander Morrison. 3rd June.—Hugh
Mackay.

GAELIC MUSICAL ASSOCIATION.—This association,
which was recently started for the purpose of encouraging the study of Gaelic music among Highlanders in Glasgow, has already made excellent progress. A large number of ladies and gentlemen have
enrolled, and the practices have been well attended.
The association meets for practice in the Waterloo
Rooms every Wednesday evening at 8, and everyone
interested in Gaelic music is cordially invited to
attend. A social meeting has been arranged for
Wednesday, 26th December, and a public concert will
be given towards the end of the season. The following office-bearers have been appointed:—President,
John Mackay, editor, Celtic Monthly; secretary, John
Mackintosh, 125 St. Vincent Street; treasurer, Miss
M. A. Mackechnie, and a committee of ladies and
gentlemen.

SURGEON-MAJOR J. MACGREGOR, M.D.

THE CELTIC MONTHLY:

A MAGAZINE FOR HIGHLANDERS.

Edited by JOHN MACKAY. Kingston.

No. 5. Vol. II]　　　　FEBRUARY, 1894.　　　　Price Threepence.

SURGEON-MAJOR J. MACGREGOR, M.D.

AMONG the many Highland Scots who have helped to shed lustre on their native land by distinguished service abroad will be found the name of Surgeon-Major John MacGregor, M.D., a native of Sandwick Hill, near Stornoway, where he was born in 1848. He was educated first at the Stornoway Free Church School, and afterwards at the University of Glasgow, which he entered in 1866. Like many other devoutly-inclined Highland lads of his generation, his first thoughts were towards the ministry of the Gospel, his aspirations in that direction being strengthened by the early deaths of three of his brothers, two of whom had been lost at sea. But a feeling of comparative unfitness and self-distrust led him subsequently to study for medicine, in which he graduated M.B. and C.M. in 1873, after a highly creditable career at school and college. We find him afterwards occupying successively the post of Medical Officer of Harris, of the Peninsular and Oriental Company, and of Morven. In 1875 he resolved to compete for the Army or Navy; and by the toss of a shilling on the London pavement in favour of the Indian Medical Service the fate of his future career was decided. Early in 1876 he passed his examinations first or second in all subjects with one exception. After the usual course he went out to India with special recommendation to the Government of Bombay for professional abilities. In 1880 Surgeon MacGregor received the degree of M.D., the subject of his thesis being the *Medical Topography of the Barren Rocks of Aden*. He was now fairly started on his career in the East, where he might be found acting in various capacities, and always with credit. He was for a while Civil Surgeon of Aden; afterwards Surgeon to the European General Hospital, and Professor of Materia Medica, Bombay, &c. At this time we were engaged in the Afghanistan War, on the scene of which he appeared, but too late to see much active service there. A genuine taste of actual war, however, he did enjoy in the late war in Upper Burmah, where he was for a long time the Senior Medical Officer with the Frontier Brigade at Bhamo, on the remote inland borders of China. Surgeon-Major MacGregor was here continually on the move with troops, and on two different occasions had his horses killed under him in action. Many in Burmah who knew and valued his services hoped he would be the recipient of the Victoria Cross; but though these hopes were not realised he was mentioned in despatches, and when the war was over he received a medal and two clasps.

After thirteen years' continuous service in the East Dr. MacGregor took furlough in 1889; and instead of taking the direct route to Stornoway he started on a somewhat lengthy wandering voyage round the world, which occupied thirteen months of his time, and yielded abundant satisfaction to his natural love of travel. The accompanying portrait represents him in Highland dress at the time of starting from India on this tour, during which he had one or two narrow escapes. He arrived at the British shores in the *City of Paris*, which was nearly lost, in 1890.

Throughout his whole career Dr. MacGregor has preserved unalloyed his native Highland spirit—Gaelic, Scotland, Scots and the Muses being the fond objects of his inexhaustible devotion. The clan that was "nameless by day" has in him a son that regards the name with almost worshipful awe and veneration. Only rare spirits kindred to himself could sympathise with his feeling as he knelt at the grave of Rob Roy. The gorgeous shrines of Eastern lands had no charms for him such as he found at the last resting-place of "Rob Roy MacGregor." A Highlander of this type is really something of a born poet; and for Dr. MacGregor to pour forth poetic thought and feeling in prose or verse is as natural as it is for the lark of his native isle to soar and sing. So in 1890 we are not surprised to find a long narrative poem from his pen—*The Girdle of the Globe*—which was well received by competent critics, followed in 1892 by a handsome volume in prose, called *Toil and Travel*, descriptive of his own personal wanderings. But what will interest Highlanders most is the fact that he has remained all along an assiduous worshipper of the Gaelic muse, as will be evident from a song in the next issue, and that we may expect a volume of Gaelic poetry from his pen at no distant date.

Surgeon-Major MacGregor is a member of various institutions and societies, such as the British Medical Association, the Society of Authors, a life-member of the Clan Gregor Society, &c.; while as an enthusiastic brother of the "mystic tie" he has advanced to the position of Grand Master of Ceremonies of all Scottish Freemasonry in India. He is in full sympathy with the Crofter Movement at home; and although at present, or until recently, in medical charge of the 20th Regiment Bombay Infantry, and Senior Medical Officer of the Nazeraba I. Command, we may any day hear of his arrival home with the retiring rank of Surgeon-Colonel. Indeed, by the time the reader is glancing over this page the subject of it "will probably be found wandering on the top of a camel through the ancient kingdom of Nebuchadnezzar."   N. MacNeill.

Camden Town, London.

SHOTTY DOOLT'S COURTSHIP.

By Reid Tait.

(Continued from page 63).

AILSA CAMERON.

HE stayed and talked to Mrs. Cameron for a while and then took his departure, looking wistfully at Ailsa's bright head as she bent industriously over her work, hardly troubling to raise her eyes when she wished him good night.

But troublous times came now to Ailsa and her mother; Mrs. Cameron was taken ill. She and her daughter supported themselves with knitting and fancy work, and now Ailsa had little time for the knitting, her mother requiring her whole attention. They had a small sum of money in the bank, and they had to live on that. Mrs. Cameron suffered a great deal, and could not eat the coarse food to which they were accustomed, so Ailsa had to procure better, and looked at their diminishing store with a heavy heart. Shotty came daily to see them, with gifts of fish or eggs, sometimes game, always something, for the invalid. Ailsa grew to like to hear his pleasant, manly voice; and as for her mother, she looked for his coming as if he had been a son.

At length came the crisis in Mrs. Cameron's complaint, and Shotty advised a physician from the neighbouring town.

"We canna afford it, Shotty," said Ailsa, mournfully. Then he pressed to be allowed to pay the fee himself, but Ailsa still hesitated.

A thought seemed to strike him.

"You needna be feared, Ailsa," he said, earnestly, "that I'll be wantin' either fee or reward for this. No reward I'll want, lassie, but what you gi'e me of your ain free will."

The girl looked up at him, and seeing the honest soul that looked through his eyes, his face seemed transfigured to her. It had a nobility and strength about it that far transcended mere regularity of feature, and she felt an odd inclination to lay her head down on his broad breast and weep. But she resisted this, and when Shotty had gone on his way rejoicing with the required permission, she said to herself, in reference to that momentary inclination—

"Guid sakes! I must be gaein' doited wi' a' the troubles."

The physician came, an operation was performed, and there was a prospect that Mrs. Cameron would soon be getting about again, and all was joy at the little cottage.

Shotty came every day still, but that was all he did to further his courtship. He said not a word of love to Ailsa, though sometimes his heart was filled with gladness when he saw she welcomed him more kindly, and seemed to look upon him as a friend.

"Have ye heard the news, Shotty?" enquired Mrs. Inkster, in the little tobacco shop, as she was serving him with his customary allowance of that article.

"What 'n news?" he asked.

"Have ye no heard it, then! Wha but Donald Fraser is comin' hame wi' his pockets full o' money to marry Ailsa Cameron. There'll be a fine, gran' weddin', I expec'."

If Mrs. Inkster hoped to see any change in Shotty she was disappointed. He was not one to wear his heart on his sleeve, and he looked at her with an impassive face.

"Aye, I daursay," he said, carelessly, and went out.

But, if his face was impassive, his heart was

not; it was beating wildly. At first he did not believe this news, but he met two or three more people before he reached his cottage and they were all full of it. Donald Fraser was not only coming home, but coming home that very night.

It was Saturday night, but Shotty went out no more, but sat thinking. He remembered how handsome Donald Fraser was, and wondered if Ailsa cared for him still. He remembered how, although she was not one to show grief at such a thing, the colour had deserted her cheek and the light had left her eye for a time after Donald had forsaken her, and how much the sight had pained him. She had got over that long ago, but still Shotty doubted if the old love would not revive again.

He went to church in the morning as usual, and heard that Donald had arrived, and was as fine looking as ever, and much grander, "wi' a gold watch and chain and a power o' money in the bank." He also heard that he was now a second mate with a "certificate."

Shotty debated within himself whether he should go as usual to the Camerons' cottage this Sunday afternoon; he hesitated about it, but finally resolved that he would. When he got near the gate he saw someone standing at the door, and recognised Donald Fraser himself. He looked bright and gay, with a most satisfied air, a flower in the button-hole of his spruce blue suit, and a fine felt hat on his head, like the hats worn by none but the gentry around. A pain struck Shotty's heart, which deepened when he saw Ailsa open the door with a smile on her face, and he turned round and went back home.

If he had only known it, that smile was for himself. Ailsa had bolted the door that afternoon, because something had gone wrong with the latch, and it would not keep "snecked," and had run to open it, thinking it was Shotty. When she saw who it really was, the smile soon faded.

Donald Fraser had come back to the girl he had deserted, having no doubt but that she would be glad to have him return. He had tired of the girl in the South. She was not nearly so pretty as Ailsa, but she had talked the English so "genteely," and she was always dressed (she was a dressmaker) in silks and velvets. She could also play (vilely, but Donald did not understand music) on the piano, and these things, combined with her most undisguised preference for himself, had flattered Donald's vanity, and he had preferred her to his old love. But he discovered that she had a temper, that she was of a jealous and exacting disposition, so he had wearied of her, and resolved to come home and marry Ailsa and take her back with him.

But Mr. Donald Fraser had a good deal yet to learn, and he learned some of it that afternoon.

Shotty, however, did not know this, and he carried a sore and aching heart home with him.

"I'm no the kind to take a lass's fancy," he said to himself as he sat by his solitary fireside. "It's no meant for me," and the fire looked blurred and indistinct to poor Shotty's eyes just then. Still he did not give up hope.

"I'll see her at the kirk to-night," he thought, "and then she'll hae to choose between us."

One of the neighbours always sat with Mrs. Cameron, while Ailsa went to church on Sunday evenings, and Shotty was there early. He saw her come in in her neat grey dress and bonnet, and thought she looked as sweet as the May-blossom outside on the hedges. Donald Fraser was there also, gold watch and all, and Shotty noticed he looked often and long at Ailsa. She took no notice of anyone, but sat with reverent face and gazed up at the old, white-haired minister, as he preached to them as he had done almost every Sunday of her life.

Shotty was determined to join her when church was over, and he thought he would soon be able to tell whether she wanted him or not. Unfortunately, this plan was upset, for as he was coming out, Mrs. Todd's Maysie, who was a great friend of his, tumbled down before him, and he was obliged to pick her up. The child put her fat arms around his neck and asked to be carried, but, to her surprise and wondering resentment, Shotty for once refused to accede to her request, and left her hurriedly. But this had detained him, and he arrived just in time to see Ailsa joined by Donald Fraser, and both walk off together.

Then Shotty gave it up, and went home, picturing to himself Donald and Ailsa walking arm-in-arm over the breezy hills, with the fragrant breath of spring playing over them, and settling when the "gran' weddin'" was to be.

Shotty walked up and down his kitchen floor, muttering to himself,

"I could a borne it better if it had come when I had nae hope," he murmured.

Sometimes he felt a wild longing to do his rival some mischief, he felt as if he could have shaken the life out of him with pleasure; as if he could not restrain his passion if left to himself.

Then, with the simple faith often found in these northern fishermen, bred up in it from their childhood, he flung himself on his knees.

It was with no meek submission that Shotty prayed at first. He supplicated eagerly, even fiercely, that this trial might be taken away from him.

(*To be concluded*).

GAELIC AIRS TO LOWLAND SONGS.

By Malcolm MacFarlane.

Continued from page 64.

7. Fear Chul-charn—Maid of Isla. I am glad to be able to testify to Knockie's correctness in this instance. A friend from Easter Ross having whistled what I felt to be a Gaelic tune in my hearing, I enquired its name, and expressed a wish to have it. He told me it was *Fear Chul-chàrn*; and between us we wrote it down. I give it here, and the reader will see that it is a marching set of "The Maid of Isla."

FEAR CHUL-CHARN.

Key D.

```
| d  : m .s | m   :  -  | s   : l .s | m   : —
| d  : m .s | m   :     | l   : s    | r   : —
| d  : m .s | m   :  —  | s   : l .s | m   : —
| d  : m .,s | m  :  —  | l ., t: d'., | l | s .m :r
| d .,r': d'., | l | s., l: s ., m | d'., r': d ., | l | s .m :r
| d'., r': d'., | l | s., l: s ., m | l ., t: d ., | l | s .m :r ||
```

8. An Caimbeulach dubh—Roy's Wife. Also called "The Ruffian's Rant."

9. Robaidh donn gòrach (*or* Robaidh tha thu gòrach)—Daft Robin. To this air, or variants of it, are sung, in Scotland "Todlin' hame," "My ain fireside," "Johnnie Armstrong," "Earl Douglas's Lament," "Carronside," "The Maid of Selma," and "The days o' Langsyne" (not "Auld Langsyne"); in Ireland, "The lame yellow beggar," "The wild geese," "Bonnie Portmore," "The boys of Kilkenny," and the beautiful and popular "The meeting of the waters;" while in the Highlands, as far as I know, we have only *Na laithean a dh' aom* and *A' Chuairt Shamraidh*.

10. Ionbhar Calla—Tibbie, lass, I've seen the day (Burns). The tune is often named "Invercauld's reel."

11. A h-uile taobh a sheideas gaoth—Of a' the airts the win' can blaw (Burns). That the Gaelic and English names translate one another is suspicious. At the same time, it is admitted on all hands that the tune is a northern one, having been perfected by Marshall, by whom it was named "Miss Admiral Gordon's Strathspey." Its simplest form is that associated with "The Lowlands of Holland." I have met in some book the Gaelic equivalent of this name, but cannot recall which. The Irish have a song of the same name, but the music differs.

12. Braigh a' bhadain—Coming thro' the Craigs of Kyle. This tune is in Bremner's Collection, 1764. It is better known as "Owre the muir amang the heather."

13. Baile nan Granndach—Green grow the rashes. I have seen a claim to this tune put forward for Ulster. But as Scottish tunes are naturally common there, its claim loses much of its force. The tunes attached to Orange songs are mostly Scottish. Indeed, it may be here noticed that "Boyne Water" is most probably a Scottish tune. It occurs in various forms in connection with the following songs:—"When the King comes owre the water," "The wee, wee German Lairdie," "To daunton me," "Lady Keith's Lament," and *O theid sinn* (see Maclean's "Songs of the Gael").

14. A h-uile fear a Muideart—Wat ye wha's in yon town. To this air are also "I'll aye ca' in by yon town," and "I'll gang nae mair tae yon town." It appears in Gunn's pipe music collection under the name, *Chu tèid mi fèin a cheitidh*.

15. An gille dubh mo laochan—Is there for honest poverty. There is in the style of this tune evidence sufficient to establish its claim to be Gaelic. Beyond this, however, a variant of the air is found attached to a song called "Donald Couper," preserved in Playford's Dancing Master, 1657. Again, in a poem by Cleland, on the Highland Host, about 1679, the following quotation occurs:—

"Trumpets sounded, skenes were glancing; Some were *Donald Couper* dancing."

But primitive as the music of "Donald Couper" is, "For a' that" is much more Gaelic in style. In some parts of the Highlands *Mo nighean dubh tha bòidheach dubh* is sung to the air.

16. Nighean donn a' chota bhuidhe—Lassie wi' the yellow coatie. These names translate each other. Rob Donn has a song, the chorus of which includes these words:—

"A nigh 'neig a' chòta bhuidhe, Dean do shuidhe cuide rium."

D. R. Mackinnon, Gaelic comic vocalist, sings a song with a similar refrain, somewhat after the following fashion :—

NIGHEAN DONN A' CHOTA BHUIDHE.

Key A.

```
. l₁| s₁ .s₁ : s₁ , l₁|s₁ ., l₁ : d ., r
A | nighean   donn  a'|chota        bhuidhe,

| m ., d : f ., m r ., d : l₁ ., 
|Dean do  shuidhe  cuide    rium ;

d .s₁ .s₁ : s ., l₁|s₁ ., l₁ : d ., r
A |nighean   donn  a'|chota        bhuidhe,

|m ., d : s ., m r : d . 
|Dean do  shuidhe  làmh rium.
```

The air given in Mayer's collection differs from the above. It has, nevertheless, points of resemblance, and would go better to Rob Donn's words than to the above.

(*To be continued*).

CLAN COLQUHOUN FIRST ANNUAL SOCIAL GATHERING.

LUSS, LOCH LOMOND—THE COUNTRY OF THE COLQUHOUNS.

DEDICATED TO SIR JAMES COLQUHOUN, BART., OF LUSS AND COLQUHOUN, CHIEF OF THE CLAN.

On! tinkle ye bells o'er the top of Ben Lomond,
    And jubilant ring o'er the land of Colquhoun ;
A gathering and union of hearts at the gloaming
    Commences to-morrow till next day at noon.

The lad and the lass of the clan and its chieftain,
    In tartan array to the music of yore,
Will dance till the heart is as light as a fountain,
    And harmony runs like a stream from its core.

The hearts never met before till this meeting
    Cemented will be in a high, loving bond ;
The night will be one of such fondness and greeting,
    As only can match with the regions beyond.

All one name, what a scene, and a curtain behind it,
    Revealing the past, to our strange, wondering eye?
Let present and future blend with it and bind it
    To hearts full of hope, and to minds mounting
        high.

For the glory, Colquhoun, is a treasure so happy,
    Unique in the annals in name or of clan,
That each when they meet o'er a wee drop of nappy
    Is proud o't as ever can be mortal man.

JOHN HAMILTON COLQUHOUN.

28th December, 1893.

THE CLAN COLQUHOUN SOCIETY.—The first social gathering of this society was held in the Waterloo Rooms, on Friday, 29th December. In the absence of the chief, Sir James Colquhoun of Luss, Bart., who was seriously ill, Mr H. Colquhoun Hamilton, M.A., LL.B., hon. secretary, occupied the chair, and delivered a most instructive address on the history of the clan, and referred to many notable men of the clan name. The Lord Provost of Glasgow (whose mother was a Colquhoun), Dr Colquhoun, and Mr. Walter Menzies, also delivered interesting addresses. A very attractive programme of song and music was successfully carried through. Col altogether the first social meeting of this, the latest clan society, was an encouraging success. An assembly followed.

THE LAST MACDONALDS OF ISLA.

By Charles Fraser-Mackintosh, F.S.A. (Scot.)

PART III.—(continued from page 68).

JAMES MACDONALD took sasine at the Castle of Mingarry of the lands of Ardnamurchan on 7th January, 1551 (the date is erroneously given as 1550), the witnesses being Angus Mak Connail, John vic Aonas Hacht, Archibald Stewart, Sir Alexander Mak Alister, rector of Kilmore, Farchard Mak-kay, Duncan-vic-Yvar-dubh, Lachlan Ban, Finlay-maol vic-Kobair, and Mr. Cornelius Omeyght, dean of Kintyre a goodly list of Highland names and patronymics. The Dean of Kintyre wrote and was witness to many of the writs connected with the Argyles and Macdonalds, and I observe in the *Origines Parochiales Scotiæ*, he is sometimes called Omay, sometimes Omey. In the sasine, which is written by him and also signed, he describes himself as Master of Arts and Clerk of Lismore.

In 1548, Master Cornelius Omey was presented by Queen Mary as rector of Kildalton. In 1550 he is rector of Kilberry, and at a later period parson of Killblane, dying prior to 1580, for in that year Donald Campbell is presented to the parsonage, vacant by the death of Master Cornelius Omay.

I do not find in the Kilmore lists the name of the before mentioned rector, who was probably son or grandson of that Charles Mak Alexander who, in 1481, received the appointment of steward of Kintyre.

It will be observed that one of the witnesses is called John son of Angus, the Isla man. The name of Isla has ever had a strong hold on its inhabitants, and the feeling is cherished at this day perhaps more warmly than ever. The very word, uttered in a strange land in Gaelic, with that soft plaintive accent peculiar to Islanders of the West, goes straight to the heart. When the old Lords of the Isles were independent, Isla in its Gaelic form was their favourite title, and down to their extinction in the person of John, last Lord of the Isles and Earl of Ross, their primary title was " de Ile," or " Yle." That it was in the Gaelic form, rather than in English or Latin, is worth noticing, and gratifying to Highlanders and Islanders. Younger sons were styled "de Insulis," and "Illis."

The next document which I have is the discharge for the price of Ardnamurchan, which, in 1723, was divided into thirty-one townships, of the aggregate value of 152 pennies, whereof Mingarry was valued at six pennies, and Ormsaigbeg, or The Point, at five pennies. Of these thirty-one, three consisted of two tenements, viz.:—Clash and Ardriminish, Daul and Gortaneorn, Ardtoe and Waterfoot. The discharge is as follows, the spelling being modernised:—" We, Archibald, Earl of Argyle, Lord Campbell and Lorne, &c., &c., grant us to have received by the hands of James Mak Coneill of Dunyvaig and Glenns, the sum of one thousand merks usual money of Scotland, in complete payment of his heritable infeftment made by us to him and his heirs, of all and haill the four score merk lands of old extent of Ardnamurchan, with their pertinents heritably, of the which sum in complete payment as said is, we hold us well content and paid, and quit claim and discharges the said James Mak Conell and his heirs and all others whom it affects for now and ever. By this our writing, subscribed with our hand, our signet is affixed at Stirling the 17th day of February, the year of God 1551 years, before these witnesses Hector Maclean of Duart, Archibald Campbell of Clachane, Master Neil Campbell, parson of Kilmartyne, Thomas Grahame of Boquhople, and John Grahame of Boquhople, and others diverse. (Signed A., Erle of Argyle)." This designation of the two Grahames brings us very close to that given by Sir Walter Scott to one of his minor characters. "The Laird of Balmawhopple." The above-mentioned Neil Campbell appears to have been vicar of Kilmartin in 1541, also dean of Lochowe, and to have been succeeded as rector or parson in 1553 by the well known John Carsewell, created in 1556 Bishop of the Isles, and, after the Reformation, Superintendent of Argyle and the Isles, by courtesy still called Bishop of the Isles.

The old possessors of Ardnamurchan, the Maclains, derived from John "Sprangaich," youngest son of Angus Mor, Lord of the Isles, this John's son Angus being the first proprietor. Four generations apparently bring us to the John Mac Iain who was rewarded with great possessions for the capture of Sir John Cathanach, as previously mentioned. He did not enjoy his estates long, and being attacked by Sir Donald of Lochalsh for the putting to death of Sir Alexander of Lochalsh, the warfare lasted from 1516 to 1518. Mac Iain was expelled from Ardnamurchan in 1517, the Castle of Mingarry razed to the ground, and in 1518 Mac Iain and his two sons, John and Angus, were slain in Morvern. Mariot, daughter of John Mac Iain, was served heir to him in 1538, and two years after Ardnamurchan fell into the hands of the Earl of Argyle; who in 1550 alienated it as above to James Macdowald, and the grant was confirmed the same year by Queen Mary. In the old castle many important gatherings took place. In 1493 (25th October), James IV. held his Court and granted a charter; and he was again there on 18th May, 1495. The subsequent history of Mingarry Castle, including a notice of the last Mac Iains, who found their final resting-place in Badenoch, will be given later. A sketch of the castle as in 1734 is here given,

A Prospect of Mingary Castle from ye Sea

and it is hoped that the intended pier will be in harmony with present surroundings.

In the titles to Ardnamurchan, the destination was limited to James Macdonald and the heirs male of his body, whom failing, to revert to the Earl of Argyle and as this prevented a sale, Archibald, the 5th Earl of Argyle, granted license to James to sell the lands, the purchasers to hold off the Earl on the same footing. This is the next document in date I have, and is endorsed, "License given by the Earl of Argyle to sell the lands of Ardnamurchan," and is dated at Glasgow, 16th January, 1563, the witnesses being Sir Colin Campbell of Buquhane, Knight; Dugald Campbell of Auchinbreck, Ninian Stuart of Kilchattan, and William Heyart, notary. Sir Colin Campbell of Boquhan was the Earl's brother and successor; the Campbells of Auchinbreck are afterwards referred to under date 1603; and Ninian Stuart was no doubt Cadet of Bute, who held the lands of Kilchattan and others in the parish of Kingarth, South Bute.

James Macdonald, in the year 1559, got the gift of the marriage of Mary Macleod, the wealthy heiress of Dunvegan, but like other good things, it ultimately fell into the hands of Argyle. Archibald, 4th Earl of Argyle, who had always befriended James Macdonald, died in 1558, and his successor, Archibald, 5th Earl, followed in this respect in his father's footsteps. In his public career, however, though his father had been a steady supporter of the policy of the Queen Regent, he threw in his whole influence with the Lords of the Congregation, became a leading Reformer and a prime favourite notwithstanding his incontinent habits, with the prominent clergy of the new order. James Macdonald was in possession of an immense estate. He purchased, in 1554, the office of Toiseachdor of all Kintyre from Macneill of Gigha; in 1558, all his charters and ancient writs which had been destroyed in time of war were renewed; in 1560, he received the Bailiary of South Argyle; in 1562 Queen Mary leased him several lands; in 1563, he was infeft in lands in Uist, under agreement with Ferchar vic Allister of Skirrehough; and, in 1564, he received a charter which included the Mull of Kintyre. His chief misfortune was a violent feud with the Macleans regarding the Rhinns of Isla, which began in 1562 and continued until James's death. The Privy Council, in December, 1563, determined in favour of James, but Maclean was dissatisfied, and, in 1565, both parties were bound down, under a penalty of ten thousand pounds each, to abstain from hostilities.

James Macdonald was so actively engaged in Scotland that his affairs in Ireland were looked to by, and the ownership practically given over to his youngest brother, Sorley Buie, a man of great energy, who not only maintained possession of the family estates, but added thereto by the expulsion of the MacQuillins from the Route of Antrim. Troubles arose, however. Shane O'Neill quarrelled with his father, with the English, and with the Scottish settlers, who desired to remain neutral. Sorley, driven to extremities, called for the assistance of his brother James, who arrived in Ireland with a large force. The Macdonalds were completely defeated, and both brothers taken prisoners. This occurred on the 2nd May, 1565, and James was confined in Castle Coreke, near Strabane. James Macdonald's release on ransom was demanded by Queens Mary and Elizabeth and the Earl of Argyle, but in vain; and, dying shortly the universal belief was that he was murdered by order of O'Neill. James's death was much regretted in the three kingdoms. Of him the Four Masters say "that the death of this gentleman was generally bewailed; he was a paragon of hospitality and prowess; a festive man of many troops; a bountiful and munificent man. His peer was not to be found at that time among the Clan Donnell of Ireland or Scotland, and his own people would not have deemed it too much to give his weight in gold for his ransom, if he could have been ransomed."

Prior to the accession of James VI., the English were exceedingly jealous of the presence of the Scots in Ulster, holding that they could not be subjects of two kingdoms. This objection in time ceased, and Sorley Buie, after two years' captivity, was restored to freedom, maintained his own against all comers, and, declaring his intention of remaining in Ireland, made his peace with Elizabeth. In 1586, he was assured in all his lands, his fourth son, Reginald, who ultimately succeeded, being created Earl of Antrim. James's widow, known as Lady Kintyre, married Torlogh O'Neill, afterwards Earl of Tyrone, and her daughter, Ineen, married Sir Hugh O'Donnell of Donegal. Their object was to strengthen the claim of James Macdonald's family to their ancient estate, which Sorley Buie, after being released, on the slaughter of Shane O'Neill, claimed as his own. Both ladies are highly spoken of. Lady Kintyre was willing to marry O'Neill, "provided she and her sons might enjoy the inheritance that her late husband and his ancestors held in Ireland for seven generations; but if not, then as long as any of the clan lived, their title to these lands would never be relinquished, or undefended." And, again, that she was "a grave, wise, well-spoken lady, both in Scots, English, and French, and well mannered." Of her daughter, Lady O'Donnell, known as "Ineen dubh," that "she possessed the heart of a hero, and the mind of a warrior."

The English did not desire the success of either Sorley Buie or of James's children, and fomented all quarrels, until at length Sorley Buie was practically left in possession. The various steps taken by him and his successor to establish themselves permanently in Antrim are full of interest, but outside the general scope of these papers. It appears rather hard that James's death assisting his brother should have been the cause of the family losing their Irish estates

Differences continued at a later period betwixt the Antrims and Angus, 8th of Isla, but in the end friendly intercourse subsisted, and a close alliance betwixt the former and Donald Gorme of Sleat, and other heads of Scottish Macdonalds. James had at least two sons—Archibald and Angus—who survived, and, dying in 1565, was succeeded by his eldest son, Archibald.

(To be continued.)

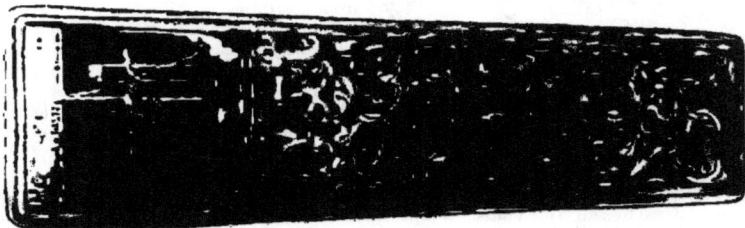

TOMBSTONE OF ANGUS MACDONALD, LORD OF THE ISLES, IN IONA.

ANSWERS TO CORRESPONDENTS.

- - -

D. R. C., Ardrishaig.—We will communicate with you in a few days. We are giving due effect to your wishes

Donald MacDonald, New York, U.S.A.—The sketch has now come to hand. We will try and find room for it in our next issue.

J. Mackenzie, London.—Sorry about the misunderstanding. Try and let us have the matter in good time for next number.

Miss Lizzie Cook, Cambridge.—Please accept our best thanks for the excellent drawing of the ancient Celtic cross at Reay. Sometime soon we may give an engraving of it in the *Monthly*.

"Ben Reay," Germany.—Your letter will appear in next issue, with engraving of the colours of the "Reay Fencibles."

Bound Copies of Volume I.

This handsome volume, consisting of 192 pages, and containing some fifty life like portraits of well-known Highlanders, and other illustrations, can now be had bound in cloth, with gilt lettering, at **4s.** post free, or in fine, strong leather, **5s. 6d.** post free.

This valuable volume is specially suitable to send as a present to a Highland friend, or as a prize in schools in the Highlands.

As only a few copies can be had, those who wish the volume should apply at once to the Editor, *Celtic Monthly*, 17 Dundas Street, Kingston, Glasgow.

ALEXANDER M'GRIGOR.

Hon. Secretary, Clan Gregor Society.

MR JOHN HILL BURTON, the historian, in his history of the proceedings against the Clan Gregor, states that it was not till the year 1775 that the opprobrium thrown on the name was removed by Act of Parliament, and he adds that, singularly enough, the clan, which was the only one to whom it was at one time prohibited to convene in numbers exceeding four at a time, was, at the date on which he wrote, the one Highland clan which strove to keep up its ancient ties and assemble together in a body in the shape of a Society.

The Clan Gregor Society which he referred to was founded on Friday, the 13th December, 1822. At first, and for many years after its foundation, its purposes were purely educational, and during its early years it did excellent work in that direction, many of the name of MacGregor greatly owing their success in life to help given them by the Society when they were struggling to raise themselves from a humble position. Its aims are now, however, widened to suit the exigencies of the times, and its purposes at present include besides education, charity, and also a provident scheme for assisting members of the Society to insure their lives by endowment policies.

We this month give the portrait of the present Honorary Secretary of the Society, Mr. Alexander M'Grigor of Cairnoch, Stirlingshire, and 13 Grosvenor Crescent, Glasgow. Mr. M'Grigor's family have been identified with the history of the Society from its foundation, his great-grandfather, Mr. Alex. M'Grigor, having been one of its original vice-presidents, and his grandfather Mr. Alex. M'Grigor, jun., having been an original director, and afterwards vice-president. The Society having become practically dormant for some years, it was on 4th May, 1886, resuscitated, when the late Dr. A. B. M'Grigor, the father of the subject of this sketch, was appointed vice-president, the late General Sir Charles MacGregor, K.C.S.I., being appointed president, and on the lamented death of the latter in 1887 Dr. M'Grigor was appointed president, which office he held till his death in 1891. It will thus be seen that the present Honorary Secretary has a connection with the Society such as few, if any, of its members can boast of, and as his son is also a life-member, the family is now represented in the roll of the Society in its fifth generation.

The number of members of the Society is at present 351, and a considerable addition is looked for in the course of this year. The capital funds administered by the Society amount to over £3000, the income being close on £250 per annum. ALEX. MACGREGOR.

27 Allison Street, Crosshill.

TO CORRESPONDENTS.

All Communications, on literary and business matters, should be addressed to the Editor, Mr. JOHN MACKAY, 17 Dundas Street, Kingston, Glasgow.

—☞—

TERMS OF SUBSCRIPTION.— *The CELTIC MONTHLY will be sent, post free, to any part of the United Kingdom, Canada, the United States, and all countries in the Postal Union—for one year, 4s.*

THE CELTIC MONTHLY
FEBRUARY, 1894

CONTENTS

TESTIMONIAL TO MR. HENRY WHYTE ("FIONN").

OUR readers will, doubtless, be glad to learn that a movement has just been inaugurated to present Mr. Henry Whyte (*Fionn*) with a testimonial, in recognition of his valuable contributions to Celtic literature, and his life-long services to the Highland cause generally. *Fionn's* name is known and respected in every part of the world where Highlanders are to be found. Few men of this generation have done as much for Highlanders, or placed their services so generously at the disposal of their countrymen without fee or reward as Mr. Whyte has done, and certainly no name is better known in connection with Celtic literature than that of *Fionn*. His personality has been in the forefront of every Highland movement, and his advice and assistance have always proved of the greatest value. His unbounded enthusiasm for everything Highland has been the means of inspiring others in the same direction. To Mr. Whyte we ourselves owe, when too young, we fear, to be of much practical use, our first introduction to a Highland Society in Glasgow, and to our acquaintanceship with him we owe in no slight measure our knowledge of matters relating to the Highlands. Hundreds have benefitted in a similar way from his encouragement and assistance. His services have been of such a nature that they could not be adequately repaid, and we know that very many will be delighted to embrace the opportunity which has now been afforded them of showing, in a practical way, their appreciation of his long and faithful services to the cause of his countrymen. We sincerely hope that the testimonial will be a handsome one, worthy of the givers and receiver. Our readers have each month been interested and instructed by his valuable contributions to our own pages, and we trust that the subscriptions from the readers of the *Celtic Monthly* will take first place in the list. We shall be very glad to receive contributions towards the testimonial fund, which we shall duly acknowledge in the *Monthly*. As the list is only to be open for a few weeks, we hope that those who intend subscribing will do so at once. Address —Editor, *Celtic Monthly*, 17 Dundas Street, Kingston, Glasgow (member of committee).

OUR NEXT ISSUE.

IN our next issue we will present our readers with a life-like plate-portrait, printed on tinted paper, of Lord Reay, G.C.I.E., D.C.L., chief of the Clan Mackay, with a biographical sketch. The portrait represents his lordship in the Highland dress. An interesting account will also be given of the Holland branch of the clan and the chief's ancestors, which will be illustrated with a number of finely engraved views of places of interest in the Reay country associated with the chiefs of the clan. Part IV., of Mr. C. Fraser-Mackintosh's valuable papers on "The Last MacDonalds of Isla" will be accompanied by *fac-simile* reproductions of a charter, dated 1509, granted by Archibald, 5th Earl of Argyll, and a full-size copy of the seal. With the continuation of Mr John Mackay, Hereford's, historical articles we will give two picturesque views in the parishes of Tongue and Durness. In addition to these, we will print several interesting illustrated papers which we have had to hold over from this issue owing to the pressure on our space. Portraits of distinguished Highlanders will also be given. Our next number promises to be the best we have yet issued.

It will interest members of the Clan Gregor Society to learn that we intend giving shortly a fine plate-portrait of Sir Malcolm MacGregor, Bart., chief of the clan, and also of the late Dr. A. B. M'Grigor. It may further be mentioned that we are arranging to give a series of sketches of the Clan MacGregor, with pictures of places of interest in the romantic country of the clan. The articles and portraits cannot fail to be of special interest to every person of the name.

CALENDAR OF MEETINGS OF HIGHLAND SOCIETIES. —We regret that owing to the demand this month upon our advertising space we have not been able to give the "Calendar" for February, but as we intend in our next issue adding four extra pages of advertising space, we will give a full list of the meetings and social gatherings for March. Our friends must excuse the omission this month.

THE DR. CHARLES MACKAY MEMORIAL FONT, which was erected by the Clan Mackay to the memory of the late clan bard, has just been unveiled in St. Paul's Parish Church, Perth. The memorial is a massive and handsome one, and we hope to give a photo. reproduction of it in our next issue.

TONGUE AND ITS HISTORIC SURROUNDINGS.

By JOHN MACKAY, C.E., J.P., Hereford.

ON the defeat of the Norsemen in Strath-naver in 1196, and the retreat of Harold into the Orkneys, Reginald in a few months pacified the distracted country, appointing three noblemen to rule the district for the King of Scots—one in the southern, one in the eastern, and another in the northern portion, Tongue, or, as it was then called, Strathnavernia. It is not very well known who was the noble he appointed to rule the northern part, but it is mentioned that he had in his army a strong party of Gallowegians, commanded by their own chief, Alexander, and his two brothers. It is very probable it was to this Alexander and his brothers that Reginald entrusted the expulsion of the Norsemen from Strathnaver and the adjoining districts; and this Alexander having executed the trust given him, was, two years thereafter, confirmed in the possession of the territory he had subdued by William the Lion, when Harold was finally disposed of by the King of Scots at Eysteindal, on the confines of Caithness, in 1198. With this warrior from Galloway began the race of the Mackay chiefs who ruled in Tongue for upwards of six cen-

KYLE OF TONGUE, FROM THE FERRY POINT.

turies, and attained to a high degree of influence by their own powers and the fidelity and bearing of their clansmen.

The Norsemen were soon expelled from Strathnaver and Tongue, their two principal settlements, yet leaving their footprints behind them in place-names round about Tongue, with which in this paper we have to do. In them we see that the names of places, however much corrupted by the lapse of ages, are, like those of the streets of a town, endowed with extraordinary vitality, frequently surviving as in this case, the race, or the nation that imposed them, and often defying alike the accidents of conquest and of time, while furnishing information of a most unexpected character.

In Tongue, there must have been a numerous colony of Norsemen, as the names of places reveal. Blandy, blanda (meeting-place); Borgie, byrgi (enclosure); Coldbackie, Kald-bakki (cold ridge); Caonasaid, Kvenna-setr (the lady's residence); Falside, fellsetr (the residence on the fell, or moor); Hysbackie, husa-bakki (houses on the ridge); Kinkiboll, kirkja-bol (kirk town) —baile-na-h-eaglais; Melness, mel-nes (the benty-grassed promontory); Modsary, meda-seyra (muddy moorland); Ribigill, ryggar-bol (the lady's home-farm)—this word in Mackay charters is spelled riga-bol and rege-bol—bal in Icelandic is in meaning equivalent to the Gaelic baile, residence, township, hamlet—setr in Norse is applied to a single residence or farm;

Scrabster, skara-bol-stadr (the outlying homestead); Skerray, skerja (isolated rocks in the sea); Skinid. sgianid, skinni (withered, bleached); Scullomie, skulda mot (court, or place where taxes, debts, dues, fines were paid to the Norse lord); Slettel, sletr (flat land or place); Taimine, talir-minn (toll-free)—this place is on the west side of the Bay of Tongue, and exactly opposite to Scullomie, which is on the east side of the bay, the one landing-place free of toll, while dues were exacted at the other, which was the more convenient to the centre of population. This is a history in words. Tongue, tunga (a narrow spit of land jutting out into the water or sea). The origin of place-names is always interesting. Those in Tongue have a peculiar historic value of their own.

The territory, being thus won by the Mackay chiefs, the people soon settled down to peaceful pursuits—the sea, the land, the river, lake, woods, and mountains were free alike to all. A Mackay then could, without let or hindrance, take a deer from the mountain, a salmon from the river, or a stick from the wood. The chiefs were then at too remote a distance to take any part or interest in the political strifes that distracted the kingdom at its centre. They were more intent on consolidating the power and influence their territorial possessions gave them, and moulding and uniting the heterogeneous

TONGUE SANDS AND BEN LOYAL, IN 1820.

mass of the people they were called to rule and guide into one compact body of clansmen. These chiefs had their reward, for very soon this wise policy bore the richest fruit. They commanded not only the reverence but the fidelity of the people, who were proud to call themselves their clansmen. They were satisfied with the power of surrounding themselves by an attached and contented tenantry, and of influencing the mind and the will, whilst the clansmen were happy to acknowledge the kindness of their chiefs by a complete devotion to their service in peace or war, and by giving so much value for the lands allotted to them as enabled the chiefs to support the dignity of their position in society with credit and honour.

Before entering further into the events that occurred about Tongue, or the various warlike affairs in which chief and clan were engaged, let us attempt to describe its surroundings.

Tongue is one of the prettiest and most romantic localities in Sutherland. The view from the bay is remarkably grand, the lofty semi-circular range of hills rises boldly and suddenly from the ocean, as it were, and sweeps all round the bay, forming the large, enclosed valley into a stupendous amphitheatre. The bay itself, on the north, seems to be guarded by a cluster of islands, whose sides are perpendicular cliffs of granite, varying in altitude from 150 to 700 feet, forming, as it were, a continuous breakwater to safeguard the noble bay, while on the west a range of hills, 1315 feet in height, runs along the rugged, trackless waste of the Moin, and terminates in Ben Hope, one of the sublimest mountain masses in the Highlands, rightly named by tourists, "Queen of Highland mountains." In the immediate distance, to the south, is seen the remains of Castle Varrick, perched on the pinnacle of a promontory, facing the Bay of Tongue, in grim watchfulness. It was founded by a Norse warrior. At the south-eastern extremity of this extensive valley, Ben Loyal starts up. The summits of this pinnacled and almost perpendicular mountain mass presents to the fancy, at one point of view, the outlines of a "lion couchant," and at another a close resemblance to the "Royal arms." On a summer morning, or after a summer shower, when the transparent mist is reposing on its bosom, or coiling among its peaks, the appearance of this mountain is very beautiful, and often fantastic. Within the mountain chain formed by this lofty mountain there are various objects which constitute marked features in the scenery of the district. The view off the mountain itself is universally admired. Starting up majestically from the end of the valley, it quickly attains an altitude of 2504 feet, presenting at its base an expanded breast of two miles, and cleft at the top into four massive, towering, and splintered peaks, standing boldly aloof from each other. The highest peak stands proudly forward to occupy the foreground, the rest recede a little, as if each were unwilling to protrude itself, from a conscious inferiority to its predecessor. As a graceful finish to its outlines, it stretches out an arm on either side, as if to embrace condescendingly the other mountain ranges, which may very well acknowledge it as chief, and which may very readily be fancied as doing it homage. On its west side, it is said, was the scene of Diarmid's combat with the wild boar, and his death. A green spot is shown as being his grave. On the same side of Ben Loyal occurred a famous clan battle, at Drum-na-Coup, of which we shall treat in another paper.

(To be continued).

GLASGOW CAITHNESS GATHERING.—This flourishing association held their annual gathering in the Queen's Rooms on old New Year's Night. Dr. J. F. Sutherland presided, and there was a large attendance. The chairman delivered a very racy address on Caithness, and referring to the Norse and Celtic elements in the country, gave it as his opinion that the Celts were the more important. Rev. Dr. W. Ross Taylor, Sheriff Birnie, and Councillor Chisholm gave interesting addresses. The assembly was well attended, and the whole proceedings were, as the Caithness gatherings always are, a very great success.

ABSTRACT OF OSSIAN'S COVALLA.*

BY LIEUT.-COLONEL CHARLES STEWART.
TIGH-'N DUIN.
Author of "The Gaelic Kingdom in Scotland, and its Celtic Church," "Killin Collection of Poetry and Music," &c.

THIS ode is of great value, not only as a glorious poetic inspiration, but also as a valuable portion of Scottish and Roman history, a touching account of touching incidents, and various references to beliefs and customs which make our Gaelic history to be of strong and special interest.

What renders its historic value of such special account is the confirmed light which it throws on a decisive part of the Roman and Scottish annals.

At the beginning of the third century the *Scots, Gaels,* or *Fians* (different names of the same race), along with the *Cruisthaich* or Picts, so worried the mid province, which was Roman, that Severus resolved upon reducing them to abject subjugation. He therefore crossed the Forth with an immense force, and marched through Pictland to the Tay, or nearly so. The Picts, however, assisted by their friends the Scots, whilst fighting no great battle, so harassed them by cutting off parties sent for various purposes, breaking and nullifying the supplies of food, and in every other way open to them, that Severus had to return after an immense loss of men and goods, as well as reputation. He was strong enough, however, to insist on a treaty, by which the mid province remained Roman, the line of Forth and Clyde being its border on the north, with the Scots and Picts, and the line of Tyne and Solway the border on the south. This occurred in the year 209.

The Scots, however, soon broke the compact, and came down on the Roman provinces, which caused Severus to assemble another great army at York, where he was taken ill and died in A.D. 211. Thereupon Caracalla, his son—called by the Gaels Carracul—proceeded northwards with the assembled host against the Albannic Gaels, and experienced the defeat related in our poem. The Roman historians, as not unusual in cases of defeat, do not mention the name of the battle, but they undoubtedly confirm the Gaelic account of it, as they acknowledge a treaty by Caracalla, in virtue of which he gave over to the Gaels that mid-province which a few years earlier was retained by Severus at such a fearful cost. By its terms also he had to retire behind the line of the Tyne and Solway. Probably the Gaels reserved this province

---

* Of course the poetry is rhythmical, and I have selected well-known Gaelic melodies which can be made easily to suit the rhythm, so that those knowing Gaelic music can read or chant them with due effect.

for its own Celtic inhabitants, the Britons, with whom they had strong sympathies in their bondage to the Romans.

I beg for a few necessary words of explanation at this point. In writing in English on Gaelic subjects I endeavour to do so as entirely in English as I can. When a Gaelic word is necessary I give its translation. Now in this paper I often use Fingal, which is the English of *Fion-Ghaidheal*.* As the *dh* is silent, and the accent on the second last syllable, the pronunciation is the same almost to exactitude. Fion,† as an adjective, means white, and Fión-Gaidheal means the "white-mieued Gael," which Fingal exceptionally was. The usage is quite common in Gaelic, as, for instance, Queen Meavy of Connaught's daughter was "Finnabhair," or "white-browed"; and her celebrated "white-horned" bull, "Finneheannach." Fingal has many other appelatives, in some of which "Fion," or one of the race, is used as a noun, but these don't concern my present enquiry, which only concerns the question whence comes the English "Fingal." The custom in Perthshire has been, and is, to use "Fion," or the "white-mieued," in reciting the ancient poetry, and "Fion Gaidheal" in some of our modern poetry, and almost always in speaking of our greatest hero. At one time I favoured the word "Fiongeal" as the Gaelic of Fingal, but had to drop it, as the accent is on the last syllable, and its pronunciation radically differs from *gal* in *Fingal*. Fion also is used as a noun in "Fion-geal," but by custom this is allowable. It has the same meaning in a different form as Fion-Ghaidheal has.

Fingal had just married Covalla, the daughter of a kingly chieftain, amongst the Western Isles, called Sarno. On his reaching Selma with his bride, he was called away to take command of his Gaelic host, and to meet Caracalla and the immense Roman host at the battle of Carron, A.D. 211. He was undoubtedly supported by the Picts, although not expressly mentioned that I can find, and, as fully and decisively stated, by a contingent of the Irish Gaels, under Cuchullin, the "son of Semo," ‡ acting as Regent during King Cormac M'Airt's minority. The date of Severus's death fixes the date of the battle.

* See "Highland Society's Report," pages 248, 232, 256; "The Stewarts," 555, &c.

† "MacAlpin's Dictionary," English and Gaelic, p. 512

‡ Cormac MacAirt ruled over Ireland from the beginning of the 3rd century to A.D. 267. This Cuchullin was the second man in the Irish Gaelic kingdom, and wa twice Regent during Cormac's minority and disability. MacPherson confounds the events of the first century surrounding the celebrated story of the "children of Maisneach," and, amongst the rest, confounds

LETTERS TO THE EDITOR.

"CHIPS FROM CAPE WRATH."

To the Editor of the "CELTIC MONTHLY."

SIR,—I think there can be no doubt that the Rev. Mr. Gunn, the minister of Durness, is quite correct in giving the true meaning of the names of the days of the week in Gaelic. But he makes a slight mistake (although no doubt it is an oversight) when he says "we have got the names of the first two days of the week from heathen times; the rest through the Church." For according to his own derivation of them three of them, viz , *Diluain*, the day of *Luna*, the moon ; *Dimairt*, the day of *Mars*, the god of war; *Diasathairne*, the day of *Saturn*, are all named after Pagan deities. But my main object in writing is to point out (what is very remarkable, viz) that while there are only *three* of the days of the week in Gaelic named after heathen gods, *all* the days of the week in English, with the exception perhaps of one, are also so named. Thus—*Sunday*, the day of the sun ; *Monday*, the day of the moon ; *Tuesday*, doubtful ; *Wednesday*, the day of Woden ; *Thursday*, the day of Thor ; *Friday*, the day of Freya (a goddess ; and *Saturday*, the day of Saturn This, I think, proves that the Celtic nations took more readily to Christianity than the Teutonic.

Apropos of this subject, could any of your readers give us the Gaelic names of the months of the year and their meaning in English? Doing so might oblige more than your humble servant.

JAMES FARQUHAR SINCLAIR.

THE MACNICOLS OF GLENORCHY.

To the Editor of the "CELTIC MONTHLY."

SIR,—Can you inform me. through the columns of the *Celtic Monthly*, to what clan the "Macnicols of Glenorchy" belong ? Have they a distinctive tartan ? If lack of space forbids the full information. kindly mention where it may be obtained. and oblige.— Yours, &c. COLIN MACNICOL.

San Francisco, California, U S.A

We regret to announce the death of Mr. Hector MacDougall, secretary, Gaelic Society of Hamilton, Canada. He was one of our earliest subscribers, and was ever ready to assist the cause of Celtic literature, and, indeed, all movements having for their object the advancement of his fellow-countrymen. He will be greatly missed by the Highlanders of Hamilton.

this Cuchullin with another Cuchullin of Dundalgan, son of Suvalta and Deitan, and one of Connor Mac-Nessa's Knights of the Red Branch at Emania. Connor died in A.D. 33. which settles the date. MacPherson actually interpolates this early 1st century history, as he knew it. into the 1st duan of "Fingal," the events of which happened circa A.D. 25-30. He was grossly ignorant of the history in this, one of the poems he collected, and one of the two principal ones, and how could he be its author ? He isplaced its date by two centuries, and what do the critics say ? We want the *Globe*'s reconciliation made level to the capacity of us poor Gaels.

(To be continued).

LIEUT.-COL. L. D. MACKINNON.

VICE-PRESIDENT, CLAN MACKINNON SOCIETY.

THE Clan Mackinnon have just held their second annual social gathering, and many members of the clan will be pleased to possess the life-like portrait which is here given of the distinguished clansman who occupied the chair on that auspicious occasion.

Lieut. - Col. Lionel Dudley Mackinnon, was born in 1850, and is the son of the late Lieut.-Col. Daniel Lionel Mackinnon, of the Coldstream Guards, who was killed at the battle of Inkerman, and brother of the present chief of the clan. His mother is a daughter of the late Major-General Sir Dudley St. Leger Hill, K.C.B. The subject of our sketch entered the Coldstream Guards in 1871, and served with the second battalion of that famous regiment in the Egyptian Campaign of 1882, including the battle of Tel-el-Kebir. He also served with the first battalion of the same regiment in the Sondan campaign of 1885.

In 1881 Lieut.-Col. Mackinnon married Elizabeth, daughter of Lieut.-Colonel Greenhill-Gardyne, of Finavon and Glenfersa, (who, it may be mentioned is to preside at the Mull and Iona gathering next month), and the Hon. Mrs. Gardyne He retired from the service in 1887 on retired pay, and is at present residing at Dochgarroch, near Inverness.

Lieut. - Col. Mackinnon is a worthy representative of a family who have always been noted for their martial prowess, and who have their names honourably inscribed in the military annals of the nation. He is proud of his name and clan, and the spirited address which he delivered at the recent clan gathering showed that above all things his "heart is Highland" and that he is inspired with the true spirit of the Gael.   DUNCAN MACKINNON.

CLAN GREGOR.—We regret to announce the death of Mr Peter MacGregor, County Buildings, Glasgow, an old and respected member of the Clan Gregor Society.

HONOURS TO HIGHLANDERS.—Mr D H MacFarlane, M.P. for Argyllshire, has been created a knight, and Mr James Lyle Mackay, the distinguished Indian financier, has been made a Knight Commander of the Indian Empire.

HIGHLANDERS TO THE FRONT.—It may interest our readers to learn that when the British (not "English" mind!) columns entered Buluwayo, the capital of Lobengula, they were headed by Pipe-Major Macdonald, late of the Royal Scots playing the "March to Buluwayo," a tune composed by himself in honour of the occasion. Mr. Neil MacDonald has truly said—

"And on the field of battle, 'mongst the bravest in the van,
You have always found him foremost, the man of Highland clan."

THE EARLDOM OF ROSS.

By D. Murray Rose.

II. *(continued from page 76).*

ALEXANDER LESLEY, Earl of Ross, by his wife Isabella, daughter of the Duke of Albany, left an only child, Euphemia, who, becoming a nun, illegally resigned the Earldom in favour of her maternal uncle, John Stewart, Earl of Buchan. The rightful heir of Ross was Lady Margaret Lesley, the wife of Donald, Lord of the Isles. Donald was not the individual to quietly submit to be deprived of the princely possessions, which formed the just inheritance of his wife. He had never been treated with much consideration by his Stewart kinsfolk, for, as a boy, in 1369,* they constituted him a hostage for the good conduct of his father. Their arbitrary dealings drove Donald and his brothers John and Alexander to act so harshly and undutifully towards their mother, the Lady Margaret Stewart, that the Earl of Fife was instructed to protect her from the violence of her sons and their dependents. This so exasperated the brothers that in same year (1398) they rose in rebellion, but were soon forced to submit, and Alexander—progenitor of the "bold Keppochs"—was imprisoned. His brother, Donald of the Isles, was appointed his keeper, and, brotherly affection overcoming loyalty to the Crown, Alexander was released in 1399, without consent of the King. As a result, Donald was cited to appear before the Parliament to answer for his conduct in giving liberty to a "robber and waster of the kingdom"—the gallant Alexander "Carrach" being thus designed by the authorities.

The Stewarts were jealous of the power of the De Yles, and through their machinations the estates of the family were divided. Donald's patrimony was still so great that they viewed with alarm his acquisition of the extensive Earldom of Ross, and determined to prevent this vast inheritance from falling into the hands of the turbulent Lord of the Isles. But such a princely possession as the modern counties of Ross and Cromarty, besides great estates in Sutherland, Caithness, Nairn, and Aberdeenshires, was not to be relinquished without a struggle, and Donald determined to make good the claims of his wife by force of arms. In 1411 he laid waste the district of Ross, defeated Angus Dubh Mackay of Far and the men of Sutherland at Dingwall, and marched to Buchan. He was met at Harlaw by the Earl of Mar, the erstwhile leader of caterans who had stormed

the Castle of Kildrummy, and in this rough manner wooed and won the Countess of Mar and her Earldom. In the contest which ensued was for a time decided not merely the rights to the Earldom of Ross but the supremacy of the Lowlander over the Highlander.

The clansmen of Ross and the Isles—armed with claymore and targe—were no match for the chivalry of the north-east of Scotland—the mail-clad barons of Aberdeen and the Mearns. The result was that Donald retired to the Castle of Dingwall, where he was besieged and forced to yield his pretensions, while the Earl of Buchan retained the titles and estates of Ross until slain at Verneuil in 1424. Donald of the Isles died in 1423, and when James I. returned from captivity he allowed the succession to the Earldom to Lady Margaret Lesley, who had two sons to the Lord of the Isles, viz., Alexander, designed "Master of Ross" during the lifetime of his mother, and Bishop Angus. She also had a daughter Mariot, married to Alexander Sutherland of Dunbeath.

Alexander, the next Earl, as "Master of Ross," in 1425 was one of the jury at the trial of the Duke of Albany. His mother, the Countess

Seal of Alexander de Yle, Lord of the Isles and Earl of Ross, 1410.

incited him to rebel; he burnt Inverness, but, being defeated soon after, was forced to sue for peace, which was refused. After holding out for a considerable time he threw himself upon the King's mercy in 1429, when he appeared before the King and Court, at the altar at Holyrood, clad only in shirt and drawers. At

* This date proves that Donald was certainly more than forty-five years of age at his death (1423). (See page 47).

the Queen's intercession his life was spared. He was confined in Tantallon Castle until pardoned in 1431; being afterwards appointed Warden of the North. In 1445 he entered into a treasonable league with the Earls of Douglas and Crawford, but died at Dingwall on 4th May, 1448, before the conspiracy was matured, leaving by his wife Elizabeth (sister of the Earl of Huntly) a son John, and two daughters, Margaret and Florence. Margaret (?) married John, Earl of Sutherland, while Florence married Lachlan Mackintosh, of that Ilk. The Earl of Ross, had also two illegitimate sons—Celestine of Lochalsh, and Hugh, the ancestor of the Macdonalds of Sleat. Their notorious illegitimacy is conclusively proved by the fact that they were of age and married while their brother John, Earl of Ross, was still a minor.

John, Earl of Ross, when in his seventeenth year, was urged into rebellion by Livingston of Callendar (who afterwards became his father-in-law), and took part in the risings of the great Douglases, creating a diversion in their favour by seizing the royal castles of Urquhart, Inverness, and Ruthven. An interview between him and the Earl of Douglas in 1453, resulted in the naval demonstration by the men of the Isles, under Donald Balloch of Islay, against Ayr. His rebellion was, however, suppressed, and the Lordship of Ross was annexed to the Crown in 1455. He was restored in 1456, and appointed Warden of the Marches, but his treason became such that it could not be tolerated. In 1462 he treated with the English King as an independent prince, and, along with the Earl of Douglas, made a remarkable treaty with Edward, whereby they became his vassals. Edward was, in return, to assist them to conquer Scotland, which was then to be partitioned between the Earls and Donald Balloch.

The Earl of Ross was not slow to act up to the letter of this agreement. He sent his illegitimate brother Celestine to plunder Inverness and Moray, which was done so effectually that large districts were laid waste. For years the north was kept constantly in the ferment of rebellion, and in 1474 energetic measures were decided upon. Ross usurped the King's authority, besieged the Castle of Rothesay, and laid waste Bute. The Earls of Huntly and Athol were therefore commanded to march against the rebels, and, driven from place to place, Ross was compelled to surrender. His Earldom was forfeited to the Crown for ever; and it was not to be alienated save to the younger sons of the Sovereign. John was created a Lord of Parliament as Lord of the Isles, and, as he had no legitimate sons, his natural sons were to be primary heirs. By his wife, Elizabeth Living-

stone, he had a daughter, Elizabeth, living in 1506.

The Lord of the Isles was still pursued by evil fortune, for he was deprived of his estates by his lawless son Angus, whose tragic end was accomplished by an Irish harper, at Inverness. (This Angus had a natural son, Donald Dubh, who set up as Lord of the Isles in 1503 and 1544). John was finally forfeited in 1493, on account of his own treason, and that of his nephew Alexander of Lochalsh son of Celestine, and thus it came about that the

" Lord of the Isles, whose lofty name
A thousand bards have given to fame,
The mate of monarchs, and allied
On equal terms with England's pride,"

died, in 1498, a royal pensioner at the Abbey of Paisley. Of his daughter Elizabeth, after 1506, nothing is known, so that the legal representation of the great Earls of Ross and Lords of the Isles devolved upon Margaret, the wife of John, Earl of Sutherland. It must be noted, however, that the name of the lady who instituted divorce proceedings against the Earl of Sutherland was "Finvol," while his relict bore the Christian name of Catherine; so that if genealogists are correct in saying that the first wife of Sutherland was a daughter of the Isles, it follows that she conveyed the representation of her family to the Earls of Sutherland.

A Dukedom of Ross was created by James III, in favour of his son James, who resigned the estates from which he derived his title in 1503; and some years later Alexander, the posthumous son of James IV, was created Earl of Ross. In 1503, Donald Dubh, natural son of Angus—the illegitimate son of the last Earl of Ross and Lord of the Isles—set up claims to the latter dignity, but was taken prisoner. After forty years' confinement he again escaped, and in 1544 rose once more in rebellion, assumed the titles of Ross and the Isles, and entered into a treaty with England, dying at Drogheda in the following year.

Between 1503 and 1544 several futile attempts were made by the family of Lochalsh, although of bastard descent, to recover the Lordship of Ross, which they plundered without mercy. The Bishop of Caithness, who, as Chamberlain of Ross, had to hold the Castles of Dingwall and Redcastle against the men of the Isles, for the better defence, secured from the south old "artailzalrie," with which to frighten the natives. The line of Lochalsh terminated with two daughters, one of whom, Margaret, married Alexander of Glengarry, the other becoming the wife of Dingwall of Kildun. As a consequence of this failure of male descendants of Celestine, Donald Gorm—the representative of the kindred illegitimate house of Sleat—appeared as the next claimant for the Earldom of Ross. In 1562, Donald followed Mary Queen of Scots everywhere, begging that he might have the Earldom. He was the great-great-grandson of Hugh of Sleat, and was so much displeased that the title was not conferred on him that he straightway entered into negotiations with the English. The Earldom was revived in 1565, for, on 25th May, Henry Stewart (Lord Darnley) was created Earl of Ross, and on 22nd July of same year the banns of marriage was proclaimed between " Harie Earl of Ross" and Queen Mary. At four o'clock the same afternoon the Earl of Ross was created Duke of Albany, so that the unfortunate Darnley was the last to enjoy the Earldom, which, for feuing purposes, was dissolved from the Crown in 1587.

Æneas Macdonell of Glengarry became a claimant for the dignity, the grounds for his pretensions being that his great-great-grandfather had married the grand-daughter of the bastard Celestine of Lochalsh. Glengarry was ready to go anywhere and do anything for Charles I., provided he were made Earl of Ross. On 30th July, 1646, he wrote to King Charles from Castle Leod, professing loyalty and obedience, " beinge only desyrus that your majesty may kno of a particulare faithful servand to receive and act your commandis." At the Restoration, on account of his services, he was created Lord Macdonell and Aros by King Charles II., who, it seems by the following petition, had granted several warrants creating him Earl of Ross. These did not take effect, the notorious illegitimacy of his descent being probably the reason. Coming to later times, about a century ago, Munro Ross of Pitcalnie made a ridiculous claim upon the Earldom, to which he had as little right by descent as had the Macdonells of Glengarry.

In our own day there are, it appears, designs upon the title and dignity of Ross, but how the gentlemen whose names have appeared in the public press, in connection with these, can advance such claims when the heirs general of the Earls of Ross are well known, it is impossible to conceive. No doubt the grounds for their pretentions would prove interesting and instructive. It is sincerely to be hoped that this historic peerage may not meet with the fate of some of our ancient Scots dignities, and be linked with names unworthy to bear the honours of the potent families of De Ros and De Yle, who so frequently measured their strength with their sovereigns.

Lord Macdonell petitioned the " King's most excellent majesty " thus :—

" Your Majesty's petitioner having, in consideration of his service and sufferings, for your crown and interest, received from your Sacred Majesty several warrants under your royal hand and signet for creating the Petitioner Earl of Ross, and bestowing upon him the rents and revenues thereof, with several other benefits promised to the Petitioner on the above considerations as they appear written by your Majesty's own royal hand or your late Secretary Sir Richard Nicholas who very well knoweth the grounds and reasons that induced your Majesty to confer the said grants upon him. That the Earl of Lauderdale, principal Secretarie for Scots affairs, being in Scotland, and the time of his return uncertain and the Petitioner very much straitened by the long-continued attendance here ; that for your Sacred Majesty's better information of the Petitioner's services and sufferings, and how far your Majesty is concerned in Honour and justice to make effectual the above warrants and promises to him, by such further authority as your Majesty shall think fit to the said Earl of Lauderdale by whom your Majesty's further pleasure in your petitioner's behalf must regularly be despatched.

" The Petitioner most humbly requests, that your Majesty would be graciously pleased to refer examination of above-mentioned warrants and others to Sir Edward Nicholas, or other Minister of State as to your Majesty shall seem meet, so that your Majesty may better understand the equity of your Petitioner's desires, and thereby with the greater ease despatch authority to the Earl of Lauderdale as shall seem meet for making effectual the said warrants and royal promises, and the petitioner will ever pray."

" Whitehall, 6th September, 1663."

NOTE. " His Majesty's pleasure is to refer examination of the above warrants to Sir Henry Bennett, Secretary of State, and report the whole matter to his Majesty, with his opinion what is fit further for his Majesty to do for making good the contents thereof."

(CONCLUDED).

CLAN MACKAY NOTES.

THE MACKAY CHIEF AND TECHNICHAL EDUCATION.—At the inaugural meeting in connection with the Scottish Association for the Promotion of Technical Education, held in Edinburgh recently, Lord Reay was elected president. His lordship has always taken a deep interest in this important national subject.

A MACKAY BIOGRAPHY.—Many Highlanders will be glad to learn that the talented sister of the late " Mackay of Uganda" has just published another interesting volume, dealing with a Mackay missionary, entitled " A. Mackay Ruthquist ; or, Singing the Gospel among Hindus and Gonds." It is published at 6s. by Hodder & Stoughton, London.

DEATH OF THE PRINCE OF WALES'S PIPER.—Donald Mackay, for twenty years piper to the Prince of Wales, died on December 30th, and his remains were interred in Kensal Green Cemetery. Donald Mackay was admitted to be the best piper of his time. He came of a family of famous pipers—his father and grandfather and five of his uncles were all pipers of repute. As we hope to give a recent portrait of this notable member of the clan, in Highland costume, in our next issue, with a short account of his career, we need say nothing further regarding him in the meantime.

CAMANACHD.

MR. HUGH MacCORQUODALE,
Hon. Secretary, Glasgow Cowal Shinty Club.

MR. H. MacCorquodale, whose portrait is given above, was born at Melfort, Argyllshire, in January, 1866. While very young he removed along with his parents to Furnace, Lochfyneside, and in this well-known nursery of shinty players he acquired that dexterity of handling the *caman* which can only be acquired by frequent practice. Coming to Glasgow in 1883, his love of the game led him to join the Cowal Club, then playing on Cessnock Park, Govan, and from that time he has always taken a leading part in promoting its interests. His play in matches, in the forward division of the team, showed him to be worthy of his place, and he has taken part in most of the club's engagements, in which he has seldom failed to score. Among the many games in which he has assisted the Cowal may be mentioned the cup ties, and various friendly matches with Glasgow Shinty Club, including that played at Glasgow Exhibition, the match at Edinburgh with Inveraray, for which he holds the silver badge, the final cup tie with Furnace, and more recently the friendly matches with Edinburgh Camanachd and Oban, the famous match with Kingussie, and, lastly, the recent match with Ballachulish. While thus assisting his club on the field, Mr. MacCorquodale also took his full share in the working and carrying on of his club's affairs. After filling the office of treasurer for two years he was elected to the secretaryship, a post to which he has been unanimously re-elected during the past four years. No small share of the success attending the club's annual concerts has been due to his efforts, and in the getting up of a club-house, which has recently been erected free of debt, he took a leading part.

Mr. MacCorquodale takes great interest in all Highland matters, and was for some years a member of the Glasgow Highland Regiment.

Glasgow.   DUNCAN MORRISON.

GLASGOW COWAL—NEW YEAR'S DAY MATCH.—The ancient custom of playing a shinty match on New Year's Day was duly observed by the members of this club. The day being fine, there was a good attendance of players, including several members of the old Camanachd Club. Teams were chosen by Messrs. John Mackay (president), and Donald MacCorquodale. The sides being well matched the game was kept up with great spirit for two hours, and resulted in a win for the Mackay team by 6 hails to 5. Thereafter the members adjourned to the new club house, where seasonable congratulations were indulged in.

LONDON NORTHERN COUNTIES CAMANACHD CLUB *versus* GLASGOW COWAL.—London Scotsmen had a treat on Boxing Day, 26th Dec., which they have not enjoyed for a number of years, and the anticipation of this may account for the large number of spectators who turned out on Wimbledon Common to witness the match between the above well-known shinty clubs. The day was all that could be desired, although perhaps a trifle too warm for the players. On the ball being thrown up it was taken in hand by the Cowal men, and it was soon apparent that they had the game in their own hands. In the first half the Cowal scored seven goals, and in the latter half increased this to ten, which gave them a very decisive victory. However, the London men played a very plucky game, but they lacked the scientific combination of the Cowal. They had evidently given little attention to " passing " in their practice games, and this defect told heavily against them in the contest. The London players are a splendid body of men, stalwart in body and fleet of foot, and it only requires the introduction of a little science into their style of play, and a few more matches with leading clubs, to make their opponents who would give a good account of themselves. It was, indeed, plucky of them to invite such a notable club to visit them in London, and we trust that they will be no way disheartened by their defeat, but prepare themselves to play the Cowal next year, when we have no doubt but the match will be more evenly contested. In the evening the London club entertained the Cowal team to dinner in the Horse Shoe Restaurant Superintendent Colin Chisholm (chief) in the chair —and a very pleasant hour was spent, enlivened with speeches and songs. For our own part, we enjoyed the trip very much, and hope that next year we shall have the pleasure of accepting another invitation from the London N.C.C. Club.

GLASGOW COWAL *versus* BALLACHULISH.—On the Saturday following the London match, the Cowal played the Ballachulish Club at Moray Park, Glasgow. During the first half the game was stubbornly contested, the " Bally " men having the benefit of the wind. Indeed, all through, the match was exciting, both teams exerting themselves to the utmost. At half-time each club had scored one goal. On sides being changed, the Cowal men, having now the advantage of the wind, soon showed their superiority, and most of the play was in the vicinity of the Ballachulish goal. The visitors, however, assisted by an excellent goal keeper, played a splendid defensive game, and several times broke away and raided the Cowal territory, but without success. The Cowal men had them latterly fairly in hand, and added two goals to their score, thus winning by 3 hails to 1. The "Bally" men proved themselves hardy and smart players, and seem quite able to give a good account of themselves anywhere. In the evening the Cowal Club entertained their visitors to supper in the Victoria Restaurant, Mr. John Mackay (president), editor of the *Celtic Monthly*, in the chair. Speeches were delivered, and Gaelic and English songs rendered by members of both clubs.

NEWS OF THE MONTH.

CALEDONIAN PIPERS' CLUB, EDINBURGH. The members of this club held their usual winter competition in the Royal Gymnasium Hall, Fettes Row, on Wednesday, 27th ult., for medals presented by the chief, P. Cameron, Esq., Corrychoillie. There was a large attendance, and the various prizes were keenly contested for. The prize-list was as follows:— *Marches, Strathspeys, and Reels* 1, Piper Robb, 1st A. and S. Highlanders; 2, T. Sutherland; 3 John Wilson; 4, M. MacRae, piper to Corrychoillie. *Dancing*—Sword Dance 1, W. Gunn; 2, D. Kerr; 3, T. Sutherland. At the conclusion of the competition dancing was engaged in by the whole company, and a very pleasant evening was spent.

CLAN MACKAY SOCIETY.—The December meeting of this society was held in the Trades' Hall, and took the form of an entertainment. Mr. Alex. Mackay, V.-P., Charing Cross, occupied the chair, and the hall was crowded. Mr. W. G. Campbell, solicitor, Edinburgh, gave a most interesting lecture on "The Mackay Country," and exhibited a large number of fine lime-light views of Lord Reay's country, and also the more southern part of Sutherlandshire. As the majority of the audience were natives of the districts described, it need hardly be said that the views shown on the screen proved of absorbing interest. He also showed portraits of a number of prominent members of the clan, each likeness being immediately recognised by the audience. The after part of the evening was devoted to a musical entertainment, in which members of the clan and friends took part. The proceedings were thoroughly enjoyed by all present, and the council intend arranging for others of a similar nature.

CLAN GREGOR SOCIETY—The monthly meeting of this society for December was held in the North British Station Hotel, Glasgow.—Mr. Alex. M'Gregor, hon. secretary, in the chair. There was a large attendance. Mr John MacGregor, solicitor, Greenock, delivered a lecture on "The MacGregor Country," illustrated by a splendid series of photographic views taken by himself. Mr. MacGregor described the extensive country which belonged at one time to the clan who were "nameless by day," and touched upon the salient points of their romantic history. A series of portraits of distinguished members of the clan was also shown on the screen; and the society's piper gave a selection of appropriate pipe music. The entertainment was greatly enjoyed, and a hearty vote of thanks was awarded the lecturer for the pleasure he had given the meeting.—THE JANUARY MEETING of the society took the form of a dinner, which was held in the N.B. Station Hotel, on January 9. Mr. Atholl MacGregor, Dunkeld (president), occupied the chair, and Captain A. Ronald MacGregor discharged the duties of croupier. After enjoying a hearty dinner, the evening was devoted to speeches and music. In proposing the toast of the "Clan Gregor," the chairman made a most interesting speech, in which he referred briefly to the society and and its work, and the toast was drunk with enthusiasm. The health of the young chief, Sir Malcolm MacGregor, Bart., was also honoured. Speeches were given by Captain A. R. MacGregor, Messrs. John MacGregor, B.L., Greenock, John MacGregor, Dr. Scott MacGregor, and other clansmen. In proposing "Kindred Societies," Dr. MacGregor referred kindly to the *Celtic Monthly*, and in replying, Mr. John Mackay, secretary, Clan Mackay, suitably acknowledged the compliment, and congratulated the Clan Gregor on the splendid work which they had accomplished, and also gave an account of the society of his own clan. A most enjoyable evening was spent.

HIGHLAND NOTES AND QUERIES.

BAYONETS AT CULLODEN.—Can any of your readers inform me in what way the bayonet was fixed in the guns used by the English and Highland armies at Culloden, as I have a gun which belonged to Fleming's Regiment, and it has not the usual catch for fixing the bayonet to, having only the small sight-point at the muzzle?—SLIOCHD ALLAN.

FRESWICK CASTLE.—As Mr. Sutherland appears to be conversant with the history of the old Sinclair proprietors of this Castle, perhaps he may be able to kindly inform me at what date the estate passed out of the hands of its previous proprietors, the Mowats; what were the Christian names of the last Mowat and first Sinclair owner; and the reason of disposal? Any information will oblige.—SLIOCHD ALLAN.

THE M'LURES.—Can you give me, through your magazine, any information as to the M'Lures; who or what were they; were they a clan by themselves, or a sept of one; were they originally Scotsmen or Irish?—KILEARNAN.

[Nothing is *positively* known as to the origin of this name. Conjectures may be made. It is not Highland; it is Galwegian. M'Cliver is the same as it. It may be derived thus—Mac Gill' iver, St. Ivar's servant. Dr. MacLauchlan, in his "Celtic Gleanings," has it "M'Gilleabhar, the servant of the book." ED.]

Is the word "baileach," on page 187, *Celtic Monthly*, correct? MacIntyre sought to convey the idea that the men, birds, and deer had *wholly* left the place. "Baileach," as I understand it, is the valley between two hills.—BALGAN-FEOLACH.

LORD REAY,
Chief of the Clan Mackay.

THE CELTIC MONTHLY:
A MAGAZINE FOR HIGHLANDERS.
Edited by JOHN MACKAY, Kingston.

No. 6. Vol. II.]　　　　　MARCH, 1894.　　　　　[Price Threepence.

LORD REAY.

THE Lords of Reay had long been silent in the land. Eric, the 7th Baron, had alienated the territory known for ages as the Mackay Country, and his immediate successors, the 8th and 9th Barons had lived so much in retirement that many people imagined that the title had either become extinct, or had fallen into abeyance. It is not necessary to enter into an account of the causes which led to this long keeping in the background, but I will simply state the fact that from the death of George, the 5th Lord Reay, in 1768, until the present peer succeeded to the title in 1875, no Chief of the Mackays had appeared on a public platform in Scotland, or taken his stand as a leader of men. The noble Lord, however, a brief sketch of whose career I will now endeavour to present, gives promise, though in a very different way, to be as famous a man in the annals of the clan as his renowned ancestor, who, with his "invincible old regiment," as Gustavus Adolphus described it, did so much for the cause of Protestantism and freedom in the thirty years' war; and, in acknowledgment of his great services, was, in 1628, raised to the peerage, with the title of Lord Reay. The first Lord Reay was a man of war, whose sphere was the battlefield; the present Lord Reay is an educationalist of the highest order, whose sphere is among the advisers of the nation.

The Right Honourable Sir Donald James Mackay, a Baronet of Nova Scotia, 11th Baron Reay of Reay in the peerage of Scotland; Baron Reay of Durness in that of the United Kingdom; and Baron Mackay of Ophemert, in Holland, is descended from Brigadier-General the Honourable Æneas Mackay, second son of John, 2nd Lord Reay, and was born in Holland, 22nd December, 1839. He studied at the University of Leyden, a seat of learning much frequented by Scotsmen in former days, and finished his course there in 1861, taking the degree of Doctor of Civil Law. After leaving the University he entered the Netherlands Foreign Office, and was for some time an *attaché* to the Netherlands Legation in London, and resided there from 1862 till 1865. From that period, until his naturalisation as a British subject in 1877, much of his time was passed in England and Scotland, and when he finally decided to settle in the latter country, it was not a surprise to his friends in Holland, though a disappointment to many of them. I will here remark that the religion and character of the people in Scotland and Holland have much in common; our educational system, too, resembles that of Holland more than it does that of England; and, from my own personal acquaintance with Dutchmen, I should say that it is as easy for a native of Holland to adapt himself to the thoughts, and ways, and habits of life in Scotland as it is for an Englishman to do so; hence it was an easy and a natural transition, on the part of Lord Reay, to come to Scotland and settle in the country. He is an out and out Scot. His own words, spoken at a meeting in Edinburgh, are worth remembering— "I should never have left the land of my birth if Scottish blood had been colder within me."

His father, Baron Æneas Mackay of Ophemert, in Holland, Minister of State and Vice-President of the Council (the King being President), succeeded to the Scottish titles, as 10th Baron Reay, on the death of his kinsman, Eric, the 9th Baron, on the 2nd June, 1875. He did not long possess the honours, however, for he died at the Hague on the 6th March, 1876, much lamented by all who knew him, for he was an eminent Statesman, a devout Christian, and a man of great benevolence.

In 1877 Lord Reay married Mrs. Mitchell (widow of Captain Alexander Mitchell of Stow), a most attractive and gifted woman, fond of science, and remarkable for her sound judgment, a brilliant conversationalist, and altogether one of the most accomplished leaders that adorn society. When not in London, Lord and Lady Reay reside at Carolside, a charming residence in the south of Scotland.

I have mentioned that Lord Reay's Scottish

title dates from 1628. In 1881 he was created a peer of the United Kingdom (which gives him a seat in the House of Lords), when he selected the title of Baron Reay of Durness, thus showing how his heart turned to the old Mackay Country, and the places famous in the history of the clan. One of the favourite residences of the old chiefs was Balnakiel, in Durness.

Lord Reay had not been long settled in Scotland before he began to take a part in public affairs, interesting himself chiefly in educational and social questions. He was much interested in the success of the Edinburgh University tercentenary celebration. His Scottishness was strongly marked on that occasion. I will give an instance. One of the delegates from France had made a speech in the language of his country, and Lord Reay was asked to reply. On rising to do so, he began by saying that he would show how *we Scots had not forgotten the old alliance with France*, and then he proceeded to return thanks on behalf of the University in French. Foreign politics are closely followed by him as well as Indian and Colonial questions.

In 1885 he was appointed Governor of Bombay, and completed his five years' term of office with brilliant success. Not long before leaving India he laid the foundation-stone of a school, to be known as "Lady Reay's Girls' School." At the ceremony one of the native princes made a speech, and among other things said "I cannot help observing that if your Excellency's tenure of office is to be grate-fully remembered for one thing more than another, it will be for the singularly remarkable fact that while your Excellency—a known educationalist yourself—is a strong supporter of scholastic and technical education for our rising youths and artisan classes, Lady Reay has been most unremitting in her pains to ameliorate the intellectual position of the gentler sex by all possible means I do not know if our Presidency ever before was so doubly fortunate." Comment on this high praise of beneficial work is unnecessary.

Lord and Lady Reay returned from India in 1890, and one of their earliest public appearances, after getting back to Scotland, was at the annual gathering of the Clan Mackay Society for that year. They received a most enthusiastic welcome; and his Lordship's address on that occasion was described in the newspapers as being "a model speech, but containing much more thought than is usually found in such addresses." But his speeches are always thoughtful, his style clear and graceful; and on any subject on which he speaks he seldom says a word more than is absolutely necessary. He takes a lively interest in all matters affecting the welfare of the people of Scotland, and especially in everything connected with his clan.

He is not a politician, but a Statesman. I would describe him as an advanced Liberal of a philosophical type, interested more in the promotion of measures that will benefit the Empire and all classes than in promoting sectional interests—one who "prefers measures

LADY REAY.

to men." For the past eighteen months he has been chiefly occupied in the working out of a plan, by a Royal Commission, for the establishment of a Teaching University in London, which has just reported to the Government. He is connected with many important societies and institutions; is President of the Royal Asiatic Society, and of the Society for Promoting Secondary Education in Scotland; Vice-President of the International Colonial Institute. The Universities of St. Andrews and Edinburgh also conferred on him the degree of LL.D.; and in 1884 he was elected Lord Rector of the University of St. Andrews. To commemorate his governorship, his statue will be erected in Bombay. It has just been finished by the eminent sculptor, Mr. A. Gilbert, R.A., who has bestowed on it a lavish amount of labour, and produced a real work of art.

The two striking portraits which accompany this sketch give a good idea of the personal appearance of Lord and Lady Reay. As Chief of the Clan Mackay, his lordship appropriately appears in the Highland dress.

Wiesbaden, Germany.   JOHN MACKAY.

CAROLSIDE, BERWICKSHIRE—RESIDENCE OF LORD REAY

CLAN MACKENZIE SOCIETY.—The annual gathering took place in the in the Oddfellows' Hall, Edinburgh—Mr. James Mackenzie, F.S.A., in the chair. The chairman delivered an address upon the past history of the clan. An excellent concert and assembly followed.

GLASGOW CELTIC SOCIETY.—The annual general meeting was held in the Religious Institution Rooms—Colonel Menzies in the chair. The directors in their report stated that relief had been given to 50 deserving applicants, and two bursaries had been awarded to Gaelic-speaking students. Vacancies in the list of office-bearers were then filled up.

THE ISLAY ASSOCIATION held their annual social gathering in the Waterloo Rooms, on the 7th ult., Mr. Arch. Sinclair, Celtic Press, in the chair. There were 1500 persons present, the Grand Hall being uncomfortably crowded. The chairman delivered an eloquent and patriotic address upon "Green grassy Islay," the latter part of his speech being in Gaelic. He received a most enthusiastic reception. Addresses were also delivered by other distinguished Islaymen. The concert was very enjoyable, and the assembly was also well attended. This gathering was by far the largest of the season, the result, no doubt, of the chair being occupied by such a popular Celt as Mr Sinclair.

SHOTTY DOOLT'S COURTSHIP.

By Reid Tait.

(Continued from page 87).

HE knelt thus for more than a hour and and the strong man's voice was broken with sobs. This was the romance of his life, the one flower in his barren existence. He had never had any near relationships, no mother or sister's tender hand had ever made life smoother for poor Shotty. On Ailsa he had lavished all the love of his strong heart, and without her he would be desolate indeed.

At length Shotty grew calmer, and a spirit of resignation came upon him.

"Thou hast taken from me the joy of mine eyes," he said, in the language of Scripture, which rose naturally to his lips, "Thou hast withheld the desire of mine heart. Even so, Lord, for so it seemeth good in Thy sight."

Shotty rose from his knees, feeling calmed and strengthened, but with a face that looked as if he had passed through a mortal sickness.

While this was passing, what were Donald and Ailsa really doing?

Donald had left the Camerons' cottage that afternoon in a passion, bitterly angry and thoroughly surprised at Ailsa for her utter rejection of his proposals. But as he thought it over he resolved to try again. He had avowed his intention of marrying her so openly that it would be very awkward for him if she refused him, and he thought it could not be possible that she really meant it. He joined her coming out of church to renew his offer, and see if he could not prevail upon her. But Ailsa would have none of him, and by the time they had reached her own gate she had succeeded in convincing Donald that she meant what she said.

"I ken hoo it is," he said, relapsing into his native tongue, and forgetting the English which he was acquiring with such pains. "I've heard aboot it. Your thinkin' o' takin' Shotty Doolt. A gran' man him, wi' not even a name o' his own to give you. SHOTTY!" and Donald Fraser expressed whole volumes of contempt and scorn in this last word.

Ailsa raised her head proudly, and her blue eyes flashed.

"I'm no ashamed o' his name," she said, "I'm trying to show how she honoured and respected the man who had been a true friend to her, she added defiantly "Its a fine name, I love it and and himsel' too," and then rather ashamed of her avowal, she ran away into the house and up to a closet which she called her own room and, although not one of the crying sort, she cried as if her heart would break, exactly why, she did not know.

Ailsa expected Shotty that evening but he did not come. Then came Monday, and she thought he would be round when he came back from the fishing, but she was again disappointed.

On Tuesday evening Ailsa thought she would go out. She understood what was the matter with Shotty and longed to put things right.

"I'm going out mither," she said to Mrs. Cameron, who sat, pale and thin, but with a look of returning health on her face, in the arm chair that Shotty had bought for her, "I'll no be lang."

"If you see Shotty, tell him I'm wearyin' for him," said Mrs. Cameron.

Ailsa went down the village street and on to the beach. It was tea time and the place was deserted. Not quite deserted though, for at a short distance she could see the figure of a man. It was Shotty, sitting beside his boat, mending a net. At least he had the net in his hands, but he was doing nothing to it, he was looking out upon the sea with a pained expression on his brown face that touched the girl.

"Shotty," she said, as she came up behind him, and he sprang up with a start.

"What's been ailin' ye that you havena been to see us lately?" she asked reproachfully. "Mither has been askin' for ye."

The gladness died out of his eyes, it was her mother then that wanted him! Ailsa saw her mistake, she had not meant to give this impression.

"I've been busy," he said, "but I'll be along to night to see her, since she wants me."

"I want ye too, Shotty," said the girl, her cheeks growing pink. Their usual position was reversed now, Ailsa was shy, but Shotty had gone through so much lately that he was lifted above such a surface emotion.

"I'm thinkin, lassie, you ha ither friends now, ye'll no be wantin' me."

"I've nae ither friends, Shotty," she replied. "I'm no sae fickle as that I hope"

Shotty came close to her and laid his big brown hand on her shoulder. No one was in sight and there was no sound but the beating of the waves on the sea shore.

"Ailsa," he said almost hoarsely, "dinna play wi' me, lass. I canna bear it!"

"I'm no playin' wi you," said Ailsa, fairly bursting into tears, and hiding her burning face on his breast, and--

Well, and Shotty Doolt's reward, full measure, pressed down and running over, had come at last.

CONCLUDED.

LACHLAN MACLEAN, COLL,

AUTHOR OF "THE HISTORY OF THE CELTIC
LANGUAGE," "ADHAMH AGUS EUBH," &c.

BY FIONN.

IT is questionable if we who live in an age when matters Celtic are in the ascendant are sufficiently grateful to those who, during the denationalising period covered by the closing decades of the past century and the opening ones of the present, drew together the dying embers of the Gaelic fire and fanned the flickering flame of Celtic sentiment. It is impossible now to make up a complete muster-roll of those patriots who were doubtless regarded, even by their friends, as a forlorn hope. Occupying a leading place in this patriotic band was one whose name at least is familiar to many, but regarding whom little else is known to the ordinary reader.

Lachlan MacLean, the author of the Gaelic work, "Adhamh agus Eubh," and several other works, was born at Arnabost, Coll, Argyllshire, in 1798. He received his education in his island home, and when quite a young man came to Glasgow, and was received into the employment of Mr. Daniel Cook, a native of Arran, who had a hosiery shop at 23 Argyle Street. When Mr. Cook retired, in 1829, Mr. MacLean purchased his business, carrying it on in the same premises till 1841. An advertisement in

ARNABOST, COLL, BIRTH-PLACE OF LACHLAN MACLEAN.

"Cuairtear nan Gleann" for June, 1841, states that Mr. MacLean, having disposed of his hosiery business in Argyle Street, had assumed as a partner Mr. James Picken, and that they had opened a clothier's shop at 92 Queen Street, under the firm of MacLean & Picken. The co-partnery, which did not prove a profitable one, ended in 1843. About this time Mr. MacLean's health gave way. He started a little bookshop in the Argyle Arcade, but it did not prove a success. Through the intercession of his friend, Dr. Norman MacLeod, St. Columba Church, and the influence of the Members of Parliament for the city, Mr. MacLean got an appointment in the General Post-Office. His health broke down, however, shortly after he entered the service, and he died at his own residence, 49 Oxford Street, Glasgow, 22nd November, 1848, and was buried in the Southern Necropolis of that city. Mr. MacLean left a widow and five of a family — four daughters and one son. The son, Norman MacLeod MacLean, and two daughters, Agnes and Jane, are still alive, and resident in Australia.

Mr. MacLean had a taste for literature, and contributed regularly to the Gaelic periodicals of his time. He also published some seven or eight separate works. His articles in the "Teachdaire Gaelach" (1829-31), "An Teachdaire ùr Gàidhealach" (1835-36)—of which he was said to be editor—"Cuairtear nan Gleann" (1810-43), will be found over such signatures as

"Mac Talla," "Eòghan Og," "An Gael anns a' bhaile," and "Am Bàirdeasach Bàn." As early as 1828 he edited a small collection of Gaelic hymns for a blind man in Skye. The work is called "Dàin Spioradail le Eoin Morison d'n Eilein Sgiathanach."[*] This work contains three original compositions by the editor, he having been allowed to insert them therein. His first literary venture was in 1833, when he published "An Historical Account of Iona." This work reached four editions. The third (1838) and the fourth (1841) editions are identical, differing materially from the first and second editions. In 1837 he published the work which secured him literary fame among Highlanders, "Adhamh agus Eubh Craobh sheanachais nan Gael." The following year, 1838, he published a little work, entitled "Sketches of St. Kilda, taken down for the greater part from the oral narration of Rev. N. Mackenzie, clergyman of the island." In 1840 he wrote "The History of the Celtic Language," being to a great extent a translation of his Gaelic work "Adhamh agus Eubh." In the same year he translated into Gaelic a little work entitled "The Life of Andrew Dunn." This work had been previously translated (1829) by P. MacFarlane.[†] In 1845 he published a pocket manual of etiquette in Gaelic, called "Maighister na' Modhannan." In the same year "The Native Steamboat Companion" was published anonymously, but there is ample internal evidence to show that it emanated from the pen of the author of "The History of the Celtic Language." It is said that he translated Dugald Buchanan's hymns into English, but the translations do not seem to have been published in a collected form. That he was well qualified for such a task is evident from the excellent translation he made of Evan Mac Coll's poem, "Màiri."[‡] He also composed several songs and poems—some in English and some in Gaelic which are to be found in the periodical literature of his day. When Dr MacLeod was minister of Campsie, he instituted, in 1828, the Glasgow University Ossianic Society, for the benefit of Highland students. Mr. MacLean was elected an Honorary Member, or Fellow, and took an active interest in its deliberations. Dr. MacLeod (Caraid nan Gàidheal) came to Glasgow from Campsie in 1835, and he soon secured Mr. MacLean as one of his most loyal supporters and hearty co-workers in the Celtic field. Mr. MacLean, who was a member of the Secession Church, left that body and joined Dr. MacLeod's

congregation, where he was afterwards ordained an elder. Dr. MacLeod found in Mr. MacLean a man after his own heart, so full of Celtic enthusiasm, and so anxious to spend and be spent in the service of his fellow-Highlanders, and his shop at 23 Argyle Street became a Celtic rendezvous, where such literary Highlanders as Dr. MacLeod, John MacKenzie, of the "Beauties of Gaelic Poetry," and Evan MacColl, the Lochfyne bard, met and exchanged views.

Mr. MacLean is described by one who knew him well as being, "if anything, under the ordinary standard, rather square and thick set, with a very pleasant, open countenance, frank, free, and hearty in his manner—a most genial and amusing companion. He had a ready wit, with a keen sense of humour." In a description of the complimentary dinner given to Dr. Norman MacLeod in 1830, contributed by Mr. MacLean to the "Teachdaire Gaelach," he refers to "Mac Talla" (himself) as follows:—Cnapairneach làidir, tuiceil de dh'fhior Ghàidheal a mhuinntir Eilean Chola mar chuala mi; agus air m' fhacal firinneach chair e dheth gu deas[*] (a strong, stout, sturdy lump of a true Highlander belonging to the island of Coll).

Mr. MacLean wrote his mother-tongue idiomatically, with great force and considerable grace of diction, while his style of English leaves little to be desired. Indeed he was one of the few who could write Gaelic as if he knew no English, and English as if he knew no Gaelic. His love and enthusiasm for Gaelic amounted to a passion, as the following incidents will illustrate:—When he lay dying intimation was sent to St. Columba Church, as was the custom, that he should be remembered in the prayers of the congregation. This intimation was intended for the forenoon Gaelic service, but by some mistake it was delayed till the English service in the afternoon. The person entrusted with this message returned home in the evening, and was asked by Lachlan if he was prayed for at the Gaelic service. When informed that it was only at the English service that he was prayed for he looked astonished, and heaving a heavy sigh exclaimed—"Cha dean e feum sam bith" (It can do no good). It is said that when on his deathbed, and so low that he was thought to be both speechless and unconscious, some one called, and spoke Gaelic in his presence. His ear caught the sound, he roused himself, and with an effort exclaimed, "Cànain mo dhùthcha chuala mi aon uair eile thu" (My native tongue, once more I have heard thy tones)—and shortly afterwards passed quietly away to join the assembly of "just men made perfect."

* Reid's "Bibliotheca Scoto-Celtica," p. 96.
† Reid's "Bibliotheca Scoto-Celtica," p. 139.
‡ Poems and Songs by Evan MacColl (Toronto, 1883), p. 111.

* "An Teachdaire Gaelach," Vol. ii., p. 188.

THE LAST MACDONALDS OF ISLA.

By CHARLES FRASER-MACKINTOSH, F.S.A. (Scot.).

PART IV.—*(continued from page 92)*

VII.—ARCHIBALD succeeded his father James Macdonald, no doubt so called, seeing the name had not occurred before, after the Earl of Argyle. In 1564, during his father's lifetime, he received a charter of the extensive barony of Bar, in Kintyre, wherein he is designed son and apparent heir of James Macdonald of Dunyvaig. This charter included the 30-merk land of Sunart. The only document I have connected with Archibald is precept of Clare Constat, signed by Archibald, 5th Earl of Argyle, in favour of Archibald Macdonald of Dunyvaig and the Glens, as heir of his late father, James, for infefting him in the lands of Ardnamurchan. The precept bears that James died in the reign of Henry and Mary (29th July, 1565-10th February, 1567). The precept is signed by the Earl, and has his seal attached, but neither place, witness, nor date, except "one thousand five hundred and sixty - —— years," the indication inferring it was prepared in the reign of Henry and Mary, and if, as is recorded, James Macdonald was taken prisoner on 2nd May, 1565, he must have survived until after 29th July of that year. The date of Archibald's death is uncertain, but in his time, as well as that of his father and grandfather, the family estates were built up anew, and seemed to be firmly re-established. Frequent mention is made of a third brother of Archibald's, no doubt the younger son (Archibald being then dead) referred to by Lady Tyrone in her negotiations with England, whom she was willing to have the Irish estates and be subject to Queen Elizabeth. On the other hand, the English, to punish Sorley Buie and frustrate his schemes, gave promises of the Glens to Angus and his son, who, however, elected to transact with Sorley, and ultimately, as I have said, Sorley came to final terms with Queen Elizabeth. Archibald Macdonald was succeeded by

VIII.—Angus Macdonald, who received from Archibald, 5th Earl of Argyle, a precept of Clare Constat, in Ardnamurchan, as heir of his father, James, signed 'Ard Ergyle,' dated Edinburgh, 16th May, 1569, of which a *fac-simile* is here given. The seal, natural size, in fine preservation, is also given. Angus also

CHARTER GRANTED BY ARCHIBALD, 5th EARL OF ARGYLE, 1569.

received a precept for infeftment in these lands, as heir of Archibald Macdonald, the propinquity being left blank. This charter is dated at Duart, 10th October, 1570, the witnesses being Dougall Campbell of Auchinbreck, James Campbell of Ardkinglass, John, Bishop of the Isles, Alexander Macnaughton of Dunondaralbie, John Stewart, and others. The seal is gone. Gregory says that Angus's name first appears in 1573, but he began making up titles, as shown above, in 1569. He succeeded to a great estate, but, pursued by ill fate, mingled with folly, died practically a beggar. The unravelment of his complicated career is too wide for these papers, and some of the more salient points only can be touched upon. Angus resolved to strengthen his influence by entering into bonds of friendship with men of consequence and septs of fighting men, extending as far north as Inverness.[*] The first date I have is one with James Lamont of Inveryne, dated Towart, 1st September, 1579, and is as follows :—

"At Towart, the first day of August, in the year of God 1569 years. It is appointed, agreed, and ended betwixt the Right Honourable persons underwritten. They are, to say, Angus M'Donill of Dunnieweg, Oge, and Glennis on the one part, and James Lamont of Inveryne on the tother part, as after follows :—That for as meikle as there has been in times past, amity, friendship, and kindness betwixt the said parties houses, and to the effect that the same may continue, in times coming amongst them, the said Angus M'Donill binds and obliges him, by the tenour hereof, to stand ane afald friend to the said James Lawmount and his house, and shall fortify, maintain, and defend them in all and sundry their just actions, causes, and debates against whatsomever in times coming, the authority, and my Lord of Argille only excepted. For the which cause the said James Lawmont, his kin and friends, and their house, binds and obliges them and their heirs to take ane afald part with the said Angus and his house, and to serve and obey him in all and sundry his and their causes, quarrels and debates, lawful and honest, against whatsomever person or persons in times coming, the authority and my Lord Erlle of Argile being excepted, and, in verifica-

tion hereof, both the saids parties, have subscribed this present contract with their subscription manual, day, year, and place above written before these witnesses Archibald vic Angus Ilycht, Johne vic Alexander of Large, Johne Lawmont of Askok Donald Campbell of Auchyrmollen, Archibald Campbell, Capitane of Dunnon, and Robert Stewart of Auchynske, with others diverse. (Signed) Angns M'Connall off Downweag, James Lamont of Inneryne."

The family of Lamont of that ilk is an ancient one, found as early as 1230 holding lands in Killinan of Cowell, and the Inveryne branch, an important one, practically supplanted the head for about a century. In 1548, the names of John Lamont, of Inneryne, and Duncan, his son and heir-apparent, appear, and in 1597 this James Lamont is served heir to his son Robert in the extensive barony of Inneryne, within the Deanery of Glassary. Referring to the witnesses, the Macdonalds of Largie, in Kintyre, descended of Ranald, younger son of Donald Balloch, long held a good position; John Lamont and Robert Stewart, both Askok and Auchynske, lay within the barony of Inneryne; in 1536, Robert Campbell of Auchymyllne, a £5 land, including the mill lying within the old Parish of Dunoon and Bailiary of Cowell, is mentioned; and, in 1571, the Earl of Argyle grants to Archibald Campbell, keeper of the Castle of Dunoon, a piece of land called "The Castle Aiker," lying near the Castle of Dunoon, with the office of steward or bailie of the town of Dunoon, the four-merk lands of Inellan, &c., and, in 1573, this Archibald is styled Captain of Dunoon.

The next bond is with the Clan Allister beg, and it is fortunate that Sir James Macdonald had endorsed the document, "Bond, Clan Allister beg, in Aran, bairnes part of gear and

SEAL OF ARCHIBALD, 5TH EARL OF ARGYLE, 1569.

---

* There was a contract of friendship betwixt Donald Gorme of Sleat, for himself, and taking burden upon him for Angus vic James Lord of Kintyre, on the one part, and Lachlan Mackintosh, Captain of the Clan Chattan, on the other part, executed at Inverness, penult May, 1587.

calpes," thereby indicating the locality, which is not mentioned in the body of the document. This document is very curious, and includes many names of the people inhabiting three hundred years ago the lands of Machrimore, Machribeg, and others on the west side of Arran and Parish of Kilmorie. In the years 1445 to 1450, Ronald vic Alister was tenant under the Crown of considerable lands, rented in all at £13 6s. 8d. and six bolls ferme, whereof Machremore and Achagallane were rented at 40s., and during all these years Ranald paid no rent. In 1455 Donald Balloch paid the island of Arran a hostile visit and some of the crimes for which John Lord of the Isles and Earl of Ross was forfeited in 1475, were stated to be depredations and slaughters committed by him in the Isles of Bute and Arran. The 20-merks land of Shisken, in Arran, was granted by Reginald, son of Somerled, in 1250, to the monks of Sagadull. In 1556, James Macdonald of Isla, who appears to have claimed or possessed these lands, infeft in favour of James, Earl of Arran; and in consideration of his being infeft in the lands of

DUNLUCE CASTLE, AN ANCIENT STRONGHOLD OF THE MACDONALDS IN IRELAND.

Sir Walter Scott, writing to his daughter regarding her contemplated visit to the North of Ireland on 20th July, 1850, says:— "You will be delighted with the Giant's Causeway, and more so, I think, with the old Castle of Dunluce."

(To be continued.)

Saddel, and keeping the place of the same, with its fees and emoluments, by James, Duke of Chatelherault, he (James) bound himself not only to refrain from invasions and slaughters in the island of Arran, but also to defend and maintain the same from invasion by others. Angus Macdonald renewed his father's obligation by bond to John, Lord Hamilton, dated at Hamilton, 20th April, 1591. By the document now given, the Clan Allister beg ("Sliochd Iain our vic Allister") appear to have sought protection of Angus. The giving of calpe was felt as a most grievous tax. I observe that on 25th September, 1591, John dhu vic Allister vic Ranald, for himself, and as taking burden on him for his sons, and his foster-child, Archibald M'Conill, son of Angus M'Conill of Dunivaig, binds himself and them as servants and obedient to John, Lord Hamilton. This sept were styled Clan Allister beg, doubtless to distinguish them from the Clan Allister of Kintyre, descended of Allister, son of Donald, the grandson of Somerled. The heads of this Clan Allister were known as the Macallisters of Loupe.

HIGHLAND NOTES AND QUERIES.

THE CLAN FRASER.—I have been told that the Fraser Clan have the right of keeping their bonnets on before the Queen of Scotland. Is it true? and why?—ELLAN.

GAELIC SONG WANTED.—Will any reader of the Celtic Monthly kindly inform me where I can procure music and words of a Gaelic song, the chorus being:—

"An chuinn thu mi mo chailin donn
Eist is thoir an aire dhomh,
Tha moran dhaoin' am barail cinn
Gur h-og an leannan donnbs' thu."

—OGANACH, Conon.

FRESWICK CASTLE.—I shall reply to "Sliochd Allan" in the order he has put his questions. The estate of Freswick passed out of the hands of the Mowats of Buchollie, and into those of the Sinclairs, in the year 1661. The Christian name of the last proprietor of the name of Mowat was Magnus, and the Christian name of the first proprietor of the name of Sinclair was William. This William was of Ratter, and a grandson of Sir John Sinclair, of

Greenland. The cause of sale was that Magnus Mowat required money to meet his obligations. It has since been in the possession of the Sinclairs.—GEORGE M. SUTHERLAND, Wick.

THE MORRISONS.—In reply to "Balgan-peolach's" enquiry in the January issue, I may say that the Morrisons are a Highland family belonging to Lewis—the famous breves or judges of Torquil of Lewis (16th century). Captain Thomas, in Vol. xii. of the "Transactions of the Society of Antiquaries," discusses them at length. The Gaelic is M'Gille-mhuire—the English is an adaptation to the real English name Morrison—Maurice's son; and on the Perthshire borders of the Lowlands doubtless that is the correct idea. The name is Scotch and English. There is no tartan that I know of—but, doubtless, one can easily be made! The Morrisons are fairly numerous.—IAN BEG.

"BAILEACH." We regret that we have been compelled to hold over two replies to "Balgan peolach" on the definition of the word "Baileach."—ED.

TO CORRESPONDENTS.

All Communications, on literary and business matters, should be addressed to the Editor, Mr. JOHN MACKAY, 17 Dundas Street, Kingston, Glasgow.

TERMS OF SUBSCRIPTION.—The CELTIC MONTHLY will be sent, post free, to any part of the United Kingdom, Canada, the United States, and all countries in the Postal Union—for one year, 4s.

THE CELTIC MONTHLY
MARCH, 1894.

CONTENTS.

A HIGHLAND CLUB.

WE are pleased to notice that a movement has been set on foot in Edinburgh to institute a club in connection with the various Highland societies in that city, which would serve as a common meeting-place for the members of the various clan, county, and other organisations. The proposal is a really useful one, and we trust that it will be heartily taken up by the associations interested.

If such a club is required in Edinburgh, how much more so is it in Glasgow, with its great Highland population, and its numerous Gaelic, clan, county, and other Highland societies. Now, it is a curious fact, that although there are so many of these institutions, few of the members of any one of them know the members of any other society. Of course, the secretaries may be personally acquainted with a few of the office-bearers of kindred societies, but, generally speaking, the members are not. Each society is in this sense exclusive. Now, we are of opinion that a greater intercourse among the members of the various societies would be of mutual benefit to all, and more in accordance with the spirit of the old Highland watch-word, "Highlanders, shoulder to shoulder!" This policy of "isolation" is detrimental to the Highland cause generally, as it is in a greater degree to the organisations interested. In the case of the many clan societies a closer communion among the different clansmen would give rise to a spirit of emulation, and each society would learn something useful in regard to the management of the others. For a long time we have advocated the institution of a club, or some place where the members of all the societies could meet together for mutual benefit. There might be a large reading-room, with several smaller rooms where monthly or committee meetings could be held. A useful library of Highland literature might also be kept here. We were glad to hear this matter discussed in a practical and sensible way at two recent meetings of the Clan Gregor Society, and we trust that it will be considered at the first meetings of the other societies—of which there are nearly one hundred in Glasgow and neighbourhood. We shall be glad to hear from our readers as to the feeling of the various associations, and will publish any short letters on the subject which may be sent to us. If there is a general opinion in favour of the proposal, a meeting of office-bearers could be called, and a suitable scheme readily agreed upon.

WE ARE INDEBTED to Mr. D. T. MacDonald, Calumet, U.S.A., and Mr J. Johnstone, Partick, for the photo-engraving which appears in connection with the sketch of "Lachlan Maclean," by "Fionn:" and also to Mr. William Gordon Campbell, solicitor, Edinburgh, Mr. D. W. Kemp, Edinburgh, and Mr. Angus Mackay, Cambuslang, for the use of negatives and prints of the illustrations to Mr. Mackay, Hereford's, article.

HENRY WHYTE TESTIMONIAL.

WE beg to acknowledge, with thanks, receipt of the following valued subscriptions towards the testimonial to our valued contributor, "Fionn":—John Mackay, C.E., J.P., Hereford, £5 ; C. Fraser-Mackintosh, London, £5 ; Colonel Charles Stewart ("Tigh'n Duin"), £3 3s ; Dr. D. MacGregor, M.P. for Inverness-shire, £1 1s ; Dr. K. N. MacDonald, Gesto Hospital, Skye, £1 1s ; Neil Macleod (the Skye bard), £1 ; Robert Fergnsson, Stirling, £1 ; Professor O'Growney, Maynooth, Ireland, £1 ; A. B., 10s 6d ; D. R. C., 10s 6d ; Dr. H. MacNicol, Dalmally, 10s 6d ; Duncan Reid, Glasgow, 10s 6d ; John MacGregor, Bearsden, 5s ; A. R. MacLeod, Stirling, 5s ; "A Highland Girl," Currie, 2s 6d ; Margaret Mackay, Glasgow, 2s 6d ; Alexander Stewart, Polmont, 1s ; Dugald MacLellan, Falkirk, 1s.

We shall be very glad to receive further subscriptions from our readers, which will be duly acknowledged in our next issue. We trust that the list will be a much larger one than the present.

OUR NEXT ISSUE.

WE will present our readers with a life-like plate-portrait of Sir Malcolm MacGregor, Bart., chief of the clan, who attains his majority in a few months. The portrait represents him in the Highland dress. We will also give finely engraved portraits, with biographical sketches, of the late Dr. A. B. M'Grigor, Glasgow ; Major A. Y. Mackay, Grangemouth ; Mr. Archibald MacMillan (better known as "Jeems Kaye"), Glasgow, chieftain of the Clan MacMillan Society. In addition to these, the continuation of Mr. C. Fraser-Mackintosh's papers on "The Last MacDonalds of Isla" will be illustrated with an engraving of the tombstone of John of Ardnamurchan, and his sister Mariot, in Iona, and fac similes of the Dunyvaig and Bute Bond, and the signatures to a document dated 1603 ; Mr. Mackay, Hereford's, next article will be attractively illustrated with fine views of the Mackay country ; and the editor will contribute a short story of the supernatural, the scene of which is laid in Sutherlandshire, which will also be suitably illustrated. Other interesting contributions and engravings will also appear in our next issue.

TONGUE AND ITS HISTORIC SURROUNDINGS.

By John Mackay, C.E., J.P., Hereford.

Part II.—(*Continued from page* 97).

THE Norsemen having now been expelled from the Reay Country, the Chiefs Alexander, Walter, and Martin successively set themselves to put in order the territory allotted them by William the Lion, and to consolidate their influence over it. They very soon acquired the goodwill and respect of their immediate retainers, and of the surrounding tribes, who, by the protection given them, soon became amalgamated into one clan. Under the sway of these chiefs order and tranquility prevailed, a very different state of affairs compared with the rule of the Norsemen, who were ever warring with each other, ever committing, on the slightest provocation, deeds of violence, assassinations, and murders.

During the rule of Martin in Tongue a great "scare" was created in 1263 by rumours of a great Norse invasion, to avenge their recent expulsion. News at length arrived from Caithness of a Norse landing there, and of a great fleet lying at anchor in Scrabster Roads, ruthless exactions, pillaging and burning of houses being threatened with merciless severity. This was the great fleet of Haco, King of Norway, on its way to disaster and defeat at Largs.

Martin and his clan round about Tongue, being forewarned, were forearmed, in the event

THE "WATCH-HILL," TONGUE—(CNOC-AN FHREACADAIN).

of a Norse invasion on their Bay of Kintail. The cattle were driven into the hills, and all men and youths able to bear arms prepared to oppose by "might and main" any landing that might be attempted. Shortly afterwards the great fleet hove in sight, seen from "Cnoc-an-fhreacadain" (watch hill). Martin had his men ready to oppose a landing and give battle for hearth, home, and country. To their great joy, no doubt, the great fleet sailed past Tongue, and came to anchor in the Bay of Durness. A landing was here effected, but no inhabitants or plunder could be found. The natives, forewarned, took themselves, their cattle, and moveables off into the adjoining hills. Foiled in their expectations of plunder, these remorseless marauders, in revenge, burned twenty hamlets, and demolished a fort on the shore, the ruins of which remain to this day, by the name of "Sean-chaisteal" (old castle). After doing all the injury they could, an injury for which they dearly paid on their return from Largs, the fleet steered away, rounded Cape Wrath, and again anchored opposite "Alisher-beg," on the west of Eddrachilis. This place is now called Old Shore-beg. A landing was here again made, but finding no prey the fleet sailed away for Skye, on through Kyleakin Sound (Caolais-Hacon) towards Mull and Kintyre, sending out parties now and again up the lochs, and everywhere committing terrible ravages. Bute, Arran, Isla, Jura, and Kintyre were ravaged and taken possession of. But their doom was approaching. Winds and storms scattered the fleet; many of the ships were wrecked and the crews drowned. The battle of Largs completed the sad disaster, and put an end to the sovereignty of the kings of Norway over the Sudereys and Hebrides.

Disconcerted with the issue of the battle of Largs, and the loss of more than the half of his fleet and army, disappointed at the repeated disasters which he met with, and crestfallen at the loss of prestige, Haco gloomily ordered a return homewards. He put into the bay now called Portree, in Skye—hence the name—and remained there some days refitting the ships left to him, and at the same time plundering the natives of Skye all round. Again the fleet was put in motion, and rounded Cape Wrath without incident, and put into "Goasfiord" (Loch Eriboll). Here it anchored for several days. A strong party was sent out into the hills to capture cattle. None could be seen. The natives had been on the watch; they drove all away into the inland valleys. The marauders pursued their way and found some in Glengollie, and began to drive them away, when they were intercepted by the natives; a fight, and the Norse rievers retreated into an adjoining valley, now called Strathmore, where they were brought to bay, and the conflict recommenced, ending with their commander, Urra, and all his men being slain, with the exception of one who fled and carried the doleful tidings to Haco. This glen was ever after named Strath-Urra-dal, in memory of the event. It is so named in charters of the 15th and 16th centuries. In recent times it came to be called

RISPOND, LOCH ERIBOLL, SUTHERLAND, IN 1820

Strathmore. Haco having received the news of this fresh disaster ordered sails to be set and steer away to the Orkneys. In crossing the Pentland Firth he lost several of his ships with all their crews; he himself landed safely at Kirkwall, but died soon after in that town.

With the exception of that scare, nothing occurred to alarm or distract the inhabitants of the North. The spirited rule of the successors of William the Lion Alexander II and Alexander III.—caused law and order to prevail in the South and North. The prosperous reign of the latter for thirty-seven years became the theme of poets. Wars, internal and external, had ceased in the land. This was the "golden age" in Scotland, when every yeoman and peasant cultivated their fields and tended their flocks in tranquility and peace; the merchant plied his trade on land and sea without dread or apprehension; commerce, home and foreign, succeeded to an extent hitherto unknown, and Scottish ships were known in almost every principal port in Europe.

The premature death of Alexander III., in the very prime of life and manhood, leaving no male issue, changed all this bright prosperity into chaos and "perplexyte." Wyntoun graphically tells the tale :—

"When Alysandyr, oure king, wes dede
That Scotland led in lawe, and le
Away wes sons of ale and brede
Of wyne and wax, of gamyn and gle.
Oure gold is changed into lede—
Christ-born into virgynyte

Succour Scotland and remede
That stodt is in perplexyte."

And so it was truly.

It was said that on this King's death by falling with his horse over a cliff near Kinghorn, a hurricane blew over Scotland, the like of which "the oldest inhabitant" had not known. Apart from natural phenomena, a political storm arose after the demise of this estimable monarch, that lasted more or less for four centuries. In the long-cherished designs of the kings of England to subject Scotland to their domination. The ambitious and powerful Edward Longshanks saw his opportunity, and grasped it, in the disputed succession to the throne of Scotland. This storm soon burst, and Scotland, even jealous of her civil and religious independence, saw itself overrun by the arrogant nobles and brutal soldiery of Longshanks.

The Scottish nobles, selfish and craven-hearted, bowed their necks to the yoke and swore fealty to Edward. The Scottish yeomen and peasantry gloomily stood aloof till, roused into uncontrollable indignation at the arrogance and oppression of the English, they were prepared to endure any misery sooner than suffer any longer the indignities put upon them by the foreigner. Just at this period uprose, like a meteor, the great patriot Wallace to lead them in a contest with the mighty Edward, to decide whether Scotland could regain its independence. The gallant attempt succeeded for a time, and might have been entirely successful, but at the supreme crisis the Scottish nobility again betrayed their country and bowed their necks to the yoke of foreign domination. Nevertheless, the noble Wallace showed the way to freedom and independence. His mantle, dyed with his blood, fell upon Robert Bruce, and he made the adventure. Foiled at first, defeated, hunted, and chased out of the country, he tried a second time, and succeeded, after many adventures, hair-breadth escapes, and hard fighting, to free Scotland from the hated domination of the Edwards, and the arrogance of the English, but Bannockburn had yet to be fought to give the *coup de grace* forever to the inordinate ambition of the monarchs of England.

Anticipating the final struggle, Bruce prepared for it by a general appeal to the country to arm for the defence of its liberty and independence. The "fiery cross" went through the land from the Mull of Galloway to Cape Wrath.

This fiery summons to all capable of bearing arms to muster at the Torwood to meet the threatening danger soon reached Tongue, and Magnus, the Chief of the Mackays, whose name betokens an affinity with the Norsemen (probably his father, Martin, married a daughter of one of the Earls of that name in Caithness, or a noble in Galloway, in the far south—a slight infusion of the old Vikingr blood in his veins was no detriment in this national crisis)—soon mustered his clan, and saw a goodly array of them ready and willing to follow their chief to the field. Choosing the ablest, he quickly made up the required contingent, and off he and they marched over moor and mountain, hill and dale, till they reached the rendezvous in the Torwood. They were brigaded with other northern Highlanders in the division commanded by the Earl of Ross, and under the orders of the brave Randolph, Earl of Moray, Bruce's nephew and trusty lieutenant, to whom he gave the command of the left wing in the subsequent battle. Here, in the Torwood, they were drilled and practised in all those military evolutions and exercises necessary at that time to make them competent to oppose the warlike opponents they were soon to encounter. During the time thus spent the Mackays of the north made the acquaintance of their brother clansmen of Kintyre and Islay, who were under the command of Angus Og Macdonald of Dunaverty, and with their other clansmen of Galloway, in the division of Edward Bruce, Robert's fiery brother. Hale, hearty fellows well met, claiming kinship as originating from one common stock, they rejoiced to meet together again after the lapse of a century or more, they renewed their acquaintance, formed bonds of friendship that stood for ages, and encouraged each other to fight like heroes in the impending contest, for—

"The storm of war was slowly rolling on,
With menace deep and dread"—

to burst on the banks of Bannock.

SCRABSTEE ROADS AND RUINS OF THE BISHOP'S PALACE, THURSO

(To be continued).

GAELIC AIRS TO LOWLAND SONGS.

By Malcolm MacFarlane.

Continued from page 88.

17. Iorram a' Gheamhraidh—Gloomy Winter's noo awa'. Here again the names suspiciously correspond. It is improbable the air, as now known, was sung to Gaelic words. The tune is known as "Lord Balgonie's favourite" in Neil Gow's collection, where it is termed "a very old Highland tune." It is also claimed as the composition of Alex. Campbell, editor of " Albyn's Anthology" (1783). Whatever its origin, it has most probably been suggested to the composer by a much simpler melody, possibly that which appears at p. 71, Vol. 1., *Celtic Monthly*. That air was given in *Harper's Monthly*, in an article treating of Cape Breton Gaels, as a specimen of their music. It was no doubt carried there by early settlers from the Highlands of Scotland.

18. Mac Dhòmhnuill dhuibh—Lochiel's awa' to France. The Gaelic name may be translated, "Black Donald's Son." "Black Donald" is a Gaelic nickname for The De'il. Parallel to this fact, in Gunn's pipe music the name is *Mac a' bhodaich ladhraich.* This, translated, is "The old hoofed-one's son." The "hoofed-one" is no doubt The De'il again. *Dòmhnull dubh* may, however, have been an historical personage, and the naming of the tune a mere playing upon the words. Burns set his song, "O wert thou in the cauld blast," to this tune.

19. An gunna cutach—Blythe was she but and ben (Burns). This tune is also known as "Andro and his cutty gun." "The cutty gun" translates the Gaelic name. This is suspicious. At the same time, tho air is decidedly Gaelic in style.

20. Bean an taighe 'san robh mi'n raoir—Wat ye wha I met yestre'en ?

21. Muinntir chridhe, Clann a' phearsoin—Macpherson's Lament. To this tune Burns wrote his song, "Macpherson's Farewell."

22. Coille Chnacaidh — Killiecrankie. The Irish claim a tune of this name as theirs. See "Hardiman's Irish Minstrelsy," p. 178, where the composer is said to have been Thomas O'Conellan, died before 1700. The Irish name is "Planxty Davis." But there are two tunes of this name entirely differing from one another. In Maver's collection, p. 126, there is a tune called "Gilliecrankie." This tune suits Dr. Rahoy's song, *Nis o'n chaidh an sgoth na h-uidheam,* and is no doubt the *Coille chnacaidh* he had in his mind when he made the song. The tune is a good one, and there is nothing about it which would invalidate a claim for its being Irish originally. But, in regard to tunes common to Ireland and the Scottish Highlands, it is impossible in a number of cases to judge by anything in the melodies themselves to which country they belong. It is quite good enough to class them as Gaelic airs as against those which are non-Gaelic.

As the air to Dr. Maclachlan's song has been asked for more than once, and as the song is such a good one, I take the liberty of writing it here :—

NIS O'N CHAIDH AN SGOTH 'NA H-UIDHEAM.

Key C.   *With spirit.*

```
| s  ., l  : s  . m | s  ., l  : s  . m |
 Nis o'n chaidh an  |sgoth na h-uidheam,|
 Now our  steady    boat is    read - y,
```

```
| r  . d : d  . m | s        : s        |
 Suidheam air a    |b-ar   -   lar ;
 Get her in - to     mo    -    tiou ;
```

```
| l  ., d¹ : l  . s | l  ., d¹ : l  . s |
 Cuir ibh oig - ear |seòlt - a  sgairteil
 Let him steer who knows no fear up-
```

```
| d¹ ., r¹ : m¹. d¹ | l         : l        |
 De chloinn Airt g'a|stiùr  -  adh.
 on the trackless    o  -  cean ;
```

```
| m¹. s¹ : r¹. m¹ | d¹ ., r¹ : m . d¹ |
 Nall am   botul  |lion an     copau ;
 Fetch the cup and fill it    up, un-
```

```
| s  ., l  : d¹ . m | s        : s        |
 Olam  -  aid le    |dùr  -  achd :
 to this toast re - spoud  -  ing :
```

```
| l  . l : d¹. d¹ | r¹. r¹ : m¹ ., |
 Deoch slàinte gach,|creutair bochd,
 The health of all, both great and small,
```

```
| ,r¹ |d¹. l ,s : d¹ ., m | r        : d        |
 Tha'n|diugh fo sprochd'san| dùth - aich.
 Now hopeless - ly do - spoud - ing.
```

The other tune, that to which Burns wrote his "Whaur ha'e ye been sae braw, lad ? " is of a rattling, martial character, and within the compass of the bagpipes.

23. Rata-murchuis—Lassie wi' the lintwhite locks (Burns). This tune is known in music books as "Rothiemurchus Rant."

24. Crodh Chailein—Can you sing Balilow ? This tune is found in several different forms. The simplest and most Gaelic-like is that in *A' Choisir-chiuil.* "My heart's in the Highlands" (Burns) is sometimes sung to this air.

(To be continued).

The Edinburgh John o' Groat Benevolent Association met in Darling's Regent Hotel, to hear a lecture from Mr. David Anderson, M.A., LL.B., on Captain Sinclair's expedition to Norway in 1612. The lecturer gave a most interesting account of this ill-fated Caithness expedition, which has given birth to so many traditions in Norway.

THE REAY FENCIBLES.

(*To the Editor of the* CELTIC MONTHLY)

SIR,—In the *Celtic Monthly* for August (Vol. i., p. 175) Mr. D. Murray Rose gave some introductory remarks regarding this regiment, based on the muster-roll, which he has taken the trouble to copy, and which appears in full in the current (January) number of the magazine.

I agree with Mr. Rose when he says that the regiment was a "mixed lot," because every regiment is so, more or less; but he writes in a somewhat disparaging strain, which may lead many people to think (notwithstanding a disclaimer which he puts in) that the Mackays did not press forward to fill up the ranks as freely as was expected, and that it was only by enlisting men in other districts, and by the bait of a bounty, "dangled before the eyes of un-

THE BANNER OF THE REAY FENCIBLES

is an interesting relic, and was placed by Lord Reay in St. Giles' Cathedral, Edinburgh, about ten years ago, when, with appropriate ceremony, so many other old Scottish regimental colours were deposited there. The flag is of sewed silk, and was made and presented to the regiment by Miss Barbara Mackay, granddaughter of James Mackay of Skerray, and daughter of Major Donald Mackay, Eriboll. Miss Mackay married Captain Mackay John Scobie, Keoldale, and during her long life was well known throughout the Reay country for her enthusiastic clan feeling, sincere piety, and great benevolence.

willing recruits," that the regiment, as he expresses it, was enabled "to take the field, and acquire laurels unfairly placed to the credit of the Clan Mackay alone."

* We are indebted to Mr. Andrew Ross, author of "Old Scottish Regimental Colours," for the use of the photograph from which the above illustration was engraved, and to Mr. John Mackay, Hereford, for its reproduction in our pages.

It is a pity that Mr. Rose made such a statement, because it conveys a false impression. When we speak of the gallant deeds of a famous regiment—the Gordon Highlanders for instance—and say "the brave Gordons" did so and so, we do not mean that it was the members of the Clan Gordon alone, who did the brave deeds; but the men, whatever their names, who formed the regiment. So when we say that "the

Mackays did nobly at **Tara Hill**," we do not restrict the praise to the Mackays alone, but give it to the officers and men who composed the regiment. Mr. Rose, therefore, should not have written that the regiment acquired laurels, *unfairly placed to the credit of the Clan Mackay alone.*

I got copies of the muster-rolls from the War Office some years ago, and arranged the names of the non-commissioned officers and privates in alphabetical order. It is not necessary to repeat the list here, but I may say, if we can judge by the predominating names, that about 600 of the men in the regiment were from the Reay country, while a large number of the non-clan names are found in the adjoining county of Caithness ; and that it was not till after the regiment was despatched to Ireland that it was recruited from the Lowlands. When embodied, the " Reays " consisted of 46 officers, 32 sergeants, 30 corporals, 22 drummers, and 670 privates—a regiment of 800 men of all ranks. Perhaps Mr. Rose did not analyse the muster-roll. Here are some of the names in numerical order—

Mackays,	.	.	209 men.*
Macleods,	.	.	63 ,,
Mackenzies,	.	.	40 ,,
Sutherlands,	.	.	35 ,,

then follow Morrisons, Macdonalds, Campbells, Munros, Rosses, Gunns, Gordons, Murrays, Calders, Hendersons, Mathiesons, Bains, &c. The roll contains in all 155 surnames, and of these, 139 are represented by 204 individuals, or 5 less that the number of Mackays in the regiment ! So its designation was perfectly appropriate—"The Reay Fencibles, or Mackay Regiment of Highlanders."

It is rather odd that no pipers are entered on the muster roll, though the names of the drummers are given. But undoubtedly there were pipers, although they do not appear on the

* The Mackays would undoubtedly have at least been double this number, but for the fact that in the previous year (1793) the third Sutherland Fencible Regiment had been formed ; and in it, according to General Stewart's "Sketches of the Highlanders and Highland Regiments," "there were 104 William Mackays, almost all of them from Strathnaver." Unfortunately, General Stewart did not state how many Mackays in all were in the regiment, but only gives the number of *William* Mackays. In the "Clan History," p. 33, it is stated that there were 33 *John* Mackays in one company of the same (Sutherland Fencible) regiment. This disposes of Mr. Rose's misleading assertion that the Mackays did not come forward "with such alacrity as is generally believed to be the case," to fill up the ranks of their own regiment. But when we consider the number that were in the successive Sutherland Fencible Regiments previous to the raising of the Reay regiment, the wonder is not that only 209 Mackays enlisted, but that so many able-bodied men of the clan were left in the district, fit for military service !

roster. I may here suggest that probably each captain had his own piper, as used to be the case in the Highland militia regiments, and may be so still. Another curious thing is, that there is no record at the War Office which mentions the uniform of the regiment. The late Miss Scobie, Keodale, who probably knew more about the regiment than any of her contemporaries, thus wrote me, only about a year before her death—" I have no doubt they had pipers. I remember an old, ugly man, a first-rate piper, and it was said that he went out with the regiment ; but when General Baillie joined he sent the man home, because he could not allow so ungainly a person to be seen with his regiment in so conspicuous a position ! . . . The uniform was similar to that of the 42nd—scarlet coats, with dark blue facings and silver lace. I am sure they had kilts." I wrote also, about three years ago, to an aged clansman at Strathy, asking about the uniform, &c., and he replied as follows :—" I knew many of the men that served in the Reay Fencibles, and my father was in the regiment. I knew one piper that was in it, but he is dead long ago. About their uniform, they wore the kilt of Mackay tartan, which was of black, blue, and green, very bonny to look at. . . . I cannot say anything about their head-dress. They wore the red coat."   JOHN MACKAY.

Wiesbaden, Germany.

ABSTRACT OF OSSIAN'S COVALLA.

BY LIEUT.-COLONEL CHARLES STEWART, TIGH-'N-DUIN.
Author of "The Gaelic Kingdom in Scotland, and its Celtic Church," " Killin Collection of Poetry and Music," &c.

(*Continued from page 98*).

BEFORE leaving, Fingal arranged with Covalla that he would send a swift-footed messenger to give her the result of the battle, and that she would meet him at a meeting-place fixed upon, where she would have a feast prepared for the host returning victorious. Defeat does not seem to have entered into their imaginations. So when the time expected came Covalla and her maidens *Dersegrina* and *Milhilcova* proceeded to the meeting-place. On reaching it, their thoughts, of course, were of the fight and Fingal. Chants "Gruagach dhonn a bhroillich bhain," or " Finnary "

MILHILCOVA.

" A deer I saw upon the ben,

By Cona's stream that gently winds,

As a great bank in shade he seemed,

Then fleetly bounded down theglen.

As night's bright arch his antlers beamed,

On the slope a meteor gleamed,

Whilst on Cona's clouds half seen,

Were those who shone in wraith hood's sheen."

DERSEGRINA.

" Ho rò! mo nighean donn bhuidheach."

" Death's spectre it is, that you seen have,

He of shield and sword matchless is slain,

On that cairn rise up, O Covalla,

Caraoul in the conflict has gained.

Shed tears, O daughter of Sarno,*

The youth who with love you enthralled,

In the midst of his strength has departed,

Soon his wraith shall be seen in the ben."

This deer seen by Millilcova is not a wraith, but an intimation by a symbol of Fingal's death. These intimations, specially of death, were believed in by the Gaels, and are so by many still, as I from my childhood well know. Covalla believed in the truth of this one, and burst into an agony of woe. In its midst Didealan, Fingal's promised messenger, arrived and, from spite to Covalla, who had at some former time refused his offer of marriage, told her the deliberate falsehood, that the Romans had conquered, and that Fingal was slain. In the agony of torture she said to the despicable author of it—

COVALLA.

Conn's chant.

" Why rehearsed thou to me the tale salsome,

That my hero had fall'n in the fight,

I would then from the hillside expect him,

And see him on crag and on plain.

I would fancy some tree was my loved one,

Coming back with acclaim from the war,

* Covalla.

Note—It must be noted that I don't give the poetry in full, but what is required to give the gist of this important episode.—C. S.

[Colonel Stewart wishes us to correct an error in the first part of his article. In the last footnote on page 98, the sentence beginning, "Macpherson," should read, "Macpherson actually interpolates this early 1st century history as he knew it, into the 1st duan of 'Timora,' the events of which happened A.D. 284," not "A.D. 25-30," as given.—ED.]

I would hear his salute midst the breezes,

Whilst his form on the slope I could spy."

At this point Fingal and his host are seen returning, but so impressed was Covalla by the symbol, and convinced by the lie, that she could not believe it was them bodily, but their wraiths. Then Millilcova breaks in—

MILLILCOVA.

"Chruagach," &c., *as before.*

" What noise on the ben, what light in the glen,

Who cometh onwards as thundering streams

In floods pouring downwards the hill-sides between,

From cairns midst quakings terrible.'

(*To be continued*).

HIGHLAND ANCESTRY OF DR. DAVID LIVINGSTONE, AFRICAN TRAVELLER.

By Rev. A. MACLEAN SINCLAIR, author of "Clarsach na Coille," "Glenbard Collection of Gaelic Songs," "The Gaelic Bards from 1411 to 1715, and 1715 to 1765."

NEIL LIVINGSTONE was born in Argyleshire. He married Mary Morrison. He had a small farm, or croft, in Ulva, but never prospered as a farmer. He left his native island in 1792, and went to live in Blantyre. When leaving he received the following certificate:—

" The bearer, Neil Livingstone, a married man in Ulva, part of the parish of Kilninian, has always maintained an unblemished moral character, and is known for a man of piety and religion. He has a family of four sons, the youngest of which is three years, and three daughters, of which the youngest is six years of age. As he proposes to offer his services at some of the cotton-spinning manufactories, he and his wife, Mary Morrison, and their family of children are hereby earnestly recommended for suitable encouragement. Given at Ulva, this eighth day of January, 1792, by

ARCH. M'ARTHUR, Minister.
LACH. M'LEAN, Elder.
R. S. STEWART, J.P."

Neil Livingstone and Mary Morrison had five sons and three daughters. The names of the sons were John, Charles, Duncan, Donald, and Neil. One of the daughters was named Mary and another Catherine. If the sons were all born in Ulva, one of them must have died before 1792. It may be, however, that the youngest of them was born in Blantyre. One of the daughters was married to a man named Laurie.

Neil, son of Neil Livingstone and Mary Morrison, was born in Ulva about 1788. He married Agnes Hunter, by whom he had three sons, John, David, and Charles, and two daughters. The daughters were living in 1891 in Ulva Cottage, at Hamilton.

John, eldest son of Neil Livingstone and Agnes Hunter, was born May 15th, 1811. He lives at Listowel, Ontario, and is an elder in the Presbyterian Church in that town. He went home to Scotland to meet his brother David in 1857. He has six sons and one daughter, Neil-Mackenzie, Henry, John, Charles, Robert, and Sarah.

David, second son of Neil Livingstone and Agnes Hunter, was the celebrated Dr. Livingstone. He was born at Blantyre, March 19, 1813. He married Mary, daughter of Dr. Robert Moffat, the eminent missionary. He had three sons, Robert, Thomas, and Oswell, and two daughters. He died at Lake Bangweolo, in Africa, May 4, 1873. He was buried in Westminster Abbey, April 18, 1874. Robert, his eldest son, lost his life in the American Civil War. Thomas died in Egypt. Oswell, who was a doctor, died in England in 1890. One of the daughters is married in Edinburgh, and the other in England.

Charles, third son of Neil Livingstone and Agnes Hunter, was a clergyman in Massachusetts. He went to Africa with his brother in 1858. He was appointed British Consul at Fernando Po in 1864. He died whilst returning to Britain in 1874. He was buried at sea. He left one son, who is a mining engineer in the United States.

Charles Morrison lived in Morvern. He married Margaret Macdougall, by whom he had four children, Hector, Neil, Mary, and Marion. He married Marion Maclean, of Ardnacross, in Mull, and had eleven children, Lachlan, Mary, Margaret, Neil, Donald, Charles, Ann, Catherine, Christy, Roderick, and John, all of whom were born in Scotland except John. He came to Prince Edward Island in 1810, and settled in Belfast. He died in 1849, in the 90th year of his age. His wife died in 1845, in the 76th year of her age.

Lachlan, eldest son of Hector Morrison and Marion Maclean, married Margaret Mackenzie, by whom he had Neil, Kenneth, Hector, John, Charles, and Donald, and two daughters. Neil, the second son, married Catherine Gillies, by whom he had Charles, Hector, John, Donald, Roderick, Murdoch, and Angus, and four daughters. Donald the third son, married Mary Macaulay, by whom he had Angus, Donald, Hector, and Charles, and six daughters. Charles, the fourth son, married Catherine Mackenzie, by whom he had Hector, Kenneth, Charles, Murdoch, and Ann. Roderick, the fifth son, married Mary Macrae by whom he had Roderick, Donald, Kenneth, John, Lachlan, and five daughters. John, sixth son of Hector

Morrison, married Elizabeth Smith, by whom he had Hector, Andrew, Alexander, Lachlan, and John, and two daughters. John is still living. Mary was married to John Macdonald, Margaret to Angus Mackay, Ann to Roderick Campbell, and Catherine to John Gillies.

Mrs. Campbell was born in 1803. She was brought up with her grandmother at Ardnacross. She was a very intelligent and amiable woman. She died May 16, 1893. I asked her one day why Neil Livingstone and his family left Ulva. Her reply was, "Cha robh ni a cinneachdainn leatha an Ulbha"—they were not prospering in anything in Ulva. It was a good thing for Africa that such was the case. Dr. Livingstone could never have received in Ulva, or even in Edinburgh, the training for his great work that he received at Blantyre.

Neil, second son of Charles Morrison and Margaret Macdougall, died unmarried. Mary was married to Neil Livingstone, and was the grandmother of Dr. Livingstone.

Belfast, Prince Edward Island.

LETTER TO THE EDITOR.

To the Editor of the "CELTIC MONTHLY."

Glasgow, 10th February, 1894.

SIR,—In Mr. Campbell's notice of Dr. Macdiarmid, in January issue, he states that to the Doctor, Mr. MacLean, and himself is due the credit of originating the Gaelic Society of Glasgow. That is not the case. They assisted in the formation of the society, but the idea had its origin with Mr. Hugh Macleod, writer, Glasgow, and it is known to every one connected with the society that, in consequence, it was Mr. MacLeod who was asked to deliver the opening address.—I am

"PALMAM QUI MERUIT FERAT."

GAELIC SOCIETY OF LONDON. The annual dinner in connection with this flourishing society was held in the St. James's Restaurant, under the presidency of the respected chief, Mr. John Mackay, J.P., Hereford. There was a large attendance, and the gathering was perhaps the most successful yet held under the auspices of the society. The toasts were entrusted to the following speakers:—The Chief, Mr. T. D. MacDonald, Rev. A. B. Bailie (of Dochfour), Dr. Matheson, Rev. Alex. MacRae, Messrs. W. C. Mackenzie, Donald C. Fraser, J. M Watson, J. T. Crowe, G. Murray Campbell (of Siam), Donald Murray, and J. Sutherland. With speeches, songs, dancing, and music a very pleasant evening was spent.

CEUD FAILTE DO M' DHUTHAICH.

Air Fonn—" Nighean fhir na Comhraich.

Ceud failte, failte, thir mo ghraidh,
Gur fada, ghraidh, bho 'n thriall mi
A nnll thar cuan bho d' bhearntan ard',
Gu dubhach, craiteach, ciannil ;
Ach ged a thriall, a riamh cha d' thraoigh
Mo ghean 's mo ghaol do 'n dt thaich
A dh-araich mi 'nuair bha mi maoth,
'S 'nuair bha mi sotram sunntach.

Os ceann gach tir an ear 's an iar
A thriall mi feadh an t-saoghail,
Bu tusa fein amhain mo mhiann,
Gun fhiaradh riamh no caochladh ;
Oir ged bhiodh tirean cein ear r nn
Gle neonach leam 'nan iaiohaidh,
Bu tusa, tusa, thir mo ruin,
An tir bu mhuirnich sgiamh leam.

Cha chuireadh beartas mor no maoin
Do raointean gorm air dichuimhn,
'S cha b' urrainn gloir no solas fa oin
Cur as do m' ghaol do d' chriochan ;
Oir cha 'n eil neach no ni fodh 'n ghrein,
Cruaidh fhorstan breun no buaireas,
A chlaonas m' aigne, ghraidh bhuat fein,
Gu sinear seimh 'san uaigh mi.

Ged bhiodh an geamhradh greannach, fuar,
Ri cuairteachadh 'nan ghleanntan
'S ged bhiodh an sneachda, mar b i dual,
Air uachdar fuar 'nam beanntan ;
Gidheadh gu 'm b' fhearr leam fhe n an sgiaml ,
'S na neoil ri 'g iathadh dluth orr'
Na tirean cein 'sam biodh a' ghrian
Cho teth 's cho dian ri ghiulan.

Leig leis na h-Innseanuaich bhi blath
Ri tamh fodh theas na greine,
'S le mnathan dubh bhi lom a ghnath,
Gun chota-ban, gun leine !
'S biodh iadsan toilicht anns an doigh
A dh-orduicheadh le Dia dhoibh,
Ach b' annsa leam-sa mhuinntir cho r
Do 'm buineadh cloth 'us bian geal.

A riamh cha d' thug mi suim no spcis
Do 'n diathan-breige neonach,
'S do 'n iodhal-aoraidh oillteil, bhreun,
Cha deanain geil gu deonach :
'S gur tric a dh-fhag e mise tinn
Bhi cluinntinn screach an canain,
Oir, oh, os ceann gach cainnt is binn,
Gur binn leam fhein a Ghaidhlig.

Thoir dhomh-sa mointeach choir an faraoich,
'S a ghaoth bhiodh fallain, fialaidh,
Ri soideadh suas tre thir nan laoch,
Le slainte sgaoilt fodh' sgiathan ;
'S biodh acasan an tirean cein
Gach euslaint bhreun a dh-innsear,
An uair bhios mise falbh leam fein,
'S mo cheum air fonn mo shinnear.

'Nuair bhiodh na naimhdean guineach, dan,
'S am Bas gun iochd mu 'n cuairt dhiom,

B' e sud an uair bu mhiann le m' lamh
Bhi fior gu brath do d' bhrnaichean ;
'S ged bhiodh a' faoileach liadhaich, fuar,
No teas 'g am bhualadh iosal.
Cha b' urrain iad gu bas toirt buaidh
Air meud mo luaidh de d' chriochan.

Ge lionmhor ceol a chuala mi,
Bha binn gu fior 'ns gleusda,
'Nuair sheideadh suas ceol mor na piob,
Co 'n ceol bhiodh binn 'n am eisdeachd ?
An sin gu 'n teicheadh each air cul,
Mar ni nach b' fhiu leam chuinntinn,
Oir, oh, b' e sud am balgan-ciuil
A thogadh surd air 'm inntinn.

Tha iomadh seorsa gearradh grinn,
'Us dathan grinn air aodaeh,
'S tha cuid cho seolta, sgiobalt, crninn,
'S tha cuid gun loinn cho slaodach ;
Ach 's aithne dhomh-sa trusgan gearr
A ruigeas bar nan ghluineau,
Bu tric a choisinn buaidh am blar,
'S a b' aluinn snuadh air urlar.

Gur fior gu 'n d' fhas mo chiamhag liath,
'S gu 'n chaill mi sgiamh na h-oige,
'S mo cheann air fas cho lan cho chiall
'S gu 'n thriall am falt ri m' bheo dheth ;
Ach 's coma leam : tha 'n cridhe blath,
Gun fhailneachadh bho thus air,
'S gur cinnteach mi gu 'm bi gu brath,
Gu 'n carar sios fodh 'n uir e.

Oh, 's iomadh bliadhna thriall a null
Bho dh-fhag mi fonn mo dhuthcha,
'S chaidh iomadh caraid caomh a chall
Bho thionndaidh mi mo chul riut ;
Tha pairt aca 's a' chuan 'nan tamh,
'Us pairt an tirean ceine,
'S och, och, nach fhaic mi chaoidh gu brath,
Am pairt a b' fhearr leam fein ac'.

Cha b' ann gu dearbh an laithean aois
A chlaon iad as gun eifeachd,
Ach gearrta sios air cuan 'us raoin,
Gu 'n chaochail iad 'nan treunachd ;
'S gur iomadh teaghlach truagh le bron
A dh-fhag iad leonta, ciannail,
Ri gul 's a caoidh na sninn a sheol,
'S nach till iad beo gu siorruidh.

Seadh dh-fhalbh iad sud, 's cha d' fhag 'nan deigh
An leithid fhein 'nan aite,
'S gur tric a bhios mo chridhe reubt'
La cuimhne ghen 'g an aireamh ;
'S air leam gu faic mi cruth nan laoch
Gu caoimhneil, caomh mar b' abhaist,
Ge cian a null bho thir an fhraoich
A dh-aog iad fad bho 'n cairdean.

Cha 'n eil, cha 'n eil iad ann ni's mo,
Gidheadh gur mor mo run sa
Do thir mo ghraidh, 's am b' abhaist leo
Bhi 'comhnuidh cridheil, sunntach ;
Ged dh' fhas mo cheum, a ghaoil, cho fann
Gu direadh bheanntamn ard,
Gidheadh sud ort, a Thir nam Beann
'S le run nach gann—Ceud Failte !

India.   Iain MacGhriogair.

NEWS OF THE MONTH.

CLAN MACKAY SOCIETY.—The January meeting of this society was held in the Oddfellows' Hall, Edinburgh—Dr. George Mackay in the chair. Mr. John Mackay, secretary, exhibited a photo. of the colours of the Dutch Mackay regiment, and referred to its history. He also made a statement in regard to a collection of music of Rob Donn Mackay's songs, which led to a most interesting discussion upon Gaelic music in general, and Reay country music in particular. The chairman gave some particulars in regard to the forthcoming social gathering, after which Mr. Donald Mackay gave an excellent rendering of a Gaelic song. The meeting was one of the most successful and enjoyable yet held in Edinburgh.

THE FEBRUARY MEETING was held in the Waterloo Rooms, Glasgow, on the 15th ult., Lieut. Wm. Mackay in the chair. There was a large attendance. A valuable paper was read—"Francis Mackay and his three sons"—contributed by Mr. John Mackay ("Ben Reay"), Germany, in which he gave an account of the eventful history of a distinguished family of the clan, since 1670, in Austria and Canada. Mr. John Mackay, Kingston (secretary), exhibited a number of beautiful colour sketches of the Mackay country, taken in 1820, and lent by Mr. John Mackay, Hereford, in connection with which he gave a description of the various places. (In this issue of the C. M. we present our readers with a reproduction of one of these—Rispond, Durness Ed.) The after part of the evening was devoted to songs and music contributed by members and friends.

THE UIST AND BARRA CONVERSAZIONE, which was held in the Waterloo Rooms, was well attended. Lieut. John Macdonald occupied the chair, and gave an account of the work of the society. Other speeches followed, after which the tables were cleared away, and dancing was kept up with great spirit till the early hours of the morning.

CLAN MACKINNON SOCIETY.—The second annual gathering of this clan was held in the Waterloo Rooms—the chair being occupied by Lieut.-Col. L. D. Mackinnon, Dochgarroch. There was a large attendance. The chairman made a most interesting speech, referring to the past history of the clan, and clansmen who had done honour to the name. He quoted Sir Walter Scott's description—

"The clan of grey Fingon, whose offspring have given
Such heroes to earth and such martyrs to heaven."

An assembly followed, which was well attended.

GAELIC SOCIETY OF GLASGOW.—A largely attended meeting of this society was held on the 30th inst., in the Religious Institution Rooms—Mr. Magnus Maclean, M.A., in the chair, who was supported by Rev. Dr. Blair, Mr. Wm. Mackenzie, Crofters' Commission; Dr. MacNicol, Dalmally; Mr. John Murdoch, and others. Professor O'Growney, May-nooth College, Ireland, gave a most instructive lecture upon "Scotland in Early Irish Literature," in which he emphasised the close relationship which existed until quite recent times between the Celtic people of Scotland and Ireland. Interesting addresses were given by Messrs. Henry Whyte, John Murdoch, and the chairman. The learned Irish Celtic professor received a very hearty reception from the Gaels of Glasgow and we trust that this will only be the beginning of a closer intimacy between the Gaelic students of Erin and Scotia.

CLAN CHATTAN ASSOCIATION.—The first monthly meeting of this association was held in the Trades' Hall, about 200 members being present. Mr. William Mackintosh, president, occupied the chair, and stated that there were 3000 members of the different septs of the clan on the Glasgow electoral roll. The secretary (Mr. W. G. Davidson) gave a short address on the aims of the society. Other meetings are being arranged for.

CLAN MACLEAN SOCIETY.—A very successful concert in connection with this vigorous society was held in the Assembly Rooms, Bath Street, under the presidency of Mr. Lachlan Maclean, vice-president, who delivered an eloquent address on the clan and its eventful history. The musical part of the programme was well sustained, and an assembly followed.

CLAN GREGOR SOCIETY.—The monthly meeting of this society was held on the 13th ult., in the N.B. Railway Hotel—Mr. John MacGregor in the chair. Mr. MacGregor Fergusson delivered a most interesting address on "Some Incidents in the Life of Rob Roy," which led to a very instructive discussion. The chairman stated that it was proposed to have a clan excursion this summer to the MacGregor country. He also advocated the opening of a Highland club or reading-rooms in Glasgow, a proposal which was very favourably received. The clan piper gave a selection of tunes on the pipes, and a pleasant evening was spent.

ANNUAL SOCIAL GATHERINGS.—We regret that owing to the pressure on our space this month we cannot notice as fully as we would like all the Highland gatherings held since our last issue. We may mention, however, that the following very successful gatherings were held, in each case the hall being crowded:—The Glasgow Cowal Society—Chairman, Lord Provost Russell; Kintyre gathering—Mr. Graham of Erins; Edinburgh Sutherland—Mr. Hew Morrison; Coatbridge Highlanders—Mr. Graeme A. Whitelaw, M.P.; Brechin Celtic Society—Mr. A. R. Maclean Murray; Glasgow Ross and Cromarty—Sheriff Johnstone; Clan Menzies Society—Colonel Menzies; Clan Mackay—Rev. Dr. J. Aberigh Mackay; London Argyllshire—Dr. H. C. Gillies.

SIR MALCOLM MACGREGOR OF MACGREGOR, BART.,
Chief of the Clan Gregor.

THE CELTIC MONTHLY:

A MAGAZINE FOR HIGHLANDERS.

Edited by JOHN MACKAY, Kingston.

No. 7. Vol. II.]   APRIL, 1894.   [Price Threepence.

SIR MALCOLM MACGREGOR OF MACGREGOR, BART.

THE young Chief of Clan Gregor, whose portrait is now given, will attain his majority this year, having been born on the 3rd August, 1873, at Edinchip, in Balquhidder. He joined H.M.S. *Britannia* as a naval cadet in September, 1886, and passed into the Royal Navy in December, 1888, third on a list of 59, and was immediately appointed to H.M.S. *Bellerophon*, the flagship on the North American station, under the command of Admiral Watson. Sir Malcolm returned to England in 1892, and served during the summer as midshipman on board the training ship at Leith. In the winter of the same year he went to the West Indies with the training squadron.

Since April, 1893, he has been going through the various classes and examinations at Greenwich for the rank of lieutenant, and in every examination hitherto has obtained a 1st class certificate. He is now at Portsmouth, preparing for the examination in pilotage.

The young chief has one brother, Alexander Ronald—now at Malvern College—and three sisters, the eldest of whom married, in June, 1892, the Hon. Granville Somerset, grandson of General Lord Raglan, the British Commander-in-Chief in the Crimea.

Edinchip, the family residence, was built in 1848, by Sir John Atholl, grandfather of the present baronet, and contains many interesting relics connected with the family and clan, and also with the Bannatynes of Kames.

Sir Malcolm is a staunch Highlander, devoted to his clan and country. His father, the late Rear Admiral Sir Malcolm MacGregor, entered the navy in 1846, when only just twelve years old, and his first voyage was in H.M.S. *Howe*, when she took Her Majesty Queen Adelaide to Madeira. After serving on different stations Sir Malcolm went to the Crimea in 1854 as first lieutenant on board H.M.S. *Royal Albert* (Captain Pasley), but was soon appointed flag-lieutenant to Admiral Sir Frederick Grey. At the end of the war, on Sir Frederick hauling down his flag, Sir Malcolm was promoted to the rank of commander. In that rank he commanded H.M.S. *Harrier* and H.M.S. *Meander*, and was a second time appointed to the command of H.M.S. *Harrier*, on the Australian station, in 1860, whence he returned on attaining the rank of post captain, at the early age of twenty-eight years. In 1864 he married Lady Helen Laura M'Donnell, only child of Hugh Seymour M'Donnell, 9th Earl of Antrim.

In the winter of 1867 he went to the West Coast of Africa in command of H.M.S. *Danae*, which command he resigned at the end of a year, affairs at home requiring his presence.

Sir Malcolm received the Crimean medal and the Turkish Order of the Mejidje for his services in the Crimea, and was awarded the medal of the Humane Society for saving the life of one of the men of H.M.S. *Danae* by jumping overboard and swimming with a life-belt to his rescue.

Sir Malcolm became a rear admiral a few months before his death in August, 1879. He was greatly beloved by all who knew him, and took the keenest interest in all matters pertaining to his own clan and to the Highlands generally.

The present burial-place of the chief's family is a mausoleum built by Sir John Murray MacGregor, in Balquhidder; the previous one is further up the Braes at Invercarnaig; and in still older days the chiefs were laid to rest on Inch Cailleach, in Loch Lomond. Among the articles of interest at Edinchip are the broadsword used at the battle of Glenfruin by Alexander MacGregor, the then chief of Clan Gregor, and a dirk given by Prince Charles Edward to his *aide de-camp*, Major Evan MacGregor, the great-great-great grandfather of the present Sir Malcolm.

THE HEADLESS SPECTRE: A SUTHERLANDSHIRE GHOST STORY.

By the Editor.

CHAPTER I.—THE GRAVES OF THE STRANGERS.

WONDER how many of my readers in their summer wanderings have visited Durness, that green and fertile land, rich in beauty of natural scenery, and the congenial home of poetry and romance. It borders on the wild Pentland Firth, and even on the calmest day the surge and roar of the ocean may be heard far inland. In this old-world place you find the quaintest relics of ancient times rubbing shoulders familiarly with the most recent developments of our modern civilisation. On all sides the eye meets objects which bring you into contact with the remote past. Every hill, stream, glen and headland has its tale of battle, love, or disaster. Indeed, if the traditions of this historical country were collected and published, they would form a volume of the most absorbing interest. I have heard many of these stories related, and it is now my intention to narrate one of the most remarkable which it has been my privilege to hear. Many of my readers who do not believe in the supernatural or "second sight" may describe it as a mere invention, or a freak of the imagination, but I have taken the trouble to verify the truth of the story in various conclusive ways, and, furthermore, there are many persons now living who remember the incidents quite distinctly, so that the facts may be accepted as being well authenticated. I shall endeavour to describe these events in plain language, exactly as I heard them related by one who was an eye-witness of them.

One day I found myself in the ancient graveyard of Balnakeil, which is certainly the most interesting spot in the whole county of Sutherland. It takes us at one step back to the time of the Culdees. In it are the ruins of a monastery, a venerable relic of the wild

"THIS PLACE IS KNOWN TO US AS THE CORNER OF THE 'ANONYMOUS.'"

days of old, when the Roman Catholic Church was a power in the land, and the strongest arm and the sharpest broadsword were the universal arbiters of what was right or wrong. In it also is the grave of Rob Donn Mackay, the Reay country Gaelic bard, covered with a rude stone bearing a brief inscription, and near it is the handsome monument erected to his memory by his admiring clansmen in 1829. The whole surface of the ground is covered with stones, many of them most beautiful examples of the sculptor's art.

I came at last to a corner of the graveyard where there were the marks of many graves, but there was not one stone erected to record the names of the persons who were buried there. I thought it very remarkable, and asked a friend who accompanied me if he could explain the reason.

"Ah," he said, "don't you know the history of this corner? It is a very strange place, and if the poor fellows who sleep there could rise and tell their histories and sufferings, they would have some weird stories to relate."

Such a reply was only calculated to provoke my curiosity, and I asked my friend to tell me what he knew of the mysterious spot.

"Well, if I could only remember all I have heard I daresay I could narrate some thrilling tales that would cause you to wonder. This place is known to us as the corner of the 'anonymous'—the graves of the strangers. Being so close to Cape Wrath, this coast was at one time the scene of the most dreadful disasters. Wrecks along these rock-bound shores were of frequent occurrence, and on many a fateful morning, when the day broke after a storm, the people have found the shore strewn with wreckage and the dead bodies of the unfortunate crew. Many a brave seaman, whose name was never known to us, has found his last long home in this peaceful corner, and no one able to convey to his sorrowing wife and family the sad news that the poor sailor had found a grave on Sutherland soil."

"But," I said, "surely the splendid lighthouse at the Cape will make a wreck here now rather a rare occurrence?"

"Wrecks do take place on rare occasions, but a serious disaster which happened many years ago created a great stir in the country, and was preceded and attended by circumstances which are likely to cause wonder for years to come. No fewer than sixteen bodies were washed ashore on the sands, and these green mounds mark the place of their burial."

"But, tell me," I asked, "what are the curious circumstances to which you refer. Was it anything supernatural?"

"I do not know what you would call it, or whether science could now explain what even to the present day the people of Durness cannot understand; but this I do know, that there are persons living here who will remember that awful shipwreck to their dying days. It seems to me that there are influences operating in our midst which can only find their origin in the spirit world. The great dark gulph which separates the living and the dead is bridged over, if only we could find the entrance. But there we all fail."

From the serious manner in which my friend spoke, I felt sure that there was some horrible story connected with these nameless graves, and that story I was most anxious to hear.

"But you have not yet told me the extraordinary circumstances you refer to," I replied. "Surely it cannot be that the living and the dead have held communion in this secluded place?"

"My dear sir, I would not care to relate to you—even although I knew the whole facts, which I do not—all that I have heard told about this disaster. Were I to do so you would think me superstitious, or that I was narrating the distorted impression of some hideous nightmare. But if you ask Joseph Morrison, who lives in the village, he will tell you all about the wreck of the *Juniper*. He was an eyewitness of the events, and I only heard the facts related, but when you have heard his story you will in some measure understand the mysteries which are associated with these green mounds."

I need hardly say that these strange remarks interested me very much. That very evening I paid a visit to the village, and found Morrison standing outside his cottage door enjoying a chat with a neighbour after his day's labours. After a good deal of persuasion I induced him to tell me the story of the shipwreck, but he assured me before he commenced that he was not superstitious—he only believed that things happen in every person's experience which no one can satisfactorily explain.

Seating himself on the dyke by the roadside, from which an excellent view of the bay, which lay right in front of us, could be had, my friend narrated the following story. I cannot do better than tell it in his own simple but graphic way.

CHAPTER II.—MORRISON ENCOUNTERS THE SPECTRE.

When I was a young lad, many years ago, the boys of this place were very fond of playing on the long stretch of sand which you see in front of us. Our favourite game was "hares and hounds," which we usually played when darkness lent an additional excitement to the game. I can remember, as if it were but yesterday, a number of us going down to the shore to engage in our favourite pastime. It was an evening just like this. The moon glimmered through a mass of clouds, yet clearly enough to permit one to recognise objects at a considerable distance. The rocks which jut out from the sand here and there cast shadows which usually proved convenient hiding-places for the poor hunted "hare."

The game was let loose, and after the usual grace time had elapsed, the "hounds" set out in pursuit. All the pack except myself took the right side of the bay, while I went in the opposite direction alone, feeling sure that I should find the hare hiding among the rocks in the distance. Unsuccessful in my search, I decided to conceal myself among the boulders, and watch the sands in the hope of seeing the object of my pursuit. It was a very lonely spot, and although I was not much given to superstitious notions, I began to feel just a little bit "queer." The cold, clammy air, and the dismal surge of the billows, combined with a sense of lonliness, helped to cool my youthful ardent spirits. My companions were now far out of sight and hearing.

I was just about to rise from my uncomfortable position when I fancied I saw in the distance a figure near the water's edge. "This must be the hare after all," I thought. "I knew I would catch him!" so I decided to remain still, and when it had come near enough to me, I would pounce upon it. I watched the figure as it passed alongside the edge of the water, and when it came nearer I could make it out a little more distinctly. I had only watched it for a short time when I felt a curious feeling coming over me. I tried to shake it off, but found I could not. The horrible idea suggested itself to me that it was a ghost! This proposition I soon put to the test. Right in front of the advancing figure was a part of the sand which was still moist and dark with water. "Now," I thought, "if this figure is a human being, his footsteps will leave a mark in the sand, which I can easily see. If a spirit—ghosts leave no marks." Trembling with excitement, I watched the shadowy figure. It reached the moist spot and—disappeared! In a second it reappeared on the opposite side, and seemed to glide along, rather than walk. I tried to scream, but I could not, my throat was parched. I strove to rise, but I was utterly helpless. Some powerful influence held me in its iron grasp, and I was unable to resist it. Oh! I shall never forget those dreadful moments.

I lay still and simply stared at the apparition.

Then I saw clearly that it had the appearance of a man with no clothes upon him except a shirt, which fluttered in the breeze. Slowly the figure approached, and soon it was quite close to the side of the rocks. It had now left the edge of the water, and was coming straight towards me. Unable to stand the strain on my nerves any longer, I overcame the feeling of weakness which oppressed me, and struggling to my feet, scrambled over the rocks towards the grassy bank which overlooked the sands. Trembling like a leaf I reached the top, keeping my face towards the sea, and dreading each moment that the unearthly spectre would clutch me.

Before flying from the scene I gave one glance behind, and there, sure enough, was the ghostly apparition gliding up the bank towards me. I was again helpless—that terrible feeling had again taken possession of me. I watched it, fascinated, and I then saw for the first time that—horror of horrors—the spectre had no head! The upper part of the head from the mouth was missing. The lower jaw only remained—the rest was a bloody cavity!

Then I found strength to run and scream. I ran as I had never run before, feeling that a horrible fiend was close behind me. Bursting into the first house I came to, that of James Mackay, I fell down on the floor in a fainting state. Hearing the frightful screams, all the the people round about ran out, and pressed into the house. When I recovered somewhat I narrated as best I could all I had seen. No one said anything to doubt the truth of my story, my pallid face and trembling limbs showed only too plainly that I had seen "something." No one suggested that it was not a ghost, but it was noticeable that the people gave the sands a wide berth after that at night. The boys no longer played "hares and hounds" among the rocks, and soon every one in the parish, and for many miles beyond, heard the story of the headless spectre of Durness Sands.

(To be concluded).

CURIOUS TOMBSTONE IN BALNAKEIL CHAPEL, DURNESS.

THE LATE A. B. M'GRIGOR, LL.D., GLASGOW.

PRESIDENT, CLAN GREGOR SOCIETY.

THIS month we give the portrait of the late Dr. A. B. M'Grigor, who was President of the Clan Gregor Society from 1887 till his death in 1891.

Dr. M'Grigor's career was one of which the society and the clan may well be proud. Born in 1827, and a native of Glasgow, in which town his great-grandfather had settled in the beginning of last century, he was the senior partner of the well-known firm of Messrs. M'Grigor, Donald & Co., solicitors, a concern whose commencement dates from well over 100 years ago, it having been established in the latter half of last century by Mr. Alexander M'Grigor, grandfather of Dr. A. B. M'Grigor, and himself in later years a vice-president of the society. From an early period in his career Dr. M'Grigor took a leading rank among those of his profession, and for twenty-five years before

his death he appeared in almost every important legal inquiry and negotiation in Glasgow, among which may be mentioned the City of Glasgow Union Railway Company, with its numerous bills and references; the Glasgow Tramway Company, the Vale of Clyde Tramway Company, and latterly the City of Glasgow Bank, in connection with the failure of which he was elected (with one other) to make the preliminary report to the shareholders, and was subsequently the chief

adviser in the liquidation and the numerous cases which arose from it. Through all of them he was identified with the best traditions of his profession, with the strictest honour, inviolate confidence and high talents. But he was more than a successful lawyer, he was also a man of wide culture and academic and intellectual attainments, and among his friends he was highly esteemed for his ready sympathy, his genial temperament, and his largeness of heart.

An omnivorous and rapid reader, he was thoroughly versed in the contents of his library, which was an exceptionally large and varied one, and there were not many better acquainted with all that was worth reading in the general literature of poetry, history, and art.

An honorary LL.D. of Glasgow University, he for many years acted as Lord Rector's assessor in the University Court, and in few places is he better remembered than in the precincts of that University which has assisted the citizens of Glasgow to record the acknowledgment of his services by the erection of a beautiful window in the Bute Hall to his memory.

A keen clansman, he was perhaps prouder of being President of the Clan Gregor Society than of any other honours which had been bestowed upon him, and his services to the society at its resuscitation in 1886 were simply invaluable. From then he took the greatest interest in its prospects and affairs generally, and its present thoroughly sound and successful position is greatly owing to him.   EDITOR.

TONGUE AND ITS HISTORIC SURROUNDINGS.

By John Mackay, C.E., J.P., Hereford.

Part III.—The Mackays at Bannockburn.

(Continued from page 117).

WHILE the Scottish forces were thus gathering together to the Torwood, the appointed rendezvous, and being drilled by companies, brigades, and divisions, under the care of Edward Bruce, Douglas, and Randolph, Robert Bruce was prudently engaged in preparing for the impending and eventful conflict by every means that military expediency, experience, and knowledge of warfare could dictate, or ingenuity and strategy could devise. As a necessary preliminary, he ordered the whole population from Berwick to Stirling, unable to bear arms, to remove with their goods and chattels to the hills, out of the way of the invading enemy. At the same time he looked out for a field of battle advantageous to his own

TONGUE HOUSE THE ANCIENT SEAT OF THE MACKAY CHIEFS.

small army to contest for the gage of victory with Edward's mighty power now advancing from Berwick—

"So wide, so far, that boundless host,
Seem'd in the blue horizon lost."

Bruce, with that intuitive strategic skill which distinguishes great commanders, selected his battlefield immediately north of the Bannock burn, having a front long enough to give the three front divisions of his small army fairplay and space for fighting, and short enough to embarrass the big battalions of his opponents in deploying for a general attack. His right front and flank were protected from cavalry charges by the steep banks of the Bannock and by a wood. His left, on the east, was posted on the high ground in front of St. Ninian, and in a measure protected by a morass, which could be turned, but, to obviate this defect, a few nights before the battle he quietly ordered parallel rows of small pits to be dug in the firm ground between the morass and his left flank and front, to disorder and bewilder the English men-at-arms in the event of their attacking him in those quarters. Stakes were placed in these pits, and he caused them to be lightly but carefully covered over to deceive the enemy.

Having thus skilfully secured a favourable field, and made all requisite preparations, he calmly abided in the Torwood for the approach of the invading army. Learning that it was advancing from Linlithgow, Bruce ordered his army to retire by divisions from the Torwood and take post on the positions assigned them in the chosen field by Bannock's banks. Edward Bruce, with his division, marched away first and took up his position on the right, Douglas followed and took up his in the centre, by Edward's left, Randolph with his division took

up the space allotted to it on the left of Douglas, while Bruce himself, with the rear division, took a central position on a rising ground behind the centre division of Douglas, in order that from this commanding position he might the better watch the phases of the fighting and order assistance to be given to any of his front divisions as necessity arose. Sir Walter Scott beautifully describes how each of these divisions was composed, and where they came from. Of the left division he says—

"North-eastward, by St Ninian's shrine,
Beneath fierce Randolph's charge, combine
The warriors whom the hardy north
From Tay to Sutherland set forth."

Having thus placed his army in position under

From Photo]   THE FIELD OF BANNOCKBURN FROM THE GILLIES' HILL.   [by Valentine.

the command of three of the best fighting generals of the age, Bruce raised his banner to the breeze, waiting for Edward's approach, which was not long in coming—

"Flashing with steel and rough with gold
And bristled o'er with bills and spears,
With plumes and pennons waving fair
Was that bright battle front!"

This was some of the foremost divisions of Edward's army, which, on the evening of the 23rd of June, came in sight of the Scottish array posted opposite to them on the other side of the Bannock. It was on this evening that Bruce's personal encounter with the De Bohun took place, and the discomfiture by Randolph of a body of English cavalry that attempted to

pass by his left to relieve Stirling. Two events successful in their results that greatly roused the spirits of the Scots and as greatly depressed the English.

Early in the morning of the eventful 24th June, 1314, both armies were astir. Bruce, now mounted on his great war-horse, and attended by his generals, rode along the whole line of his front division, encouraging one and all to stand firm, and addressed them in those stirring terms so well paraphrased by Burns. The enthusiasm was immense. Generals, commanders and men took up the theme, and responsive swore—

For Scotland's freedom, king, and laws
That day "to do or die."

The battle began by the advance of a formidable body of English archers from the left, who fiercely assailed with their artillery Edward Bruce's division, inflicting considerable damage upon his men. The fiery Edward could scarcely restrain himself from advancing to attack them. Meanwhile his more prudent brother ordered Keith with his men-at-arms to make a detour and fall upon the archers in flank and rear. This movement was completely successful. The archers were so cut up that they fled the field, and gave no more trouble that day The fighting now became general all along the line from west to east.

> "Unflinching foot 'gainst foot was set,
> Unceasing blow by blow was met,
> And slaughter revell'd round."

Yet the fighting went on fast and furious. The King of England, provoked by the sturdy and obstinate resistance of the Scots, ordered a division of his mail-clad cavalry to advance and make a furious charge on Randolph's and Douglas's divisions, partly posted behind the pits. This grand charge, from which so much was expected, soon ended in disaster and complete overthrow.

> "Down ! down ! in headlong overthrow,
> Horsemen and horse, the foremost go
>   Wild floundering on the field.
> They came like mountain-torrent red,
> They broke like that same torrent wave
> When swallowed by a darksome cave."

The terrible failure of this grand cavalry attack disconcerted Edward and his commanders and dispirited his whole soldiery, still, English tenacity would not yield. Fresh divisions from the rear were brought to the front to sustain the fight. Bruce from his vantage position anxiously yet calmly watched the phases of the dreadful conflict ; he intently scanned its ebb and flow, and admiringly beheld how valiantly his men were contending with much superior numbers, now and again re-enforced. Edward's superiority in number of men enabled him to renew the battle after every repulse. The Scots, animated by their brave commanders, and cheered by their gallant king calling to them in confident tones—

> "My merry men, fight on !"

redoubled their efforts, did fight on, and eventually were gaining ground, when Bruce's eagle eye, perceiving that the crisis of the battle had at last taken place, shouted —

> "On them, men ! on them ! they fail ! they fail !"

Wheeling his war horse round, he rode to the rear division, hitherto held in reserve, but burning with impatience to have a part in the fray, and ordered it to advance. Then, rising in his stirrups and brandishing his great claymore, exclaimed—

> "Follow me ! one effort more, and Scotland's free."

Then directing Angus Og MacDonald, with his west Highlanders, who formed the right wing of this division, to wheel to his right and assist his brother Edward, he addressed him in these words :—

> "Lord of the Isles ! my trust in thee
>   Is firm as Ailsa Rock ;
> Rush on with Highland sword and targe,
> While I with my Carrick spearmen charge.
>   Now ! forward to the shock."

Bruce personally led his Carrick spearmen and the rest of his division to the assistance of Douglas and Randolph. These reinforcements arriving so opportunely gave a fresh impetus to the Scots, and dismayed the front ranks of the English. At this critical moment the baggage-guards and camp-followers appeared on the English commander on the horizon, marching over the Gillies' Hill, like an army arriving to the assistance of the Scots. Confounded at this spectacle, the tenacity of the English gave way, and Bruce, at once judging that the supreme moment had come, like Wellington at Waterloo, ordered a general advance to be made, which soon swept the Plantagenet and his myrmidons off the field, and Bannockburn was won ! A glorious field of fight, creditable alike to the noble Bruce, to his brave lieutenants, and to every gallant Scot, Lowland and Highland, who contributed to the victory.

The consequences of it were of the highest importance to the king and the country, politically, morally, and socially. It asserted the independence of Scotland, secured for it twenty years of internal peace and tranquility after twenty years of internal wars and commotions ; raised the character of the Scots, while it equally depressed the arrogance and ambitious motives of the English and their kings.

Bruce afterwards gratefully acknowledged his obligations to those who aided him in his adversity or contributed to his prosperity. He endowed his chiefs with large estates, and amongst the yeomen classes whose services to him in his days of adversity did not go unrewarded were the Mackays of Kintyre, who harboured and befriended him after the fight and flight at Methven, and the dispersion of his followers by MacDougall of Lorn. To these he gifted lands in Mid Kintyre, where they prospered greatly, for in the 17th century there were not less than twelve territorial lairds of the name Mackay in that district.

To the Mackays in Galloway he was equally liberal. Some of these assisted him after the dispersion of his patriot band by Aymer De ably brothers. Leases of this old date are always valuable, and this one forms no exception. While the landlord warrants the possession, he also maintains and defends the tenant, and, on the other hand, the tenant not only pays rent but gives service. It should be remembered, to Angus's credit, that he did not raise the rent, leaving the same as by use and wont. The period of endurance is indefinite, and is important in ascertaining what the real position of tenant and occupier was of old. Though the spelling is modernised the language is so rude that the meaning is occasionally doubtful. I have not hitherto observed the name of this clergyman of Eilean Finan parish, now united with Ardnamurchan. The old church stood in a small island lying towards the south-east of Loch Shiel. Neither have I observed the name of John MacGhey, vicar of Kildalton, who was probably the writer of the document.

"Be it kenned to all men by these presents, me, Angus M'Conall of Dunywag and Glenis, &c., grants to have set in assedation for farm duty, and service letting, and by the tenor hereof sets, and for farm duty and service sets to my loving servitours, Donald Mac Inuis Mac vic Finlay, minister of Ilan-Inan and to Finlay Macdonald maol Mac vic Finlay, all and haill the ten-merk land of the farm land of Rescholl, with the pertinents thereof, lying within the land of Smart, and sheriffdom of Tarbert, the said Donald and Finlay, their heirs and assignees, paying to me, the said Angus, and my heirs and assignees, yearly, the ferme of old use and wont, their entry being at the Whitsunday afore the day and date hereof, and this ferme to be paid every year at the Whitsunday term. This ten-merk land, before named, of farm land shall be enjoyed, bruiked, and possessed by the saids Donald and Finlay, their heirs and assignees, as long and during the true, leal, affaild service done to me, the said Angus, and my heirs :—And in like manner I, the said Angus, binds and obliges me, my heirs and assignees, to assist, warrant, and defend the saids Donald and Finlay against all manner of men whatsoever, during their true service done to me, the said Angus, and my posteretheis (successors?) against all manner of men whatsomever,—And attour, when the ferme is paid yearly at the term, the officer's part to be allowed. In witness, and for more verification of this letter of tack, we, the saids Angus, and Donald, and Finlay, our heirs, subscribes this present letter at Ardtelwa, the 17th day of August, 1595, before these witnesses—John Oig Macleod, John Og Mac Iaine, and Iou M'Ghey, wicar and minister of Kildalton, &c. (Signed) Angus M'Connall off Dunwaig, Donald Mac vic Finlay, minister of Ellanfyuan, Finay Macdonald Mowill, officer of the saidis lands foirsaid, with my hand on the pen."

SIR JAMES LYLE MACKAY, the distinguished Indian financier, has decided to contest Plymouth at next election.

LORD ARCHIBALD CAMPBELL has presented Miss J. N. MacLachlan with a beautiful clàrsach, or harp, the first of several manufactured by Mr. R. Buchanan, jun., Glasgow.

DEATH OF DR. MACDONALD, LATE M.P. FOR ROSS-SHIRE.— Dr. Roderick Macdonald, late member of Parliament for Ross-shire, died on Friday afternoon, 9th ult., at his residence in Camden Road, London. The deceased gentleman had been ill for some months, and underwent a serious operation, which has just terminated fatally. Dr. Macdonald lost his wife some time ago, and never seemed the same man afterwards. The deceased was the son of a crofter, and was born in the island of Skye. He became a tutor, and subsequently studied for the medical profession at Edinburgh, where he took his degree as M.D. On removing to London, he practised in the East End. When the Middlesex district was divided, about seven years ago, he was elected to the Coronership, for the north-east portion, a post worth £1600 per annum. We understand that he has left handsome bequests to several Scotch charitable institutions in London, and to a few personal friends. His property amounted to £28,000. Dr. Macdonald was one of the earliest subscribers to the *Celtic Monthly*.

HIGHLAND NOTES AND QUERIES.

CLAN MACKAY.— I believe the words "wig worgan" (mhic Morgan) are used by the Clan Mackay. Can you inform me what this means? If it is the "son of Morgan," who was he? how was the name derived? and what does Morgan mean? —J. MACLACHLAN, London.

MACINDOE.—Having read in various Highland magazines particulars regarding the origin of Highland surnames, I do not find any reference to the name Macindoe. I have been told it signifies "the son of black John," as *Mac Ian Duibh* testifies this. Perhaps some of your readers could say whether this is correct or not.—JOHN MACINDOE, Glasgow.

THE CLAN FERGUSON SOCIETY celebrated their second annual reunion in the Trades' Hall, on 8th ult.—Mr. James Ferguson, jun., of Kinmundy, in the chair. The attendance was good, the programme was excellent, and the proceedings passed off with great *éclat*.

GAELIC SOCIETY OF GLASGOW.—At the last meeting, the Rev. Dr. Blair, Edinburgh, delivered a lecture on " Aiteal de sheann nithean Gàidhealach " (A glimpse of old Highland matters), which was greatly enjoyed by the members, as all Dr. Blair's Gaelic addresses are.

THE LEWIS AND HARRIS ASSOCIATION met in the Waterloo Rooms on 6th March—Mr. Malcolm Macleod, president, in the chair. Mr. Henry Whyte (*Fionn*) delivered a most amusing lecture on " Highland Wit and Humour," which clearly proved that the Celt has as keen a sense of humour as his southern critic.

EDINBURGH SUTHERLAND ASSOCIATION.—At the March meeting of this association, Mr. D. W. Kemp, J.P., gave some interesting notes on the schools and schoolmasters of Sutherland of past generations, and stated that he was preparing a work on that subject, and invited members to assist him in collecting material for the "Fasti."

MAJOR A. Y. MACKAY, GRANGEMOUTH.

THE ancestors of Andrew Younger Mackay, of Lea Park, hailed originally from the neighbourhood of Tain, Ross-shire. His grandfather, Andrew Mackay, was a man of distinguished scientific attainments, and, in addition to a professorship of mathematics, held the responsible post of examiner for Trinity House, London, and also for the East India Company; and his father, George Gray Mackay, in conjunction with an elder brother (John Selby Mackay), took a principal part in founding the Grangemouth Coal Company.

Grangemouth has had an almost phenomenal growth, having, within living memory, more than quadrupled its population and risen into considerable importance as a sea-port town. The two brothers referred to above grew with its growth helped, indeed, to make it what it is — and, until their death a few years ago, filled an honoured and very conspicuous place in the life of the young community.

The subject of this sketch was born in Grangemouth in 1845, where he still resides. After completing his education at Dollar Academy, he entered the office of the Grangemouth Coal Co., of which his father was manager. In 1868 he went over to Germany, and was for eleven months in a large shipowner's office in Rostock, and on his return he passed into the employ of George G. Mackay, steamship owner and iron merchant, where he remained till 1883. Thereafter, with a cousin as partner, he started the firm of A. & A. Y. Mackay, steamship managers

and commission merchants, and is still engaged in carrying on this business in its different branches.

Mr. Mackay's aims have never been selfish. As a volunteer, he is an enthusiast, and is almost entitled to be called a *veteran*. Joining the 1st Stirlingshire—now known as the 12th Coy. of the 1st Fife—Volunteer Artillery as far back as 1861 as a gunner, he has passed in succession through the various grades up to the rank of honorary major and commander of the company, and last spring received the volunteer decoration as a tribute to his long and faithful services. As a civilian he takes more than his full share of public work, in proof of which it will be sufficient to state that he is a Burgh Commissioner, is sitting for the second time as a Councillor for the County of Stirlingshire, and is completing his sixth year as Chairman of Grangemouth School Board, a position which he has filled to the entire satisfaction of his coadjutors.

Mr. Mackay has, since its formation, been an enthusiastic member of the Clan Mackay Society, and a liberal contributor to its funds.

Born and bred in the Free Church, he is still one of her staunch and generous supporters.

Warm hearted, open-handed, in all things above suspicion and reliable to the last degree, Mr. Mackay is serving his day and generation according to the will of God. There may be more eventful careers than his; there is not any more honoured or useful. It is through such men that the life of a community is kept fresh and sweet.　　　　S. M. RIDDICK.

GAELIC AIRS TO LOWLAND SONGS.

By Malcolm MacFarlane.

(Continued from page 118).

Songs by Burns to Gaelic Airs.

Some of these are given in the preceding list, and need not be repeated.

25. Gala Water. "From time immemorial," says Dean Christie in his 'Collection of Ballads,' "'Richie's Lady' has been a favourite in Buchan; and no wonder that 'Cam ye by Athol,' by Neil Gow, jun., became such a favourite with the populace, seeing that its first strain is little more than 'Gala Water' turned into 6/8 time." "Richie's Lady" is a set of "Gala Water." The air is replete with Gaelic feeling, and is a perfect example of Gaelic style, except the coda to which "Braw, braw lads" is sung; and this has apparently been added to please the Lowland ear. For Gaelic tunes ending similarly on the suspended notes | l : s | see *Giullan nam bo*—The Cow-boy, and The Highland Widow's Lament.

26. Bonnie Peggy Alison. The Braes o' Balquhidder. There are two tunes named "The Braes o' Balquhidder." One has an older name, "The Three Carles o' Buchanan," is called Gaelic in Maver's collection, and is suggestive of *Cruachan Beann.*

27. From thee Eliza. Gilderoy. "Gilderoy" is the Englished form of *Gille ruadh*—The red-haired lad.

28. Gordon's Welcome Hame. Out over the Forth.

29. The Banks of the Devon. Bannarach dhonn a' chruidh.

30. How long and dreary is the night.

31. Bonnie Castle Gordon. Mòrag.

32. Highland Harry. The Highlander's Lament. Burns writes:—"'The Highland Watch's farewell to Ireland' is the oldest title I ever heard to this tune." It is in Gunn's pipe-music, and is named *A' bhainead ghorm*—The blue bonnet.

33. Musing on the roaring ocean—Druimfhionn dubh. The Irish have a song with a similar name, but the music differs.

34. Ae fond kiss. Rory Dall's Port.

35. My heart's in the Highlands. Fàilte na miosg.

36. Kenmure's on and awa. *Tha boin iul bheag, bhiorach air Alasdair garbh* is the name given to this bagpipe tune in Gunn's collection.

37. Fair Eliza.

38. Willie Wastle. The eight men of Moidart. Wha'll be king but Charlie. The Gaelic words to this air, in some parts, are as follows:—

"A null am monadh, a null am monadh,
A null am monadh gu Tearlach," &c.

39. Farewell thou fair day. Oran an Aoig.

This tune is in Patrick MacDonald's collection. This song was afterwards adopted to "My lodging is on the cold ground," an Irish air. The Scottish "I lo'e nae a laddie but ane" is a variant of the latter air, and "The 78th Highlanders' Quickstep" is another.

40. My lady's gown, there's gairs upon't. Gregg's pipes. The Gaelic name of this pipe tune is *Chaidh an cuthach 'sa bhanarach.*

41. Lovely Polly Stewart. Ye're welcome, Charlie Stewart.

42. Blythe ha'e I been on yon hill. Liggeram Cosh. Burns states, on the authority of "an old Highland gentleman, a deep antiquarian," that this is "a Gaelic air, known by the name of *Gliogram chos.*" It is generally known as "The Quaker's Wife." The air is Gaelic-like beyond a doubt.

43. Whistle and I'll come tae ye, my lad. Burns says—"This I know, Bruce (John Bruce, a fiddle player in Dumfries), who was an honest man, though a *red wud* Highlander, constantly claimed it (the tune), and by all the old musical people here he is believed to be the author of it." R. A. Smith, on the other hand, seems to allow a claim by Ireland for it, under the name, "Noble Sir Arthur." However that may be, it seems to me to be an elaboration of the Scottish Gaelic set of *Robaidh donn goroch,* sung to *Na làithean a dh' aom* (see *The Celtic Lyre,* No. 38). It is not improbable that Bruce based his composition on the set referred to.

44. Behold the hour. Cuir a chinn dìleas. This tune is common to Scotland and Ireland. The Irish name is *Ceann dubh dìleas.* It may be interesting to give the fragment preserved by Hardiman in his "Irish Minstrelsy"—

" A cheinn dhuibh, dhilis, dhilis, dhilis !
    Cuir do làmh mhin-gheal thorm a nall !
A bhéilin mheala, bh-fuil boladh na tìme air,
    Is duine gan chroidhe nach d tiùbhradh duit gràdh.
Ta cailineadha air an m-baile-se air builleadh
    's air buaidhreadh,
Ag tarraing a n-gruaige 's da leigeann le gaoith,
Air mo shon-sa, an seafaire is fearr san tuaithe,
Acht do threiginn au meid sin air rùn dhil mo
    chroidhe.
        As cuir do cheann dìleas, dìleas, dìleas," &c.

It may be remarked that the preceding, unlike most Irish Gaelic songs, is defective in rhyme. The chorus is practically the same as the Highland one. The air, as found in books of Burns's songs, is in the minor mode, has two parts, and is Irish-like. The air in *A' Choisir-chiùil,* is in the "lah" mode, is simpler, true to the Scottish Gaelic style, and has only one part. The Highland words make a complete song, and have the appearance of being old ones, the meaning of the allusions being in some cases obscure. In Tiree, from which the latter form of air comes, the words are *Cuir a ghaoil dìlis.*

(To be continued).

ARCHIBALD MACMILLAN, F.S.L.A.
("Jeems Kaye").
CHIEFTAIN, CLAN MACMILLAN SOCIETY.

ALTHOUGH Mr. Archibald MacMillan, or rather "Jeems Kaye," has for several years back been delighting the readers of *The Bailie*, our local *Punch*, with humorous and entertaining letters on passing events, he is not so well known to Celts as he ought to be.

Mr. MacMillan was born in Greenock in 1843, his father being a prosperous merchant in that town. He came to Glasgow when fourteen. Getting into a situation as clerk he rose steadily step by step till he now conducts a large business on his own account as commission agent.

While a boy many of his holidays were spent at Kilmalcolm, and opposite Otter Ferry, Lochfyne, where he acquired a good smattering of Gaelic. He herded the "kye" and spent nights at the herring fishing during his six weeks' school holidays, and he always declares that he owes his good health to his yearly Highland sojourn, where he was fed on the plainest, and ran about half naked with the boys of the clachan.

Mr. MacMillan, as his writings show, is geniality and good humour personified. He is a thorough master of the doric, and can write it with great force and freedom. His articles are not the laboured efforts of serious study, but rather the natural outflow in leisure moments of one who is a keen student of men and things, and who can give a decidedly humorous turn to his every saying. He has contributed to numerous papers under various names, but it is chiefly as the author of the "Jeems Kaye Papers" that Mr. MacMillan's reputation as a writer rests. These "papers" deal with various subjects, and not a few of them make fine readings, the humour of which is never vulgar. A first collection of the "Jeems Kaye Papers" was published in 1883, and so popular has the work been that over twenty-seven thousand have been sold. A second series was issued in 1886, and in 1888 a third appeared, both of them being accorded a hearty welcome and a ready sale.

It may be stated that Mr. MacMillan was among the first to join the volunteer force, being a member of the 17th (Accountants) Company, which company ultimately became part of the 1st Lanark Rifles, and when the "Glasgow Highlanders" was afterwards raised it was a grief to him that he had not waited and joined that corps, as he is fond of the kilt and tartan, and thinks pipe music the finest in the world.

Mr. MacMillan assisted in the formation of the Clan MacMillan Society, of which he is a chieftain. He delights in travelling in the Highlands, and makes himself thoroughly at home among the peat reek. *Sanghal fada dha!*

ARCHIBALD MACMILLAN.

Overnewton, Glasgow.

HIGHLAND WIT AND HUMOUR.

By "FIONN."

IT has been frequently asserted that the Highlander is very deficient in wit, and utterly lacking in humour. Of course it is but natural that the Lowlander should find little wit in a language which he does not understand, and no humour in the man who speaks a "barbarous language," as our mother tongue has been frequently designated. Of course every Gaelic-speaking Celt understands that many good Gaelic stories and jokes lose their point and edge when presented in Lowland garb. Instead of attempting a definition of "wit," or an analysis of "humour," let me rather submit a few examples, and leave the reader to assort them.

It has been asserted by a Highland sheriff that it is next to impossible to convey to the Celtic mind a correct idea of the "rights of property." This, if true, may be the result of "heredity," for we know that in the "brave days of old" more than one clan prided itself on its *creachs*, and more than the Clan MacFarlane were prepared to take up the words of the gathering tune, "'*Thogail nam bò dhèid sinn.*" "The man who steals a sheep," said my honest countryman, "is a mean thief, but the man who 'lifts' a score of cattle is a gentleman drover." A similar Highland idea of the "rights of property" is represented in the following dialogue :—

DUGALD.—Did you hear that Sandy MacNab was taken to prison for stealin' a coo?"

DONALD.—Hoot, toot, the stupit ass. Could he no bocht it and no paid for't?"

There is rather an amusing story told of a Highlander who was visited on his death-bed by a clergyman, who, knowing Donald's cattle-lifting proclivities, began to exhort him to reflect on the long, black catalogue of his sins before it was too late, otherwise he would have a tremendous account to give on the great day, when all the crimes he had committed here would appear in dreadful array against him, *as evidence* of his guilt. "Och, sir," said Donald, "and will all the sheep and all the black cattle that Donald lifted be there, too?"

"Undoubtedly," replied the clergyman.

"That will be all right, then," said Donald, with considerable relief, "just let every man take back his own, and Donald MacGregor will be an honest man again."

A certain noted poacher and smuggler in the West Highlands was being reprimanded by his "spiritual overseer" for his habits—the priest winding up by saying in Gaelic, "*Fhaic thu Eòghan, mur sguir thu dheth, thèid thu dh' ifrinn cho cinnteach 'sa' chaidh Colla Ciotach ann*" ("Look here, Hugh, if you don't drop it you will go to hell as sure as Coll Citto went there"). "*Colla Ciotach!*" arsa Eòghan, "*ma bhitheas esan is mise an sin còmhla, cumaidh sinn darna taobh an teine dhuinn fhèin*" ("Coll Citto!" said Hugh, "if we two are there together we will keep the one side of the fire to ourselves").

Let us return to the drovers and shepherds. Who could find fault with the idea of the relation that should exist between master and servant as set forth in the following :—"He was a guid maister, the laird," said Donald, "and he keepit min' o' me till the last, for in his will he said—'I leave to my son Willie the twa black-faced yowes that were lost last week, if they're foun' oot. An' in case they're no foun' oot, I leave them baith to my faithful servant Donald.'" The benevolent expression on Donald's countenance deepened as he added, in a sighing undertone, "An' I hope they're no foun' oot."

A Highland—and evidently a Highland-looking—drover attending Falkirk Tryst was accosted by two Lowland scamps, who wanted to have some fun at Donald's expense—"Well, Donald," said the more forward of the two, "what will she do wi' the coos the year?" "We'll do that to the fat," said Donald, as he felled him to the ground with his fist, "and we'll kick the lean to the grass," as he gave the second a "rise in the world" with the toe of his tackety shoe.

A clergyman, crossing the moor, met a Highland shepherd who happened to be calling his dog "Moreover," "Moreover," "Moreover." Accosting the shepherd, he remarked that it was surely a strange name he had for his dog. Was it the same as Rover? "No, no," said the owner, "I like to call all my beasts *Scripture names.*" "But where do you find that one in Scripture?" The shepherd expressed great astonishment at the clergyman's ignorance, and asked if he had never read the Bible story of Lazarus, and how "Moreover the dog came and licked his sores." This reminds one of the gamekeeper who called his first-born Nimrod—"because he was a mighty hunter." In due time a second son appeared, and the gamekeeper, with a fine ear for euphony, named him "Ramrod."

"SECOND TO NONE."

(The motto of the Second Dragoons, Royal Scots Greys).

CHARGE OF THE SCOTS GREYS AT WATERLOO; AND FRENCH "EAGLE" CAPTURED BY
SERGEANT EWART.

[The above spirited picture is reproduced from W. & A. K. Johnston's excellent work on the "Royal Scots Greys,"
which we heartily recommend to our readers.]

Scotland for ever! hark, it is ringing,
　Down the long vista of echoing years ;
Shrill and triumphant the cavalry trumpet
　Sounds "To the charge," amid deafening cheers.
"Sensere gigantes," * the giants have felt it,
　Jove's thunder falls powerless on Scotia's shield :
The pride of a nation, untouched by a foeman,
　The white standard-bearer to Scotland must yield.
Hurrah for the lads of the white plume and thistle !
　Their fame lives for aye, in the deeds they have done ;
Where danger lies thickest, and stout hearts are needed,
　Look there for the lads who are " Second to none."

Scotland for ever ! grey steed and sabre
　Flash as the foam on a storm-beaten rock,
Back, driven back on their haunches, the Frenchmen
　Tremble and reel 'neath the terrible shock.
"Fight for the standard," † brave son of the mountains,
　The Waterloo eagle is linked with thy name ;
More leaves for the laurel entwining the standard,
　Already o'erweighted with Scotia's fame.
Hurrah for the lads of the white plume and thistle !
　The lads of " the bonnets of Bonnie Dundee,"
Long may they flourish, our pride and our glory,
　For the dread of their foes are the "devils o' Dundee."

Scotland for ever ! the " Greys " to the rescue
　(Long shall the Frenchman remember the cry)—
They were two thousand, the Gordons two hundred,*
　Charged them with bayonet, to conquer or die.
Oh ! the wild clash they made, grey steed and tartan,
　Hand on the stirrup, and face to the foe :
Scotland for ever ! their columns are scattered
　As trees are borne down by a torrent in flow.
Hurrah for the lads of the white plume and thistle !
　Resistless in battle, or courtesies charms ;
Long shall the land that so proudly hath borne them
　Ring with the tale of the brothers in arms.

Scotland for ever ! grey steed and scarlet,
　The clank of the spur, and the tuck of the drum ;
" Second to none " in their dash and their finish—
　Welcome our gallants wherever they come.
On guidon and sabretache see the French eagle,
　The grey steed clasped fast on the bearskin behind ;
On stirrup or saddle, where'er the eye glances,
　Some record of valour be sure you may find.
Hurrah for the lads of the white plume and thistle !
　Their fame lives for aye, in the deeds they have done.
Honour and welcome to Scotia's darlings,
　The bonnie " Scots Greys," who stand " Second to
　　none"

ALICE C. MacDonell.

London.

* At Dettingen the Greys captured from the French
the white standard, which bore in the centre a thunderbolt, with the motto, " Sensere gigantes."
† During the retreat to Waterloo, Sergeant Ewart, of
the Greys, captured the eagle of the 45th French Infantry, immortalised in art as "The Fight for the
Standard."

* The 92nd Gordon Highlanders, reduced to 200,
charged with the bayonet 2000 French. As they broke
into it, the Greys rode up in support, the Highlanders
holding on by their stirrups.

LETTERS TO THE EDITOR.

THE REAY FENCIBLES.

To the Editor of the "CELTIC MONTHLY."

London, 9th March, 1894.

SIR,—Controversy in these columns would be reprehensible ; yet permit me, in self-defence, to say that I make every allowance for the clannish zeal which prompted Mr. Mackay's remarks on my notes about the Reays. This zeal has unfortunately led Mr. Mackay to make assumptions and deductions totally inconsistent with facts, so that without more conclusive proof, I cannot accept him as a better authority—on the raising of these famous Fencibles—than Colonel Mackay Baillie and his recruiting officers. Consequently I adhere to my statement " that the Mackays did not come forward with such alacrity as is generally believed to be the case."

Mr. Mackay's references to the " Gordon Highlanders " are not relevant, for that regiment was raised as the " Gordon Highlanders," whereas neither in army list nor muster-roll can be found a regiment designed "The Reay Fencibles, or *Mackay Regiment :*" so that those who write in this connection about the achievements of the " Mackays " at Tara Hill or elsewhere are guilty of an unwarrantable assumption.

In conclusion, let me say Mr. Mackay should not rely on the fictions of Stewart of Garth, nor the fables of the Mackay historian when accusing anyone of making " misleading statements." So far from there being (as Mr. Mackay avers on above authority) " 104 William Mackays in the Sutherland Fencibles, and 33 John Mackays in one company of the same," there were not 104 *Mackays in the whole regiment !* The muster-roll, which is surely the most reliable author ty, only gives 16 Johns and 13 William Mackays—so thus these oft-quoted fables are exploded.—Yours, &c.

D. MURRAY ROSE.

THE HIGHLAND CLUB.

SIR,—I am glad to see that you are endeavouring to establish a Highland Club, where all Highland societies could come together for mutual intercourse, and yet not interfere with their individual objects and interests.

I am sure there are many like myself, who are descendants of old Highland families, though they may not be of the Clans MacGregor or Mackay, but are true-hearted Scotsmen, and miss the pleasure of the company of like-minded men. Therefore I hope that when your endeavours achieve success through the medium of your excellent magazine the privileges and pleasures of such a club, with its reading-room and library, will be extended to us also. J. GILCHRIST MARSHALL.

" BAILEACH.'

SIR,—I notice in the February issue " *Balgan-peolach*" inquiring as to the correctness of the word " *baileach*," used by M'Intyre in his " *Cead deireannach*." This word, in the instance quoted by your correspondent, is a provincialism for " *uil-*

each," which means wholly, totally. In the Perthshire Highlands it is almost invariably pronounced with the " a " sound, and M'Intyre, born and bred contiguous to that county, and often wandering through it, would be familiar with the Perthshire rendering, and used the one or other as the exigencies of rhyme required.

He uses the " a " sound in *Màiri bhàn Og* as follows :—

" Na'n cuireadh i ciil ruim 's diultadh baileach
Bu chuis domh abart a's uaigh "—

while in *Oran nam Briogaisean* he finds the " n " sound suitable—

" Smachdaich iad gu baileach sinn
Tha angar a's duilichinn
'San am so air iomadh fear," &c.

The Gaelic term for a valley between two hills is " *bealach*," an entirely different word and differently pronounced.—Yours, &c.

ALEXANDER STEWART.

Polmont, Stirlingshire.

SIR,—I notice in your " Notes and Queries," page 104, that " *Balgan-peolach* " is in a mistake about the word " *baileach*." The poet is right enough. " *Baileach*" and " *buileach* " are synonymous, the latter more commonly used in the West Highlands, while the former is oftener used in Perthshire and the immediate neighbourhood. The Gaelic for " valley between two hills" is *bealach*, and not *baileach*, as " *Balgan-peolach* " thinks.

A. MACGREGOR.

MY LOVE'S ASLEEP.

DEAR, tender dawn, that bids the world arise,
Break not too soon upon my loved one's eyes,
Wake her not rudely, let sweet darkness keep
    My love asleep.

Oh ! wind of Dawn, breathe softly as you may,
Waft not a single silken tress astray,
Nor stir the lashes on her downy cheek
    When she's asleep.

Sing soft, ye little birds, that so my dear
May think that in her dreams she hear
Sweet music ; sing of all that's sweet
    While she's asleep.

Bright day, new born, be gentle with my love,
Shower on her joys and blessings from above.
And when she wakes, oh ! give her dreams as sweet
    As when asleep.

RITA RICHMOND.

THE sketch on " Highland Wit and Humour " is taken from " Thistledown "—an excellent collection of Scottish wit and humour, published by Alex. Gardner, Paisley.

WE regret that owing to the pressure on our space this month, we have been compelled to hold over the continuation of Col. Charles Stewart's interesting article on " Covalla," and reviews of " Urquhart and Glenmoriston," by William Mackay ; " Manners and Customs of the Highlanders," and " Irish Gaelic Journal."

NEWS OF THE MONTH.

CLAN MACKAY SOCIETY.—The annual social gathering in connection with this society was held in Edinburgh last month—Rev. Dr. J. Aberigh-Mackay in the chair. There was a large attendance. Addresses were delivered by the Chairman, Sheriff Mackay, LL.D., Colonel A. Forbes Mackay, and Messrs. Alex. Mackay, LL.D., and Hew Morrison. The concert, which was essentially Highland in its character, was ably sustained by a number of talented artistes. The whole proceedings were very enjoyable, and show that the Clan Mackay is in a flourishing condition. We understand that a surplus of about £10 has been realised from the gathering. THE MARCH MEETING was held in the Oddfellows' Hall, Edinburgh, on Thursday last—Mr. Thomas A. Mackay in the chair. The Secretary read a letter which he had received from a clansman, offering to contribute £100 to the Bursary Fund if other members contribute £200. It was resolved to issue a circular to members inviting subscriptions. Collections of pictures of the Reay country, and MSS. containing a large number of melodies of Rob Donn Mackay's Gaelic songs were exhibited, as well as photographs of celebrated clansmen abroad, which gave rise to a very interesting discussion. It was proposed to arrange an excursion to the country during the summer, for the benefit of children of the clan. A very pleasant evening was spent. There was an unusually large attendance.

PERTH GAELIC SOCIETY.—The fourteenth annual festival was held on the 9th ult., in the City Hall, Ex-Bailie MacGregor in the chair, and was supported by the Lord Provost and a distinguished company of gentlemen. Addresses were delivered by the chairman, Rev. Hugh Ross, Glasgow, and Mr. Hew Morrison, Edinburgh. An excellent programme of music was sustained by the Glasgow Gaelic Musical Association, whose efforts were enthusiastically applauded. This was considered the best gathering the society ever held.—AT THE FEBRUARY MEETING—Mr. John A. Stewart, solicitor, in the chair—a paper was read on the "Children of Uisneach, first Duan of Fingal, and the two Cuchullins," contributed by Colonel Charles Stewart (*Tigh'n Duin*). Like all the gallant colonel's literary work, the paper was scholarly, and an able exposition of an interesting period in early Celtic history.

THE GLASGOW COWAL SHINTY CLUB held their annual concert in the Waterloo Rooms, on 7th ult.—Dr. David Ross, M.A., B.Sc., in the chair. The chairman advocated that Highlanders should engage in the old Highland game of camanachd, as it was superior to football or any other game. The concert was sustained by a number of talented artistes, all of whom gave great satisfaction. The dance was attended by over sixty couples.

THE CLAN GREGOR SOCIETY.—The March meeting of this society took the form of a smoking concert, which was held in the North British Station Hotel. Speeches were made, and songs and pipe music rendered by members of the clan, and a very pleasant evening was spent.

AIRDRIE HIGHLAND ASSOCIATION met in the rooms on the 7th ult.—Mr. MacNab, president, in the chair. Mr. John Collie, read a paper on the "Depopulation of the Highlands, and compared the census of the Highlands in 1831 and 1891. He deplored the decrease of population, and advocated legislation on the subject.

THE GAELIC CLASS CONVERSAZIONE was held on 13th ult.—Colonel James Menzies in the chair. The hall was crowded with members and friends. Speeches were delivered by friends, a first-rate programme was sustained by students of the class, and dancing was carried on till morning. Mr. Duncan Reid, the able teacher of the class, deserves to be congratulated on the high marks taken by his scholars at the examination, and on the success of the social gathering.

GAELIC SOCIETY OF LONDON.—At the February meeting of this society,

Mr. John Mackay, Hereford, read a most instructive paper on "Gaelic Laments," and at the March meeting he contributed another paper on "Satires," taking Rob Donn as his special understudy. Both papers were greatly appreciated by the members, and gave rise to most interesting discussions.

THE PAISLEY GAELIC CLUB celebrated their annual reunion in the Good Templars' Hall, on 2nd March—Rev. Alex. MacMillan in the chair. The hall was crowded, and the whole proceedings proved a great success. The Chairman's speech was particularly good, and raised great enthusiasm among the audience. A dance followed.

CLAN MACLEAN SOCIETY.—A meeting of this society was held in the Assembly Rooms, on 1st. ult.—Mr. Magnus Maclean, M.A., in the chair. A paper was read on "General Maclean," contributed by Professor J. P. Maclean, U.S.A., giving a biographical account of this distinguished clansman, and the after part of the evening was devoted to Gaelic and English songs by members and friends.

GLASGOW SUTHERLANDSHIRE ASSOCIATION.—The March meeting was held in the Assembly Rooms—Mr. Alex. Bruce, vice-president, in the chair. Mr. D. W. Kemp, delivered a lecture on the "History of the Municipality of the Royal Burgh of Dornoch," which led to a very interesting discussion.

THE GOVAN HIGHLANDERS held their annual conversazione in the Broomloan Hall, on 9th March—Mr. Edward E. Henderson acting as M.C. There was a good attendance, and dancing was kept up with great spirit till a late hour in the morning.

THE MULL AND IONA GATHERING was presided over by Colonel Gardyne of Glenforsa, who delivered a very instructive address on the habits and customs of our forefathers in the Highlands a century ago. He considered the conditions of life had greatly improved since then. The concert was very enjoyable, and the dance was well attended.

DAVID REID CROW, F.R.C.I,
Vice-President, London Argyllshire Association.

THE CELTIC MONTHLY:

A MAGAZINE FOR HIGHLANDERS.

Edited by JOHN MACKAY, Kingston.

No. 8. Vol. II.]   MAY. 1894.   [Price Threepence.

DAVID REID CROW, F.R.C.I.,

VICE-PRESIDENT, LONDON ARGYLLSHIRE ASSOCIATION.

A MORE worthy Highlander than the subject of our sketch this month it would indeed be difficult to find. Mr. D. Reid Crow was born at Lochgilphead, Argyllshire, and there received the education which so well fitted him for his afterwards varied and active life. His father, Mr. David Crow, was in his day a well-known architect in Glasgow and the West of Scotland.

At an early age our friend made his *debût* in commercial life in Glasgow, but after a time he exchanged that centre of industry for London. There, amidst the bustle of a business career, Mr. Crow, who wielded a facile pen, found time to devote himself to press matters, and many of the newspaper columns of a generation ago are indebted to him for his able contributions. His knowledge of the affairs of the day would soon have brought the young Scotchman into public eminence, but about this time his health gave way, and he was advised to go abroad.

Selecting South Africa as his new abode, he arrived in Natal in 1869. Here he met the Rev. Mr. Newnham, M.A. Cantab., now a rector in the south of England, and both being deeply interested in the subject of education, they founded Hilton College, Natal, which has since remained one of the leading educational institutes in the colony.

In military matters also Mr. Crow showed great skill. When war broke out, and the colony was assailed on the north and west by the powerful Zulu tribes, he raised a battalion of volunteers — known afterwards as the Hilton Carabineers. This company, which formed a valuable auxiliary to the regular forces, he commanded in person, his knowledge of the country rendering him peculiarly suited for the duty. On the annexation of the Transvaal to the British Crown in 1877, Mr. Crow, along with the celebrated novelist, Mr. Rider Haggard, and Mr. Clarke, R.A. (now Sir Marshal Clarke, governor of Basutoland), were appointed to the staff of Sir Theophilus Shepstone. After the pacification of the country he was placed on the Commission of the Peace and appointed a Special Commissioner. At Heidelberg, Mr. Crow had the honour of first officially hoisting the British flag.

Again, in the Transvaal War of 1880-81, he distinguished himself in the military operations at Potchefstroom. During this exciting period, however, many of his comrades fell. Mr. Crow and his old friend Col. Clarke became prisoners of war until peace was restored, when they regained their liberty.

After these eventful times, Mr. Crow again turned his attention to business, and settled down in Pretoria. Here he was one of the earliest and most successful merchants. His connection with the London markets necessitated his opening an office there, which he conducted himself, taking periodical visits to the Transvaal.

Notwithstanding his eventful career, Mr. Crow always cherished the warmest interest in his fellow-countrymen and anything pertaining to his native country. When, in 1890, the London Argyllshire Association was formed, he was unanimously elected president. To this post he has been re-elected every year, till last session, when, owing to his leaving London, the Association had to reluctantly accept his resignation. He was, however, elected an honorary vice-president.

Mr. Crow is a Fellow of the Royal Colonial Institute, a member of the National Liberal Club, and holds a high position in the Masonic fraternity. Though yet in the prime of life, he has retired from business, and, like a true Highlander, has selected Ardrishaig as his place of residence. That he may live long to enjoy the fruits of his well-earned leisure will be the heartfelt wish of all his numerous friends.   NEIL MACMILLAN.

London.

THE HEADLESS SPECTRE: A SUTHERLANDSHIRE GHOST STORY.

By the Editor.

CHAPTER III.—THE SPECTRE AGAIN SEEN.

A YEAR passed. As the weeks rolled on, and nothing more was seen of the spectre, I sometimes wondered if it could be all real. Was it possible that I had fallen asleep on the rocks, and dreamt what I had seen, and awakening in the midst of my excitement, had imagined it all true? No; I was too sure about the reality of my experience. I saw the ghostly figure as clearly as I see you now before me, and I shall not forget its horrible appearance as long as I live.

Twelve months had passed away, and people were beginning to remember the occurrence as an old and curious story. It seemed likely soon to be looked upon as one of the many weird "traditions" of the district. However, it was brought fresh to their memory in rather a strange manner.

One night the village shoemaker was working in James Mackay's house, making a pair of boots for one of the children. In the midst of work he found that he required a tool which he had forgotten to bring with him, and he asked his younger brother, John Gordon, to go across the river to his house for the instrument. John departed on the errand, accompanied by his companion, Sandy Munro. The road winds round the edge of the sands, as you can easily see from here, then across the river, and up the hill above the shore towards the great cave of Smoo. The sand reaches right around to the cliffs on the other side.

Well, it was a very pleasant night, and there was light enough to see the great expanse of sand quite clearly. The lads soon reached the house, procured the required tool, and started on their way back. As they came chatting along the road, Gordon suddenly stopped speaking, and looked out towards the sea, as if watching some object.

"EVERYTHING WAS WRAPPED IN MYSTERY."

After a little he stood and said :

"I wonder what that man out there can want at this time of night?"

"Where?" exclaimed Munro, surprised.

"Why, out there. Don't you see him?" said John Gordon, pointing out towards the sands. "He is standing in the water. Surely the fellow cannot be bathing?"

Munro looked out, then rubbed his eyes and looked again, but said he could see nothing.

"You must be very blind," said John. Then putting his finger to Munro's right eye, in telescope fashion, he added : "Now, look straight down my finger, and you will see a man. He is now coming over this way."

Munro had to confess that he could see nothing except the water and the sand. Not a living being was in sight.

Up till this point neither of them had thought for one moment of anything supernatural, but now Munro began to feel somewhat scared.

For some little time John stood motionless, his eyes rivetted on some object which they seemed to follow. Then, in awe-struck voice, almost a whisper, he said :

"Sandy, it's a ghost! It has only a shirt on, and it is quite close to us—just down there," meaning the sands which lay below the embankment upon which they stood.

"Oh, John, don't stand there so quiet ; let us run to the village," exclaimed Munro, who was now greatly agitated.

"I can't, Sandy ! I can't move! I feel as if I were bound hand and foot," John said, slowly and quietly, as if he only spoke mechanically.

"And oh, Sandy !" he suddenly shrieked, "it has no head! It's James Morrison's ghost. Run and bring my father, or it will carry me away !"

Munro needed no second bidding. He fled on the wings of fear. As he rushed across the bridge he heard a frightful unearthly scream, and glancing back he saw John Gordon throw up his arms and fall heavily on the road. Terror-struck, Munro ran into James Mackay's house, and breathlessly related all that had passed. Mackay, Gordon's brother, and one or two men who were in the house enjoying a chat, started to their feet at once, and rushed out of the house. Munro said he would not venture outside again that night for his life.

On the edge of the road they came across the motionless body of Gordon. His face was so that of a corpse, and they thought at first that he was dead, but soon found that he was in a faint. They lifted the poor lad tenderly, and carried him to the house. It was long before he became conscious, and no one could induce him to relate all that he had seen that night. He simply said that he had looked upon the remains of the dead, and that such things only came upon us as a warning.

A party of men made a thorough search of the sands, hoping to find some clue to explain this ravelled mystery. Every nook and corner was explored, but all without result. No human being was to be found, and no glimpse could be had of the disturbing spirit. The sand even below the place where the body was found was closely examined, but no trace could be seen of a footmark. Everything was wrapped in mystery. The searchers went home feeling that some horrible fiend was abroad at their very doors, and they were unable to protect themselves from its unwelcome attentions. All they could do was to wait and see how it was to end.

CHAPTER IV.—THE MYSTERY SOLVED.

It may seem strange that intelligent people should accept these ghostly visitations as only an earnest, a destinct warning, indeed, of some great calamity which was to happen sooner or later in their neighbourhood. They believed that there was a purpose in these things, but in what form that warning was to find expression, or who the sufferers were to be, they could make no satisfactory conjecture. . . . The next generation may know more about the supernatural world than we do. Science and commonsense may accomplish what scepticism has failed to teach us.

At any rate, there was one thing which we in this parish were sure of—the spectre had disappeared from the sands, and it was fondly hoped that its absence would be a permanent one. Very nearly a year had come and gone and no one had seen the dreaded spirit, which, truth to tell, no one really wanted to see ! The weather had been beautifully fine at the season I speak of, and it seemed likely to continue so for several weeks to come. One memorable night, when the people had retired to rest, the moon was shining brightly, and there was hardly a breath of wind to ruffle the surface of the water.

In the early hours of the morning the good folks of the village were suddenly awakened by the roar of a great hurricane which swept over the land, threatening to tear the roofs off the houses. At short intervals bright flashes of lightning illumined the landscape, while the thunder kept up a continual crash overhead. The dashing and moaning of the stormy sea could be heard at a great distance. Indeed, such a wild night had not been experienced for many years in Durness.

In the morning, when the day had dawned, the people came out to see if any damage had been done to their property. The morning was so quiet and serene that one could hardly believe that only a few hours before such a wild storm had raged.

A man happened to go down to the shore, and what a sight met his eyes! A large ship had gone to pieces on the rocks, and the sands were covered with a mass of wreckage. The news quickly spread, and soon the whole population were gathered on the beach, saving from the waves the debris of the wreck. Not a soul on board the ship was saved, the bodies of sixteen drowned sailors being found strewn among the rocks. Many others were carried out into the deep Pentland, and were never recovered.

But what sent a thrill a horror through the spectators was the appearance of one of the bodies which was found far up on the sands, just below the spot where John Gordon had fainted. This corpse had no head! Through some curious accident the upper part of the head had been wrenched off, the lower jaw being all that remained. It had no covering except a shirt of the usual length. Not a word was said as the remains were carefully lifted up on to the road, and placed in a large box which was procured for their reception. To the minds of those present the discovery of this body had solved a mystery,

BALNAKIEL GRAVEYARD AND CHAPEL, DURNESS.

for the corpse was placed in the coffin on the very place where the ghost had been seen. It was a most remarkable coincidence—if I could call it that. And it exactly answered the description which both Gordon and myself had given of the spectre, even in regard to its scanty clothing.

The remains of the sixteen sailors were interred in the graveyard at Balnakill, in the right hand corner opposite you as you enter. Many a poor drowned seaman was buried there before, and several have been placed there since. A great number of the people of the place attended the funeral, and saw all that was human of the "headless spectre" placed under the sod.

Now that is all I have to tell you regarding the wreck of the "Juniper," and the strange circumstances connected with it. If you can explain to me by any rule of science or reason how I saw that man's spirit two years before his death, or why Gordon saw it twelve months before the body was found, I shall be obliged to you. To me the memory of these events is not a pleasant one. How could it be otherwise?

When Morrison had finished his weird story I looked down at the beach, which was close at hand. There was not a cloud in the sky, and the long stretch of pure white sand was bathed in a flood of moonlight. Away in the distance the great cliffs rose out of the water, and cast a dark shadow. The whole expanse of sand and water could be scanned as far as the eye could reach—a perfect fairyland to those who were not acquainted with its gruesome associations.

Turning to my friend, who was preparing to go indoors, I said :

"Was nothing ever found out about the identity of this man—his name, position, or history? There must surely have been some strange story connected with his career?"

"Nothing, absolutely nothing, was ever found out about him. The bodies were never identified,

although full particulars regarding the vessel and crew were afterwards ascertained. The ship was homeward bound from India for the Clyde. People said that the man must have committed some great crime, and that justice had overtaken him in the storm. But it is getting late, and you have some distance to go up the strath, so good-night, and a safe journey to-morrow across Erribol."

"Good-night," I answered, "and the best wish that I can express is that you may see no more headless spectres on Durness Sands."

(Concluded).

OUR MUSICAL PAGE.

FAILTE DHUIT, SLAINTE DHUIT.

To Lord Archibald Campbell, on his coming to preside at the second Mòd of the COMUNN GAIDHEALACH *at Oban, in September, 1893.*

Sèisd.   KEY E♭.   *Lively, beating twice in the measure.*

Cha'n ionann 's na h-uaibhrich mach tigeadh gu tuath,
Ach a mharbhadh 'sa ruagadh feadh chruach agus chàrn ;
Ri losgadh 'us leònadh air creutairean bòidheach,
'Se crùnadh an sòlais 'bhi còmhradh mu'n bàs.
Ach 'b feàrr le Gilleasbuig toilinntinnean eile,
Cruit-chiùil a bhiodh deiseil gu freagairt nan dàn.
Ag èisdeachd nan òran gu h-aoibheil 's a' chònmhlan.
'S a' chainnt a tha ceòlar an òrdugh nam bàrd.

Gur math thig an deise thug buaidh air gach sgeudach,
Mu d' chom a tha eireachdail deas air a' bhlàr ;
'S a' bhoineid a direadh tha iteag an fhìor-eoin
Crios-guaile nan riomhadh fo ghrian lannair bràisd.
Cirbean a' bhreacain a bualadh air gartain,
Glasgow.

'S do ghluasad air faiche, am maise, thar chàich.
Gur iomadh fuil uasal ag còmhail a d' ghruaidhean,
'S tha Inntinn nam buadhan 'an suaireeas gun stràic.

Cha d'fhuair thu le cheannach bhi cruadalach smearail,
Ach dùchas nan seanar nach leanadh an tràill.
A' chòmhsaicheadh rìghrean an aobhar na firinn,—
'Chum còirichean cinnteach na rìogh'chd o gach nàmh.
Cha'n ioghnadh leam t-aogasg 's fuil Dhiarmaid a' d' aodan,
'O cheannardaibh laoch a bha daonnan na'n sàir.
Gur fàillein thu 'n chraobhaig a dh'fhàs am Bun-aora,
'Leig slos an fhuil chraobhach 's thug saorsa o thàir.

JOHN MACFADYEN.

REV. DONALD H. O. D. MACKINNON, M.A., F.R.G.S.

HON. VICE-PRESIDENT, CLAN MACKINNON SOCIETY.

REV. DONALD H. O. DIMSDALE MACKINNON, M.A., F.R.G.S., is the eldest son of the late Major-General Daniel MacKinnon, a distinguished officer, who served in the 16th (Queen's) Lancers throughout the first Afghan war of 1838-9, and the Sikh campaign of 1845-6, for which he received two medals with clasps for Ghuznee, Sobraon, and Aliwal, in which latter battle he had his horse shot under him, and in which, although a subaltern, he commanded a squadron throughout the day, and at the end of which he was almost the only officer of his corps fit for duty when he had to bury the dead throughout the ensuing night. Mr. MacKinnon's mother was the daughter of the late Honourable Thomas Robert, 4th Baron Dimsdale, and his great-grandfather was William, thirty-third chief of the Clan MacKinnon, who succeeded, on the death, in 1808, of the last male representative of the Kilmorie, or direct line. On William's death, in 1809, the chieftainship passed to his eldest grandson, William Alexander, whose brilliant Parliamentary career extended over a period of forty-six years.

The subject of our sketch was educated at Haileybury and Exeter College, Oxford, whence he graduated in 1871, and proceeded M.A. in 1873. He was ordained deacon in 1872, and was assistant minister of Quebec Chapel, St. Mary-le-bone till 1879, when he took charge of Speldhurst, in Kent, of which he became rector in 1889, as such holding the patronage of Rusthall and Langton vicarages, and the chapelry of Groombridge. In early life he devoted himself to athletics, being a member of his College boat for three years, and gaining several prizes for running, jumping, &c. After his marriage, in 1875, with Jemima, daughter of James Macalpine-Leny, of Dalswinton, Dumfriesshire, an officer of the 8th (King's) Hussars, he spent much of his leisure time in travel, having visited most parts of Europe, and latterly the Cape. He explored the Arctic regions of Lappmark in 1887 with his wife, who is one of the first British ladies who penetrated so far, and he subsequently published a book entitled, "Lapland Life," which reached two editions. Mr. MacKinnon is a Free Mason of Apollo Lodge (Oxford Univ.). He has always taken the keenest interest in all matters connected with the Highlands, and in 1882 published the only "Memoirs of Clan Fingon." Mr. MacKinnon has long advocated the formation of a clan society, and the wish of his heart has now been happily realised. He has three sons—George (midshipman, R.N.), Alaister, and Lachlan.

From a photo. by Fex & Mundl, London.

Glasgow.   DUNCAN MACKINNON.

THE LAST MACDONALDS OF ISLA.

By CHARLES FRASER-MACKINTOSH, F.S.A. (Scot.).

PART VI.—(continued from page 137).

THE last of the documents I have connected with Angus Macdonald is a bond of friendship by Dougall, afterwards Sir Dougall Campbell of Auchinbreck, dated 25th August, 1603, the signatures to which, being those of men of some consequence, are given in *fac-simile.* In a singular old MS. genealogy of the Argyles, done by Advocate Campbell, styling himself "Bailie of Argyle," and which terminates with John, second Duke of Argyle, who succeeded in 1703—No. 40 of the line—I observe from my copy, which is not very legible, that, beginning with "Smerrie Mor," who married a sister of King Aiden of Scotland, (crowned Anno 542), the chronicling bailie in due time reaches No. 28, viz., Duncan, father of the first Auchinbreck. Here is the account :—

"28. Duncan-an-aigh is said in France to have killed a boar, for which reason the family has a boar's head in their arms ; he married Marjory Stuart, daughter to Robert, Duke of Albany, Governor of the Kingdom under his brother, King Robert the Third,

SIGNATURES TO AUCHINBRECK'S BOND OF 1603.

second king of the Stuarts. This King Robert was he that was called John Harnyear? So his wife was King Robert's niece, and grandchild to King Robert Bruce, daughter to King Robert Bruce, by whom the crown came to the Stuarts. This Duncan begat on this noble lady two sons and a daughter, viz , Archibald Roy and Colin, afterwards Sir Colin Campbell of Glenurchy, called Colin-dubh-na-Roinuh, who married Margaret Stewart, eldest daughter to the Lord Lorn. She built Castle Kilchurn, in the head of Loch Ow in her husband's absence at Rome. On his return he became tutor to Argyle, his nephew ; built the tower of Inveraray. He married four times, and lived 100 years. Duncan an Aigh's second marriage was with Margaret Stuart, daughter to Sir John Stuart of Ardgowan, now called Blackhall, a natural son of King Robert, and had many sons of her, viz., Duncan Campbell of Auchinbreck, whose offspring were called Sliochd Donchy ; (2) Neil Campbell, of whom the Laird of Ellangireg ; (3) Archibald, the first Laird of Ottar, in Cowal. This Duncan an Aigh was cotemporary with King Robert the Third, second king of the Stuarts, crowned anno 1390, and with King James 1st, crowned 1424."

I may mention that Duncan-an-Aigh is stated to have been so called, being fortunate in his life, while his feeble-minded brother John, predecessor of Barbreck, had the significant appellation of "Annain." Sir Dougall Campbell of

Auchinbreck was a leading man among the Campbells betwixt the years 1592 and 1625.

"Be it kenned to all men by these present letters, We, Angus M'Connald of Dounavaig, and Dougall Campbell of Auchinbreck, understanding the ancient, honourable, and mutual bond, and the great friendship that was, and is, betwixt the house of Kintyre and the house of Auchinbreck, and now we, the saids Angus M'Connald and Dougall Campbell of Auchinbreck, being of that same good mind that our predecessors was to others, and willing to renew the said ancient and honourable bond, I, the said Dougall Campbell of Auchinbreck to be bound and obliged, like as I, by the tenor hereof, binds and obliges me for myself, and the haill House of Auchinbreck, and all others my vassals, friends, servants, tenants, and dependers to fortify, assist, maintain and defend the said Angus M'Connald of Dounavaig, his friends, vassals, servants, and dependers in all his and their honest, honourable, and leisome affairs and adoes whatsoever contrar, whatsoever person or persons (His Majesty and the Earl of Argill except), and shall not by myself, or by any of my house or any dependers, hear or see the said Angus

MACDONALD OF THE ISLES

"The figure represents one of the Lords of the Isles sitting in judgment on the Tom Mold, or Law Hill, in Eillean Comhairliech, with his barons around him. He wears the habergeon, or shield of mail, underneath, the sleeves of a leather doublet are seen, and the legs and arms exhibit the appropriate breacan of Lord MacDonald. The clogaid, or skull-cap, is of the form worn by the old Gael. As a regal head-piece, it is ornamented with a circlet of Cairngorm stones, or topazes, and the "eagle's wing," which Ossian tells us distinguished a chief, is fixed on the apex amid the badge of lovely heather. The sword represents the old claidheamh of the Highlander.—M'Ian's "Clans of the Scottish Highlands"

or any of his house or dependers hurt, or skaith, either in body, lands, or goods, without it come by His Majesty, or by my Lord Earl of Argill, but I shall stop and latt the same to my power, and make the said Angus and his friends to be foreseen hereof, in so far as I and my said friends may by any moyan either by sea or land, and to corroborate the former bond and this new bond. Likeas has given a solemn private oath to perform the same, and shall renew the same *toties quoties* if I be required thereto. In witness whereof I have subscribed this bond with my hand, as likeways the said Angus has subscribed the like bond to me, at Skipnish, the 15th day of August, 1603 years, before these witnesses, Colin Campbell of Kilberrie, Neill M'Neill of Thynis, Malcolm M'Neill his brother, Alexander Macdougall Persone of Kildaltane, Hector M'Neill, fiar of Thynis; and Cuthbert Adamsoun, Commissar of Argyll. (Signed) Dougall Campbell of Achinbreck, Colin Campbell of Kilberrie, witness; Neil M'Neill of Thynis, witness; Alexander M'Dougall Persone of Kildaltane, witness; Cuthbert Adamson, witness.

Without some account of the desperate feuds betwixt the Isla family and the Macleans the story of Angus Macdonald's life would be incomplete. In place of attempting to summarise matters, and committing myself to either side, I purpose to transcribe the account given by the historian of a northern clan unconnected with either by close ties, but friendly to the Macdonalds. This history has not been published, was written about 150 years ago, is conceived in easy and concise language, and the part now given was introduced as a matter of general importance in Scottish history of the time :—

"Here it may be observed that, by undue influence, King James was in 1588 induced to confirm to

Hector Maclean certain lands in the Rinns of Isla, stating that they at one time pertained to his predecessors.

"There had been a quarrel of an old standing between the M'Donalds of the Western Isles and the M'Leans, which was like to prove fatal to either sometime. As far back as the year 1586, Donald Gormmor of Slait, intending to visit his brother, Angus M'Donald of Kintyre, he embarks in the Isle of Skye, but was driven by contrary winds on the Isle of Jura, which was divided betwixt the M'Donalds and the M'Leans. He happened to land on the side of the island belonging to the M'Leans.

"About the same time that Donald Gorm landed, two gentlemen of the name of M'Donald who had a quarrel with him arrived in the island with a company of men, who, understanding that he was there, they secretly, under silence of the night, seized a number of cattle belonging to the M'Leans and carried them off in their boat, knowing that Donald Gorm and his retinue would be blamed, and that the M'Leans would revenge the loss of their cattle upon them, which accordingly happened.

"Sir Lachlane M'Lean being alarmed, presently raises his men, and under silence of the night marches and attacks Donald Gorm and his company and killed 60 of his followers dead upon the spot. Donald himself and the rest escaped to a ship that stood in the harbour waiting a fair wind.

"Angus M'Donald of Kintyre hearing of this unhappy affair betwixt his cousin Donald Gorm and his brother-in-law, Sir Lachlane M'Lean—for he was married to Sir Lachlane's sister—he resolved to lose no time in setting out for the Isle of Sky, to wait for Donald Gorm, and to offer his good offices to make up a peace betwixt two such near relations.

"Having stayed some time in the Isle of Sky with his cousin, he returns home, and in his way lands at Mull, and went to Dowart, M'Lean's principal residence, though his two brothers, Coll and Ronald, used their utmost effort to dissuade him from seeing Sir Lachlane at that time, but rather to make an appointment with him to meet him in some proper place, and at the same time to acquaint him that though Donald Gorm was so greatly injured by him, yet he was disposed to have matters amicably adjusted. But Angus had such confidence in his brother-in-law that nothing could dissuade him from seeing him then, upon which his brothers left him, but his cousin Ronald accompanied him to Dowart.

"Sir Lachlane at first received him with a show and appearance of great civility, but at length Angus was seized with his men and secured in prison. His cousin Ranald narrowly escaped that night, but Angus was detained close prisoner till he renounced his title and right to the Rinns of Islay, which was the heritage of the M'Donalds by donation from the king for their personal services. Angus in the end was forced to consent or die. He gave James, his eldest son, and Ranald, his brother, as hostages for the performance, to remain at Dowart till Sir Lachlane was put in possession of the Rinns, which being done they were set at liberty.

"Angus, full of resentment at the injuries done to his cousin and himself, meditates how to be revenged. In order to which he sends a kind invitation to Sir Lachlane to come to Islay to finish their agreement, and to get the sasine of the Rinns. Sir Lachlane

accepts the invitation, and leaving Ranald, one of the hostages, in fetters at Dowart, he brings the other, James, who was his own nephew, along with him to his house, promising to make him as welcome as his heart could make him while his provisions lasted.

(*To be continued*).

SON OF THE GAEL.

To "FIONN."

Son of the Gael, I will lilt thee a ditty—
Well art thou loved in the glen and the city,
Loved for thy diction so powerful and witty,
  Loved for thy fealty so fearless and bright:
    Long may health cling to thee,
    While I now sing to thee—
Blessings on "Fionn" the fair—brave Henry
  Whyte !

Son of the Gael, could I warble thy praises
With all the sweet freshness and beauty of daisies,
Then would I cheer thee, 'mid mystical mazes,
  While you teach Gaelic by day and by night:
    Long may you praise the tongue
    Which your own mother sung—
Blessings on "Fionn" the fair—brave Henry
  Whyte !

Son of the Gael, sure thy heart's in the Highlands,
Twined round the tight little, storm-beaten islands,
Thinking no country in foreign or nigh lands
  Equals in grandeur thine own, and thou'rt right:
    Long may you love the glens,
    Corries and heath-clad bens —
Blessings on "Fionn" the fair— brave Henry
  Whyte !

Son of the Gael, where the pibroch is screaming,
There with the mem'ries of old thou art dreaming—
Dreaming of martyrs who, heedless of scheming,
  Fought 'gainst the darkness of Error for Light:
    Long may you love to praise,
    Men who have won their bays,
While we bless "Fionn" the fair—brave Henry
  Whyte !

Son of the Gael, may thy faith never falter,
Till from the Highlands you loosen the halter,
Till on a pinnacle thou shalt exalt her.
  To reign o'er a kingdom untrammelled by
    might:
    Then every Gael shall sing,
    While all the Highlands ring.
Blessings on "Fionn" the fair— brave Henry
  Whyte !

Manchester.   DUNCAN MACLEAN.

TO CORRESPONDENTS.

All Communications, on literary and business matters, should be addressed to the Editor, Mr. JOHN MACKAY, 17 Dundas Street, Kingston, Glasgow.

TERMS OF SUBSCRIPTION.— The CELTIC MONTHLY will be sent, post free, to any part of the United Kingdom, Canada, the United States, and all countries in the Postal Union—for one year, 4s.

THE CELTIC MONTHLY

MAY, 1894.

CONTENTS.

A HIGHLAND REGISTRY.

WE are glad to intimate that the long talked of Highland Register is actually about to become an accomplished fact, and girls coming from the north and west to our great city will, in a short time, not only find friends to help them, but a "Home" to receive them.

The Highland societies have had the subject before them for a long time, and have discussed it again and again without any practical result. Now, however, a few ladies in Edinburgh and Glasgow have put their heads together, and behold the thing is done! They have formulated a plan, and in a few weeks we are told that they intend to open a Highland Home in our city, and, in connection with the Home, propose to have a Register for all Highlanders, a Restaurant, and a Depot for home industries. We confess that this at first appeared to us rather a large order, but after an interview with one or two of the energetic ladies of the committee we came away convinced that the scheme is quite practicable, and that, if once fairly started, can be made, after a short time, self-supporting.

The establishment must be on a small scale to begin with, and only six or eight girls can be accommodated. The restaurant will be a means of training the girls and supporting the establishment, and the depot is going to be a parcel-post arrangement; to encourage old and young to make and send marketable articles, and help to revive the art of spinning, weaving, and knitting again in the Highlands.

We must, however, impress upon our readers that such an undertaking requires funds to start successfully, and we hope they, as well as our Highland societies, and all interested in the Highlands, will help with the good work.

We understand that a Gaelic concert, under the distinguished patronage of the Lord High Commissioner for Scotland and the Marchioness of Breadalbane, will be given in Edinburgh, during the meeting of Assemblies, in its behalf.

Secretaries—Mrs. Carmichael, 7 St. Bernard's Row, and Miss Hay, Merchiston Avenue, Edinburgh.

We shall be glad to receive and acknowledge subscriptions on behalf of the "Highland Home."

OUR NEXT ISSUE.

WE will present our readers with a life-like plate portrait of Mr Donald N. Nicol, of Ardmarnock, a gentleman well known and greatly respected in all parts of Argyllshire, which will be accompanied with an interesting biographical sketch. We will also give finely engraved portraits of Mr. A. Stewart MacGregor, vice-consul at Christiania, Norway; Mr. A. MacNab, president, Airdrie Highland Association; and Messrs. Thomas H. Murray, and Neil MacMillan, joint-secretaries, London Argyllshire Association. Mr. C. Fraser-Mackintosh will continue his valuable series of papers on the "Last MacDonalds of Isla," which will be illustrated with fine engravings of several of the crosses and ancient churches of Islay, and a fac-simile of a MacDonald bond. Mr. John Mackay, Hereford, gives a graphic account of the career of Angus Dubh, the Mackay chief, and the eventful battle of Druim-na-cupa, in connection with which two beautiful views of the Reay country will be given. In addition to these, "Fionn" will contribute another paper on "Highland Wit and Humour,"Mr. James Ferguson a very interesting article on "Highlanders in the Archer Guard of France," and several other attractive contributions in prose and verse will appear with suitable illustrations. We also hope to be able to publish the result of the John Mackay, Hereford, Prize of £10, offered by the Gaelic Society of London, with the successful song set to music.

HENRY WHYTE TESTIMONIAL.

WE beg to acknowledge, with thanks, receipt of the following additional subscriptions:—Mr. Alex. Mackay, 63 Renfield Street, Glasgow, £1; Miss Stobo, Green Knowe, Bridge of Allan, 5s; John Mackintosh, secretary, Comunn Gaidhealach, 5s; Messrs. Macpherson, Ivy Cottage, Easdale, 5s. Total, £26 4s.

TONGUE AND ITS HISTORIC SURROUNDINGS.

By John Mackay, C.E., J.P., Hereford.

Part IV.—Assassination of Iye Mackay—Battle of Tutem-Tarrach.

(Continued from page 133).

MAGNUS, the Mackay chief who led his clan contingent in Randolph's division at Bannockburn, died in 1315, the year after that event, whether or not from the effect of wounds received in the battle history does not record. He was succeeded by his son Morgan, who ruled the clan for fifteen years. Such names as Alexander, Walter, Martin, Magnus, Morgan, were at the time foreign to the North Highlands, but were common enough in the south of Scotland; in Strathclyde and Galloway the probability seems to be that these names were imported from that district of Scotland from which these chiefs came, and these names seem to corroborate the supposition. The Gallowegians were a mixed race of Picts and Britons from Cumberland and Westmoreland, who penetrated as far north as the Clyde, and took possession of Dumbarton, as the signification of that word implies—Dun-nam-Breatunnaich, the fort of the Britons—the more ancient name of which was Al-cluyd, or Al-cluith (ail-cluith), the rock of, or at, the Clyde. There

is a river Clwyd in Denbighshire North Wales.

Morgan is not a Saxon, nor a Pictish, nor a Scottish name, but it is, even now, very common in Wales, where the descendants of the ancient Britons now exist. It is very probable that the Britons, who kept possession of the south-west of Scotland for several centuries, and intermarried with the natives, would leave a name common to them behind. They were not expelled by the Scottish monarchs who subjected them to their rule, turbulent as they were they remained. Magnus, Morgan, Martin, were names common in Galloway, amongst gentle and simple, and imported thence by the Mackay chief, as we afterwards find Donald and Iye imported from Kintyre. It has been stated that the Mackays were called the Clan Mhorgan from this chief. That is simply a misconception. It was only his direct descendants who were called Clainn Mhic Mhorgan. The name Morgan became extinct amongst the Mackays in about a century. In the same way the families of Farquhar, Paul, Angus, Neil, Thomas—sons of Mackay chiefs—were nicknamed Mhic Ercher, Mhic Pol, Mhic Angus, Mhic Neil, Mhic Thomas, eventually Anglicised into Farquharson, Polson, Macangus, Nelson, Thomson.

Morgan was succeeded by his son Donald, who, in his father's lifetime, sought for himself a wife amongst his kindred in the south. It is

MACKAY.

"The figure wears a flat bonnet, on which the clan badge is displayed, and an eagle's feather. The doublet, or jacket, is of strong cloth formerly much worn, to which a dull red colour was imparted by a native dye. The tartan is that recognised as peculiar to the Clan Vodh, the brogues made chiefly of hide, from which the hair is not removed; the sword and targe are of the forms in common use among the Highlanders." James Logan, in R. R. M'Ian's "Clans of the Scottish Highlands."

possible he may have been with his father and grandfather at Bannockburn, and there became intimate with his Gallowegian, Kintyre, and Isla relatives, and on his return visited those in Kintyre, where he met Miss MacNeil, a daughter of Iye MacNeil, chief of Gigha, whom he married and took with him to Tongue to share with him the amenities of the north.

This chief seems to have lived a quiet and peaceable life, and died in 1340, leaving a son and successor, named Iye (Aodh, Hugh), after his grandfather of Gigha. This is another instance of the relationship that then and previously existed between the Mackay chiefs of the north and those of the south.

Iye Mackay had during his rule serious differences with William, Earl of Sutherland. The earl did not feel himself sufficiently powerful to take the law into his own hands, and was the more disinclined to do so as the Sutherland men were the aggressors, though they dearly paid for it by the retaliations they provoked. The earl, unwilling to admit that his men were the aggressors, proposed to the Mackay chief to submit their differences to the Lord of the Isles and others for arbitration at Dingwall. Iye Mackay consented. The parties met at Dingwall and submitted their relative cases to the arbitrators. It would appear that the Mackay chief seemed likely to get the best of it. The earl sought for an interview with Iye and his son Donald, who accompanied him, and in the heat of discussing the question in hand the earl drew his dirk and killed father and son, and at once rode off to Dunrobin, pursued by the Mackay retainers who accompanied their chief, but the earl with difficulty got safely to Dunrobin. Sir Robert Gordon, as usual, in recording incidents dishonourable to the Earls of Sutherland, does not tell the truth, for in this instance he states that the earl's name was Nicolas, whereas it ought to be William, and gives the date 1395, when it ought to be 1380, the year of the arbitration and assassination. This was the commencement of the feuds and

conflicts which lasted for upwards of two centuries between the Mackays and the Earls of Sutherland.

Donald, the only son of Iye Mackay killed at Dingwall, left three sons—Angus, who succeeded his grandfather as chief, and Hugh and Neil. This Donald is stated to have been the founder of the name Mackay in the north, from being the son of Iye—Mack-Iye, Mack-aoi. This is a mistake, for the name Mackay was known in Galloway and the south of Scotland as early as the reign of David I. Besides this, the name MacKie, MacKai appears in charters previous to 1340, notably in charters granted by Bruce, who died on the 7th June, 1329.

Angus, the eldest son of Donald, and grandson of Iye, succeeded. He married a daughter of MacLeod of Lewis, had two sons—Angus Du, or the swarthy, and Ruari-gallda, or Roderick, the foreigner, from his having been reared out of his father's family amongst his mother's relatives in Lewis. He died at an early age, leaving his family and estates in the care or tutorship of his brother Hugh, who proved himself to be worthy of the trust reposed in him.

During his tutorship, the mother of the young chief, Angus Du, desired to have some share in the management of the estates, and probably a larger allowance than her husband set apart for her. Hugh declined to agree to these demands. She then complained to her brother, MacLeod of Lewis, who came to Tongue with a large company of men, with the resolution of compelling Hugh, either by entreaty or force, to comply with his sister's demands. Finding Hugh inflexible, and that he would not be cajoled by fair words, nor overawed by force, he departed in high dudgeon, and on his way back drove off a great number of cattle from the Mackays' lands. This being reported to Hugh, he and his brother Neil at once collected their men and pursued the Lewis men. Having overtaken them at Tutem-tarrach, in Strath Oykel, Hugh immediately attacked the Lewis men, and, says

HOPE FERRY, DURNESS, SUTHERLAND.

Sir Robert Gordon, "a terrible battle was fought," in which the islanders were annihilated, one only finding his way back to Lewis to relate the woful tale. Hugh Du died two years after this event, and his brother Neil died shortly before or after him, leaving three sons—Thomas, Neil, and Morgan—who, as we shall see in the next chapter, played an important part in the story of the great Mackay chief, which led to the terrible conflict of Druim-na-cupa, the "Bannockburn" of the Mackay territory.

LOCH HOPE, LOOKING TOWARDS STRATHMORE.

MANY of our readers will be glad to learn that the handsome prize offered by *The Scottish Congregationalist*, for the best essay on "Benefits of Attendance on Public Worship," has been awarded to Mr. John S. Mackay, Thurso, the local secretary of the Clan Mackay Society.

WE have to express our thanks to Mr. Donald Mackay, Town and County Bank, Thurso, for kindly giving us the use of his interesting collection of negatives of views of the Reay country. We reproduce two of them this month in connection with Mr. Mackay, Hereford's, article. We shall be greatly obliged to any of our readers who can assist us with photos. of places of interest on the north coast from Reay to Bettyhill; and also of Mingarry, Ardlamont, and Toward Castles, Argyllshire.

THE HIGHLAND DRESS.—We have just been favoured with a copy of Messrs. Rowan & Co.'s new illustrated price-list, which contains a great deal of information which should prove valuable to parents anxious to know where to get good value in boys' suits. Messrs. Rowan make a specialty of the Highland costume, and supply all the dress accoutrements. Their catalogue contains a list of nearly 180 clan tartans which they are in a position to supply. Owing to the rapid increase in this department of their business they have been forced to add a handsome saloon to their extensive premises. There is no dress which becomes a boy better than the Highland costume when correctly made and of good material, and at Messrs. Rowan's establishment customers may depend upon being well satisfied in this respect.

CLAN MORGAN, OR MACKAY.—Morgan means "mawr-gàn," large capacity—the same as the Gaelic "ceann-mor" means big head, or a man with large capacity. Mhic Mhorgan means the son of Morgan, who was a chief of the Mackays in the 14th century, and only applied to his descendants, who for less than a century preserved the distinction, and soon became extinct.—MACAOIDH.

MR. THOMAS SINCLAIR, M.A , Falmouth, has a new work in the press—"Caithness Events"—which will be published shortly by the *Northern Ensign* Office, Wick.

"RAINING'S SCHOOL MAGAZINE" continues to do credit to its editors and contributors. The recent issues have been specially good, and we wish the magazine every success. We are glad to notice that the shinty club is so prosperous.

MUSIC.—We are indebted to Miss Katherine Mackay, Fort-William, Belfast, for a copy of Mr. J. G. Callcott's "March of Brian Boru." The composer has done excellent justice to his subject, the music being tuneful and masterly. It is published by Mr. John Blockley, 3 Argyll Street, London, W.

"THE GAELIC JOURNAL." (Dublin).—The February and March numbers are to hand. Not the least interesting feature of the present issues is the commencement of a series of easy lessons in Irish, conducted by the learned and active editor, Professor O'Growney. We also note with pleasure that it is contemplated to issue the *Journal* monthly instead of quarterly. We hope the conductors will be encouraged to make this change, and thus give a fresh impetus to the national language and literature.

HIGHLAND WIT AND HUMOUR.

By "FIONN."

AT a fishmonger's window, in Glasgow, a Highland drover, accompanied by his faithful collie, was admiring the large silver salmon, the splendid lobsters, and huge crabs displayed on the window sill, which projected slightly into the street. By some unchancy accident the collie wagged his tail into the claws of a crab, which instantly closed on it. The dog gave a dreadful howl and bolted along the street, the crab holding on with commendable tenacity. On seeing his crab disappear, the fishmonger rushed to the door, and observing the owner of the dog shouted, "Donald, Donald! cry back ye'r dog." "D——n you," exclaimed Donald, at his leisure, "cry you back ye'r *partan*."

A Highland parish minister, who was ever anxious to magnify his office, took some dislike to a poor herdboy who was employed by a neighbouring farmer. This boy was the son of a poor widow woman, and received some help from the parochial authorities—usually a suit of moleskin clothes once a year. One day the minister driving with his "man" in the gig espied the herdboy near the roadside, wearing a new suit which his reverence knew had been supplied by the parish. Anxious to tease and humble the boy, he stopped the machine and said—"Well, my boy, who gave you that splendid suit of clothes?" "O, just those that gave you yours—the parish," was the boy's cutting reply. The minister felt he had been caught, and drove off in a hurry. After a little reflection, he felt to be so humbled in presence of his "man," and addressing him, said—"Go back and ask the boy if he will come and be my fool." The minister's "man" went back in glee to the boy and said, "My master sent me back to ask if you would come and be his fool?" "Are you going to leave him?" asked the boy. "No," replied the minister's "man" in astonishment. "Well," said the boy, "go back to your master and tell him that I think his stipend is small enough to support *two fools*, without engaging a third." The minister avoids that boy now.

An English doctor came to reside in a Highland parish. Being fond of flowers, he sowed a large variety of them, and, true to nature, the weeds also grew up alongside of them. Enquiring if there was any handy man in the village whom he could employ to weed his flower-beds, he was directed to a man somewhat weak in the intellect, but who was accustomed to garden work. They went to the garden together, and the doctor showed him his flower-plots, adding—"But, Donald, I am afraid to trust you with the work—are you sure you know the *flowers?*" "No, sir," replied Donald, "but I know the *weeds.*" "Very good, very good, Donald," was the doctor's reply, "that is all I want."

A certain man of mean and stingy manners sent his man-servant, with whom he had often quarrelled for not carrying out his orders to the very letter, to weed a bed of onions, with the instruction—"*Na fàg nì air uachdar talaimh*" (Leave naught above the ground). Coming back in a short time he found that his servant had carried out his behests to the letter, with the result that onions and all had disappeared. "*Rinn thu so mar a dh' iarr mi ort*" (You did this as I told you). "*Bha mi 'feuchainn ris*" (I was trying to do so), was Dugald's reply. "*Nach tu seirbheiseach an Diabhail*" (Aren't you the Devil's own servant)? "*Tha mi creidsinn gur mi, ach tha mi dol g'a fhàgail aig an Fhèill-Màrtainn*" (I daresay I am, but I am going to leave *him* at Martinmas). He had given his master his warning.

SHINTY—COWAL *v.* KINGUSSIE.—This great shinty match, which was played at Cathkin Park on the Spring Holiday ended in a win for Cowal by 2 goals to 1.

A VERY large circle of our readers will learn with very deep regret of the death through pneumonia of Miss Macpherson, eldest daughter of the venerable Major-General Macpherson, of Fortwilliam Park, Belfast. Miss Macpherson's labours in the cause of philanthropy are known and appreciated all over the north of Ireland.

DONALD MACDONALD, New York, U.S.A.

SECRETARY, NEW YORK CELTIC SOCIETY.

THE subject of this short sketch imbibed an intense patriotism with his mother's milk. It needed neither fortuitous influences, nor that distance which lends enchantment, to develop the deep love for kith and native country, which are leading elements in his character.

Born in the island of Tiree in 1858, he is in the full prime and vigour of manhood, with a promise of opportunities before him to add much to that which he has so well accomplished already in the Gaelic world. At the age of fifteen he left the paternal roof for the city of Glasgow, where he served his term of apprenticeship in the carpenter trade, coming out as a highly skilled and versed artizan. His next venture forth was to England, the busy centres of Manchester and Newcastle being among the places where he wooed and won fortune's sunny smiles. A position of responsibility opened for him at Neilston, Renfrewshire, and while here he became connected with the 3rd Lanarkshire Rifle Volunteers, remaining with that corps for about four years. Again he took up residence in Glasgow and met with unqualifying success. He was a member of St. Columba Church and of its famous Gaelic choir, and during the remainder of his stay in Scotland took a deep interest in matters affecting or pertaining to his native Highlands, whether social, political, or religious.

It is now about seven years since Mr. Macdonald crossed the Atlantic. At that time there was an awakening among the Toronto Highlanders, and he stepped at once into the ranks of the most active workers. It was not long before his usefulness was seen in the success which attended the society, of which body he was appointed recording secretary. He was the soul of the society; no more popular member or officer was connected with it. He was especially successful in planning and carrying out arrangements for entertainments, to which he personally contributed not a little. He combined a keen ear with a sweet, well-trained voice, and was a favourite singer of Gaelic songs. He did much to infuse a love for, and knowledge of, Gaelic song among his countrymen in Toronto.

While Mr. Macdonald's memory will long be green in Toronto, it looks as if he had found the true sphere of his labour for the Gael in the city of New York. Bearing with him laurels which few young men could have won so well in so short a time, and worn so modestly, it was but the matter of a few months after his arrival in New York when the New York Celtic Society, of which he is the founder and the father, was formed. He was appointed its first secretary, and that post he still holds.

Mr. MacDonald loves his tight little native island dearly, and his love for his native Gaelic is equally great. He always spoke Gaelic fluently and correctly, and has acquired an extensive knowledge of its literature. This love is contagious, and wherever he goes he has the happy faculty of imparting to others much of his own sentiment and enthusiasm. *Buaidh 'us piseach leis 'sgach deagh obair.*

Toronto.   ALEXANDER FRASER.

GAELIC AIRS TO LOWLAND SONGS.

BY MALCOLM MACFARLANE.

(*Continued from page* 139).

45. Ca' the yowes to the knowes. Whatever the origin of this tune, it would be hard to find one more Gaelic-like. (?)

46. Contented wi' little. "Lumps of Pudding" is the old name of the tune. When sung in the Ray mode, as it ought to be, it is of the style of which *Air faillirinn illirinn* is a type. (?)

47. Address to the Woodlark. Loch Erroch Side.

48. Last May a braw wooer. The old name of this tune is, "The Queen o' the Lothians cam cruisin' tae Fife," a ballad song with a fal-de-ral lairo chorus. It is impossible to overlook the similarity of this tune to *C' àite 'n caidil an ribhinn an nochd*, once the attention has been drawn to it.

49. Aye waukin', O. This tune is certainly Gaelic-like, and is practically the same as *Oran Mulaid*, No. 14, "Celtic Lyre."

50. Come boat me owre to Charlie. "Owre the water to Charlie" is called a Gaelic air in Maver's collection.

51. Whistle owre the lave o't. This tune is said to have been composed by John Bruce, Dumfries (see 43). On the other hand, it is said to have been in existence before his day. Whoever composed it made a tune which is Gaelic in every note. It is to this tune, played on the bagpipe, that *Seann Triubhas* is usually danced.

52. There's a youth in this city.

53. The Battle of Sheriffmuir. Cameronian Rant. This is a Highland reel tune. It is called *Buail na bodaich à Culfhodair* in Gunn's book.

54. Rattlin', roarin' Willie. *Am port crom* is the name given in Gunn's book.

55. Eppie Adair. My Eppie. This tune is the same to which *Am bard luideagach* made his song *Cha téid mise tuilleadh a shealtainn na cruinneig*. See Maclean's "Songs of the Gael," No. 10. See also Fraser of Knockie's collection, p. 26, where it is called *Crodh laoigh nam bodach.*

56. The Highland Widow's Lament. The air to this song was picked up by Burns on the occasion of his trip to the Highlands. It is given with harmony in a recent number of "The National Choir."

57. The tither morn. The editor of "Albyn's Anthology" says *Mo nighean dubh* is the tune to which this song is adapted. But the best known air for *Mo nighean dubh* is not that given to Burns's song. It bears a slight resemblance to it, and is of the same kind of measure.

58. I ha'e a wife o' my ain. Naebody. *Chaidh mi gu banais mo ghaoil* is the name given to the air in Gunn's book.

59. As I was a wandering. *Rinn m' fheudail mo mhealladh.* There seems to have been two different tunes of this name. See Maver's collection, p. 52, for "My darling has deceived me," and Knockie's collection for the other melody to which Burns made his words.

60. The Lass o' Ecclefechan. Jacky (or Jocky) Latin. The Gaelic name of this tune in Gunn's book is *Cuir do chuid air fire faire.* I have myself heard words which suit this tune, beginning as follows :—

> "Bidh fir a' bhaile farumach,
> Bidh fir a' bhaile sunndach,
> Bidh fir a' bhaile farumach,
> Bidh fonn air Banais Dhùghaill."

61. Bannocks o' Barley. The Killogie. In Gunn's book there is a tune named *Bonnaich mhin eorna*, which suits not only Burns's song but that of Duke John of Argyle. The tunes given to both these songs by Maver differ from Gunn's. One of them is not unlike the pipe set.

62. O saw ye my dearie. Eppie MacNab. Maver's collection, p. 104.

63. I gae'd a waefu' gate yestreen. The Braes of Bushbie. This is called a Gaelic air by Maver; and Gunn's name for it is *Port siubhail Dhiùc Chat*—The Duke of Sutherland's quick-step.

64. O, bonny was yon rosy brier. The wee wee man. This air is named in Gunn's book *Crodh laoigh nam bodach*, and also "Bundle and go." Dr. MacLachlan of Rahoy's song, *Cha'n òl mi deur tuilleadh*, is adapted to it. It is not unlike the Irish "Garry Owen."

65. Scots wha ha'e. When Burns submitted this song to his publisher Thomson, the latter thought the air "Tuttie Taitie" to which Burns had set it, and to which it is now sung, unworthy of the words, and he caused it to be adapted to "Lewie Gordon." In "Lewie Gordon" I recognise *A huro mo nighean donn* (see Sinclair's "Oranaiche," p. 15), which was very popular at the Bath Street Gaelic concerts several years ago.

66. A Highland lad my love was born. O, an ye were dead, guidman. The White Cockade. This latter, as the words evince, is a northern tune. The Irish also claim it as "Clarach's Lament," and the Irish Gaelic words do suit the air. Further, there is an Irish lullaby, composed by Owen Roe O'Sullivan, a poet of last century, Englished thus, "Sho-ho, baby, weep no more," the air of which was taken down from the singing of David Condon, Bally Organ, County Limerick, by P. W. Joyce, collector and editor of "Ancient Irish Music." Although it is not remarked by the editor that the air given by him is "The White Cockade," there can be no mistake about its being it. I would not call it a good set of the melody. The air, "White Cockade," is familiar in the Highlands as *Port nam pòg*.

The late COLONEL CHARLES STEWART, J.P.
(Tigh'n Duin).

COLONEL CHARLES STEWART, TIGH 'N DUIN.

THE name of Colonel Charles Stewart, Tigh'n Duin, is a household word in the Highlands, especially in the district of Killin, where the greater part of his life was spent. He was a direct descendant of the famous Donald Stewart of Invernahyle, who fought with distinction at the battle of Pinkie, in 1517, and whose sword and dagger, of Andrea Ferrara fame, he was proud of having in his possession, as well as many other interesting relics of the Appin Stewarts.

Colonel Stewart was born at Glenlyon House, Fortingall, and was the youngest son of Donald Stewart of Glencripesdale, who was a large landed proprietor, and was a celebrated breeder of blackfaced sheep and Highland cattle. He was educated at the University of Edinburgh, and was originally intended for the legal profession, but his health and other circumstances caused him to abandon the idea and live in the country. Being a man of great intellectual ability, of wide knowledge of the Highlands, and of large-hearted sympathies, his influence became widely felt all over Perthshire, where he was universally esteemed and beloved. He threw himself heart and soul into everthing pertaining to the welfare of the Highlands and Highlanders. He was a J.P. for the county of Perth, a director of the Killin Railway, and at all the agricultural and social gatherings he always occupied a foremost place. By his lamented death the extensive district of Breadalbane has lost a valuable friend and counsellor.

Col. Stewart was warmly attached to the Breadalbane family, and was a welcome friend and visitor at Taymouth. By the nobility and agriculturists alike his advice was held in high esteem.

He was thoroughly conversant with the Gaelic language, its folk-lore and music, its archæology and monuments, and the dearest object of his life was to help to conserve the grand old Celtic race, its history and literature. As a keen antiquarian Colonel Stewart stands in the foremost rank of investigators, and contributed many important papers to the "Proceedings of the Society of Antiquaries," of which he was a Fellow.

As chief of the Perth Gaelic Society many will remember his stirring and eloquent addresses at the meetings at Perth, where he and his celebrated "Killin Gaelic Choir," of which he was the voluntary conductor, were deservedly popular. He was an accomplished musician, Highland music being one of his hobbies, and often spoke of the "mesmeric effect" of Gaelic music, which, he said, when played with the real "diel," stirred his patriotism when nothing else could. His "Killin Collection of Gaelic Songs" is well known, and the interest and value of the book is enhanced by the historical and critical notes he affixed to each song. Col. Stewart was a warm supporter of the Church of Scotland, and his "History of the Celtic Church" shed a new light on its early ecclesiastical history, and was acknowledged to be a monument of patient research.

Owing to enforced absence in the South, on account of his health, his stately form has been missed for some time from its accustomed place — nevertheless, love of country, the distinguishing mark of the true Gael, remained undimmed to the last. Up to the day of his death he was busily engaged with Celtic literary work. He was an earnest student and translator of the Ossianic poems, and has left many valuable manuscripts, which will be published in course of time. He was also the author of a celebrated work, "The Gaelic Kingdom in Scotland." Most of his published Celtic literary work during the past year was written specially for the *Celtic Monthly*, in the success of which he took the keenest interest. The paper on "Covalla," which we hope to conclude next month, was perhaps the last contribution he made to Celtic literature.

One of his favourite subjects was the religion of the ancient Gaels, and their belief in the immortality of the spirit, and this same belief was the mainspring of his own spiritual being. During his short illness of an hour and a half's duration he was calm and conscious, and able to tell of the happiness and repose he felt in resting entirely upon his Saviour.

He passed peacefully away, in the full assurance that death is no break, but only a transition from the growing life of faith and love *here* to the full fruition yonder. Colonel Stewart was laid to rest in Killin Churchyard on the 11th of April by a large gathering of sorrowing friends, and the funeral, which was a representative one, was the largest that has taken place in that district for many years. He leaves a widow and two children.

We have great pleasure in presenting our readers with an excellent plate portrait of this distinguished Highlander, from a photograph taken four years ago. It is very appropriate that a likeness of his little daughter—Miss Minnie Grace Annan Stewart, commonly known as "Gracie"—should appear beside him, as a strong and unusually deep attachment existed between father and child.

REVIEWS.

"URQUHART AND GLENMORISTON: OLDEN TIMES IN A HIGHLAND PARISH." By William Mackay. Inverness: *Northern Chronicle* Office. —We have been looking forward with great interest to the appearance of this work, and now that it is before us we fear we cannot say sufficient in its praise. It is a large and handsomely bound volume of 600 pages, embellished with a number of fine engravings of places and objects of historic interest, and it contains within its covers the result of the many years which Mr. William Mackay devoted to the collecting and preparing of material for this exhaustive history of his native parish. Urquhart and Glenmoriston, so full of rich, historic associations, has been singularly fortunate in its historian, for no one was better fitted to undertake this pleasant, though arduous, duty than the patriotic Highlander who has presented us with this valuable volume. Mr. Mackay's literary work has always the stamp of "thorough" upon it. He tells the story of the parish from the beginning, its earliest history being of the usual legendary character. Then the Picts and Norse appear upon the scene, and Conachar, the ancestor of the Forbeses, Mackays, and Urquharts, settles in Urquhart. The period up to 1362 is devoted to an account of the conflicts between the English and the native inhabitants, in the struggle for national independence, after which the clan period begins, with its feuds and forays. The story of the Solemn League and Covenant is one of perpetual commotion, followed by the wars of Montrose and the revolution period. In these Mr. Mackay's own ancestors come pretty frequently upon the scene, losing their lands and regaining them, and through all these centuries it is pleasant to learn that Mr. Mackay's ancestors have been identified with the old place —Achmonie. Perhaps the most interesting pages in the book are those devoted to an account of the "Seven Men of Glenmoriston" who so nobly accompanied Prince Charlie in his wanderings; and disdained to accept the bribe of £30,000 offered for his head. A portrait is given of Patrick Grant, one of the "seven." The '45 uprising brought misery and desolation to these glens, and since that period "change has followed change in rapid succession; and now, almost literally, old things are passed away, and all things are become new." Three interesting chapters are devoted to the church history of the parish, which are followed by an account of Education and Culture, Folk-Lore, and Industrial and Social Life in the historic glens. There are also appendices which are certainly not the least interesting feature of this attractive work, that dealing with the bards of the parish being specially valuable. We need say nothing further

in the meantime regarding Mr. Mackay's "Urquhart and Glenmoriston" except that is perhaps the most exhaustive and readable history of a Highland district that has ever been published, and it is a work which ought to have a place in every Highlander's library. In its publication the author has done a service to his native parish the value of which cannot be over estimated, and the volume will remain a monument to his patriotism and literary ability. We trust that this beautiful book will have a large sale, and we heartily recommend it to our readers.

"A BRIEF ACCOUNT OF THE CLAN DONNACHAIDH," by David Robertson, F.S.A., Scot., has just come to hand, and will be duly noticed in our next issue.

PRESENTATION TO HENRY WHYTE ("Fionn").

OUR readers will be glad to learn that the testimonial to our valued contributor, "Fionn," was presented on Wednesday, 18th April, in the Royal Restaurant, West Nile Street, Glasgow. There were between fifty and sixty gentlemen present — several of them from a distance, and Mr. Hugh MacLeod read letters of apology for absence from many prominent Celts. The meeting, which was thoroughly representative' was presided over by Mr. Wm. Graham of Erines, who, in a few apposite remarks, referred to the object of the meeting, and concluded by calling on Mr. Magnus MacLean, M.A., to make the presentation. Mr. Mac-Lean, as convenor of the committee, stated that the result of the movement was that in three months they had collected a sum of £160 from representatives of every class, creed, and clan, which showed how much "Fionn" was respected by all. Mr. MacLean went on to enlarge upon Mr. Whyte's estimable qualities of head and heart, and his valuable labours, ungrudgingly given, for the advancement of the Celtic people, their language, and literature, and concluded by presenting him with a purse of sovereigns and a gold watch, which bore the following inscription :—"Presented, along with a purse of sovereigns, to Mr. Henry Whyte ("Fionn") by numerous friends, in recognition of his valuable services to Celtic literature. Glasgow, April, 1894." *An là 'chì 's mach fhaic.*

Mr. Whyte, who was loudly cheered, thanked Mr. MacLean for the kind manner in which he had spoken regarding him. There was nothing enhanced the testimonial more than the fact that it was the spontaneous gift of people representing every sect and party. Other short addresses, interspersed with songs, followed, and during the course of the evening Mr. Neil Ross recited the poem, "Son of the Gael" (see p. 153).

LETTER TO THE EDITOR.

THE REAY FENCIBLES.

To the Editor of the "CELTIC MONTHLY."

Wiesbaden, 3d April, 1894.

SIR,—Mr. Rose's reply to my remarks in the March number of the magazine may be summed up in one short sentence : he seems to bear a grudge against the Clan Mackay. I do not like controversy, but as he has made a disingenuous assertion to the effect that the regiment known as the Reay Fencibles never appeared in an army-list, I beg permission to make a few further remarks, in order that those who are not acquainted with the facts may have a correct understanding of the matter. Here are Mr. Rose's words : "Neither in army list nor muster-roll can be found a regiment designed 'The Reay Fencibles, or *Mackay Regiment*.'" I fancy, in making this statement he was hitting at my having drawn attention to the fact that there were 209 Mackays * in the ranks of the regiment when the first muster-roll was drawn up [there were also, at the same time, 11 Mackay officers], and to my having added, "So its designation was perfectly appropriate, The Reay Fencibles, or Mackay Regiment of Highlanders." It is true, *Mackay Regiment* does not appear in the official, that is, the War-Office list, but the REAY FENCIBLE REGIMENT does; and if that regiment was not the Mackay regiment, what was it? Perhaps Mr. Rose can tell.

On the 4th November, 1894, the cousin and heir-presumptive of the then Lord Reay addressed a letter to the tacksmen in the Reay country requesting their assistance in the raising of a new regiment for the Government. In that letter he asked (I quote his own words) "that the names of the men who engage in THE MACKAY FENCIBLES," should be transmitted to him. This was probably the designation which had been suggested for the new regiment, though the warrant which Colonel Baillie received merely authorised him to raise "a regiment of fencible men"—no title being given. As soon as it was embodied, however, it was inscribed in the War-Office list as THE REAY FENCIBLE REGIMENT. It was placed on the establishment 10th June, 1795, and shortly afterwards proceeded to Ireland, where it served with distinction, and was known as "Lord Reay's Highlanders." Why was it so called? Because it was raised in Lord Reay's, or "the Mackay country." Mr. Rose says that it is an "unwarrantable assumption" to write about the achievements of the Mackays at Tarahill or elsewhere;" but I stated distinctly that we did not restrict the praise to the Mackays only, but accorded it equally "to the officers and men who composed the regiment." Is it not, therefore, a perversion of facts on his part to assert that the regiment acquired "laurels" which were "unfairly placed to the credit of the Clan Mackay alone?" The merest tyro in the study of history could scarcely be guilty of such a

blunder. In bringing this part of my remarks to a close I will quote a few words by James Logan, author of "The Scottish Gael." Logan furnished the letterpress to M'Ian's "Clans of the Scottish Highlands," and in the latter work says—"In 1795 the Reay Fencible Regiment, or *Mackay Highlanders* were embodied." . . . The "signal defeat of the rebels at the Hill of Tara" was "accomplished by the Mackays in gallant style." As a historian, Logan was here stating a fact. Was it an "unwarrantable assumption" on his part to do so ? I trow not. So much for Mr. Rose and *his* "unwarrantable" allegations.

Another thing. Mr. Rose would fain make us believe that the statements in General Stewart's "Sketches" are *fictions*, and the figures which are given as facts by Robert Mackay in his clan history are *fables*. This is trying the credulity of the readers of the *Celtic Monthly* a little too far. If what is recorded by these two authors about the number of Mackays in the Sutherland Fencibles is wrong, it is rather remarkable that no one before this has drawn attention to the error. As I have not seen the muster-roll of the regiment, I, of course, cannot vouch for the correctness of the figures; but I will hold that General Stewart's statements, as well as those given in the "History of the Clan Mackay," are neither "fictions" nor "fables," but *facts*, until Mr. Rose has furnished proof that his own assertions are correct. Pray, pardon the length of this communication.— Yours, &c.

JOHN MACKAY.

A KISS OF THE KING'S HAND. *

It wasna from a golden throne,
Or a bower with milk-white roses blown,
But mid the kelp on northern sand
That I got a kiss of the king's hand.

I durstna raise my een tae see
If he even cared to glance at me ;
His princely brow with care was crossed
For his true men slain and kingdom lost.

Think not his hand was soft and white,
Or his fingers a' with jewels dight,
Or round his wrist were jewels grand
When I got a kiss of the king's hand.

But dearer far tae my twa een
Was the ragged sleeve of red and green
O'er that young weary hand that fain,
With the guid broadsword, had found its ain.

Farewell for ever, the distance gray
And the lapping ocean seemed to say—
For him a home in a foreign land,
And for me one kiss of the king's hand.

SARAH ROBERTSON MATHESON.

* There is an old pipe tune "I got a kiss of the king's hand."

CLAN MACMILLAN.—Our readers will regret to learn of the death of Mr. C. S. MacMillan, National Bank, Govan, who has acted as treasurer for the Clan MacMillan Society since its inauguration.

* There were seven Murrays and one Rose in the regiment. I wonder if they constituted the "unwilling recruits" who were tempted to enlist at Tain by the "bait" of 'a bounty of two guineas," dangled before their eyes by "the patriotic . . . civic authorities of the ancient burgh!" (See D. Murray Rose on *the Reay Fencibles*, in this magazine, Vol. I. 175).

NEWS OF THE MONTH.

CLAN MacKINNON SOCIETY.—A largely attended meeting of this Clan was held in the Waterloo Rooms, Glasgow, on 29th ult. Mr. William MacKinnon, hon. vice-president, presided. The president, Mr. Duncan MacKinnon, read a long paper on the origin and early history of the clan, tracing them back to the 9th century, showing their close connection with the MacGregors, MacNabs, and other branches of the Alpine race of kings of Scotland. He also described their migrations to Mull and Skye, and referred to various conflicts in which the clan took part, their septs and branches, the disasters of 1745, and the later history of the clan.

GLASGOW SKYE ASSOCIATION.—The following gentlemen were elected office-bearers for the ensuing session:—Chief, Capt. Macleod, Dunvegan; Hon. President, Mr. Macdonald of Skaebost; President, Mr. R. Mackinnon; Vice-President, Col. Williamson; Secretary, Mr. Hugh Macleod (writer); Treasurer, Mr. Duncan Finlayson; Directors—Messrs. Macdonald, K. Macdonald, M. Nicolson, D. Maclean, A. Robertson, K. D. Mackenzie, J. Macintyre, M. Nicolson, L. Mackinnon, and A. W. Macleod. Temporary assistance was voted to two deserving cases. The secretary's statement showed a very satisfactory condition of the society, notwithstanding the frequent calls on its funds during the last year.

CLAN DONNACHAIDH SOCIETY.—The second annual general meeting of this society was held in the Merchants' Hall, George Square, on Wednesday, 4th ult.—Col. J. Leslie Robertson, C.B., of Butterglen, in the chair. The Chairman having intimated an apology for the absence of the Lord Justice General, who, he said, was with them in spirit, alluded to the conspicuous position taken by Robertsons throughout the world. He had never met, after travelling the greater part of the world, a Robertson who asked him for pecuniary aid, except in New York, but on further inquiry he found this one to be an Englishman. (Laughter.) Mrs. Sarah Robertson Matheson, Dunfermline, general secretary, stated that the membership since the inauguration of the society in 1891 up to date was 435, and the funds in hand were £106 11s 8d. During the evening the Right Hon. W. E. Gladstone was proposed and unanimously accepted as an honorary member of the society; whilst Mr. J. Logie Robertson (Hugh Haliburton) was appointed bard to the clan. A capital concert followed.

PERTH GAELIC SOCIETY. The annual meeting of this Society was held in the Guild Hall. Ex-Bailie MacGregor, the Chief of the Society, presided. Mr. J. MacKenzie, the Secretary, submitted the annual report, from which it appeared that the past year had been the most successful that the Society had ever seen. The membership had been well maintained, and during the year 25 new members had joined. There were 3 life members, 40 honorary members, and 228 ordinary members. Office-bearers for the ensuing year were elected, ex-Bailie MacGregor being re-appointed Chief.

CLAN MACKAY SOCIETY.—A concert of this society was held in the Sauchiehall Rooms on Tuesday, 10th ult., Mr. Alex. Mackay, Charing Cross, presided, and there was a crowded attendance. Among members of the clan present were Messrs. Charles Mackay, John Mackay, Celtic Monthly; Lieut. William Mackay, and others. Pipe-Major John Mackay, A. and S. H., Paisley, and Mr. W. Henderson. Govan, played stirring selections while the company was gathering. The chairman, after a few remarks on the objects of the society, suggested the confederation of the Highland Societies in Glasgow for the purpose of organising a Highland Club. A capital concert programme was sustained by Miss Flora Donaldson, "Scottish Troubadours," Miss Williamson, Miss Sinclair (pianist), Messrs. G. Morrison, John Sinclair, and others. Messrs. E. E. Henderson and W. Henderson gave the Highland dances with great spirit. A dance, which was largely attended, followed.

AIRDRIE HIGHLAND ASSOCIATION.—On Thursday evening, 6th ult., in the Association Hall, Bell Street, the members of the above society and friends were treated to a high-class lecture and musical entertainment on "The Songs and Poetry of the Highlands," by Mr. John Mackay, Glasgow, editor of the Celtic Monthly. There was a good turnout. Mr. Wm. Thomson occupied the chair, and briefly introduced the lecturer and Miss Lizzie B. Mackay, Glasgow, and Mr. J. Mackintosh, secretary, Glasgow Gaelic Musical Association. Mr. Mackay touched upon Celtic love songs, humorous love songs, poems on Nature, songs that dealt with the desolation of the Highlands, boat songs, laments, sacred songs and hymns, marching songs, drinking songs, fairy and nursery songs, and patriotic songs, all of which he dealt with in a creditable manner, and evoked hearty applause. The musical part was ably sustained by Miss Mackay (a coming vocalist), Mr. Mackintosh, and the lecturer, who sang the Gaelic and English versions (with piano accompaniments) to the delight of those present. Altogether the entertainment was a most enjoyable one. Mr. MacDonald (vice-president), and Mr. MacNab (president), awarded a hearty vote of thanks to the entertainers, and one of the most enjoyable meetings was brought to a termination at a seasonable hour.

DR. LIVINGSTONE'S ANCESTORS.

To the Editor of the "CELTIC MONTHLY."

SIR,—I read with considerable interest the article on David Livingstone and his relatives in your issue for last month. I should feel obliged if you would put a query in next month's number, in order, if possible, to see whether Dr. Livingstone was in any way related to the Livingstones of Crogan. By doing so you would much oblige.—Yours, &c. JAMES LIVINGSTONE.

D. N. NICOL, of Ardmarnock.

THE CELTIC MONTHLY:

A MAGAZINE FOR HIGHLANDERS.

Edited by JOHN MACKAY, Kingston.

No. 9. Vol. II.]   JUNE, 1894.   [Price Threepence.

DONALD N. NICOL.

THE subject of our sketch this month; Mr. Donald Ninian Nicol of Ardmarnock, will scarcely require an introduction to many of our readers. A resident in his native county of Argyllshire for many years, his name has become familiar as one who has its interests and welfare deeply at heart.

The only surviving son of the late Dr. Nicol of Ardmarnock, he received his early education at Merchiston Castle School, and Glasgow University. Proceeding afterwards to Queens College, Oxford, he took the degrees of B.A. and M.A. and having been called to the English Bar joined the Northern Circuit. Although he has ceased the active practice of his chosen profession, his early study of law has proved of excellent service to him. A fluent and ready speaker, he is able to grasp the salient and material points of his subject and to communicate them to an audience in a telling and effective way. Since 1855 Mr. Nicol has resided on his Argyllshire estate with the exception of a brief visit to London during the winter months. At an early period he began to take an active interest in local affairs. A Justice of the Peace and Deputy Lieutenant of the County, he was the Convener of the Finance Committee under the old regime of the Commissioners of Supply, and when they were superseded by the County Council, he continued to hold that position and has proved himself an able guardian of the Exchequer. In presenting his annual Budget to the Council, Mr. Nicol displays a masterly command over the intricacies of his subject, and has the rare ability of imparting to it a vivid interest which is seldom found amidst the dry bones of statistics. He was also Chairman of the Valuation Committee, and is also a member of several other Committees of the County Council. As a

member of the Lunacy Board he has been prominent in the movement to modify the excessive control exercised by the Central Board in Edinburgh. He is also Chairman of the Parochial Board of his own Parish of Kilfinan, which he represents in the County Council.

In 1874 Mr. Nicol married the daughter of Sir Edward Bates, Bart., late M.P. for Plymouth, and he found congenial work in taking a leading part in successive contested elections for that constituency. Since the retirement of Colonel Malcolm he has been chosen as the Unionist Candidate for Argyllshire. Mr. Nicol's talents deserve a wider scope than the somewhat contracted sphere to which his energies have hitherto been devoted, and his ripened experience, ready tact and intimate and discriminating knowledge of local and imperial affairs fit him in an eminent degree for a seat in the supreme Legislative Council of the Kingdom.

This brief sketch of Mr. Nicol's career would be incomplete without some mention of his warm sympathy with the cause of higher education in the Highlands. As Joint Honorary Secretary of the Highland Society of London he has taken an active interest in the provision of bursaries for the assistance of students in the outlying districts. These bursaries are awarded not by competitive examination but after a careful comparison of the merits of the applicants with special regard to the difficulties under which they have pursued their studies. Many a poor student has been assisted by this means to overcome the initial obstacles in his way and to enter upon a successful career in one of the professions. The personal knowledge which Mr. Nicol gained during his study at Glasgow University of the disadvantages under which Highland students are placed has led him to devote a very considerable amount of time and trouble in working out the details of a scheme which has proved so fruitful in its results.

Mr. Nicol is a member of the Kintyre Club, Glasgow Cowal Society, London Argyllshire Association, and other county organizations, in the welfare of which he takes a keen interest, and his presence at the recent Annual Social Gatherings in Glasgow was very heartily welcomed by the members. It may be also mentioned that as a native of Cowal he naturally takes a special interest in the well-known Glasgow Cowal Shinty Club, of which he is a patron.

Glasgow. JAMES MACKELLAR.

GAELIC AIRS TO LOWLAND SONGS.

BY MALCOLM MACFARLANE.

FROM ALBYN'S ANTHOLOGY (1816).

(Continued from page 160).

67. Banarach dhonn a' chruidh. The auburn-haired bonnie dey—being an imitation of the original Gaelic song. "Hail to the Chief," by Sir W. Scott, "Hill of Lochiel," by James Hogg, and "The Banks o' the Devon," by Burns, were adapted to this air or variants therof.

68. Guma slàn a chì mi. Blythesome may I see thee—by the Editor. A translation by Professor Blackie is given in "The National Choir" vol. 2, page 202; an original song to the same air by Joseph M'Gregor at page 156; and another by Thomas Hood at page 157.

69. Soraidh slàn do 'n Ailleagan. I still may boast my will is free—by the Editor.

70. Tha mi sgìth 's mi leam fhìn. Why should I sit and sigh—by James Hogg. The following remnant of the Gaelic words, differing somewhat from those given in part 3 "Celtic Lyre," is worth quoting :—

"Tha mi sgìth, 's mi leam fhìn,
H-uile là an Cnoc-na-beannachd ;
Tha mi sgìth, 's mi leam fhìn,
H-uile là a 'm ònar.
H-uile là an Cnoc-na-beannachd,
H-uile là a 'm ònar ;
H-uile là an Cnoc-na-beannachd,
'S ni fhear tigh'nn g' am fheòraich.
Cùl an tomain, beul an tomain,
Cùl an tomain bhòidhich ;
Cùl an tomain, beul an tomain,
H-uile là a 'm ònar.

71. Caidil gu lò. Hush thee my baby—by Sir Walter Scott. Fraser of Knockie, in a footnote at page 73, writes " This tune supposed to be composed by the roving King James, would spread among all his subjects as his production ; but I find the best set of it preserved in the Highlands and sung to Gaelic words." Patrick MacDonald, in his collection of Gaelic Air, calls it a Skye Air. Knockie's set is the simplest of the three and I give it along with as much of the Gaelic song as is preserved in Albyn's Anthology :—

CAIDIL GU LO.

Key E.

'S e m' fheudail am fleasgach
Ghabh air talbh air an fheasgar;
O, tha mi fo bhreislich
Ma sheasas an ceò.

Dol a null air an fhaoghailt,
Gu 'n deanadh mo roghainn ;
Bhiodh càch air a dheaghaidh
'S mo roghainn air tòs.

72. Hé 'n clò-dubh. Like lightening gleams —by James Douglas.

73. Gura thall ann Sothaidh. It was o'er in yon Soa—translation by Editor.

74. An gille guanach. I've made a vow—by Mrs. Gray. This is the well-known *Seinn an duan so* by Dr. MacLachlan of Rahoy. The Editor gives the following fragment of the original song which, it will be seen James Munro worked into his fine song to this air (see *Am Filidh* page 16—An t-òigear uallach):—

A ghille ghuanaich o hì o rò,
A ghille ghuanaich o ho ì,
A ghille ghuanaich nan leadan dualach,
Tha mi fo ghruaim o'n dh' fhàg thu 'n tìr.

75. Bealach a' ghàraidh. O, my love, leave me not—by Mrs. Grant. This air is best known as "Mackintosh's Lament." The Gaelic words given in Albyn's Anthology differ from those given by Lachlan MacBean in his "Songs of the Gael," and are worthy of quotation here :—

Ochain, a laoigh, leag iad thu (3 uairean)
Am bealach a' ghàraidh.

'S truagh nach robh mis an sin (3 uairean)
Us ceathrar gach laimh domh.

An leann thug iad gu d' bhanais (3 uairean)
Air t' fharaire bhà e.

'Nam bhreidich 's 'nam ghruagaich (3 uairean)
'S 'nam bhanntraich 'san aon là ud.

Gun chron air an t-saogh'l ort (3 uairean)
Ach nach d' fhaod thu saogh'l buan fhaotainn.

76. Soraidh slàn do 'n Ailleagan. The Spring for me revives in vain—Gray. This tune is a variant of that to which Morison's spiritual song *An Cath* is adapted (See No. 30 MacBean's "Songs and Hymns of the Scottish Highlands"). Entirely different airs of the same name appeared in the Gael Vol. v. page 22, and in the "The Highlander," No. 164.

A · SHINTY · MATCH · IN · SUTHERLAND ·

Stewart Orr

CAMANACHD.

Times have changed in the North of Sutherland, and with them the habits and customs of
the people have undergone an alteration also.
The amusements of the winter months are still
indulged in, but not so heartily, I fear, as they
were in the days of long ago. Shinty was a
favourite game on the sands at Balnakeil, o'er-
shadowed by the fine baronial residence of the
Lords of Reay, and on New-Year's Day the
game is still played. It may not prove un-
interesting to the readers of the *Celtic Monthly*
to describe a New-Year's Day Shinty Match as
it was played on these beautiful sands many
years ago.

It is a fine clear morning, with a touch of
frost in the air sufficiently keen to add zest
to the exertions of the day. The players having
arrived, the Shinty is thrown down, and boys,
lads, and men play merrily for half-an-hour
without drawing sides, like the first flourish of
fence before beginning in earnest.

The crowd thickens, old men appear upon
the ground, and young wives and maidens also,
as spectators, come dressed in their best attire.
A murmur goes round that it is time to begin: it
gets louder, and they collect in a group. The
company having assembled, it was proposed,
and unanimously carried, that the game be
commenced in earnest. Retiring to the middle
of the sands, two persons are chosen to draw
sides, and a club is tossed in the air for the first
call. The chosen one standing out in the ring
looks around for his companion-at-arms, who
modestly holds back until called by name, when
he advances, not unconscious of the honour

conferred on him, but with affected humility,
perhaps finding fault with his principal for
having made such a bad choice. His opponent
next selects his man, and so proceed, at first
cautiously, each party consulting together as to
whom they would choose. At times both call
out a favourite player simultaneously, and then
the battle wages long and loud. But they now
get impatient, and the names are called out
still faster, until none are left save a few half-
grown boys too young to join the strife of heroes,
and too old for entering the battle of the
pigmies. A hole is then made in the sand, the
ball is dropped into it, men are seen stripping;
shoes, stockings, bonnets, clothes are left in the
custody of some daughter or fair favourite, or
upon a sand hillock.

Two field marshals are appointed, who take
their stations; the ball is tossed out of the hole,
each man firmly grasps his club, each eye is on
the alert, up it ascends, and then begins the
fight of heroes. All else is forgotten, brother
comes against brother, father against son, for
their blood is up. Now they seem all in a knot,
next instant they separate, they press in a body
upon one end, and they then diverge like mountain streams; but though many they are one,
for they have a common object, though only a
piece of wood three inches in diameter. The
fair ones, gentle and simple, group along the
shore, while many a loving look is exchanged,
no doubt stimulating some to greater exertions.
The running of one is beautiful, another's
playing is awkward, that of a third superb, of
a fourth ludicrous. The masculine exhibition
on that sea shore is really fine. What flashes
from that young man's eyes as he strikes forward
the ball! What a proud step after he has

done it! What attitudes that field marshal puts himself into as the ball is deliberately fixed on a fulcrum of sand before him! Conscious of the gaze of a thousand eyes, he retreats a few steps, and, measuring the object with the eye, clutches more firmly the club, and comes down with it in a circular sweep, hitting the ball beautifully, and following it with his eye as it rises into the clear blue sky. No rest being allowed, the ball is at times by mistake thrown into the sea, into which, though the surge should be considerable, a dozen stalwart fellows leap, and even midst the breakers struggle for it. As a tribute to this bravery, the one who finds it is permitted to strike without molestation, a sufficient reward, he considers, for his ducking.

But look at that group who support a fainting man. From an accidental stroke of the club on the temple his skull is laid bare. He is deadly pale as they carry him out of the melee. Women also surround him, among whom is the young man's sweetheart. Pale and trembling, she takes the handkerchief off her neck, and binds it round his head. His eyes open; that look she gave him has acted like a cordial. The warm blood once more mantles his face, he says he is quite well, and wishes again to enter the melee, but is kept back by a beseeching look from the maiden, and the tears by which it is backed have more weight with him than the remonstrances of a thousand tongues.

But we see another and a larger group, but it is difficult to wedge one's way into it. There is a ring and loud words, inside are two fellows with brawny arms, pale with anger, collaring one another, while others try to hold the determined fighters back. 'Let them alone,' cries a sensible old man, and, left to themselves, they see what a ridiculous figure they cut; they look at each other, shake hands, and set off once more in their pursuit. Sometimes, however, they are not so easily separated, and blood flows ere they desist from fighting. But see that poor limping dog which has faithfully followed his master, and for his fidelity has got a broken leg. What has so suddenly dispersed that female group? The ball has effected this with as great expedition as a shell falling among a party of troopers. Off it goes, however; that handsome young fellow who eyed it intently had a design upon it, and now is his time, beautifully does he send it along, never missing, and as skilfully does he out-manœuvre his adversary, who meets him; he waits, strikes it, and passes him. With the ball at his foot, a false step and all would be lost, for he is hotly pursued, the whole field being in full cry at his heels. But he knows his power, and reserves his strength to the last. Forward he

goes, only now pursued by two or three, and, out-distancing all, he is cheered by his own party, while the opposition only sullenly growl. Reaching now the goal, he strikes the ball against the rock, while a triumphant hail rises from a hundred voices, and meets him gratefully as again he draws breath. By this time it is almost dark, and as each youth, weary with the day's exercise, returns home in the gloaming, he looks out for the girl he loves best, and engages her as his partner for the evening dance.

London.   ROBINA FINDLATER.

AG AMHARC AIR AIS.

Air tulaich ghuirm ri taobh na tràigh,
Fodh sgàile tlàth nan creagan lom;
Tha m' inntinn mar gu 'm biodh i snàmh,
Ag éisdeachd gàirich throm nan tonn.

'S mi cuimhneachadh nam bliadhn' a thriall,
Mar bhruadar diomhanach nach till,
'S mo chàirdean lionmhor, gràdhach, fiall,
'Tha cnàmh a 'n diomhaireachd na cill.

Có 'bheir an sgeula dhuinn air ais,
No 'm bi sin glaiste uainn gu bràth?
Am faic sinn tuilleadh gnùis am mais',
A phaisgeadh ann an glaic a' bhàis?

An cluinn sinn tuilleadh cainnt am beòil,
A sheòladh sinn le 'n còmhradh glic?
Au caidil iad a chaoidh fodh 'n fhòid,
An dorchadas a bhròin fodh 'n lic?

An lean an saoghal-so gu bràth,
A bàrcadh air 'us dheth an t-sluaigh!
'S 'g an iomairt mar na tuinn air tràigh,
An uine gheàrr a bhios au cuairt.

Tha linn an deadhaidh linn gun tàmh,
Mar abhuinn làn a ruith do 'n chuan,
'S mar lusan maoth a thig fodh bhlàth,
'S a bhàsaicheas 'n uair 'thig am fuachd.

Tha caochladh sgriobht' air gnùis gach nì,
'S cha bhuain' an righ no 'n duine bochd;
An glòir 's an ionmhais cha toir sìth,
'S iad aig a chrìch gun bhrìgh gun toirt.

Ach tha ar dùil ri tir is feàrr,
Far am bheil fois do 'n ànrach sgìth;
Far nach bi dealachadh gu bràth,
'S far nach tig bròn no plàigh 'g ar claoidh.

Ach fàgaidh sinn e aig an Triath,
Am breitheamh ceart nach fiar a' chòir,
'Thug dhuinn ar tùs, 's dha 'n aithn' ar crìoch,
'S a bhios gu suthainn siorruidh beò).

N. MACLEOID.

LONDON ARGYLLSHIRE ASSOCIATION.

THOMAS HUNTER MURRAY and NEIL MACMILLAN,

JOINT SECRETARIES.

THOMAS HUNTER MURRAY, though born in Glasgow, is of Argyleshire parentage, his ancestors of several generations rest in the beautiful old church-yard of Kilmun, his father's and mother's home being separated only by the Holy Loch. His father's family still possess the pleasant summer residence of Finnart Bank, Kilmun, and his maternal grandfather was John C. Turner of Dunloskin, a man well-known and greatly respected, who gave much time and voluntary labour to all the interests of the County. Joining the stream of young life which flows towards the great Metropolis, he entered the Firm of Macmillan & Co., Publishers, Strand, where he has been for twelve years, rising gradually in position and respect. Two years ago he became Secretary of the Argyleshire Association, a friendly society, through which new comers may find a welcome, and older members may feel, from time to time, the strength of the united centre, the fellowship of early days. Being originated in 1890, the Association is still in its infancy, but has every prospect of developing a vigorous manhood in the years to come, unless its existence is effaced by the time that's "comin' yet" "when man to man the world o'er, shall brothers be, an a' that;" the advent of which is materially helped forward by such Societies. Genial and upright, he bears about in him amid all the toil of business life, the pure atmosphere of his native hills.

NEIL MACMILLAN was born at Bowmore, Islay, and is the son of Captain Donald Macmillan of that village. On the maternal side he can trace his ancestors as far back as "Traigh Ghruinard," while paternally he comes of a well-known seafaring family. His grandfather, the late John Macmillan, was one of most respected and hospitable men in the island. The subject of our sketch began his education at the village school, and afterwards studied at Glasgow for the Civil Service. At a competitive examination held in London in the beginning of 1891 he took a high place on the successful list, and was immediately called upon to take up his appointment in London.

After nearly two years service in a Government Office, he resigned it in favour of the more active pursuits of a commercial career, having received an appointment with Messrs. E. D. Sassoon & Co., one of the foremost East India Merchants.

True to his warm Highland sympathies he early became a member of the County Association, and on the resignation of one of the Secretaries he was unanimously elected to fill the vacancy, the duties of which he discharges with credit and satisfaction. He is a member of the 12th Middlesex (Civil Service) Volunteer Corps, and also belongs to the Service Rugby Football team, and plays a good game in the forward division. In every respect Neil Macmillan is a worthy son of "Green grassy Islay."

TONGUE AND ITS HISTORIC SURROUNDINGS.

By John Mackay, C.E., J.P., Hereford.

Part V. The Battles of Dingwall and Harpsdale, and Slaughter of Mowat of Freswick.

(Continued from page 157).

WE have now arrived at an eventful and momentous period of Highland and Mackay history during the Rule of Angus Du Mackay in Tongue. As we have seen in the last chapter, this young chief was a minor at his father's death. During his minority the clan was ruled by his elder uncle Huistean Du (swarthy Hugh), a man of great resolution, determination and bravery, manifested by his opposition to the demands made upon him by the MacLeods of Lewis, and the quick retaliation he inflicted upon them at Tutimtarrach. Whether his young nephew accompanied him on that expedition, as very probably he did, we are not certain, yet there cannot be a doubt that his martial uncle instructed him in all the necessary accomplishments of the period, to govern and to lead men in peace and in war. On his uncle's death two years after the battle of Tutim-tarrach Angus Du assumed the reins of government, and proved himself to be a real

KIRKIBOL CHURCHYARD, TONGUE.

leader of men. From the associations he had formed, and the influence he had acquired in the earlier years of his rule we find him to have been a young man of the highest capacity, attaining within the three northern counties an ascendency second only to the Lord of the Isles, when that potentate rebelled against the Regent of Scotland to assert his assumed right of succession to the Earldom of Ross during the long imprisonment of James the First in England.

The Munros, Rosses, and other clans in that Earldom, were on the side of the Regent, and were not well inclined to the Lord of the Isles. They preferred to be loyal to the government of the Regent, and to have his son as their superior. Probably enough instigated by the Regent Albany, these clans formed a confederacy to resist the pretensions of the turbulent and disloyal Lord of the Isles, who had been plotting with the Kings of England to re-subject Scotland to their domination and partition it between them. Angus Du, being the more influential and powerful of the confederates, was chosen to be Commander-in-Chief to resist him. The Lord of the Isles was informed of this confederacy, and at once resolved to force these refractory clans into submission. For this purpose he collected an army in the Isles and invaded Ross, to take forcible possession of the Earldom and reduce these clans to acknowledge him as their over Lord. The confederates under the leadership of Angus Du hastily assembled their forces in time to meet the invading army of the Isles at Dingwall, as Sir Robert Gordon tell us. A bloody battle ensued, the confederates being defeated with great loss of men. Angus Du was taken prisoner, his young brother Rorie Gallda slain, but no mention is made of the Chiefs of other clans killed, or taken prisioners by the Lord of the Isles This battle, severe as it must have been, is assumed to have taken place in the same year as that of Harlaw, 1411. It is much more likely to have happened two or more years previously, and for the simple purpose of reducing the clans of the Earldom of

Ross to his submission before undertaking the more serious object of contending with the Regent for the superiority of the Highlands beyond the "*Garbh-chrioch*"—an event well fixed by "The Day of Harlaw,"—and which Donald, Lord of the Isles failed to accomplish by his want of tenacity of purpose, and by the stern resistance he met with that day.

Angus Du, "the leader of 4000 men," taken prisoner at the Battle of Dingwall, was kept in bonds for a few months in Caisteil-tirrim, under the guardianship of "Alastair Carrach," "Lord" of Lochaber, and brother of Donald, Lord of the Isles. Donald was politic enough to make terms with so powerful a Chief as Angus Du. He

LORD REAY'S PEW, TONGUE CHURCH.

proposed to him, now, that the confederacy was subdued, and the refractory clans had given in their submission, to give him his liberty to return to his own country and clan, to give him also, his sister in marriage, and grant him as her dowry, the superiority of lands in the south west and north east of Sutherland, which he possessed in right of his wife the Countess of Ross.

An agreement upon these terms was come to, Angus Du, married the sister of Donald of the Isles, obtained his liberty, and as "Sir Robert" says, "carried her away with him to Tongue."

From the fact of this Mackay chief being imprisoned for a few months in Caisteil-tirrim by the Lord of the Isles, he was ever after nicknamed by his clansmen "Enneas-a-phriosan, (Angus of the prison) erroneously given as "Enneas-en-Imprissi," (Angus the absolute) absolute and masterful he undoubtedly was, but the words "en-imprissi," is neither Gaelic, Latin, nor Greek, but a corruption of "a-phriosan" as above ; a similar epithet was afterwards applied to his eldest son who was kept in ward in the Bass for nearly ten years.

The Lord of the Isles, faithful to his treaty with Angus Du, conveyed to him and his wife Elizabeth, the superiority of a large stretch of property in Ross and Sutherland, extending from the Church lands of Skibo to the confines of Assynt and the whole of Strath Halladale. On

taking possession of these lands by virtue of a
charter (1414), Angus Du, leased them to his
three cousins Thomas, Morgan, and Neil, the
sons of his uncle Neil, and brother of Huistean
Du. This extensive acquisition of territory
adjoining his patrimonial estates gave the
redoubtable Mackay chief a preponderance of
influence and power greatly superior to the Earl
of Sutherland. To him this was a great eyesore,
and a greater grievance for the Mackay territory
now encompassed his on three sides, making in
reality Angus Du in Sutherland, "Angus the
absolute." Thus the Earl became extremely
jealous of the influence and power attained by
the Mackay chief; he felt himself powerless to
counteract the effect, yet what he could not
accomplish by policy or force he tried to do by
treachery and fraud in fomenting quarrels and
disturbances in that lawless age of continuous
contentions. He found willing instruments in
the Murrays, the chief of whom was Angus of
Pulrossie, a wadsetter or lease holder of Thomas
Mackay, the cousin of Angus Du, referred to
previously.

This Thomas, to whom Angus Du had allotted
Strath Halladale, Pulrossie and Creich, had a
dispute with Mowat, laird of Freswick in Caithness, and was refused satisfaction. Hearing of
Mowat passing into Ross with a retinue of men,
he speedily pursued him, and overtaking
him at Tain, demanded redress, and not obtaining
it, words culminated in blows. The Mowats
were worsted and took refuge in St. Duthus'
Chapel, which was considered a sanctuary. The
infuriated Mackays unable to get at the Mowats,
set fire to the chapel, and either burnt or slew
them. Complaint was made to the Regent
Albany. The crime was brought before the
Council, the fact of the atrocity of a Saint's
chapel being burnt was enough. Without
further investigation, Thomas Mackay, called
Neilson from his father being Neil, was forfeited
and a decree was issued to apprehend him, his
lands, goods and chattels to be the reward for
his apprehension.

The difficulty was who would or could apprehend so powerful a man, for Angus Du would not
like to forfeit the esteem of his clansmen by
bringing his cousins to justice if he were called
upon. The Earl of Sutherland was afraid of
Angus Du whom he thought it was not politic
to offend. The apprehension of Thomas lapsed
for some time. The Earl consulted Angus
Murray and urged him to do the deed. Angus
was not loathe to undertake it on the promise of
protection if he failed.

Angus Murray had two daughters of whom
the younger brothers of Thomas Neilson Mackay,
Morgan and Neil were enamoured. Angus
Murray persuaded these miscreants to assist him

in apprehending their elder brother by giving
them his two daughters in marriage and
promising to share their brother's property with
them, which was now forfeited to the crown,
and promised as reward for the apprehension.
The unnatural brothers yielded, Thomas was
apprehended and executed at Inverness, and the
three villains received the promised reward.

In the meantime the Caithness people, indignant at one of their Lairds being slain by Thomas
Mackay, made several raids upon Thomas' lands
in Strath Halladale, but after his execution and
Strath Halladale being conveyed by Charter to
Angus Murray, they extended their raids into
Strathnaver. Angus Du was not the man to
permit such deeds to be done on his own lands
with impunity. He convened his men and
marched into the heart of Caithness, unmolested
till he came to Harpsdale within a few miles of
Thurso, where the men of Caithness met him
and a furious battle took place attended with
great slaughter on both sides. The men of
Caithness getting the worst of it they made
loud complaints to King James the first of
Scotland, who had within a year or two been
released from his captivity in England. The
affair was much magnified to the King and
Council. James since his return had many
similar reports from other quarters in the Highlands. He determined to go to Inverness and
personally inquire into the atrocities complained
of. He summoned the Highland chiefs to meet
him at Inverness. Angus Du, amongst the
rest obeyed the King's command, and gave the
King such good reasons for his conduct that he
was allowed to return on condition of sending
his eldest son to his Majesty as a hostage for
good behaviour in the future.

OUR MUSICAL PAGE.

C'AITE 'N CAIDIL AN RIBHINN?

Key F.   Harmonised by H.C.

O, c'àite 'n caidil an ribhinn au nochd? O, c'àit-e 'n caidil an ribh-inn?
O, where art thou, my love, to night, Where sleepest thou my dear-ie?

Far an caid-il luaidh mo chridu; Is truagh nach robh mi fhin ann.
Where'er thou art, my la-dy bright, O would that I were near thee.

2 Tha' ghaoth a' séideadh oirnn o'n deas,
   'S tha mise deas gu seóladh,
   'S na'n robh thu leam air bhàrr nan stuagh;
   A luaidh, cha bhithinn brònach.

3 Bha mi deas 'us bha mi tuath,
   'S gu tric air chuairt 's na h-Innsean,
   'S bean d' aogais riamh cha d' fhuair mi am
   No samhladh do mo nigh'naig.

4 'S ann ort féin a dh' fhàs a' ghruag,
   Tha bachlach, dualach, riomhach,
   Fiamh an òir a's bòidhche snuadh
   'S e dol 'n a dhuail 's na cìrean.

5 Cha tog fiodhull, 's cha tog òran,
   'S cha tog ceòl na pioba,
   'S cha tog briodal nigh'naig òig,
   Am bròn 'tha 'n diugh air m' inntinn.

6 'Se dh' iarrainn riochd na h-eala bhàin
   A shnàmhas thar a' chaolais,—
   'Us rachainn féin troimh thonnaibh breun,
   A chur an céill mo ghaol dhuit.

7 Tha nis gach ni a réir mo dheoin,
   Gach aefhuinn 's seòl mar dh' iarrainn;
   'S gun mhaille théid mi air a tòir,
   'Us pòsaidh mi mo nigh'nag.

2 My ship is floating on the tide,
   And prosperous winds are blowing;
   If thou wert only by my side
   My tears would not be flowing.

3 I long have braved the stormy sea,
   To distant lands oft sailings;
   No maiden have I seen like thee;
   Thine absence I'm bewailing.

4 How fair thy locks are to behold
   When in the sunbeams shining;
   In colour they will vie with gold
   That oft has stood refining.

5 In song or dance I take no part,
   And music cannot cheer me;
   Nor maiden's smile can raise my heart
   Since absent from my dearie.

6 If like the swan I now could sail
   Across the trackless ocean,
   Ere break of day my love I'd hail
   And prove my heart's devotion.

7 My sails are set; blow, breezes blow,
   All thoughts of danger scorning;
   Where dwells my love I'll quickly go
   And wed her in the morning.

Translation by "Fionn."

TO CORRESPONDENTS.

All Communications, on literary and business matters, should be addressed to the Editor, Mr. JOHN MACKAY, 17 Dundas Street, Kingston, Glasgow.

TERMS OF SUBSCRIPTION.— The CELTIC MONTHLY will be sent, post free, to any part of the United Kingdom, Canada, the United States, and all countries in the Postal Union—for one year, 4s.

THE CELTIC MONTHLY

JUNE, 1894.

CONTENTS.

A HIGHLAND REGISTRY.

We are glad to be able to intimate that the proposal to form a Highland Registry has been so favourably received that the directors have decided to open an Office in Glasgow, for the purpose of providing employment for the great numbers of young Highland men and women who crowd into this city continually in search of remunerative work. That the Registry will be a positive boon is admitted by all. We understand that the responsible position of manageress has been offered to, and accepted by, Miss Annie Mackay, a lady whose intimate knowledge of the working of such institutions will prove of great service. Steps are now being taken to secure suitable rooms in some central part of the town, and we hope to be able in our next issue to give full particulars. Meantime, we trust that the many Highland Societies in the district will give the " Highland Registry " their hearty support.

OUR NEXT ISSUE.

We will present our readers with life-like plate portraits of Mr. John MacMillan, J.P., of Glencrosh and Holm, Dumfries-shire ; and Mr. D. W. Kemp, J.P., of Trinity, Edinburgh, whose name is so familiar to our readers. Interesting biographical sketches will accompany the portraits. We will also give finely engraved portraits of Dr. K. N. MacDonald, Gesto Hospital, Skye, editor of the " Skye Collection " of Highland Reels and Strathspeys, Mr. W. MacGregor Stoddard, London, and Mr. George MacKay, Sanitary Inspector for Perthshire. In addition to these a *fac simile* will be given of the famous bond of the " Men of Islay " in favour of the forfeited Lord of the Isles, and a number of views of places of interest in Islay will also appear as illustrations to the next part of Mr. C. Fraser-Mackintosh's interesting papers on the MacDonalds of Isla. Mr. John MacKay, Hereford, contributes a valuable article on " Ian Abrach," the young hero chief of the Clan MacKay, which will be suitably illustrated with views of historic places in the MacKay country. We also intend giving *fac similes* of several of the beautiful plates which appeared in the Queen's magnificent work on the " Highland Clans." The article on " Highlanders in the Archer Guard of France," held over from this issue, will also appear, in addition to the following interesting contributions,— " Domhlach odhar nan creach's encounter with the Men of Assynt " (illustrated), by George Morrison. " An old Highland Moderate Minister," by Rev. P. Macleod, " Three rare Gaelic Books " by Rev. Dr. Masson, " How a Provost was made in Wick nearly two centuries ago," by Geo. M. Sutherland, F.S.A., Scot.; " The Auldest Native," a humorous Highland reading, by Mr. Duncan Maclean : besides other attractive contributions in prose and verse. We hope to make our next number the best we have yet issued, both in regard to the literary matter and beautiful illustrations. We want to prove that Highlanders can produce a Magazine which will compare favourably with any published in Britain at the price. Every Highlander should buy a copy of next month's *Celtic Monthly.*

The Clan MacKinnon.—Our next issue will contain contributions relating to this clan which will prove of great interest to clansmen. Communications on the disputed chiefship will also appear.

We have to express our indebtedness to Mr. Arthur MacKay Morrison and Miss Margaret J. Morrison, Laurel Bank, Partick, for the use of a large number of negatives of views of Islay, several of which we reproduce in this issue. We hope to give reproductions of several other scenes in Islay from Mr. Morrison's unique collection.

Death of a Distinguished Sutherlander.—Many of our readers will regret to learn of the death of Mr. George Munro, Bolton. Mr. Munro was a native of Evelix, Dornoch, and although absent for thirty four years from his native parish he took a deep and practical interest in every project which was intended for the benefit of his fellow countrymen.

Shinty—Inveraray v. Oban.—This important contest which took place at Oban on 26th April, resulted in a win for Inveraray by 5 goals to 2.

The Highland Emporium.—What has long been a felt want in Glasgow is now likely to be supplied —we refer to the establishment of a Gaelic Bookseller and Stationer in Glasgow. Mr. Henry Whyte (Fionn) has just taken over an old established business at 4 Bridge Street—at south end of Glasgow Bridge—where he intends to carry on the business of Gaelic Bookseller, Stationer, News Agent, and Tobacconist. Mr. Whyte's acquaintance with Gaelic Literature generally, and his knowledge of the wants and requirements of his Celtic brethren in this line, ought to secure him a large share of Celtic patronage. We bespeak for him the support of all Highlanders.

PORT - ASKAIG.

LIGHT HOUSE. PORTNAHAVEN

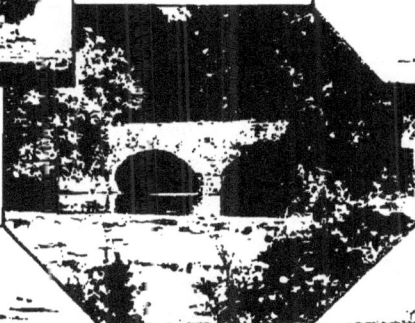

BRIDGEND.

LOCH GRUNARD.

PORT-CHARLOTTE.

THE LAST MACDONALDS OF ISLA.

By Charles Fraser-Mackintosh, F.S.A. (Scot.).

Part VII.—*(continued from page* 153*).*

'IT was a custom among the Highlanders to visit from house to house making merry while the provisions lasted, then they would carry the master of the last house with them to the next and so on. Angus said he did not choose to demean himself in such a way thro' Ilay, as he had not the least doubt but he would be fond of a proper opportunity to revenge the treatment he had given him. But Angus protested that he meant to live in the greatest friendship with him as a brother. But besides had he not the dearest pledges he could give him in the world already. Add to all this it was his sister's house, who would neither countenance nor suffer the least wrong to be done to the nearest of her relations, and far less to her brother. In fine Sir Lachlan was prevailed upon to go with him which he did without any fear or suspicion, accompanied with eighty of his relations and kinsmen besides servants, to Angus' house, where they were entertained at a very high rate. Sir Lachlan kept James his hostage with him every night in his bed-chamber in case of any attack.

"Angus had privately warned all his friends in the Island to be in full armour at his house about midnight and to wait his signal resolving to kill them all the very first night after their arrival.

After supper M'Lean, at his own desire, lodged with all his men in a long strong house that lay at a little distance from the rest of the houses in the town, keeping still his hostage James with him. About midnight when it was thought all were asleep, Angus surrounded the house with 400 men in arms. He came himself to the door, and called upon Sir Lachlan to rise and let him in that he might give him his sleeping drink which he had forgot to give him before he went to bed. Sir Lachlan thanked him but told him he wanted none then. Angus, however, insisted that he should come out and take it. Sir Lachlan suspecting the worst rose and went to the door, carrying James his hostage and nephew in his arms. The boy seeing his father with a drawn sword in his hand at the door, and others in the same way about it, cried for mercy to his uncle, which was granted, and M'Lean retired with him to a private room till morning. About daylight Angus M'Donald called to all that were with M'Lean, that such of them as wanted to save their lives should come out and surrender themselves which all did except two, who refused to come out and were therefore burnt in the house. Next day there was a report spread through all Ilay that Sir Lachlan's friends at Dowart had caused Ronald, Angus' brother, the other hostage, to be put to death. Though this was a false alarm, yet Angus desired no more than to be revenged on the M'Leans, for the very next day he caused sixty of M'Lean's followers to be beheaded in couples.

"The Earl of Argyle being informed of these outrages acquaints the King and Council with it, upon which a herald was despatched to summon Angus to deliver Sir Lachlan M'Lean to the Earl of Argyle. But the harbour at which the herald should land was blocked up so that he could not land but was obliged to return without doing anything. But after a great deal of pains and travail by Sir James Stewart the Chancellor and others, and after imposing very high conditions, Sir Lachlan was released, and Ronald his brother and the other hostage set at liberty, and further Sir Lachlan was obliged to give his own son and M'Leod of Harris' son as hostages to Angus M'Donald and thus matters were adjusted between them at that time.

"Some time after this Angus M'Donald being obliged to go over to Ireland upon some affairs of importance, Sir Lachlan M'Lean no sooner came to know this than he invaded Ilay in a hostile manner, and burnt, killed, pillaged all before him without

the least regard to his own faith or the safety of the hostages. Angus M'Donald having returned from Ireland never troubles the innocent hostages for the outrages committed in his absence, but in great rage convocates his men and in a hostile manner enters Tyree, belonging to the M'Leans, and with fire and sword kills all the inhabitants and cattle that was for the use of man, without exception or distinction, and from that proceeded to Mull, killing all the M'Leans that came in his way at his pleasure.

"Sir Lachlan in the meantime enters Kintyre with fire and sword and lays it waste. Thus for a while they ruined one another till both their countries were desolate. At length Sir Lachlan to detach John M'Iain M'Donald of Ardnamurchan from Angus M'Donald's party, he invited him to Mull promising him his mother, to whom he had formerly been a suitor in marriage. John M'Donald accepts

SANCTUARY CROSSES OF ISLAY.

KILCHOMAN.

KILDALTON.

ARDNAVE.

of the invitation, goes to Mull and was married, but it being whispered that he could not be detached from Angus M'Donald's interest and party, a few nights after the marriage, the chamber where John M'Donald lay was forced open. He was violently dragged out of bed from his wife and made prisoner and eighteen of his followers killed on the spot, nor would they accept of his eldest son as hostage for him. At length Sir Lachlan M'Lean and Angus M'Donald were both charged with a herald to compear before the King at Edinburgh, under pain of forfeitry. Both compeared and were committed close prisoners to the Castle of Edinburgh, at length they were both reconciled and got remissions and a severe penalty imposed upon the first that would break the peace.

"A considerable time after this Sir Lachlan M'Lean resolves to strike at the root of the M'Donalds of South Isles, having borrowed or purchased an action against the whole Isle of Islay, the

ancient inheritance of the M'Donalds. He thought it a very proper time to accomplish his design when his brother-in-law and famous antagonist Angus M'Donald was laid aside by old age and infirmities, and Sir James M'Donald his nephew and the right heir was but young and inexperienced. He therefore raised his men and enters Isla with an army to take possession of it by virtue of his pretended claim.

"Sir James M'Donald being informed of the preparations made by his uncle endeavours to be as ready as he. Accordingly they entered Isla much about the same time, several offering their good offices to adjust matters, and to make up the difference between them. Sir James being the more reasonable of the two was willing for peace, to let his uncle Sir Lachlan to possess the half of Isla during his life, provided he would hold it of him, as the Macleans his predecessors, held of his ancestors, the Macdonalds, and offered to refer the whole dispute to the King's Majesty, or any other Arbiter. But nothing less than the whole would please Sir Lachlan, whereupon they parted, and both parties prepare to decide the controversy by the longest sword,—Sir James having fewer men, but better trained, a most bloody battle was fought, —Sir Lachlan M'Lean with eighty of the gentlemen of his name and two hundred common soldiers were killed on the spot, his son Lachlan was severely wounded and he and all that remained of the M'Leans were chased to their vessels. There were sixty of the M'Donalds killed and as many wounded, Sir James being dangerously wounded, shot through the body with the arrow and left for dead most of the ensuing night among the slain.

"The King being incensed with these broils, and finding that the original Right of Isla and Kintyre was at his own disposal, he gave the whole land in feu to the Earl of Argyle, who apprehended Sir James and imprisoned him within the Castle of Edinburgh where he was confined a long time."

From the Extract Clan History before given, it will be seen that Angus had two brothers, Coll and Ronald. In the Kalendar of State Papers of Queen Elizabeth, Scottish Series, there is a memorandum in the hand-writing of Sir Robert Cecil, circa 1602, regarding Angus Macdonald's family and connection with the Irish Macdonalds. The English Queen's representatives and correspondents in Scotland spied out and reported the most trivial events, and her advisers had the great Scottish families pedigrees, connections, quarrels, etc. minutely before them. Sir Robert Cecil gives James Macdonald, 6th of Isla family, as (1) Archibald who died without issue; (2) Angus of whom we are now treating; (3) Ronald or Randal; (4) Coll who died without issue; (5) Donald Gorme, and (6) Alexander whom he styles "Carrach" and must not be confounded with the first Keppoch.

Angus married Fynvola, daughter of Hector Oig Maclean of Duart, who is not named in the Baronage unless indentical with the Florence therein mentioned, who is said to have married Hector Roy Maclean of Coll; and if so, Angus Macdonald was her second husband.

One of the charges against Sir James Macdonald, when indicted in 1604, was that in January, 1597, by the desire of the Laird of Loupe, then at great enmity with the Tutor of Loupe who happened to be visiting Angus Macdonald at Askomell, two miles distant from Simereby, where Sir James lived, he, Sir James with a large party, on refusal of Angus to surrender the Tutor or open the doors, set fire to the house, to the imminent danger of those within. The lady is described as calling out "Thiefe will thou burn thy mother," altogether a shocking occurrence. The word "thief" was of old a general term of opprobium much extended from its primary signification, and probably in this case signified "Devil" or "Spirit of Mischief." In the times when witchcraft was reputed as common in the land, the ladies who wished to lay the wind, which they had raised in the Devil's name, if they failed in the first instance to do so, called upon "our Spirit" and said to him,

"Thieffe Thieffe! conjure the wind,"

etc. With regard to Angus Macdonald's lawful children, besides Sir James, notice is found of Angus Oig, who was executed in July, 1615, for taking and holding of the Castle of Dunyvaig, notwithstanding his life was promised on his surrender. Angus Macdonald had also a daughter, Margaret, whose hard position in 1617 when the Privy Council gives her "special license to resort at her pleasure to her friends, to solicit their help notwithstanding her having visited her brother Sir James Macdonald in Kintyre during his rebellion" seems inaccountable. Margaret had married Archibald Macdonald, younger son of Sleat, with issue Donald who succeeded his uncle in 1616, was served heir in 1617 and was the first Baronet of Sleat; Mary who married a younger son of Clanranald; also a son Hugh, who though one of the worst Macdonalds known in their history, occupied a good position. Why it was necessary for the poor lady to "solicit the help of her friends" is, as I said, inaccountable.

Angus Macdonald had at least two natural sons, Archibald and Ronald Oig. Angus seems to have made appeals to the King in the years 1605 and 1606, without effect. These are couched in the most humble terms, and the state of the proud chief had indeed become low when he could get himself to pen them. He says he paid all the Crown rents and dues of Isla and Kintyre and promises to pay them for the future, except for the part that are waste, and he makes the significant offer to find sufficient caution *within the lowlands* that he would be obedient to the laws of Scotland, and to that effect should compear before the Council upon lawful premonition wherever they sit. Upon 10th September, 1606, he sent a final letter to the King through the Bishop of the Isles whose intervention he sought, stating among other things and beseeching "your Majesty for the cause of God to respect my age and poor estate and to let me know your Hignness' own mind signed with your Majesty's own hand, and if it please your Majesty to continue me in the possession of these kindly rooms which my forbears and I have had of your Majesty, and your Highness' Royal progenitors, I shall not only pay the duties and maills used and wont herefor; but also shall find sufficient security for obedience to your Majesty's laws in all points, and in all time coming; or otherwise that it may seem good to your Majesty to let me know how and whereupon I shall live."

A. STEWART MACGREGOR,

British Vice-Consul, Christiania.

THE subject of the following sketch was born in Wales. His father, Mr. Alexander MacGregor, a Civil Engineer, died in India; and when only two years of age the boy was taken to Scotland. He received part of his early education at Windsor Lodge Academy, Portobello, and afterwards attended private classes in Edinburgh. We take the following extract from a testimonial written regarding him by the Rev. A. Barron, M.A., then Head Master of the School referred to. "At the closing competitions of his last year with me he stood at the head of every class (six) which he had attended during the Session."

When he left school Mr. MacGregor had himself a preference for the Church, but, not being very robust, he was advised to give up continuous hard study, and to seek healthy, if possible out-door employment. With a view to carrying out this idea he devoted himself to farming, first at home and subsequently abroad. At Edinburgh University in session 1870-71 he took first-class honours in Agriculture and obtained one of the two grants of books presented to the class by the Highland and Agricultural Society of Scotland.

He then visited Denmark and Sweden, and while in the former country having a thorough knowledge of the language with other co-editors, he published Danish Notes on two of Shakespeare's Plays. Archæology has great attractions for him; several years ago, he was elected Member of the Society of Northern Antiquaries at Copenhagen, and to him was entrusted the translation of the eminent Danish Antiquarian, Professor Worsaae's last work:— "The Industrial Arts of Denmark." This little book was written in Danish, but published in English for the South Kensington Museum, London. It is an interesting manual on the beginnings of Danish Art in the Stone, Bronze, and Iron Ages. Since residing abroad Mr. MacGregor has taken every opportunity of re-visiting Scotland, for which he has an intense affection. He lost both parents while he was still quite young, but most fortunately had been placed by his father under the care of two true-hearted old Highland ladies, Misses Stewart, from Appin, Argyllshire. This may perhaps partly account for the fact that the Highlands have ever possessed for him a wondrous charm. Though these ladies, like so many other Highlanders, were intensely loyal, they had something of the old romantic admiration for Prince Charlie, and an interest in everything connected with the stirring incidents of the '45. While Mr. MacGregor was at Copenhagen the then British Vice-Consul there retired; the vacant post was offered to him. He was there for several years as Vice-Consul and was then nominated by the Marquis of Salisbury to the Vice-Consulship at the Norwegian capital, subject to his passing the usual Civil Service Examination. This Mr. MacGregor did. Since

ALEXANDER KENDALL MACKINNON.

1890 he has been British Vice-Consul at Christiania, and upon several occasions during the absence of the senior officer, he has discharged the duties of Acting British Consul-General. Notwithstanding all his foreign experiences, comparing him with genuine Highlanders at home, he has said it himself and it may most truthfully be said of him:—"His heart is in the Highlands, and his love to the old country is no less than theirs."

Crosshill, Glasgow.   ALEX. MACGREGOR.

ALEXANDER KENDALL MACKINNON.

AFTER the decease of Alexander Mackinnon (of whose remarkable life we may be able hereafter to give an account), at Buenos Ayres, on the 17th of November, 1815, his son, Charles Villiers Mackinnon, settled at Montevideo, in Uruguay, as a merchant. He married on the 22nd February, 1823, Miss S. Kendall, daughter of P. Kendall of Alfreton, Derbyshire. Of this marriage were two sons, Alexander, the the subject of our sketch, and Charles Duncan who died at Brighton on the 16th January, 1879.

In 1843 Mr. Charles V. Mackinnon brought his family to this country to attend to the education of his sons, but died soon after at Reading on the 19th May, 1850.

Mr. Alexander K. Mackinnon received his professional education of Civil Engineer and Architect by private tuition, and afterwards, at University College, London.

In 1851 he married Emiley Netherwood (who died on the 29th April, 1860), eldest daughter of Christopher Netherwood, Esq., late of Cliffe Hall, Keighley, Yorkshire, by whom he had two daughters and two sons:—the eldest died, the second son, Alexander G. Mackinnon, is at Buenos Ayres.

Mr. Mackinnon married again in 1869 to Miss T. Gomez, daughter of the late P. A. Gomez of Montevideo, by whom he has living one daughter and two sons—Frederick Alexander and Albert Edward Mackinnon.

In 1851 he proceeded to Montevideo and commenced the practice of his profession, and was appointed by the Buenos Ayres Government on an important Commission. He left this country again in 1861 to continue the practice of his profession at Montevideo. He carried out some important works for the Municipality there, and was afterwards appointed Director General of Public Works by the Government.

The country was then in its infancy, as far as Public Works were concerned. Mr. Mackinnon, in the carrying out of an ambitious programme, found an earnest supporter in President Flores.

The laying out of the new city, new roads, gas works, the pioneer railways, water works, lazaretto, fireproof warehouses, reclamation of lands by the construction of a sea-wall more than 2000 metres long, and other public works, all of which were either designed or assisted in their realization by Mr. Mackinnon.

In 1869 the Government sent Mr. Mackinnon to this country as Special Financial Commissioner, and also to contract the realization of his fireproof warehouses, both of which missions he carried out successfully.

In 1889 he presented designs for Port Harbour Works at Montevideo, a matter still under consideration. Mr. Mackinnon is a Member of the Institute of Civil Engineers, and also F.R.I.B.A., F.G.S., and F.I.I.

DUNROBIN.

A REMINISCENCE OF A VOLUNTEER REVIEW.

With round dark eye aglow with watchfulness,
    A redbreast on the path soft -sudden—dropt,
    And boldly round our very footsteps hopped
In happy freedom. We stood still to bless
    Its confidence ; then fed it and passed on
To where, 'mid richest flowers, the fountain rose
Into the irised sunshine,—thence to those
    Whose martial fire the day had caused to don
The flowing tartan. Rattling rifles rang ;
    And weighty guns sank in the peaceful sward
Their wheels; while brazen-throated trumpets sang
    "The Huntsman's Chorus!" On the wind each chord
Wavered: around, the writhing banners flew,
And over all the sky spread summer's softest blue.

                                JOHN HOGBEN.

A LOCK OF PRINCE CHARLIE'S HAIR.

Mr. A. Stewart MacGregor has many curiosities, and among the things which he treasures most is a little locket containing a piece of the Prince's hair. Regarding this souvenir the following history has been written by Mr. MacGregor himself. "It was given to Miss Ann Stewart, a sister of the Appin Stewarts (Miss Jessie and Miss Flora - referred to on page 178), by a daughter of Colonel Campbell, Lochend. Miss Campbell got it from a grand-daughter of Flora MacDonald's, the Campbells, Lochend, then being tenants of Kingsburgh, Skye. This same Miss Ann Stewart afterwards became Mrs. MacBride, wife of the Minister of the Parish of Little Dunkeld. For a most interesting account of the way in which the lock was cut, see "The Book of the Noble Englishwoman" by Charles Bruce ; W. Nimmo, Publisher. The only thing difficult to understand is how anyone could call Flora MacDonald an Englishwoman!"

HIGHLAND WIT AND HUMOUR.

By " Fionn."

A HIGHLAND boy went with his mother to Inverness to get his first pair of boots. Returning home with his boots slung round his neck, and feeling as proud as a chief, he paid little attention to his steps. Suddenly he struck his big toe against a stone with a terrible shock. Stooping down he began to hold his toe in his hand, while with a rueful countenance he showed the pain he was suffering. Brightening up suddenly he turned to his mother and exclaimed — "*Taing do'n Fhreasdal nach i a' bhròg ùr a fhuair siud*," (Providence be thanked that it was not the new shoes that got yon.)

A deer-stalker after a series of inexcusable misses, remarked to his gillie — "Well, Donald, whose fault was it that time?" Quoth Donald —" Well, he wasn't more than a hundred yards, and it's not my fault you missed him ; and it's not the fault of the stag, for he stood still enough ; and it's not the fault of the rifle, for I ken well it's a right good one ; so I'll just leave it to you to think it over, and find out whose fault it was.'

This reminds one of the Highland lady who sent her son—the young laird—for the first time to the shooting, under the charge of old Sandy the gamekeeper. On their return in the evening with rather a light bag the fond mother asked Sandy how the laird got on in the hill—and if he was a good shot. "He shot real pretty," was Sandy's reply, "but Providence was kind to the birds "

Two Highlanders were benighted, and lay down to sleep on the side of a mountain. After they had lain a little one of them got up, but soon returned again. The other asked him— "What's this, Donald? What have you been about?" Donald replied—"I was only bringing a stane to put under my head." Duncan started up and cried—"Man, but you're unco pernickety! Canna ye sleep without a stane aneath your head?"

Gaelic epitaphs are but seldom met with, but some of the English attempts to convey to the reader an idea of the virtues of departed Celts, are very funny. Take the following for example—

Here lies Andrew MacPherson
Who was a peculiar person,
He stood six foot two
Without his shoe,
And was slew at Waterloo.

It is not every epitaph that is so painfully true as the following :—

Here lies interred a man o' micht,
His name was Malcom Downie ;
He lost his life ae market nicht
By fa-in' a1l his pownie.   Aged 37.

On a stone not far from Rob Roy's grave at Balquhidder, the following ludicrous inscription may be seen—

Beneath this stane lies Seonaid Roy,
Shon Roy's reputed mother,
In a' her life, save this Shon Roy,
She never had another.
'Tis here, or hereabout, they say—
The place no one can tell ;
But when she'll rise at the last day
She'll ken the stane hersel.

The fact of a man being a good shot is not usually included among "tombstone virtues," but in the churchyard of Fort-William we find the following—

"Sacred to the memory of Captain Patrick Campbell, late of the 42nd regiment. He died on the 13th of December 1816. A true Highlander, a sincere friend, and the best deerstalker of his day."

In a churchyard not far from Glasgow there is a stone evidently erected by a Highlander— The confusion of ideas in the epitaph is rather extraordinary—Erected by Hugh MacMillan in memory of his father Donald MacMillan who died, etc., then we have this line from Gray's "Elegy in a Country Churchyard"—

"He gave to misery (all he had) a tear,"
followed by this extraordinary coda—
Also my son Hugh.

It reminds one of the inscription over some youth who was "shot by a blunderbuss, one of the old brass kind—"For of such is the Kingdom of Heaven"!

It is wonderful what havoc the misplacing of part of a sentence, or even a comma makes on the sense, as will be seen from the following— "Erected to the memory of John MacDonald who was shot by his brother as a mark of respect." The members of this family must have had rather a peculiar way of showing their respect for one another.

A certain Captain MacPherson was about to proceed on a long voyage, and his wife sent a request to the church to which they belonged desiring an interest in their prayers. Poor body, she doubtless wrote—"Captain MacPherson going to sea, his wife requests the prayers of the congregation." The announcement made to the congregation was—"Captain MacPherson going to see his wife, requests the prayers of the congregation." If Mrs. MacPherson was present her feelings may be easier imagined than described.

ABSTRACT OF OSSIAN'S COVALLA.

BY THE LATE LIEUT.-COLONEL CHARLES STEWART,
TIGH-'N-DUIN.

Author of "The Gaelic Kingdom in Scotland, and its Celtic Church,"
" Killin Collection of Poetry and Music," &c.

(Continued from page 121).

COVALLA, in answer to this question, first supposes it was the World-King's son (Caracalla) and his host; but then suddenly she changes, and says—

COVALLA.
Conn's chant.

" But no ! 'tis my Fion's wraith, surrounded

By those of his host that are slain :

O why hast thou come, my beloved one,

To fill me with grief and with pain.

Fingal arrives and thus addresses the bards—

Iain chridhe.

" Mouths that duans chant, each your voice raise,

Of Carron's host, sing loud the praises ;

Fled, my swords shrive ! Caracul and his host have,

Across the plain, and over the height tops.

As wraiths of the night, in their shining vestures,

Over the slope, they as lightnings cusped,

Neath the soft breezes, that blew from the westward,

With woods in bright beams, of light round about them

Hush ! is yon, a voice I am hearing,

Or a sweet sound, of gladdening breezes

That down from grey cairns, are softly breathing

Thro' my own glen, with its winding hillsides.

Covalla now for the first time realises that it is Fingal in all his manhood who is near her, and she thus addresses him—

COVALLA.
Conn's chant.

" My chief, with fame great returning,

Who hast my fond heart all thine own,

O joyfully take me beside thee,

To where we will find our repose."

Fingal replies—

Iain chridhe.

- " Yes, my own loved one, come thou with me,

Sped has the storm, and aglow are the sunbeams,

Come thou where, we find repose will,

Huntress bold, of the high forest's cold ben."

COVALLA.
Conn's chant.

" Then come thou hast, my brave darling,

With a name that afar is renowned,

Thy arm fast holds me in love's clasp,

My hero, my champion, my own.

Under thy shade I will rest me,

Behind thy fond sheltering form,

Till hither my spirit return makes,

That from fear is now floating around. *

In tuneful strains the most joyous

The harp's strings cause gaily to sound,

And ye maidens of eyelashes fairest

Duans raise to ennoble his fame.

DERSEGRINA.

" Ho ró ! mo nighean donn bhòidheach."

" On the heath by Covalla three deer fell,

On high in the breeze a bright fire burns,

To the maiden's spread feast joyful come, then,

King of Morven of wood-claden cairns.

* This has mostly been translated as. "from fear that is swimming around." This, however, is nonsense, and the above is evidently the correct one. It is of no importance as to the fact of her spirit being absent from her body and soul, as either equally shows that to have been the case. The Gaelic, " A null," is decisive as to this.

(To be continued).

MACCRORIES OR RORISONS :—

CAN you tell me if the "M Crorie's " are a distinct Clan, and if the " Rorison's " are a connection of same? Greenock. T. D. RORISON.

LETTERS TO THE EDITOR.

THE CHIEFTAINSHIP OF THE CLAN MACKINNON.

'S RIOGHAIL MO DHREAM.

"Sliochd nan righribh duthchasach
Bha shios ann an Dùn-staighineis,
Aig an robh crun na h-Alba o thus,
'S aig a bheil dùthchas fathast ris."

Junior Constitutional Club,
London, W., 9th May, 1894.

Sir,—I shall be obliged if you will allow the insertion in your interesting Magazine of a few lines in reply to Mr. Duncan Mackinnon's article on the above subject. It is lamentable, but no less a fact, that there are five or six claimants to that honour. It is manifestly an impossibility that they have all a right to the distinction of Chief of the Clan. It is desirable that all interested in this subject should come to an agreement to settle it once for all. A divided house is most deplorable.

The Clan Mackinnon is increasing and multiplying to such a degree that we may look forward ere long, if not already arrived at that point, of wishing possibly to raise a regiment of the Clan to fight for Queen and Country, as our forefathers did in times long ago. But we must have the Chief, whom we shall agree to follow as the legitimate head.

I, in common with others, am unable to follow the premises laid down by Mr. Duncan Mackinnon, or the interesting and able work of the author on "Clan Fingon." Others have written on the same theme, and altogether diverse opinions have appeared, proving that there is a great hiatus to be filled up before we can settle the disputed point. At all events let us in a friendly spirit endeavour to solve this question as soon as possible, and in accord with justice and right, without attacking anyone, till we have found truth, which surely will not elude our grasp.

With the view of making a beginning let me say what I know, which the circumstance that a large number of documents, papers, and letters of an ancient character came into my possession not long ago, bearing on the "trunk," enable me. Now, none, so far as I am aware, has ever disputed the direct descent of the Chiefs which had their home in the Isle of Skye. Without going further back let me name my great great grandfather, John Mackinnon of Mackinnon, of Strathaird, and Mishnich. His son, who succeeded him in the Chieftainship, was Charles Mackinnon of Mackinnon, who married Alexandra, daughter of John MacLeod, younger of MacLeod, and sister of Colonel, afterwards General MacLeod, of Dunvegan Castle, Skye; of this marriage were a daughter, Mary Emilia (who married my grandfather, Alexander Mackinnon, Banker at Naples, during the time that Sir William and Lady Hamilton were there), and John, the Chief on the death of his father in 1808, in London, and who had made an effort to recover the estates. This very interesting document is in the possession of a member of our Clan.

Mary Emilia Mackinnon was married to Alexander Mackinnon at Edinburgh, on the 5th of October, 1792; of this marriage was my father, Charles Villiers Mackinnon, who when quite a lad, accompanied his father to Buenos Ayres.

Going back to Charles Mackinnon of Mackinnon, I have printed documents of the time, where is set forth his title of Chief in Courts of Law in Scotland, and no one attempted to question the point. But in fact the above author agrees to the issue of the direct line of my family; and even the late Mr. William Alexander Mackinnon respected it, for we find he did not register his patent of Chieftainship at Edinburgh till 1811, *after* the death of my great uncle, John Mackinnon of Mackinnon.

Having said so much I would suggest that all claimants should agree to submit their claims to experts, with all documentary evidence, and resolve to abide by their decision.

Yours truly,
ALEX. K. MACKINNON.

LORD REAY AND THE CUTTIE STOOL.

Sir,—At page 91 of Vol. I. *Celtic Monthly*, the Rev. Donald Masson, M.D., states that the Rev. Murdoch MacDonald, of Durness, "made the Lord Reay of his day do penance on the cuttie stool." It is a pity that the Rev. gentleman did not verify his statement before aspersing the character of a nobleman unique in his character of charity and mercy, and of whom Rob Donn—the Juvenal of the Highlands—could say :

"'S iomadh buille bha cràiteach,
A rinn am bàs thoirt dhuinn,
Air chosd gheugan do theaghlaich,
Gun athadh bonn do na cinn ;
Ach cha deach' uiread do throcair
A chur fo 'n fhòd ri mo linn,
'S a chaidh chàradh 'a an tòma,
'S e Morair Domhnull MacAoidh."

Lady Reay sought to coerce the Rev. Mr. Mac-Donald to relax the discipline of the church in favor of one of her maids, whose frailty had come prominently before the parish, but the stern disciplinarian was immovable, and Sheriff Forbes was instructed to enforce compliance with her Ladyship's demands. The good man heeded the Sheriff as little as he did Lady Reay, when the purity of the churches ordinances was assailed, and the frail damsel did the required penance before she was allowed to cover her folly by the matrimonial veil. Lord Reay needed no such expurgation as the Rev. writer implies.

The memory of the Lords of Reay is still dear to Durness men ; the family traditions have been woven into their very being ; they are looking hopefully to the time when a democratic Legislature shall restore the soil of the British Islands to its original owners, and re-establish the Lord of Reay in his ancestral home to rule over the remnant of his people. The peasantry will then take up the words of Rob Donn and sing with all the enthusiasm of a re-invigorated patriotic fervor, of a time when prosperity favoured the straths and glens, once teeming with loyal and devoted adherents, (now, unhappily, the home of sheep and deer, and of south country shepherds and game protectors)

"Bha barran trom tir againn,
Bha toradh fridh is fairg againn."

Yours truly,
(Captain) W. MORRISON.

London.

REVIEWS.

HISTORY OF THE MACKENZIES, by Alexander MacKenzie, M.J.I., new, revised and ex ended Edition. Inverness: A. & W. MacKenzie.

The fact that a new edition of this work has already been demanded goes a long way to prove its historic value and importance as a book of reference. But this is not only a new edition, but virtually a new book containing as it does over two hundred pages more than the former issue. The origin of this clan has long been a matter of dispute, but Mr. MacKenzie in this edition completely refutes the Irish origin of the clan, tracing it to the famous family of the Earl of Ross. As might be expected in elucidating the history of the clan the author throws considerable light on the actions of other clans, as well as upon various historic incidents connected with the Highlands. In this way the work before us is such as cannot be overlooked by anyone who would study the history of the Highland people thoroughly. The question of chiefship is discussed at some length and disposed of in a satisfactory manner, the dignity belonging to Mr. James Fowler MacKenzie of Allangrange. The work as a whole is a monument of perseverance, for the amount of labour and research entailed in producing such a history must have been enormous, and the task which Mr. MacKenzie set before him has been performed with wonderful accuracy and faithfulness. In addition to a copious index we have an excellent portrait of the author and a coloured reproduction of the MacKenzie tartan. We cordially recommend the volume not only to members of the clan but to all who are interested in matters Celtic.

SUMMER TOURS IN SCOTLAND by David MacBrayne's Royal Mail Steamers.

The Official Guide for this Royal Route has just been issued for the present season. It contains a vast amount of reliable information regarding places of historic interest in the Highlands, as well as valuable hints and carefully compiled sailing-tables setting forth how and when these places can be reached. We have several clearly printed maps, and a large number of excellent views, while the printing and general get up of the Guide is all that could be desired. To the thousands who patronize Mr. MacBrayne's Steamers the work must prove invaluable, being at once a pleasant as well as a reliable companion.

A BRIEF ACCOUNT OF THE CLAN DONNACH-AIDH, WITH NOTES ON ITS HISTORY AND TRADITIONS, by Davidson, F.S.A., Scot.—The author explains that this work was read at a meeting of the clan society, and was published at the desire of the members. It contains a brief history of the clan, in which its salient points are emphasised, and a light thrown upon matters which were before obscure. Some curious facts are given which are no doubt new to most Highlanders. The author quotes a tradition to the effect that what historians have described as a body of camp followers whose presence on Gillies Hill decided the Battle of Bannockburn, were really the clan Donnachaidh, who had hastened to take part in the great contest. Altogether the book is a most interesting one, the illustrations and covers of the clan tartan being very pretty. It is a work which we have every confidence in recommending to our readers.

THE CLAN CAMERON, by John Cameron, J.P., —This handsome volume consists of a brief sketch of the history and traditions of the Cameron clan, with short notices of eminent clansmen. Mr. Cameron devoted a great deal of time and research in preparing this contribution to the clan's history, and he has managed to condense into a limited space a great deal of curious and valuable information. Almost every topic of clan interest has been touched upon, tradition, poetry, antiquities, etc., all receiving attention. The book contains fourteen full page portraits of distinguished members of the clan, which add a special value to it. Mr. Cameron deserves to be congratulated on the valuable contribution which he has made to the literature of his clan, and we feel sure that it will be read with interest by Highlanders of all clans, for it is a work which should be on every Highlander's bookshelf.

NEWS OF THE MONTH.

AIRDRIE HIGHLAND ASSOCIATION.—The usual monthly meeting was held on 2nd ult., when it was arranged that the annual trip was to take place on 21st June, to Aberfoyle. A large turnout of members and friends is expected.

CLAN MACLEOD SOCIETY.—The third annual social gathering of the Clan Macleod Society was held in the Athenæum Hall, Macleod of Macleod, Chief of the clan, presided, and there was a large attendance. In the absence of the president (Rev. Donald Macleod), the secretary (Mr. Peter MacLeod), presented an address of welcome to the Chief. Macleod of Macleod, who had a most cordial reception, in reply said he was not going to say much about the Highlands. The society was a non-political one, but he desired to say that the Macleods must all have an immense interest in the country with which they had been connected for hundreds of years. It was a beautiful but poor country, and they had to search for fame and fortune elsewhere. He had a very great regard and respect for the people who lived in that country.

He was himself born at Dunvegan, and he hoped to spend his later years there. A programme of music was gone through, and other addresses were delivered.

EDINBURGH SUTHERLAND ASSOCIATION. — The monthly meeting of the Association was held on Friday, 4th May, when there was a large turn-out of members to hear a most interesting paper from Mr. Alexander Mackay, upon his early recollections of Sutherland. These recollections dealt with many of the customs and manners of the people of Sutherland in the first part of this century, customs which have now considerably changed. Mr. Mackay's paper was characteristic throughout, and was much appreciated.

At the previous meeting in April the paper was upon "The Ancient Forests of the Highlands" by Mr. George Morrison, which was also an interesting and instructive contribution. An important report by Mr. Hugh Mackay, M.A., the educational secretary, in regard to the present position of the Association's efforts to assist education in the county, was further considered.

GLASGOW COWAL SOCIETY. — The 29th annual general business meeting of this society was held in the Religious Institution Rooms on Friday evening—the chair being occupied by Mr. John Black, president. From the secretary's report it appears there are at present 350 members on the roll, being an increase of 32 during the year. The treasurer's statement indicated that the income for the year amounted to £120 7s 6d, and the expenditure to £95 4s 6d, of which the sum of £86 5s was paid to pensioners, who at present number 22. The capital of the society now amounts to £854 13s 6d, being an increase of £25 3s during the year. The following are the office-bearers for the ensuing year : Hon. President, Mr. Jas. Waddell, Invereck, Kilmalcolm ; president, Mr. Thos. Dunlop; vice-president, Mr. James MacKellar ; treasurer, Mr. Donald Murray, 152A Stobcross Street ; secretary, Mr. Robert Murray, 103 Kent Road ; and nine directors.

AN COMUNN GAIDHEALACH. — A meeting of the executive council of this association took place in Oban. Among the more important business was the appointment of judges for the coming Mod, to be held in Oban, in September next, the adjustment of the prize list, conditions of competition, and list of part songs and solos therefor. Competitors (except in choral competition) who have already taken first prizes two years in succession, are excluded from competition at this Mod. Besides the usual prizes by the association, the following special ones have been offered :—Two Gold Medals, value £5, by the burgh of Oban, for best male and female soloists ; £5 5s by the Highland Society of London for best original Gaelic prose composition ; £5 5s by Mr. John Mackay, C.E., Hereford, for best original Gaelic poetry ; £10 by Lord Archibald Campbell for solos accompanied by the Highland harp or clarsach ; £4 4s by Mr. C. Fraser-Mackintosh, and £2 by Mr. William Birkmyre, M.P., Ayr Burghs. It was arranged that a number of the prizes should be given in the form of books. It was also agreed that the Mod should take place on the day preceding the Highland Games, and that a concert should be held in the evening as usual. The Mod promises to be a success in every way.

CLAN MACMILLAN SOCIETY. — The annual meeting of the Clan Macmillan Society was held on Thursday, 26th April, in the Christian Institute, Mr. Daniel Macmillan, president, in the chair. The secretary and treasurer submitted their annual reports, which showed the Society to be in a flourishing condition. Rev. Dr. Macmillan, LL.D., Greenock, was re-elected chief, and Rev. Donald Macmillan, M.A., Kelvinhaugh Parish Church, chaplain. Messrs. Arch. Macmillan, Saltcoats ; James Macmillan, Vulcan Ironworks ; ex-Provost Macmillan, Rothesay ; and Frederick Macmillan, publisher, London, were re-elected chieftains. Mr. Daniel Macmillan was re-elected president ; Mr. Archd. Macmillan, secretary ; and Mr. Donald Macmillan, was elected treasurer.

ARCHIBALD MACMILLAN,
CHIEFTAIN, CLAN MACMILLAN SOCIETY.

SMITH & SEE

JOHN MACMILLAN, J.P

THE CELTIC MONTHLY:
A MAGAZINE FOR HIGHLANDERS.
Edited by JOHN MACKAY, Kingston.

No. 10. Vol. II]　　　　JULY, 1894.　　　　| Price Threepence.

SKETCH OF THE FAMILY OF MACMILLAN OF BROCKLOCH.

THE time at which the Macmillans came to the South is a matter of controversy. One writer thinks they came into Galloway from Argyllshire after the death of Alexander III. (A.D. 1286), but it is probable they were located there previous to that date. When Malcolm IV. broke up some of the clans about the year 1260 the Macmillans were shifted from Morayshire, and it is generally believed a branch of the clan was sent direct into Kirkcudbrightshire, where they acquired large possessions. They originally held their land by the tenure called "Manrent," but afterwards King Robert the Bruce created the chief, Baron of Ken, and gave him a charter of his lands to be held "Blanche of the Crown." The chief was Macmillan of Brockloch, in the parish of Carsphairn, and Mr. Macmillan of Holm of Dalquhairn in Carsphairn and Glencrosh, in Dumfriesshire, is the representative of this old family.

The estates of Holm and Brockloch were united in 1741 by the marriage of David Macmillan of the former and Marion Macmillan of the latter. Brockloch remained in the possession of the family till 1831, when it unfortunately passed into other hands.

The most important of the cadet branches of this family is that connected with the property of Laidloch in Carsphairn. In 1803 Thomas, third son of David Macmillan of Brockloch, acquired by purchase the lands of Laidloch and Drumanister. He married Miss Jean Boyle. He died in 1831 and was succeeded by his only son James, who purchased the lands of Changue Loxton, and Craigmulloch, in the parish of Barr, Ayrshire, and Corridow in Dumfries-shire. He married in 1835 Catherine, daughter of the Rev. William M'Call of Caitloch, Dumfriesshire, by whom he had issue, five sons and one daughter, viz:—Thomas of Changue and Loxton; William of Lamloch; Samuel of Carridow; James of Craigmulloch; David of Drumanister; and Katherine.

Thomas Macmillan of Changue died in 1873 and was succeeded by his elder son David, who is a Justice of the Peace for Ayrshire. William Macmillan of Lamloch is also a Justice, and County Councillor for the parishes of Carsphairn and Kells in Galloway.

The last recorded appearance of the South-country clan was in assisting James, Earl of Douglas, against James II., anno 1445. About the year 1662 John Macmillan of Brockloch was fined £360 for non-conformity to Prelacy and adherence to the National Covenant, which was then declared unlawful. In Carsphairn Churchyard are many old Covenanting Gravestones. One of them believed to belong to the Macmillans runs thus:—

M. M.

YOV . TRAVLERS . AS . YOV . PASS . BY
　COME . READ . AND . DO . NOT . FEAR
FOR . DOVN . BELOV . THIS . STON . DOTH . LY
　TRYTH'S . CHAMPION . BVRIED . HERE
ALTHOVGH . HIS . BONS . BELO . THIS . STON
　DO . PICE . AND . PICE . DECAY
HIS . SOVL . IN . HEAVEN . OF . GLORY . SHAL
　ANE . DEDM . VEAR . FOR . AY.

The inscription of another Gravestone is headed by the Macmillan Family Arms and runs thus :-

I. M. : K. L.

BROKLOCH . M'MILLAN . WHO . DID . DIE
UNDER . THIS . STONE . HIS . BODY . DOTH . LY
HIS . SOVL . AT . HEAV'NLY . WORK . ABOVE
WITH . THEM . WHOSE . FAITH . HERE . WROVGHT
　BY . LOVE
MOST . USEFUL . WAS . IN'S . DAY . AND . STATION
IN . DEFENCE . OF . OUR . REFORMATION
GREAT . PROOFE . HE . GAVE . AT . ALL . FIT . TIMES

FOR . THEM . THINGS . ONCE . CALL'D . HIGHEST
CRIMES
NOU . HE'S . GONE . UP . ON . JACOB'S . LAD'R
TO . PRAISE . KING . CHRIST . THE . MEDIATOR
CLOTH'D . IS . HE . NOU . IN . A . WHITE . ROBE
WITH . THEM . THAT . STILL . SING . PRAISE . TO . GOD

VIRTUS . EIUS . POST . FUNERA . VIVIT.

OBIT . 28 . FEB : 1725 . ANNO . EIUS.
.ÆTATIS . 61.

John Macmillan of Brockloch and Holm died
in 1830 leaving Holm to his eldest son Robert,
and Brockloch to his younger son John. Robert
Macmillan married Mary Goldie, daughter of
James Goldie of Stonehouse and Marbrack, and
great-great grand-daughter of Bonnie Annie
Laurie. He died in 1858 and was succeeded by
his elder son John, whose portrait accompanies
this sketch. He was born in 1833 and was
educated at Glasgow High School. He is a
Justice of the Peace for the Counties of
Dumfries and Kirkcudbright.

The Arms of the Family are "Argent on a
Chevron between three Mullets, sable ; as many
Besants, or"

Crest—A Lion rampant, bearing in his hand
a bloody dagger.

Motto—"Age aut peri."

Glasgow.   ARCHIBALD MACMILLAN.

LETTERS TO THE EDITOR.

THE CHIEFTAINSHIP OF THE CLAN MACKINNON.

SIR,—If the letter of Mr. Alexander Kendall
MacKinnon published in the June number
of the "Celtic Monthly" is intended to infer that
he considers himself to have a claim to the Chiefship of his Clan, it would be better at once to tell
him briefly that his position is quite untenable and
this on his own shewing. I do not desire to point
this out in an unfriendly spirit, and doubtless Mr.
A. K. MacKinnon's long residence in South America
may have put him a little out of touch, so to speak,
with the subject of Clan pedigrees. He traces his
descent from Charles, last Chief but one in the
direct line. Charles had a son John, the last direct
Chief, who died at Leith in 1808 (not in London),
and unmarried. Charles had an only daughter,
who married Alexander MacKinnon of Naples, a
clansman having no place on any recognised tree
or claim to the Chieftainship. The Lady was Mr. A.
K. MacKinnon's paternal grandmother. Plainly,
therefore, Mr. A. K. MacKinnon can have no claim
to the dignity since he traces through the female line.
The late Mr. W. A. MacKinnon, M. P., "respected"
the direct line of Mr. A. K. MacKinnon's grandmother's family because until the Chief John,
above alluded to, died, the Antigua branch of
which he became head, had naturally no title.
A slight inaccuracy on the part of Mr. A. K.

MacKinnon must here be set right. The late
Mr. W. A. MacKinnon succeeded his grandfather,
William, who died at Binfield, Berks, in 1809,
aged 77 years, and who thus was actually Chief
for one year after the death of John, 1808,
but for obvious reasons he would not have registered his patent. Mr. A. K. MacKinnon seems
to doubt the rights of the Antigua family. Besides
the patent allowed in 1811, there is the testimony
of six trees ranging from the early part of last
century to the time of Donald Gregory. All these
agree in tracing the Antigua family to Donald or
Daniel, second son of Lachlan Mor, which is all
that is wanted to establish the claim. Lachlan
Mor, who lived in the reign of Charles II., for
whom he fought at the Battle of Worcester, 1651,
and Donald, who was taken prisoner, emigrated to
Antigua on his liberation, and from whom the
Antigua family is descended, and William Alexander, who registered his patent of "Ensign
Armorial" as Chief, granted three years after the
death of John already alluded to, might be sufficient
to remove all doubt on the subject, the necessary
documentary proof having been admitted by the
Lord Lyon, in whose office the Certificates of
Births and Marriages up to Lachlan Mor can be
examined. In Bath Abbey there lies a slab stone
on which is a Coat of Arms, viz :—that of
"MacKinnon" (with the bordure and crescent for
difference). "To the memory of William Mac-
Kinnon, Esq., son of Daniel MacKinnon, second
son of Lachlan Mor MacKinnon, Chief of
MacKinnon, who died, October the 8th, 1767, aged
70 years." This gentleman was father of William
MacKinnon, who became Chief in 1808 on the
failure of the direct line, and great-great grandfather
of the present Chief's father, William Alexander
MacKinnon, Esq., of Acryse Place, Folkestone, Kent.
I trust these few notes may satisfy Mr. A. K. Mac-
Kinnon, for I am not anxious to disturb the harmony
which is annually becoming more and more marked
among the members of the Clan, principally through
the instrumentality of the newly formed Clan
Society, of which I am happy to say Mr. A. K.
MacKinnon is a member.

Glasgow.   DUNCAN MACKINNON.

DESCENDANTS OF ALLAN CAMERON.

SIR,—Can any of your readers state, authen-
tically, whether Allan Cameron,—who married
Jean M'Gregor in 1666, brother of Ewen afterwards
Sir Ewen XVII. of Lochiel, had any children,
and if so, their names and what became of them.

D. C.

THE MACRITCHIES, MACCROSTIES, MACGUFFIES, AND GORRIES.

SIR,—Could you or any of your readers tell me
anything in regard to the Ritchies or MacRitchies,
MacCrosties, MacGuffies, and also the Gorries?
Are they Highland Clans, or septs of Clans? The
first is a pretty common name in the Long Island,
in Perth, and Argyllshire. I shall be glad of any
information as to their origin.

Yours truly,

Glasgow.   LEOD.

THE LAST MACDONALDS OF ISLA.

By CHARLES FRASER-MACKINTOSH, F.S.A. (Scot.)

PART VIII.— BOND OF THE MEN OF ISLA: AND
THE MACDONALDS OF ANTRIM.

(*Continued from page* 177).

"FOR it shall be known, i shall seek no other
rafuge but only your Majesty's clemency,
nor no other living, but that which your
Majesty's princely liberality, it shall
please your Highness bestow upon me as a more
length, the bearer
will inform your
Majesty, and so I
beseech God to bless
your Highness with
a long and prosper-
ous reign, your
Majesty's most
humble servant,
(Signed), Angus
M'Connal of Duni-
vaig. From Iylaye,
the tent of Septem-
ber, 1606."

About this per-
iod the following
affecting supplica-
tion was sent to
the Council,
whereof a *fac-sim-
ile* is given. The
spelling is modern-
ized :—

"My Lords of
Secret Council,
please your Lord-
ships to understand
that we the tenants
and under sub-
scribers testify and
approve to your
Lordships that
Angus M'Connell
of Dunivaig and his
forbears have been
native superiors
above us under His
Majesty's hands
and grace. Now
therefore we crave
of your Lordships'
grace in respect of

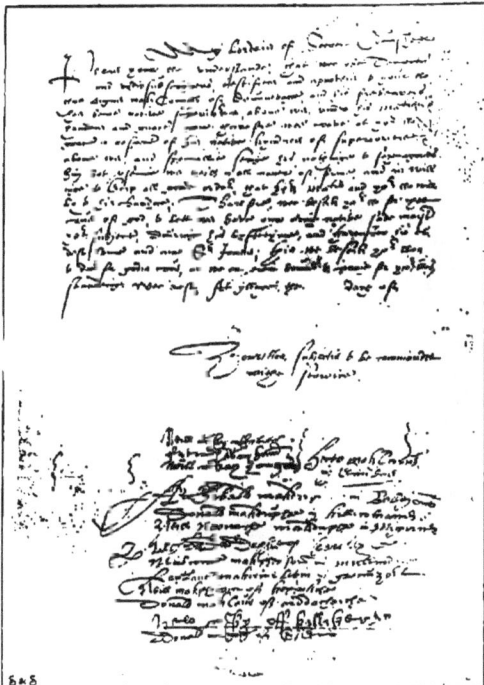

BOND OF THE MEN OF ISLA.

his native kindness of superiority over us, and
specially seeing has nothing to say aga nst him, but
using us well, in all manner of form, and is willing
to keep all good order that his Majesty and your
Lordships will lay to his charge, therefore we
beseech your Lordships for the cause of God to let
us have our own native said Master your subject
during his lifetime, and thereafter his eldest son
and heir Sir James. This we beseech your Lordships to do for God's cause, as we are ever bound
to pray for your Lordships standing. We rest at

Yllaye the   day of   . Your
Lordships subjects to be commanded with service,
(signed), Neil M'Ky, Officer of the Rinns, with my
hand ; Neil M'Kay, younger ; Hector Maclavish in
Kinibos ; Archibald Makduphee in Ballijonen ;
Donald Makduphee in Killicolmane ; Neil Neonach
Makduphee in Migirnes ; Archibald Makduphee
of Skerolsay ; Malcolme Makphersone in Mullin-
drie ; Lauchlane Makirini levin in Gronozort ;
Neill Makphetera of Kepposiche ; Donald Maktav-
ish of Ardacheriche ; Hew M'Ky of Killikeran ;
Donald Maktioin of Esknis."

No satisfactory reply was made. Angus'
name appears occasionally thereafter at meetings
of Western High-
land Potentates,
and heading the
Lists. But restora-
tion was not to be;
and baffled and
unsupported
Angus Macdonald
on 1st January,
1612, for the
trifling sum of
6000 merks re-
nounced in favour
of Sir John Camp-
bell of Calder all
his rights to Islay,
and dying shortly
thereafter, is re-
ferred to in 1614,
as "umquhile
Angus Macdonald
called of Duny-
vaig."

MACDONNELLS OF ANTRIM.

Although in
part anticipating
events, a brief
account of the de-
scendants of Sorley
buie may be
given. He had
by Mary, daughter
of Con, first Earl
of Tyrone, several
sons, the eldest,

Donald was killed in 1585; the second, Alexander was subsequently taken prisoner, executed
and his head placed over one of the gates in
Dublin. The father having occasion to go to
that City, an English officer cruelly brought him
to this gate and pointed to the head, whereupon,
alluding to the power and influence of his family,
Sorley said with dignity "my son hath many
heads." The third son was James, the fourth

Randal, fifth Angus, and sixth Lother. Mary O'Neill died 1582, and Sorley died in 1590, succeeded by his third son James, afterwards Sir James Macdonnell, who married Mary O'Neill, daughter of Phelim of Claunaboye. This Sir James came to Scotland and made some claims to the Isla Estates in 1597. He was well received by James VI. by whom he was Knighted, and received a grant of twenty-two merks of land in the south-west of Kintyre, of which the principal messuage was Cullelungart. These lands formed part of the Isla possessions. In an old Chronicle it is said of Sir James, he was "ane bra man of person and behaviour, but had not the Scots tongue, nor nae language but Erse." It is reported of *Rory Mor Macleod of Macleod* that when he either paid a visit, or was summoned to appear in London before King James, he like Sir James Macdonnell had no English, and the conversation between them was carried on in Latin. It turned out satisfactory, perhaps Rory complimented the Royal pedant in his mastery of the language but be that as it may, Rory departed from the Royal audience as Sir Rory. Sir James died Easter Monday 1601, not without suspicion of being poisoned, and according to the Four Masters "the most distinguished of the Clan Donnell, either in peace or war." Altho' Sir James had several sons, his brother Randal was immediately recognised as chief. Having been fostered and brought up in Arran he was known in Ireland as "Arranach" and being more of a politician than a soldier, became a warm supporter of the English interest after Elizabeth's death. King James conferred the honour of Knighthood; and

re-granted, and on 26th May, 1603, confirmed him in upwards of 300,000 acres of land in Antrim. He married, about 1604, Alice O'Neill, daughter of Hugh, Earl of Tyrone and niece of the Earl of Tyrone, and surrounded by enemies he had great difficultly in maintining his position. He was confirmed in the Kintyre lands of his late brother, and had a tack of seven years of Isla, receiving no benefit. Always favoured by King James, he in 29th June, 1618, was created Viscount Dunluce, and on 12th December, 1620, Earl of Antrim. The Kintyre Estates of the Macdonalds fell into the hands of James Campbell, son by his second marriage of the "Apostate" Earl of Argyle, created Lord Cantire in 1622. Like his relative Calder, in the case of Isla, Lord Cantire soon found that their acquisitions were unprofitable, and desired to get rid of them. Lord Cantire first offered the lands to his senior half-brother, Lord Lorn, who declined to purchase. The Earl of Antrim then came forward, agreed with Lord Cantire and paid down £1500 sterling of the price. Upon this coming to the ears of Lord Lorn, he was furious, took forcible measures to stop the Earl being infeft in the lands, and used every exertion and remonstrance within his power with the ruling powers in Scotland to prevent the Earl of Antrim from getting possession. The Earl however was infeft on 16th January, 1635; and in answer to Lord Lorn's threats stated that he was one of the remainder men under Queen Mary's Charter to James Macdonald of Isla, was the successor of his brother Sir James who had possession of part of Kintyre, and he had bought them when for open sale

SECOND EARL AND FIRST MARQUIS OF ANTRIM.

GEORGE MUNRO

by Lord Cantire. In reply to a specific charge
by Lord Lorn, that if he got possession he would
be representing, nourishing and maintaining the
ancient papists, and troublesome Macdonald
Islanders, who had been happily suppressed,
Lord Antrim stated that he and his predecessors
had welcomed and given shelter to Scottish
people on his Irish Estates, not enquiring as to
their religion; and as regarded Kintyre and the
Macdonalds that there had been such wholesale
evictions and clearances, since the Campbells
acquired possession, that only two three Macdonalds, in very humble circumstances remained.
But all was of no avail, Lord Lorn now Earl
afterwards Marquis of Argyle, worthy son of
him regarding whom it was said

"Now Earl of Guile, and Lord For Lorn thou goes
Leaving thy Native Prince to serve his foes;
No faith in plaids, no truth in tartan trews,
Chameleon like, they change a thousand hues."

was up till 1660 all powerful, and the dismemberer
of the great County of Inverness, easily defeated
Lord Antrim. By the time of the restoration,
it was too late to recover Kintyre. The first
Earl of Antrim died at Dunluce, 10th September,
1636, leaving two sons and six daughters, and
by the kindness of the present Earl of Antrim,
I am enabled to give the portrait of the second
Earl and first Marquis of Antrim, preserved at
Glenarm Castle, to whom reference will be made
later on. This great man, born in 1609, was in
use to relate himself, that he wore neither hat,
cap, shoe, nor stocking till seven or eight years
old, being bred "in the old Highland way."

THE LATE GEORGE MUNRO,
BOLTON.

THIS notable Sutherlander was born at
Evelix, in the Parish of Dornoch, in
1832, and was educated at Rosehall
School, his parents having removed to the farm
of Invernauld in that district. At the age of
nineteen, when still undecided as to his future
career, his uncle, Mr. James Hall, who had
made a considerable fortune in the Sugar
Plantations of Jamaica, returned home to
Sutherland, and through his intervention Mr.
Munro obtained his first situation with Messrs.
Findlater and Mackie of Manchester, and soon
raised himself to a position of trust by his
ability and application.

In 1860 he started business on his own
account, and so successful did the venture soon
become that in five years he was able to
purchase the property in which his place of
business was situated. At this time he was
ably assisted by his schoolfellow and friend
Mr. Alexander Ross, now of Leicester, who
after leaving Mr. Munro has had a very successful career. No keener sportsman than Alec Ross
is known on the moors and rivers of his native
county, and his friend Mr. William Black, the
celebrated novelist, has instanced him in several
of his works as the model of a true sportsman.

In 1864, in partnership with his cousin Mr.
John Forsyth, a branch of the business was
successfully established in Blackburn, and a
further extension was made two years later,
when the present large and important concern
in Hanley was commenced. In this latter
enterprise he was fortunate to secure as partner
a fellow clansman, Mr. John Munro, a native
of Clashmore, Dornoch, who now, as surviving
partner, possesses the Staffordshire portion of
the business.

In politics Mr. Munro was an ardent Liberal,
and for three years, 1886-9, represented the
Exchange Ward in the Bolton Council Chamber, and was the respected Chairman of the
Ward Liberal Association. He was also a
member and generous supporter of the St.
Andrews Presbyterian Church. Mr. Munro
always cherished a strong attachment to his
native county, and was a life member of the
Edinburgh Sutherland Association, to whose
Jubilee (Victoria) Bursary Fund he contributed
a very handsome donation.

In 1863 Mr. Munro married Miss Isabella
Waugh of Lochmaben, Dumfries-shire, and had
three sons and four daughters, who survive him.
In this lady Mr. Munro found in the highest
sense a helpmeet: who by her gentle consideration, and readiness to help and comfort
all with whom she came in contact, endeared
herself to a large circle of friends.

On the Sunday following Mr. Munro's funeral,
the Rev. T. B. Johnstone of St. Andrews Church,
in addressing his mourning congregation said—
"after a long and painful illness our dear friend
Mr. George Munro, who has been so honourably
connected with this congregation for over thirty
four years, during the greater part of which
time he was member of the Deacons' Court and
Treasurer of the Church, has been removed by
death, and a heavy blow thereby falls on all
who knew him, and were associated with him."

Frank and open in all his dealings, simple
minded, generous, and sincere, Mr. George
Munro has left behind a name for amiability
and goodness of heart that will not readily be
effaced from the minds of the inhabitants of
the Town of Bolton.

Hanley.   JOHN MUNRO.

FAMOUS HIGHLAND BARDS.

No. I.—IAIN LOM.

BY W. DRUMMOND-NORIE.

THE MacDonells of Keppoch, like their kinsmen, the MacDonalds of Glencoe, have from the most remote period of their history been justly celebrated for their distinguished heroism in the field, and for their skill in the art of versification ; two apparently opposite characteristics, but in reality quite in harmony, for had there been no heroes to inspire the bards by their deeds of valour, there would have been no bards to hand down to posterity the famous achievements of their kings and chieftains. Had Agamemnon never lived and fought at Troy, or had Fingal preferred a pastoral existence among the hills of Morven to the glorious career of a warrior, the grand epic of the immortal Homer would never have been written, and the voice of Ossian would have been mute.

Foremost among the many talented bards of the family of Keppoch, and for the matter of that, among Highland bards generally, Iain Lom's striking personality stands conspicuous. The exact date of his birth is uncertain, but it probably occurred during the early years of the reign of Charles I. He was of gentle blood, being descended from Iain Aluinn, IV. Chief of Keppoch, who lived in the 15th century, and was consequently related to the head of his family and occupied a position of some importance in the clan.

Born amid the romantic scenery of Lochaber, with the great mountains of Ben Nevis and Ben Chlinaig looking down upon him as he lay in his cradle, and for his lullaby the music of the turbulent rivers Roy and Spean, it is scarcely to be wondered at that poetical instinct should have been early awakened in his breast. Of Iain's boyish days little is known, but a tradition is extant that owing to his marked predilections for study, he was sent to the great Catholic seminary at Valladolid in Spain to receive his education at the hands of the scholarly clerics who directed the studies at that celebrated establishment ; and that, having incurred the anger of his tutors by some breach of discipline or youthful escapade, he returned to his native land to avoid the chastisement he probably deserved, but which his proud Highland blood could not brook. There is great probability of truth in this story, as it is a matter of history that Ranald, the eldest son of "Alasdair nan clens," X. Chief of Keppoch, was living in exile in Spain at this time, and it was no doubt under his protection that young Iain lived while prosecuting his studies at Valladolid.

Upon his arrival in Lochaber, Iain found his clan ready to take up arms in the cause of their rightful King, Charles I., under the leadership of his relative and chief, Donald Glas of Keppoch, and the renowned Montrose, against the forces of the Covenanters, headed by the astute Argyll. Iain, who hated the Campbells with a deadly enmity, hereditary in his blood, and begotten of many an ancient feud in which his clan had suffered from the cruelty and rapaciousness of the race of Diarmid, threw himself vigorously into the warlike preparations that he found going on around him, and roused his fellow clansmen to fresh exertions by his stirring poetry. He placed himself in communication with Montrose, who received his overtures gladly, and a friendship was cemented between the Highland bard and the famous general, which only ended with Montrose's death. In February, 1645, the Highland army, having wreaked its vengeance upon the Campbells by a six weeks' raid among the Argyllshire glens, had retired along the shores of Loch Lochy and Loch Oich to Cille-Chuimein (now Fort Augustus), and lay in camp there awaiting fresh developments. Meanwhile Argyll, exasperated at his late reverses, and burning with a desire to wipe out the insult he had received at the hands of his enemy Montrose, hastily mustered an army of three thousand Campbells, and followed stealthily along the road taken by the Royalist troops, destroying and wasting the lands of the MacDonalds and Camerons as he went. Arriving at the old castle of Inverlochy in Lochaber, he determined to halt and commence a fresh series of depredations in that district before proceeding further. Iain Lom got wind of this movement and hastened to Montrose with the news. It is not certain that he actually saw Montrose on this occasion, for there is a story in existence that when the bard arrived at Cille-Chuimein he was received by Alasdair MacColla (MacDonald of Antrim), who was in command of the Irish contingent. MacDonald listened to Iain's account of Argyll's arrival at Inverlochy, and appears to have doubted the truth of the story, for turning to the bard, he threatened that if he had told an untruth he would hang him on the first tree he met. Iain replied angrily, "Unless you shall find the Campbells all here, for certainly they are in the country, before this time to-morrow, you may do so."

Whether this is a correct version of what really took place is, of course, uncertain, but there is little doubt that Iain Lom not only was the first to bring the tidings of Argyll's presence at Inverlochy to the Royalist camp, but that he personally led the army of Montrose through the secret mountain passes to Glen Nevis, and that it was in a great measure due to this strategic movement, so rapidly carried out, that Mac-Cailean Mór and his marauding Campbells were utterly routed by the shores of the river Lochy on Sunday morning, February 2, 1645. The bard took no personal part in the fight, having excused himself, when offered a claymore by MacDonald of Antrim, on the ground that if he fell in battle there would be no one left to sing the praises of the victors.* There was no gainsaying this argument, so Iain Lom was left to witness the engagement from the safe vantage ground of one of the towers of Inverlochy Castle, from whence he amused himself by hurling abusive epithets at the discomfited Campbells. The poem, entitled "Latha Inbher-Lochaidh," in which he describes the events of the battle, is probably one of the most powerfully descriptive in the Gaelic language. Every detail of the fight is brought before the reader with marvellous distinctness and accuracy, and it is easy to conjure up in the imagination the whole of the stirring scene that was enacted under the shadow of giant Ben Nevis more than two centuries ago. Throughout the whole poem there is a current of biting sarcasm and almost savage jubilation at the expense of the hereditary foes of Clann Donuill ; in fact, so bitter and caustic are the bard's satirical utterances that they are quite untranslatable into the English tongue. It was this inveterate hatred of his enemies, this vein of sarcasm in his nature, that earned for John MacDonell the nickname of Iain "Lom," *lom* signifying in the Gaelic *bare*, and it was probably bestowed upon the bard on account of his skill in laying bare the faults and weaknesses of those whom he lashed with the whip of his stinging satires.

After the battle of Inverlochy little is known of Iain's movements, until we find him taking an active part in avenging the dastardly murder of his young chieftains, Alastair and Ranald, about the year 1663. Space will not admit of a history of the Keppoch murder being given here ; it was a cold-blooded crime of the worst description, prompted by jealousy and avarice, and it is some satisfaction to know that to Iain Lom belongs the credit of tracking the murderers and meting out to them the punishment they so richly deserved. This event is vividly described with all its ghastly details in his poem "Mort na Ceapach"; an extraordinary work full of pathetic interest and horrible realism. A curious memorial of the bard's terrible vengeance on the slayers of his kinsmen, is to be found in the monument erected by Colonel Macdonnell of Glengarry, in the year 1812, near the well in

which the seven murderers heads were washed, before being laid at the feet of the chief. The spot is locally known as "Tobar nan Ceann" (" the Well of Heads "), and may be seen by all who travel to Inverness by the Caledonian Canal when passing through Loch Oich. Several poems were composed by Iain Lom about this period relating more or less to the Keppoch murder. "A bhean leasaich an stop dhuinn," " Oran do Shiol Dughaill," and " An Ciaran Mabach " were all inspired by that atrocious crime, and, powerful as they are, there is something so repugnant to our feelings in the poet's exultation over the dying agonies of the criminals when he had them at his mercy that it is impossible to refrain from an expression of regret that he should have so lowered himself. It is a relief to turn from these blood curdling horrors to the scathing sarcasms of the "Oran air Righ Uilleam agus Ban-righ Mairi" (Ode to King William and Queen Mary); here Iain is at his best, and we see in him the staunch adherent of the Royal Stuarts, as with fearless pen he castigates the the usurping William of Orange and his Dutch followers ; or if we want pathos and tender sentiment we may find it in the " Marbhrann do Shir Seumas Mac-Dhonuill " or the " Marbhrann do dh' Alasdair Dubh Ghlinne-garaidh," both good specimens of the old Highland laments in vogue at that period, and full of real poetical feeling.

Iain lived to a great age, and died in the reign of Queen Anne about the year 1710. He sleeps among his native mountains in the ancient burying-ground of St. Cyril, on Dun-aingeal, in the Braes of Lochaber, where a suitable monument has been recently erected to his memory by the munificence of Charles Fraser-Mackintosh, Esq., of Drummond.

CLAN MENZIES.—The Members of this Clan have decided to commemorate in some fitting manner the fiftieth year of Sir Robert Menzies' occupation of the position of Chief of the Clan.

THE CLAN CAMPBELL SOCIETY had their Annual Excursion to Lochgoilhead on the Queen's Birthday. There was a large turn-out of members and friends, and a most enjoyable day was spent.

THE ST. COLUMBA GAELIC CHOIR also had their Annual Outing on that day to Kelly Glen, Wemyss Bay, which proved as pleasant and successful as those of former years.

OBITUARY.—Many of our readers in all parts of the world will regret to learn of the death of Rev. James Cumming, Melness, Sutherland, who for over forty years officiated as Free Church Minister in Melness and Eriboll. We are also sorry to intimate the death of Mr. Archibald Maxwell Macdonald of Glencoe, whose remains were interred in the family burial place in St. Munda's Island on 15th June.

---

* The actual words used by the bard on this occasion were, it is said, "Cha-u e sin mo ghnothuch, cath-aichibh sibhse 'us innsidh mise."

THE MACKAY (Hereford) PRIZE SONG.

The Prize of Ten Guineas offered by Mr. John Mackay, Hereford, for "The best original and unpublished Gaelic Song, written on a Patriotic theme" and suitable to be sung to the Music which gained The Charles Fraser-Mackintosh Prize of £20, has been awarded to Mr. Malcolm MacFarlane, Elderslie, whose song we give below. The Judges were Messrs. John Whyte, Henry Whyte, and Archibald Ferguson. It will be readily conceded that the task of composing words to the music was no easy one, as the call for rhyme necessary to the requirements of Gaelic style, was excessive. The theme is a happy one, and one which Highlanders would do well to take to heart, and not be content with singing it only but acting up to it.

NA GAIDHEIL AN GUAILLIBH A CHEILE.

(HIGHLANDERS, SHOULDER TO SHOULDER.)

Music by J. LINDSAY MACKAY, M.A., LL.B.   *Words by* MALCOLM MACFARLANE.

KEY A♭. With spirit.

Do lamh dhomh a charaid, Oir 's Gaidheil a th'annainn, D'an còir a bhi 'tarruing ri cheil e;

Is braithrean sinn uile, S'cha dean e feum tuilleadh Bhi roinnte 'nar buidhnean end mhor;

KEY E♭ t.

'Nar buaireadh air uairibh Do'n choimheach mhi-shuairce Tha 'g iarraidh le cluain a thoirt beul oirnu;

Ar sreathan air fuasgladh An aite bhi 'glusadh Mar bu dùth dhuinn, An guaillibh a cheil e.

CHORUS—KEY A♭ f.

Thugaibh o robha hiuraibh o eil e Air Gaidheil an guaillibh a cheil e!

KEY E♭ t.

Air Naile! Cha smarach Am feachd iad a' gluasad mar 's dùth dhoibh an guaillibh a cheil e.

KEY A♭ f.

Thugaibh o robha hiuraibh o eil e Air Gaidheil an guaillibh a cheil e;

Rall.

'S gu'n ruigeadh ar glaoth Gach Gaidheil 'san t-saoghl'l, 'S gu'n togadh gach aon diubh an seisd leinn.

Tha 'chuiseag so-aomaidh
Do 'n oiteig a's faoine
Thar monadh 'us raon a bhios seideadh :
Ach seall oirre snìomhte
Am meadhon an t-sìomain—
Gu 'm bacadh a righnead an steud-each.
Sud leasan bu chòir dhuinn
'Bhi 'g aithris an còmhnuidh
'S a' tarruing as eòlas 'chum feum dhuinn—
Ma 's math leinn bhi buadhmhor,
Is fheudar bhi 'gluasad
Mar 's dùth dhuinn, an guaillibh a chèile.

Tha eachdruidh ag innseadh
Mu mhòrachd ar sìnnsre'
'S gu 'n robh iad 'nan linntibh-san treunmhor ;
An cliù a thaobh dìlse
Cha leigear air dhìochuimhn'
Gus an sguirear de sgrìobhadh 's de leughadh.
Ach 's beag ni e dh' fheum dhuinn
Mur bi sinn fhein gleusda 'chum euchdan,
Ar giùlan fìor-uasal,
Ar n-onoir gun truailleadh
'S ar gluasad an guaillibh a chèile.

'S i tìr nam beann àrda,
'San d' fhuair sinn ar n-àrach,
An dùthaich a's àille fo 'n ghréin leinu ;
'S i 'Ghàidhlig a' chànain
A dh' ionnsuich sinn tràthail
Ri briathraibh ar màthar ag éisdeachd ;
'S e 'n fraoch bharr a' mhonaidh
Ar suaicheantas dosrach.
Cò 'n Gaidheal nach nochdadh mòr-spèis da !
Gach àbhaist a's dual dhuinn,
Ma 's airidh iad, suas leò !
Ach gluaismid an guaillibh a chèile.

Nis leanmaid mìothlachd
'Us togamaid fìor-ghradh,
'Us cleachdamaid dìcheall 'us geur-chuis
A rèiteachadh cùisean
Ar cinnidh 's ar dùthcha,
Gun smaointinn air tionndadh no geilleadh ;
E mar bhloid 'us mar bhriath'r'r dhuinn,
Ma 's tràill no mo 's triath 'th' ann
'Tha 'bagairt no miannachadh bend oirnu,
Gu 'n cas sinn a suas ris,
'Toirt buaidh as gach cruaidh-chas
Le bhi 'gluasad an guaillibh a chèile.

DANIEL WILLIAM KEMP, J.P.

DANIEL WILLIAM KEMP.

NO better proof can be given of the vitality of a movement than its power of assimilating elements from the outside. Judged by this test the Celtic movement is in a very fair way. The voice of the syren still floats down from our mountains and up from our shores, and the unsuspecting wanderer comes and hears and is conquered. Sometimes the friendliness is merely sentimental, but in the case of the subject of this sketch it is a spring of beneficient activity.

D. W. Kemp was born at Wrexham in 1844. He was educated at the Grammar School of that town and afterwards at an Edinburgh Academy. Although born in the Principality he is of pure Scottish descent, the Kemps being an old Lowland family. Nor is the Highland strain awanting, for among his immediate ancestors are a MacAlister, a MacPhail, a Davidson, and a Donaldson.

Mr. Kemp is a man of many-sided and remarkable activity. Business, politics, literature, science, art, antiquities, volunteering and philantrophy all claim his attention, and it is truly surprising how they all receive it. At an early age he gave indications of the drift of his talents. When only fourteen he wrote an essay on Hydrogen which was published with illustrations in the Annual of his school in Edinburgh. The scientific interest manifested in youth became with manhood a leading impulse. He is a life Fellow of the Royal Scottish Society of Arts and has been awarded several medals by this society for papers on original subjects. In 1870 he suggested the formation of the Edinburgh Association of Science and Art. On attaining its majority in 1891 the association presented him with a Diploma of Distinction as its Founder, and in recognition of the eminent services which he had rendered to the association throughout the whole period of its history.

In the early days of volunteering Mr. Kemp threw himself with characteristic enthusiasm into the movement. He was largely instrumental in raising the 5th Highland Company of the Queen's Own Rifle Volunteer Brigade, and was its first Ensign. At that time the Highland companies wore the kilt.

Whether or not it was in this connection that his blood "warmed to the tartan" we do not know, but about this time we find him visiting the far north, and forming a strong attachment to the romantic county of the 93rd and Reay Fencibles. He soon made himself intimately acquainted with the history, topography, and antiquities of Sutherland, and in extent and accuracy, his knowledge of these matters is outstanding, if indeed it is not unequalled. Already he has published a number of works bearing on the county of his adoption. These include an edition, with valuable notes and illustrations, of "Bishop Pococke's Tours in Sutherland" in 1760, published for the first time from the original MSS. in the British Museum, and forming the second volume of the "Sutherland Papers" (1888); "Notes on Iron Smelting in Sutherland" (1887); "The Democracy of Sutherland" (1890); and "An Eccentric Sutherland Dominie" (1892). Other works not yet published, but, we believe, in an advanced stage of preparation are the "Endowments of Sutherland," "The 'God's Acres' of Sutherland," "Fasti Scholae Sutherlandianae," etc. In connection with the endowments of the northern county it may be mentioned by the way, that one practical result of Mr. Kemp's researches was his discovery of a forgotten School Fund which had lain in a Highland Bank for twenty years unclaimed. On the formation of the Scottish History Society in 1887 he was requested to undertake the editing of its first volume—a complete edition of "Pococke's Tours in Scotland, 1747-1760."

Mr. Kemp possesses probably the largest and most complete collection of Sutherland books extant. What Sutherlander, as he reverently handled those treasures, but secretly sighed for a brief recall of the good old "lifting days!"

Mr. Kemp has been for many years a moving spirit in the Sutherland Association (Edinburgh), and it may be said with strict justice that the Victoria Bursary Scheme and the Publication Scheme of that Society owe their origin and success mainly to him.

In recognition of his services to Sutherland he has been appointed a J.P. of the County. The Ancient City and Royal Burgh of Dornoch has also bestowed upon him the privilege of its "freedom," and he has on several occasions represented this Burgh as its Assessor at the Convention of Royal Burghs.

In politics Mr. Kemp is a progressive Liberal. He is President of the Leith Liberal Club, an office which he has held for several years.

He is still a comparatively young man, this being his Jubilee year, and it is therefore legitimate to hope that the best of his career in business, science, letters and affairs is still before him.

This sketch would seem inadequate to anyone who has been a visitor at Ivy Lodge, Trinity, near Edinburgh, Mr. Kemp's surburban home, unless reference were made to the kindly hospitality of the amiable and accomplished lady who presides over his household. Mrs. Kemp is a descendant of a Sutherland family, and accords to her husband's guests a true "Highland welcome."

Forfar.   DONALD MACLEOD, M.A.

TO CORRESPONDENTS

All Communications, on literary and business matters, should be addressed to the Editor, Mr. JOHN MACKAY, 17 Dundas Street, Kingston, Glasgow.

⟶✦⟵

TERMS OF SUBSCRIPTION.— The CELTIC MONTHLY will be sent, post free, to any part of the United Kingdom, Canada, the United States, and all countries in the Postal Union—for one year, 4s.

THE CELTIC MONTHLY

JULY, 1894.

CONTENTS.

CLAN MACKAY SOCIETY.

BURSARY COMPETITIONS.—This Society has now made a practical start in giving effect to one of its most useful objects, namely the encouragement of higher education. Two Bursaries for MACKAYS are to be competed for in Sutherland and Caithness early in August, full particulars as to Rules, subjects, etc., will be found in our advertising columns. There is one feature of these competitions which deserves special notice, and which does credit to the thorough "Highland" spirit of this society. Gaelic Grammar and Composition are made one of the essential subjects in these competitions, so that before a young Mackay can presume to seek higher education in the English language, he must first prove that he has a thorough knowledge of his mother tongue. It is only by the preservation of the native language that Highlanders can hope to preserve their individuality as a race.

A GENEROUS OFFER.—In response to Mr. John Mackay, (Hereford's) offer to contribute £100 if Members of the Clan will subscribe other £200, so as to increase the capital to £700, the following donations have been already intimated:—John S. Mackay, LL.D., Edinburgh Academy, £10; Rev. J. Aberigh Mackay, D.D., Bridge of Allan, £5 5s; George J. Mackay, J.P., Mayor of Kendal, £5 5s; Dr. George Mackay, 2 Randolph Place, Edinburgh, £5; John Mackay (Ben Reay), Wiesbaden, Germany, £5; William Mackay, F.S.A., Scot., Solicitor, Inverness, £3 3s; Dr. W. Murray Mackay, North Shields, £1 1s; R. G. Mackay, Berriedale, Stamford Hill, London, £1 1s; Eric Mackay, 7 Royal Ex-change, London, E.C., £1 1s; P. M. Mackay, Villa Dilred, Hilversum, Holland, £1; Provost W. W. Mackay, Isabella Villa, Dunoon, £1.

A BRIEF ACCOUNT OF THE CLAN DONNACHAIDH.—We regret that in the review of this interesting work in our last issue a mistake was made in regard to the authorship. Mr. David Robertson, F.S.A., Scot., is the author and publisher.

THE HIGHLAND REGISTRY.—We are glad to be able to state that suitable premises have now been secured at 19 Park Road, near Great Western Road, and that Miss Mackay is now prepared to assist Highland girls coming to Glasgow to secure suitable employment. We trust that it will receive the hearty support it deserves from our countrymen and countrywomen. Members' tickets are now being issued, and can be had on application at above address.

"FIONN" AT THE GLASGOW HIGHLAND CROSS.—As we anticipated, the premises which Mr. Henry Whyte recently opened at 4 Bridge Street, have already proved a most encouraging success. Mr. Whyte deserves great credit for his enterprise, and we are glad to find that Highlanders have acknowledged this by bestowing upon him their patronage. He has already laid in a large stock of books in Gaelic and English on the many subjects in which Highlanders are interested. We are glad to congratulate our talented contributor on the well-deserved success which has attended his venture.

═══════════════

OUR NEXT ISSUE.

GRAND SUMMER NUMBER.

OUR next issue is to take the form of a Grand Summer Number, which will be specially attractive both in regard to its literary contents, and fine illustrations. With it we will present our readers with five life-like plate portraits of the following gentlemen—Messrs. William Graham of North Erines, President, Kintyre Club and Argyllshire Society; Captain James Mackay, Trowbridge, vice-president, Clan Mackay Society; Atholl MacGregor, Dunkeld, President, Clan Gregor Society; Provost George J. Mackay, Kendal, (a distinguished Caithnessian), and Thomas Greer, London, of the Clan Gregor. These portraits are of a larger size than those we usually give, and are engraved by the best known process.

In addition to these we have arranged for several articles of exceptional interest. Mr. John Mackay, Hereford, contributes a valuable paper on "The Highland Brigade at Waterloo," which will be suitably illustrated. A complete list will also be given of the number of officers of each clan name present at the battle, and other interesting information. Mr. Fraser Mackintosh will give part IX of his papers on the "Last MacDonalds of Isla," and reproductions will be given of the MacDonald plate from the Queen's book on the clans, and a fac-simile of the Clan Neill Bond. Besides these several very attractive contributions will appear, in prose and verse, and no trouble or expense will be spared to make our "Summer Number" worthy of Highland literature.

Owing to the Glasgow Fair Holidays our next issue (being the August Number), will appear about the middle of July.

TONGUE AND ITS HISTORIC SURROUNDINGS.

By John Mackay, C.E., J.P., Hereford.

Part VI.—Ian Abrach, and the Battle of Drum-na-Cupa.

(Continued from page 172).

THIS was a dodge of the King to get the heirs of the principal Highland chiefs into his custody, to civilize them in the South of Scotland and near his own court as he himself had been educated and civilized in England. In this affair Angus Du succeeded admirably in spite of his traducers. The King saw that he was more sinned against than sinning.

CLANS SUTHERLAND AND MACKAY.
From "Highlanders of Scotland," by Kenneth Macleay, R.S.A., (The Queen's Book of the Clans), published by Mr. Mitchell, London, in 1870.

(1). James Sutherland, born in 1833, at Doll, Brora, Sutherland; was sergeant in the Sutherland Rifle Volunteers.
(2). Adam Sutherland, born in 1843, at Knockarthur, Rogart, Sutherland.
(3). Neil Mackay, born in 1830, at Achvoulderock, Tongue Ferry, Sutherland; now Ferryman at Hope, parish of Durness.

The truculent and cowardly Earl of Sutherland still plotted against his powerful neighbour, Angus Du, though shorn of the territory given him by the Lord of the Isles as the dower of his wife, by the unfortunate action of his cousin Thomas. It was seen by the Earl that Angus Du was getting into years and was deprived of his son and heir who might never return. He again had recourse to Angus Murray of Pulrossie to try to persuade his sons-in-law, Morgan and Neil Mackay that they now were the successors of Angus Du, his son Neil being taken away by the King, and that John the younger son had not so good a title to the territory or the chiefship, as they had. No doubt these young ruffians had by the apprehension of their brother Thomas incurred the high displeasure of Angus Du. The knowledge of this made them more readily the tools of the Earl and Angus Murray and to fall into the farther plot of weakening Angus Du, and if successful become possessed of his territory.

The demand was made, and Angus Du no doubt refused compliance. The plotters were impatient, and at last determined to obtain possession by force. In this determination they were encouraged by the Earl of Sutherland, even by the admission of Sir R. Gordon, that they had "Earl Robert his attollerance." Angus Du, desirous of preserving the King's peace, sent his cousins a message informing them that he would surrender them all his possessions, except Kintail, now Tongue. His cousins would have all. The aged hero was astonished, consulted his youthful son John Abrach, as his clansmen called him from having been reared amongst his mother's relatives in Lochaber. He consulted too his chief men. The resolution come to was, to defend the territory, and the honour of their chief and clan, or die in their defence. The resolution was conveyed by the fiery cross from hamlet to hamlet of the Mackay country and every preparation made to meet and resist the threatened invasion.

Angus Du, though aged and infirm, had yet much of the fire of youth when aroused. When he ascertained the determination of his youthful warrior son and the leading men of the clan to die in his defence and the freedom of their country hitherto so well preserved and defended he rose to the occasion, scouts and spies were sent into Sutherland to observe the doings and movements of the enemy, and to report upon all they heard and saw, especially to ascertain in what direction the threatened invasion would be made. It was soon known that throughout the whole of Sutherland men were preparing for some warlike expedition; there was no concealment as to its purpose and intent, and that full encouragement was given to one and all by the Earl to take part in the invasion and assist Angus Murray, who was also bringing men from Ross and Assynt, promising them all the plunder they could capture. Angus Du was kept well informed of all that was going on, and he and his young son and head-men were at the same time devising means and making every possible preparation to meet so formidable an invasion. Councils were daily held with the old veteran chief, who knew the lie of the land, and the advantage of choosing the field of strife for a defensive battle, which should be as near Tongue as possible. He pointed out Drium-na-Cupa as offering the greatest disadvantage for attack, and the greatest advantage in resisting it. This ridge slope is two miles from Tongue, on the west side of Ben Loyal, having a narrow boggy valley at its foot, trending westward to Kinloch and northward to Tongue. On the south side of this valley the land rises to the same level as Drium-na-Cupa, with a narrow pass quite close to the foot of Ben Loyal. Thro' this pass the road track to and from Tongue went, and it was anticipated, if Tongue would be the point of attack, this would be the route the invaders would prefer, being shorter by some miles than the other route by the east side of the mountain. Besides these advantages of position, it was not lost sight of, that the further the Sutherland men had to march the more tired they would be in the fight. There was a doubt as to which of the routes the invaders might adopt, and to ascertain this a strong party of Mackays was posted in ambush on the south front of Ben Loyal to watch the advance of the enemy and report as to the route. From this point of view they could see over many miles in their front. It was observed that the invaders were coming in by the west end of Lochnaver and making for the west side of Ben Loyal. This being reported the Mackay commanders took post on the slope of Drium-na Cupa ridge, while at the same time a detachment was sent forward into the pass

THE VILLAGE, TONGUE.

DR. KEITH NORMAN MACDONALD.

and ambush themselves in a copse wood growing in the slope of the pass, and when the greater portion of the invaders had passed to cut into their flank. The party posted on the south face of the mountain were ordered to follow up the rear of the invaders and skirmish with them as best they could till the flank attack had taken effect, when they were to fall in with might and main. These arrangements being made Ian Abrach and the other commanders advised the aged chief to keep out of the battle and retire to a knoll in the rear, where he could survey the fight and be out of harm's way. He consented and gave Ian Abrach the command. The invaders confident in their superiority of numbers came on through the pass in a disorderly manner, leaders in front. On emerging from the pass, the Mackays were seen right in front in a compact body, posted on the slope of the opposite ridge.

Judging them to be very inferior in numbers one of the Sutherland leaders said, "come on, we shall soon shackle these calves," to which another replied, "take you care of yourself, these calves may jump too high for you to shackle them."

The invaders as they emerged from the pass rushed across the valley, and came up the slope in a straggling manner for the onset. They were firmly and fiercely received by Ian Abrach and his men. In the meantime the flank attack was made upon the rear portion of the invaders, straggling and hurrying confusedly through the pass. They were soon thrown into disorder, and the scouting party which followed in the rear coming up, the annihilation of this portion of the invaders was complete, the few fugitives that escaped ran on to the main body causing dismay and terror, pursued by the ambuscade men, who advanced and attacked the left rear and flank of the invaders. The Sutherland men fought resolutely and bravely but they were out manœuvred, still they continued the fighting. Their left wing was soon turned and doubled up on the centre, they had to fight in front and rear, and their commanders Angus Murray, Morgan and Neil Mackay were slain in the front of the battle. At last falling into disorder, the survivors fled from the fatal field by the passes at the west end of Ben Loyal pursued by the infuriated Mackays, who gave no quarter, for several miles till the last man was slain at Athcharrie, where a stone was reared to commemorate his fall and the close of the chase.

The fighting over on the field of battle, and none left on it but the dead, the dying, and the wounded, the old chief Angus Du came upon the ground to view the slain and see if he could find amongst them the bodies of his unnatural cousins. Having found them, and as he was leaning on his staff looking at them and bemoaning the carnage of which they were the cause, he was shot dead by an arrow from the bow of a Sutherland man lurking in a bush, who had come too late, or had been too much of a coward to take part in the fight. He immediately decamped and got safely home, to fall another day by the hand of Angus Du's grandson.

So momentous was the issue of the battle and the utter annihilation of the invaders that Sir R. Gordon is forced to record in his history two centuries thereafter.—"The memory of this skirmish remaineth in that country (Mackay country) with the posterity unto this day." The memory of it remains to this day, and to this day the graves of the slain on the ridge slope of Drium-na-cupa may be seen and counted in parallel rows.

(To be continued.)

DUNROBIN CASTLE SEAT OF THE DUKE OF SUTHERLAND.

W. MACGREGOR STODDART, LONDON.

THE Stoddarts were originally a Renfrewshire family, but like most Scottish names it is now to be found in all parts of the world. Among those who left their native land to win fame and fortune in distant parts was Admiral Stoddart, who, with Admirals Keith and Gordon, was one of the founders of the Russian Navy.

It is from this gallant Scotsman that the subject of our present sketch is descended. Mr. W. M. Stoddart was born near Edinburgh, where his parents were staying for a time, but he looks upon the MacGregor country as his native spot, having spent many years in that romantic district. His love for Perthshire may be better understood when we state that on his mother's side he is descended from Rob Roy, her grandfather, James MacGregor, being the grandson of Rob's third son James, who died in Paris, where he fled after the '45 and was buried in Père La Chaise. Though the third son he was the most famous; it was he who led the clan at Prestonpans, where he greatly distinguished himself by his bravery.

Mr. Stoddart has been in London for the last ten years, during four of which he has occupied the position of Headmaster of St. Stephen's School. It is, however, as a Highlander that he is best known in the Metropolis, and there are few Celtic Gatherings in which he is not a moving spirit. He is Captain of the L. N. C. Camanachd Club, member of the Gaelic Society of London, and the Highland Balls Committee. He also acts as Hon. Secretary for the Paddington and District School Sports Association, and for the Society for the Extension of University Education. He has rendered good service in the cause of Gaelic Music, having harmonised most of the melodies rendered by the Gaelic Choir at their recent Concert, and has acted as Accompanist since its formation. He takes a special interest in the success of the Clan Gregor Society, of which he is a life member.

In conclusion, it may be said to his credit that although he has travelled a good deal abroad he has always made it a rule to do so in the Highland costume, and our readers will, we feel sure, agree with us when we say that he could not have chosen a more graceful dress, and there are few who do it better justice. Mr. MacGregor Stoddart is considered one of the best all round Highland dancers in London, and for several years past has acted as Master of Ceremonies at the Highland Balls held under the auspices of the Shinty Club and the Highland Balls Committee.

London.   JOHN MACGREGOR.

DR. KEITH NORMAN MACDONALD, F.R.C.S.E., EDINBANE, SKYE.

DR. MACDONALD, or to give him his full designation—Dr. Keith Norman Macalister MacDonald, is the third son of the late Charles MacDonald, Ord, Sleat, Skye, and grandson, on the maternal side, of Captain Neil MacLeod of Gesto, and therefore a true son of *Eilean-a'-cheò*. He received his early education by private tuition, and went to study Medicine in the Edinburgh University in 1854. After completing his curriculum he practised for some time in Skye, and then sought, in 1860, a wider field, under the glorious shadow of Ben Nevis—among the genial and hospitable Highlanders of the Braes of Lochaber, where his Jacobite instincts found full scope. Leaving Lochaber he removed to North Wales where he acquired considerable experience, but finding the work too heavy he took charge of a Hospital in Bath for a time, so that he might recuperate and study. He soon afterwards proceeded to India and after a time was appointed by the Government of India to the Civil Surgeoncy of Prome, and it was when in charge of this station where he had a Hospital, Dispensary, and three hundred convicts under his charge, that he undertook to translate the practice of Medicine among the Burmese from original palm-leaf manuscripts which he procured, after a great deal of trouble, from the native doctors, but which could not be purchased at any price, as they had been handed down from father to son for countless generations, something after the manner of the oral teachings of the Asclepiades. This work was afterwards published, with a historical sketch of the progress of Medicine from the earliest times. Dr. MacDonald's success at this station was considerable and his name was frequently mentioned in the Government Blue Books, and his sanitary reports and the great good he had affected in the interests of the public health of Prome, were very favourably received and acknowledged by the Government. Considerations of health, however, blighted his bright prospects at this time, and he was obliged to return to Europe in 1869, and he has practised at home ever since. During his long experience he did not neglect the splendid opportunities that such a varied and wide field of practice placed before him. He has contributed between thirty and forty papers of scientific interest to the literature of his profession, and has encroached on the Sister Art of Music by publishing a "Skye Collection of Reels and Strathspeys" which many good judges consider second to none, and has also added some Fantasias for Violin and Piano, on Scotch and Irish airs. As the Editor of "Musical Scotland" * remarks, Dr. MacDonald is one of the "most worthy representatives now living of the leisured amateur whose sympathies extend warmly to professional musicians, as well as amateurs, all being "brothers in art!" In 1872 Dr. MacDonald married Miss Niblett of Erneston, near Edinburgh, and has two sons and three daughters. It may be here stated that Dr. MacDonald is a M.D. of St. Andrews, a Fellow of the Royal College of Physicians, Edinburgh, and Licentiate of the Royal College of Physicians, London. He is at present Resident Medical Officer, Gesto Hospital, Skye — enjoying the love and attachment of his fellow-islesmen. *Saoghal fada dha.* FIONN.

* "Musical Scotland" by D. Baptie, Paisley: J. & R. Parlane, 1894.

HIGHLANDERS IN THE ARCHER GUARD OF FRANCE.

BY JAMES FERGUSON, GLASGOW.

SOME years ago, a well-known American monthly gravely remarked that the portion of Scotland North of the Forth had contributed little or nothing to the greatness of the Scottish Race. That was amusing; and to anyone who possessed the most elementary knowledge of Scottish History and Ethnology it must have seemed surprising that an assertion so remarkable should have found its way into the pages of an intelligent and impartial Journal. Yet, upon consideration, the matter is, perhaps, not so wonderful after all. Your Saxon is a fine fellow; but he has never been very keen to do justice to his Celtic brother. There is no part of the British Empire on which the Celt - Scottish, Welsh, Irish, or Cornish,— has not set an indelible mark. His name meets us everywhere. The History of our connection with India, both civil and military, for example, is besprinkled with Highland names as freely as the battlefields of that Country have been bedewed with Gaelic blood; the muster roll of the Canadian Parliament is like that of a gathering of Representatives of the Highland Clans; and the number of men bearing Highland names who have been Prime Ministers or have occupied other positions of distinction in the Colonies is amazing when one considers the relative size of England, and the Country from which they sprung. Men like Sir Alexander MacKenzie, the Pioneer Explorer of the North American interior; Livingstone, the Ulva Crofter's son; Henry Morton Stanley, the Welshman; MacKinlay, the Cowal man of

Australian fame; and many others in whose veins the warm blood of the Celt predominated, have done far more than their share in the arduous task of filling up the blanks on the Map of the World. But all that does not avail with your modern Anglo-Saxon chronicler. English politicians tell us, without a stammer, that England alone has built up the Empire; and we have become accustomed when we pick up Cockney Journals of a certain class to find the inferiority and supineness of the Celt dilated upon with an unfailing zest. Possibly, therefore, the American Writer was a student of the Cockney Press and took his notion of the Scottish Celt second hand. If so, it is not to be wondered at the Saxon element should bulk so largely in his view that the Celt should be crowded out, or, at best, should appear but dimly in the background, a mere humble accessory to the glowing portrait of the great, ruddy, jolly Saxon in the foreground.

There were, it is said, more Irishmen and Welshmen than Englishmen in the victorious army at Crecy; but what English Historian dilates upon the little fact?

The silence is significant—and typical! The Celtic student of history has encountered it elsewhere and often.

A distinguished Scottish Historian recently told the present writer that, in his opinion, "the History of Scotland, as far as the Celtic people are concerned, has often been misinterpreted and misrepresented." Every Celtic student of History will agree that, unfortunately, the work of misrepresentation still goes merrily on. Possibly it is the outcome of insufficient knowledge; for John Bull, despite his prejudices and with all his limitations, is, in the main, an honest fellow. It is none the less unpleasant however: especially when we call to mind that the English saying demands that even the devil shall get his due.

Not long ago, an English Military Journal published an article on the Scots in France, in which, of course, the writer took occasion to let it be understood that the Scottish Adventurers whose gallantry redounded so much to the credit of their Native Country were entirely recruited from the Saxonised districts of Scotland. In answer to that somewhat sweeping assertion—your Saxon is always sweeping in his assertions—one might remind the writer in question that Rabutin, for instance, (*Coll. Petitot*, vol. xxxi, page 67) thus describes a body of Scots in the French service about 1551. " Most of them, mounted on small spirited horses, were rather scantily armed, *wearing Kilts* and red bonnets."

Did the lowland Scot of the year 1551 wear the Kilt?

One might also hint that a century later, the *first* Company of the Royal Eccossais wore the Highland dress.

It may be useful, however, to inquire more particularly into the composition of the stream of adventurers who continued from the year 1419 to pour out of Scotland to fight Scotland's ancient foe on foreign soil.

The first event of consequence in their history is the Battle of Beaugé in which the Duke of Clarence fell before the onset of the Earl of Buchan. The Duke received the *coup de grace* (according to the Book of Pluscarden) at the hands of a Highlander named MacAusland, one of Buchan's retinue. Under Stewart, Earl of Buchan, there would of course be many North Countrymen, and in this instance we find a Gael in the thick of the fight.

Again at the Seige of Cravant, in 1423, where the Scots made a glorious stand, two Knights named respectively Cameron and Davidson were among the slain. When Knights so named fell, in those feudal times, they fell amid their clansmen; so we may rest assured that the Gaelic slogan was heard in the thick of the fight at Cravant. The Account of the Seige of Verneuil brings us to a most interesting and significant episode. Here there were 10,000 Scots under the Earl of Douglas. Verneuil was strong and Douglas had recourse to a stratagem. He sent a large number of his men "who could speak English," says the Chronicler, and to them the gates were opened by the defenders, the latter imagining that the new comers were Englishmen. An interesting question occurs here. If the Scots were all Lowland-men, as we are asked to believe, why should it have been necessary to say that the men who were selected to carry out the stratagem "could speak English?" Or how did it come about that the enemy, whom bitter experience had already made well aware of the presence of Scots in the opposing army, were deceived by their speaking English? One must, at the same time, bear in mind that, even as late as the days of James VI. "a great part," as George Buchanan tells us, of the district between the Clyde and the Solway was still Gaelic-speaking, and many of the inhabitants were probably, owing to the gradual spread of Lowland Scottish, bilingual, like the Highlanders of to-day. We know, also, that Gaelic was still spoken at this period in many other districts which are now termed Lowland. It is, for instance, an open question whether it was not alive in Fifeshire in the middle of the 18th century; and it was certainly spoken in the Ochils at that time. So that even if the Scots adventurers were all from Lowland districts (which they certainly were not) a large proportion of them might still be Gaelic-speaking Celts.

(To be concluded.)

GEOFGE MACKAY.

GEORGE MACKAY,

SANITARY INSPECTOR OF PERTHSHIRE.

MR. GEORGE MACKAY was born in the Parish of Applecross, Ross-shire, where he received his early education. He was teacher in that parish for two years, but desirous of seeking a wider sphere of activity he went to London in 1857, and from thence to Glasgow, where he was appointed a Detective Officer in the Central District. When the Sanitary Department was incepted in 1863 Mr. Mackay rendered valuable assistance in its organization. To perfect his knowledge of sanitation he entered Glasgow University, and studied Chemistry and Physiology In 1882 he was appointed Sanitary Inspector for Govan where he quickly altered the insanitary condition of that populous burgh, and rendered public services which were tangibly acknowledged on his securing the important post of Chief County and District Inspector for Perthshire in 1890. The Provost and Magistrates presented him with a Solid Silver Tea and Coffee Service, and his daughter with a handsome Gold Present, as an expression of their good wishes towards him, and their regret at losing such a valuable public servant. There were 300 applicants for the Perthshire appointment, but Mr. Mackay's qualifications for the office were so high, and his certificates so incomparable that he was selected almost unanimously. That his appointment was a happy one has been since evidenced by the excellent work he has already performed in the cause of sanitation in Perthshire. It may be also mentioned in this connection that he an Examiner in Sanitary Science, a Member of Council of the Sanitary Association of Scotland, and held the position of Secretary of the Association for four years, ending July, 1890. He is frequently consulted by various local Authorities and Sanitary Officials in both England and Scotland.

In 1863 Mr. Mackay married a daughter of the late Alexander MacGregor, Shipowner, Applecross, and has one daughter.

Mr. Mackay is well known as an enthusiastic Highlander, and a good Gaelic scholar. He naturally takes a special interest in the Clan Mackay Society, of which he is a councillor, and with which he has been connected since its formation in 1888. We trust that he may be long spared to take part in the work of that flourishing society, and to complete the valuable scheme of sanitation to which he is devoting his best energies in Perthshire.

Edinburgh.   ALEXANDER ROSS MACKAY.

REVIEWS.

AN UISEAG (The Lark).—A Collection of Gaelic Songs in two-part harmony for the use of Schools. Glasgow: Henry Whyte, 1 Bridge Street.

When we mention that this little work is compiled by Mr. M. MacFarlane, and Mr. Henry Whyte ("Fionn") our readers will be satisfied that the preparation of such a work could not have been placed in better hands, and that the book is likely to supply adequately a decided want in the educational literature of the Celt. The *Uiseag* contains sixteen carefully selected songs, in two-part harmony. Many of the airs are already popular, while we have three original ones to excellent songs, which have hitherto had no airs associated with them This is the first time that a Gaelic Song Book in two-part harmony has been given to the public, and we trust that School Boards and teachers will give it a trial, and so render still more popular the native music of the Celt. Junior Choirs intending to compete at the annual *Mòd* will find this book exceedingly serviceable. The book is neatly got up and carefully edited, and is without doubt an excellent threepence worth of Gaelic music.

THE MACPHAIL BURSARIES.

WE are glad to observe that a movement is set on foot to recognise the services of Rev. Dr. James Calder MacPhail, Pilrig, on the occasion of the Semi-Jubilee of his Scheme of Grammar School Bursaries for Gaelic-speaking youths. A Meeting of Highland Ministers and others who had benefited by the Scheme was held in Edinburgh during the time of the Assembly, and resolved to raise a fund, the interest of which is to be devoted to the formation of additional Bursaries to be known as "The MacPhail Bursaries," in honour of its originator. We need hardly refer to the large number of Highlanders who now occupy distinguished positions, and who are indebted to these Bursaries for the means by which they were enabled to equip themselves for the professions in which they are now engaged. A small Committee was appointed to carry out the above proposal, of which Rev. Peter Macdonald, M.A., Edinburgh, is Convener, and Rev. Adam Gunn, M.A., Durness, Sutherlandshire, Secretary. Mr. James Macdonald, W.S., 21 Thistle Street, Edinburgh, has kindly consented to act as Treasurer for the fund, and will be glad to receive contributions towards this deserving object.

GAELIC SOCIETY OF INVERNESS.—The Annual Concert in connection with this Society, takes place in Inverness on 12th July (the evening of the Wool Market), Mr. Charles Fraser-Mackintosh, Chief of the Society, in the Chair. A very attractive programme has been arranged, and the proceedings promise to be specially interesting this year.

DONNACHADH ODHAR NAN CREACH'S ENCOUNTER WITH THE MEN OF ASSYNT, SUTHERLANDSHIRE.

IT is not more than two or three centuries ago since the Borders of Scotland were the happy hunting-grounds of cattle-raiders, and there are to-day several esteemed and well-to-do families in the south of Scotland whose ancestors belonged to that questionable class of the community. The midland Counties of Scotland suffered severely for many generations from the predatory incursions of these raiders. The Lothians were such fertile counties and the cattle being considered superior to any others, they suffered much accordingly. These raiders were petty chiefs or despots on the Borders, who kept a number of servants or retainers, and paid them generally according to the success of each raid or according to their valour. When a large pillaging incursion was contemplated, two or three of the raiders joined with their men so that any opposition to such a number was out of the question. When the spoil was brought home, it was equally divided among the various raiders who had taken part in the foray. The cattle were kept on each man's ground and were used as required, or were driven to the market towns of England and there disposed of to the best advantage. The raiders were chiefly tall and able bodied men who could use the sword as easily as the whip and to the same effect, and would kidnap a fair maid as soon as lift a cow. Indeed, it is said that the Lothians lost several fair daughters, who were unceremoniously carried on horse-back across the Pentlands or Lammermoors behind their fathers' and kindred's cattle to their future homes among the Border hills and valleys. Oral tradition has it—that the Mid-Lothian people united and commenced to build a huge dyke having a large ditch on the one side—with the view of keeping back the Border thieves and preventing them getting the cattle across. Until lately a part of some ancient dyke and ditch was visible near Balerno, which was said to have been the Border robbers' dyke. But although the Borders were the locus of the raiders, yet the Highlands had their *creachadairs*, who have been quite as famous or infamous as their brethren of the South when the geographical conditions were suitable. Indeed there are some families in the Highlands who pride themselves on their clan's name or connections, and whose ancestors have frequently marched to the strains of the gathering tune—" *Thogail nam bo théid sinn*." I believe that the raiders or *creachadairs* considered this method of cattle lifting a more honourable way of making a living then, than buying a cow without paying for her, is to-day considered. The Highland humorist insinuates this very strikingly in the following colloquy:—

Dougal.—"Did you hear that Sandy MacNab was taken to prison for stealin' a coo!" Donald.—"Hoot, toot, the stupid ass, could he no bocht it and no paid for 't!"

Donnachadh Odhar nan Creach, or Dun Duncan of the raids, which designation seems to be very appropriate according to his description, was a native of Lewis, and depicted as a man of six feet and a half, with long shaggy dun hair and whiskers; a complexion rather unusual in Lewis, and which indicates an admixture of Norse blood in his veins. He wore a dim tartan kilt, whose shortness violated all the rules of etiquette, but was favourable to his mode of life; he had a dun sporran made of the skin of a calf; a large claymore adjusted by a belt made from a hide of the same colour, and a stout stick from a well smoked rowan tree, attached to which was a strong hide thong, and which served the double purpose of a staff and whip as required. After he had subdued all the other *creachadairs* in the island, and finding the Park Hills rather too narrow a scope for his calling, he furnished himself with several boats or galleys and made frequent incursions to the West Coast of Sutherland. Ross, and Inverness-

BEN SUILVEN, ASSYNT.

shire, which afforded a wider field for his operations. He made several successful raids on Assynt, which incensed Macleod of Assynt so much that he swore by all that was holy that if *Donnachadh* made another raid he would have him hanged to the walls of Ardvreck Castle and left there until he became as black as he was dun. *Donnachadh* was equally aggravated at the Macleod for depriving him of a splendid *creach*, during which he nearly lost his life at Lochinver, on one of his incursions upon the coast of Assynt. He determined to be up-sides with the chief and his men. *Donnachadh* equipped himself and his retainers with the best arms that could be got, and set sail for the main-land. He landed somewhere on the North Coast of Lochbroom, some have it at Cean-chaoilis and others at Coigach, but more probably between both, according to the route taken by him, at a place called *Bad-na h-airach*, a small creek at the foot of Craigmore. Day was breaking on a fine summer morning when *Donnachadh* and his men landed, and looking around him, he stood motionless for a short time, as if reflecting on past errors, or speculating on future mishaps, or perhaps entranced with the wild and rugged sight before him.—

"It was a barren scene and wild,
Where naked cliffs were rudely piled."

His reverie over he left one or two men in charge of the boats and marched up *Glaic-bad-na h-airach*, along Drumminie and into Elphin, Assynt.

This part of the extensive parish of Assynt is termed Ard-Assynt, and is the most fertile district on the West Coast of Sutherlandshire and the cattle bred here had long been known to *Creachadairs* as the best to be found at any season of the year. The sublime scenery of this place is picturesque and romantic; the mountains lofty but not rugged, and the green straths at their base famous for their fertility. This district was inhabited by man from a very early period, which is proved by the various old buildings and quaint structures of the ancients. It was but early in the morning when *Donnachadh* and his men arrived on the top of a small hill overlooking the whole district. He could not resist the beauty of the scene; so he stood and gazed around him to view the magnificent spectacle. The sun was then clearing the shoulder of Benmore, whose serrated edges and quartziferous formation threw a dazzling brightness over the scene and Ben Suilven seemed in the distance engulfed in a sea of indistinct haze showing the summit clear and like an island afloat in the air—the lazy smoke from the scattered houses rising straight, but slowly as there was not a breath of wind to aid it in its

upward course, and the cattle were spreading themselves out over the plain, while the lark began its carol in the sky. But as *Donnachadh* was more a lover of the *creach* than of nature, he resisted the charms of the latter and betook himself to the rougher and harder work which he had in view. He gave express orders to his men how to proceed and how to act in case of emergency. The men executed his commands as directed and in a very short time a large drove of cattle was collected, all in prime condition. So satisfied was *Donnachadh* with the drove that after getting it on the track for Lochbroom, he began singing the "*Creachadair's return*." He raised his hoarse voice to its highest pitch, either from joy at his success or as a defiance to the Assynt men, so that each hill re-echoed in its turn. The inhabitants of the distant hamlets were aroused from their accustomed quiet by the shouting of men and the bellowing of cattle, and on looking abroad saw to their dire loss the majority of their cattle driven at a rapid rate beyond their marches. A cry got up from house to house that *Donnachadh Odhar nan Creach* was driving away their cattle. What was to be done? The chief with the best men and arms was either away on a similar expedition or was settling some feud on the borders of the county. However, the brave men of Ard-Assynt were not dismayed; both young and old took up the nearest available instrument, however rude and unwarlike, and gave chase to the *creachadairs*. They overtook them at *Blair-lochan-ashe*, now almost a small tarn between Drumminie and Elphin. Here a fierce struggle took place between *Donnachadh's* men and the men of Assynt, who were led by *Uilleam Mac Thormaid Mhic Ailein 'ic Iain Mhoir*. The Lewis men were completely routed leaving behind all the cattle and several of their companions dead or dying on the plain. The cattle were driven back by the victors, but a party of the more desperate of them thought of pursuing *Donnachadh* and his men with the view of despatching them or seeing them clear away from the coast. The raiders without looking behind made all haste to gain their boats, knowing that they were pursued by the infuriated Assynt men. On reaching the upper end of *Glaic-bad-na h-airach*, and in sight of where their boats lay, they turned round and to their amazement saw that they were pursued by only a dozen men instead of two or three score as they had thought.

The Lewis men, enraged at the loss of their *creach* and at so many of their companions being injured, faced their pursuers and a bloody fight took place with the result that all the Assynt men were killed except one who escaped up the burn-side. *Donnachadh* and his men reached their boats and made all speed for home, disappointed at the loss of the *creach* and several of his men, but on the other hand, overjoyed at the later result which had proved so fatal to his pursuers.

Glaic-bad-na h-ùrach is a long narrow glen that intersects Craigmore from the sea to almost its extremity. It terminates at a point nearly surrounded by steep heathery braes and perpendicular cliffs, with a craggy cascade over which flow the waters of a muddy and mossy rill, fed by the overflow of several tarns in the district. Of the many mountainous regions of the Highlands, with which I am familiar, I do not know of another that is so entirely destitute of drinkable spring water as the vast mountain-district of Craigmore. This of course could be explained by geological agency, but which explanation doth not concern the theme of my story. It was at the end of this glen or corrie where the struggle took place that ended so fatally to the brave warriors of Assynt. On a semi-green and heathery mound beside the burn is a cairn of stones, said to mark the spot where the Assynt men fell, or to cover their remains. This corrie has been ever since called *Coire-fhir-Assynt*.

One tradition has it that *Donnachadh* was slain at *Bhir-lochan-ashe* when the first fight took place; another that he and his men were wrecked in the Minch on their way home and all drowned, a severe storm having sprung up at the instigation and intercession of a noted Assynt witch; a third again says that he was gored to death by an infuriated bull on the Park Hills in Lewis. The latter imputed end seems to be the most correct, as it is related that he was seen, many years after this, making a considerable depredation on Eddrachillis, a district of the West Coast of Sutherlandshire, where he was designated as *Donnachadh Odhar nam bò*. It is also said that he visited the West Coast of Ross-shire and Inverness-shire after the Assynt incident from which he took considerable *creachs* and was known as *Creachadair mor Leòdhais*.

During my enquiries regarding this notorious personage, I found that he is not much known in parts of Lewis, and that he seems to be confounded with another *creachadair*, or that he had a different name. *Donnachadh Mac Rob ic Alastair dhuibh* is said to have been a noted *creachadair* who was very successful in all his expeditions, on which account, it is said, that he was in league with His Satanic Majesty. He was found killed under mysterious circumstances on the Park Hills, and that the marks of the hoofs of the scaly monster were around where he was found, which circumstance indicates that his term of compact had expired. He was said to be very eccentric in his dress and was of very fair complexion; this is probably the same individual. The dates I received as to the time at which he lived, had considerable variations, so much so that I consider it prudent not to give them at all, but as all oral traditions are the same, it is better to restrict them to between centuries rather than to be confined to certain years. Therefore it appears that *Donnachadh Odhar nan Creach* lived sometime in the sixteenth or seventeenth centuries.

The good old days when "Right was Might" are gone; they have vanished like vapours before the rising sun. Education has converted the ancient motto: –

> "That they should take who have the power,
> And they should keep who can."

to the modern one: —

> "That they should give who have the will,
> "And they should help each on."

Edinburgh. GEORGE MORRISON.

NEWS OF THE MONTH.

GLASGOW COWAL SHINTY CLUB.—Mr. William Robinson, who for several years has acted as Goal-keeper for this Club, was on 5th June presented with a handsome Marble Timepiece by his Club-fellows on the occasion of his marriage. Mr. John Mackay, Kingston, President of the Club, made the presentation in the presence of a large attendance of members and friends, and an enjoyable evening was afterwards spent.

EDINBURGH CALEDONIAN PIPERS' CLUB. The usual Summer Competition of this Club was held in the Royal Gymnasium Hall, Fettes Row, on Saturday Evening the 22nd inst. There was a very good turnout of Competitors, Members, and Spectators. One of the principal features of the meeting was the competition for the Silver Medal presented by Councillor Hay for Marches, Strthspeys, and Reels. The coveted Prize was finally carried off by Piper William Robb, Argyll and Sutherland Highlanders, who had won it on two previous occasions. The handsome Challenge Cup which decides the Championship of the Club was secured by a young Member Piper, C. Dunbar, Glencorse. The Pipe-Major's Medal which carries along with it the honorary office of Pipe-Major of the Club for the ensuing year, was deservedly won by Murdo Macrae, Piper to Mr. P. Cameron, Corrychoillie, Chief of the Club. At the conclusion of the competition dancing was heartily engaged in by the whole company present and a most enjoyable evening was spent.

The following is the Prize List:—*The Club's Challenge Cup*, Piper Charles Dunbar, Glencorse; *The Club's Challenge Medal for Amateurs*, J. A. Center; *Gardner Medal for Pibrochs*, D. C. Mather; *Hay Medal*, Piper William Robb; *Pipe-Major's Medal*, Murdo Macrae, Piper to the Chief; *Medal for Highland Fling*, D. C. Mather; *Medal for Strathspey and Reel*, D. C. Mather.

WILLIAM GRAHAM, North Erines.

THE CELTIC MONTHLY:
A MAGAZINE FOR HIGHLANDERS.
Edited by JOHN MACKAY, Kingston.

No. 11. Vol. II.]   AUGUST, 1894.   [Price Threepence.

WILLIAM GRAHAM, J.P., OF NORTH ERINES.

THE subject of our sketch was born in Glasgow, and is the youngest son of the late Patrick Graham, Merchant, who was one of the Grahams of Kittochside. His mother was a Miss Lang, whose father used to boast that as a boy he was fondled by Prince Charlie when passing the Lees, Stirlingshire, the family residence. Mr. Graham was educated at the High School and University of Glasgow. He afterwards entered the office of his brother, John Graham, C.A., with whom subsequently he became a partner under the firm of J. & W. Graham (now Grahams & Co.), and carried on a large and successful business as Chartered Accountants. In addition to the many important trusts and audits which he conducted, he held various responsible public appointments. He was officially connected with the Burgh of Cove and Kilcreggan, where he resided during the summer months for twenty-seven years, and where he is still held in high esteem for his public and private services to the community.

He retired from active business about ten years ago, and has since largely devoted himself to charitable and educational pursuits. He has been for a long time an active director of the Glasgow Eye Infirmary, and last year was unanimously elected Chairman of the Glasgow General Education Endowments Board in succession to the late Sir Michael Connal. He is also a Governor of the Logan and Johnston School of Domestic Economy, and an ex-Preses of the Graham Charitable Society, whose motto is—"For Grahams and Grahams' bairns, and all who sleep in Grahams' arms."

In 1883, Mr Graham purchased the small residential estate of North Erines, Tarbert, Lochfyne, which property he has greatly improved and beautified. From his professional experience he has rendered useful services to the county of Argyll, formerly as a Commissioner of Supply, and until lately as a County Councillor. He is Chairman of the Parochial Board of South Knapdale, which he also represents on the Mid-Argyll District Committee. He is a J.P. of the County and Commissioner on Income Tax.

Since he purchased North Erines he has heartily interested himself in Highland affairs, lending invaluable assistance to many of its charities. At the present time he happens to be the President of two of the premier Societies connected with Argyllshire—the Kintyre Club and the Glasgow Argyllshire Society—a position unique in itself and not likely to occur in the experience of another. He has joined the Gaelic Society of Glasgow, the Celtic Society, and the Argyllshire Gathering, and is a member of the Royal Highland Yacht Club. From his genial disposition and urbanity of manner he has made himself popular with all sorts and conditions of Highlanders. As a director of the West of Scotland Bible Society, he has been largely instrumental in propagating the circulation of both the Gaelic and English versions of the Scriptures all over the Western Highlands. For thirty years he has been a devoted office-bearer of the Church of Scotland. He was one of its lay Representatives at the Pan-Presbyterian Council held at Philadelphia in 1880. He is an elder of the Tarbert Parish Church, of which he laid the Memorial stone in 1885. He has done much to encourage Young Men's Mutual Improvement Societies both in Glasgow and Argyllshire, by giving lectures, and otherwise.

We trust that he may be long spared in health and strength to enjoy his beautiful residence in Knapdale and to interest himself in every matter relating to the Highlands. All who listened to his interesting address as Chairman of the recent Re-union of the Natives of Kintyre in Glasgow, must have felt how warmly he sympathizes with those, who by force of circumstances have left

"that school-boy spot
We ne'er forget, though there we are forgot,"

and how deeply he longs for the enforcement of the Small Holdings and Allotments Acts, in the hope of preserving, if possible, to the High-lands a remnant at least of our rural peasantry —of those "hardy sons of rustic toil," from whom old Scotia's greatness sprung. EDITOR.

THE LAST MACDONALDS OF ISLA.

By CHARLES FRASER-MACKINTOSH, F.S.A. (Scot.)

PART IX.—SIR JAMES MACDONALD; AND BOND OF THE CLAN NEILL.

(Continued from page 177).

SIR JAMES MACDONALD succeeded his father Angus, and was the last of the Macdonalds of Isla.   Prior to his father's death, he had for years been taking the leading part in family affairs, and may be said to have been nurtured and reared among scenes of violence and blood.

The first document I have connected with him, is a Bond of the Clan Neill, wherein he is described as Apparent of Dunyvaig, dated at Killeonane, 18th July, 1594, of which a *fac-simile* is now given. The following is a modernized copy:—

"At Killeonane, the 18th day of July, 1594 years, the which day Hector Macneil, Donald Dhu Macneill, Lachlan Mor Macneill, John vic Eachin vic Neill, and John vic Gilliechallum Macneill has granted and also conferred, as by the tenor hereof, grants and confesses themselves and every one of them to have taken the Right Honourable James MakConili of Simereby, Apparent of Dunyvaig, their foster maintainer, defender and master above any man, Angus MakConill being excepted. And

CLAN NEILL BOND, 1594.

by the tenor hereof, the present persons, and every one of them with all the remanent of their kin and surname of the offspring that they are come off, promises truly and faithfully to be fosters and foster fathers to the said James, and do their duty to him in all things that becometh them, and as they are bound to do. For the which doing, the said James promises truly and faithfully to maintain, fortify, warrant, assist, and defend the foresaid persons, and all their surname, defenders and kindly tenants in all their doings, and in all things as becometh a foster to do to such fosters and foster fathers. In token whereof both the said James and the foresaid persons has subscribed these presents with their hands as follows. At Killeo-nane, the 18th of July, 1594, before these witnesses, Neill Buie M'Neill, Donald Makayne, Tormoyde M'Neill, Donald Madder M'Neill, and John Stewart, with other diverse. (Signed) Ja. M'Connall of Simerby, Hector M'Neill of Carskey with my hand, day, year, and place aforesaid. We Lachlan Mor M'Neill, John M'Aichan vic Neill, John M'Gillie Callum vic Neill, Donald M'Clery vic Neill, Mulmorie M'Neill, Gillie Callum M'Neill, with our hands led on the pen. I, Donald Dhu M'Neill, son to Hugh M'Neill, with my hand touching the pen. John Stewart, as witness and writer hereto."

Sir James in some documents is descri æd "of Simereby" in Kinchousland, in others "Master of Kintyre," and followed his father's course in endeavouring to strengthen the position of the family by means of Bonds of Manrent and friendship. Killeonane was a two merk land, situated within the old Parish of Kilkerran, now incorporated with the modern Parish of Camp

belltown. The Bond was granted by the Macneils of Carskey, Cadets of the ancient house of Gigha. Hector, the principal subscriber, was doubtless the same person appointed in 1618 as interim keeper of the Castle of Kilkerran in the absence of Argyle.

Between 1594 and 1596 James Macdonald received the honour of knighthood, as in the

CLAN MACDONALD
From ' Highlanders of Scotland," by Kenneth Macleay, R.S.A., (The Queen's Book of the Clans), published by Mr. Mitchell, London, in 1870.
(1). Farquhar MacDonald, born in 1831, in the Island of Scalpa.
(2). Lachlan MacDonald, born in 1836, at Elligoll, Strath, Skye.

following Bond, dated 19th January, 1596, he is designed Sir James Macdonald of Knockransay, Master of Kintyre. The deed granted by Gillespic Makduffie, indweller in Isla, and John Gromach Mac vic Eachan, indweller in Colonsay, is as follows, modernized:—

"At Glasgow, the 19th day of January, the year of God, fifteen hundred, [four score, and sixteen years, the which day we Gillespik Makduffie, in-

dweller in Isla, and John Groiame Mac vic Eachene, indweller in Colonsay, grants and confesses us by the faith and truth of our bodies to have taken and accepted Sir James MakConell of Knockrynsay, Knycht, Master of Kintyre, as our only Lord and Master, and promises faithfully never to leave the said Sir James during our lifetime, and shall maintain, assist, fortify, and defend the said Sir James, contrar all men whatsomever to the uttermost of our power, in all things and at all times herafter.

For the which doing, I, the said Sir James promises, as also grants me to have received the foresaid persons in my maintenance, protection, and defence, and shall defend and assist them in all their lawful adoes in contrar of all men whatsomever. In token whereof we have subscribed these presents with our hands as afterfollows day, year, and place foresaid, before these witnesses, Alexander Makdongall, Parson of Kildaltone, Johne M'Cay and John Stewart, servitors to the said Sir James, with others diverse. (Signed) Sir J. M'Connall of Knockransay, Knyt; J. Gillespie Makduphie in Ilay, with my hand touchand the pen, day and year, and place foresaid. I, Johne Groiame Mac vic Eacbeane in Colonsay, with my hand touching the pen, day, year, and place foresaid."

Sir James married Margaret Campbell of Calder, and although there are references to a proposed divorce in the year 1621, after Sir James' return from abroad, they seem to have been a devoted couple. He frequently refers to Margaret in his letters, and she at his trial in 1607, for the affair of Askomell formerly referred to and other crimes, exerted herself vigorously to get Mr. John Russell, Advocate, to compear for her husband, going to him personally, and making protest at his declinature. Sir James had to defend himself notwithstanding a warrant by the Lords of Secret Council, allowing Counsel to appear for him; and to his eternal disgrace, and contrary to universal custom and etiquette of the bar, "The said Mr. John Russell refused to compear." Sir James was found guilty and sentenced to death. The sentence was not carried into effect, and Sir James who had been confined for upwards of two years, first in Blackness and afterwards in Edinburgh, lingered in prison until 1615. Several of Sir James' letters have been preserved, from which some extracts may be given. To the Duke of Lennox, 27th June, 1607:—

"I am willing to accept what His Majesty will bestow on me, either in his own kindly room, or in any other part of his kingdoms, and shall find caution for my obedience, which I beseech Your Grace to report to His Majesty, and that Your Grace will get me that favour as to be banished, rather than I be in this misery."

To the Earl of Caithness from Ila, 2nd July, 1615:—

"And I beseech your Lordship so far as you can, stop the Campbells to get any employments against me, for they care not how much they trouble the country, and put His Majesty to charges needless."

Sir James made his escape from Edinburgh Castle, being informed that Calder had got warrant to put him to death. In a letter to the Earl of Caithness, without date, he says:—

"Gif the Council be curious to know whom it was that Calder said to he had the warrant for taking my life,—the Prior of Ardchattan, and Macdougall his son Allan Macdougall, is my authors, and they will not nor cannot deny it. Also Calder's

own agent, James Mowatt, made no secret thereof, for he told it both to the Earl of Crawfuird and Mackintosh."

In a letter to the Bishop of the Isles, 3rd June, 1615, Sir James says of the Campbells:—

"Wha crawis ever to fish in drumly waters"— (who ever crave to fish in troubled waters),—an expression characterized by Pitcairn, as a "well merited though bitter sarcasm."

In another letter to the Bishop, Sir James says:—

"Therefore I beseech Your Lordship, seeing my Race has been ten hundred years kindly Scottish men, under the Kings of Scotland, and were I willing to live upon any poor part of that which our forbears had, and I to find security for all that becomes loyal subjects to do, both for myself and my whole kin that follows me, that Your Lordship will, as you ever do, intercede for me at His Majesty's hands to see what grace or favour Your Lordship may obtain for me, and in particular to see given without diminishing His Majesty's commoditie. I may have the Island to myself, and my kin to sustain us,"—and again—"if Your Lordship may get me any favourable conditions by His Majesty, you may assure yourself I will give you the House (of Dunyvaig), providing it be in your hands, and none of the Campbells to get it."

In a letter to the Earl of Crawford, dated Dunyvaig, 3rd July, 1615, Sir James Macdonald, who then held it, says:—

"I trust in God that all the Campbells in Scotland, without His Majesty's power, shall not receive it so long as they live."

A BRAVE HIGHLAND GIRL.

AMONG other admirable traits of character once peculiar to the Highlanders, but, alas! fast disappearing, was that of fidelity of servants to their employers.

In my young days it was quite usual for servants to stay ten, fifteen, or even twenty years with the same family—all that is changed now.

Talking of servants, reminds me of the story of a very faithful girl who had been many years with an old couple who lived in a lonely part of the Highlands. This servant was so faithful and courageous that, several times, she had been left in entire charge of the house, although it was known to contain much valuable silver plate.

One one occasion, she was thus left alone. During the day she was so occupied with household affairs that she did not feel the time pass. At night, however, she felt an "eerie" feeling creep over her, as she sat knitting at the fireside. Presently she heard a rustling movement outside, and, looking up, saw, in the moonlight, the shadow of a man's figure pass the window.

CAPTAIN JAMES MACKAY,
1st V.B. Wiltshire Regiment.

Seizing an axe that lay near, she ran upstairs into the room where the valuables were kept. Standing at the window, she saw a ladder placed directly under it and a man ascending. Her first impulse was self protection, but her sense of duty constrained her to stay there and protect her master's property. So she stood quietly behind the window curtain till there was a crash of glass, then a man's head and shoulders were thrust in. Springing forward, Mary struck him on the side of the head with the sharp side of the axe. Muttering a deep imprecation, the robber disappeared.

Next day when her master and mistress returned, Mary told them her story. Going upstairs, they discovered one of the robber's ears on the floor, where it had been cut off by the blow from Mary's axe. They were loud in their gratitude and praise of Mary for her bravery and faithfulness.

The story of this adventure became widespread in the neighbourhood, when one day a well-dressed good-looking young man called, and, asking to see Mary, said he had come a long distance to see one who had done such a meritorious act. Poor Mary, in her quiet uneventful life, was so unaccustomed to compliments or attentions from young men, that she was quite taken with this fascinating stranger. He became a frequent visitor at the house, and, at last, proposed to Mary. She could hardly credit that such a "grand gentleman" should wish to marry a poor servant girl. However, he assured her he really was in earnest, so she consented to go with him. She knew nothing of his family or circumstances further than that, in order to get to his home, they must drive many miles through thick forests. So, bidding a tearful farewell to her friends, after the marriage ceremony, they drove away. For the first few miles her husband was kind and attentive to her, till they entered a dark wood when Mary noticed a scowling look in his face and his manner become short and snappish. She sat quietly beside him, till a gust of wind blowing right in their faces blew the man's unusually long hair away from the side of his head, when, to her horror, she discovered he had only one ear! For many miles they drove on in silence, when a shrill whistle resounded through the wood, followed by the appearance of a dark fierce-looking ruffian, who, in a low voice, muttered a few words to the other man, and without appearing to notice Mary, jumped into the conveyance. At last they came to a small wayside inn, when, giving his horse in charge to his companion, Mary's husband hurried her into the inn. A servant girl then took her into a small back room, where she was left alone for some time. Presently she heard the two men come in from the stable.

"Does she know yet who you are, Bill?" she heard the ruffian ask. "No," her husband's voice answered, "but she will know soon to her cost who I am, she shall pay me for my ear with her life. There is no time to be lost. Let us go now into the thickest part of the forest to dig a grave for her." Suiting the action to the word, she heard them both walk away. She sat for sometime thinking how best to escape. If she attempted running away by the road on which they had come, she knew they could easily overtake her on horseback, while, if she hid in the forest she was sure to lose her way. The only means of escape, for her, she thought, was to take the horse out of the stable and harness it as quietly as possible, while her would-be murderers were digging her grave. She found that by raising the lower sash of the window she could easily get out that way, which she did, and, finding her way to the stable, harnessed the horse and led it along at slow pace till out of hearing, when she drove furiously. This she continued doing till daybreak brought her in sight of her old home, where she told her adventure, to the horror of the listeners. When the horse was unharnessed, the conveyance was found to contain a box with an enormous sum of money in it. Search was made in all the surrounding country for the robbers, but no trace of them was to be found.

As the robber had married Mary legally and was therefore bound to provide for her, it was decided that she had every right to her husband's money, so she became heiress to many thousands, but continued to live with her old master and mistress, as friend and companion till the end of their lives.

Many years after, an old tramp was found dead at the roadside with only one ear.

Strontian, Loch Sunart.   (Mrs.) D. MacLean.

CLAN MacLEAN.—A Committee Meeting of this Association was held on Friday, 6th July, Mr. John MacLean, Vice-President, in the Chair, when arrangements were made that the Annual Clan Gathering be held in the Waterloo Rooms, on Friday, 26th October, Sir Fitzroy Donald MacLean, Bart., Chief of the Clan, in the Chair.

IN 1745, at the time of the rebellion, the Duke of Argyll gave a grand ball in honour of the Kintyre men who had taken up arms on the side of the government. The Duke danced to the playing of MacLeolan, a famous piper. When His Grace had finished, he said to the musician, "You are the sweetest player ever I heard, and you are the most ill-looking man I ever saw." The piper immediately replied, with a touch of irony, "I think it was the same tailor that shaped us both." Even a Duke finds at times that he is only human after all, and that the "clothes" make all the difference.

CAPTAIN JAMES MACKAY, F.S.A.

THE Parish of Latheron, Caithness, can claim as natives a larger share of distinguished professional, military, and successful business men all over the world than any other in the North. This because here chiefly settled the Celts from Sutherland, and their qualities were improved and intensified by the blend with the restless energy, frankness, and sturdy independence of the native sons of the Viking.

A typical specimen of this happy mixture of Celtic and Norse blood is the subject of our sketch. His pedigree is easily traced. His ancestors, even among a hospitable people, have been famed for their hospitality and frank generosity. To no family may the well-known proverb "A' h-uile fear a th'id a dhulaidh, gheobh i dolar o Mhac-Aoidh," be more justly applied.

Over a hundred years ago his great grandfather James, descended from the Bighouse branch of the Clan Mackay, settled in Berriedale. He had several holdings in the Langwell Strath —

by his premature death. She was a great beauty, and is the heroine of the well-known song—"Is boidheach am boirionnach Seònaid Guine, a-ro-horo is nich horo." His father Donald settled in Braemore, and he took for wife Jane Macivor, niece of the then local factor, and whose pedigree can be traced to the Macivors who came to Caithness with "Glenorchy," but unlike him settled in the Norse or Lowland part of the County.

Captain Mackay is the fourth son of this union, and his career has been worthy of his forebears. Receiving his early education from the late J. W. Mackay, afterwards Town-clerk of Wick, he entered the office of William Miller, *Primus*, Wick, —theablestlawyer produced by Caithness. With a good literary education and a thorough grounding in method and business habits, he "held South." Practical Cloth manufacture he learned at Stroud, Gloucestershire, thereafter he accepted a share in the firm of W. H. Tucker & Co., Trowbridge, where an elder brother was already a partner. It will be enough to state that the business has been conducted and developed with credit and considerable success.

Fixity of tenure even in a degree has only quite recently become a reality in the North. His grandfather William had the important holding of Borgue and afterwards occupied Bracleit in Braemore, and it was here he brought home as wife Janet Gunn of the Kildonan MacHamishes, whose engagement with the famous Allister Gunn, Tacksman of Dalnaglatan was broken off

Captain Mackay is a many sided man. His ancestral martial ardour has found fitting outlet in Volunteering, and even apart from his admirable tact and knowledge of men, his commanding appearance and bearing are enough to demand the enthusiastic respect in which he is justly held by his Company of the 1st Wiltshire Regiment

Antiquarian, Archæological, and Literary pursuits are to him most congenial, and many a well earned holiday has he spent trying to unearth the forgotten story of the Picts. Several communications, particularly about a Pict's House opened by him in conjunction with the Duke of Portland, at Ousedale, have appeared in the *Transactions of the Society of Antiquaries*, of which he is a Fellow.

In 1877 Captain Mackay married Ellen Florence, daughter of Mr. John Broomhall, J.P. for Surrey, who although she was born in India takes as much interest in, and has as much love for the Highlands and Highland traditions as even her husband has.

In his Clan, and in the people and things of his native Caithness and Sutherland he has always taken a lively, warm, and substantial interest. Last year he was Vice-President of the Clan Mackay Society, of which his oldest brother, Alexander, is now President. His hearty welcome, absolute frankness, and abounding generosity,—in which in his wife he has a very meet companion,—either at Trowle, Trowbridge, or at the picturesque Highland Home of his brother at Ousedale, Caithness, makes the heart even of the greatest stranger "warm to the TARTAN."

Dunbeath. ADAM MACKAY.

GAELIC AIRS TO LOWLAND SONGS.

BY MALCOLM MACFARLANE.

FROM ALBYN'S ANTHOLOGY (1816)

(*Continued from page 166*).

77. Robi dona gòrach. Leave thee, loth to leave thee—by the Editor. This air has already been referred to (see page 88, Vol 2). There it is named "Robaidh *donn* gòrach" according to the spelling usually found in song-books. But the word in italics is also found *dònna*. *Donn* seems to be an error, as the following verse taken down from the singing of Miss MacLeod of Roudle in Harris in 1815, testifies:—

KEY F. ROBI DONA GORACH.

```
}  . |f  .m  :r  .d |l₁ :d .l₁ |s₁ :l₁ .d |r :r .
|    Robi    dona gòrach  an còmhnuidh 'gam iarraidh,
{ .m|s .m :r .d |l₁ :d .l₁ |s₁ :l₁ .d |d :d .
  Gu 'n d' innis mi g'am dheoin  duit nach pòs mi an bliadhna,
}  . |f .,m :f .s  |l  :s .d'|s .,m:r .m|s :l .
   'S mor gu 'm b'annsa Tearlach a ghnath an cois an t-sliabh e
{ .d'|s .m :r .d |l₁ :d .l₁ |s₁ :l₁ .d |d :d .|
   Na Robi dona   gòrach  a dh' òladh a   lèine.
```

78. Cha teid mis' a chaoidh. Nora's vow—by Sir Walter Scott, being a free translation of the original.

79. Ma 's tu mo mhàthair. Now Winter's wind—by the Editor. This air is united to an Ossianic ballad.

80. Faill ithill o ró. I'll ne'er return more—by the Editor. A St. Kilda melody.

81. 'S e do mholadh. Our Heroes return—by William Smith.

82. Creag ghunnach. The hawk swhoops on high—by the Editor. This song is given in "The Killin Collection" to a different air, page 74.

83. Tha 'ghaoth an iar cho caithreamach. O sing ye children of the brave—by Fairbairn.

84. Gur muladach tha mi. The Royal Sufferer's farewell—by the Editor. This song is better known as *An Talla 'm bu ghnàth le MacLeòid*, and is given along with the music slightly differing from that in Albyn's Anthology, at page 85, Vol. 5 of "The Gael."

85. Tha tighinn fodham èirigh. Rise and follow Charlie.

86. Ribhinn àluinn 's tu mo rùn. Come my bride—by the Editor. This air is referred to at page 118 of this volume, number 17. It is universally known as "Gloomy Winter's noo awa." The air and the words of the Song are claimed by the Editor in a footnote which I here quote :—

The Editor, in thus claiming an early composition of his own, feels a mingled sensation of diffidence and satisfaction in venturing to insert it in a Selection such as the present. But as the title in question has been honoured with public approbation for many years past, and has been considered by many, nay even professional men, as one of our oldest Tunes, it becomes the duty of the Composer to state briefly, yet distinctly the fact, and leave it thus on record. In the year 1783, while the present Writer was studying counterpoint and composition, and turning his attention to National Music, he made essays in that style, one of which was the Melody to which he has united Gaelic and English verses of his own, written for Albyn's Anthology. It was originally composed as a Strathspey; and in the year 1791 or 92, it was published and inscribed to the Rev. Patrick M'Donald of Kilmore, the Editor of the "Collection of Highland Airs" mentioned in the Preface of the present Work. In Mr. Nathaniel Gow's Collection, this Strathspey is called "*Lord Balgowny's Delight*," and pointed out as a "very ancient air." It has since been published by Mr. J. M'Fadyen of Glasgow, under the title of "*Gloomy Winter's now awa,*" a Scottish Song, written by R. Tannahill, with Symphonies and Accompaniments by R. A. Smith. Wherefore, it being now reclaimed, this indispensible egotism will freely be pardoned by every liberal and candid mind, when a Writer, in order to do himself justice, embraces a fair opportunity, as in the present instance, of doing so.

HIGHLAND WIT AND HUMOUR.

By "FIONN."

OF late years Cockney and Lowland Tourists have invaded the fortresses of the Gael, nor has the incursion been resisted beyond the impost of a swinging tax in the shape of hotel bills and charges for guides. Hotelkeepers and guides are inclined to consider Tourists their special prey, and many stories are told of the stratagem practised by both to fleece the *Sassunnach* whose pockets are supposed to be lined with gold.

A Cockney having reached Arran, determined to climb Goatfell without a guide. Reaching the foot of the mountain, he informed the guides who offered their services of his intention. The guides could not see the fun of being deprived of a day's work, and so they forthwith proceeded to warn the Tourist that his project was a mad one, that he might lose his way and that he would certainly miss some of the finest sights. All was of no avail, the Cockney although somewhat alarmed was determined to keep to his resolution. "Well," says Donald, as he pretended to withdraw—"since you will not have a guide, good luck to you. Mind you don't miss the *Clach-bhodhar,*—or Deaf-stone."

"What stone?" demands the Cockney.

"Oh, on the top of Goatfell," replies Donald, "there is a stone that might well be called enchanted. When you stand upon that stone, no sound can reach your ears."

"Really?" says the Cockney, gaping.

"Aye a thunder storm might burst over your head and you would not hear it," added Donald, with feigned concern.

"Most wonderful," exclaimed the Tourist. "How shall I know the stone? Do tell me."

"Not very easily," replied Donald, "it is only known to guides. However as a favour I will try and explain to you where it is."

Here Donald entered into an explanation that sounded like Greek to the Cockney—who capitulated at once and told Donald to "come along."

Near the top of the mountain they came to a large boulder which Donald declared was the enchanted stone. The Cockney at once took up his position on it, and begged the guide to stand a few steps off and to shout at the top of his voice.

Donald began to make all sorts of contortions, placing his hands to his mouth as if to carry the sound; but not a whisper reached the ears of the Tourist. Donald began to get blue in the face.

"Take a rest Donald, you will make yourself hoarse. It is most wonderful. Not a sound has reached my ear. Now you go and stand on the stone and I will shout."

They changed places. The Cockney shouted with all his might. Donald did not move a muscle.

"Don't you hear anything?" cried the poor Cockney.

Donald was not so silly as to fall into the trap. He simply demanded the Cockney to shout louder.

"It's wonderful," remarked the Tourist, as he sat down to take a rest. "I never saw anything so remarkable all my life," and putting his hand in his pocket he drew out a golden guinea and placed it into Donald's hand, adding "I would not have missed this on any account."

Sitting beside the Driver of a Highland Coach a Tourist remarked, "Dear me, Donald, are there no milestones on this road?" "Hoch yes," was the reply, "the last milestone was a big tree, and the next is an inn where they keep a good dram." Donald got his dram!

Ronald accompanied an English sportsman who was a wretched shot. After each shot the gillie considered it proper to make some remark to soothe the feelings of the sportsman. These remarks took the shape of "Yon one got a big fright," "If he stayed yonder he got it" or "Yon one will know a gun again." Such observations only exasperated the Cockney who turned on the gillie saying, "Stop your infernal clatter, what would it matter to you if I blazed a ton of powder into the air," to which Donald meekly replied, "You would not need a gillie to do that."

ATHOLL MACGREGOR.

ATHOLL MACGREGOR, DUNKELD.

ATHOLL MACGREGOR, President of the Clan Gregor Society, whose portrait we now present to our readers, is second son of the late Sir John Atholl MacGregor by Mary Charlotte, daughter of the celebrated Admiral, Sir Thomas Hardy.

Sir John, his father had served in the Austrian Cavalry, and was noted for horsemanship among those who were then considered the best riders.

For some years Curator on part of the Atholl Estate, he settled on family property and built the present house of Edinchip.

A thorough Highlander and an enthusiastic sportsman of the old type, he was a general favourite among all classes in the Perthshire Highlands, and his feats on mountain and moor, in Glenartney, Glen Tilt, and Rannoch are still quoted by the older inhabitants. His premature death at the age of forty, a few weeks after assuming the Governorship of the Virgin Islands, was regretted by a wide circle of relations and friends.

The subject of our sketch proceeded from Haileybury in 1855 to join the Madras Civil Service, visiting *en route* the Crimea, where hostile shots were still being exchanged.

Arriving in India shortly before the great Mutiny he was detached to an insolated post, seventy miles from head quarters, to watch the lawless Clans on the Madura coast, and later was deputed as Special Magistrate to hold in check the Malabar Moplahs, a tribe of fanatical Mahometans, who related to those in the Soudan, and numbering nearly half a million, had recently murdered the Chief Magistrate. During the nine years he served among them only one outbreak occurred, which was quelled the same day, his measures receiving the approval of the Madras and Home Governments. When in 1870 Local Government was extended to the Madras Provinces Mr. Mac-Gregor, as Chief Civil Officer of Malabar, was able to carry to completion a system of Roads and Bridges, Elementary Education, and Town Conservancy throughout this, probably the largest District in India, where his long previous experience had given him a thorough insight into the character and requirements of the people and country.

Of his twenty-five years service the last five were spent in the coveted post of British Resident in Travancore, and retiring in 1881 he settled in Perthshire where he still serves his countrymen in various capacities, as Member of the County Council for the Dunkeld Division, Chairman of the Lunacy Board, and Bench of Magistrates, Governor of the Royal School,

Representative for St. Mary's in the Episcopal Church Council and Member of its Clergy Fund, etc., and last, but not least, as President of the Clan Gregor Society, in connection with which he has done most excellent and useful work. Under his Presidentship, to which office he has just been re-elected for a further term of three years, the Membership of the Society has not only been much increased, but chiefly on his initiation a special branch has been added, by which deserving persons of the Clan Gregor can be assisted in making provident arrangements by way of effecting insurance on their lives for the benefit of themselves or their families, or for provision for themselves after a certain age, or in case of sickness, or by giving aid in cases of exceptional necessity. This important branch is now in complete working order and is credited with considerable funds. It is therefore hoped that it may result in great benefit to those for whose assistance it was inaugurated.

The numerous trophies of large game which adorn the walls of Eastwood bear evidence of the keenness with which he pursued sport in the intervals of business, and but for an outbreak of cholera which prevented H.R.H. the Prince of Wales from carrying out the intended sporting tour on the Travancore Hills he might possibly have emulated the deed by which his ancestor won the Clan motto and armorial bearings. He married, in 1878, Caroline Mary Stewart, eldest daughter of Sir Robert Menzies, a lady who by her kindliness of heart, wide sympathies, and gracious bearing has, in the neighbourhood of her home, as well as in Travancore, and in a more extended sphere, during the last two years at the Palace of Holyrood House, won golden opinions from all sorts and conditions of men and women.

Grosvenor Crescent, Glasgow.

ALEXANDER M'GRIGOR.

BOUND COPIES OF VOLUMES II.—As we will be able to supply only a very limited number of copies of this handsome volume, those who wish any are requested to apply to the Editor at once. The prices are—Bound in strong leather, with gilt lettering, 8/-; Cloth, 6/6.

CLAN MACKAY SOCIETY BURSARY.—We beg to remind clansmen who intend competing for this, and the St. Andrews University Bursaries, that the examinations are to take place in Sutherland and Caithness early in August, and those who intend competing are requested to communicate at once with Mr. Thomas Mackay, 40 Henderson Row, Edinburgh, *Educational Secretary.*

We understand that a new volume of the "Waifs and Strays of Celtic Tradition" by the late Rev. J. Gregorson Campbell of Tiree, is in preparation for the press.

TO CORRESPONDENTS.

All Communications, on literary and business matters, should be addressed to the Editor, Mr. JOHN MACKAY, 17 Dundas Street, Kingston, Glasgow.

TERMS OF SUBSCRIPTION.—The *CELTIC MONTHLY* will be sent, post free, to any part of the United Kingdom, Canada, the United States, and all countries in the Postal Union—for one year, 4s.

THE CELTIC MONTHLY

AUGUST, 1894.

CONTENTS.

OF INTEREST TO OUR READERS.

WITH our next issue we will complete the second volume of the *Celtic Monthly.* It will, we trust, be conceded that the promise which we made at the beginning of the volume to steadily improve its literary and artistic departments has been most amply fulfilled, and our ideal of what a thoroughly patriotic Highland magazine ought to be is pretty nearly attained in the present number. It will, we think, compare favourably with any magazine published at the price. However, we intend making some further improvements in the second volume, not the least important of which will be an attractive cover, embellished with appropriate Celtic ornamentation, which is being specially designed by a Highlander of repute in artistic circles. We are at present engaged in arranging a prospectus of contributions for next volume, and we hope in September issue to place a most interesting programme before our readers. All the gentlemen whose valuable contributions appear so frequently in our pages have promised to continue their support, and their names alone is a sure guarantee that the high reputation which the *Celtic Monthly* has already achieved will be fully maintained. We intend, further, giving special attention to the artistic department, which has become one of the most attractive features of the magazine. However, next month we will be better able to lay before our readers a complete statement regarding our future arrangements.

Having on our part promised this much we expect our large circle of readers will continue to extend to

us their hearty support. We depend largely upon our Annual Subscribers, who are to be found in every quarter of the globe, and to them we again confidently appeal. *We are most anxious to complete our List of Annual Subscribers for next volume, and will esteem it a favour if those who intend renewing their subscriptions for another year would kindly fill up the enclosed order form, and forward it, with postal order for 4/-, to the Editor, Celtic Monthly, 17 Dundas Street, Kingston, Glasgow, at once.* We trust that our readers will give this matter their immediate attention.

A TITLE PAGE AND LIST OF CONTENTS for the present volume will be given with next number.

WE have to express our indebtedness to Mr. Graham of North Erines for kindly providing the charming views which accompany the article on " Dunaverty ;" and to Mr. Millar (of Messrs. William Cross & Co., 45 Montrose Street), for permitting us to reproduce the two plates representing the Clans MacDonald, Sutherland, and Mackay from his copy of the Queen's Book of the Scottish Highlanders. Mr. Millar possesses one of the finest collections of rare Highland books and curious prints we ever had the pleasure of viewing.

MACMILLAN HUNTING TARTAN.—We are living in a time when the clan spirit of former days has been quickened, and every clansman aspires to do something to add to the good name of his clan. Messrs. MacMillan of Partick have done their clan a service and that in a practical way. They have designed for their clan a new Hunting Tartan, which in every respect is a decided improvement upon the older tartan. It is modest in its colours, and yet sufficiently bright and artistic to produce a most pleasing effect. The designers have shown good taste in their work, and we have no doubt but the tartan, which they euphoniously call " Breacanscilgmhicghillemhaoil," will become very popular among members of the Clan MacMillan. We desire to congratulate Messrs. MacMillan on the success of their design.

OUR NEXT ISSUE.

WE will present our readers with life-like plate portraits of Sir Charles A. Cameron, M.D., F.R.C.S.I., Dublin, Chieftain of the Clan Cameron, who will be appropriately represented in the Highland dress; and Messrs. A. K. Sandison, Southampton (a notable Caithnessian), and A. W. Martin, Secretary, Gaelic Society of London. In addition to these a large variety of contributions will appear, which will be profusely illustrated, and portraits will also appear of well-known Gaels. Our next number will be as attractive as any we have yet issued.

The following new works of Highland interest have reached us just as we go to press, and will be reviewed in our next number :—" Transactions of the Gaelic Society of Inverness;" "Tales of the Heather" by Emma Rose Mackenzie ; "A Visit to Staffa and Iona" by Malcolm Ferguson ; and also the " Irish Gaelic Journal."

The following Elegy to the Respond Family is by Rob Donn, the Sutherland Bard :—

The Respond Family consisted of two brothers who lived together in single blessedness. They were mean, sordid misers. They had a stock of sheep and cattle on the hills. They amassed gold, and like the man in the parable, hid it in the earth, in a spot it is said where from their house window they could see its hiding place. They had a housekeeper. In the dead of winter, and late on a Saturday night, a poor woman came to their door for shelter, but they closed it in her face, an act, which at that time, and for at least one hundred years subsequent was in those parts looked upon as a heinous crime. Before that night week the three were dead. The house-keeper first and the brothers within a day and a night of one another. The trio were borne to their last resting place by the same company of men and laid together in mother earth. It is possible, though we have no account of it, that remorse for the act they had been guilty of, might have accelerated their end ; at any rate the Bard, the teacher,—may I not add the "Preacher of Righteousness !"—made it the theme of his Poem.

ALEXANDER MACKAY, Edinburgh.

MARBHRANN CHLOINN RUSPAINN—THE RESPOND FAMILY ELEGY.

Gaelic Words by ROB DONN MACKAY. *Translation by* MISS SCOBIE, Keoldale, Sutherland.

KEY D. *Slowly with feeling.*

```
:d ._,r | m ._,s :   m ._,r | d ._,r    m .m | m ._,s :   d' ._,t | l :—.
 'Nan  luidhe     so  gu  h-iosal,    far  na  thiodhlaic  sinn  an triùir,
 Quite hale and  strong and hearty  at  the  opening    of   the  year,

:l_,t | d' .m    s ._,l | d' ._,t :   d' .l | s ._,m :   r ._,m | d :—.
 Bha  fallain,   lài lir,  inntinneach 'n uair dh' inntrig a' bhliadhn' ùr ;
 Were the three whom we have buried  and now lie  so   lowly  here ;

: .s | d' ._,r' :   m' ._,r' | d' ._,l :  s .l | d' ._,r'   d' .t | l :—.
 Cha  deachaidh   seachd fhathast   ach deich  latha   dhith o  thus,—
 Ten days have    only   passed as  yet since  the new  year  began,—

: .d' | s ._,m :   s .l | d' ._,t :   d' .l | s .m    r .m | d :—.||
 Ciod fhios nach   tig an teachdair-s' oirnn, ni's braise  na ar  dàil !
 Who know when    this dread messenger may call for  any   man ?
```

Am bliadhna thiom' bha dithis diubh,
  Air tighinn o'n aon bhroinn
Bha iad mar na companaich,
  O'n choinnich iad na'n cloinn ;
Cha d' bhris an t-aog an comunn ud,
  Ged bu chomasach dha 'n roinn,
Ach gheàrr e snàthainn na beath' ac',
  Gun dàil ach latha 's oidhch'.

Daoine nach d' rinn briseadh iad
  Le tiosrachadh do chàch ;
'S cha mhò a rinn iad aon dad,
  Ris an can an saoghal gràs ;
Ach ghineadh iad, is rugadh iad,
  Is thogadh iad is dh' fhàs—
Chaidh stràchd de 'n t-saoghal thairis orr',
  'S mu dheireadh fhuair iad bàs.

An dèigh na rinn mi rùsgadh dhuibh
  Tha dùil agam gun lochd,
'S a liuthad focal firinneach
  A dhirich mi 'n ur h-uchd,
Tha eagal orm nach èisd sibh
  Gu bhi feumail do na bhochd ;
Ni 's mo na rinn na fleasgaich ud
  A sheachduin gus a nochd.

Within the circle of a year
  Were two of these men born ;
Closest of comrades ever were
  Since days of life's gay morn ;
Ev'n death, who heeds not closest bonds
  No separation made,
For in the space of one brief day
  He both in silence laid.

No wrong had they to any done
  Judging by human ken ;
But neither had they helped in aught
  Their needy fellow men ;
And all that can be said of them
  Is—they were born--survived
Some years upon this earth—and then,
  The hour of death arrived.

But after all that I have said
  The whole of which is true,
(For in this song most faithfully
  I've told but what I knew),
I fear you will not heed my words,
  Nor help the needy more
Than those poor fellows who last week
  Were buried at our door.

The above Music was taken down by the late John Munro, a native of the Reay country, and is now published, we believe, for the first time.

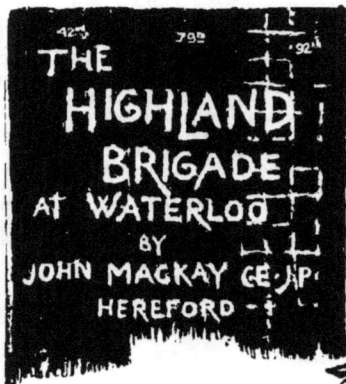

THE HIGHLAND BRIGADE AT WATERLOO BY JOHN MACKAY CE.JP HEREFORD

PART I.

" The last time France stood British fire
  The Brigade gained glory at its cost,
At Quatre Bras and Waterloo
  Three dreadful days they kept their post ;
Two thousand there, who formed in squares
  Before the close, a handful grew,
But the little phalanx never flinched
  Till " Boney " fled at Waterloo.

SOLDIER'S DITTY.

" Agincourt may be forgot
And Cressy be an unknown spot
  And Blenheim's name be new,
But still in story and in song
For many an age remembered long
  Shall live the towers of Hougomont
  And field of Waterloo.

SCOTT.

Waterloo, like Inkerman, was essentially a soldiers' battle. Never on the plains of the Peninsula, had the British soldier better shown with "what a majesty he could fight." The Great Moltke said that Waterloo was one of the finest instances of defensive warfare in all history, and no other than the British soldier could have withstood the fiery assaults of the French for so long without flinching. The Highland Brigade was decimated on the Pyrenees and the fields of Orothes and Toulouse, and its ranks, on its return home in 1814, were filled with the newest of recruits, who for the most part had scarcely emerged from their teens, when sent to Flanders to form the immortal squares, upon which the Gallic fury broke like waves of foam upon their native coasts. Yet young as they were in this campaign, which terminated so gloriously at Waterloo, the martial youths of Scotland evinced a steadiness, a courage, and audacity worthy of the best days and deeds of their country.

No country in Europe is so proud of its gallant national regiments as Scotland. No country manifests so much pleasure and delight in receiving into its midst, one or other of its gallant corps, on returning from a campaign, or long foreign service. The Metropolis of Scotland has never forgotten nor neglected its sense of the duty owing to the brave warriors she sends forth to defend the rights, and vindicate the honour of their country. Happily for Scotland her soldier sons are easily distinguished in the field or in garrison by their national uniform, which attracts attention, and spreads terror. It was at Waterloo Napoleon for the first time saw this warlike uniform before him in martial array. He knew who wore it. He heard too for the first time the wildly animating pibroch notes that sounded that fearful charge which confounded a whole division of his grand soldiers, inured to warfare and vastly superior in numbers, drawing from him the appreciative exclamation, " Ces braves Ecossais," but he did not know that those other grand soldiers mounted on gallant grey steeds, were also "Ecossais" who, when their kilted countrymen by their furiously sustained charges threw this division into disorder, came galloping up from the rear, and fell like a thunderbolt into the disordered ranks, ploughing through them, cutting, slashing, stabbing, piercing them through and through, annihilating or taking prisoners the whole division. The sight was terrible; Napoleon winced, saying, " Qui sont terribles, ces chevraux gris" (How terrible are these grey horses), yet these infantry and cavalry corps were both "Ecossais." The one had a distinctive uniform, the other had not.

GEORGE J. MACKAY.

Should successive governments be permitted to efface so distinctive and distinguished a uniform !

The regiments which composed the Highland Brigade at Waterloo, Alma, and in India, with other equally national Scottish corps, from the day they were first enrolled to the present time, have conferred the highest honour and glory upon their country by their bravery and manly conduct in the field, and by their equally ex-cellent behaviour in quarters. They well deserve the hearty welcome, the affectionate greetings, the kindly embraces of their "auld mither," whenever they are permitted to meet her. Between Scotland and her gallant soldier sons exists a vein of affection, respect and regard, wholly unfelt, unknown, in other countries. Her sons are delighted to visit the old country. The "auld mither" is charmed at the expecta-

THE "BLACK WATCH" REPELLING A FRENCH CAVALRY CHARGE
AT WATERLOO.

The above spirited Picture is reproduced from Messrs. W. & A. K. Johnston's excellent work on the "Black Watch," which we heartily recommend to our readers.

tion of again seeing and meeting with her martial sons returning to her with credit and honour, and the reception she prepares for them, and accords to them with such spontaniety and enthusiasm is nowhere else witnessed. Long may this continue!

The soldier's ditty often heard "sixty years since," well describes the position of the allied armies in the eventful month of June, 1815.

On the 16th day of June, my lads, in Flanders where
        we lay
Our bugles did the alarm sound, before the break of day,
Our British, Belgians, Brunswickers, and Hanoverians
        too,
Brussels we left that morning for the plains of Waterloo.
    *   *   *   *   *   *   *
At Quatre Bras we met the French, their shape to us
        seemed new,
For they were in steel armour clad for the field of
        Waterloo

The Highland Brigade were in the gallant Picton's fighting division, encamped at Brussels. On the night of the 15th June Wellington had intelligence from the Prince of Orange, who was posted with a division of Dutch, Belgians, and some English regiments around Quatre Bras, in touch with the Prussians to his left at Fleuris, that Napoleon was approaching Charleroi. Orders were at once issued to prepare to march. By midnight more precise intelligence was received that the French had beaten the Prussians in front and around Charleroi, and taken possession of it in great strength. There was no longer any doubt as to Napoleon's real points of attack, nor as to his plans for future action. He had been well informed of the scattered position taken up by the forces of Wellington and Blucher. He as well concealed from them the movements of his own troops till he had collected them at one point, and by overwhelming forces to thrust himself like a wedge between the two, to defeat the Prussian first, then turn upon Wellington, defeat him and get possession of Brussels, when he thought Belgium and Holland would declare themselves in his favour.

Wellington about midnight of the 15th,

having received the above intelligence, at once gave orders to Picton to march with his divisions in advance to Quatre Bras to the assistance of the Prince of Orange, in case he might be attacked by the French advancing from Charleroi. At the same time he sent orders to the other divisions of infantry, cavalry, and artillery to march and converge on Quatre Bras as quickly as possible. Then there was seen in and around Brussels the mustering squadrons and the clattering cars pouring through the echoing streets, and drum and bugle summoned horsemen and foot soldiers to their places in the ranks for war. Byron, in his immortal "Childe Harold," grandly depicts the scene that night in Brussels, and in the early morning when the 79th left for Quatre Bras along with the other regiments in Sir James Kempt's brigade of Picton's division.

Sir Walter Scott says, "Our two distinguished Highland corps, the 42nd and 92nd, were the first to muster. They assembled with the utmost alacrity to the sound of the well-known pibroch, 'Come to me and I will give you flesh,' an invitation to the wolf and the raven, for which the next day did, in fact, spread an ample banquet at the expense of our countrymen, as well as of their enemies. One could not but admire their fine appearance; their firm, collected, steady, military demeanour as they went rejoicing to battle, with their bagpipes playing before them, and the beams of the rising sun shining upon their glittering arms. The kind and generous inhabitants assembled in crowds to witness the departure of their gallant friends, and as the Highlanders marched onward with a steady and collected air, the people breathed many a fervent expression for their safety."

Picton's division was composed of two brigades, the first commanded by Sir James Kempt, comprised the 79th, 28th, 32nd, and 95th regiments; the second commanded by Sir Dennis Packe was composed of the 42nd, 92nd, Royal Scots, and the 44th regiments, all infantry, arrived at Quatre Bras at 2 p.m., having marched 21 miles, at a most critical time, when the French under the command of Marshal Ney, "the bravest of the brave," had defeated the troops of the Prince of Orange, and were

GUARDING THE COLOURS OF THE 79th CAMERON HIGHLANDERS.

pursuing them past Quatre Bras. Picton's division were at the time marching through fields of tall wheat and rye, obscuring them from the enemy, and obscuring the enemy from them. The Prince of Orange made and was still making a gallant resistance. His Dutch and Belgians fought well, but they could not resist the impetuosity of the French. The Belgians were the first to give way. The 42nd were the first to emerge from the rye fields into a field of clover. Seeing the retreating Belgians' order was given to open ranks and let them pass through, to form in the rear. In an instant the ranks were closed when the pursuing French were seen right in front. The French were staggered at the sudden appearance of the Highlanders. The order was at once given the 42nd to fire, advance, and charge. The wild terrifying yell of the Highlanders was enough. The French immediately faced right about, fled and fell before this impetuous charge, and were pursued for some distance towards the main body. Marshal Ney was not the man to permit such audacity to go unpunished, if he could. Instantly ordering a regiment of lancers to advance from the Wood of Bossu where they lay concealed, and attack the 42nd before they could complete their formation to receive cavalry. Imagining these lancers to be Brunswickers coming to cut up the retreating French, the 42nd were unprepared for the shock. They had to do with angry foes instead of friendly Germans. Speedily perceiving the mistake, a rallying square was formed to meet the fierce Polish Lancers, but two companies were unable to come in, and one side of the square was open when the lancers burst upon them, and here they speedily found an entrance. The two companies were soon cut down to a man, fighting back to back. In this perilous crisis the 42nd were true to their ancient fame, and with marvellous steadiness completed their formation, hemmed the lancers within their square, shot and bayonetted the most of them, making prisoners of the rest, while the restored front battled all the efforts of those outside to penetrate to their comrades' succour. Finding every effort useless, and losing men from the fire of the square, the lancers retired after receiving a dreadful volley from the 42nd, which laid low many a man and horse. The fight was hot, though brief. In the space of a few minutes the command of the regiment devolved upon four officers in succession—Sir Robert MacAra, killed ; Lieutenant-Colonel Dick, severely wounded ; Major Davidson, mortally wounded ; and Major Campbell.

(To be continued.)

GEORGE J. MACKAY, J.P., KENDAL.

GEORGE J. MACKAY was born in the Parish of Mey, Caithness, on 5th September, 1845, and was removed when four years of age to Olrig. He was educated at the Parish School, Castletown, where he was considered the cleverest boy in his classes. His first start in business life was made with Mr. Sinclair Bain, Ironmonger, Thurso, and he afterwards occupied situations in Leith, Glasgow, and Whitehaven (Cumberland), at which latter place he married. He went to Kendal as manager and traveller for the present Mayor, Alderman William Bindloss, J.P., D.L., and after remaining in his worship's employment for some time he started business on his own account as Horse Clothing Manufacturer, and built the finest mills in the district. He has also an old established factory at Chatteris (Cambs), which was burned down recently, and is now being replaced by mills of much larger dimensions. Mr. Mackay holds large contracts from H.M. Government, and does a large export business to the Continent and Colonies.

Mr. Mackay has for many years past taken a considerable interest in municipal affairs, and was Chairman of the Finance Committee, and member of several others. In 1890 he was elected Mayor of Kendal, and in the following year was created a J.P. for the County of Westmorland. During his term of office he had the honour to receive and entertain Her Royal Highness the Marchioness of Lorne, and other distinguished visitors. On completing his term of office the Corporation entertained him to Dinner, and presented his wife with several valuable ornaments, etc.

The subject of our sketch takes a very deep interest in the Masonic craft, and was initiated in the Union Lodge, Kendal, in December, 1872. Since then he occupied various offices, and until recently acted as Right Worshipful Provincial Grand Master of Cumberland and Westmorland. He is a Past D.P. Grand Master of the Royal Order of Scotland, and filled various offices in the Order of Knights Templar. Mr. Mackay is also Vice-Patron of the Royal Masonic Benevolent Institution for aged Freemasons, the Girls' and Boys' Schools, and has collected large sums on behalf of those noble charities. He is also a Member of 32 Degree.

Mr. Mackay has led a very active and laborious business life, and is now considering the propriety of retiring, and seeking rest and recreation in a voyage round the world. At last election he "narrowly escaped" being elected a Member of Parliament. He was invited to represent Whitehaven, but being engaged at the time in assisting the local candidate, Mr. Morley's telegram did not reach him until too late.

Like a true clansman Mr. Mackay takes a special warm interest in the Clan Mackay Society, of which he is a Life-member, and has contributed liberally to its various educational and other schemes. He also attended the grand reception given by the Clan in Glasgow to the Chief, Lord Reay, on his return from India, and delivered on that memorable occasion an eloquent address. He is a Life-member of the Glasgow and London Caithness Associations.

Although himself born in Caithness, Mr. Mackay's parents were both natives of Lord Reay's country in the north of Sutherland.

We trust that with greater leisure at his command Mr. Mackay will be soon able to take even a larger interest in matters relating to the mountain land from which he sprung, and upon which he has reflected credit.   EDITOR.

HIGHLANDERS IN THE ARCHER GUARD OF FRANCE.

(Continued from page 199).

AT the battle of Verneuil, the Earls of Buchan, Mar and Moray were slain ; and large numbers of the common soldiers must of necessity have been North Country Celts.

As long as the war with England continued, the hereditary enemies of the Saxon never ceased to pour into France and gather unfading laurels. The English hated them with a deadly race-hatred. Quarter was given to all "save the men of Wales and Scotland." No quarter for the Celt, who had battled the Saxon advance at home and now battled it abroad ! Thirty Scots were hanged in cold blood at the siege of Melun. At the battle of Verneuil nearly 9000 Scots fell. "The cause of this implacable slaughter" says one writer, "was the pride of the Scots, who would neither give nor take quarter."

After twenty-five years' hard fighting we find the Scots Guard instituted. A hasty survey of the muster roll of this famous body shows that the English military writer was scarcely correct when he assured us that the Highlanders had no share in its glory.

The rolls are somewhat difficult reading and many of the names, after passing through the alembic of a French brain, cannot be identified even as Scots, much less Highland or Lowland. The orthography, as one might expect 15th century orthography to be, is execrable, and one is frequently staggered by such names as Hourdela, Nyssuenain, Doyel, Yon, Houlphell, and

Neuserich. The Lowland Scottish names must have been comparatively easy writing for the French penman ; but one can easily imagine his difficulty with the Gaelic ones and the process by which M'Lellan might become Leolain ; or Dughal, Doyle ; or Iain, Yon. We trace a certain Doincamp through the rolls of several years until, to our surprise we find the name resolve itself into "Duncan": Doincamp being the frantic attempt of the clerk to spell "Donnachadh." Other Highland names are more easily identified. Moureau is plainly Munro ; Macrat, Macrae ; Maclaclem, MacLachlan ; and so on. We have no difficulty with Joe Maguy, who appears on the list in 1449.

In studying the Muster Rolls one is struck by their brevity, running as they do from 14 to 170 names. It must be kept in mind, however, that only the names of the gentlemen are entered, no notice being taken of the common archers. Each Highland name infers a Highland following; so that, at times, there must have been a considerable contingent in the Archer Guard. For example, on the Roll for 1449, we have, among other names which are indistinguishable, at least 33 unmistakably Celtic names. Each of these must, at the lowest computation, have had five Celts at his back, and, without doubt, men of his own clan : so that, to mention a few names, there would be 36 Stewarts, 12 Frazers, 18 Robertsons (or Donnachies), and of Rosses, Mackays, Gordons, MacDugals, Macleods, Sinclairs, MacMillans, and Macleans, 6 each, in the Guard of that year. There must have been plenty of Gaelic spoken in the barrack room of the Archer Guard in the year 1449.

A cursory survey of the lists up till about 1500 gives us the names of the following Highland Clans, some of them slightly disguised by the French spelling—others only to be guessed at :—

Cameron, Campbell, Comyn, Davidson, Frazer, Forbes, Fullarton, Graham, Grant, Gordon, Lamont, Mackay, Maclean, MacDugal, MacLachlan, MacDonell, Macrae, MacCallum, MacMillan, MacLay, Macauslan, MacKinlay, MacMorran, Maclellan, Menzies, Munro, Robertson, Ross, Sinclair and Stewart. Loude (the same man appears as Patrick Loude and Patrick Clou) is, no doubt, Macleod ; Mag Nyn may be MacKinnon ; Fagozil, which, traced through the rolls of successive years, becomes Fargozilles and finally Fergouzil, is probably Ferguson.

Many of the men seemed to have been entered under names which refer to some personal characteristic, such as "Le Petit," "Le Roy," &c.

There is one very interesting and most significant instance of this on the Roll for about 1450, viz : John Coquenen, *called the Saxon*. It

THOMAS GREER, J.P.

is hardly probable that a guard composed of Saxons would confer such a title as a distinctive name. The fact is that most English writers have exaggerated the Saxon element in Scotland; and few of them recognise the fact that what is now an English-speaking district may still be in the main Celtic. The Archer Guard in which John the Saxon found himself cannot have regarded itself as very much akin to the English, yet there were many Lowlanders in it.

It was not for nothing, it may be added in conclusion, that Sir Walter took his famous Archer from North of the Tay and sent the immortal Quentin out from Glenhoulakin,—"The Glen of the Midges" as Durward himself translated it—in the Braes of Angus.

Glasgow. JAMES FERGUSON

THOMAS GREER, J.P., F.R.G.S.

IT is an interesting study to trace the changes which have taken place in several of the Clan names, and those in connection with the Clan Gregor are perhaps as varied and interesting as any. This month we give a life like portrait of a gentleman who bears a name familiar to Scotsmen, and yet few are aware of its Highland origin.

Thomas Greer of Sea Park, Carrickfergus, was born in 1837, and is the eldest son of Alfred Greer of Dripsey House, Co. Cork, and grandson of Thomas Greer of Rhone Hill and Tullylagan, Co. Tyrone, who died in 1840.

Their ancestor, Henry Grier of Rock Hall, Alnwick, removed to Redford, Co. Tyrone, in 1653, and died in 1675. His father, Sir James Grier, Kt. of Capenoch, Dumfries-shire and Rock Hall, Alnwick, adopted the name of Grier instead of Grierson, and was the fifth son of Sir William Grierson, Kt. of Lag and Rock Hall, Dumfries-shire, seventh in descent from Gilbert Gregorson of Lag, son of Malcolm the lame Lord of MacGregor and brother of Gregor Anulich.

This Gilbert had a Charter from George Dunbar, Earl of March, to himself and heirs male, called by the name of Grierson, early in the fifteenth century; the lands of Lag were conveyed to him by a Charter from his cousin, Henry Sinclair, second Earl of Orkney, dated 6th December, 1408. The present representative is Sir Alexander Grierson, ninth Baronet of Lag, to whom Mr. Greer of Sea Park is seventh cousin. Mr. Greer was High Sheriff of Carrickfergus in 1870 and for Co. Tyrone in 1876, and M.P. for Carrickfergus from 1880 to 1886. He was the last Representative in the Imperial Parliament for that Ancient Borough. Mr. Greer married in 1864 Margaret, only child of the late John Owden of Brooklands, Co. Antrim, and niece of the late Sir Thomas Scambler Owden, Lord Mayor of London. Mr. Thomas Greer is J.P. for Co. Antrim, and a F.R.G.S., F.R.Z.S., F.R.B.S., and M.R.I.A.

Dunkeld. A. G. MURRAY MACGREGOR.

THE CHIEFTAINSHIP OF THE CLAN MACKINNON.

SIR.—I confess that the reply of Mr. Duncan MacKinnon to my communication of the 9th May is unsatisfactory. He does not attempt to deal with the schism existing, nor of the different claims to the Chieftainship, or accept my proposition to bring about a conference with the view of setting the matter at rest definitively. He cannot be unaware of the adverse feeling there exists in and out of the Clan MacKinnon Society on this topic.

It is to be lamented that Mr. D. MacKinnon has not seen my grandfather's name in the pedigrees before him. His great grandfather was of Strath, Skye, but he left it for Arran. His son, father of Alexander MacKinnon, was named Ian og MacKinnon of Corrie-Crevie. He completed his education in Glasgow, and was a pupil of Dr. Adam Smith. Then he left for Leghorn and was articled to Mr. W. Orr of that place from 1780 to 1785. Subseqently he established a Banking House at Naples; was Purveyor to the British Fleet in the Mediterranean and Admiralty Agent for Prizes, during an anxious time with regard to the War with France. I have a large collection of letters from the highest members of the aristocracy showing how much he was esteemed, including a most friendly one from H.S.H. Prince Frederic, Duke of Sussex; from Lord Andross, Secretary of State; Lord Gardenstone, etc. The latter refers to him in flattering terms in his published travels in Italy (q. v.).

I press for another opportunity to give some further facts regarding this remarkable man, up to his arrival at Buenos Ayres, that country then suffering from the effects of the Capitulation of the British Forces under General Whitelocke.

His merits were soon found out, for we find that about a dozen British Merchants there named him spokesman in the communications with the Home Government, and the nearest Minister resident at Rio de Janeiro, in the struggle against the arbitrary proceedings of the then Spanish Viceroy. These, with my grandfather, were the pioneers of British Trade, which has since been enormously extended.

Well, I do not claim the Chieftainship through him, but through my grandmother, the daughter of Charles MacKinnon of MacKinnon. There are several clans that are now represented through the female line.

I, nevertheless, keep an open mind, and, if it should be found on a careful examination that the other claimants of the branches cannot establish their pretention, and that the present Chief remains unmoved by the ordeal, then I am quite prepared to "lower my colours" and make my *salaam* to them.

Surely it is desirable to endeavour to take up this matter, and settle it once for all, and, then, "all shoulders to the wheel," to work to make the Clan MacKinnon Society a success, which it deserves.

In the meanwhile I consider myself entitled as representing the main line to sign myself, with becoming modesty, as Chief of the Clan MacKinnon.

London.   ALEX. K. MACKINNON.

SGEUL NO DHA MU DHONNACHADH BAN.

THA iad so mar a chuala mise iad :—'N uair a bha Donnachadh Bàn a' dol feadh na dùthcha a' trusadh ainmeannan na feadhnach a bhitheadh toileach a leabhar a ghabhail 'nuair a bhitheadh e deas aig na clò-bhuailtearan, thachair dha a bhi latha 's an Oban Latharnach. B' e Di-Sathuirne a bh' ann. Am feadh a bha Donnachadh a' spaidsearachd mu 'n cuairt thachair e-fhéin agus Uilleam Dubh Mac-an-t-Saoir air a' chéile. Bha soitheach aig Uilleam d' am b' ainm an "George." agus bha i air an latha sin anns a' phort. Chaidh an dà charaid còmhla do Thigh Clach-a'-gheòidh, tigh-òsda a bh' aig fear Iain Mac-an-t-Saoir. Bha Iain a' stigh, agus chuir an triùir beagan ùine seachad 'an cuideachd a' chéile. An déigh dhoibh siola no dhà a chur as an t-sealladh catorra, thubhairt Uilleam Dubh gu 'm bu mhaith leis iad a dhol comhla ris do 'n "George" agus gu 'n gabhadh iad sgrìob a mach leatha. Bha Iain agus Donnachadh toileach sinn a dheanamh, agus gun dhi-chuimhneachadh botul a dh' uisge-beatha a thoirt leo, chaidh iad air bòrd, agus sheòl iad a mach. An déigh dhoibh tilleadh thàinig an

oidhche orra mu 'n d' fhuair iad air tìr. Chaidh iad a rithist do Thigh Clach-a'-gheòidh. Bha dà leaba cas ri cois anns an t-seòmar, agus air do 'n chuideachd a bhi sgìth, cadalach, chaidh iad a laidhe. Bha Donnachadh Bàn agus Uilleam Dubh anns an aon leaba, agus ghabh Iain agus a bhean tàmh anns an leaba eile. Bha latha na Sàbaid gu maith air aghart mu 'n d' rinn iad dùsgadh. B' e Donnachadh an ceud fhear a mhosgail, agus ghlaodh e a mach, "Hò fheara! Ciod e an saod a th' oirbh an diugh ?" Fhreagair Iain, agus thubhairt e :—

    " Cha chuir mi mo chas 'am bàt',
    'S cha tèid mi gu bràth air muir,
    Oir leis na dh' òl mi 'n raoir de 'n dram
    Is truagh 'tha mo cheann an diugh ;
    Mo mhìle mallachd do Dhonnachadh Bàn
    'S mar a's feàird do Uilleam Dubh !"

B' e an t-Iain Mac-an-t-Saoir so a rinn an t-Oran Molaidh a tha 'n deireadh leabhar Dhonnachaidh Bhàin.

Bha Donnachadh air a' cheart thurus do 'n taobh tuath, agus a' dol thairis air Caol-reithe, 'n uair a fhuair e 's a' bhàta, dh' fhaighnich e de ghille-an-aisig. "Cò a's àirde air a' bhàta so ?"

Fhreagair an gille, "Thà an crann, 'n uair a tha e 'n a sheasamh !"

"Cha 'n e sin a tha mi a' ciallachadh," thubhairt Donnachadh, " 's ann a tha mi a' ciallachadh, Cò a's maighstir oirre ?"

"Thà an stiùir," thubhairt am balach, " tra bhitheas i oirre !"

'N uair a fhuair iad air tìr thug am balach Donnachadh leis do thigh 'athar a chur seachad na h-oidhche; 's thuit a mach gu 'm b' e buntàta-pronn a bh' aca gu 'n suipeir, mar bu chleachdta leo 's an dùthaich 's an àm, 's dh' fhaighnich bean-an-tighe de Dhonnachadh, " Ciamar tha 'm buntàta-pronn a'còrdadh ruibh ?"

"Bhitheadh e duilich a thoileachadh, am fear nach còrdadh am buntàta ris," thubhairt Donnachadh, "am fear leis am bu mhaith leis pronn e, gheibheadh e pronn e, agus am fear leis am bu mhaith cnapach e, gheibheadh e cnapach e !"

Is dòcha leam gu 'n robh am bùntata air a dhroch phronnadh, agus gu 'n robh cuid dheth mìn, agus cuid garbh.

Dh' fhaighnich bean-an-tighe dheth an sin, "An tusa Donnachadh Bàn nan Oran ?"

"'S mi," thubhairt esan.

"Is tusa 'rinn Beinn Dòrain !"

"'S e Dia a rinn Beinn Dòrain, ach is mise a mhol i !" Fhreagair esan.

"Is duilich nach robh an dà theanga agaibh !"

"Na 'm bitheadh an dà chànain anns an té a th' agam, dheanadh i 'n gnothach," thubhairt Donnachadh.

D. MAC ISAAC.

DUNAVERTY & ITS TRADITIONS

❊ BY ❊

J·HAMILTON·MITCHELL

PART I.

EARLY HISTORY

ON a rocky promontory in the south end of Kintyre, with a precipitous sea-wall and only to be approached from the mainland by a narrow isthmus, are the few visible remains of what was once one of the most important fortresses in Western Scotland. At what period of our history Dunaverty Castle was built we have no definite information, but it undoubtedly is of great antiquity, and comes into notice early in the annals of Scotland. Mention of it is made so far back as the time of the Danish invasions on the Scottish coasts, and there is reason to believe in its existence at an even earlier date, for we find the name of Dunaverty—though perhaps not the castle— associated with the Dalriadic or Scoto-Irish settlement on the shores of Argyle in the beginning of the sixth century. These Scoto-Irish appear to have been a branch of the great Celtic family, generally supposed to have found their way into Ireland from the western shores of North Britain, and to have established themselves in that portion of the island now known as Ulster. There they appear to have divided themselves into two different tribes or clans, the most powerful of which got the name of Cruithne (eaters of wheat), from the fact that they were addicted to agricultural pursuits. The quarrels between these rival tribes were frequent, and about the middle of the third century rose to such a height of violence, as to call for the interference of Cormac, King of Ireland at that time. Accordingly his general and cousin, Cairbre Riada, conquered a territory in the north-east part of Ireland which was possessed by the Cruithne. This tract was granted to him by the King, and denominated Dal-Riada or the portion of Riada over which Cairbre and his descendants ruled for many generations, under the protection of their more powerful relations, the Sovereigns of Ireland. The Cruithne of Ireland and the Picts of North Britain, being of the same lineage and language, kept up a constant communication with each other, and it would appear to be clearly established that a colony of the Dalriads had settled at an early period in Argyle, from which, however, they were afterwards expelled and driven back to Ireland, about the time of the Roman abdication of North Britain, in 446.

THE DALRIADIC SETTLEMENT IN ARGYLE.

In the year 503, a new colony of Dalriads or Dalriadini, under the leadership of three brothers, Lorn, Fergus, and Angus, the sons of Erc, the descendants of Cairbre Riada, came over to Argyle and settled in Kintyre. As to the causes of this settlement, which afterwards proved so important in the annals of Scotland, history throws but little light and it is doubtful whether it was obtained by force or by favour, but, as the invaders met with feeble opposition from the native tribes, the latter supposition is probably the correct one. Their chiefs had each his own territory and tribe. Lorn took possession of the district of Argyllshire, which still retains his name; Angus is supposed to have acquired away over Islay, for it was enjoyed by his son Murdoch, after his decease; and Fergus, who landed at Dunaverty, took possession of Kintyre, and on his brother Lorn's death, added his territory to his own, and so became the sole monarch of the Scots, and has ever since been recognised as the head of our Scottish kings. Dr. Skene writing on the subject, says: "The Firth of Clyde is universally allowed to have been the boundary which separated the Dalriads from the Strathclyde Britons, and consequently it follows that Dalriada, or the territory of the Scots in Britain, must have been confined to South Argyle, or that part of the country lying to the south of Linne Loch; and the Scots appear to have maintained their possession of a territory so inconsiderable in comparison with that of the Picts, partly by the strong natural boundaries and impervious nature of the country itself, and partly by the close connection which they at all times preserved with the Irish"—("Highlanders of Scotland," Vol. I., p. 33). The same author also says of the three tribes of Lorn, Cowal, and Kintyre, "that of Kintyre attained to so great power as eventually to obtain the supreme authority over all Scotland"—(Vol. II., p. 9).

From Cairbre Riada or Ruadh, Kintyre and the adjacent lands got the name of Dalruaidh or the portion of Ruadh; the Scots were called Dalruadhini; and their capital or seat of Government, Dalruadhain, which was afterwards changed to Campbeltown. For nearly three centuries and a half this town continued to be the seat of Government and the capital of the Scottish kingdom, until 843, when Kenneth the Second, having finally subdued the Picts, merged into one the two kingdoms of Picts and

TARBERT, LOCHFYNE.

Scots, and transferred the seat of Government to Forteviot, in Perthshire.

DANISH INVASIONS.

On the seat of Government being thus changed, Kintyre became a prey to foreign invaders and an asylum for pirates. The Danes and Norwegians had already got firm possession of the vast portion of the Western Isles, and making frequent incursions into the very heart of the kingdom, put it entirely out of the Sovereign's power to pay any attention to the frontiers. They fortified the Castle of Dunaverty, and made it their principal stronghold on that part of the coast; and during their rule, the neighbouring country suffered the same fate as the other islands with which it was classed.

It is, however, at a later period, that we come to the history proper of Dunaverty. As the author of "Glencreggan" remarks: "Where you come upon the track of a Lord of the Isles you may feel pretty sure that you are upon the footsteps of war and violence; and as Dunaverty Castle was one of the great strongholds of the Macdonalds, who were Lords of the Isles and Lords of Cantyre, we may be certain that this rocky promontory formed no exception to the peaceful rule." No, not by any means an exception as we shall afterwards see, but meantime it may not be out of place to say something here about this illustrious family who owned Dunaverty, and who for so long were the ruling power in the Western Highlands.

(To be continued).

SIR CHARLES A. CAMERON.

THE CELTIC MONTHLY:
A MAGAZINE FOR HIGHLANDERS.
Edited by JOHN MACKAY, Kingston.

No. 12. Vol. II.]   SEPTEMBER, 1894.   [Price Threepence.

SIR CHARLES ALEXANDER CAMERON·

SIR CHARLES ALEX. CAMERON is the youngest and only surviving son of the late Captain Ewen Cameron, a Highlander who served with distinction in the Peninsular Wars and was wounded severely eight times. Captain Cameron married Belinda Smith, an Irishwoman, which no doubt accounts for the fact that their son was born in Dublin and not in Lochaber. Sir Charles received his early education in Schools in Dublin and Guernsey. He was intended for the army, but his father dying when his son was only thirteen years old, this intention was abandoned on the ground of expense, as in those days an Ensign's commission cost £400 to purchase, beside the expense of an outfit. Sir C. Cameron has devoted himself to Science in several of its departments, more especially Chemistry, Geology, Agriculture, and Hygiene. As a Student in Germany he gained the esteem of the celebrated Chemist, Baron Liebig, to whom he dedicated one of his works. Sir Charles Cameron is the author of a large work, entitled "A Manual of Hygiene and Compendium of the Sanitary Laws;" and of several works on Food, Sanitation, and Agricultural Chemistry. He edited six editions of Johnston's well-known Agricultural Chemistry (Blackwood, Edinburgh), and wrote the treatise on that subject in Cassells' Technical Educator. His *opus magnum* is the History of the Royal College of Surgeons in Ireland, which, however, is really a history of the healing art in Ireland since the earliest ages. It contains three hundred biographies of eminent Irish medical men. Sir Charles has translated a Volume of Poems from the German, and in his earlier days was a constant contributor to the newspaper and serial press. Sir Charles Cameron is a D.P.H. and ex-Examiner in the University of Cambridge, and is Examiner in the Royal University of Ireland. He was this year re-elected President of the Society of Public Analysts of Great Britain and Ireland, and

[SIR CHARLES A. CAMERON.

for four years was President of the British Institute of Public Health. He was President of the Royal College of Surgeons in Ireland; of the Irish Medical Association; of the Metropolitan (Dublin) Society of Medical Officers of

Health : and of the Surgical and Public Health Sections of the Academy of Medicine. He is an Honorary Member of many Societies, for example, the Swedish Academy of Medicine ; the Hygienic Societies of France, Belgium, Paris, Bordeaux ; the State Medical Society of California ; the Royal Hibernian Academy. which corresponds to the London Royal Academy and the Scottish Society of Arts.

He presided in 1892 at the Sanitary Congress (at Portsmouth) of the Sanitary Institute, and his address formed the subject of leading articles in scores of Newspapers in the United Kingdom, India, and the Colonies. The *Times* devoted nearly a page to it. Sir Charles holds numerous appointments. He is Professor of Chemistry and Hygiene ; R.C.S.I. Lecturer of Agricultural Chemistry to the Commissioners of National Education. He is the Chief Medical Officer of Health of Dublin, and the whole Sanitary department of that city is directly under his control. He is Consultant for various Government departments, and Public Analyst for the greater number of the Irish Counties and Cities. He is a Member of the Army Sanitary Committee, and has been a Member of various Commissions and of the Juries of International Exhibitions.

Sir Charles was married in 1862 to Lucie, daughter of John Macnamara, an Irish Lawyer: who died in 1883, leaving seven children. "Men and Women of the Times" and "Contemporary Medical Men," etc., contain memoirs of Sir Charles Cameron.

To Highlanders Sir Charles is known as an enthusiastic Cameron, and the hearty reception which was accorded to him two years ago when he presided at the Annual Social Gathering of the Clan in Glasgow showed the high respect in which he is held by his Clansmen and by Highlanders generally.

Kirkintilloch.   JOHN CAMERON, J.P.

A MINOR POET.

AT the close of an Autumn day, which had begun in brilliant sunshine, and was closing in mist and driving rain, a belated traveller found refuge in the smoky mystery of a Highland farmhouse kitchen.

He was a man of evident culture, with a handsome shrewd face, framed in snowy hair ; and, as he and the old farmer talked together, in the grateful glow of the peat fire, they found many points in common.

In the background, a sturdy short-gowned lass was washing dishes, and scouring pots. A young man sat well back in the shadow, listening intently to the conversation, and frowning impatiently at the girl, who, in a spirit of mischief, was squirting water on him from her tub.

"Have ye suppered the brown quey, Donal'?"

The farmer swung round on his chair, and darted the question at the young man in the corner.

A muttered, inarticulate answer came out of the darkness ; Donald then advanced, and took down a lantern from over the fireplace, in sullen silence.

"It is a glorious country, this of yours!" continued the traveller. "It would make a poet of a man, whether he would or no."

"God save us from poets, sir, we've too many poets here ! It is honest, dependable men we're in sore want of—not paper and pencil 'Amadain'."

As he spoke, the old man glowered wrathfully on Donald, who made a hasty exit, amid the suppressed tittering of the herd lad who had just come in, and the giggling of the girl.

"Well, Donald Mackenzie, I hear you are a poet."

Donald, hard at work cleaning out the byre in the morning, looked up with a crimson face and a quick suspicious glance. He was a broad-shouldered, well-knit youth, with an aquiline type of face, and large light-blue eyes, which kindled and darkened under excitement.

His eyes fell, under the grave, kindly inspection of the belated traveller of the night before, and he stood awkwardly leaning on his grape.

"Would you mind guiding me to the nearest station, if I got you a day's holiday to do it in, Donald?"

Donald was electrified. "Indeed, sir, I will be very proud to do it," he responded eagerly. He gripped the barrow-load of manure blocking the doorway, trundled it out of the way, and stood outside, cap in hand.

"Well, then ; will you be ready to start in an hour's time?"

"I will, sir."

The stranger made his way to the house. Donald hauled the overturned barrow out of the midden, and resumed his byre cleaning in a frenzy of haste.

"Well, now, Mackenzie ; what about this poetry?" questioned the stranger, when they had left the farm about a mile behind them.

Once more the young man blushed like a girl. For answer, he pulled a bulky package from an inner coat-pocket and handed it to his questioner, with a hand which slightly trembled.

They were passing through a fir wood. "We will stop here and consider the matter," said the gentleman, seating himself on a fallen tree, and undoing the package, with great deliberation.

Donald watched the examination of the package with pathetic anxiety. He leant against a tree, his lip trembling, his colour coming and going, as one after another, his precious papers were skimmed over, and laid aside.

"There is far too much of Donald Mackenzie here," said the gentleman at last, raising his eyes and looking straight into Donald's face. "Don't write another line of verse for the next two years, if you want to write anything worth reading."

The young man took the parcel without a word, and walked on by the stranger's side, his lip firm, but his face ghastly pale under the sun tan.

His companion had been attentively watching him. "Donald," he said, "I have not given you your death-blow, though that is what you are thinking. I have been through it all before you, man, and I tell you it rests with yourself, whether you make a spoon or spoil a horn. You are only twenty-three; give up dreaming; put your poetry into your work; and gather grit and backbone, man."

"The papers have printed some of them."

"The papers print a deal of rubbish."

"I may as well be dead and buried at once, if I am to live the life of a clod!" Donald burst out, fiercely, after a long pause.

"That is quite true."

He turned a puzzled, suspicious look on the face of the stranger; but it was calm and meditative.

"Did it never strike you, young man, that your heart could never be nourished on waterfalls and mountains, sunsets and sunrises? What is a poet worth, if he does not take his share of the burden of humanity—if he does not feel and suffer, with and for, his fellow creatures! Leave the rocks and the mountains alone for a time; and try, in the next twelve months, what you can do to make those around you happier and better, and never fear, all the poetry in you will have scope enough."

Still the youth shambled along by the stranger's side, with blank despair in his downcast countenance. His gait had lost all the easy spring of the true Highlander, his shoulders drooped, and his step was heavy.

"Donald Mackenzie! are you a selfish coward after all?"

Donald started out of his gloomy reverie, and faced round on his adviser, in angry surprise, at this stern demand. He subsided before the other's steady gaze, and muttered, resentfully, "A man must have time to gather himself up, when his house is levelled on the top of him."

They had reached the crest of a hill. Below them lay a well-watered valley.

"Is that the station?" asked the stranger, pointing to a faint haze of blue smoke, about two miles off.

"It is, sir."

"Then I can find my way. Now, Donald Mackenzie, if I'm alive and well I'll look you up next year. And don't forget, that there is grander poetry in your own old bible—lying neglected in the bottom of your trunk, perhaps—grander poetry, I say, than you or I could ever write."

"I'm not one that can turn round and lick the hand that thrashes me," Donald jerked out, when they parted, "but I'm not without sense, sir, and I'll come to it in time—I'll come to it in time."

But his literary vanity and ambition died hard. He sat on a rock for hours, gazing with blank eyes over the moor, with the wild Highland cattle and sheep sniffing and stamping round, at intervals. "Fool! fool!" he shouted, as he thought of his mad exultation on receipt of his first proof-sheet. And as the cattle scampered away, snorting and tossing their heads, he flung himself, face downward, on the heather, and wept like a four-year-old boy.

But in the still hours of the night, he swung himself down from his sleeping loft overhead, uncovered the "smoored" kitchen fire, and watched his air castles vanish in smoke and flame.

On the morrow, he faced the future, empty of everything but the sacred purpose which led him, in the end, by a way that he knew not, to an honoured place among the good men of the earth.

Pitlochry.   K. S. CAMERON.

DESCENDANTS OF ALLAN CAMERON.

Sir.—I note no one has replied to a query in the July number by D. C. as to the descendants of Allan Cameron. The following are all the facts known, viz:—

Allan Cameron (Ailean Mac Iain Duibh) XVI. Chief of Lochiel, who died about the year 1645, married a daughter of Stewart of Appin by whom he had issue.—1st. John, who married in 1626 Lady Margaret (daughter of Robert Campbell of Glenfalloch, who in 1640 succeeded his brother Sir Colin in the estates and baronetcy of Glenorchy, and became father of the first Earl of Breadalbane), with issue; 1st Ewen (the famous Sir Ewen Cameron of Lochiel); 2nd Allan, who married in 1666 Jean, sister of James Macgregor of Macgregor. He was a man of many parts, but died early and there is no record of any issue of the marriage.

W. D. N.

A MILITARY CONTRAST.—Last year, the total number of recruits for the whole of Scotland was 2485. This is a paltry number when compared with the 40,000 men who were raised in the Highlands alone, in six short years, from 1793 to 1799.

THE HIGHLAND BRIGADE AT WATERLOO BY JOHN MACKAY C.E. J.P. HEREFORD

PART I.—(*Continued from page 219*).

CAPTAIN MENZIES, a tall, powerful man, and an excellent swordsman, fought outside the square like a hero of antiquity, but his good claymore was no match for the long Polish lance. He received a severe wound in the chest which unhorsed him. Lying on his back he saw another lancer aiming a thrust at him. Quickly rolling himself round to avoid the blow, he grasped the foot of the lancer and pulled him off his horse. The foe fell on the top of him; another lancer riding by, saw the struggle, and made a thrust at the gallant Menzies, who instantly grasped the lancer and placed him in a way to receive the thrust. The enemy was killed and Menzies freed himself of his weight. After being unhorsed a drummer boy got hold of the horse. A private of his company (grenadier) Donald Mackintosh, came to Menzies' assistance. He was immediately mortally wounded. The little drummer seeing Donald fall, left the horse to come to his assistance. A lancer noticing the horse unattended, thought him a fair prize and made a dash to capture it. This did not escape the watchful and keen eye of the dying Highlander, who, with all the provident spirit of his country "ruling strong even in death," groaned out, "Hoot, man, ye manna tak that beast, it belangs to oor Captain here." The lancer understanding nothing of this remonstrance and respecting less the writhing gesture it provoked, seized the horse, and was making off with it, when Donald loaded his musket for the last time and shot him dead—and the next moment fell back, and expired content. Another private of his company now came up, and asked his Captain what he could do to assist him? "Nothing, my good friend, but load your piece and finish me." "But your eye still looks lively" (said the devoted grenadier) "If I could move you to the 92nd fighting yonder I think you would yet do well." With the aid of a fellow grenadier he was moved, and soon seen by Colonel Cameron of the 92nd, who instantly ordered him every possible needful aid. Four men carried him in a blanket to the rear. While they were raising him Colonel Cameron exclaimed, "God bless you, I must be off,—the devils (meaning the French) are at us again—I must stand up to them." He did so, and in a few minutes thereafter, the brave and gallant Cameron of the 92nd was wounded and stretched upon the field. It is a pleasure to add that the gallant Captain Menzies of the Grenadier Company of the Black Watch survived for some years, to wear the honourable decorations and marks of *sixteen wounds* received in this arduous and unequal conflict. Still the battle reeled hither and thither in the throes of mortal desperation. In vain Ney's splendid cuirassiers and lancers dashed upon the 42nd. They might as well have ridden against a wall of iron. For more than two hours the Black Watch unflinchingly bore the hurstling storm of the French artillery and the repeated charges of cavalry and infantry, repelling every attack in square, or in a more extended formation, till reinforcements came up towards 5 p.m. In the next chapter we shall deal with the deeds of the 79th and 92nd round Quatre Bras, and afterwards with the doughty deeds performed at Waterloo by the Highland Brigade.

"For those are deeds which must not pass away,
    And names that must not wither, though the earth
Forgets her Empires with a just decay,
    The enslaver, and the enslaved, their death and
        birth."

PART II.—THE 79TH CAMERON HIGHLANDERS.

The 79th Cameron Highlanders, like the 42nd, were fearfully cut up at the Battle of Toulouse. Out of 494 officers and men who took part in that action, only 263 came out unwounded, showing a loss of 231 officers and men, while the 42nd lost 321 officers and men. The importance of the positions carried by these two regiments was so great, that their capture decided the fortunes of the day and compelled the French to retreat and abandon Toulouse. The behaviour of these regiments was so gallant and intrepid that they won special commendation from the Duke of Wellington, being two of the four regiments particularly mentioned in his despatch of 12th April, 1814. The 79th landed in Cork on the 26th July, 1814, where its shattered ranks were filled by a large draft

DEPARTURE OF THE HIGHLAND BRIGADE.

from the 2nd Battalion. In February, 1815, it set sail for America, but was driven back by contrary winds. It again sailed for the same destination on the 1st of March, when providentially it was also driven back by the same cause, and was then sent to Belfast. Here in May it was called upon to take part in that fierce and final struggle with Napoleon at Quatre Bras and Waterloo, and assist in putting an end to his bloody machinations against the peace of Europe. The 79th joined the army of Wellington at Brussels, and was brigaded with the 28th, 32nd, and 95th, under the command of Sir James Kempt, in Picton's division.

On the dread night of the 15th June, 1815, the alarm rapidly spread that the French had crossed the frontier and were rapidly approaching. The 79th were the first to muster ready for the march to meet their old opponents, and by 4 a.m. were on the road to Charleroi, provisioned for three days. Byron, in a stanza of "Childe Harold," thus refers to the Cameron Highlanders.—

"And wild and high the Camerons' Gathering rose,
The war note of Lochiel, which Albyn's hills
Have heard, and heard too, have her Saxon foes:—
How in the noon of night that pibroch thrills
Savage and shrill! But with the breath that fills
Their mountain pipe, so fill the mountaineers
With the fierce native daring which instills
The stirring memories of a thousand years,
And Evan's, Donald's fame rings in each clansman's ears."

The gallant Camerons marched on through the forest of Soignes, past Waterloo towards Genappe, hearing on their way the roar of cannon and the rattle of musketry, towards Quatre Bras, within half a mile of the enemy, from whom the column was separated by a rising ground. From this position a full view was obtained of the French, obliquely to the left, and in movement to their front. The 79th formed the extreme left of the division, which after a very short halt broke off to the left, lining the road to Namur, the banks of which were here ten to twelve feet high on each side. The ground had scarcely been so taken up when the enemy advanced in great force, sending out "a cloud of sharp-shooters." The light companies of the first brigade, with the 8th company and marksmen of the 79th, were sent forward to meet them. These gallant men maintained their ground bravely for an hour in spite of the constantly increasing numbers of the enemy, but as the French sharp-shooters had by this time picked off nearly all the artillerymen serving the only two British guns that had come into action, and most of the officers, and as the French were in such force in front Wellington directed Picton to detach a regiment to the front to cover the guns, and drive the enemy from his advanced position. Kempt thereupon rode up to Colonel Douglas, telling him that upon the Cameron Highlanders would devolve the honour of executing his Grace's orders. Gallantly was this order obeyed and performed. At a bound the regiment cleared the banks in its front, fired a volley, and immediately charging with the bayonet drove the French advanced troops with great precipitation and in disorder to a hedge about a hundred yards in their rear, where they attempted to reform, but were followed up with such alacrity that they again gave way, and were pursued to another hedge about the same distance, from which they were again driven in confusion upon their main column, which was formed in great

strength upon the rising ground opposite. The 79th now joined by its detached companies began firing volleys upon the enemy from behind the last mentioned hedge, and in the course of fifteen minutes expended nearly all its ammunition. Whilst in this exposed situation it was ordered to retire, which it accomplished as if on parade, although it had a broad ditch to leap and the first hedge to repass, when it formed line about fifty yards in advance of its original position. Being here much exposed to the fire from the enemy's guns it was ordered to lie down, and so continued for nearly an hour, when it was again directed to resume its first position in the Namur road, and form in column as circumstances might require. Being afterwards repeatedly threatened by cavalry it formed and moved forward in square, but without being attacked.

(*To be continued*).

W. A. MARTIN,
SECRETARY, GAELIC SOCIETY OF LONDON.

THE subject of this sketch is a young Highlander, well and favourably known for his earnest and practical enthusiasm in the matters Highland of London. A Lewis man by birth and a true Gael in heart, Mr. Martin received his early education, first in the Free Church School, and afterwards in the Nicholson Institution, in his native town, Stornoway. He completed it at King's College, London, and afterwards joined the staff of Messrs. Gray, Dawes & Co., Merchants, and London Agents to the British India Steam Navigation Company, Limited. Here he remained for over seven years, when he left them (a year ago) for an appointment with the New Zealand Shipping Company, Limited.

As already stated, Mr. Martin takes an active part in all the Highland movements in London. He is Joint Honorary Secretary of the Gaelic Society of London; a Member of the London and Northern Counties Camanachd Club; the London Highland Amateur Athletic Club; the London Ross and Cromarty Association, and of several other Highland Societies. He is also an enthusiastic volunteer, and is a non-commissioned officer of that deservedly popular corps, the London Scottish Rifle Volunteers; and F. Company, over which Captain Glynn Smith holds command, shows no one with a more soldierly bearing than the subject of this sketch.

Mr. Martin is not yet thirty, and has therefore a life before him. Let us wish him, then, a long and happy one, with health and strength to make his mark in the world that lies before him. *Lean gu dluth ri cliu do shinnsir.*

London.   T. D. MACDONALD.

W. A MARTIN

DUNAVERTY & ITS TRADITIONS
* BY *
J. HAMILTON-MITCHELL

PART II.

THE LORDS OF THE ISLES.

According to Towry's "Clanship and the Clans," the founder of the family of the Isles was Gillebride MacGille Adamnan, who had the ill fortune to be expelled from his possessions by the Norwegians, and sought refuge in Ireland. Having received assistance from the MacQuarries and MacMahons he afterwards undertook an expedition for the recovery of his territories, but was unsuccessful; and it was left to his son to retrieve the fortunes of his house. This son was Somerled—the "mighty Somerled" of Scott. Putting himself at the head of the inhabitants of Morven, he expelled the Norwegian invaders, and soon became Master of Morven, Lochaber, and Argyle; and in order to secure the Isles for his posterity, he carried off and married the daughter of Olaf, Norwegian King of the Isles. By her he had three sons, Dougall, Reginald, and Angus.

Somerled having so far been successful, now sought a wider sphere for his operations. After an attempt to secure the Earldom of Moray for his grandsons, his next great aim was to depose Malcolm IV., in favour of the "Boy of Egremont" (William, grandson of Duncan, a son of Malcolm Canmore); but after many conflicts he was ultimately repulsed by Gilchrist, Earl of Angus, and a treaty of peace was concluded in 1153, held to be of such importance that it formed an era in dating Scottish Charters. The fiery spirit of this warrior, however, once again asserted itself, and in a second rising in 1161, Somerled with his army appeared at Renfrew,

on the Clyde, where he was met by the Steward of Scotland with a large force, and slain along with Gillecallum, a son born of a previous marriage. Gillecallum's son, Somerled II., then succeeded to his grandfather's possessions in the Highlands, while Dougall, above mentioned, acquired sway over the Isles.

Somerled II. remained in undisturbed possession till 1221, when he took part in an insurrection which caused Alexander II. to march against him. Collecting an army in Lothian and Galloway, the Scottish King sailed for Argyle, but was overtaken on the way by a storm and driven into the Clyde. A second attempt, however, proved more successful, and Somerled was compelled to retire to the Isles. At the same time, Argyle was raised into a Sheriffdom, with Gillespie Campbell of Lochawe as hereditary Sheriff.

In the Sagas, under the name of Sundereyan Kings, appear the two sons of Dougall—Dougall Scrag, and Duncan. On these Princes refusing to yield even a nominal homage to Norway, King Haco despatched his commander Uspac, with a fleet to reduce them to obedience; but the leader of the expedition was in reality a brother of the two men he had been sent to subdue, and abandoning the service of Haco, united himself to them. Upon this Haco himself advanced against them, and ultimately slew Dougall Scrag and his ally Somerled II. Uspac and Duncan escaped, but the former was afterwards slain in Bute. Duncan subsequently reasserted his authority, and founded the Priory of Ardchattan in Lorn. His son and successor, Ewen, continued his allegiance to Haco.

DUNAVERTY ATTACKED BY THE NORWEGIANS.

The troubled state of the Isles at this period and the wavering allegiance of many of those northern chiefs who were the acknowledged vassals of Scotland, were a source of continual annoyance and anxiety to the Scottish monarch (Alexander II.) and it became necessary for him to devise some means to maintain his superiority over this portion of his territories. Accordingly, when all efforts to come to a compromise with Norway had failed, the chiefs whom he had completely bound over to his interest, were commissioned to attack the more steady adherents of that nation, and ravage their dominions by fire and sword till they were thus reduced to such a state of misery and weakness, as to be glad to supplicate for forgiveness and embrace the friendship of the Scottish King. Acting under the influence of this policy, Allan, Earl of Galloway, a faithful vassal of Scotland, with a fleet of a hundred and fifty ships set out in 1228 and attacked and conquered the dominions of Olave the Black, King of Man. To revenge this insult Haco despatched an expedition to the Western Isles in 1230, and succeeded in re-establishing his vassal, Olave, in his kingdom of Man, though in other respects his expedition did not meet with much success. The Norwegians were violently opposed in Islay, and again in an assault on Dunaverty Castle, they lost three hundred of their men. The castle on this occasion was bravely defended by one of the chiefs of the Stewarts; and when Haco's soldiers afterwards attempted a descent on Kintyre on

SALTPANS AND MACHRIHANISH BAY, KINTYRE.

their return from Man, they were repulsed with much loss and compelled to return to Norway. Haco, however, notwithstanding this defeat peremptorily refused to acknowledge the property of the Scottish Crown in the Western Isles and indignantly rejected a subsequent proposal of Alexander to purchase their surrender by payment of a large sum of money. The Scottish monarch had now no other course open to him than to resort to arms, and having assembled a powerful fleet he declared that he would conquer the Isles and plant his standard on the cliffs of Thurso, Caithness at that time being a Norwegian province. Death, however prevented the accomplishment of these designs for the King had not proceeded farther than the little island of Kerrera off the coast of Lorn, when he was seized with a mortal illness and died on 8th July, 1249. The account of his death as it is given in the Norwegian Chronicle, is striking and romantic: "King Alexander," it says, "then lying in Kiararey Sound, dreamed a dream, and thought three men came unto him. He thought one of them was in Royal robes, but very stern, ruddy in countenance, something thick, and of middling size. Another seemed of a slender make, but active, and of all men the most engaging and majestic. The third, again, was of very great stature, but his features were distorted, and of all the rest he was the most unsightly. They addressed their speech to the King, and enquired whether he meant to invade the Hebrides. Alexander thought he answered, that he certainly proposed to subject the islands.

The genius of the vision bade him go back, and told him no other measure would turn to his advantage. The King related his dream, and many advised him to return, but the King would not; and a little time after he was seized with a disorder, and died. The Scottish army then broke up, and they removed the King's body to Scotland. The Hebridians say, that the men whom the King saw in his sleep, were Saint Olave, King of Norway; Saint Magnus, Earl of Orkney; and Saint Columba."

Alexander III. on attaining his majority, resolved to complete the designs of his father, and sent the Earl of Ross against the Isles. Haco collected an army and assisted by many Highland chiefs, determined to oppose the forces of the Scottish King, and if possible assert his supremacy over the territories in question. In 1263 both armies met at Largs where, as we know, the Norwegians were totally routed and Haco's hopes for ever blasted. Ewen who during the hostilities had changed his mind and remained neutral, died without male issue, and the Lordship of the Isles then passed to the descendants of Reginald, second son of Somerled I. This Reginald was a more powerful Prince even than his father, and it was from him that those Macdonalds of Kintyre who in other days ruled with Princely state at Saddell and Dunaverty, were descended. Kintyre paid the Lords of the Isles a yearly tribute of five hundred cows. Islay contributed another five hundred, and the other isles a like proportion.

ROBERT BRUCE VISITS THE CASTLE.

One of the Macdonalds surnamed Angus Og, was the friend of King Robert the Bruce in his adversity and sheltered him at Saddell and afterwards at Dunaverty whence he crossed over to Rathlin after his defeat at Methven in 1306. This chieftain was the selfsame

" . . . heir of mighty Somerled,
Ronald, from many a hero sprung,
The fair, the valiant, and the young,
Lord of the Isles, whose lofty name
A thousand bards have given to fame;"

the true name of the hero as Sir Walter Scott explains in a foot note being exchanged for Ronald euphoniae gratia. It was to this Angus also, on his arrival at Torwood, near Falkirk, that Bruce addressed these words still borne as a motto by the lineal descendants of the Lords of the Isles: "My hope is constant in thee." The monarch had waited long and anxiously and was even beginning to suspect the chieftain's allegiance, for Edward II. of England with a mighty force was fast approaching and the battle which was to decide the fate of Scotland was at hand. Angus, however, like a true Highlander proved as good as his word and nobly repaid his monarch's confidence by his valiant bearing at

Bannockburn. It is to that juncture indeed that the poet transfers the words of Bruce:—

" Lord of the Isles, my trust in thee,
Is firm as Ailsa Rock;
Rush on with Highland sword and targe,
I, with my Carrick spearmen charge;
Now, forward to the shock!"

Upon the failure of the line of Reginald by the slaughter of Ronald in 1346, the Lordship of the Isles was inherited by John Macdonald, Chief of the Clan Donald, who had married his third cousin Amy, sister of Ronald; and in this family it remained until the failure of the direct line by the death of Donald Dhu in 1545.

James IV. ascended the Scottish throne in 1488 and in the sixth year of his reign thrice visited the Highlands and the Isles, and having penetrated as far as Dunstaffnage and Mingarry, reduced most of the refractory chiefs to obedience. The Lord of the Isles, however, refused to submit and the King not being then in a condition to attack him in his strongholds with any prospect of success, returned to Edinburgh, where he assembled a Parliament which declared the title and possession of John, then Lord of the Isles, to be forfeited to the Crown. Since that period the title has been borne by the heir-apparent to the Scottish throne.

CAPTURED BY JAMES IV.

When proceeding on his first expedition, James landed at Tarbert, Loch Fyne, and having repaired the fort originally built there by his great ancestor Robert the Bruce, he provided it with artillery and skilful gunners. On his return in July he also seized the Castle of Dunaverty and placed a garrison in it for the purpose of reducing to submission the rude and turbulent chiefs of the district. This act gave great offence to Sir John Macdonald of Islay who it is said had nourished the hope of regaining possession of Kintyre which at one time had belonged to his family. On the first favourable opportunity the infuriated chieftain collected his followers, laid siege to the Castle and being successful showed his contempt for the royal authority by hanging the governor over the wall in sight of the King and his fleet. This savage revolt took James completely by surprise, but as most of his followers were absent on another expedition, he was unable to take immediate steps to punish the rebel chief. But so promptly were measures taken for the vindication of the royal authority, that in a short time Sir John and his four sons were captured and conveyed to Edinburgh where they were found guilty of high treason and executed on the Boroughmuir, a huge tract of land in the neighbourhood of what is now known as the district of Bruntsfield.

(To be continued.)

TO CORRESPONDENTS.

All Communications, on literary and business matters, should be addressed to the Editor, Mr. JOHN MACKAY, 17 Dundas Street, Kingston, Glasgow.

🙶

TERMS OF SUBSCRIPTION.— The *CELTIC MONTHLY* will be sent, post free, to any part of the United Kingdom, Canada, the United States, and all countries in the Postal Union—for one year, 4s.

THE CELTIC MONTHLY

SEPTEMBER, 1894

CONTENTS.

OUR NEXT ISSUE.

As we begin our third volume with the October issue we intend making it a specially attractive number. With it we will present our readers with life-like plate portraits of Mr. Alexander Mackay, J.P., Wilts, President of the Clan Mackay Society; Lieut. Colonel Duncan Menzies, J.P., of Blarich, Commanding the 1st Sutherland Highland Rifle Volunteers; and Alderman Thomas Bantock, Wolverhampton, a distinguished native of Golspie. In addition to these a number of very interesting contributions will appear, which will be profusely illustrated.

To Subscribers.—We beg to remind our readers that the Annual Subscriptions for Volume III. are now due We are most anxious to complete our list of Annual Subscribers for next volume, and will esteem it a favour if those who intend renewing their Subscriptions for another year would kindly forward a postal order for 4/- to the Editor, *Celtic Monthly*, 17 Dundas Street, Kingston, Glasgow, at once. We shall feel greatly obliged if our readers will give this matter their immediate attention.

Bound Copies of Volume II.—As we will be able to supply only a limited number of copies of this handsome volume those who wish any are requested to apply to the Editor at once. The prices are Bound in strong leather, with gilt lettering, 8/-; cloth, 6/6. Post free.

Gaelic Society of Inverness.—The Annual Concert in connection with this flourishing Society was held in Inverness on the Evening of the Wool Market, Mr. C. Fraser-Mackintosh, Chief, occupied the Chair, and was supported by a large number of notable Highlanders. The Concert was a brilliant success, the programme being a specially attractive one. The popular chairman delivered a most interesting address on Gaelic music, and urged on Highlanders to cultivate more the beautiful melodies of their own land. Miss Lizzie B. Mackay, Glasgow, was the leading vocalist, and received a hearty reception from the audience.

Mr. T. D. MacDonald, London, whose name is familiar to so many of our readers has, we understand, accepted the management of the Rideau Club, Ottawa, Canada, and leaves for the Dominion in September. Mr. MacDonald is a thorough good Highlander, and has taken an active part in all the great national, social, and literary Highland movements for many years past, and we are glad to learn that his countrymen intend presenting him with a handsome testimonial as a mark of their esteem. Mr. W. A. Martin, 24 Beauclerc Road, London, W., acts as Secretary, and will be glad to receive subscriptions from Mr. MacDonald's many friends. We trust that his valuable services will be adequately acknowledged. He has our best wishes for his prosperity in the land of his adoption.

We have again to acknowledge our indebtedness to Mr. Adam Millar (Messrs. William Cross & Co., 45 Montrose Street, Glasgow) for the use of several valuable engravings for reproduction in the *Celtic Monthly*. He has kindly placed his splendid collection of Highland books, prints and paintings at our disposal for engraving purposes, and we hope to give fine copies of these from time to time.

We are also indebted to Mr. William Graham of North Erines, and Mr. John Cameron, J.P., Kirkintilloch, for two of the plates used in this issue; and to Mrs. Ramsay of Kildalton, Islay, for a photograph of Dunyvaig Castle of which we give an excellent reproduction.

The Mod or Gathering of the Highland Association takes place in Oban on 11th September. We trust that as many as possible of our readers will attend. Full particulars will be found in our advertising pages.

The Glasgow Cowal Shinty Club have recently been making themselves useful in contributing to the success of the Highland Sports at Edinburgh and Dunoon. At both these gatherings this famous club sent two picked teams who gave a spirited exhibition game of shinty, which on each occasion aroused great enthusiasm among the spectators, and proved the most exciting item on the programme. They are still open to send teams to other sports, in the hope that in this way they may revive an interest in the grand old Highland game.

The Corry MacKinnons.—We are obliged to the lady of the MacKinnon Clan who kindly sent us a copy of the pamphlet stating the claims of the Corry branch of the Clan to the Chieftainship. We have read it with much interest.

Dr. Archibald Campbell, Captain of the Glasgow Cowal Shinty Club, has just taken his degree at Glasgow University, and the interesting event was duly celebrated at a Social Meeting of the members, when the Doctor was heartily congratulated on his success.

THE LAST MACDONALDS OF ISLAY

BY CHARLES FRASER-MACKINTOSH, F.S.A.(Scot)

DUNYVAIG CASTLE ISLAY

PART X.—PRIOR OF ORONSAY'S BOND; TROUBLES OF SIR JAMES MACDONALD; AND DESTRUCTION OF DUNYVAIG CASTLE.

THE next document I have of Sir James Macdonald's is a Bond by Ronald M'Connald vic Iain of Iland, which is as follows, modernized :—

I have not identified the granter, unless he were owner of the Isles at the mouth of Loch Kilkeran, sometimes called "Island Davaar," and have some doubt where Knockransay is situated, probably in Loch Ranza of Arran, or the five merk land in South Kintyre called "Knockreanoch." The Witnesses were all men of note.

"Be it known to all men by these present letters, the Ronald M'Connald of Iland, vic can to have granted, confessed, and accepted as by these presents grants, confesses and accepts the Right Honourable Sir James M'Connald of Knockransay, Knight, as my superior Master and Foster, and therefore by the tenure hereof binds and obliges me to fortify against and defend the said Sir James with all my whatsoever force, strength, and might, that I can or may have, either of men or gear, in all his actions, errands or business in whatsoever places he have or shall have to do, contrar and against all deadly or mortals without any exception in all times hereafter, and for the more verification of all and sundry the premises the said Ronald has sub-

scribed these presents with my hand as follows. At Knockransay the 9th day of March, 1597 years, before these witnesses, Gorrie vic Allister of Lupe, Archibald M'Connald of Largie, and Archibald M'Allister of Crossage, with others diverse. I Ronald M'Connald with my hand at the pen led by the writer under written because I could not write myself. (Signed), Johne M'Kay, writer hereof as witness, etc."

The next and last of my original documents is most interesting referring as it does to Oronsay, that Sacred Isle adjoining Colonsay, where by tradition Columba first set foot on Scottish soil. Oronsay in the ancient Parish of Kilchattan or Kilduran was a five merk land and belonged to the Priors instituted it is said by Columba, and carried on till 1555 when Robert Lamont, probably the last Catholic Prior was presented to the Priorate, vacant by the death of Donald Macduffie. The remains of the Church and Cloisters are still considerable, with fine crosses and handsome tombs, all connected with the ancient family of Macduffie otherwise Macphee. Of this Bond a *fac simile* is given, and with the spelling modernized is as follows:—

"Be it known to all men by these presents me Sir James M'Conill of Knockrinsay, Knight, to have taken and by these presents takes my loving servitor and native kynd man Donald Makduphee Pryor of Oronsay in my maintenance, warrand and life safe guard, and promises faithfully to warrand

and defend, fortify and assist the said Donald in all his lawful adoes in contrar all men—the King's Majesty being excepted. For the which doings, I the said Donald grants and confesses me to have taken the said Sir James my chief master, and promises to wair myself goods and gear in the maintenange of the said Sir James during my lifetime, so long as the said Sir James does his lawful duty to me. And for more of verification and shewing of my obedience to the said Sir James, I by the tenure hereof grants me to have given upon myself and my brethren and our heirs ane bairn's part of gear to the said Sir James and his heirs for ever; and the said Sir James to do all duties that he ought to us, and ours for the same. In token whereof both I, the said Sir James, and the said Donald, has subscribed these presents with our hands as follows :—At Simerby the 3rd of July, 1597, before these witnesses—Gillespic Mac vic Allister of the Largie, John Mac Gillespie vic Cay, John Oig Mac MareNis, and John Steward, writer, hereinto with others diverse. (Signed), Sir J. M'Connall of Knockransay, Knyt, I, Donald M'Duphie, hes subscryssit, this present

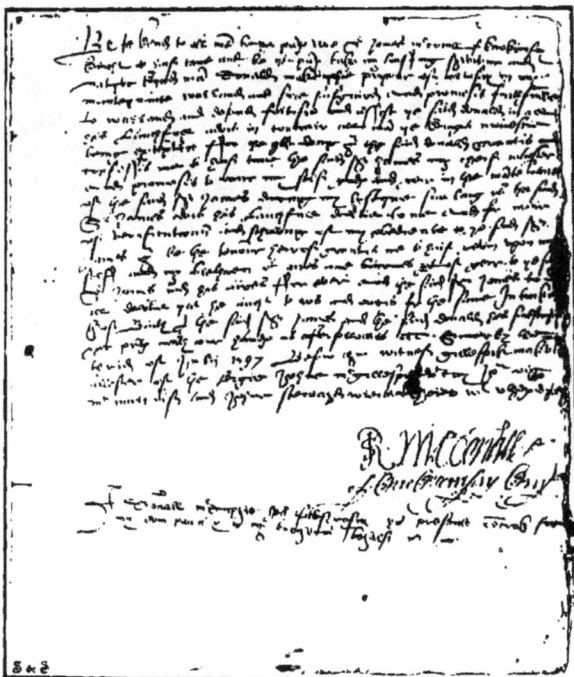

PRIOR OF ORONSAY'S BOND.

contrak for my own part, and in my brother's behalf."

Sir James M'Donald was taken prisoner as early as 1601, and after one attempt of escape which failed in consequence of his being kept in irons, whereby he fell and was injured, finally escaped in May, 1615. Prior to this Dunyvaig, which had been occupied by the Bishop of the Isles, had been suddenly seized by Angus Mac-donald, and some of the Bishop's family held in security. Information being conveyed to Sir James that the time was favourable for his re-appearance, and he having also heard that the King had secretly given the Earl of Argyle power to carry out the old sentence, made a determined and successful attempt to escape. Accompanied by Keppoch and others he moved rapidly through Perthshire and the Islands, and arrived in Isla, where we find him at Dunyvaig, given up by the Campbells. At first many flocked to his standard but gradually melted away, and it is clear by his letters from Dunyvaig that he wished to be restored to his estates peacefully. Later on he had to flee to Ireland and thence to Spain. Meantime, his followers were mercilessly pursued and hunted down, his base brother Angus, who took Dunyvaig, and surrendered on promise that his life would be safe, being tried and executed. A reward of £5000 had been offered for the apprehension of Sir James; of £3000 for Keppoch and Coll Gillespie; and of three thousand merks for others, by the Privy Council. Mr. Cosmo Innes says of Sir James, "though his early exploits show him reckless of blood, in later life he was not cruel, and sometimes spared his enemies when in his power. His letters, many of which are preserved and have been printed, show a touch of feeling and self respect, and of what was due to his ancient race; with a straightness and manliness of expression that contrast favourably with some of the lawyer's letters among which they are found."

Sir James had a warm friend in Sir Lachlan Mackintosh, long his fellow prisoner in the Castle of Edinburgh. Now what was Calder's position? He had attained what for years he had plotted for, shed blood, sold his plate, and dilapidated his great grandmother's ancient Estate of the Thanedom of Cahier, all to carry out his objects, and the end was not worth the candle. By 1619 he could not pay the Crown Duties, was put to the horn, and friends and relatives assembled in council to extricate matters, if they could. In 1623 Calder had resolved to sell the illgotten grand Estate of Isla; but the family managed to pull through until about the year 1726—the island never having paid its way, and been retained with difficulty. Notwithstanding the Welsh marriage. Rumours of the Sale not only of Isla, but even of Calder, reached the North causing great consternation among northern friends and particularly its representative Sir Archibald Campbell of Clunes. He implored his nephew that if a Sale was necessary it ought to be of Isla, and that the first offer of Isla and Muckairn ought to be made to the Duke of Argyle, and that it was well worth £20,000 stg. Sir Archibald was mistaken as to the rumoured Sale of Calder, and writing to his nephew on 17th June, 1726, he says:—

"I own my mistaking your affairs for which begs pardon, and desires to be gratefully thankful for your valuable resolution of leaving this your North Country Estate free to your posterity, which I wish as heartily as I can do anything in time, and hope if your dear bought lands in Argyleshire be gone, that better may come in their place, and be

annexed to the ancient honourable Hawthorn Tree, as formerly."

In 1631 John Fiar of Calder asked the Privy Council to sanction the destruction of Dunyvaig which was granted, and tho' it has since been a ruin, it stands out an imposing warning to its umquhile Campbell possessors for the mean and shabby opinion and spirit displayed for its being destroyed. It is no surprize to find this Calder cognosced as a lunatic in 1639.

It would rather appear that Sir James' appeals to the King, formerly referred to, had never been forwarded, for we find that after several years absence he was recalled by King James from Spain, received into favour, and a handsome pension given him. He was not allowed to return to Scotland, and his history from 1616 to 1626 when he died is as yet in obscurity. Doubtless some notices are to be found in English Records. He left no male issue, and the representation was claimed by the Earl of Antrim who desired to acquire both Isla and Kintyre.

NOTES AND QUERIES.

SEANN ORAN :—Dh' ionnsaich mi na rannan so 'n uair a bha mi 'n am bhalachan ann an Uithist. Cha 'n fhaca mi riamh ann an leabhar iad. Tha mi 'g an cur do 'ur n-ionnsuidh anns an dòchas gu 'm faigh sinn tuilleadh mu tha còlas aig leughadair 's am bith air an òran no air có a rinn e.—A MacIsaac, Clachan-an-diseirt.

Ged nach 'eil mi ach òg
'S beag m' àbhachd ri spòrs ;
Rinn m' àrdan 's mo phròis
      Mo thrèigsinn.

Dol dha 'n arm g' am cheart dheòin
'S mi chaidh iomrall 's a' chèò :
'S e mo chall-sa 'bha mòr
      'N a dhèigh sin.

Thug sinn turus dà uair
Gu Righ Lochlainn mu thuath ;
'S ann da rioghachd 'bu chruaidh
      A's sgeula ud.

Chuir sinn 'aitreibh 'n an gual,
Chuir sinn gaisgeadh 'n a sguaib,
'S thug sinn creach as le ruaig
      Beinn-sgeithe

'S iomadh clàr agus bòrd
Air 'n a chàradh mo lòn
Bho 'n a chaith mi 'cheud chòta
      Is lèine.

Cha 'n 'eil cearn 's an Roinn Eorp'
'S nach 'eil làrach mo bhròig
Eadar tràigh is tir-mòr
      'S na sleibhtean.

GEORGE DUNCAN SHEARER,

PRESIDENT, AIRDRIE HIGHLAND ASSOCIATION.

THE subject of the following sketch is a North-country-man, embued with all the love of fatherland and pride of birth contained in that word. He was born in the Orkneys and his childhood was spent on those rock bound isles, his father having been ruling Magistrate in Stromness for the long period of fifteen years. Mr. Shearer was partly educated at a private tutorial School in Orkney before he proceeded to Glasgow University, where he completed his education, and passed as a Solicitor in 1885. He thereafter commenced the practice of his profession in Airdrie, where he has been eminently successful, his genial tact and gentlemanly bearing winning the respect of all classes of the community. His success he owes to his natural ability and admirable legal training in one of the largest offices in Glasgow, and also to the thorough earnestness and energy he brings into all his work. He is known (but will only admit it on provocation) to occasionally contribute to one of the Glasgow papers, and has even thrown himself with fervour into warfare with those who favoured the despoilers of those lovely straths in our Highlands now the haunt of the deer. Mr. Shearer is a bit of a sportsman and is frequently seen with his gun. He is one of the Presidents of the Airdrie Highland Association, which along with the sister Association in Coatbridge seeks to keep alive the best traditions of the land of the 'brown heath and shaggy wood.' The Association is managed by an able committee and is making itself a powerful factor in the Monkland district for bringing together the affections of the "children of the mist," and in preserving by Evening Classes and frequent communications, the language of their race. During the last winter session Mr. Shearer presided over one of the largest and most successful Concerts of the Society ever given in Airdrie. We learn that County gentlemen, members of well-known Highland clans, are realising the disinterested motives of its patriotic promoters, and are identifying themselves with the Society, which is not yet very old, but success seems so assured that the establishment of a Highland Institute building is being considered.

Presided over as this Society is by such an able and energetic leader as the subject of our present sketch we fear not but that many residenters in Airdrie will investigate into their ancestry and discover some long forgotten Highland forefather who will entitle them to a claim on its Membership.

L. GRANT.

ANDREW KEY SANDISON.

ANDREW KEY SANDISON.

MR. A. K. SANDISON was, until he left London some years ago, perhaps one of the most popular Scotsmen in the city. He was born at Pulteneytown, Caithness, where he served his apprenticeship in the office of the *Northern Ensign*, Wick, then edited by the late Mr. John Mackie.

Intent upon following an active commercial career Mr. Sandison went to the Metropolis in 1869, and obtained an appointment upon the staff of the "Public Ledger," the oldest existing London daily newspaper. His connection with this journal lasted till 1884, when he was appointed Visitor and Collector to the London Scottish Corporation, at which time Mr. George Henderson was Secretary. While acting in this capacity Mr. Sandison rendered valuable services to many of the Highland Associations in London, including the Caithness, Morayshire, and Inverness-shire, all of whom retain a keen sense of appreciation and gratitude for the practical interest which he took in their prosperity. On retiring from his position with the Scottish Corporation he was appointed to a responsible post on the staff of the celebrated "Le Dansa," Southampton, on whose behalf he now does yeoman service in all parts of the British Isles.

Although Mr. Sandison bears a name which is probably of Scandinavian origin, he is on the maternal side closely allied to the Clans Stewart and Mackintosh, so that the Celtic blood flows freely through his veins. He prides himself in being a Highlander, although it is not often that a Caithnessian will claim connection with the Gael! Immediately on his arrival in London he joined the Caithness Association, and has ever since continued an active member, and has contributed not a little to its success. He is also a Life Governor of the London Scottish Corporation.

Mr. Sandison has a large circle of friends, for he makes friends wherever he goes. Naturally of a genial disposition, and gifted with a rich vein of Scotch humour, he is at all times a delightful companion. He is always ready to help forward Highland movements; and we have frequently heard the Editor of the *Celtic Monthly* express his indebtedness to Mr. Sandison for introducing the magazine to so many Highlanders whom he met in his travels in all parts of the kingdom.

Mr. Sandison, as will be seen from the excellent portrait, is still in the prime of life, and has yet the prospect of many years of usefulness before him. Through his patriotic services on behalf of the Highland cause he has already earned an abiding place in the affections of his countrymen.

London. NEIL MACMILLAN.

OUR CANADIAN LETTER.

ENTHUSIASTIC GATHERING OF THE CLAN FRASER.

PERHAPS the event in Highland circles so far this summer has been the Gathering of the Clan Fraser in Toronto. The example was set by the Clan MacLean, who gave a reception to Sir Donald Fitzroy MacLean of Duart last fall, after the great gathering at Chicago. One result, as has been said, was the Fraser Clan Banquet, and if there was no hereditary Chief or Chieftain present to evoke enthusiasm, there was genuine Clan sentiment in abundant measure, and no more loyal Clansmen ever assembled to honour Clan name and tradition. It is now long ago since the Clan Fraser organized in Canada; so long ago that Keltie was able to avail himself of a good notice of it in his History of the Clans, an account which must be familiar and interesting to most of your readers. At the time the Clan was then organized there were over 12,000 men of the name in Canada, not one of whom was a day laborer, and all of whom were in comfortable circumstances. In Nova Scotia the country is teeming with Frasers, while they are numerous all over the country.

With the view of bringing the Members of the Clan once more together and considering the formation of a Clan Society, the Clan Dinner was held. Over three hundred letters were received conveying greeting from Clansmen who could not be present, and invitations were accepted from many parts of Canada. A goodly company sat to dinner, which was served in excellent style. Mr. Alexander Fraser, Toronto (of the Clann 'le Fhionnlaidh branch), presided, the vice-chairs being occupied by Mr. Robert Lovat Fraser, barrister, Toronto, and Mayor Fraser, Petrolea. The dining-room was neatly decorated. Among the things that lent interest as well as beauty to the room were a finely poised Royal Stag's Head (the Crest of the Clan), draped with Fraser Clan Tartan, Mezzo-tint Pictures of Simon, Lord Lovat, beheaded on Tower hill, of Brigadier-General Simon Fraser, killed at Saratoga, kindly sent by Mr. B. Homer Dixon, a Water-colour of the Coat-of-Arms of the Clan, a Map of Inverness-shire, showing the Clan possessions, a Life-size Copy of Hogarth's Picture of Simon, Lord Lovat, the "last of the Martyrs," a Life-size Copy of an Engraving of Sir Alexander Fraser, of Philworth, founder of the University of Fraserburgh.

The project of forming a Clan Association was heartily received and a Committee, with Alexander Fraser, Toronto, as Chairman, was formed to carry out the work of organization.

Toronto, Canada. SGIAN DUBH.

BOUND COPIES OF VOLUME I.—We have now only a few copies of this handsome volume left, which can be had from the Editor at the following prices—Bound in strong leather, 6/6; cloth, gilt lettering, 5/-. Post free.

FAMOUS HIGHLAND BARDS.

No. II.—"Rob Donn" Mac Aoidh.

By W. Drummond Norie.

FAR away in the rugged north and within sound of the angry billows of the North Sea lashing themselves into fury against the precipitous rocks of the Sutherland coast, Robert Mackay was born. His parents, who were in a humble position of life, resided at Allt-na-caillich in the beautiful and picturesque district of Strathmore, one of the most lovely spots in the celebrated "*Diathaich Mhic Aoidh*" (country of the Mackays), and it was here that sometime during the winter of the year 1714, the future bard made his entrance into the world. Donald "Donn" Mackay, his father, does not appear to have had any poetical or literary tastes, and it was probably from his mother that Rob Donn derived his love of poetry, for we are told that she was a woman of more than ordinary ability and possessed talents of a very high order. She could recite with the greatest ease long poems descriptive of the Ossianic heroes, and other metrical stories relating to the ancient traditions of her native country, and it is therefore only reasonable to conclude that she would take every opportunity of encouraging her son's natural inclination in the direction of verse-making as soon as it became apparent, which if the following story is to be credited, it did, at a remarkably early period of his life. His biographer informs us, that when Rob was quite an infant his father had occasion to slaughter two oxen, one of which on being prepared for curing, was found to be considerably inferior to the other. Small-pox was raging in Strathmore at the time, and by way of a joke (surely a very grizzly one), Donald Mackay turning to his children, who were watching with childish curiosity

MONUMENT TO ROB DONN "MACKAY, IN BALNAKIEL GRAVEYARD, DURNESS.

the process of salting the meat, remarked, "Now, the best of this beef is not to be touched until we see who survives the small-pox to share it." Rob, who like his brothers had been deeply interested in the proceedings, suddenly exclaimed in childish accents "'*S olc a' chuid sin do 'n fhear a dh' fhalbhas*,"—(He who departs will have a bad share of it then!) "True my boy," replied his father, somewhat surprised at his child's precocity, "and yours will never be a bad share, while you remain able to use it."

Another instance of the youthful bard's genius is recorded of him, when he had attained the mature age of three. It was the custom at that period to dress children in a short frock fastened tightly round the waist and buttoned at the back. Rob's mother had procured one of these garments from the village tailor, and on the morning after it had been sent home, the child proud of his new acquisition, and anxious to exhibit it to his brothers and sisters, endeavoured to put it on himself, but all his efforts to fasten the buttons at the back were in vain. Angered at his failure he ran out of the house perfectly naked, and met his mother just returning from some of her farm duties; she was naturally annoyed at seeing her son in such a state and probably administered a little maternal correction to him on the spot. Rob's pride was hurt, and young as he was he composed the following lines as an outlet for his feelings :—

"'S maith dhomhsa bhi 'n diugh gun aodach,
Le slaodaireachd Mhurchaidh' 'ic Néill,
Mo bhroilleach chur air mo chùlthaobh,
'S nach 'eil a dhùnadh agam fhein !"

About three years later, when Rob Donn had reached the age of six years, he fortunately attracted the attention of Mr. John Mackay of the family of Skerray, a gentleman of cultivated tastes, who in addition to his many other attainments, was an accomplished poet. He apparently took a great fancy to the child bard of Allt-na-caillich, and found a place for him at his farm of Musal, where he employed him to herd calves and fulfil other light duties about the place, leaving him ample leisure to follow his favourite occupation. It was whilst living at Musal that Rob Donn first began to give real evidence of his powers as a poet, and even at this early stage of his career, his verses possess considerable merit and argue a keenness of observation, and knowledge of human nature remarkable in one so young. Nor was humour wanting, as we shall find on reading " *Am fear liath* "—(The Grey Man); an amusing production written out of spite, because he was not allowed by his master to attend the wedding of a neighbour who went by that appellation.

Rob, like most of his brother bards, was no stranger to the tender passion, and as he approached man's estate he fell a victim on more than one occasion to the shafts of love shot from the dark eyes of the Highland maids of Strathmore. His first love was Ann Morrison, and it was in her praise that he composed the finest of his love poems, commencing

> " 'S trom leam an àiridh,
> 'S a ghàir so a th' innt,
> Gu 'n a phairt sin a b' abhaist,
> Bhi 'n dràsd air mo chinn ;
> Anna chaol-mhalach, chìoch-chorrach,
> Shlip-cheannach, ghrinn,
> 'S Iseabail a bheoil mhilis,
> Mhanranaich, bhinn."

The Isabel referred to in the above verse, was the daughter of his employer, and after Ann had proved faithless, he consoled himself for her loss by attuning his lyre afresh and singing the charms of Isabel Mackay. One of the bard's most characteristic productions is a song of which this lady is the *motif*. It is entitled " *Piobaireachd Iseabail Nic-Aoidh* " and is written to the well-known pipe tune " *Failte Phrionns* "—(The Prince's Salute). In this song we have ample evidence of Rob Donn's rythmical powers, for the difficulty of closely following all the variations of the Highland *piobaireachd* in verse, as he has successfully done, must be palpable to all those whose knowledge of the intricacies of pipe music, enables them to form an opinion on the subject. Whether Isabel Mackay reciprocated the bard's passion is not known, probably the fact that he was in her father's service, and consequently inferior to her in social position, deterred her from encouraging his advances, as marriage between them was out of the question. Nothing daunted by his failure in this quarter, Rob looked elsewhere for consolation, and soon found it in the society of Janet Mackay, the daughter of a small tenant farmer of Durness parish,

whom he eventually married, and she being a woman of good sense and of the most amiable disposition, their domestic relations were of the happiest description,

The first few years of Rob Donn's married life were spent at Bad-na-h-achlais, a farm belonging to his old friend and patron Mr. John Mackay, and here he became known as one of the most expert deerstalkers in the neighbourhood. It was due to his skill as a hunter, rather than to his fame as a poet, that brought him about this time under the notice of his chief Lord Reay, who provided him with a small croft at Allt-coire-Fraisgil, on the eastern shore of Loch Erribol, where he was employed in the congenial duty of supplying his Lordship's table with venison, and his own at the same time. As time went on, so many deer had fallen to Rob's gun, that Lord Reay gave strict orders that no more were to be killed without his direct command. Little heed however was taken of this injunction by the bard, who like the rest of his class in the Highlands, looked upon wild game as the property of the people ; a feeling expressed in the following Gaelic proverb " *Is ionraic a' mhèirle na fiadh* "— (Righteous theft is *(the killing)* deer). At last Rob's notorious disregard of his chief's orders got him into trouble, and he was summoned before the Sheriff Substitute to answer for his disobedience, He set out for the Court accompanied by his wife and with his favourite gun on his shoulder. They had not proceeded far, when Rob espied a small herd of deer quietly browsing on the hill side, and with utter disregard of the consequences, he took a steady aim and brought down two fine stags. His wife was terrified when she saw what he had done, and commenced to upbraid him for his recklessness. His only reply was " Go home and send for them; if I return not you shall have the more need for them ; but fear not, it shall go hard with me if I am not soon with you again to have my share." His words were soon verified, for he was so popular in the district that no one could be found to bear witness against him and he was let off with a caution. Shortly after this episode he was appointed Lord Reay's bow-man at Baile-na-Cille, a farm close to the sea coast within a few miles of Cape Wrath, where he remained for the greater part of his life, with short intervals of other employment elsewhere. One of these occurred, when, probably at the request of his chief he enlisted in the 1st Regiment of Sutherland Highlanders, raised in 1759, in whose ranks he made many friends both among the officers and men. His military duties do not appear to have been of a very arduous character, a fact which was probably due to his popularity with the officers of the regiment. One day he was strolling listlessly about in the neighbourhood of the barracks, when an officer who had only recently been appointed enquired somewhat curtly of him "to what company do you belong?" "To every company" replied the bard and passed on, leaving the officer standing aghast at his apparent impertinence. The incident was reported to the commanding officer, and after explanations had been made the matter ended. In 1763 the regiment was reduced, and Rob Donn once more returned to his ordinary avocations. A slight difference with his employer, which is thought to have been occasioned by some satirical verses in which Lord Reay was held up to ridicule, caused a temporary breach in their otherwise amicable relations, and Rob removed with his family to Achmore in the same parish ; but after a brief interval returned to Baile-na-Cille where he remained until his chief's death. A touching tribute to the many estimable qualities of that nobleman will be found among the bard's poems. After Lord Reay's death the place of Baile-na-Cille was managed by Mackay of Skibo, and afterwards became the residence of Colonel Hugh Mackay, the son of Rob's old patron. An amusing anecdote is told of a meeting which took place in Lochaber between Rob Donn and MacDonald of Achatriochadain, who were at that time quite unknown to each other. The bard had missed his way and meeting MacDonald asked him if he could direct him to his destination. Having done so, and noticing the northern accent in Rob's Gaelic, Macdonald remarked "I perceive by your dialect you belong to the north,—what part there?" "To Lord Reay's country," replied the bard. "O then you must know Rob Donn!" "Yes I could point him out to you in a crowd." "Pray inform me then what like a person he is, of whom we hear so much?" "A person, I fear of whom more has been spoken than he well deserves." "You think so, do you?" returned MacDonald with some sharpness, for he was something of a poet himself and considered the stranger's answer argued a want of appreciation. The conversation then lapsed for a few minutes until they came in sight of Ben Nevis, when pointing to its cloud enveloped summit, MacDonald enquired "Were you ever, my man at the top of yon mountain?" "I never was," said Rob. "Then you have never been so near Heaven." "And have you yourself been there?" "Indeed I have." "Then what a fool you must have been to descend," retorted the bard, "are you sure of being ever again so nigh?" This witty reply fairly took away MacDonald's breath, and turning to his companion he exclaimed "I'll be shot if thou be not thyself Rob Donn." The bard modestly

admitted that such was the case, and a friendship was struck up between them on the spot.

Owing to his wife's failing health preventing her from continuing her duties about the farm, Rob Donn removed to a small croft at Nuybig, where she shortly afterwards died. The bard himself never recovered from the shock, and only survived her a few months. He died on the 5th of August, 1778, at the age of sixty-four years, beloved by all who knew him and mourned by the whole country side. Although we cannot claim for Rob Donn the highest place among the Gaelic bards, it would be no exaggeration to say that few excelled him. His satire was keen without being vindictive; his humour (except in a very few instances) racy, without being indelicate, and his wit natural and unforced. In private life he was a fond and faithful husband, a good father, and a staunch friend. His only failing was an occasional over indulgence in the national beverage, a fault which most of his fellow countrymen will readily excuse, on the ground that "people who live in glass houses mustn't throw stones." Some years after his death a subscription was raised and with the money thus collected a handsome monument was erected over his grave in Durness Church-yard, with an inscription in Gaelic, English, Latin, and Greek, by the Rev. Alexander Pope, Minister of Reay.

Note.—As I happen to be spending a few days in Durness (Rob Donn's birth-place) when the proof of Mr. Drummond-Norie's excellent article reached me, I take the liberty of adding a few lines by way of supplement. To-day I visited the ancient churchyard of Baile-na-Cille, and saw the massive monument which was erected to his memory in 1827. The English inscription is as follows, "In memory of Rob Donn, otherwise Robert Mackay, of Durness, The Reay Gaelic Bard. This tomb was erected at the expense of a few of his countrymen, ardent admirers of his native talent and extraordinary genius, 1827." The monument was carved from one large boulder of granite which was found in the glebe of the parish minister of the time. The bard's remains lie under a plain slab somewhat sunk in the ground, a few steps in front of the entrance to the graveyard. The stone bears the simple inscription "Robert Donn, 1777. M K" In the engraving of Balnakiel on page 148, Rob Donn's grave may be seen immediately to the right of the engravers' name. The railing surrounding the monument is rust-worn, and the carving and inscription are partly covered with moss. I trust that some patriotic clansman will see the matter remedied.

Durness, 4th August, 1891.   Editor.

OUR MUSICAL PAGE.

MARAICHE NAN TONN—THE SAILOR LADDIE.

Gaelic Words Old. — *Translation by* "FIONN."

KEY F. *Moderato.*

|m ., r : d . d | r ., m : | d' | t ., l : l . d' | t . l : s

Seisd.—Hithill - en, na hillean   l, Hithill - en na hillean ó;
Chorus.—O, my heart is fu' o'   pain, Sighing daily a' my lane.

|m ., f : s ., s | l ., t : d' | .l | l . s, m : r . d, r | m . d .-: d ||

Fàill-ill éile 's l ó - ro   l, Mo thruaighe mi mar fhaigh mi thu!
For my love that's o'er the main, My ain dear sailor laddie O!

Tha mi 'n so mar dhruid an crann,
An déigh a cuid eòin a chall;
Seachran air dol a'm' cheann,—
  'S ged thig an t-àm cha cl aidil mi.

"Thasgaidh mo chridhe 'us mo chléibh,
Chuireadh tu air feadan gleus
Dhànnsadh tu air ùrlar réidh
  Gu lùghor eutrom, aighearach.

Dh' fhàg thu mise dubhach, trom,
'S thaobh thu crannagan nan long,
Ged a bhiodh do phòca lom,—
  Gun mì gun fhonn gu'n gal hainn thu.

'S e mo cheisd fear a' chùil bhàin,—
B 'aotrom do cheum air sràid
O'n a chaidh thu null thar sàil'
  Tha mi o'n là sin aeanach.

Fhuair mi do litir a nall,
Air a sgrìobhadh leis a' pheann,
Thàin' an Nollaig 's dh' fhalbh an t-àm
  O'n gheall thu tighinn 'am amharc-sa.

Tha mi gun airgiod 'us gun òr,—
Cha 'n e so a rinn mo leòn,
Ach nach fhaic mi thu ri m' bheò
  A seòladh taobh an fhearainn so.

Like the thrush on yonder thorn,
Wi' her offspring frae her torn
Here I'm sittin' a' forlorn
  Lamentin' sair my laddie O !

O, my love is young and gay,
He can dance and he can play,
So be wiled my heart away—
  My rantin' sailor laddie O!

He has left me sad and drear,
Since he sailed awa frae here,
Still my choice, tho' lackin' gear,
  Wad be my sailor laddie O!

He is young and he is fair,
Wi' a wealth o' gouden hair,
O, it pains the heart fu' sair—
  The absence o' my laddie O!

Once you wrote me, weel I min'
That you'd come and mak me thine,
But the time has gane langsyne,
  Yet nae words o' my laddie O !

Goud an' siller I hae nane,
'Tis na that that gies me pain,
But that I shall ne'er again
  Behold my sailor laddie O !

TALES OF THE HEATHER, by Emma Rose Mackenzie (A. & W. Mackenzie, Inverness). This is a second and enlarged edition of what in our opinion is one of the most fascinating collections of Highland short stories extant. The tastefully got up volume reached us just as we were leaving for a brief holiday at the coast, and before the evening was closed we had read it from beginning to end. The tales are admirably told, in a graceful easy style, and there is not a dull one in the book. Above all we were delighted with the intense *Highland* atmosphere of the stories; they took us in imagination to the heathery mountain side, with the fragrance of the peat wafted on the breeze The printing is excellent, the binding is tasteful, and altogether the "Tales of the Heather" ought to be on every Highlander's bookshelf.

THE IRISH GAELIC JOURNAL for August has just come to hand and is an excellent number. Under Professor O'Growney's able editorship the *Gaelic Journal* improves with every issue. We wish it success.

REVIEWS.

A Trip from Callander to Staffa and Iona, with brief descriptive sketches of the route by sea and land, and the sacred rock-bound Isle of I-colm-kill, by Malcolm Ferguson (John Leng & Co., Dundee).—This is undoubtedly the best of the many excellent volumes which Mr. Ferguson has contributed to our Highland literature. In it the author takes his reader on a pleasure trip from Callander to Iona, giving a most interesting account of the historical and other associations of the various places passed *en route*. Curiously, the volume reached us just as we were leaving on a visit to the Western Highlands and Islands, and we followed the route so well described by Mr. Ferguson. The volume proved a most useful and interesting companion, and we heartily recommend it to those of our readers who purpose making a similar trip. It is nicely bound, and contains a number of fine plates illustrative of places and objects in Argyllshire and the Islands. Copies can be had from Mr. Henry Whyte, Bookseller, 4 Bridge Street, Glasgow.

Transactions of the Gaelic Society of Inverness, Volume XVIII., 1894.—This bulky Volume embraces the work of the Society from Mid-summer 1891 till the Mid session of 1893, and is of more than average interest. A glance at the contents shows that the papers have been contributed by well-known Celts whose names are a tower of strength to the Society. "The Apparitions and Ghosts of the Isle of Skye" form the subject of a paper by Mr. Norman Matheson. Mr. Fraser-Mackintosh contributes two valuable papers on "Minor Highland Families" and we have "Some Highland Fishermen's Fancies" by Mr. A. Polson, Dunbeath. There is a paper from the pen of the late Hector MacLean on "The Ibernians"—probably the last complete treatise penned by this gifted Son of Islay. Rev. John MacRury, Snizort has a suggestive paper on some of the byepaths of Gaelic Orthography, while "General Monks Campaign in the Highlands in 1654," is successfully dealt with by Mr. William Mackay. Mr. Alexander MacBain, M.A.—the learned Rector of Raining's School—contributes two most valuable papers. To the Student of Gaelic his article on "The Dialect of Badenoch" cannot fail to be interesting, while he has done a piece of excellent work in his paper on "Ptolmey's Geography of Scotland." Mr. William MacKenzie's article on "The Gaelic Incantations and Charms of the Hebrides," is of permanent value—and displays much learned research. The indefatigable Celt—Mr. John Mackay, J.P., Hereford—contributes two exhaustive papers on "Sutherland Place Names," while Mr. A. Mackintosh Shaw, London, deals with "Some Clan Chattan MS. Genealogies and Histories." "The Early History, Legends, and Traditions of Strathardle" are treated in a popular manner by Mr. Charles Ferguson, Fairburn, and the well-known Gaelic *Seanachir*, Rev. A. Maclean Sinclair, Nova Scotia, makes an interesting contribution to Clan history by giving a sketch of "The MacIntyres of Glenoe." Mr. Paul Cameron, Blair Athole, contributes a second paper on "The

Gaelic Songs of Perthshire and their Composers." We cordially recommend the Volume to all who are interested in the Celt, his language and literature, confident that they will find much in it to instruct and interest.

THE CHIEFTAINSHIP OF THE CLAN MACKINNON.

Sir.—I hope you may allow me a small space in the *Celtic Monthly* in reply to Mr. A. K. MacKinnon's letter in this month's issue. Mr. A. K. MacKinnon on his own admission, cannot be Chief of MacKinnon. His statement, without giving instances, that sometimes Chiefs of Clans hold the position through the female line, is absurd. Supposing his paternal grandmother, Miss Mary Emilia MacKinnon, through whom he claims the Chieftainship, having married Michael O'Brien, instead of Mr. Alexander MacKinnon, Mr. A. K. MacKinnon's grandfather, their descendants (say Bernard O'Brien, their grandson), according to this arrangement, would still have claimed the Chieftainship of the ancient Clan Fingon. Mr. A. K. MacKinnon states that I cannot be unaware of the adverse feeling there exists in and out the Clan MacKinnon Society regarding the Chieftainship. I am not aware of such feeling existing, and I cannot see any reason to introduce any ill feeling. I am quite content to abide by the decision arrived at by competent authority nearly a century ago, when Mr. William Alexander Mackinnon, head of the Antigua branch of MacKinnon, a direct male descendant of Lachlan Mor of Strathaird became Chief on the death of John MacKinnon in 1808, a brother of Mr. A. K. MacKinnon's grandmother, and through whom he claims the Chieftainship. The present Chief of MacKinnon, William A. MacKinnon, of Acryse Place, Folkeston, is worthy of the honour, and both himself and his relatives have proved themselves an honour to the race, and served their Queen and country as statesmen, and gallantly as officers in the British army. Mr. A. K. MacKinnon wishes a conference to decide the question, I have no objection, but I cannot see Mr. A. K. MacKinnon's ground of argument in favour of his claim through the female line, because such claim is bad in theory, in custom, in practice and usage, amongst the ancient Scottish Clans, and all history bearing on the subject is against it. The custom amongst the Clans in ancient times was when a Chief died or was killed on the field of battle, without male issue, to elect the nearest direct male heir to the Chieftainship, and the present Chief is the nearest male direct heir on the death of John already alluded to, and all the Scotch historians of any standing recognise him as such. I have nothing to say against Mr. A. K. MacKinnon's respectability, and am proud of himself and his forefathers as worthy and honourable Clansmen, and I should be very sorry to disturb the harmony amongst the Clan since the formation of the Society. Should Mr. W. A. MacKinnon still persist with his claim, I shall be glad to correspond with him by private letter.

Glasgow.   Duncan MacKinnon.

END OF VOLUME II.

www.ingramcontent.com/pod-product-compliance
Lightning Source LLC
Chambersburg PA
CBHW020509270326
41926CB00008B/801